D1108086

SOCIOLOGY

rules, roles, and relationships

THE DORSEY SERIES IN ANTHROPOLOGY AND SOCIOLOGY

Editor ROBIN M. WILLIAMS, JR. *Cornell University*

ANDERSON *Sociological Essays and Research: Introductory Readings*

BARNOUW *Culture and Personality*

BELL *Marriage and Family Interaction* rev. ed.

BELL & STUB *editors* *The Sociology of Education: A Sourcebook* rev. ed.

BREER & LOCKE *Task Experience as a Source of Attitudes*

GAMSON *Power and Discontent*

GEORGES *editor* *Studies on Mythology*

GOODMAN *The Individual and Culture*

GORDEN *Interviewing: Strategy, Techniques, and Tactics*

GOTTLIEB & RAMSEY *The American Adolescent*

HAGEN *On the Theory of Social Change: How Economic Growth Begins*

HSU *editor* *Psychological Anthropology: Approaches to Culture and Personality*

JACOBS *Pattern in Cultural Anthropology*

JOHNSON *Crime, Correction, and Society* rev. ed.

KNUDTEN *Crime in a Complex Society: An Introduction to Criminology*

KNUDTEN *Crime, Criminology, and Contemporary Society*

KOHN *Class and Conformity: A Study in Values*

LE MASTERS *Parents in Modern America*

MARIS *Social Forces in Urban Suicide*

SALISBURY *Religion in American Culture: A Sociological Interpretation*

SHOSTAK *editor* *Sociology in Action: Case Studies in Social Problems and Directed Social Change*

WARRINER *The Emergence of Society*

WILSON *Sociology: Rules, Roles, and Relationships* rev. ed.

SOCIOLOGY

rules, roles, and relationships

EVERETT K. WILSON

Professor of Sociology
The University of North Carolina

Revised edition 1971

THE DORSEY PRESS
Homewood, Illinois

IRWIN-DORSEY LIMITED, *Georgetown, Ontario*

HM
51
.W48

© THE DORSEY PRESS, 1966 and 1971

All rights reserved. No part of this publication may be reproduced, stored in a retrieval system, or transmitted, in any form or by any means, electronic, mechanical, photocopying, recording, or otherwise, without the prior written permission of the publisher.

Revised Edition
First Printing, January, 1971

Library of Congress Catalog Card No. 73–135768
Printed in the United States of America

Acknowledgments. For reproduction of all photos, except the ones indicated below, acknowledgment is made to Magnum Photos, Inc.
For other photographs, acknowledgment is made to Bettmann Archive: pages 12 and 133. Boy Scouts of America: page 443 bottom left. FPG: page 236 top. Historical Pictures Service, Chicago: pages 24, 342, and 422. Newberry Library, Chicago: page 443—Baskerville Bible top right, Complutensian Polyglot Bible center right, Gutenberg Bible bottom right. Photo World: page 33 top right, page 594 top. Wide World Photos: page 256 center, page 549 bottom left.
The constructions on pages 29, 221, and 457 were designed by David Battle.

Foreword

Among sociologists, introductions to the field have never been the most celebrated activity. Yet, apart from the fact that so many people are involved, there are reasons for thinking this lowly genre important.

Every text in sociology is a somewhat different effort to frame a complex field intelligibly. If by some divine criteria such attempts at synthesis must fall short, they nonetheless promote a continuing conversation about analytical elements of the field, their connections and boundaries.

Nor is it simply a matter of letting a thousand flowers bloom. There are interaction effects, a dialectic that constantly reworks the public and professional face of sociology.

There is pedagogical profit, too. An adequate text provides an intellectual structure that can liberate more than it constrains. It frees the student from a degree of mental indigestion to which more fragmentary strategies condemn him. Because it discloses itself, it invites criticism and revision. And while it provides a useful anchorage, a text obviously does not preclude the use of complementary materials—for example, several of the good paperbacks that report sociological research. (A list of these, geared to chapters in this book, is provided in the *Instructor's Supplement.*)

The aims of the earlier edition guided this revision. First, I sought a simple and sensible scheme of organization: *building, sustaining,* and *changing* human groups. Flanked by Prologue and Epilogue and crosscut by the three *R's* in the title, this simple structure should lend coherence to the book.

The first *R* (the rules) is our cultural legacy. The rules define our roles. Since roles are continuously vacated, the group must, to the extent that it persists, replenish its losses (the subject of Chapter 2). Infants and migrants must acquire, willy-nilly, the culture of

30318

the group (discussed in Chapter 3). Picking up the rules of the game is not a happenstance affair. It occurs through a process called socialization (Chapter 4) at the hands of the elders, who have enormous leverage on the relatively impotent newcomer (Chapter 5). There is a dual outcome, discussed in Chapter 6: a person is created and the group is constantly recreated.

These concepts, and this process, are what the artist means to convey by the design introducing Part One. The cubes represent roles, the elementary unit of analysis in sociology, the building blocks of the social structure. A slight indication of the vast variety of roles is given by the different designs on the cube faces: father, mother, daughter, son, priest and communicant, worker and boss, governor and governed—and a host of others. The rules are seen, in this scheme, as the squares in which the cubes fit—never so neatly or rigidly as is suggested here. But there *are* tolerance limits in the performance of roles. The incompetent employee is fired. The parent, performing outrageously, loses his child under court order. The disinterested nonvoter reads himself out of the citizen role. Thus the cut-out squares represent requisites and limits in role performance. Finally, the lines joining the roles (cubes) indicate social *bonds,* the relationships that interlock to form a group. They obtain only insofar as performance in roles follows the cultural prescriptions (suggested by the cut-out squares) that define appropriate roles. And since groups are always losing people—by death, resignation, retirement, or movement of some sort—there must be a constant input of persons to replace the losses. These are the ideas implicit in the first theme-design.

The design fronting Part Two stresses structure. Structure simply means an arrangement of parts. There are all sorts of structures, but in this case, since we are dealing with social structures, the systematically arranged parts are roles and relationships. In this design, both the symmetry and the stability of the structure are purposely exaggerated. If, somehow, we could see a social unit subtly changing its form and boundaries, yet retaining an identity, and all the while displaying an inner dynamism—this would be a more accurate representation of a social system. Keep in mind, then, as we examine this structure, that the graphic metaphor is hyperbole. Yet it is a statement purposely overdrawn to stress the necessary order in the arrangement of parts. This order is revealed in the demographic structure, in the spatial and temporal arrangement of human relationships, in the way we organize relationships in business and factories and schools and committees (Chapter 7). It is revealed in the class structure (Chapter 8) and

Part one,
Building the group

Part two,
Sustaining the group

Part three,
Changing the group

in the relational structures that we institutionalize (Chapters 9, 10, and 11).

But just as a chemical compound is altered when new elements are introduced, so is the social order constantly transformed, slowly, inexorably, as new rules emerge to define new roles and the relationships built out of them. Thus the shifting pattern is represented in the rearrangement of roles and relationships presented in the design introducing Part Three. Our task, of course, is to try to understand how these social changes come about. Sometimes, as in the case of revolutionary movements, the explanation seems simple. But this may be deceptive. For example, many of the initial changes in the U.S.S.R. have now been reversed or modified. Revolution-induced change may not be so dramatic as, at first, one might have thought. Sometimes change is foreshadowed in rising rates of crime, or dependency, or affluence, or drug use—or by overt rebellion against traditional authority (Chapter 12). But the deepest tides of social change, induced by forces as remote as lunar gravitation, creep up on us unawares. Such change we see in our society's drift from rural-agrarian past to urban-industrial and postindustrial present (Chapter 13).

Of course, some change is planned. And in planned change the sociologist plays a quite special role. This is a matter considered in Chapter 14.

This, then, is the first objective: an intelligible structure that is, at the same time, faithful to the field.

A second aim is to show sociology's central place in the liberal arts tradition. An introductory exposure should liberate—first, by cultivating curiosity about the customary and a skepticism of common explanations. And second, by liberally exploiting other disciplines: mathematics, other languages, and other of the sciences. For the few readers who become sociology majors, more narrowly defined preprofessional work can come later. But for most—those having but a single go at sociology—the important thing is to see the mutually fructifying influence of sociology and their other intellectual interests. One would hope for the result suggested by the rector of Justin (in the Auchincloss novel)—but with sociology added to the list.

> An equation, a Keats ode, a Gothic cathedral, a Mozart aria, the explosion of gases in a laboratory, they should be seen by [students] as related—and divine.*

Sociology promises most when skills are added to insight. So a third aim is to exemplify the interplay between ideas and their testing. This requires a few sorties into methodology. The discussion of research methods is not technical. For those who wish to dig a little deeper an occasional invitation is offered to explore one of the "Asides on Methods."

These "Asides" may be bypassed if that seems indicated. But it is most important for students to come to realize that our knowledge is only as sure as the methods used to acquire it. In the past, and especially in American secondary schools, the methods used to acquire knowledge in the social studies have ranged from inadequate through ingenuous to inexcusable. The unsystematic exchange of atypical personal experience, directed at fuzzily formulated questions, infused with emotion and morality, and leading to no verifiable conclusions, has made the social studies into a spongy bag of marshmallows. Such a diet is not good for growing things.

So it is worth suggesting that there *are* ways of acquiring reliable knowledge about social phenomena. And this is about as far as I will go in this book. These brief references to methods are no substitute for work in symbolic logic, calculus, and mathematical statistics. But there are certain fruits of an exposure even as fleeting as that offered in these "Asides on Methods."

First, some minimal intuitive grasp of methods is necessary for literacy in sociology. It doesn't make sense to read $p < .001$ without knowing that the writer thinks his findings ought to be taken seriously because such a concurrence of social events as he is reporting is most unlikely to have occurred by chance. Or to read that Hollingshead analyzed his data by means of a chi-square test

* Louis Auchincloss, *The Rector of Justin* (Boston: Houghton Mifflin Co., 1964), pp. 285–86.

—without understanding that he was comparing his observations on class and adolescent behavior with what would have been the case were there no relationship between class and, say, school grades. Or, to read that Weber used the ideal type without understanding that this unreal distillation of social experience is simply an intellectual device that provides a bench mark from which we can measure what actually occurs in men's organizations. Or, to read that a certain variable was controlled in a piece of research —without understanding that otherwise the possible connection between two other variables would be confounded and our answer less sure, our knowledge less illuminating.

Beyond literacy, there is a second yield, a revelation of possibilities of discovery that a more pessimistic common sense would rule out. For example: so many influences converge to affect human behavior that common sense (erring, as usual) would indicate the impossibility of untangling them in order to assess the influence of one variable. Even a brief brush with sociology's methods of inquiry will be reassuring on this score. It is not very commonsensical to think that an apparently biological characteristic like the sex composition of one's family can be controlled. Is it possible? Does it happen? There are methods that allow us to answer these questions. Common sense might suggest that in sociology, in contrast to the biological and physical sciences, the investigator must affect the data—human responses—that he gathers and manipulates. Does this indeed happen? If it does, can we discover to what extent it occurs? If we can identify the sources of error and measure them, can we correct for the error introduced by the influence of the investigator himself? Again, there are methods that give us hope of identifying, measuring, and correcting for the error of "the chemist in his own test tube." So, in short, we come to be more hopeful, recognizing that methodological ingenuity can sometimes overcome the specious barriers that ignorance erects.

A third reason for such detours into methodology is this: Some concern for methods of inquiry lies at the heart of education in any field. Presumably one seeks an education to get answers, however tentative, to significant questions. But if one doesn't know *how* to get an answer, there is little point in posing the question. Thus the motive for learning disappears.

It may be objected that the stress on reason—on intellectual knowing, or finding out—is exclusionary. Some would allege that the expansion of consciousness and the "aha!" moments that suddenly illuminate our worlds can be induced by other means: religious insights, sensitivity training, fasting and spiritual discipline, drugs. Doubtless there are various ways of generating hot flashes. Whether they yield reliable knowledge is at least debatable. In any case, we are dealing here with the methods of reason, ways of gaining knowledge that have had certain demonstrable outcomes. They have vastly increased our control over the unknown. They have extended our range of options. In doing so, they have enhanced our freedom. There are possibilities in our world that, in the absence of reason (as represented in methods of problem solving) would not exist. These are not all good possibilities, obviously. Knowledge always opens up the moral range, as it does the aesthetic and intellectual range of options. Thus as they open our worlds, carefully designed methods of inquiry lie close to the heart of a liberating education.

* * * *

I owe much to the expertise of colleagues who reviewed and improved the manuscript in many ways: Professors Marvin Bressler of Princeton, Thomas Drabek of the University of Denver, Charles M. Grigg of Florida State, Charles Nanry of Rutgers and Robin Williams of Cornell. It is such sociologists and teachers that account for the exponential growth of the field. Dorsey's sociology editor, Professor Robin M. Williams, Jr., continues his yeoman services to American sociologists. Profession, publishers, students, and the writer are lucky to have the protection of this man, standing between author and the damage that might otherwise be done in print.

It is time, too, for thanking the people at Dorsey: Frank Griffin, Bill Barnes, Tom Rusinek, and Jack Byrnes. Harry Bingham, a Dorsey editor, really represents the crew: generous in praise, gentle in rebuke, a skillful guardian of the student's right to intelligibility.

Textbooks don't merit dedications. But they might well prompt apologies for the absenteeism occasioned by academic moonlighting. These I offer: to EOW, AOW, and DKW. My warm thanks go to the many students who read the first version and helped, through their instructors, to improve this one.

EVERETT K. WILSON

Chapel Hill, North Carolina
January, 1971

Contents

part one
Building the group

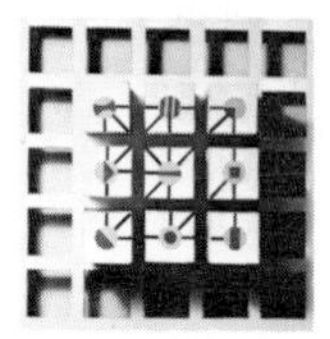

part two
Sustaining the group

prologue: The nature of the field

chapter 1 Sociological inquiry: the focus, means, and yield

Independence? That's middle class blasphemy. We are all dependent on one another, every soul of us on earth.
George Bernard Shaw, *Pygmalion,* Act V

Nothing exists from whose nature some effect does not follow.
Spinoza, *Ethics* Part I, Proposition 36

Invited, as you are, to explore unknown terrain, you are surely justified in raising some questions. *What are we looking for? How shall we go about it? Why bother?* So let us start with questions such as these. The answers will help us chart our course, giving us a first fix on where we are and where we're going.

These questions could be curtly answered in three sentences. The realm we will explore is that of men's relationships—the social structures that we build. As to the question: How? our answer is, through sociology, its tools, insights, and findings accumulated through the years. To the question: Why? we answer, because human nature is, for us, the most important part of nature; and human nature is preeminently social.

But these answers may be more mystifying than enlightening. If we are to know where we are going, we had better dwell a bit longer on each of them.

What are we looking for? What realm will we explore?

We shall be studying social structures—the way they are formed, sustained, and changed. But what do we mean by the term "social structure?" A building is a structure. A sentence, with its subject and predicate has a structure. A machine, the solar system, our government—all these have structures. That is to say, they have a discernible arrangement of parts—parts not randomly but systematically connected.

So also with a social structure. Certain rules (standards of behavior written in law or known in custom) define the roles we take, the relationships we form, endowing the groups built of these relationships with a certain tangible, structural quality. A family, a congregation, a work group, a school—these groups are social structures whose elements fit together in some coherent whole. Such social structures are our targets of inquiry.

But we cannot deal with social structures taken as a whole. If we look at a physical structure, like a building, we may ask about its floor area, percent of wall space in glass, or the loadbearing capacity of its beams. Thus when we examine a physical structure, we analyze dimensions appropriate to it. So also with a social structure: there are dimensions peculiar and appropriate to it. Sometimes the newcomer to sociology has trouble identifying appropriate dimensions of analysis because he doesn't know what they're dimensions of.

What is that social structure that we call a group? It is *not* a collection of individuals. Indeed, sociology does not investigate people, as they are commonly conceived. It focuses on the bonds *between* people, not the persons themselves who are bound in one another's destinies. On first encounter this is a difficult conception. For almost invariably we tend to focus on the individual—his behavior, motives, attitudes. This preoccupation with the individual deflects attention from the underlying social structure, the target of sociological inquiry.

As a result, some people misunderstand the nature of the field and its dimensions. Were the group simply the sum of its individual members it would seem to distort reality to say, as demographers* do, that "the American family of today has 3.6 children."[1]

* Demography is a subfield of sociology. Demographers describe and explain differences in the growth and composition of human populations.

For of course there is no family with six tenths of a child.

But the reference here is not to *an* American family but to *the* American family. Groups can be characterized decimally, fractionally. Few if any individuals ever had, precisely, the median rate of income ($8,274 and $5,141 for whites and blacks, respectively, in 1967). None ever had an average level of grade achieved, a birth or a death rate, a net reproduction rate, or a distribution of attitude scores. None ever had a delinquency or recidivism rate, a percent voting the Socialist ticket, a psychosis rate, or percent belonging to the Church of the Latter Day Saints. None ever had a measure of density, or of cohesion, or of moral integration. But groups do.

If human groups have unique dimensions it is for this reason: as people join to love and work, to learn and worship, fight and play, they create something new—invisible structures of relationships. It is in their joining, in the combination of elements, that a new order of phenomena emerges. Seventy-five years ago the French sociologist Émile Durkheim put it this way.

> Whenever certain elements combine and thereby produce, by the fact of their combination, new phenomena, it is plain that these new phenomena reside not in the original elements but in the totality formed by their union. The living cell contains nothing but mineral particles, as society contains nothing but individuals. Yet is is patently impossible for the phenomena characteristic of life to reside in the atoms of hydrogen, oxygen, carbon, and nitrogen. . . . Life [cannot] be thus separated into discrete parts; it is a unit. . . . The inanimate particles of the cell do not assimilate food, reproduce, and, in a word, live; only the cell itself as a unit can achieve these functions.
>
> . . . The hardness of bronze is not in the copper, the tin or the lead, which are its ingredients and which are soft and malleable bodies; it is in their mixture. The fluidity of water and its nutritional and other properties are not to be found in the two gases of which it is composed but in the complex substance which they form by their association.[2]

So, also, with human groups. It is not men as individuals, but the social structures they create—patterns carved out of a rich repertoire of possible human relationships—that constitute the realm we will explore.

We shall be studying social structures . . . What is that social structure that we call a group?

. . . we tend to focus on the individual . . .

This preoccupation . . . deflects attention from the underlying social structure, the target of sociological inquiry.

". . . The hardness of bronze
is not in the copper,
the tin or the lead,
which are its ingredients
and which are soft
and malleable bodies; it is
in their mixture." (*Durkheim*)
So, also, with human groups.
It is not men as individuals,
but the social structures
they create . . . that constitute
the realm we will explore.

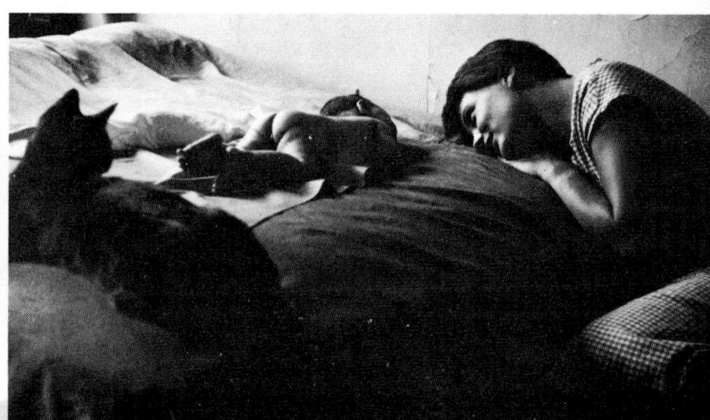

How shall we go about it?

Our aim is to learn something about the social structures that men build. All well and good, but how? Through sociology. But what is that?

Common definitions of the field are such as these: The scientific study of society (or of human behavior or social relationships or of the structure and function of society). Such definitions are acceptable, but still are rather ambiguous. We can be more specific, at the same time suggesting the procedures that characterize sociological inquiry, if we define the field this way: *Sociology is the controlled observation and interpretation of differing patterns of human relationships—their sources and consequences.* Let us consider the terms of this definition, one of which (patterns of human relationships—i.e., social structure) points to the *subject* of inquiry, while the others bear on *methods* of inquiry. First, then, for the process celebrated by Dr. Johnson:

> Let Observation with extensive view
> Survey mankind from China to Peru.[3]

Controlled observation

What is implied by this term? One aspect of controlled observation is that it has *focus*. It deals with certain things to the exclusion of others. It bars the irrelevant. First attempts at careful inquiry into human behavior are characteristically diffuse, global, and mushy. They include much that is irrelevant and so confound the hypotheses* which might be tested, making it impossible to get clear-cut and reliable answers. Sometimes we justify this sort of approach by contending that we want to get the whole picture, see society whole, or see the whole man. But neither in ordinary life, nor above all in scientific inquiry, do we "see things whole." Nor, indeed, do we wish to. The physician sees his patients as patients, the lawyer deals with clients, the teacher with students, the storekeeper with customers. Each of these views is very partial. Even our intimate friends we are far from seeing as whole persons. And

* A hypothesis (hypo = *under,* as in *hypo*dermic, under the skin—in this case, under or derived from the thesis) is a statement asserting a determinate relationship between two variables under stated conditions. Thus we might wish to test this hypothesis: Among white males aged 15–19, the lower the race-and-nationality standing of the groups they belong to, the higher the high school drop-out rate. Such a statement follows—is derived from—a more general line of thought.

in sociological inquiry we contrive a clear and specific focus by isolating those aspects of behavior which are relevant in testing our ideas about the nature of men's relationships with one another.

Controlled observation also implies a *clear-cut definition* of terms. Any body of knowledge is built through the use of abstract words called concepts. These must refer unambiguously, in the social sciences, to forms of behavior and methods of analysis. There must be no question about what we refer to when we use such words as *role, relationship, class, culture, relative deprivation,* and the like. If we are to see clearly, we must be able to communicate accurately about the things seen.

Concepts permit another feature of controlled observation, the *ordering* of the data. It is unthinkable that we could deal with our various worlds and the infinity of stimuli which pour in upon us daily if we did not organize and classify them. Whenever we use categorical terms like "women," or "the establishment," or "the administration," we are putting a number of people in certain pigeonholes on the basis of observed (or reputed) characteristics. Controlled observation requires that this be done in meticulous fashion with the criteria of classification carefully specified. Linnaeus' classification of biological forms—species, genus, family, order, class, phylum—represents such an ordering of observations. So, too, does the Periodic Table, classifying elements of the physical universe. Similarly, the sociologist may assign persons to classes differing in prestige, privilege, and power. To do so he will use such criteria as type of occupation, amount and source of income, place of residence in the community, or level of education achieved. Careful ordering of the data is an invariable aspect of controlled observation.

Another feature of controlled, in contrast to casual, observation is the development of increasingly adequate and refined *tools,* both for "seeing" and for analyzing what is seen. Adequate sampling provides such a tool, since it allows us to make observations about the whole from knowledge of the part—and within measurable and specified limits of error. Thus a probability sample of some 3,000 persons can predict how Americans will cast their votes—within the span of sampling error. (This last can be crucial as in the Truman-Dewey presidential race when the sampling error was greater than the percentage gap between the candidates.) Questionnaires, interview schedules, attitude scaling devices, measures of social affinity and social distance, probability statements, measures of relationships—these and similar instruments, and ever better ones are needed for controlled observation.

But the model of controlled observation is the *controlled experiment.* This is a way of so organizing our attack on a problem that we can identify with some assurance an influence which promotes a given outcome. Ordinarily we are too cavalier in our assumptions that such-and-such, a given "cause," produces something else which we call the result. Consider an example. We assume that the experience of taking a certain course will result in an increase in a specified kind of knowledge. In reality, several outcomes are possible. It is at least conceivable that the student might emerge from the experience quite unaffected in any perceptible degree. It is also conceivable that the course might be so confusing that he knows less at the end than he knew at the beginning. So also with his attitudes: he may be less favorably disposed toward the subject matter; or he may have been intrigued by it, stimulated, eager to pursue problems in the field long after the course has been concluded.

We can enter the same warning about commonplace assumptions about any behavior assumed to have certain "obvious" consequences. Does a spanking set the child's feet in paths of righteousness, or may its only outcome be to relieve the emotions of an infuriated parent? Does greater contact with persons of other races, nationalities, and ethnic backgrounds promote friendly attitudes, or does it increase hostility? Does the work of minister, priest, or rabbi promote moral behavior and enhance sensitivity to ethical issues, or is it a tranquilizer enabling the parishioner to persist in his iniquities with peace of mind? Do fines or imprisonment prevent the criminal from repeating his violations and deter others from doing so? Or are the results quite otherwise? How do we know?

Now it would seem obvious, to take the first example, that if we discover through a test that students entering the course know little about the subject, and by a posttest that they know considerably more, the intervening experiences in the class have "caused" the student to learn. Teachers seem to operate on this assumption. But clearly, taking a course is a very complex experience. Greater knowledge might be due to the teacher's brilliant exposition. It might be due almost exclusively to assigned reading in the course. It might result chiefly from bull sessions and similar experiences that are no part of the formal program of learning in this course. Across the span of a semester or an academic year many other influences have been playing upon the student. He has read books, newspapers, and magazines. He has talked and listened to others, both fellow students and instructors in other courses. He has listened to radio and watched television. He may even have corresponded with his parents touching on intellectual as well as financial problems. How can we attribute the change in learning (represented by the difference between his posttest and pretest scores) to the experience within that course?

The fact is that unless we attack this problem with something approaching the strategy of a controlled experiment, we cannot know. And the fact is, further, that in most of those daily-life situations where we assume that *A* causes *B*—parents train children, salesmen induce customers to buy, politicians influence voters—we do *not* really know. We take it on faith. *In any rigorous sense it is accurate to say that we do not know what we are doing.*

How might we know? We must somehow be sure that, in our illustration (Figure 1.1), the increased learning is not attributable to some out-of-class influence. We can get such assurance if there is another group of comparable students, subject to the same range of influences *except* that they are not taking the course in question. Such a group is known as a *control group.* If, in the gain from pretest to posttest, there is not much difference between the control group and the group actually taking the course (the *experimental group*), then we must conclude that the course had little influence on its unhappy subjects.[4] The control group must, of course, be like the experimental group in all relevant respects except for the presumed causal influence, or stimulus. Often our casual observations are quite wrong because the two groups compared are *not* alike in relevant respects.

For example, in every major American city we find depressed areas with slum housing and a large Negro population. A casual observer might think the Negro extremely prolific, for the streets and alleys and yards are full of children. This would confirm stereotypical propositions about the Negro which you may have heard: He is sexually promiscuous and an excessive breeder. By implication, Negroes are more fertile than whites. We are comparing differing patterns of human relationships (one dimension of the marital relationship) among whites and Negroes. Are the groups compared alike in all factors relevant to fertility excepting the experimental variable of race? The answer, of course, is that they are not.

But if we were to "make" them so by comparing the fertility of these Negroes with whites *in the same income category,* we would find the differences in fertility fading out. And income is not the only factor known to be related to fertility. Age, education, reli-

Figure 1.1
A model for controlled observation of differing patterns of human relationships

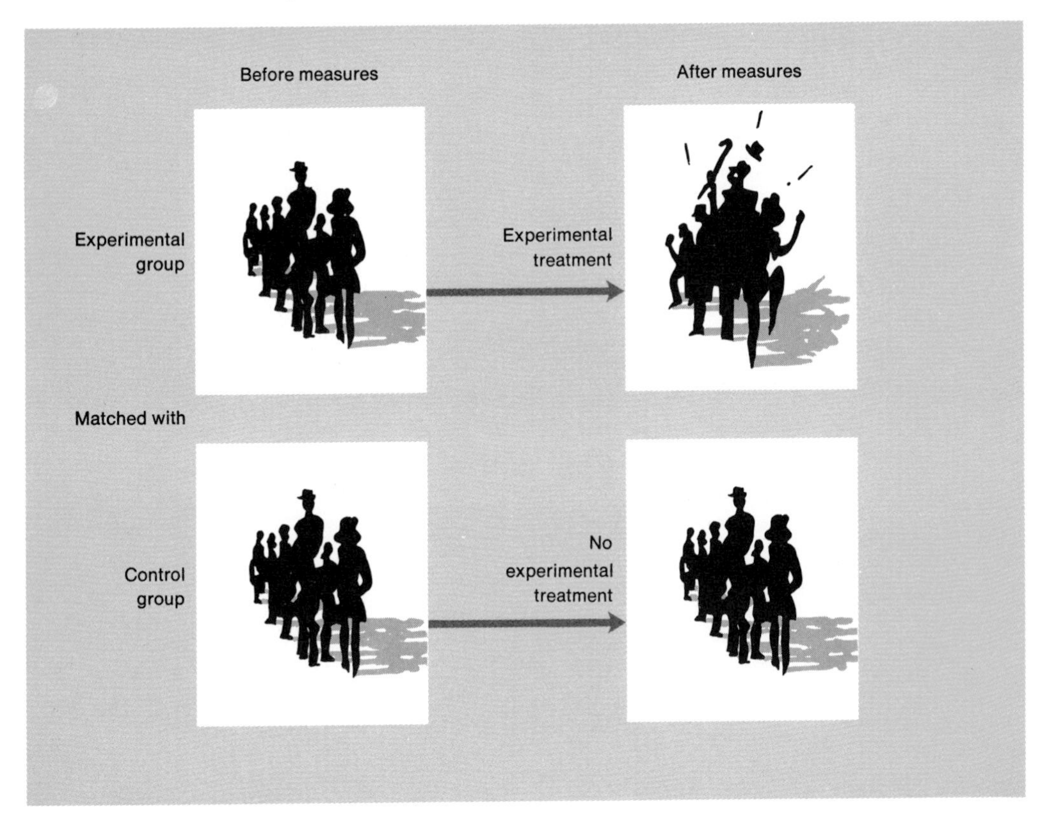

gious affiliation, and nativity are also factors which should be alike in both groups if we are to assess the influence of race on fertility. When these factors are controlled—made comparable in both groups—we find that our original observation about the excessive fertility of Negroes is quite wrong.

This process of making the control and experimental groups sufficiently alike (except for the experimental variable) is called "holding factors, or variables, constant"; or sometimes it is called "controlling the variables." A variable, incidentally, can be defined as any characteristic, any dimension of a social relationship that can take on differing values—i.e., any attribute or characteristic that varies. The distribution of such values may be either continuous, as in the distribution of numbers from zero to infinity; or it may be discrete, as in an either-or classification (white-Negro, male-female), or as in, say, a "high-medium-low" sort of classification.

There are a number of procedures for making the experimental and control groups comparable on the relevant variables. Sometimes we can control simply by eliminating irrelevant variables. For example, assume that we are testing the hypothesis that measures of the husband's authority in the household (over wife and children) decline when he is unemployed. Now in this case employment-unemployment is the independent variable, and *depending* on his employment status is some measure of his authority in the household (the dependent variable).* But it might well be that the stability of a relationship between husband and wife or between father and child varies with race, or by religion, or by level of education of the couple. In order to test the influence of unemployment in altering a man's relationship to wife and child, we *must eliminate these other possible influences.* Hence we might compare employed and unemployed who are white, Protestant, and have 12 years of education, eliminating all others.

To control by *randomizing* we follow a procedure that aims to make control and experimental groups comparable by distributing various attributes randomly (entirely by chance) as between the two groups. Suppose we were trying to assess the influence of a propaganda film on attitude toward birth control. Now certain variables such as education and religion are known to affect this attitude. Therefore we want so to distribute such variables as to make their impact the same on control and experimental groups. (In effect, their influence as between the two groups would then be canceled out.) This we could do by listing all persons alphabetically, numbering them, and then assigning all the odd-numbered (or even-numbered) persons to the control group and the others to the experimental group, which would be subjected to

* A *dependent variable* is one whose differing values we wish to explain. (For example, scores on an instrument measuring anti-Semitism range from high to low. We want to understand what makes for bigotry toward, or acceptance of, Jews.) The *independent variable* is, or represents some causally prior influence. (If, for example, we argued that exposure to different cultures reduces ethnocentric bias, we might use a measure of foreign contact as the independent variable, expecting it to vary inversely with measures of anti-Semitism.)

† Auguste Comte (1798–1857) was a French mathematician and scientist who coined the term *sociology.* (He would have preferred *social physics* had not the Belgian, Quetelet, already preempted these words as the title of one of his books. Comte is often thought of as the father of modern sociology. He saw man's understanding of the world evolving through history. The final mode was *positivism,* explanation based on controlled observation.

the supposed influence of the film. Having pretested both groups on the subject matter of the film, if on the posttest the experimental group showed greater change in attitude, we might then conclude that the film had had some influence.

In precision control, a person in the experimental group having a given cluster of traits—male, college graduate, Protestant, etc.—is matched in the control group by a person having the same attributes.

In control by frequency distribution, the frequency with which a given trait appears in the experimental group is made approximately the same as its frequency in the control group. Thus, if in the experimental group 20 percent are Catholics and 40 percent are college graduates, the same percentages must characterize the control group. But this does not require that *the same person* be both Catholic and a college graduate. In precision control, the attributes of one individual are matched by those of another. In the second case (control by frequency distribution), it is the group as a whole which is matched with another.

Sometimes we combine methods of control. For example, we might match one 70-year-old Catholic with another (precision control, and similarly with our other subjects), then flip a coin to determine who goes to control, who to experimental group. Thus we would randomize, and neutralize the distribution of unidentified variables which might otherwise confound the test of the hypothesis.

Interpretation

But sociology does not stop—nor indeed does it begin—with controlled observation. It also involves interpretation. For what is seen is always affected by the see-er. What is known is transformed by the knower. "No man," says Benedict, "ever looks at the world with pristine eyes. He sees it edited by a definite set of customs and institutions and ways of thinking."[5] And so it is that neither in everyday life nor in disciplined inquiry do "facts speak for themselves." They must be interpreted. And this is where imagination enters. Nearly two centuries ago Saint Simon remarked that there are two sources of knowledge: observation and imagination. He deprecated imagination because he thought men's minds were clouded by shoddy theological fantasies. And Saint Simon's secretary, August Comte,† systematically developed the idea that man had undergone an intellectual evolution in the course of which undisciplined imagination gave way to hardheaded observation of the facts of social life. Here is Comte, speaking:

> . . . In my inquiry into the whole course of intellectual development from its simple beginnings up to the contributions of our day, I believe I have uncovered the underlying law that, by an invariant necessity, governs the development of men's minds. This law states that each of our major ideas, every branch of knowledge, passes through three different theoretical stages: the theological (or fictitious), the metaphysical (or abstract) and the scientific (or positive). . . . Hence three sorts of philosophies or three mutually exclusive conceptual systems. The first is the necessary point of departure for the human mind. The third is its clearly destined state. And the second stage is peculiarly suited to serve as transition between them.[6]

The words "positive philosophy" and "positive method" are ambiguous ones in English. Comte used the term *natural philosophy* synonymously with *positive philosophy.* He meant that we should regard and investigate human behavior as natural phenomena; that theory ("interpretation" in our definition) was the handmaiden of observation and subject to its test; and that the notion of the *relative* was to be substituted for the old *absolutes,* testable hypotheses for unquestioned dogma.

Yet despite the emphasis on observation, Comte's position should not be construed as being hostile to interpretation, to the development of theories and those sub-theses we call hypo-theses.

> . . . if all positive theory must necessarily be based on observation, it is equally clear that, if the mind is to make anything of what is observed, it must be furnished with some sort of theory. Were we to deal with phenomena without promptly linking them with some abstract categories not only would it be impossible to combine disparate observations (and, consequently, to make any use of them) but we would be utterly incapable of remembering them. Indeed, for the most part we could not see things right under our noses.*

To celebrate the imaginative—i.e., the interpretive, or theory-building—aspect of sociology is not to minimize the first term in

* See Original Texts, Note 1.1, following Selected Supplementary Readings at the end of the text.

† The words *empirical* (adjective), *empiricist* (noun) refer to the way an *empiricist* looks at the world and knows what is there: through direct sensory experience with things. Near antonyms are *theoretical, theory, theorist.*

our definition, *observation*. Upon occasion there have been spurious, sterile, even acrimonious debates between those who thought that one or the other of these aspects of inquiry was being overdone. Those stressing tough-minded observation, treating social phenomena rigorously (as though they were things—"*comme des choses*," in Durkheim's words) have sometimes appraised the theorist as a woolly-headed dreamer, out of touch with reality, while the latter, in his turn, has spoken derisively of raw empiricists,† figure-fiddlers, and machine manipulators.

But I think we must agree with Bacon. Each of these positions is wrong because each rejects its essential complement. As he put it, "Neither the naked hand nor the understanding left to itself can effect much."[7]

> Those who have handled sciences have been either men of experiment or men of dogmas. The men of experiment are like the ant; they only collect and use; the reasoners resemble spiders, who make cobwebs out of their own substance. But the bee takes a middle course; it gathers its materials from the flowers of the garden and of the field, but transforms and digests it by a power of its own . . . experience, when it wanders in its own track is mere groping in the dark, and confounds men rather than instructs them. But when it shall proceed in accordance with a fixed law, in regular order, and without interruption, then may better things be hoped of knowledge.[8]

Of course, it is an easy resolution and a counsel of perfection to recommend the bee as model. Sociologists differ in capacities and preferences. But here we are speaking of sociology, not sociologists. And from the perspective of sociology, observation and interpretation are twin necessities. If for the moment we are stressing the importance of *interpretation*, the second term in our definition, it is because the popular view tends to minimize the part played by disciplined imagination. Science is reduced to routine formulas and techniques employed by passionless, white-coated robots with the aid of esoteric gadgets. But it is an utterly false notion that imagination is alien to science, especially to social science. The truth is quite the contrary. The theoretical aspect of sociology involves the insightful and imaginative treatment of observations. For this reason poetry, literature, and philosophy are closely related to first-rate scientific work.

But to assert that the imaginative, yet disciplined, interpretation of things observed is a *sine qua non* for sociology is simply to state a virtue. We should ask in the good American tradition how virtue pays off. What good is theory? For theory is what we build and use in interpreting a set of observations. And there is the prior question: What is meant by theory?

> In sociology, as in most scientific fields, theory is an intellectual creation, explaining the sum of the observed facts by means of a general principle from which these observations can be deduced as consequences. Theory, furthermore, provides the guidelines for future research.*

What sort of intellectual creation is this? A theory consists in a set of logically linked, general propositions which interpret the phenomena under investigation in such a way as to lead to testable hypotheses. These general propositions result from describing, ordering, and relating classes of concrete events.

This aspect of sociological inquiry is most important for the following reasons. First, it requires a public statement of the assumptions underlying a study and so makes appraisal and criticism possible. It leads to endless revision of theory, sometimes to outright rejection. Thus Freudian theory emphasizes the crucial importance of the child's early years, especially the struggle which ensues as imperious biological impulses are confronted with the repressive demands of culture. The battlefield lies within the framework of the mother-father-child triangle. Related propositions suggest that an affectionate, permissive, and supportive relationship takes much of the devastating edge off this conflict, leading to a better adjusted personality in the child. Such a relationship might be expressed in easy and late toilet training, breast feeding, avoidance of corporal punishment, and so on. We will consider Professor Sewell's test of these notions in Chapter 4. Here it is only necessary to note the use to which the theory is put: it gives rise to a testable hypothesis which states that, as between two groups of comparable children, those treated in one way will differ significantly in their personal adjustment, in their subsequent relationships with others.

Second, theory provides us with a set of categories, concepts,

* See Original Texts, Note 1.2.

† It is futile to pretend to be *au courant* by seizing on fashionable labels. In this book black and Negro simply mean U.S. citizens of African ancestry. (Of course even the word *black* is fuzzy, since it may apply to a person who, by sheerly perceptual—rather than conceptual—criteria is white.

and questions with which we confront a problematic world. It is, as it were, a pair of glasses through which we select and inspect relevant social events, classifying and relating them in such a way as to enhance our understanding of them. What we see through these glasses is governed by the key terms in a theory, those words we call concepts. These are abstract terms which summarize a rich variety of concrete beliefs and behaviors. Sociological theory makes frequent use of such concepts as culture, role, status, class, stratification, bureaucracy, attitude, mobility, structure, and institution.

Third, since theory involves general propositions, it is both economical and powerful in its interpretive capacity. It is economical in saying much with few symbols. To say that social class affects life chances is to embrace a world of events touching all age categories across a broad spectrum of experiences. Theory is powerful to the extent that its general propositions allow us to predict to a wide variety of specific instances. If, for example, we can make a general statement about minority group members, it means that we can predict what will happen, under specified conditions, not only in the case of Negroes but also where Catholics, Puerto Ricans, Jews, or orientals are involved.†

Fourth, sociological theory, the interpretation of social phenomena, is useful because it helps us see the similarities in apparently unlike events and the dissimilarities in apparently similar events. Max Weber, in *The Protestant Ethic and the Spirit of Capitalism,* develops a theory which finds a necessary feature of capitalist enterprise at the heart of a church doctrine. Durkheim's theory of suicide bridges the family, the military, and the church—i.e., finds the same causal factors operating in these disparate social settings. Later on I shall have occasion to remark about the similarities between child rearing and brainwashing. A theory of effective induction into a group may reveal similarities between boot training, entering a convent, becoming a prison inmate, or joining a business organization. To the extent that interpretation of apparently disparate events allows us to embrace them in a single theory (the rusting nail and the burning wood, both cases of oxidation), our understanding is enhanced. Adam Ferguson, a Scottish sociologist put the point well about 200 years ago:

> . . . the degree of sagacity with which [a person] is endowed is to be measured by the success with which [he] is able to find general rules applicable to a variety of cases that seemed to have nothing in common, and to discover important dis-

> tinctions between subjects which the vulgar are apt to confound.[9]

A final note—something that must be obvious in discussing the essential part played by theory: It is in theory that the work of many people from different times and places is distilled. There would be no science were the ideas and findings of various investigators scattered, separate, never being joined together or mutually confronted for the building of a structure of knowledge. Knowledge necessarily is general. And theory is the pool of general knowledge—general both in the sense of being abstract and in being a common storehouse. Theory—interpretation, explanation—is the beginning and the end of inquiry.

Differing

If there isn't any difference, it doesn't make any difference. Problems arise out of differences. This term is emphasized as a reminder that the controlled experiment is simply a way of analyzing the factors which make for such differences. In Greenwood's definition:

> An experiment is the proof [meaning "test"] of an hypothesis which seeks to hook up two factors into a causal relationship *through the study of contrasting situations* which have been controlled on all factors except the one of interest, the latter being either the hypothetical cause or the hypothetical effect."[10]

That is to say, we manipulate a situation so as to induce differences in one group while a comparable group is not so manipulated. Or, if we are unable to manipulate the situation, we may simply observe differences in behavior between two groups or categories of persons, proceeding then to ferret out another factor which *differentiates* the two groups and which might, therefore, be regarded as causal (the groups remaining comparable in other respects).

> . . . if you want to improve your understanding of something you will observe it as it changes [i.e., as *differences* emerge] and preferably as it changes under conditions that you yourself have created. . . .[11]

It may well be that the rapid development of sociology in recent decades is due to our increased exposure to differences. Both in space and in time, contrasts are now more apparent than ever before. Change occurs so rapidly that within the span of a person's lifetime there are sharp points of contrast. Whereas "around the world in 80 days" was one a breathtaking feat, as many hours would, today, be onerously slow. Hence the comparison of different forms of social organization has become frequent, easy, and inevitable.

Yet, most of us are so deeply immersed in the familiar forms of our own societies, or even restricted segments of them, that it is not easy to detect the differences. There is, therefore, an injunction involved in this term of our definition. Sociology requires us to sharpen our capacities for asking, especially with respect to customary, taken-for-granted behaviors: *"Why this instead of that?"* "Why this type of relationship rather than a different one?" We are asked to cultivate a heightened sensitivity to the existence and meaning of differences.

Patterns

This term in our definition suggests two characteristics of social phenomena: recurrences in time and concurrences in (social) space. If we try to explain differences, they are patterned differences. Different patterns of relationship—employer-employee, priest-communicant, parent-child, buyer-seller, governor-governed —persist through time. And yet we may be blind to the pattern woven by myriad individual actions. For these recurrences in social life are forests that we often fail to see for our preoccupation with the individual trees. We love and marry, a friend dies, an acquaintance is arrested. These are not marriage or mortality rates, or federal judicial statistics. We do not see them as threads in the pattern of social life. Thus through our short life-span the sequence of personal experience promotes the illusion of novelty and inconstancy.

But the condition of the social order is stability through predictable recurrences. In sociology we ask what recurrent conditions yield predictable effects. This concern with regularities in conduct does not, of course, distinguish sociology from other scientific disciplines. None of them is concerned with the unique, the idiosyncratic. Even in applied psychology, in diagnosing and prescribing for the unique individual, the therapist does so only against the background of a general knowledge of those *patterns* of individual behavior described in psychological theory. All knowledge is general and so implies patterns in the phenomena dealt with.

From another perspective, the patterning of conduct is seen in the interconnection of complementary forms of behavior. Effective induction into an organization may go along with low turnover. Ordeals and tests of physical fortitude for the young may go along with a rejection of corporal punishment of children. A high level of participation in decision making may be associated with low rates of absenteeism. Adverse attitudes toward minorities may be linked with conventional religious orientations. Restricted access to male roles in a female-dominated group may be associated with delinquency among juveniles. In all these examples there is an interweaving of behaviors in the social order that reveals a pattern. It is these differing patterns (social structures) that we try to identify and understand.

Human relationships: their sources and consequences

In defining the field of sociology I used the term *human relationships* rather than *social relationships,* to emphasize their identity. For outside a social context, the attributes we call human do not develop or mature. *These are the objects of our inquiry: the building, maintaining, and changing of human relationships.* And certainly nothing could be of greater personal concern to us; for aside from sheerly visceral pleasures, all the satisfactions of life are bound up with making, maintaining, and sometimes breaking, human relationships.

But here our interest is in the scientific rather than the personal significance of human relationships. This being the case, it is well to suggest more exactly what the concept means. A relationship is an inference derived from the behaviors of two or more people. We can represent it not by person *A* or person *B,* but by the double-headed arrow joining them and indicating its existence. This inferred bond grows out of the interaction of persons in roles: student-teacher, husband-wife, worker-employer. Roles, then, may be regarded as the unit elements in a human relationship. Here role means the performance, following culturally prescribed rules, expected of any person occupying a certain social position. It is legitimate to infer the relationship only on the basis of direct or indirect observation. That is to say, our inference may be based on the behavior of the persons as they deal with one another in their respective roles; or it may, for example, be based on our reading of a job description which states the expectations of and by employer and employee.

To state the polar roles involved in a relationship is only a beginning, and a crude one at that. The same roles (parent-child roles, for example) may be defined quite differently by different groups (Israeli Kibbutz and French peasant family); and by different categories (U.S. middle- and lower-class families). Moreover, we may analyze performance in these roles along various dimensions. The range of claims that *A* may make of *B* may be very great (as in the child's relationship to its mother), or quite restricted (as in the relationship between patient and physician). The role may be infused with emotion, or coldly calculated. The right to perform in the role and appraisal of the performance may be based on demonstrated capacity (passing a civil service examination) or on factors unrelated to performance (knowing the right person). The roles may be carried out face to face, or remotely, unwittingly, anonymously. They may be analyzed as they range from conflict to reciprocal support. Matters are further complicated because two people may be related in one pair of roles, only (a refined division of labor) or in a number of roles: employer-employee, teacher and student may also be father and son, as in the early American rural family.

Of course, no relationship stands alone. For example, the parent-child relationship is woven into larger patterns touching—and affected by—relationships at work and worship, those at school and those defined by one's role as citizen. Patterns, we call them; yet they are fluid, shifting like the images in a kaleidoscope. They differ from place to place and time to time. These differing patterns the sociologist describes. He traces their connections, seeks out their sources and their outcomes. For man is not like the lowly mule, without pride of ancestry or hope of posterity. Human relationships have both ancestry and posterity. They derive from antecedent relationships. (The husband-wife relationship is significantly shaped by each partner's antecedent parent-child relationship.) And they have consequences. (How does the relationship between husband and wife affect their child's relationships with teachers and peers?) And whether investigating sources or consequences of a given pattern of relationship, we always ask: Why this way, rather than some other way? (Why is the child rebellious, the student-teacher relationship tense rather than a fruitful teaching-learning relationship? Why are husband and wife alienated rather than harmoniously related?) There is always the contrast, implicit or explicit, with a *different* structure of relationships.

We have dealt, now, with two of your three questions: Where

are we going? and How do we get there? Now for the third: Why bother?

To what end? Why study sociology?

Sociological inquiry offers a high yield. We learn about the most important of all social objects, our self. We learn about the environing social world in which that self is nurtured. We learn how to learn. (And this is not so easy. For social patterns have obscure and complex causes. And they're obscured the more because misleading folklore has it that the workings of the human group are transparently self-evident.) And we learn, if we are action oriented, what must be known if we're to shape the world closer to our heart's desire. For it is not possible to get where you want to go if you don't know where you are. This is why the man of action needs to collaborate with the man of knowledge—especially since these are aspects of the same person. And this is the connection between social or civic problems, and sociological problems. Sociology is the logical link between social purpose and social program. Let us dwell a bit on these four answers to the question, Why bother?

The self

While it has little or nothing to do with the single individual, sociology can help us understand who we are. Indeed, just because it deals impersonally with group data, it helps us find our self. For to understand others' influence is to avoid one or more implicit falsehoods: that one is a creation without a creator, or the no less false but more flattering notion that the exclusive author of the self is one's self. We are, in fact, preeminently social. Hence the study of social phenomena helps us grasp the nature of that self. We discover our identity as we learn that a person is a fabrication, a social artifact made largely in other times, at other places, by other people.

The social world

This, of course, is the focus of our study—connections between the parts of that vastly intricate web of relationships that constitutes the social order. Perhaps excepting anthropology, sociology has no peer in opening the mind's door to the deceptively familiar world of men's social arrangements.

About that world we learn two things: what is, and why it is that way. Which is to say, we *describe* and we *explain.* Our descriptions disclose the framework of our social structure. And seeking explanations, we look for connections between the parts of that structure. We look for links between the rules that dominate our roles in church and work. We ferret out connections between patterns of governing and levels of literacy. We look for reasons underlying the curious ways that men divide their spoils, assign rewards and punishment. We trace a tie between the social structure of the family and mayhem in the streets. We uncover the ways in which social divisions produce unity. And in our explanations we attend particularly to the hidden linkages, the unintended, undetected outcomes of our social patterns.

Learning how to learn

Sociology is in a strategic position to sharpen skills of inquiry. It is a humane discipline, for it studies that humanity which can only emerge from man's life among men. Yet at the same time its tools of observation and analysis place it with the other sciences. Thus it brackets "two cultures, the scientific and humanistic, [using] the methods of science to explore the affairs of humanity."[12] The study of sociology stimulates a critical appreciation of logic and tools of inquiry characteristically lacking in the realms that bracket it. "For in the humanities the scientific method plays no part and in the sciences it is taken for granted. It is especially in sociology that it rises to the level of awareness and becomes a matter of conscious application and employment." If the humanities, especially philosophy, chiefly stress the *strategy* of inquiry, they typically shortchange the grubbery of *tactics,* the artful collection and meticulous analysis of data. If, on the other hand, the biological and physical sciences are long on tactics and the hardware of inductive research, they tend in their training to short-suit problems of strategy, the epistemological underpinnings of inquiry.* Sociology offers a special opportunity for cultivating

* Practitioners in these older disciplines are likely to pick up their epistemological assumptions—beliefs about ways reliable knowledge is gained—all unwittingly, in exposure to laboratory work. Perhaps, as Bierstedt suggests, the tardy emergence of their discipline prompts sociologists to confront more challenging epistemological questions than is true of those in the biophysical sciences whose roots press deeper into the past. So it may be that sociology profits from what Trotsky called "the privilege of historical backwardness" (Leon Trotsky, *The History of the Russian Revolution* [Ann Arbor: University of Michigan Press, n.d.], p. 4).

sensitivity to problems both of strategy and tactics of disciplined inquiry.

Informed action

The civic role requires a constant concern and occasional action in the public interest. What acts promote the general welfare is not always clear. But this we surely know: informed action is more likely to advance our ends than remedies applied to an unknown or misconceived society.

Reliable knowledge about that society is the sociologist's quest. While he is not a professional reformer, to know the sociologist's findings is a condition of effective reform. *"Voir pour prévoir,"* said Auguste Comte a century ago. And Herbert Spencer, writing a little later, noted that hardly a law is passed that is not meant to patch up an inadequate law.* He was asserting that the loftiest motives are not enough if reform is based on erroneous views of man and his society. The man of knowledge and the man of action must somehow collaborate if social change is to be effective. (Examples, in the case of the sociologist, are given in Chapter 14.)

Sociology, then, helps us learn about our selves and about our social world. It helps us learn both how to learn and how to act—not omnisciently, yet more effectively than we could in ignorance of the field.

So much for prologue and some first answers to three important questions: What are we looking for? How shall we look? And why? The rest of our work will help us expand these answers. Let us look at what's ahead.

Preview

Having discussed the nature of the field we turn to three general problems: How are human groups built? What is the makeup of the social structure that's been built? And how is that social structure changed?

Human groups—families, businesses, football teams, societies—continuously lose their members. Places are vacated in the

* Herbert Spencer lived from 1820 to 1903. Like Comte he can be regarded as a founding father of sociology. The French phrase from Comte means: See in order to foresee or, more adequately translated, Know in order to predict. A keen sense of methodological problems, a theory of social evolution, and a conviction of the need for a science of society marked Spencer's writings.

social order as people move away, die, resign, are fired, promoted, and demoted. Hence any enduring group must have replacements, a regular input of persons (Chapter 2), who are shaped to the culture (Chapter 3), through a process called socialization (Chapter 4), under the auspices of the group, family and school being chief agents (Chapter 5), resulting both in the creation of a person and the renewal of the group (Chapter 6).

In Part Two we ask: What's the makeup of this social structure that dies a little every day and daily is reborn? There are many dimensions of social structure: the age, or sex, or ethnic composition of a group; its racial or religious makeup; the composition of the labor force; the distribution of marital statuses; the structure of beliefs and political preferences. But two dimensions, in particular, are significant for our understanding of society. These are the *class structure* and the *institutional structure.*

The study of social stratification highlights inequalities in society—differences in the possession or achievement of things valued by the group. This aspect of social structure is crucially important, for it points to differences in social ancestry, differences in style of life, and for the future, differing life chances. Knowledge of class enables us to predict, for it captures a complex cluster of variables that create "different basic conditions of life at different levels of the social order."[13]

If class conjures up the image of horizontal layers (Chapter 8), we might conceive of institutions as pillars of the social edifice, supporting the social structure (Chapters 9, 10, 11). They represent the rather fixed ways of answering persistent questions: How can we depend on others to fulfill their obligations? How shall we make adults out of infants? How shall valued things be divided among us? What is to be valued? To what and to whom do we owe allegiance? How shall we resolve the inevitable differences that threaten group integrity?

The other side of the coin, social change, is the focus of inquiry in Part Three. We ask not "What sustains the social structure," but "What social factors make for changes in the group?" We will try to understand social change better by asking when, if ever, deviant behavior is a signal of social change (Chapter 12), what changes in the social order were wrought by the shift from a rural-agrarian to an urban-industrial society (Chapter 13) and how, sometimes, change is consciously contrived (Chapter 14).

An epilogue on sociology as a profession (Chapter 15) concludes our work.

Now it is time to begin.

References

TEXT

1. Jacques Barzun and Henry F. Graff make this statement in their book, *The Modern Researcher* (New York: Harcourt, Brace & World, Inc., 1962), p. 224.
2. Emile Durkheim, *The Rules of Sociological Method,* ed., George E. G. Catlin, trans. Sarah A. Solovay and John H. Mueller (Chicago: University of Chicago Press, 1938), pp. xlvii and xlviii, *passim.*
3. Samuel Johnson, "The Vanity of Human Wishes," *Rasselas,* chap. x.
4. The foregoing is an application of J. S. Mill's method of difference: "If an instance in which the phenomenon under investigation occurs, and an instance in which it does not occur, have every circumstance in common save one, that one occurring only in the former; the circumstance in which alone the two instances differ is . . . the cause . . . of the phenomenon" (John Stuart Mill, *A System of Logic* [New York: Longmans, Green & Co., Inc., 1884]).
5. Ruth Benedict, *Patterns of Culture* (New York: Mentor Paperback, 1952).
6. This isn't quite true. He spoke, of course, in French. If the reader would like to see how Comte *really* said it, he should refer to Original Texts, Note 1.

   I would like to step aside, occasionally, to let better informed, more literate, and more distinguished persons speak to the reader, even when they speak a different language. A university is a place of many ideas and many tongues. Important ideas are better conveyed in their own tongue than through the awkward intervention of an interpreter. Where the student can do so independently, or with another's help, he is urged to read the original statement, given at the end of the text, following the Selected Supplementary Readings, rather than, or in addition to the translation provided in the text.
7. Francis Bacon, *Novum Organum,* "Aphorisms Concerning the Interpretation of Nature and the Kingdom of Man" (London: George Routledge & Sons, New Universal Library, n.d.), pp. 60, 64.
8. *Ibid.,* p. 121. Dualisms are dangerous, and this as much as most. In reality, the "men of experiment" do not pose their problems or select their data in random fashion. Nor are "men of reason" able to divorce themselves from the concrete events in which they are implicated. The former are theorists by default; the latter empiricists because they are sensate, more or less integrated beings. Whether desirable or not, I doubt that we can achieve that schizoid separation of interpretation from observation implied in the statement attributed to Darwin: "It is a fatal fault to reason whilst observing, though so necessary beforehand and so useful afterward" (*The Autobiography of Charles Darwin 1809–1882,* ed. with an Appendix and Notes by his granddaughter Nora Barlow [New York: Harcourt, Brace & Co., Inc., 1959], p. 159).

   About 30 years later the American sociologist, Charles Horton Cooley resolved the theorist-versus-empiricist opposition this way. He wrote: "A little detailed research quickens insight; too much paralyses the imagination. One must flee both extremes and must alternate generalizations with close observation" (*Journals,* Vol. 10 [1895], p. 28 and cited by E. C. Jandy, *Charles Horton Cooley: His Life and His Social Theory* [New York: Dryden Press, 1942], p. 232).
9. Adam Ferguson, *An Essay on the History of Civil Society* (8th ed.; Philadelphia: A. Finley, Publisher, 1819), p. 49.
10. Ernest Greenwood, *Experimental Sociology* (New York: King's Crown Press, 1949), p. 28.
11. Theodore M. Newcomb citing the late Professor Kurt Lewin, *The Acquaintance Process* (New York: Holt, Rinehart & Winston, Inc., 1961), p. 3.
12. This and the following quotation are from Robert Bierstedt, "Sociology and General Education," in Charles H. Page (ed.), *Sociology and Contemporary Education* (New York: Random House, Inc., 1964), pp. 54 and 45 respectively.
13. Melvin Kohn, "Social Class and Parent-Child Relationships," *American Journal of Sociology,* Vol. 58, No. 4 (January, 1963), p. 471.

part one

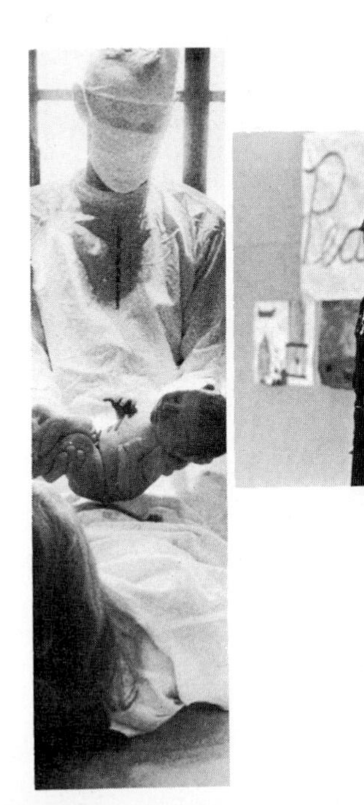

Building the group

The cubes are roles, the building blocks of social structure—priest, thief, student, wife, and a host of others. Roles are defined by rules (the squares) which shape and limit performance in them. Connecting the roles are lines, the relationships that form a group. The group itself is constantly changing as those moving and dying are replaced by newcomers.

2. *Newcomers: creating members and replacing losses*
3. *Rules for newcomers: the cultural framework of the social order*
4. *Process of cultural transmission: socialization*
5. *Agent of cultural transmission: the group*
6. *Product of cultural transmission: the person and the group*

chapter 2 **Newcomers: creating members and replacing losses**

chapter 2 Newcomers: creating members and replacing losses

Come Malthus, and in Ciceronian Prose
Show how a rutting population grows
Till all the produce of the soil is spent
And brats expire for lack of aliment.
Science finds out ingenious ways to kill
Strong men, and keep alive his weak and ill,
That these a sickly progeny may breed,
Too poor to tax, too numerous to feed.
A journalist contemporary of Malthus

The common conception of a group is misleading. It is not a collection of people.* But if a group does not consist in people, it nonetheless requires them. And since men are both mortal and migrant, group survival requires continuous replacement.

The sociologist studies population, then, because a regular input of individuals is needed to man the ship—of state, or any other sector of the social order; to staff a business, factory, or

* A group consists of one or more relationships whose boundaries are marked by the interlocking of differentiated roles and a common mission. Teams, clubs, businesses, worshippers, political organizations have these characteristics. Groups may exist regardless of the particular set of persons in various roles. (Think of the constantly shifting population of a university.) But they cannot exist apart from a given arrangement of roles and relationships.

The concept *group* is often loosely used to include anything, in size, from a couple school, a team, a club, or a community. Hence we can think of demography (the study of population growth and composition) as treating the raw materials, the newcomers who, through socialization,† are transformed into group members.

Obviously variations in size and sort of input affect the human group. (As Hitler began to ravish Europe in the 1930's, his military strength was diminished for lack of males not born during World War I, 1914–17.) Thus a first problem is this: What conditions are set for the social order by demographic phenomena? We must look, then, to the general effects on society of changes in births, deaths, and migration rates. Along with changing length of life and composition of the population, these are the variables that affect group survival. In passing we shall touch on the disruptions of the system resulting from over- and underreplacement.

But the problem of system maintenance is more complex than this. For if we look at the occupational structure of a community, its division into men and women, religious classifications such as Catholic, Jew, and Protestant, categories like Negro and white—with these and scores of other categories, the problem of replacement becomes enormously complex. Replacement is not a matter of gross numbers, but a continuous filling of finely differentiated social roles having different weight and meaning for the social order. (How do we rebuild our fading force of shepherds? Senator McCarran saw to the importing of Basques, just as previous statesmen had seen that Chinese were imported for unskilled labor on western railroads. How do we continually fill the roles of teachers, or physicians? In part by encouraging the upward mobility of middle- and lower-class males.)

But beyond the sheer quantity of persons available to man a group's roles, there is the effect of numbers on the quality or character of interaction. How do changing numbers affect the nature of the social bond?

It is not only the case that population changes affect the group. Group differences make for different demographic outcomes. Thus we must look at the other side of the coin: the impact of the social order on population variables. We have only to think of Catho-

to a nation. Sometimes it is used when the words *category*, or *aggregate* would be more precise. A category is a classification of persons whose boundaries are set by the fact of sharing one or more traits in common, for example, males, aged 15–19. An aggregate is a set of individuals whose boundaries are set by their occupancy of a certain area, for example, the population of Westchester county.

† Socialization is the process of group renewal as newcomers are transformed into full-fledged members. Socialization is the subject of Chapter 4.

lic and communist doctrines which agree, for quite different reasons, in opposing contraceptive techniques that would limit population growth. In our society, level of income and of education have been social characteristics inversely associated with fertility. In India, a rigidly stratified society, low levels of literacy, a highly developed religious life, a weak central government, subservience to foreign interests, subsistence agriculture—these social characteristics contributed, in the past, to high birth and death rates.[1] With the help of Davis and Blake,[2] we shall consider the many points at which the social order sets conditions for fertility and, thus, for replacement of losses. On the same theme, we shall look at two other studies that point to social and cultural influences on population. In one, we find evidence that certain elements of our culture prompt people to manipulate the boy-girl balance in their families.[3] A second study asks whether, and to what extent, diffusion of urban values lowers fertility rates.[4]

Now let us turn to the first of our two problems: How do population variables affect the social order?

Demographic conditions affecting the social order

The crucial notion in understanding the link between demographic and social phenomena is this: an input of human organisms (presently to be socialized) is essential to staff the system. For human groups, like organisms, die a little every day. And daily the group must be rebuilt. People—culture carriers—must be fed into the system in appropriate numbers, balancing losses from death and emigration with births and immigration. Furthermore, they must be fed into appropriate sectors of the system; for how they are to be socialized depends in large measure upon whom they are born to. So it is that birth and death, immigration and emigration, become important considerations for the maintenance of the group.

When we have a fair match between input and output, we have a basic condition for a stable system. When a community's population grows markedly and rapidly—or declines—strains are introduced. These are periods of rapid change. The contrary system, a stable social order, can be oversimply represented by a football team. A condition for its continuance as a group is the regular replacement of lost parts. There are 11 distinct roles. (Were we to classify ends, tackles, guards, and halfbacks together we might settle for seven roles.) Fatigue, injuries, and graduation, like deaths and migration in the larger social order, *require re-*

2. *Newcomers*

. . . since men are both mortal and migrant,
group survival
requires continuous
replacement. . . .
an increase in numbers,
in size of group,
can transform
the nature
of human relationships.

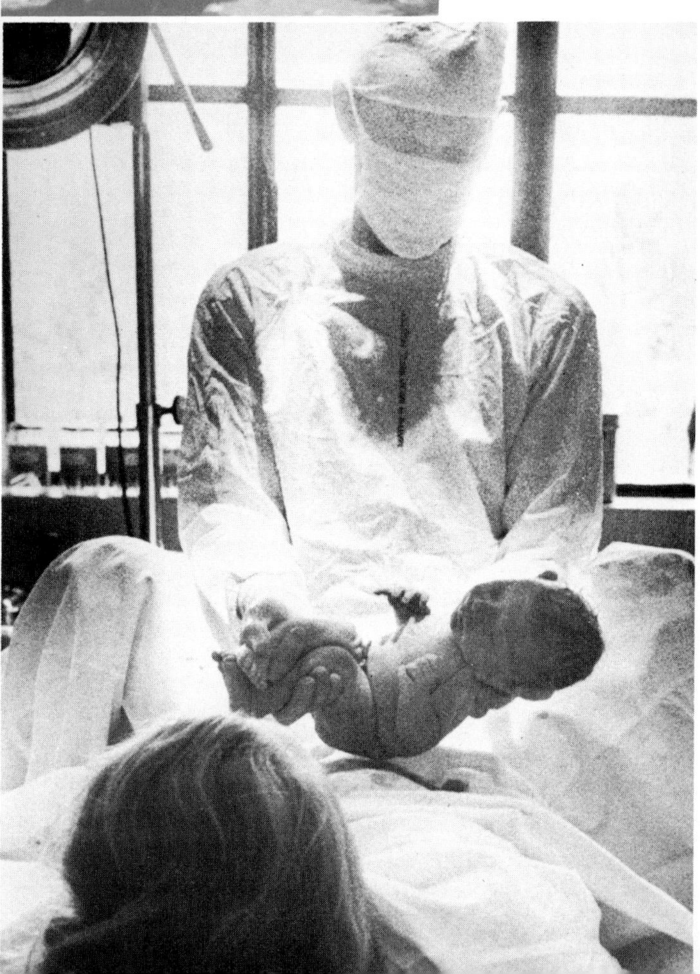

With three instead of two. . . .
the possibility of mediation,
arbitration, as the third seeks to resolve
some difference between the two. . . .

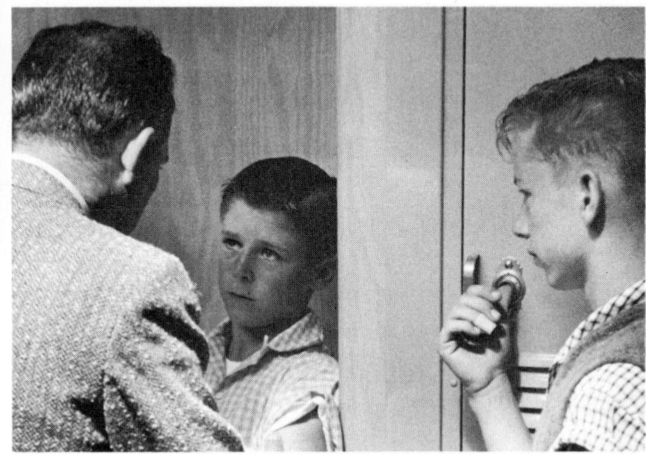

. . . the mortar of human relationships
comes to be people's interdependence
based upon differences
rather than their common cause
founded in likenesses.

placements, part for part. If this proves impossible, the team falls apart. The group is destroyed.

Similarly our labor force in American society requires regular replacements for its maintenance. But beyond this, if the order is to sustain itself, *as is,* we must have a regular recruitment and replacement of Catholics, Protestants, and Jews; Negroes and whites; old, middle-aged, and young; men and women; foreign- and native-born; the law-abiding and criminals of various sorts. . . . Let us take the last category as an example. If we are to maintain that web of relationships represented in a police force of given size, insurance salesmen and the customers they protect against losses from theft; the Pinkerton people and sundry "private eye" outfits; all those employed in the lock, bolt, and safe business; tool and weapon, car and radio manufacturers; lawyers, judges, and the clerical apparatus of the courts, and the taxpayer who supports them; prison personnel and the sociologist specializing in criminology—if we are to maintain the relationships implied by these role labels, then we must have a regular input of criminals into the social order. (Regular replacement of our criminal population is, of course, different from sheer replacement of bodies through birth. But the former entails the latter.)

This immediately suggests that a social system is never literally maintained. Quite aside from unplanned change, we are always trying to alter certain aspects of it deemed by some to be undesirable. Stability of the system is not necessarily to be viewed as a good in itself. But from the sociologist's point of view, the unreal condition of a stable system is a most useful heuristic device (a thinking tool). For it provides a base point, a point of comparison. We can then ask the question: How much does what we observe differ from what would have occurred under conditions of stability, of a balanced input and output? And then the second and intriguing question: What accounts for this difference?

The general problem of population replacement

Births and deaths

The extent of balance between input and output in a human population can be crudely measured by the rate of natural increase (disregarding net migration for the moment). The crude rate of natural increase (CRNI) is given by the difference between the crude birth rate and the crude death rate (CBR − CDR = CRNI).

The CBR is measured by dividing the number of births in a given community over a period of one year by the number of persons living in that community.* This gives us a statement of births per person. It is typically modified to make it a more intelligible and manipulable figure by changing it to births per thousand persons. So the CBR is defined, for a given community, as

$$\frac{\text{Number of births in a year}}{\text{Population of given community}} \times 1{,}000$$

The death rate (the CDR) is similarly defined. The difference between the two, then, is a measure of input, of natural increase. For the United States in 1968 the CBR was 17.4 and the CDR was 9.6. Thus the CRNI was 7.8 or 0.78 per hundred (about three fourths of 1 percent per year).

These rates, incidentally, are called crude because they represent unrefined and possibly misleading observations. If we compare two communities, observing that in one the CBR is 30.0 and the other 0.0, we are likely to miss the boat—despite the fact that the observations are "correct"—if we blithely accept popular explanations: differences in race, or leisure time, or fecundity.† We cannot begin to interpret differences in population input until we have controlled or taken account of variables that affect fertility—differences in age distribution, religion, median income, occupational structure, and education to name a few. For the hypothetical communities cited, we might find, in the first, people who are predominantly between ages 17 and 35, and in the second—say, a war-ravaged community—only the very young and the very old. For this reason it is common to gather age-specific data. Thus, when we compare two populations, we can be sure that differences in fertility are not simply due to differences in age. That is to say, we control the variable of age.‡ And so, also, with other variables that must often be controlled for adequate interpretation of demographic data.

When input exactly matches output—i.e., when CBR − CDR = 0 —we have a stable population of a special sort: a *stationary* one. (A population may also be stable when the rate of growth or de-

* Since this number changes from time to time throughout the year, the number of persons estimated to be residing in that community, state, or nation at year's midpoint is often taken as the denominator.

† Fecundity means biological capacity to reproduce. Fertility, on the other hand, means the rate of reproduction actually observed in a group.

‡ See Aside on Methods, Number 1: "A Way of Controlling Certain Demographic Observations," page 610.

cline persists from generation to generation. Social conditions may then be geared to regular change rates in population.) The situation of a stationary population, where input provides precisely and continuously the personnel necessary to man the social structure, may be viewed as a theoretical limit which does not, in fact, occur. Normally, growth exceeds or falls short of demands or resources of the social order. This is what exercised the Reverend Thomas Malthus, "a kindly, gentle, sensitive and sincere Christian minister [whose name nonetheless] stands for a cruel, mechanical doctrine of despair."[5] He saw population growth constantly threatening to outstrip resources. Responding to what he deemed an almost irresponsible naïveté on the part of a fellow cleric, William Godwin,[6] Malthus felt it imperative to confront the reality of man's two primal, and irreconcilable, biological drives, sex and hunger. He wrote:

> . . . the power of population is indefinitely greater than the power in the earth to produce subsistence for man.
>
> Population, when unchecked, increases in a geometrical ratio. Subsistence increases only in an arithmetical ratio.[7]
>
> . . . .
>
> Taking the population of the world at any number, a thousand millions, for instance, the human species would increase in the ratio of—1,2,4,8,16,32,64,128,256,512, &c. and subsistence as—1,2,3,4,5,6,7,8,9,10, &c. In two centuries and a quarter, the population would be to the means of subsistence as 512 to 10: in three centuries as 4096 to 13, and in two thousand years the difference would be almost incalculable, though the produce in that time would have increased to an immense extent.[8]
>
> . . . .
>
> By that law of our nature which makes food necessary to the life of man, the effects of these two unequal powers must be kept equal.
>
> This implies a strong and constantly operating check on population from the difficulty of subsistence. This difficulty [of matching reproductive performance and available food] must fall somewhere and must necessarily be severely felt by a large portion of mankind.[9]

The "constantly operating check(s)" were those disasters that periodically decimate populations: war, plague, famine. Malthus held out little hope that another sort of check, a preventive one called "moral restraint," would ward off the catastrophic knife thrusts of the positive checks. We could predict then, that any population, given a certain subsistence base, would increase, at first slowly and then with increasing speed until, reaching the point of saturation, numbers would level off, before long being cut back to size through disease and death. The picture Malthus paints is much the same as the often demonstrated growth of the fruit fly, *Drosophila melanogaster* on a limited subsistence base. The growth curve that emerges was first given prominence mathematically by Raymond Pearl and Lowell J. Reed. It looks like Figure 2.1, and it may indeed represent the situation of culturally crude accommodation of organism to environment. *X* marks the spot in this figure at which malnutrition, epidemics, the aggressive ravaging of foreign territories occur, decimating the population, which then begins, slowly, to repeat the cycle.

So far as we can estimate past populations—and the data are poor—over most of the centuries past, world population has remained sparsely distributed and at a low level. If, among most human groups, culture was little elaborated, approaching, to a degree, the condition of nonhuman organisms, Malthus' conception of a miserably monotonous and monotonously miserable pattern of population growth and decline may have had some substance. Sounding this somber note and insisting that no conceivable advances in agriculture could possibly offset the ultimate curse of man's reproductive propensities, Malthus elicited the twitting verse that heads this chapter.*

Whether a theory of population growth is somber or distasteful is irrelevant. The sociologist cannot prefer the "sweet mirage" to "bitter, barren truth."[10] We have to ask: Is it accurate? (Not: Is it pleasant?) Does it fit our observations? Or, under what condi-

* Perhaps you will recall Jonathan Swift's answer to the Malthusian dilemma (although he saw its source in an evil English colonialism rather than in irremediable biological impulses). His solution for a population so burgeoning as to entail death and deprivation for the Irish is found in *A Modest Proposal for Preventing the Children of Poor People in Ireland from Being a Burden to Their Parents or Country, and for Making them Beneficial to the Public* (1729):

"It is a melancholy object to those who walk through this great town [Dublin] or travel in the country, when they see the streets, the roads, and cabin doors, crowded with beggars of the female sex, followed by three, four, or six children, all in rags and importuning every passenger for an alms. . . .

"I think it is agreed by all parties that this prodigious number of children in the arms, or on the backs, or at the heels of their mothers, and frequently of their fathers, is in the present deplorable state of the kingdom a very great additional grievance; and, therefore, whoever could find out a fair, cheap, and easy method of making these children sound, useful members of the commonwealth, would deserve so well of the public as to have his statue set up for a preserver of the nation. . . .

"I do therefore humbly offer it to public consideration that of the 120,000 children

Figure 2.1

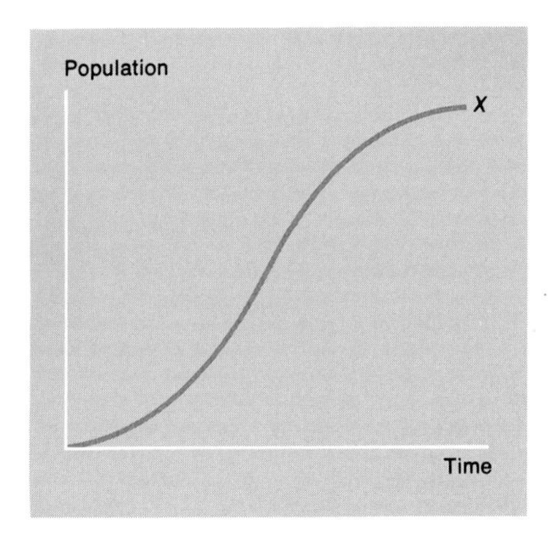

tions is it true? And when not true? For example, does the Malthusian model fit our estimates of world population growth over the last three and one-half centuries? (Figures 2.1 and 2.2). Or consider the growth of population in the United States (as Malthus himself did, noting that the population was doubling every 25 years). How does it happen, then, that this population on a virgin continent has not continued to expand at the rate predicted by Malthus' theory (see Figure 2.3); or that it has not been cut back to size despite a fairly sizable growth? How does one explain the fact that Eire's population is today half of what it was 100 years ago, yet without the intervention of Malthus' positive checks? Is it due simply to gut and glands that certain Americans who threatened to vanish are no longer "vanishing Americans" but are re-

already computed, 20,000 may be reserved for breed, whereof only one-fourth part to be males . . . one male will be sufficient to serve four females. That the remaining 100,000 may, at a year old, be offered in sale to the persons of quality and fortune throughout the kingdom; always advising the mother to let them suck plentifully in the last month, so as to render them plump and fat for a good table. A child will make two dishes at an entertainment for friends; and when the family dines alone, the fore or hind quarter will make a reasonable dish, and seasoned with a little pepper or salt will be very good boiled on the fourth day, especially in winter. . . .

"I believe no gentleman would repine to give 10 shillings for the carcass of a good fat child, which, as I have said, will make four dishes of excellent meat, when he has only some particular friend or his own family to dine with him. Thus the squire will learn to be a good landlord, and grow popular among the tenants; the mother will have 8 shillings net profit, and be fit for work till she produces another child" (Taken from Paul Robert Lieder, Robert Morss Lovett, and Robert Kilburn Root, *British Poetry and Prose* [New York: Houghton Mifflin Co., 1928], pp. 495–99, *passim*).

Figure 2.2
Estimated world population for selected years, 1650–1970

Figures for these nine years are: 0.5, 0.7, 0.9, 1.2, 1.6, 2.4, 3.0, 3.7, and 6.3 billion respectively.

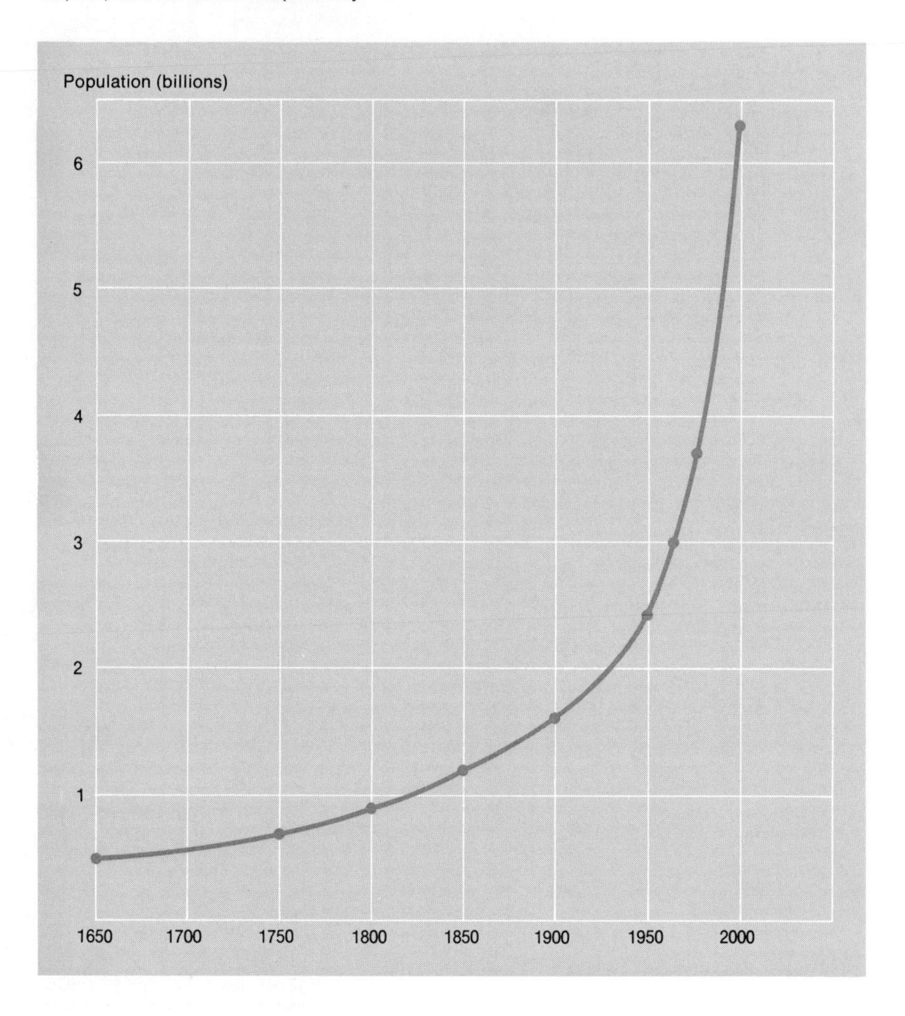

producing at a rapid rate? Why does it happen that peoples with about the same reproductive potentials and having available similar resources vary so emphatically in their population growth?

Our general answer must be that Malthus' interpretation of population growth neglects social variables. Commonsense might confirm his notion that inflated fertility rates would gobble up the gains in agricultural productivity enabled by science. (And this comes close to being the situation in India.) But it is pre-

Figure 2.3
The growth of U.S. population, 1790–1970

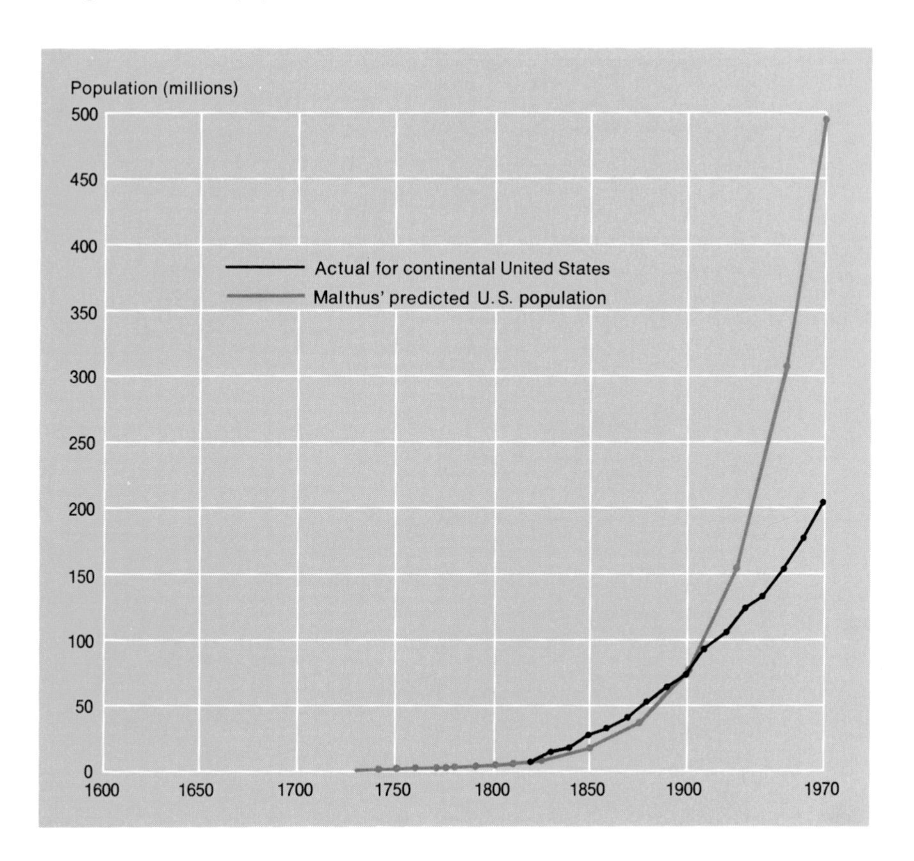

Year	U.S. census	Malthus' formula	Year	U.S. census	Malthus' formula
1650	0.05		1825		9.6
1660	0.08		1830	12.9	
1670	0.1		1840	17.1	
1680	0.2		1850	23.2	19.3
1690	0.2		1860	31.4	
1700	0.3		1870	39.3	
1710	0.4		1875		38.6
1720	0.5		1880	50.2	
1730	0.6		1890	62.9	
1740	0.9		1900	76.0	77.2
1750	1.2	1.2	1910	92.0	
1760	1.6		1920	105.7	
1770	2.2		1925		154.5
1775		2.4	1930	122.8	
1780	2.8		1940	131.7	
1790	3.9		1950	154.2	309.0
1800	5.3	4.8	1960	179.3	
1810	7.2		1970	204+	494.4
1820	9.6				

cisely where such gains have been greatest that fertility has declined. Lower birth rates seem to go along with advances in science and technology and with the generally high level of educational achievement that underlies such advances. Fertility is low where there is a relatively high standard of living, a fair degree of upward mobility, values that go beyond traditionalism (when they do not actively oppose it). And, speaking of values, certainly non-Malthusian possibilities emerge when we look at the changed distribution of children per family in Great Britain, contrasting the situation in 1860 with that in 1925. The data are presented in Figure 2.4.

The flat curve in 1860 suggests the random influence of a number of unknown factors influencing the growth of population (and excluding, generally, the intent of the marriage partners). But the dramatically different curve for 1925 showing that 67 percent of British married couples had one, two, or no children reveals purpose and planning. Such general limitation of family size means commonly held values—a standard of living to be maintained, a status to be achieved, the desire to invest more in fewer children, general support given medicine and biological science, so reducing mortality and making possible three survivors out of three births rather than three out of six, and so on.

Let us put it this way: rate and type of population growth reflect people's values. People's values reflect the nature of the social order. The fact that actions or decisions bearing on population growth are individually made tends to obscure both their cumulative social effect and their source in the conditions of society. Even in groups where no *preventive* measures are commonly undertaken to control the growth of population (contraception, postponement of marriage, esteem of celibacy) or where there are practices unplanned but promoting control (protracted military service, hazardous male occupations, like fishing, that promote an unbalanced sex ratio) *curative* measures may be practiced: abortion, infanticide, and the like. Very generally, that is to say, the link between population and the social order is tacitly acknowledged in behaviors that have the latent function of adjusting input to system requirements.

But such an adjustment is a matter of extraordinary intricacy —more so than this formula suggests:

$$\text{Population} = \frac{T \times R}{LL}$$

Figure 2.4
Distribution of family size in England and Wales (1860) and in Great Britain (1925)

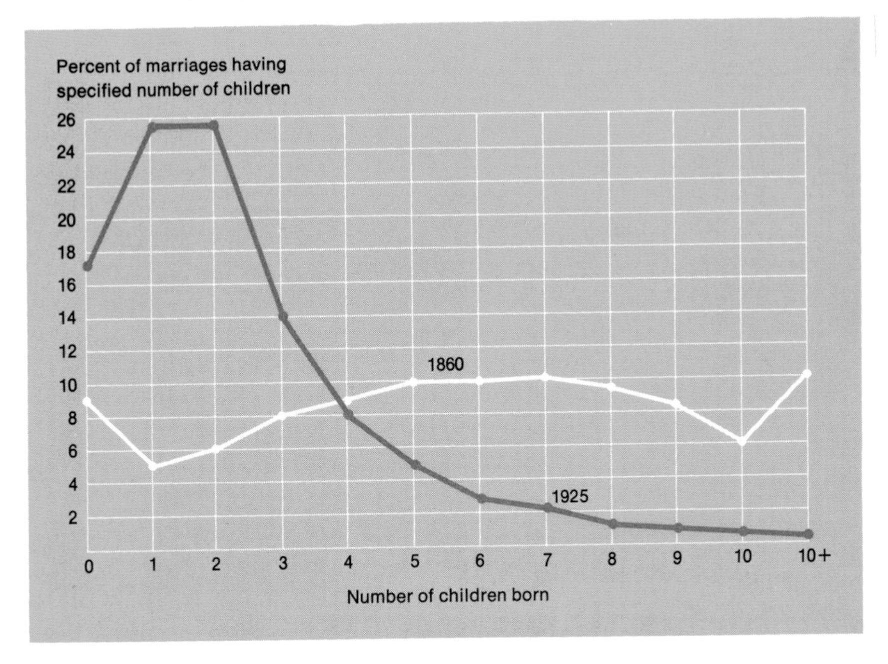

(where T means technology, R stands for resources, and LL refers to level of living). Thus, to maintain the balance between the two sides of the equation, an increase in population would require an increase in the value of T or R or both. Conversely—and this is more clearly seen if we convert the equation to

$$LL = \frac{T \times R}{P}$$

—a decline in population enables an increase in the level of living. (One is reminded of Carlyle's statement: "The fraction of life can be increased in value not so much by increasing your numerator as by lessening your denominator. . . . Make thy claim to wages zero, then; thou hast the world at thy feet."[11]

But what is implied in such a formula? Both T and R depend on the rate of savings and investment, on invention and scientific work, and these upon the available cultural backlog and the means and interest in diffusing scholarly knowledge. All of these depend on the extent and quality of education. Education will vary depending on the level of economic development and the complexity of the culture. The level of economic development is linked with the form of government, with modes of production and distribution.

In Marx's view, these were so fundamental that we cannot properly speak of population problems, but rather of problems of economic organization. Various modes of economic organization have population problems peculiar to them. In his own day he insisted that:

> The laboring population . . . produces—along with the accumulation of capital produced by it—the means by which itself is made relatively superfluous [i.e., it creates of itself a surplus population]—and it does this to an always increasing extent. This is a law of population peculiar to the capitalist mode of production; and, in fact, every special historic mode of production has its own special laws of population, historically valid within its limits alone. An abstract law of population [like Malthus'] exists for plants and animals only, and only in so far as man has not interfered with them.[12]

In recent years Communist China has vacillated between this orthodox Marxist position and the desperately felt need to limit the growth of the largest nation, now numbering about a quarter of the world's population.

Marx's correction of Malthus lies not only in stressing the error of a sheerly biological view of population growth but also in asserting that variations in the biological realm are themselves outcomes (as well as reinforcing sources) of the social order. But if it is right to assert that population input is influenced by the nature of the economy, it is wrong to regard the economic subsystem as the only one bearing on population problems. The socializing institutions, family and school, the church and the values there affirmed, the political system, the extent and mode of institutionalizing scientific development—all of these institutions with everything they imply, including their complex interweaving, affect and are affected by rate of population growth.

Now the supply or replenishing of a social order is clearly not a mere matter of input, of balance between birth rate and agricultural productivity. Nor, indeed, is it a matter solely of social factors conditioning the birth rate. The maintenance of a social order depends upon length of life or, more grimly, upon death. If 10 men remain on the job in one factory for 10 years but in a second factory the average tenure is 5 years, then, other things being equal, we will need 20 men—twice as many—to staff the second plant. We need to double the birth rate to compensate for a doubled death rate. It makes a difference, in staffing a society, that the infant mortality rate is over 150 in Egypt and under 20 in Sweden. It makes a difference that, at birth, a male child in the United States may expect to live better than 20 years longer than his counterpart in Guatemala.* Deaths as well as births, mortality and longevity as well as fertility, must be taken into account as we study the continuous rebuilding of groups.

Imagine a society in which men were immortal, each role permanently, and with consistent competence, filled by the same person. Obviously, this society would require no input. We would have a stable, an unchanging social order. This limiting case is not closely approximated in reality.

But why not? Because of death, emigration, and internal role-shifting. Our attention here is focused on death (or on any disability rendering a person incompetent to perform as parent, worker, communicant, citizen, learner, and so on). Death or disability represent output. Birth is the input counterpart.

Now one might suppose that where the death rate is high, there must likewise be a counterbalance in the birth rate if the role structure is to be maintained (apart from migration or some internal rearrangement of roles). "Must," that is, if the group is to sustain itself. For either lack or oversupply of role incumbents places stress on the social network. An oversupply may mean such things as unemployment, schools operating in shifts with inadequate facilities and hastily certified teachers, erstwhile-teachers-then-mothers leaving their families in response to a flood of school-age children, inadequate housing, a strain on public services. An undersupply may entail the flight of factories, a loss of tax base for public services, redefinition of parental and spouse roles, an emphasis on technology to supply mechanical hands to substitute for the missing human hands, and a score or more of other outcomes. Thus the tendency would be, one might suppose, for birth rates and death rates to vary together. Certainly, if there is any tendency toward equilibrium in a social system, or conversely if there is any stress induced when certain roles fail to be fulfilled (or are oversupplied), then we would expect that birth

* See, for such data as these, the *Demographic Yearbook* published annually, in New York, by the statistical office of the United Nations.

and death rates would not vary randomly but would tend to move together. Figure 2.5 suggests that this has been so in the United States. Assuming that death rates for the first three decades were in fact higher (the only data available for this period were those from Massachusetts, which probably enjoyed lower mortality rates than the country as a whole) and that birth rates for the 1945–65 period would have been lower were it not for making up for marriages and births deferred during depression and early war years, then we have roughly parallel declines in these rates. A measure of the relationship between birth and death rates at 43 time points from 1860 on gives us a correlation coefficient (r) of +.79.* This is a fairly strong relationship. (A perfect relationship would be 1.0, meaning that for every unit of change in one variable a predictable change occurs in the other variable. We square this figure to learn what part of the variance in the death rate can be predicted from knowledge of the birth rate. The figure is 62 percent.)

In general, demographic findings suggest some fit between the level of these vital rates and the social and economic conditions of community or society. Where fertility is high, mortality rates are likely to be high, also, as in isolated rural communities depending on extractive industry: agriculture, mining, forestry, or fishing. In urban commercial and industrial settings, on the other hand, both rates are likely to be low.

The historical shift has been from the high to the low, and oftentimes we find a period of transition between the two conditions. This period of demographic transition is one in which better control over death is achieved, dropping mortality rates while fertility continues high. As a result, the rate of natural increase is

* We will run across the correlation coefficient from time to time—one among a number of measures of association between variables. When we come to An Aside on Methods, Number 7, you may wish to get better acquainted with it.

† This is a good place to remind ourselves that the group need not be maintained exclusively by a balance of births and deaths. In a moment we will turn to immigration and longevity as they affect the staffing of the social order. But in addition, it may be that an imbalance in one social sector may offset a complementary imbalance elsewhere. For example, a relatively low death rate and continuing high birth rate in one category may supply the blue-collar workers that low birth rates in another category fail to provide. Thus the very fact that there is not a stable input-output relationship in one sector of the population could be a prime factor in maintaining balance in the system as a whole.

‡ Relating daughters to mothers is simpler and gives about the same value for generational replacement as though we had used daughters + sons related to mothers + fathers.

Figure 2.5
Birth and death rates, United States, 1860–1967

Mortality data for 1860 through 1890 are for Massachusetts only and are doubtless understatements of the U.S. death rates.

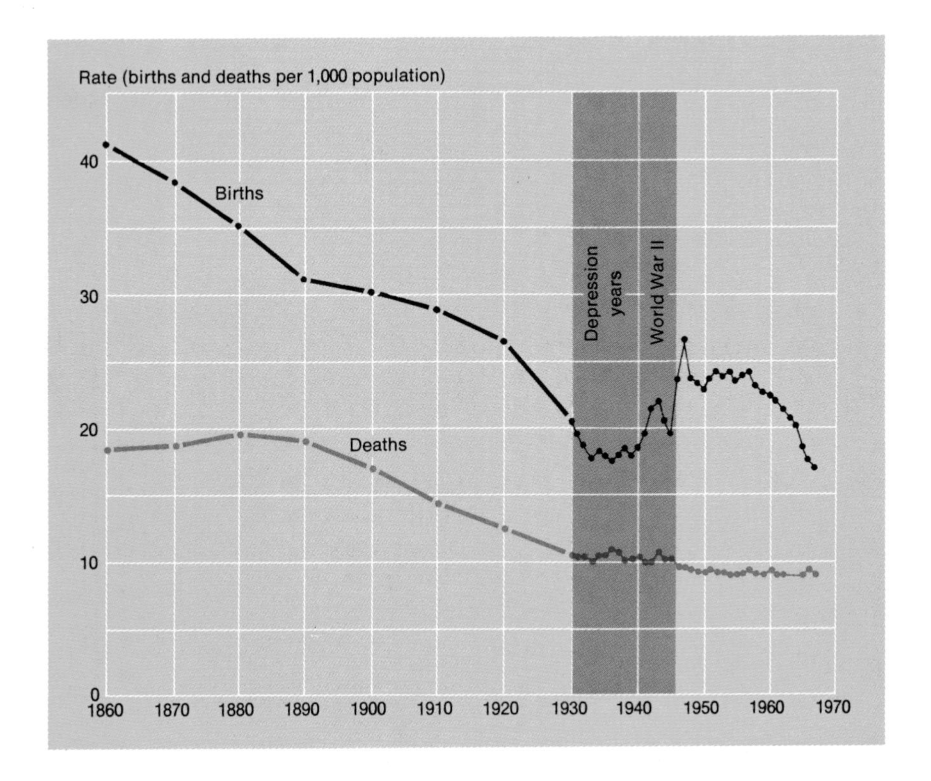

higher during this period than in preceding or succeeding stages. There will be more than enough sons to replace the fathers.

The extent to which birth and death rates are so adjusted that the deaths of the fathers are offset by the births of sons† (and mothers replaced by daughters) is measured by a demographic device called the net reproduction rate (NRR). It tells us the extent to which one generation is replaced by its successor (assuming that birth and death rates persist over a period of time). Exact replacement gives us a net reproduction rate of 1.00. That is to say, at *N* years after their birth (the number of years being the average age of their mothers at the time they gave birth), the number of daughters will equal the number of mothers, so that the one divided by the other equals 1.00.‡ This, as you might expect, is seldom the case. Table 2.1 illustrates the calculation of the NRR with data for 1965. These data indicate a 38 percent excess over exact replacement between generations (on the assumption that the conditions then prevailing would persist over several decades).

Note the assumption. In interpreting these figures we must remember that they are projections, indicating *what would happen if* the birth and death rates then obtaining—and related conditions like age composition, marriage, and divorce rates—were to continue over a period of years. But with this caution in mind the NRR yields useful clues to the ebb and flow of population, the challenges to stable role replacement inherent in the current demographic situation. For growth or decline of populations is the common case, just as change—social change—is the chronic condition. And the two, population change and social change, are certainly connected. Rapidly increasing numbers impose new, sometimes excessive, demands on the existing role structure. Declining numbers render existing roles useless or obsolete.

We saw in Figure 2.4 how sharply our birth rates increased after World War II. In ways you can readily imagine, this affected education, the labor force, recreation and leisure, government, and other sectors of the social order. Such overreplacement can be absorbed in a growing economy and an adaptable social system. (Of course the Russian position is that it can be absorbed in any case, under communism. Nonetheless, the U.S.S.R. has recently withdrawn its support of illegitimate children, is cutting family allowances and, once again, is making abortion legal.)[13] But in some nations continued rapid input creates the situation Malthus gloomily foresaw: poverty, hunger, threat of war and death. And so, for example, Pakistan budgeted $12 to prevent each of 5 million births in the period 1965–70 by making birth control techniques available to fertile couples.

Other countries face problems of underreplacement. In 1969, and almost annually on Republic Day, officials exhort white South Africans to have larger families. (On the other hand, as the *Times* reports it, "efforts are being made to persuade the 19.1 million non-whites to limit their families.")[14] Similarly, Japan has a low growth rate—1 percent or less, as compared with the 2 to 3 percent annual increase for India and China. Hence Japan's Demographic Research Institute reports serious labor shortages due to 10 years of very effective birth control (contraception and abortion).

In anticipating strains on the social order due to changing population input (either over- or underreplacement), the NRR is a useful device. In the Depression years the NRR was commonly

Table 2.1

Computing the net reproduction rate: United States, 1965

Age (1)	Birth rates per 1,000 (2)	Female life table population ($_5L_x$) (3)	Percent female births (4)	Number of female births (5)
10–14	0.8	486,446	49.2019	191
15–19	70.4	485,454	48.5339	16,587
20–24	196.8	483,929	48.6890	46,370
25–29	162.5	482,046	48.7093	38,155
30–34	95.0	479,522	48.9320	22,291
35–39	46.4	475,844	49.1672	10,856
40–44	12.8	470,419	49.2878	2,968
45–49	0.8	462,351	48.3312	179
				137,597

Net reproduction rate $= \frac{137{,}597}{100{,}000} = 1.376$ or 1,376 per 1,000

Notes:

Col. 3: 100,000 women, age 10, will live, between ages 10 and 15, 500,000 years minus the years not lived by those who die between these ages. Total years lived is 486,446.

Col. 2: For each of these 486 thousand years lived, the birth rate for women aged 10–14 is 0.8, or just under 1 for every 1,000 women.

Col. 3 × Col. 2 = 389 births, both boy and girl babies. But since we are dealing with the replacement of mothers by daughters, we have to cut this figure approximately in half. Of those 389 births, 49.2019% (Col. 4) were girls.

Col. 4 × 389 births = number of female births produced during the years lived (486,446 years) by women between ages 10 through 14.

Following the same procedure for all the childbearing years, we come up with a total of 137,597 girls born to an original cohort of 100,000 women.

below unity in European and North American countries. In the United States it was 0.96, or 4 percent below replacement level in 1940. In France, the Scandinavian countries, and England a similar situation obtained. And in our urban areas in this country, the threatened decline was even more marked, with the NRR at about 0.75, or a potential deficiency of 25 percent. By contrast, the *United Nations Demographic Yearbook* reports a NRR for Israel, in the same year, of 2.17!

Immigration and emigration

But a social order does not live by births alone. A second source of supply for staffing the group's role structure is immigration. Emigration is the output counterpart. Endowed with great natural resources, enjoying a standard of living based in part on a growing population (a growing market), stressing optimism, inventiveness, and enterprise as a triad of prime virtues, our society has welcomed immigrants in the past. An expansionist immigration policy fitted very well the requirements of a burgeoning industrial society. Immigrants were typically youthful, therefore low in mortality and high in reproductivity as well as productivity. And their coming and going was well geared to the economic conditions of our society. For example, during the depth of the Depression years, 1932 through 1935, more persons left than entered the United States.

A similar link between input through immigration and economic roles and rewards is seen in Figure 2.6. But note that, although there is an association between the variables (the higher the percent foreign born the higher per capita income), this should not be taken as a causal relationship. Commercial and industrial activities in urban coastal regions might account both for higher per capita income and higher percent of immigrants. In any case, entering and leaving American society has adapted itself remarkably well to deficits and surpluses in our population. And as Figure 2.6 suggests, immigrant labor has filled empty and newly created slots rather than displacing natives.

Note, finally, the input through immigration as it has operated in the United States from 1921 through the revision of the National Origins scheme up to 1968 (Table 2.2).

The percentages in the right-hand columns hint at the way our legislators tried to arrange for input to match output, for the future to match the past. (The death of persons of West European background was to be compensated for by admitting similar others, in disproportionate share, under our quota system.)* Indeed this was the central notion underlying our national origins system of immigration. The Senate Judiciary Committee in supporting our Immigration and Nationality Act of 1952 wrote:

> Without giving credence to any theory of Nordic superiority, the subcommittee believes that the adoption of the national origins formula was a rational and logical method of numerically restricting immigration in such a manner as *to*

* Actually many more aliens are admitted to the United States than are suggested by our immigration quotas. Of the 3.6 million aliens who came in 1968, about nine tenths were nonimmigrants: students, foreign government officials, exchange visitors, and the like. The law also provides for special categories of immigrants in addition to those subject to quotas. These include refugees and escapees, immediate relatives of U.S. citizens, and others. Hence the total number of immigrants in 1968 was 454,448 persons of whom about 35 percent came in under the quota system.

Figure 2.6
Immigration and per capita income

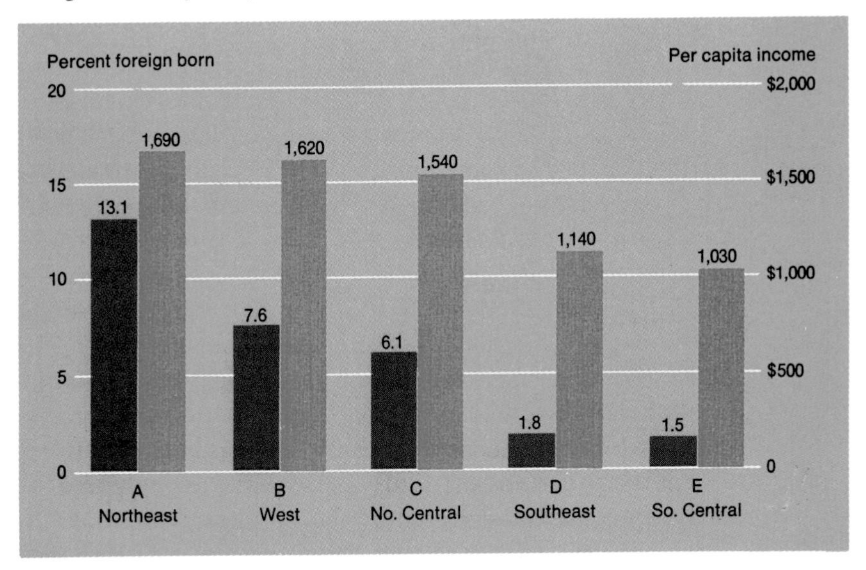

Table 2.2
Input through immigration, 1921–68

	1921 act*	1924 act†	1929 National Origins Act‡	1952 Immigration and Nationality Act		Quotas effective January 1, 1968	
	N	*N*	*N*	*N*	%	*N*	%
Total	375,803	164,667	153,714	154,657	100.0	158,261	100.0
Asia	492	1,424	1,423	2,990	1.9	3,590	2.0
Africa, Oceania	359	1,821	1,800	2,000	1.3	4,974	3.0
Europe	356,952	161,422	150,491	149,667	96.8	149,697	95.0
Northwest Europe:							
Great Britain, North Ireland, Germany, and the Irish Free State				108,931	70.0	108,931	69.0
Belgium, Denmark, France, Netherlands, Norway, Sweden, Switzerland, and others				17,200	11.6	16,700	10.6
Southeast Europe							
Austria, Czechoslovakia, Greece, Hungary, Italy, Poland, Portugal, Rumania, U.S.S.R., Turkey, Yugoslavia				23,536	15.2	24,066	15.4

Notes:
*1921 act set quotas at 3 percent of that nationality resident in the United States in 1910.
†1924 act set quotas at 2 percent of that nationality resident in the United States in 1890.
‡1929 National Origins Act set the quota for a given country as that part of a total of 150,000 represented by the percent that nationality constituted of the white population of the United States in 1920.

best preserve the sociological and cultural balance in the population of the United States.[15]*

Length of life

There is a third demographic factor, length of life, that affects the maintenance of a social order. The longer a person's life, the greater his span of parenthood, the longer his period of employment, the more votes he will cast (and otherwise act in role of citizen), the longer his participation as a communicant in some religious group, the less the need, to maintain the social order, of input through births. It's likely that a society having great longevity (other things equal) will have achieved solutions to problems of survival, will have fixed its roles and institutionalized its relationships. Its turnover is slow. It can rely on answers given in tradition, can indoctrinate, or socialize, slowly and surely. An everyday contrast is offered by the summer camp that admits new groups every two weeks to a strange way of life. Here socialization† must be swift, clear, intense, systematic—and will often be ineffective. And so longevity has much to do with the character of the social order.

Wherever we have records of birth and death, they show man's longevity increasing through the years. From these records we know that out of a given number—say 100,000—so many will survive to any specified age. Knowing, then, the number who live to each age we can calculate the total number of years lived. Dividing by the number of persons living those years gives us average life expectancy. For example, five persons die at ages five, six, seven, eight, and nine for a total of 35 years lived. Average life expectancy is 35 ÷ 5 or 7 years. (Insurance companies depend on such calculations, of course, for determining the premiums charged to cover their risks.)

As Table 2.3 indicates, longevity varies greatly in time and space. In 1967, at age 20, males might expect to live an additional 50

* The 1970 data show a shift in immigrant origins, reflecting legislation that came fully into force in 1968. The new law replaces national with hemispheric quotas: 170,000 for Asia, Africa and Europe and 120,000 for the Western Hemisphere. Latin America, southern Europe, and the Philippines are displacing Canada, Britain, Northern Ireland, and Germany as chief sources of immigrant populations. Preference is given to those with relatives in the United States, to scientists, artists, and skilled laborers in short supply. Thus there is still an effort to gear this input to the particular needs of American society: to the family, economy, and polity.

† Socialization is the process of transmitting the group's culture to newcomers. It is the subject of Chapter 4.

Table 2.3
Average number of years of life remaining, at specified ages, United States, 1900–1902 and 1966

Age at beginning of year	Average number of years of life remaining		Increase in average remaining lifetime (in years)
	1900–1902	1966	
Birth	49.2	70.1	20.9
1	55.2	70.8	15.6
5	55.0	67.1	12.1
25	39.1	48.0	8.9
65	11.9	14.6	2.7

years, on the average, females 57 years. While in Shakespeare's day, life expectancy at birth was about 35 years (the average being reduced by heavy infant mortality), today's newborn can expect to live 67 years, if a boy and 74 years, if a girl.

We have been considering how several demographic factors—fertility-mortality, immigration-emigration, and longevity—affect the social order taken as a whole. But this oversimplifies matters. For any given social arrangement requires *differential replacement.* The metropolitan labor force absorbs more women than do smaller communities. It also requires more foreign born with special talents in language, crafts, and culinary arts. Overreplacement affects particular sectors of society. The post–World War II baby boom created repercussions that started with diaper services and continued with a host of effects: new schools to be built, bond issues to be floated, more school architects, builders, and suppliers—and, of course, teachers, counselors, and administrators—a boom in the jewelry industry (class rings), and more business for school photographers and suppliers of caps and gowns. Music, clothing, and magazines were adapted to the juvenile market as there emerged a youthful peer culture stronger in numbers than ever before. And then, at 1945 plus 17 the demographic wave rolled on to colleges and universities.

Overreplacement is always relative to social need. Changing social needs alter the structure of the labor force and, therefore, the rate of needed replacement. For example, output per man-hour in farming quadrupled in the 50 years following 1910. From 1957 to 1968, productivity doubled again. Hence an overreplacement, relative to need, in the farm population. While 37 percent of the labor force was employed in agriculture in 1900, 69 years later it was down to 4.3 percent. A highly fertile farm population, over-replacing itself, requires a shift of its young to different sectors of the system. The farmer's boy goes into insurance. The Welsh miner's son becomes a professor of physics.

Thus differences in fertility may enable or require compensatory shifts in the role structure. For example: *How does differential fertility entail certain characteristics in the social order* (mobility, in this case) *that contribute to the rebuilding of the group?* Now in the United States the upper classes have typically had reproduction rates below replacement.[16] Assuming that their roles must be replenished if the system is to be maintained, it becomes necessary for such categories of persons to be supplied from other sources. Table 2.4 gives us some notion of the significance of social mobility in offsetting inadequate population replacement by the upper classes. In this illustrative table, upper and upper-middle classes have NRR's of 0.80. So they are deficient by 20 percent in replacing themselves.

Numbers and patterns of interaction

I have been trying to show how population factors—birth and death rates, length of life, the ebb and flow of migrants, shifts from one sector of the population to another—affect the continuous process of building the group.

But important as this is, there is another critical matter: the effect of numbers on the quality or character of interaction. For, as population increases, there is a change in the structure of relationships that constitutes a group. This is the matter to which we now turn, drawing, first of all, on Simmel's discussion of two- and three-person groups, and then raising the question: What is it about population increase that accounts for these changes in the social network?

This, then, is the first point: an increase in numbers, in size of group, can transform the nature of human relationships. But then we must ask: How so? What is it about population increase that accounts for such changes? To answer this question I shall point to three outcomes of population increase: a disproportionate increase in the number of relationships, an increased heterogeneity or diversification of roles and finally, a significant increase in the proportion of coordinating roles—administrative, supervisory, mediating.

We betray some sense of the significance of numbers for human relationships when we deplore the impersonality entailed by the growth of a business, a club, or a college; or, conversely, when we

Table 2.4

Differential fertility, by class

If structure is to be maintained necessary replacements are recruited from the next lower class. Estimates based on fertility conditions existing 1920–40

				If proportions are to remain the same			
Social class 0	Number in every 100 adults i	NRR* ii	Number in next generation if no mobility occurs iii†	Number needed in next generation iv‡	Number who must be upwardly mobile v§	Percent in each class who are upwardly mobile vi‖	Percent of total mobility deriving from each class vii#
Upper	3	0.80	2.4	3.3	0	0	0
Upper-middle	8	0.80	6.4	8.7	0.9	14	7
Lower-middle	30	1.00	30.0	32.6	3.2	11	24
Upper-lower	39	1.15	44.9	42.4	5.8	13	44
Lower-lower	20	1.25	25.0	21.7	3.3	13	25
Totals	100		108.7	108.7	13.2	12	100

* The estimates of column ii are derived, one supposes, from known differentials in fertility by occupation, income, and other class-related variables. The net reproduction rate (NRR) is a rate that takes age-specific fertility and mortality into account, estimating the survivors to the next generation on the assumption that the birth and death rates used in the calculation continue to apply over that period.

† Columns ii × i.

‡ Column i × 108.7.

§ Columns iv − iii plus mobility losses from next higher class.

For example, if the net reproduction rates give us, from 100 persons (i) a total of 108.7 in the next generation (iii); and if these 108.7 persons are distributed among the several classes as were their forebears in the preceding generation (i), then we would have 3.3 persons in the upper class, 8.7 in the upper-middle, etc. But they do not distribute themselves in this way because the fertility of the several classes differs and the upper classes fail to reproduce themselves. The extent of this under- or overreproduction is indicated by the difference between columns iv and iii. Thus the number of upper-class persons needed (3.3, column iv) minus those available (2.4 in column iii) gives us the number that must be recruited from the next lower class if the upper class is to maintain its position in the structure (3%, column i). This is simply 3.3 minus 2.4 in the case of the upper-class category, indicating that 0.9 persons must be recruited from the upper-middle category to compensate for their failure to reproduce themselves. In the case of the upper-middle class the discrepancy is 2.3 (8.7 − 6.4) to which must be added the 0.9 lost to this category as a result of their movement into the upper-class category—i.e., 2.3 + .09 or 3.2 represents the number who must be upwardly mobile from the lower-middle class to fill out the ranks of the upper-middle class, etc.

Column vi suggests that it may be the upper-middles who tend to be most mobile (14%); although the difference between them and the lowers is certainly not great. Indeed the surprising thing here is the comparative equality of upward mobility due to differential fertility among the several classes.

Taking all who are mobile, 13.2, as the base we find in column vii that 44% of all those who are upwardly mobile are the upper portion of the lower class, followed by the lower-lower and the lower-middle classes, each of these accounting for about a fourth of the total upward mobility.

‖ Columns v/iii. It is important to remember that upward mobility may be due to factors other than differential fertility which is the only matter we are considering here.

Number mobile in given class related to the total of 13.2 movers.

shudder at the goldfish-bowl character of the small community where one's innermost secrets may be ruthlessly broadcast through the rumor-gossip network; or when we savor the comfortable anonymity of a large city; or when Reinhold Niebuhr speaks of *Moral Man and Immoral Society*[17] (the moral individual and the amoral mass); or when Georg Simmel* associates with the increased membership of a religious or reform organization an erosion of unqualified commitment to its cause.[18]

Simmel was especially intrigued by the way relationships change as numbers increase. He asks us to consider the nature of a two-person group, a dyad.[19] It has this peculiar characteristic shared by no other group: the loss of one member destroys it. This extreme vulnerability, the complete dependence of each upon the other for the maintenance of the group, may explain why (in addition to society's obvious interest in the protection and appropriate rearing of offspring) the husband-wife relationship is hedged about with conventional and legal prescriptions. Being such a fragile relationship, this dyad requires the support of socially devised buttresses.

But, Simmel says, note what happens when the dyad is increased by one. The conversion to a triad (a three-person group) makes possible a majority: two against one. Also, there is the possibility of delegating authority and responsibility. With three instead of two we have a more refined division of labor. There is the possibility of mediation, arbitration, as the third seeks to resolve some difference between the two, playing one off against the other. Thus the shrewd child advances his interest by pitting parent against parent, and the student by contriving differences between teachers to his own advantage. Nor need it be a matter of an individual manipulating two others. A special case of the *tertius gaudens* (the third who profits—at the expense of the other two) is that of "divide and rule" (*divide et impera*) as where a colonial ruler creates or encourages factional disputes among the ruled. Thus the unbridged gulf between Moslem and Hindu in India made it possible for the English Raj to sit more firmly on the imperial throne.

* This perceptive German sociologist, a kind of intellectual window-shopper (among contemporaries one is reminded of Erving Goffman), lived from 1858 to 1918. His essays dissect the social nature of conflict and of secrecy, the role of the stranger, the meaning of the metropolis for human relationships, patterns of authority and submission, and the dilemmas of social cross pressures.

Simmel speaks suggestively of the difference numbers make as between small and large groups. Here is a sample of his thinking on this matter:

> . . . socialistic societies . . . have been possible only in very small groups and have always failed in larger ones. The principle of socialism—justice in the distribution of production and reward—can easily be realized in a small group and, what is surely quite as important, can be safeguarded there by its members. The contribution of each to the whole and the group's reward to him are visible at close range; comparison and compensation are easy. In the large group they are difficult, especially because of the inevitable differentiation of its members, of their functions and claims.[20]

Distinctive religious groups, too, can preserve their identity only so long as their numbers remain small.

> Where dogma forbids oath, military service and occupancy of offices; where very personal affairs, such as occupation, daily schedule, and even marriage, are regulated by the community; where a specific dress separates the faithful from the others and symbolizes their belonging together; where the subjective experience of immediate rapport with Christ constitutes the real cohesion of the community—in such situations, extension to large groups would evidently break the tie of solidarity which consists to a large degree precisely in the position of being singled out of larger groups and being in contrast to them.[21]

Or again, with an increase in population size, ideas held in common must be reduced to their simplest terms. For ". . . large masses can always be animated and guided only by *simple* ideas: what is common to many must be accessible even to the lowest and most primitive among them."[22] Or conversely, if the beliefs that distinguish a group, that establish its cultural identity and define its boundaries are to be maintained, then its population must not get out of bounds. This is especially so with deviant or radical groups. For:

> It is the unconditional solidarity of elements on which the . . . possibility of radicalism is based. *This solidarity decreases in the measure in which numerical increase involves the admission of heterogeneous individual elements.* For this reason, professional coalitions of workers, whose purpose

> is the improvement of labor conditions, know very well that they *decrease in inner cohesion as they increase in volume.* . . . on the other hand, the numerical extension has the great significance of freeing the coalition, through each additional member who joins it, of a competitor who might otherwise have undersold it and thus have threatened its existence.[23]

In such seminal remarks as these, Simmel raises important questions about the connection between population size, on the one hand, and the effective functioning and maintenance of the group on the other. Is it through some subconscious appreciation of this connection that the Hutterites limit their settlements to about 100 persons? Is it this connection that we sense when we make our estimates for the optimum size of the classroom group under specified conditions? How large should a department be? A working group in a factory?

The group is not simply reconstituted, it is altered when increases in its population change the nature of the relationships that define the group. But the significant question is: How? How do increases in population alter the nature of relationships and thus jeopardize the maintenance of the group? Let me suggest three ways in which this occurs: (1) by increasing disproportionately the number of relationships to be articulated in the social structure of the group, (2) by increasing the heterogeneity of the group, and (3) by increasing the division of labor, or specialization, entailing an increase in coordinating or administrative roles.

First, an increase in numbers entails a disproportionate increase in relationships—the parts that are to be shaped into a whole social structure. We can illustrate what happens, as population increases, by noting how many simple, bilateral relationships we have with two persons, three persons, four, five, six, and so on (Figure 2.7).

Figure 2.8 is another way of representing this elementary idea about the linkage between size of population and number of simple relationships. The connection between numbers and complexity of relationships can be expressed algebraically in the following formula.[24] (X = number of actors-in-roles and Y = number of simple, two-way relationships.)

$$y = \frac{x}{2}(x - 1).$$

Figure 2.7

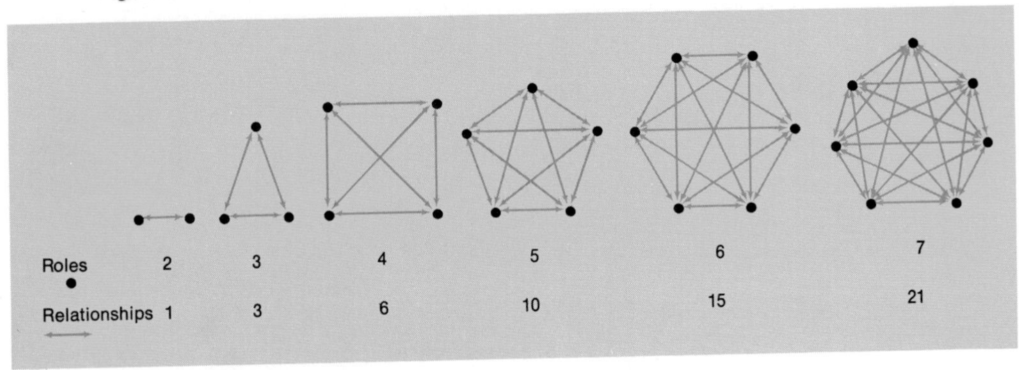

Figure 2.8
The relationship between increase in numbers of persons (size of population) and simple, bilateral social relationships

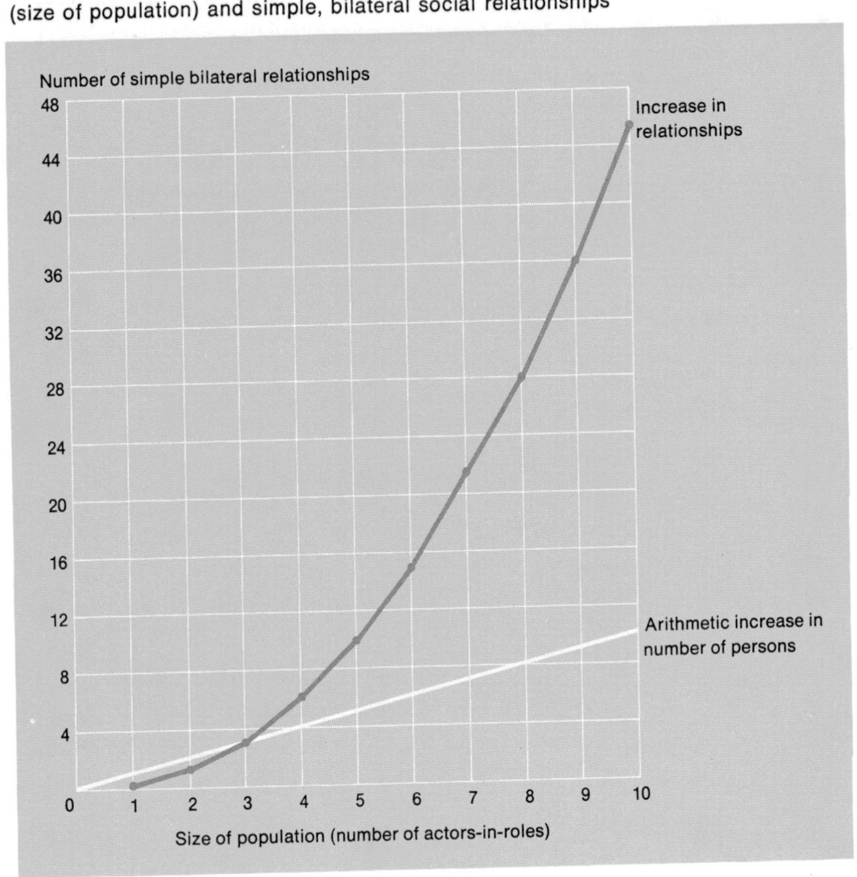

Thus, where we have a group of six persons, we evaluate the formula as follows:

$$y = \frac{6}{2}(6 - 1) = 15.$$

If a student were living in a fraternity house or a dormitory section numbering 20 men, we would see, by evaluating this formula, that he was involved in a network of 190 simple, bilateral relationships.

But this is a minimum statement of the way in which number and complexity of human relationships increase with a growth in population. For obviously, in a three-person group there is the possibility not only of bilateral relationships between A and B, B and C, C and A, but also of A leading B and C (or mediating between them, or being in a minority position vis-à-vis their majority), or of B confronting a united A and C, or of C differentiated somehow from A and B. Which is to say, once again, that the shift from a two- to a three-person group opens up a richly varied set of possible relationships. And while we have six bilateral or symmetrical relationships with four actors-in-roles (A ↔ B, A ↔ C, A ↔ D, B ↔ D, B ↔ C, and C ↔ D) there are, in addition four combinations, four three-and-one permutations suggesting leader-led, alliances, majorities or divisions-of-labor: (A,B,C) ↔ D; (BCD) ↔ A; (C,D,A) ↔ B; (D,A,B,) ↔ C. But beyond this there are the two-and-two combinations (contending factions, collaborators in teams of two, split votes, etc.): (AB) ↔ (CD), (AC) ↔ (BD), (AD)↔(BC).

This, then, is the first point: as population grows, the number and form of potential human relationships are vastly elaborated at a rate far in excess of the sheer increase in number of persons.

Now heterogeneity comes into the picture in two ways: culturally and socially. First, other things being equal, the greater the number of persons, the greater the cultural range likely to be represented within the group. Thus American society includes scores of religious groups: denominations, sects, and cults. In America's major metropolitan centers we find more than a hundred religious groups ranging from the "big seven" (Catholics, Jews, Lutherans, Baptists, Methodists, Presbyterians, and Episcopalians) comprising most of the city's church membership to the rare and esoteric groups whose membership taken together make up but a fraction of the total. So, other things equal, the larger the population, the broader the sampling from this religious spectrum.* And so, too, with other aspects of social life.

But increase in numbers entails social as well as cultural diversity. In his book *The Division of Labor in Society,* Durkheim traces a whole sequence of social effects having their roots in an increase in numbers. Assuming no extension of the area occupied, increase in numbers means increased density. Increased density increases the likelihood of interaction with one's neighbors. Through such interaction, common commitments are buttressed. Physical density thus leads to "moral density." This awkward term means a binding together through the regular reaffirmation of shared views and values. But as a result of the "moral density," competition arises. For since "moral density" implies similarities in skills and occupations and the values attached to them, people are unwittingly brought to compete by the same means for the same limited supply of food, fibers, and frivolities. A social mechanism then emerges, taking the sharp edge off competition and conflict: *differentiation* occurs, a fragmenting of blocks of behavior. Such differentiation, or specialization, or division of labor contrasts with the relatively undifferentiated antecedent state of "mechanical solidarity." It diminishes the *conscience collective,* beliefs and values held in common. Men's relationships are increasingly regulated by formalized legal codes. Increasingly the mortar of human relationships comes to be people's interdependence based upon differences rather than their common cause founded in likenesses.

But let us turn to an empirical test of this notion that an increase in population affects the social structure of the group. As one significant social effect of increasing numbers, let us consider the division of labor between that part of an organization carrying out the coordinating, or supervising, or administrative role, and all other sectors of the organization. Frederic Terrien and Donald Mills pose the problem: When numbers increase (in this case, numbers of persons involved in the operation of school dis-

* Things are not, of course, equal. Such an assumption would suggest the random selection of persons from some larger whole to swell the population of a designated group. But populations do not grow, either "naturally"—as we erroneously put it—or by migration on a random basis. It is not a chance matter that Detroit has the largest Lebanese population outside of Lebanon; or that there are better than half a million Puerto Ricans living in New York City. Yet, even despite the fact that groups—associations, communities—tend to select their newcomers and that newcomers sort themselves into comfortable and appropriate niches, there is strong empirical evidence for an increase in heterogeneity with an increase in population size. This is an important matter, as it effects changes in the group; and we shall have to pay some attention to it in Chapter 13 when we raise the question: What are the sources of change in patterns of human relationships?

tricts), what happens to the size of the administrative component?[25] They start with the assumption represented in Figure 2.8 showing the link between increased population and number of relationships.

> If the point be taken as axiomatic that the number of potential intra-group relationships increases at a greater rate than does the size of the group, then it would seem logical to suppose that those relationships would require at least a moderately increasing amount of supervision.[26]

Let us be clear: what an administrator administers is relationships, not persons. He helps define appropriate roles to achieve the group's mission; and he tries to link these roles in productive relationships—productive of whatever the group seeks to achieve: health, wealth, happiness, or, in this case, informed children. And since relationships increase, disproportionately, with numbers, the investigators put this hypothesis for testing: ". . . the larger the size of the containing organization, the greater will be the proportion given over to its administrative component." They got their data from a sample drawn by (1) taking just under half of the state's 58 counties, rank ordered in eight strata according to total yearly budgets; and (2) adding all districts having an average daily attendance of 2,000 or more students, where such districts were not already in the sample. Thus the larger districts were overrepresented; and this is especially so since districts having fewer than 10 employees were not dealt with. Their findings for three types of districts are summarized in Table 2.5.* Note especially the drift of the data in columns (1) and (3).

Of course, it would be absurd to suggest that the disproportionate increase in administrative roles is simply a consequence of increased population. What the division of labor shall be, how much of the total pool shall be vested in coordinating roles, depends as well on other factors. If the school district administrators are extending their adult education efforts, strenuously cul-

* Table 2.5 may have some symbols unfamiliar to you. $\overline{X}$ is the symbol for the *mean*, commonly called the average. It is one of three frequently used summarizing measures. (They summarize some characteristic of a group.) Thus, among 264 small elementary school districts, the average percent of all employees working in administrative roles was 9.5 percent.

σ, on the other hand, is a summarizing measure for a group telling us how much range (or spread, or deviation) there is from some central tendency. Thus there is more spread from the mean among the 178 small districts than there is among the medium-sized and large districts.

If you wish to nail down these ideas more clearly and securely, see Aside on Methods, Number 2.

Table 2.5
Average size of the administrative component* in California school districts that varied in number of employees
(1951–52 school year)

Type and number of districts	Size of organization (personnel)† (1)	*N* (2)	Average ($\bar{X}$) size (%) administrative component (3)	σ (4)
	Small	178	9.5	4.1
264 elementary school districts	Medium	60	12.6	3.2
	Large	26	13.9	3.0
	Small	55	11.4	4.0
96 high school districts	Medium	25	12.3	4.4
	Large	16	17.6	4.9
	Small	31	13.7	3.7
68 unified and city school districts	Medium	27	14.3	2.5
	Large	10	15.6	1.7

* Administrative personnel were defined to include "the superintendent, his assistants and immediate staff, principals, business managers, and the like."

† An elementary school district organization was classified as small if it employed 10–49 persons, as medium sized if employees numbered 50–149, and large if there were from 150 to 626 employees. Somewhat different cutting points were set for high school and city districts. Among the latter, for example, "large" meant having from 1,000 to 4,624 employees.

tivating PTA concerns, wooing the service organizations in the county, and stepping up public relations programs in anticipation of a bond issue—then the administrative component may be increased for reasons other than internal growth in the organization. Or it may be that with the electronic processing of data and the proliferation of ingeniously contrived business machines, the administrative component can decline despite an increase in size of organization. Again, it might be that people have an ingenuous conception of democracy and bureaucracy. Maybe they deprecate empire building and define organizational size in terms of persons rather than in terms of an increasingly intricate tangle of roles and relationships. Perhaps they emphasize Jacksonian conceptions of government by laymen rather than specialists—or "participant democracy" in which every man is, among other things, an administrator. Such views as these might lead to a stable or declining administrative component despite increase in population size.

Indeed, later research has turned up instances in which size of administrative component decreased as size of organization increased.[27] (This is the course of the intellectual detective story that sociological inquiry is: theories, clues checked, found wanting, revised and refined, and retested.) These studies suggest that size may be confounded with complexity—the number of different tasks performed or the number of separate places at which they're performed. And organizational size may be related to members' morale or to the power of its representatives in dealing with other organizations. In any case, whether in itself or mediated through some other variable, size (population) has an effect on behavior in human groups.

Before leaving this matter of changes in the structure of relationships stemming from increases in the size of the group, let us take one more case, the link between variations in city size and measures of police protection. For cities of different sizes, small (10,000 to 25,000) to large (over 0.5 million), the median number of police employees per 1,000 population goes like this: 1.5, 1.5, 1.6, 1.7, 1.8, and 2.2. And some years ago a sociologist inquiring into optimum size of cities discovered a nice gradient in per capita expenditures for police: the larger the city the larger the per capita cost.[28]

Now common sense would suggest that such findings are to be explained by the iniquity of the city. And the investigator does say that "the large city not only experiences a greater relative amount of crime, but also pays proportionately more heavily for it."[29] But he also notes that the differences between cities of differing populations, differences in police effort and expenditure, are greater than the differences in most sorts of crime. In any case, to establish the relationship is not to explain it. To speak of the evil city is to revert to unenlightening epithets.

I would suggest that an increase in population leads, as we have seen, to an enormously increased complex of relationships and that this development has two plausible outcomes. First, there is the impossibility of knowing all the others with whom one's destiny is linked. Relationships become increasingly superficial, specialized, and anonymous. In smaller groups people will be treated as *social* objects, as self-determining ends-in-themselves. In the mass society, people tend to use one another as *physical* objects, as useful instruments in the achievement of their ends. (The two sorts of relationship are not exclusive. In urban civilizations the second form is superimposed on the first.)

But beyond this, there is a vastly more complex set of relationships that must be coordinated, chiefly through the marketplace, the exchanges, the agencies of government. This coordination can be seen as an important function of the police, standing as in-between agents: between driver and pedestrian, driver and driver, between Birch Society rightists and left-wing pickets, between union members and the management they condemn, between law-abiding and criminal, between local criminals and those who would muscle in on their territory.

* * * *

Thus we begin to see how demographic matters bear on the building of the social order. Birth and death, in- and out-migration, changes in the length of life—these mean changes in numbers available for role replacement. The incessant need to rebuild the group means that output is more or less offset by input.

But demographic and social events are linked in other ways. It is not merely a matter of filling (or over- or underfilling) a role structure. As a result of increases in population, changes may be wrought in the nature of the group itself. As we have seen, Simmel commented perceptively on this. The triad, he suggested, is not as vulnerable to dissolution as the dyad. With the advent of the third—and more—the possibilities of a majority, of a more refined division of labor, of leadership, mediation, arbitration, and of the instrumental use of others to promote one's own purpose—these possibilities emerge.

Finally, complexity (a disproportionate increase in relationships), heterogeneity, and a more refined division of labor (along with the ever greater significance of the white-collar, coordinating role) may be outcomes of increasing numbers.

Social conditions affecting demographic variables

Now let us reverse the perspective. I have been pointing to variations in demographic factors that generate repercussions throughout society. But the reverse is true. Social and cultural variables promote population changes. Births, deaths, migration, and longevity have their sources, as well as their effects, in aspects of the social order. Let us see how social influences are revealed in certain demographic data (Figure 2.9).

Take birth rates which, in Western Europe and the United States, declined from various points in the 19th century to a low point in the mid-1930's.

This general decline has been recapitulated in countries like Bulgaria, Poland, and Czechoslovakia, the change being compressed within a much shorter time period. Now why this decline over the past 75 to 100 years? Our evidence suggests that, except in Ireland, it cannot be attributed to lower marriage rates or an increase in age at marriage. Nor can it be attributed to a change in age distribution such that there were fewer women in the reproductive age period. Other speculations seem inadequate to explain the decline: an increase in veneral disease, sybaritic living, dietary changes inhibiting conception, or the practice of women bathing with soap (a spermatocide).[30] Most of the decline appears to be due to the increasing and increasingly effective spread of contraception. In a landmark study of family planning in the United States, Freedman, Whelpton, and Campbell found that in a national sample of 2,713 married women, aged 18 to 39 inclusive, 65 percent who had been married for 15 or more years (and 70 percent of all women) had used some measure to prevent conception.[31] Among fecund couples the figure was higher: 83 percent for all fecund couples and 92 percent for those who had been married 15 or more years. But such data then require us to rephrase the question: How account for the spread of contraceptive practices? Or, to put it in terms of our second major question in this chapter: *What underlying social influences are reflected in the decline in fertility* (*or mortality*) *in our society?*

Social factors promoting a decline in fertility

To answer this question let us inspect the data on those categories of American society registering the lower rates and the larger declines, raising the question: What do these low fertility categories have in common that might explain their smaller families? During the few decades that we have had adequate data on these matters, the results have been quite consistent. Urban dwellers have had lower fertility rates than rural nonfarm residents, and the latter lower rates than farm populations. Rates for higher-income, white-collar workers have been lower than for poorer, blue-collar workers. Higher levels of education are associated with low fertility. The fertility of Jews has been quite consistently lower than that of Protestants, and Protestants in turn, have had lower fertility rates than Catholics.

Some years ago Samuel Stouffer found both Catholic and non-Catholic fertility declining in certain midwestern cities, the former at a faster rate than the latter, suggesting a point of convergence at some future date.[32] Freedman, Whelpton, and Campbell found that the Catholic women in their national sample were married, on the average, 1.5 years later than the Protestant wives.[33] Furthermore, "thirty percent of all Catholics . . . had adopted either withdrawal or appliance methods [of birth control], that is, methods unacceptable to the church."[34] This would support the expec-

Figure 2.9
Crude birth and death rates, United States, 1800–1965
(rates are five-year averages centering on year indicated)

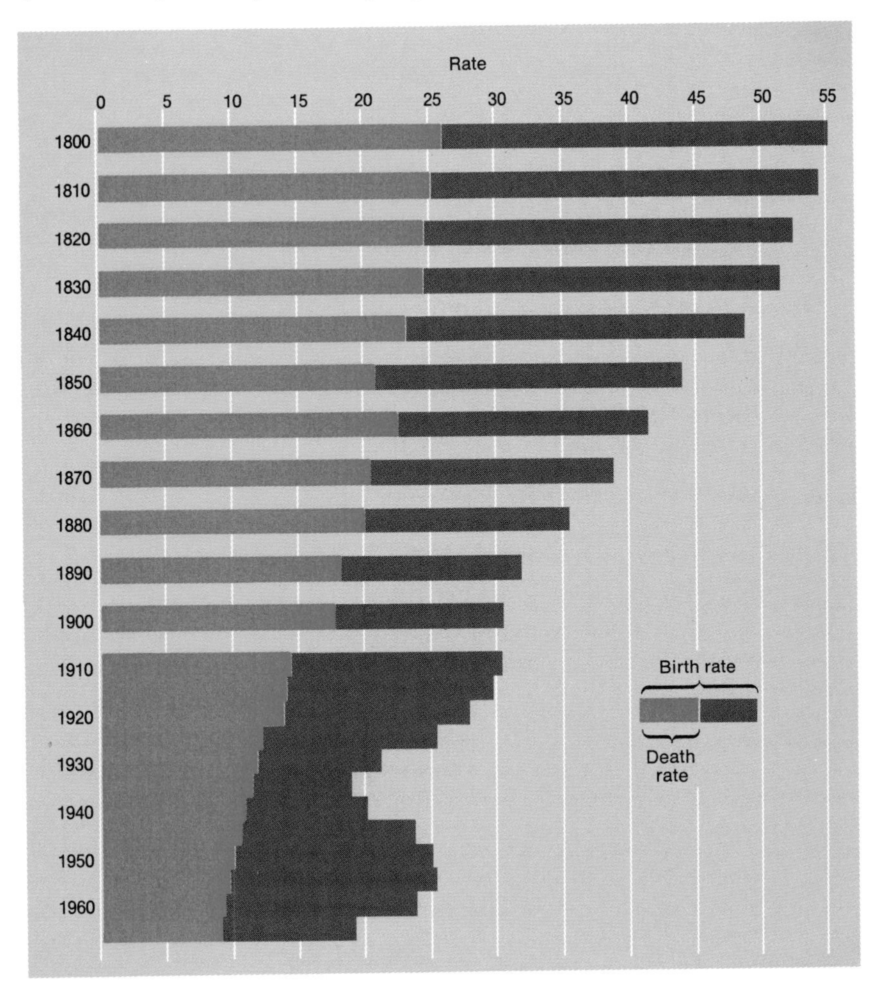

tation of converging rates anticipated in Stouffer's study. Yet despite delayed marriage and fairly extensive control of conception (among fecund Catholics 70 percent practiced some means of control), Catholic wives in this national sample expect and have more children than their Protestant counterparts—but not as many more as their favorable attitudes and expectations would indicate. Why is this so? There is, of course, the underlying instruction of the church, adjuring mechanical and chemical means of contraception. Further, there are fewer divorces among Catholics, and although most divorced women remarry, they do not have as many children as their nondivorced counterparts. Also, births to Catholic women are more closely spaced: between marriage and first birth an average of 23 months for Catholic women and 27 months for Protestant women, between first and second births 33 months for the former and 36 for the latter.[35] While reduced, the Catholic-Protestant-Jewish differences in fertility persist.

Second, we find in the Freedman study a confirmation of the inverse relationship between years of schooling and size of family. Women of lower educational attainment expect and have more children than those with more extensive education. If it were assumed that advanced education is related to superior mental ability, then the inverse relationship between fertility and education achieved would suggest a decline in the general level of problem-solving ability in the United States. Indeed, it has been argued that the offspring of the well-born and able are being supplanted by those of the ill-born and incompetent. The reproductive failures of Vassar girls and Princeton men are viewed as alarmingly dysgenic. But I think there is no evidence that the less educated have not been able to provide, from among the children in their larger families, enough capable offspring to meet the demands for professionals, executives, and technicians, demands unfulfilled by highly educated but underreproducing parents.[36] This is one reason, of course, why public in contrast to private and familial agencies of education are so significant in our society. But this is not to deny that "better educated parents are likely to provide a more stimulating and more constructively oriented environment for their children than are the less educated."[37]

Differences in fertility are also registered between different income and occupational categories. Both the number and spacing of children tend to be planned more among high-income than lower-income families, although differences in the number of children they expect to have are slight. The relationship between income and family size is strongest for the older persons, weaker among the younger, suggesting that this differential may disappear in time. Occupational differences, too, are less marked for younger than for older families, suggesting, again, a narrowing of differentials. The average number of births in the 2,700 families studied by Freedman *et al.*, broadly classified as to type of occupation, was as shown in Table 2.6.[38] Among wives who were working, there was an inverse relationship between length of time worked and number of children expected or had.

Another persisting differential is that between the fertility of

Table 2.6

Type of occupation*	Average number of births at time of interview (1955)
Upper white collar	1.9
Lower white collar	1.9
Upper blue collar	2.1
Lower blue collar	2.2
Farmers	2.7

* Families were classified as follows by husband's occupation:
Upper-white-collar workers: Proprietors, managers, officials and professional workers
Lower-white-collar workers: Salesmen, and clerical and kindred workers
Upper-blue-collar workers: Craftsmen, foremen, and kindred workers
Lower-blue-collar workers: Operatives and kindred workers, service workers and laborers (nonfarm)
Farm workers: Farm managers, and farm laborers, farmers

urban and rural residents. The progression of the average number of births by place of residence as Freedman found it in 1955 was as follows: for the 12 largest cities, then other large cities, small cities, suburbs of the largest cities, other suburbs, rural nonfarm residents, and farm families: 1.7, 1.9, 1.9, 2.1, 2.1, 2.3, and 2.8, respectively. Essentially the same differentials were found as to the expected total number of children to be born. Again these investigators observe that the differentials appear to be narrowing. There is ". . . a rising trend in the expected fertility of wives living in urban and suburban areas and a downward trend in the expected fertility of farm wives."[39]

In our cities, differences in fertility between income, educational, occupational, and race categories are often disguised place-of-residence differentials. For migrants to the city carry their fertility patterns with them. Among families who have lived in Detroit at least two generations, there are only insignificant differences in fertility between different social and economic categories.[40] It is the migrant to urban communities (a rural-agrarian import: poorer whites and Negroes from the South, Irish Catholic immigrants to major cities, and others) who accounts for the link between high fertility, and low level of education achieved, unskilled occupation and distinctive institutional patterns.

Now let us return to the question: What social characteristics, what aspects of the social order are revealed in the general decline in fertility and the differences in fertility rates between such categories as those I have mentioned? We are now moving from observation to interpretation. This is to live, to think, rather more dangerously. And I shall be outgeneralizing the data. Yet there is something to Professor Bruner's statement: "Better to be flat-footed and wrong than guardedly indeterminate."[41] To be as flat-footed as possible, let me say at the beginning that I interpret these changes in fertility as revealing a revolution in culture and a dramatic transformation in the social order. The cultural revolution consists, first, in changed conceptions of what *ought* to be. In the physical realm, it seems we should not regard ourselves as limited by our provincial atmospheric envelope. So entrancing are our lunar fantasies that we're willing to invest vast amounts in sending migrants to the moon. In the biological realm, we think it good to uncover the meaning of the genetic code, to unlock the secrets of ribonucleic acid. So far have we moved from submission to instinct and bodily needs as to plan to achieve our genetic preferences.

So, too, we seek to bend life and death to our purposes. Whereas the flood and ebb of population was a matter, once, of ill-controlled mortality, it is becoming a matter, chiefly, of well-controlled fertility. And few would question the goodness or oughtness of these advances in control over our destiny. Socially and psychologically the decline and differentials in fertility seem to mean not merely a sense of the possibility and practicality in balancing income and output but of pride in supplanting quantity with quality (calories, clothing, and college for a few, rather than a thinner gruel distributed among more children).

The cultural transformation consists, further, in changed conceptions of *what is*. The exponential rate of development in all the sciences, and their derivative technologies, provides both the impulse ("better things for better living") and the means (biochemical knowledge and contraceptive techniques) of fertility control. As we view these cultural accretions, we see man progressively banishing the gods of indeterminacy. Not for us the "bludgeonings of chance." The child of the late 20th century can say, with evidence beyond Henley's conceiving: "I am the master of my fate; I am the captain of my soul."[42] (But he had better note at the same time, with Donne, that he is so "involved in mankind" that apparently private matters are increasingly clothed with a public interest; and self-determination, taken literally, is a dangerous illusion.) Our studies of fertility suggest, then, that man is shaping his world so as to match personal demands with changing cultural norms* by means of innovations—sometimes artfully contrived, more often not—in social organization.

What of his social organization? What changes in it are revealed by these fertility data? The high-fertility society (and such remaining high-fertility groups as the Hutterites, or the Catholics of rural Quebec with an average family size of better than 10 children) was a rural one. It was sparsely populated. Its people were in agrarian occupations. They profited from many "hands." For not only were large numbers required to counterbalance a heavy death rate; many children were also needed because there was almost no other form of productive energy save for low-efficiency domestic animals. Their education was chiefly, if not exclusively, outside the classroom. It provided a near-perfect fit for the world of work: direct relevance, honest motivation, learning on the spot and at the moment of necessary performance, role models readily available, emotional involvement and bodily participation in the learning process, alternative paths closed or unknown. It was a traditional society. Answers to persisting problems were simply and strongly given within the institutions of the church, the extended family and traditional practices. Family, school, church, civic participation were woven together on the loom of blood ties. Religious model and communicant, teacher and pupil, father and son, employer and employee, elder statesman and younger citizen—these were the *same two persons*. Thus were beliefs and behaviors continuously reinforced, and without contending or distracting alternatives.

These are traits, somewhat exaggerated, of groups having high fertility and mortality. The contrasting low-fertility groups are typically those living in cities, or under the far-reaching influence of urban centers. Such populations have increasing proportions employed in industry, commerce, the professions, and service trades. Their energy is multiplied by mechanical, electrical, and chemical processes, and with the matter of crude power or energy well in hand, more attention is accorded social inventions—the corporation, the holding company, the stock exchanges—to match machine efficiency with that of collaborating humans. The employment of women rises, that of children declines. Legislation precluding child labor, required school attendance outside the home for longer periods of time and at great cost, and higher standards of nutrition and medical care have made children increasingly costly. A reduction in family size accords with these social changes, especially since large numbers of children are not re-

* In support of their values (conceptions of the good) men develop rules of conduct. Such rules, stipulating behavior commonly expected in a given role, are norms. Fixed in custom and convention, the norms of everyday life are less articulated in the mind than rooted in the heart.

quired to offset high mortality rates. In short, increased control over his physical, biological, and social worlds is reflected in modern man's declining fertility.

Points at which social and cultural factors influence fertility

But we can be more specific than this. If we refine the notion of fertility, isolating those points at which social and cultural factors can influence the reproductive rate, we are in a better position to pinpoint the conditions of rise and decline in birth rates. This is what Davis and Blake have done in their discussion of what they call the "intermediate variables."[43] These are the social and cultural factors, present in all societies, that affect the probability of (1) intercourse, (2) conception, and (3) successful gestation and bearing of the infant. The following outline of these variables gives us some conception of the many points at which changes in fertility reflect social and cultural influences.

The Intermediate Variables
(Factors through which varying cultural conditions effect variation in fertility)

I. *Intercourse variables* (factors affecting exposure to intercourse):
   A. Those governing the formation and dissolution of unions in the reproductive period.
      1. Age of entry into sexual unions.
      2. Permanent celibacy: proportion of women never entering sexual unions.
      3. Amount of reproductive period spent after or between unions:
         a) When unions are broken by divorce, separation, or desertion.
         b) When unions are broken by death of husband.
   B. Those governing the exposure to intercourse within unions.
      4. Voluntary abstinence.
      5. Involuntary abstinence (from impotence, illness, unavoidable but temporary separations).
      6. Coital frequency (excluding periods of abstinence).

II. *Conception variables* (factors affecting exposure to conception):
      7. Fecundity or infecundity, as affected by involuntary causes

8. Use or nonuse of contraception.
   a) By mechanical and chemical means.
   b) By other means.
9. Fecundity or infecundity, as affected by voluntary causes (sterilization, subincision, medical treatment, etc.).

III. *Gestation variables* (factors affecting gestation and successful childbirth):
   10. Foetal mortality from involuntary causes.
   11. Foetal mortality from voluntary causes.[44]

Consider, as an example, cultural prescriptions as to age of marriage (or, more generally, age of union—I, A, 1, above). In our nuclear family the age of union depends in some measure on the young people's command over minimal property, their independence of kin and elders. This is not the case where the group is organized on a clan basis. When the clan controls the property, "marriage is in no way made contingent on the possession of separate property by the newly married pair."[45]

Other cultural influences may press for early marriage. When marriages are arranged by the parents, they may do so before the puberty of the partners, thus lowering age of entry into sexual unions. Or, if the residence pattern is patrilocal, a mature but unmarried daughter may be regarded as disrupting the division of labor between her brother and his wife (or wives) and otherwise being in an anomalous position. Hence the inclination to see that she is married early.

On the other hand, in an agrarian group where marriage is neolocal* and subdivision of land holdings is either prohibited or known to be injudicious, unions may be deferred until one son can inherit the farm, the others making their way elsewhere in other occupations. (This is the situation in Ireland, accounting, in part, for an average age, at first marriage, of 27 for brides and 31 for grooms, according to the 1951 census.)

In general, Davis and Blake suggest, where the marital bond is subordinate to the filial bond, marriage does not depend upon economic independence and occurs early. Where the marital bond has primacy, symbolized in neolocal residence, independence and marriage occur at later ages.

* *Neolocal* means, literally, new place. Applied to marriage it tells us that the couple, rather than living with the wife's family or tribe (matrilocal) or with the husband's (patrilocal), sets up an independent household in a new location.

Singleness and celibacy operate in varying degree to lower fertility. While it could not be the prevailing practice (in any group save religious orders who recruit "migrants" as new members), it is more widespread than might be assumed, even outside the religious realm. Among Irish women aged 50, one fourth, in 1951, had never married. Comparable data for a few other countries are given by Davis and Blake: a fifth of Swedish women (1945), a fifth of Swiss women (1941), and, earlier, 17 percent of the women in England and Wales in 1931 and 13 percent of the women in Belgium (1930).[46]

The practice and effectiveness of contraception vary widely. Again this intermediate variable depends upon social and cultural factors: limits of biological and chemical knowledge, religious prohibitions defining destruction of the fertilized cell as homicide, social theory that insists that population problems stem from erroneous ways of organizing production and are, therefore, solvable by altering modes production, a changing view of woman's role that increasingly opens to her the hitherto male world of work *in addition to,* or instead of child rearing, attitudes toward divorce—all those influence the practice of contraception and, therefore, fertility.

For most of the world the prevailing cultural traits are such as to lower the practice and effectiveness of contraception, operating in a way to increase fertility. This is fortunate (if survival is deemed good) since such groups have, characteristically, high mortality rates. Indeed, the conditions making for the one promote the other: elementary cultural development (limited physical and biological science and technology); hunting and gathering, pastoral or subsistence agriculture as the economic base; communal property, clan, or extended family organizations; a pervasive sense of the sacred supporting traditional patterns and militating against change.

Social and cultural influences reflected in population pyramids

Features of the social order are revealed, partially, in a device we call the population pyramid. Such pyramids (see Figure 2.10) simply depict the distribution of persons, by age and sex—and sometimes, additionally, by race and nativity—characterizing a given group at some point in time. Age categories are represented vertically, numbers (or percent) of persons, by sex, in given age categories, horizontally.

Figure 2.10
Pyramids showing five-year age groups, by sex, for Alaska 1939, and Germany 1946

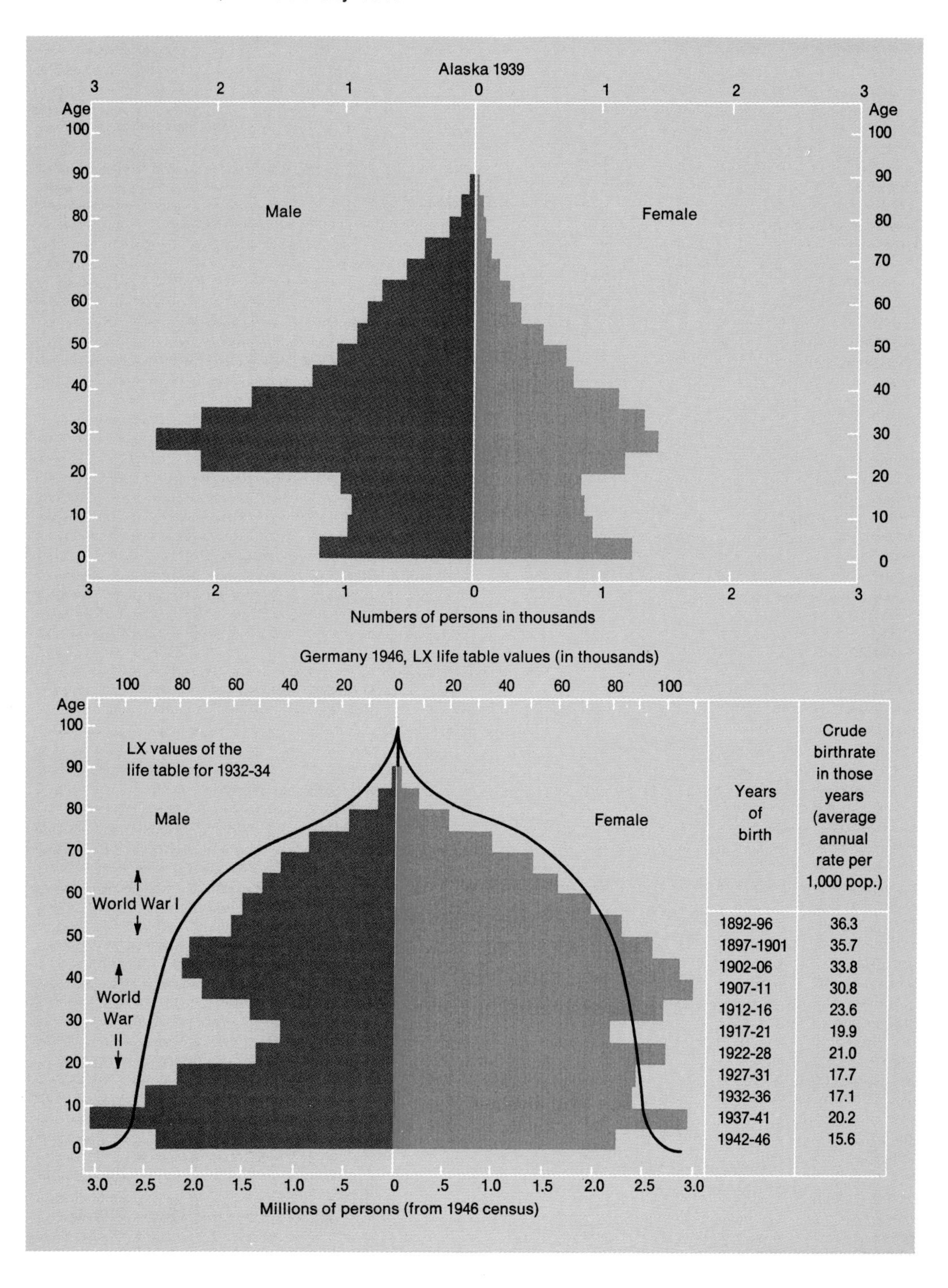

Years of birth	Crude birthrate in those years (average annual rate per 1,000 pop.)
1892-96	36.3
1897-1901	35.7
1902-06	33.8
1907-11	30.8
1912-16	23.6
1917-21	19.9
1922-28	21.0
1927-31	17.7
1932-36	17.1
1937-41	20.2
1942-46	15.6

Let me highlight two significant features of the Alaska pyramid that lead to useful inferences about the nature of this society: (1) the excess of males, especially between the ages of 20 and 40 and (2) the fact that such a disparity must be attributed to in-migration. This is typical of what we might loosely call a pioneer community. Its effects are felt in the family, in relations between men and women (or their absence), in modes of governing and administering justice, in religious practices, in its economic system (work in extractive industry—fishing, mining, oil, agriculture—predominates).

The distribution of the German population in contrast reveals an excess of women. They have survived the ravages of two world wars. Notice in World War II the marked deficiency of both men and women who might have been expected to be born in the period 1917–21. These children are missing because their parents are missing. And these are missing because of the disruption of the German family during World War I. So do "the gods visit the sins of the fathers upon the children."[47] The demographic facts of life carry a delayed punch. Or, more accurately, the characteristics of a given social order, registered in growth and composition of population, have social repercussions remote in time.

As a final example, consider the 1969 population pyramid for the United States (Figure 2.11). Here we find our social history recorded in the age-sex composition of the population. One comes to realize how many suggestive clues can be teased out of such a population pyramid if he asks questions such as these: How will education be affected in the next two decades by the age structure of population in the United States? When will the next bulge occur at the bottom of the population pyramid? What effect would you predict on the labor force in the next twenty years? What sorts of businesses will be especially favored—or hurt—by the age structure of the population? What part of the pyramid represents those who were available for service during World War II? Does the sex ratio* in this age category tell you anything about our losses during that war?

* The sex ratio is measured by dividing the number of males by the number of females and multiplying some constant—100, or as is becoming conventional, 1,000. The formula, then, is:

$$\text{Sex ratio} = \frac{\text{Number of males}}{\text{Number of females}} \times 1{,}000 .$$

In frontier areas the sex ratio tends to be very high. In commercial and urbanized areas, long settled, the sex ratio tends to be low. In 1969, the sex ratio for the total population of the United States was 964 (males per thousand females). For the age category 20–29 it was 1,007, and for those over age 65 it was 742.

Figure 2.11
Composition of the population of the United States, by age, sex, and race, July 1, 1969
(Median age was 27.7 years)

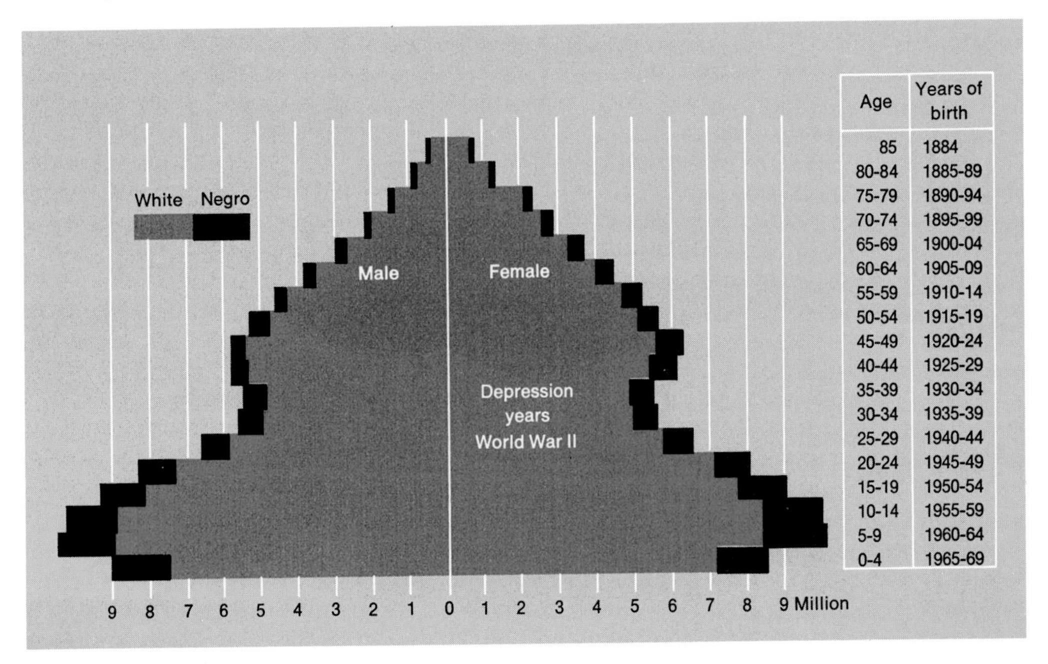

Age	Years of birth
85	1884
80-84	1885-89
75-79	1890-94
70-74	1895-99
65-69	1900-04
60-64	1905-09
55-59	1910-14
50-54	1915-19
45-49	1920-24
40-44	1925-29
35-39	1930-34
30-34	1935-39
25-29	1940-44
20-24	1945-49
15-19	1950-54
10-14	1955-59
5-9	1960-64
0-4	1965-69

Cultural influences on the sex ratio

Age and sex are significant axes for role differentiation. Since critical roles are geared to age and sex, marked shifts in the demographic structure of a group mean shifts in role structure—which is to say, in the social order. Consider the sex dimension.

In a monogamous society some numerical balance between the sexes is necessary. Whether such a balance is achieved—and if so, how—is a matter of some interest to the sociologist. Do we achieve such a balance? The answer is, overall, yes. But the sex ratio varies considerably from group to group. (Cities tend to be on the female side, especially white-collar, commercial, governmental cities, like Washington, D.C., which had, in 1960, a sex ratio of .86. But to suggest that we "achieve" a balance of sexes consonant with our monogamous pattern of courtship, marriage, and family life is to fly in the face of everyday experience: our inability to determine the sex of our children. Indeed, we do not even know whether

American parents do, somehow, come to prefer families in which both sexes are represented.

Raising this question allows us to place in evidence an ingenious piece of demographic detective work. It will also give us an example of empirical research.[48] The case in point is a study of the extent to which the preference for at least one child of each sex influences the size of the family. Or we could put it this way: Do parents achieve some control over the sex ratios in their families by altering family size? Or, a final formulation: Do parents prefer balanced-sex families, so acting as to achieve this balance within their families and thus providing for the larger group a sex ratio approximating 1.00, consonant with the legal, familial, and religious requirements in our social order?

The plausibility of such a preference ought first to be established, since we do not come to understand our world by haphazardly chasing notions of zero plausibility. The notion of preference for at least one child of each sex might be supported by three assertions. First, each parent gets satisfaction from recapitulating, savoring, improving on, his own childhood experiences through the agency of a child of his own sex. Second, although neither parent might be able to articulate it, each is aware, if dimly, that children are bridges to satisfying associations with other adults and children; but a boy leads to different interests and activities than does a girl. Taken together, they expand the circle in which parents can be rewardingly implicated. Third, a parent may get compensatory satisfactions from enjoying, vicariously, a childhood much of which was denied him because he was of the other sex.

Now to test whether parents do prefer two-sex families, and the demographic effects of such a preference, the investigators raise these questions: What would people expect to do and how, in fact, would they act if this were their aim? The answer is given in their first formulation of the hypothesis: "If such differential satisfactions are enjoyed by couples with any given number of children, those with children all of the same sex will be more likely than will others to have an additional child."[49]

The first test of the hypothesis has to do with expectations. Table 2.7 reports the responses of 888 couples (345 with children of just one sex and 543 with children of both sexes) as to whether they expected to have another child.[50] The differences, as we see, are small but consistent.[51]

But let us turn from expectations to actual behavior, comparing the sex distribution of completed two-child families with that of

Table 2.7
Expectations of additional children for couples with children of both sexes or all one sex

Number of children already born (1)	Couples expecting an additional child: Families with children of just one sex — Percent (2)	N (3)	Families with children of both sexes — Percent (4)	N (5)	Differences in expectation of additional child between one-sex and both-sex families (6) (col. 2 – col. 4)
Two	63	259	59	261	4
Three	61	69	53	197	8
Four	76	17	49	85	27
		345		543	

Table 2.8
A comparison of the sex composition of completed families

Type of family by size and completion	Sample size	Percent having children of the same sex	Percent difference
Completed two-child families	203	47	8
First two children in three-child families	266	55	
Completed three-child families	119	23	8
First three children in four-child families	102	31	

the first two children whose parents went on to have a third. And we can do the same with completed three-child families and the first three children in families whose parents had a fourth. The results are summarized in Table 2.8. We see that with actual behavior as with expectations, *having two or more children of the same sex is related both to expecting and having an additional child.*

Now the investigators raise the question whether other factors known to be related to fertility might alter this apparent link between sex composition and having additional children. So they repeated the five comparisons I have reported above, holding constant the duration of the marriage, wife's religion and education, and the extent of her work experience (in years). In no case was the *direction* of the relationship altered and in only one case, religion, was the *extent* of the relationship affected. The relationship is more tenuous for Catholics. "It seems that a desired sex distribution is more important to Protestants than it is to Catholics."[52]

So it is a fair inference that families in the United States prefer having both boys and girls among their children. And they seek, through the addition of children, to rectify a sex imbalance. So does modern man adapt himself to the dual character of a social order in which distinctive cultural prescriptions stipulate sex-linked roles. And so it is that the social order is reflected in demographic data.

Cultural diffusion, urban-rural, and effect on fertility

Social influences on births, deaths, and migration can be traced with some precision. One final illustration is seen in the inquiry of Nathan Keyfitz, an inquiry bearing on the cultural diffusion of urban influences tending to depress fertility.[53] As family size varies, Keyfitz argues, we get some index of exposure to, and the influence of, those social conditions and cultural characteristics that tend to depress birth rates. And when family size varies with some consistency along a given dimension, values along this dimension become useful indicators of degree of cultural diffusion: diffusion of knowledge and values and, in this case, the confronting of traditional orthodoxy with urban heterodoxy. Distance (from cities over 30,000 in population) becomes the dimension, the independent variable, number of children the dependent variable.[54] "We suppose," Keyfitz says, "that for a new element of culture the point of entry into a society is not only the rich, better-educated, urban population but also that, as among the rural population, those closer to cities are earliest affected."[55] His data show that

> . . . family size on French farms near cities, when all other accessible variables have been controlled [these were age at marriage, education, income, age and whether area was mixed French-English or not so mixed] is smaller than on French farms far from cities and we infer that the current of diffusion is from the city outward. On the other hand, no significant difference in family size is shown according to residence near or far away from English-speaking people. We infer that the influence of the English-speaking world upon the French-Canadian farmer is via the French cities.[56]

* * * *

Any enduring human group must replace its losses. That is the central theme of this chapter. Without the individual, obviously, we lack the makings for a person. Without the person, we lack the makings of the group. And a continuous loss of persons (deaths, emigration, role-shifting) requires a regular input through births and immigration. These newcomers are the natural resources of an enduring group, resources that are then shaped to the requirements of a given culture.

But it is not a matter, simply, of balancing total output (dead and departing) with total input (infants and migrants). Certain sectors of the social order still overreproduce (rural dwellers, Catholics, miners, the lower classes) and others underreproduce (urban dwellers, the upper classes, professionals). And the ranks of the latter must be filled from those of the former. Thus we saw how differential fertility implies upward mobility if a given class structure is to be maintained.

Demographic factors also carry significant implications for the social order beyond the matter of staffing the system and its differentiated parts. Increased numbers entail an exponential increase in relationships, alter the give and take among men, promote social and cultural diversity, giving rise to different patterns of social control. Here Simmel and others provided useful illustrations.

This was only one side of the coin, the other being the way social factors affect demographic variables. This effect is registered in the vital rates of different religious, occupational, class, and ethnic categories. It is reflected in the age and sex composition that we represent in population pyramids. Blake and Davis help us see the impact of social influences at the many points where they touch on intercourse, conception, and gestation. And unlikely as it might at first blush seem, we find couples in our society realizing a culturally conditioned preference for children of both sexes—through control of family size. Finally, we noted, in Professor Keyfitz' study, the influence of the city on family size in rural Canadian communities.

Now the raw material must be transformed, the newcomer made privy to the ways of his group. The individual becomes a person. Sheer behavior, aimless and normless, becomes conduct. For this to happen, infant and immigrant must learn the rules that define roles and relationships. In short, the newcomer must get culture. What this is, that he gets, and how he gets it are the matters dealt with in the next two chapters. First, then: What is this culture that the newcomer must acquire?

References

TEXT

1. The interplay of demographic and social factors is splendidly brought out by Kingsley Davis in his *The Population of India and Pakistan* (Princeton, N.J.: Princeton University Press, 1951).

   Demographic studies typically use social phenomena for one variable, dependent or independent, and demographic phenomena for the other. Since births, deaths, numbers, density, and migratory movements have sources and consequences in aspects of the social order, the sociologist is disposed to consider population phenomena either as intrinsically social, in themselves, or as indexes of significant social variables. I take the latter position, making two observations. First, demographic data are particularly potent as indexes, because they point to phenomena indispensable for maintaining a social order and because they deal with events of central importance to the person. (They have high social and psychological relevance.) Second, using these data as indexes, any complete sociological study must at least acknowledge both the social sources and social outcomes that flank the demographic event.
2. Kingsley Davis and Judith Blake, "Social Structure and Fertility: An Analytic Framework," *Economic Development and Cultural Change,* published by the University of Chicago Press, Vol. 4, No. 3 (April, 1956), pp. 211–35.
3. Deborah and Ronald Freedman and Pascal K. Whelpton, "Size of Family and Preference for Children of Each Sex," *American Journal of Sociology,* published by the University of Chicago Press, Vol. 66, No. 2 (September, 1960), pp. 141–52.
4. Nathan Keyfitz, "A Factorial Arrangement of Comparisons of Family Size," *American Journal of Sociology,* Vol. 58, No. 5 (March, 1953), pp. 470–79.
5. Kenneth E. Boulding in his "Foreword" to Thomas Robert Malthus, *Population: The First Essay* (Ann Arbor, Mich.: University of Michigan Press, 1959), p. v.
6. Godwin's *Enquiry Concerning Political Justice* (1793) reflected a yeasty optimism that pervaded his times, supported in part by social Darwinism and the heady political climate of the American and French Revolutions. It was clear, Godwin thought—as did Condorcet, in France, sketching out the *Progress of the Human Mind*—that man had the world by the tail on a downhill drag. His ideal society, an anarchistic one, was grounded in equality, cultivated individualism and, through the ascendance of reason, would eliminate error, vice, and violence. Percy Bysshe Shelley, Godwin's son-in-law, echoed these sentiments in poetry and pamphlet.
7. Malthus, *op. cit.,* p. 5.
8. *Ibid.,* p. 9.
9. *Ibid.,* p. 5.
10. William Wetmore Story, "Girolamo, Detto Il Fiorentino, Desponds and Abuses the World," in *Poems* (New York: Houghton Mifflin Co., 1896), Vol. I, p. 115.
11. Thomas Carlyle, *Sartor Resartus,* in Paul Robert Lieder, Robert Morss Lovett, and Robert Kilburn Root, *British Prose and Poetry* (New York: Houghton Mifflin Co., 1928), p. 959.
12. Karl Marx, *Capital: A Critique of Political Economy* (Chicago: Charles H. Kerr & Co., 1921), pp. 692, 693.
13. Dael Wolfle, "Soviet Population Theory," *Science,* Vol. 158, No. 3804 (November 24, 1967), p. 1.
14. *The New York Times,* Sunday, May 19, 1969, p. 2.
15. President's Commission on Immigration and Naturalization, *Whom We Shall Welcome* (Washington, D.C.: U.S. Government Printing Office, 1953), p. 89. Italics mine. I cannot forbear signalizing this sloppy and erroneous use of the word *sociological.* The good senators have fallen into the common illiteracy of substituting "sociological" for "social." The first refers to a field of inquiry. The second refers to a class of phenomena, a class to be distinguished from psychological, biological, physical phenomena. While for pomp and circumstance "sociological" has the advantage of four syllables, it has the disadvantage of the wrong referent and of obscuring the meaning.
16. While this was the characteristic situation in the past, there is some evidence that the long-standing inverse relationship between breeding (cultural) and breeding (biological) is weakening. Professor Freedman's data suggest a convergence on an ideal family size with the rich having more, the poor fewer children. (Ronald Freedman, Pascal K. Whelpton, and Arthur

A. Campbell, *Family Planning, Sterility, and Population Growth* [New York: McGraw-Hill Book Co., 1959], pp. 402–4.)

17. Reinhold Niebuhr, *Moral Man and Immoral Society* (New York: Charles Scribner's Sons, 1932).
18. Georg Simmel, *The Sociology of Georg Simmel*, trans., ed., Kurt Wolff (Glencoe, Ill.: Free Press, 1950), pp. 89, 90, 94 *et seq*. The whole section "On the Significance of Numbers for Social Life" bears on the way the quality of human interaction is affected by numbers.
19. *Ibid.*, Part II, chaps. iii, iv.
20. *Ibid.*, reprinted with permission of Free Press. The reference here is not to "socialism" as the term is used in the U.S.S.R., but rather to the sort of communal group represented by the Hutterites or various utopian groups. That it be small is not, of course, the only relevant criterion for group survival, as Robert Owen's experience at New Harmony, Indiana, indicated.
21. *Ibid.*, pp. 89, 90.
22. *Ibid.*, p. 93.
23. *Ibid.*, Part II, p. 95. Italics mine.
24. This is the formula expressing what the sociologist James H. S. Bossard called "The Law of Family Interaction" (*American Journal of Sociology*, published by the University of Chicago Press), Vol. 50 [January, 1945], pp. 242–94). This he stated as follows: "With the addition of each person to a family or primary group, the number of persons increases in the simplest arithmetical progression in whole numbers, while the number of personal interrelationships within the group increases in the order of triangular numbers." Bossard was especially impressed by the increased potential for tension with the disproportionate increase in relationships as families grew larger. He reports on the case of one youngster "who at five years of age, appears nervous, high strung, and over-stimulated, with spells of nervous vomiting. Helen is an only child, but in her two-and-a-half-story home of moderate size there live, in addition to her father and mother, two grandparents, one paternal, the other maternal. Also two servants are in the house daily. With seven persons in the house, there are twenty-one sets of personal relationships. In at least ten of the twenty-one, there is some emotional strain and tension. Helen is the most constantly present person in the household [and hence most regularly exposed]." Clearly, there are dimensions other than numbers that might be relevant in understanding this child's behavior: number of generations present, employer-employee as well as intrafamilial relationships, and so on. Yet we must agree with Bossard that an increase in population involves a disproportionate increase in the potential heterogeneity of the group and in potential tensions.

    Baker and Traphagen, with whose work Bossard was apparently unacquainted, suggested some years earlier the significance of this dimension in analyzing personality and problems of adjustment (Harry J. Baker and Virginia Traphagen, *The Diagnosis ànd Treatment of Behavior Problem Children* [New York: Macmillan Co., 1936], pp. 284–85). Baker and Traphagen deal not with a relationship between two people but with the orientation of each toward the other. Hence, where there is one relationship there are two orientations, and their formula would read $Y = x(x-1)$.
25. Frederic W. Terrien and Donald L. Mills, "The Effect of Changing Size upon the Internal Structure of Organizations," *American Sociological Review*, Vol. 20, No. 1 (February, 1955).
26. *Ibid.*, p. 12.
27. Theodore R. Anderson and Seymour Warkov, "Organizational Size and Functional Complexity," *American Sociological Review*, Vol. 26, No. 1 (February, 1961), and Richard H. Hall, J. Eugene Haas, and Norman J. Johnson, "Organizational Size, Complexity, and Formalization," *American Sociological Review*, Vol. 32, No. 6 (December, 1967).
28. See U.S. Bureau of the Census, *Statistical Abstract of the United States* (Washington, D.C.: U.S. Government Printing Office, 1969), Table 220, p. 147; and Otis Dudley Duncan, "Optimum Size of Cities," in Paul K. Hatt and Albert J. Reiss, Jr. (eds.), *Cities and Society* (New York: Free Press of Glencoe, Inc., 1959).
29. *Ibid.*, p. 761.
30. United Nations, Department of Social Affairs, Population Division, *The Determinants and Consequences of Population Trends* (New York: United Nations, 1953), pp. 74–75.
31. Ronald Freedman, Pascal K. Whelpton, and Arthur Campbell, *Family Planning, Sterility, and Population*

Growth (New York: McGraw-Hill Book Co., 1959), Table 3–2, p. 65.
32. Samuel A. Stouffer, "Trends in Fertility of Catholics and Non-Catholics, "*American Journal of Sociology*, Vol. 41, pp. 143–66.
33. Freedman, Whelpton, and Campbell, *op. cit.*, p. 281.
34. *Ibid.*, p. 182.
35. *Ibid.*, pp. 281, 282.
36. There is "no simple linear correlation between fertility and intelligence," as Bruce Eckland points out in "Genetics and Sociology: A Reconsideration," *American Sociological Review*, Vol. 32, No. 2 (April, 1967), p. 182. A principal reason is that "although the least intelligent groups produce more children within marriage, they are the least likely to marry." Evidence suggests that despite differential fertility, average levels of competence have not been lowered.
37. Freedman, Whelpton, and Campbell, *op. cit.*, p. 288.
38. *Ibid.*, p. 306.
39. *Ibid.*, p. 313.
40. David Goldberg, "Family Role Structure and Fertility" (Unpublished Ph.D. thesis, University of Michigan, 1958).
41. Jerome S. Bruner, "Theorems for a Theory of Instruction" (Dittoed working paper, n.d., received 1963).
42. William Ernest Henley, "Invictus," in Arthur Quiller-Couch, *The Oxford Book of English Verse, 1250–1900* (Oxford: Clarendon Press, 1921), p. 1019.
43. Kingsley Davis and Judith Blake, "Social Structure and Fertility: An Analytic Framework," *Economic Development and Cultural Change*, published by the University of Chicago Press, Vol. 4 (April, 1956).
44. *Ibid.*, p. 212.
45. *Ibid.*, p. 212.
46. *Ibid.*, p. 218.
47. Euripides, *Phrixus* (trans., Morris Hickey Morgan), fragment 970.
48. Deborah Freedman, Ronald Freedman, and Pascal K. Whelpton, "Size of Family and Preference for Children of Each Sex," *American Journal of Sociology*, Vol. 66, No. 2 (September, 1960), pp. 141–52.
49. *Ibid.*, p. 141.
50. These couples are a subsample of a national probability sample of families in the United States in which the wife was white, between ages 18 and 39, and living with the husband (or temporarily separated because of military service). This subsample establishes additional limits and controls. It includes only fecund women, in their first marriage and having borne, to date, two, three, or four children, all of them still living.
51. So are the *N*'s small, especially for the families having three and four children of one sex. The reason for this is given by the investigators: "Given the current norm of two, three, or four children in American families, it is inevitable that [the desire to have a child of each sex] will affect only a small percentage of the families; by virtue of the nearly equal sex ratio at birth, most families will have children of both sexes in the course of having the moderate size of family they desire. On a chance basis, about 50 percent of the two-child families [note the *N*'s for two-child families in Table 2.7: 259 and 261!] 75 percent of the three-child families, and 87 percent of the four-child families, will have at least one child of each sex" (Freedman and Whelpton, *op. cit.*, p. 142).
52. *Ibid.*, p. 145.
53. Nathan Keyfitz, "A Factorial Arrangement of Comparisons of Family Size," *American Journal of Sociology*, Vol. 58, No. 5 (March, 1953), pp. 470–80.
54. This is a shorthand statement. The distance from each county in Quebec to each of the five cities having a population greater than 30,000 was calculated. This city's population was divided by the square of the distance to a given county. Since there were five cities, there were five such quotients for each county. These five quotients were added to yield an index of closeness to or distance from urban influences.

    I should also add, in explanation, that Keyfitz' chief interest was in the method of analysis rather than in the findings on which I concentrate here. Read the article for some sense of the care and sophistication of the method used.
55. *Ibid.*, p. 478.
56. *Ibid.*, p. 479.

TABLES

2.1 Arthur A. Campbell, Chief, Natality Statistics Branch, Division of Vital Statistics, Public Health Service, Department of Health, Education, and Welfare.

2.2 Report of the President's Commission on Immigration and Naturalization, *Whom We Shall Welcome* (Washington, D.C.: USGPO, 1953), pp. 76, 77, Committee on the Judiciary, U.S. House of Representatives, *Immigration and Nationality Act with Amendments and Notes on Related Laws* (Washington, D.C.: USGPO, 1966), especially pp. 203–6, and Bureau of the Census, *Statistical Abstract of the United States, 1969* (Washington, D.C.: USGPO, 1969).

2.3 U.S. Department of Health, Education, and Welfare, *Toward a Social Report* (Washington, D.C.: USGPO, 1969), p. 1.

2.4 Adapted from Robert H. Havighurst and Bernice L. Neugarten, *Society and Education* (Boston: Allyn and Bacon, Inc., 1962), Table 16.5, "Relations between Natural Population Increase, Differential Fertility, and Upward Mobility (Estimates)," p. 422. The table title is changed here, column vii is added along with column-identifying numbers and explanations of derivation of the figures in columns iii through vii.

2.5 Frederic W. Terrien and Donald L. Mills, "The Effect of Changing Size upon the Internal Structure of Organizations," *American Sociological Review,* Vol. XX: No. 1 (February 1955).

2.6 See Freedman, Whelpton, and Campbell, *op. cit.*, p. 306.

2.7 Deborah and Ronald Freedman and Pascal K. Whelpton, "Size of Family and Preference for Children of Each Sex," *American Journal of Sociology,* Vol. 66, No. 2 (September, 1960). Adapted from Table 1, p. 143.

2.8 *Ibid.* Table built on data reported on p. 144.

FIGURES

2.2 For 1650–1950, *The Determinants and Consequences of Population Trends* (New York: United Nations, 1953), p. 11, Table 2. For 1960 data, *United Nations Demographic Yearbook, 1961* (New York: United Nations, 1962), Table 2. The 1970 figure is the author's extrapolation, assuming a 2 percent growth rate from 1960. The estimate for the year 2000 is from, *The Future Growth of World Population* (New York: United Nations, 1958).

2.3 Bureau of the Census, *Historical Statistics of the United States, 1789–1945; Continuation to 1952 . . .* ; and *United States Census of Population, 1960: United States Summary* (Washington D.C.: USGPO, 1949, 1954, 1961), Tables B 1–12 in first two sources, pp. 25 and 1; and Table 42, p. 1–143 for 1960 data. The 1970 figure is an extrapolation from "Estimates of the Population of the United States to October 1, 1969," *Current Population Reports,* Series P–25, No. 434, November 18, 1969 (Washington, D.C.: USGPO, 1969).

2.4 Based on data reported in Dennis H. Wrong, *Population and Society* (New York: Random House, Inc., 1961), p. 53, and coming originally from Table XVII of Command Paper 7695 *Royal Commission on Population* (London: His Majesty's Stationery Office, 1949), p. 26.

2.5 Bureau of the Census, *Historical Statistics of the United States,* Series B–20 and B–130, pp. 23 and 6, respectively, together with *Continuation to 1962,* Series B–20 and B–130, pp. 4 and 6, respectively (Washington, D.C.: USGPO, 1965). *Statistical Abstract of the United States* (Washington D.C.: USGPO, 1969), Table 55, p. 48, Table 69, p. 55.

2.6 Report of the President's Commission on Immigration and Naturalization, *Whom We Shall Welcome* (Washington, D.C.: USGPO, 1953).

2.9 Ronald Freedman, Pascal K. Whelpton, and Arthur Campbell, *Family Planning, Sterility, and Population Growth* (New York: McGraw-Hill Book Co., 1959), p. 4, and U.S. Bureau of the Census, *Pocket Data Book: U.S. 1967* (Washington, D.C.: USGPO, 1966), Table 25, p. 55.

2.10 A. J. Jaffe, *Handbook of Statistical Methods for Demographers* (Washington, D.C.: USGPO, 1951), p. 88.

2.11 Bureau of the Census, "Estimates of the Population of the United States by Age, Race, and Sex: July 1, 1969," *Current Population Reports,* Series P–25, No. 428, August 19, 1969 (Washington, D.C.: USGPO, 1969). Adapted from Table 2, p. 2.

chapter 3 **Rules for newcomers: the cultural framework of the social order**

. . . ideas, no less than the living beings in whose minds they arise, must be begotten by parents not very unlike themselves, the most original still differing but slightly from the parents that have given rise to them.
Samuel Butler, *The Way of All Flesh*

As with a building, a social structure has exits and entrances. Since members exit constantly, they must be regularly replaced. But those entering are raw recruits. They must acquire the skills and values appropriate to their society and its subgroups. This is a condition of group survival. So, once at hand, the newcomers—infants, immigrants, entering students, new employees, rural-urban migrants—must learn and meet (within certain tolerance limits) the group's requirements.

These requirements—let's call them rules—are embedded in our culture. There are complicated sound-making rules that allow us to communicate with one another. There are rules that say what we must do to feed, clothe, and shelter ourselves. Others tell us how to resolve conflicts and make decisions. These and a thousand other rules represent our common understandings about what is and what ought to be. They constitute the core of culture, and that is what we must look to in this chapter. For this is the logical next step: after an input of raw material, it is shaped to cultural prescriptions.

We can frame our inquiry around three questions: What's the connection between the rules (culture) and roles and relationships? What, precisely, do we mean by culture? And finally, how can this concept, culture, be used as a tool of inquiry?

Rules underlie roles and relationships

The significance of rules lies in the relationships they create. A set of relationships is not a happenstance thing. It is contrived, an artifact, the most significant of all human artifacts. Thus a group, which is a structure of relationships, is a creation. And an enduring group is a continuous re-creation. For as we've seen, it must be continuously rebuilt.

We do not commonly conceive the group as a structure of relationships built out of interlocking roles, these being defined by the rules peculiar to a given culture. Instead, we're likely to think of it as as collection of individuals. But this simple view of the group diverts our attention from its essential and significant characteristics. For if we think of the group simply as two or more persons, we neglect certain facts of overriding importance. First, the group may outlast a given membership and so have an existence independent of particular persons. Second, in any single group "the whole person," whatever this misleading cliché may mean, is only partially involved. Third, membership means learning to perform in a particular role which is then meshed with others' roles. Fourth, membership requires and presupposes shared understanding of what is and what ought to be in members' dealings with one another. Fifth, it follows that, on the basis of such understandings, there is a predictable interplay between the *roles* which comprise the *relationships* that constitute the *group*.

Even apparently simple groups—families, gangs, college roommates—involve an intricate network of understandings which require certain learnings before a person can become a full-fledged member. The newcomer must understand and accept the group's goals and the agreed-upon means for achieving them. Until he learns the obligations of membership—accepting certain aims, acquiring requisite skills (language, for example)—he cannot be considered by others a normal or legitimate group member. In the vernacular, he doesn't know the score.

Knowing the score means acquiring the group's *culture.* Linton[1] conveys the meaning of this term by suggesting that society (or a group) is an orchestra in which the musical score represents culture. Each musician (each of us) must learn and follow the score in his particular role. Of course, our performance may not be wholly predictable from the score. For we have our own interpretation, due largely to the idiosyncrasies of our particular background (training). At a given moment in time we are the repository of a set of experiences, and we stand at the center of a network of relationships which, in their combination, have never been duplicated anywhere else or at any other time. So we may improvise a bit. Yet we cannot so depart from the score, from the expectations of conductor and fellow musicians as to jeopardize their collective effort. Should this happen, we will be dropped from the group. But it is worth noting that we must be replaced. For the rules (the score) require our part (role) if the music is to be realized. Conversely, it is impossible for us to produce the score independently. For the score is realized only in concert: culture emerges only within the framework of human relationships. It is not a case of a C and an E and a G, but of a chord which results only from collective effort and common purpose.

Thus the rules—the shared understandings about what is and what ought to be—embodied in culture make a social relationship possible. Indeed, a social relationship can be said to exist only when, *as a result of their common culture,* one person's behavior elicits a dependable and expected response from another.[2] Were it not so—if in answer to A's query or greeting B might respond in any way, randomly, from coitus to combat—human life would be utterly impossible. Human beings cannot live without order.

> A system of ordered relationships is a primary condition of human life at every level. *More than anything else it is what society means.* Even an outlaw group, a pirate ship, a band of brigands, has its own code of law, without which it could not exist.[3]

However unpalatable it may be to those who imagine themselves completely free to follow vagrant whims of the passing moment, human society depends for its existence on recurrences and continuities. Lacking the order which enables prediction, a relationship founders. To reply in anatomical detail to a person's casual query, "How are you?" is, at the least, to put the questioner off. Such a response reveals a divisive lack of common understandings. But culture, as Ruth Benedict has put it, is "that which binds men together" rather than separating them. A society is an ordered or organized set of relationships maintained by common adherence to the culturally specified rules, and roles, of the game. We have to know them if we are to enter the group.

For the human group is to be conceived as a system of relationships sustained by generally shared cultural prescriptions. A culture is the condition of a social system. This term, *system,* is often used to convey the idea of differentiation and unity—unity through the dovetailing of differentiated parts.[4] It is in this sense that we speak of an atomic system, an economic system, a molecular system, a cultural system, a political system, a social system. They are often represented as in Figure 3.1.

The unity of a social system, and of other systems, is an outgrowth of differentiation of parts, interdependence between the parts, and predictability in the connections between the parts. Consider as an example of a social system a family of four. We might represent the system of social relationships in some such fashion as shown in (*d*) in Figure 3.1. The lines represent relationships; the circles, roles. Each of these persons is linked with three others by common understandings, reciprocal obligations, and privileges. Whether the wife is to be decorous, docile, and an adornment for her husband or a career woman commuting to work while her children are consigned to the care of a sitter depends largely on the role prescribed by the culture inherited by members of her group.* Her conceptions of the wife's obligations, her notions of beauty, and even her idea of a desirable weight are culturally conditioned. And so, also, with the is's and ought's of her relationship to son and daughter. The integrity of a social system is rooted in the rules embedded in a culture.

So, thinking about our first question, we see that the constant rebuilding of the group requires the transmission of the rules (culture) that define our roles and relationships. For building that structure of relationships that is society, or a family, a team,

* In a society so complex as ours the wife's role will vary, of course, by subcultures. Different regions, different classes, rural and urban settings may represent subcultures differing in conception of the woman's role.

a community, a union or a civic organization, requires that the newcomer believe and feel "properly." Only when we know the score—when we get culture—can we articulate our behavior effectively with others.

The meaning of culture

Now we had better dwell a bit on this concept, culture. For culture embodies the rules that define the roles which make the relationships that make the group. Hence we must be clear about its meaning.

Definition

The commonest and simplest definition of culture consists of two words: *social heritage* (or *social legacy*). It is ". . . the total life way of a people," says Kluckhohn, ". . . that part of the environment that is the creation of man."[5] But "social heritage" and "life way" are spongy phrases, conveying just enough meaning to engender a premature sense of having grasped an idea, yet not enough to put it to use. And the notion of a man-made environment conveys the false notion that culture consists in perishable hardware. I find the classic definition of culture by Tylor rather more satisfactory, yet not so from another point of view. In his *Primitive Culture,* Tylor wrote:

> Culture or civilization, taken in its wide ethnographic sense, is that complex whole which includes knowledge, belief, art, morals, law, custom and any other capabilities and habits acquired by man as a member of society.[6]

While this seems a good beginning for grasping the meaning of culture, it makes a bad ending. For it is an enumerative definition. (What is a mammal? A mammal is Sophia Loren, an opossum, a whale.) The question remains: What is it that all these things have in common? That which all manifestations of culture have in common, I suggest, is knowledge; and I propose, therefore, this definition: *Culture is socially shared and transmitted* knowledge *of what is, and what ought to be, symbolized in act and artifact.*

Characteristics

That is to say, first of all, culture is learned: it is socially transmitted from parents to child, from elders to youth, from drill

Figure 3.1

Representations of systems

(*a*) atomic, (*b*) information and data processing systems, (*c*) a molecular system, (*d*) and (*e*) microsocial systems

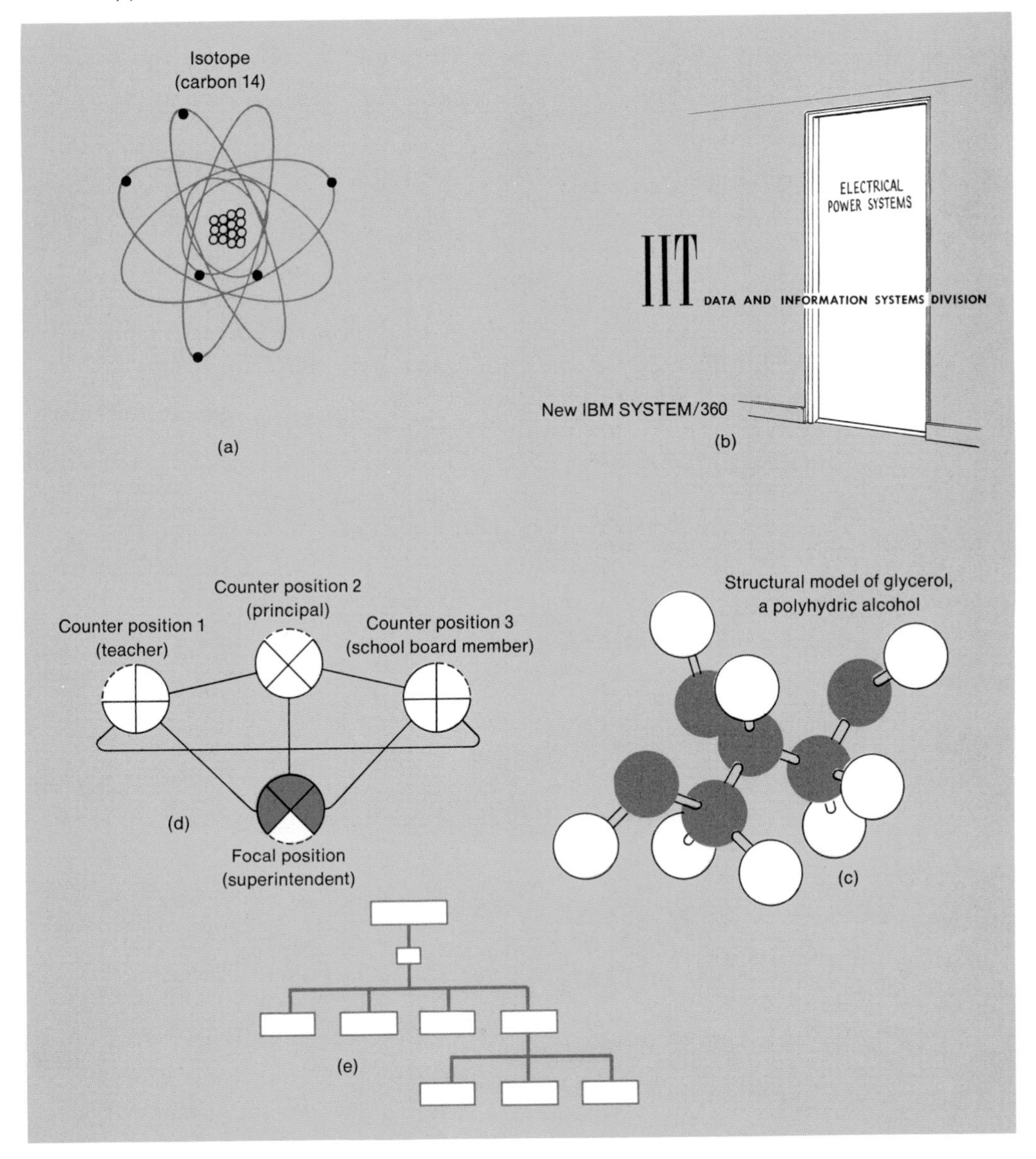

sergeant to inductee, from priest to novice, from generation to generation.*

> Every new generation has to learn to accommodate itself to an order which is defined and maintained mainly by the older. Every society imposes some sort of discipline upon its members. Individuals grow up, are incorporated in the life of the community, and eventually drop out and disappear. But the community, with the moral order which it embodies, lives on.[7]

Now what is learned is, in one way or another, taught. What is generally taught to the young is what is commonly thought to be *necessary*. Culture is forcefully inculcated. There is a mandatory element in it. It is not a *comme ci, comme ça* affair. As we are instructed in *South Pacific,*

> You've got to be taught, before it's too late
> Before you are six, or seven, or eight
> To hate all the people your relatives hate,
> You've got to be carefully taught.[8]

One *must* learn his mother tongue. He must learn enough arithmetic to do the shopping, pay the bills, and balance a checkbook. He must become domesticated. Culture has this coercive element. Being generally shared, culture represents the expectations that large numbers of powerful adults have of the newcomer. It exercises constraint upon him. It has the characteristics of what Durkheim called the "social fact": *generality, exteriority,* and *constraint*. This may seem a dismal doctrine, denying what must seem apparent to every casual observer, that man is an active innovator rather than a passive conformist. One need not gainsay man's creative capacity to assert that culture sets the conditions for creativity.

> Man makes his own history, but he does not do so independently or under conditions of his own choice. The tradition of all past generations weighs like a mountain on the mind of the living.†

* The following discussion of the meaning of culture is cast in the frame suggested by George Peter Murdock in his *Social Structure* (New York, Macmillan Co., 1949).

† See Original Texts, Note 3.1.

What is taught requires a teacher, whether or not formally designated as such—which is to say that the transmission of culture is a social matter, as is the fact of its being shared. The social character of enculturation must be set over against geographical and biological factors. Culture is not determinatively linked to a geographic base or to such biological factors as race, age, or sex. Manhattan is not a fishing village despite its location. And so far is culture from being biologically rooted that it would be more plausible to reverse the relationship, suggesting that biological characteristics stem from cultural factors.

Professor Stanley Garn illustrates the point: "In what other animal does a railroad track serve as an effective barrier to gene flow?"[9] He goes on to point out that what is eaten, how much and how often, is affected by our culturally conditioned eating patterns. Again, as we saw in past pages, level of fertility in a population may be affected by social factors that influence mean age at marriage and the culturally conditioned extent of sexual activity, including ritual taboos. Garn gives further illustrations: The ". . . middle class American child, reared by moderately authoritarian and relatively apprehensive parents, is protected from overexertion"—play periods, naps, and so on. There is sufficient contrast with lower-class behavior, on this score, so that even if caloric intake in the two groups were comparable, "the caloric expenditure is not. And the difference, caloric intake minus caloric expenditure, represents the energy reserve available for tissue maintenance and growth."

When in our definition we say that culture is knowledge of what is and what ought to be, we emphasize its *ideational* character. Culture is not to be confused with the acts and artifacts that symbolize it. Buttons, bowlers, and bikinis are not culture—they are indexes of culture. They symbolize the extensive knowledge in agriculture, manufacture, chemistry, animal husbandry, merchandising, advertising, metallurgy, bookkeeping, accounting, and corporate organization which enable their production. Not only do they symbolize the *what is* sort of knowledge. What *ought to be* is implicit in the choice of this garment over another (trousers instead of a kilt); and the implied constraint when, for a given occasion, this clothing is preferred to that. We cannot, therefore, speak of material and nonmaterial culture as though they were coordinate categories. This jumbles together jet planes, toothbrushes, steel and concrete, the ideal of monogamous marriage, baked beans, razor blades, and the commitment to decisions by majority vote. Such a bifurcation, material and nonmaterial, confounds the concept.

Again, what these things have in common is the ideational element. Act and artifact are symbols of common understandings which include: (1) discrimination of the object, and knowledge of its meaning; (2) knowledge of the techniques of production and/or use; (3) knowledge of its worth. Nor would I say that the rate of growth in material culture outstrips that of the nonmaterial culture. This is an Alice-in-Wonderland race between creatures of different realms. A better statement would be that the accumulation of culture (knowledge) is irregular: sporadic in time and uneven as between various realms of human activity. The result is that elements of culture are variously distributed. In some cases, they may differ to the extent of being incompatible, even contradictory.

If culture is ideational, if it resides in our knowledge of what is and what ought to be, then it must be conveyed symbolically. "Of all aspects of culture, it is a fair guess that language was the first to receive a highly developed form and that its essential perfection *is a prerequisite* to the development of culture as a whole."[10] The significance of language in and for culture is stressed by Dewey. "Society not only continues to exist *by* transmission, *by* communication, but it may fairly be said to exist *in* transmission, *in* communication. There is more than a verbal tie between the words common, community, and communication."[11] The sense and reality of a common culture are given in language. The objects of life and our experiences with them are shaped by a prefabricated system of symbols, a legacy from the past, influencing both perceptions and conceptions. The terms, the gestures, the inflections and associated affect, the range and richness of vocabulary—these vary with age and sex, time, place, and circumstance.[12]

The shared definitions of the situation implicit in language have both a selective and a directive influence on man's conduct. Relevant objects are indicated to the exclusion of other objects: a piece of obsidian, a carburetor, cow dung, manioc. But the symbol also embraces the social meaning of the object. The obsidian is for a knife, useful among other things in competitive destruction with rival Indians. The carburetor is an essential part of our civilization on wheels, providing an air-and-fuel mixture for controlled explosions in most internal combustion engines. The dung is to be made into patties to be burned as fuel, in India; or in the U.S.A., to be loaded on the manure spreader to fertilize the fields. The

... the rules
... embodied in culture
make a social relationship
possible.

... Culture
is socially shared
and transmitted knowledge
of what is,
and what ought to be,
symbolized
in act and artifact.

. . . Culture is not
to be confused with the acts
and artifacts
that symbolize it.

. . . since all enduring groups
have beliefs
and ways of life they cherish
arrangements must be made
for conserving them
in the face of changing personnel
and changing circumstance.

manioc is to be eaten although, being poisonous, it must be artfully leached to render it edible.

The word, its inflection, the frequency with which it is used, the number of words used to describe an object—these give us some clue as to its importance to those who use the object, speak the word. The more language devoted to a given object, the greater its cultural significance for the group. Cases in point are the great number of terms for buffalo and parts of this animal among the Plains Indians; the great number and diversity of terms referring to maize and its uses among the agricultural Indians; or the highly refined discrimination between kinds of snow among Eskimo groups. Thus language, the chief carrier of culture, reveals its symbolic and ideational character.

To mention three such groups as the Pueblos, the Plains Indians, and the Eskimos is to remind ourselves of the enormous variation between cultures—and of certain related matters: the process of diffusion as a way by which cultures are *diversified,* the *ethnocentrism* displayed in rejecting other varieties of culture, and the *inconsistencies* likely to emerge in a variegated culture or between subcultures. Let us consider these matters briefly.

People's behavior—and the products of their behavior—reveal the great range of the cultural spectrum: from the queer conduct of the Nacirema[13] to our own cultural patterns which seem so much more plausible to us, from our alleged monogamy to others' polygyny and polyandry, from our "conspicuous consumption" to the conspicuous destruction of Kwakiutl and Tlingit, from our cult of romance and cheesecake to unions quite terrestially ordained by parents (sometimes before the birth of one of the partners), from snakehandling Protestant sects to Zen Buddhism, from space ships to Missouri mules.[14]

But cultural diversity can be seen even within our own country. There is marked regional variation revealed in dialect, habits, and preferences. The D.A.R. has taken special interest in one variant, the culture of small Appalachian enclaves where isolation has preserved in purer form the Anglo-Saxon heritage. Some are convinced that culture, in the vulgar sense of the term, is bounded on the west by the Hudson River; and that the center from which refinement radiates is "the home of the bean and the cod" where the Lowells, the Cabots, and God form an exclusive trinity. In any case, many traits vary widely within the United States. For example, East and West Coast dwellers were found by Stouffer[15] to be more tolerant than Midwesterners of atheism, communism, and socialism. City dwellers have been shown to vary quite consistently in their beliefs and behavior from rural residents. It is at least conceivable that modes of life and norms of conduct so differentiate urban from rural that we have here, symbolized in space, some crucial contradictions of contemporary life: the split between an expressive and an instrumental orientation, between the world of the heart and that of the head, between giving and getting, between a world of social and one of physical objects.[16] But the contrast, exaggerated here, is diminished with greater mobility, extension of mass media, and national standards and controls.

Our cultural diversity results largely from imports—and this despite a propensity to view our beliefs and behaviors as indigenously American (or French, German, Irish, or Russian), ours by ordinance of God and nature. Conversely, other peoples' ways are often seen as unnatural and barbarous. This tendency to depreciate others' ways and to appreciate our own is called ethnocentrism. Ethnocentrism is doubtless a universal characteristic, a function of isolation and a concomitant of the loyalty which is necessary for self-identification and persistence of the group. In the United States, ethnocentric predispositions are likely to be revealed in our esteem of 100 percent Americanism.

> There can be no question about the average American's Americanism or his desire to preserve this precious heritage at all costs. Nevertheless some insidious foreign ideas have already wormed their way into his civilization without his realizing what is going on. Thus dawn finds the unsuspecting patriot garbed in pajamas, a garment of East Indian origin; and lying in a bed built on a pattern which originated in either Persia or Asia Minor. He is muffled to the ears in un-American materials: cotton, first domesticated in India; linen, domesticated in the Near East; wool from an animal native to Asia Minor; or silk whose uses were first discovered by the Chinese. All these substances have been transformed into cloth by methods invented in Southwestern Asia. . . .
>
> On awakening he glances at the clock, a medieval European invention, uses one potent Latin word in abbreviated form, rises in haste, and goes to the bathroom. . . . But the insidious foreign influence pursues him even here. Glass was invented by the ancient Egyptians, use of glazed tiles for floors and walls in the Near East, the porcelain in China, and the art of enameling on metal by Mediterranean artisans of

> the Bronze Age. Even his bathtub and toilet are but slightly modified copies of Roman originals. The only purely American contribution to the ensemble is the steam radiator. . . .
>
> [And so on, through his dressing, his breakfast, his dishes, to the point of his departure for the commuter's train.]
>
> Breakfast over, he places upon his head a molded piece of felt, invented by the nomads of Eastern Asia and, if it looks like rain, puts on outer shoes of rubber, discovered by the ancient Mexicans, and takes an umbrella, invented in India. He then sprints for the train—the train, not the sprinting, being an English invention. At the station he pauses for a moment to buy a newspaper, paying for it with coins invented in ancient Lydia. Once on board he settles back to inhale the fumes of a cigarette invented in Mexico, or a cigar invented in Brazil. Meanwhile, he reads the news of the day, imprinted in characters invented by the ancient Semites by a process invented in Germany upon a material invented in China. As he scans the latest editorial pointing out the dire results to our institutions of accepting foreign ideas, he will not fail to thank a Hebrew God in an Indo-European language that he is a one hundred percent (decimal system invented by the Greeks) American (from Americus Vespucius, Italian geographer).[17]

Of course, it would be surprising if, in a culture so diverse in its origins, so complex and so rapidly changing, certain inconsistencies and antitheses did not appear. Professor Lynd highlights some of these antithetical elements in the culture of the United States[18] with their opposing directions illustrated in Figure 3.2. One such antithesis in our culture presented the problem, the theme, and the title of Gunnar Myrdal's important volume, *An American Dilemma.*[19] The dilemma was created by allegiance to contradictory principles: (1) all men are created equal; and (2) the white man is genetically superior (and, *sotto voce,* should be accorded, in custom and in law, privilege consonant with his superiority).

Such discrepancies—in this case *de jure* equality versus *de facto* inequality—imply stress. When we are conscious of inconsistencies, we feel constrained to iron them out. (The Supreme Court decision on school integration is an example of this tendency to resolve discordant elements in a culture.) As William Graham Sumner suggested in his classic work, *Folkways,* there is a strain toward consistency in the mores.[20]

LEWIS AND CLARK COLLEGE LIBRARY
PORTLAND, OREGON 97219

Thus we do find prevailing themes, certain motifs that thread their way through the score of a culture. In her *Patterns of Culture,* Ruth Benedict[21] tried to isolate just such basic cultural configurations, summarizing them in single words: Dionysian (for the Kwakiutl) and Apollonian (for the Pueblo Indians). Such brave attempts to crystallize, with conceptual parsimony, the diversity of a complex culture suffer the defects of hyperbole. Yet they may have the primary scientific virtue of being sufficiently provocative to stimulate significant research.

Sociologists prefer verifiable statements about the cultural context of American society. This is why they are amused and disheartened, if sometimes enlightened, by the sweeping and confidently proclaimed generalizations about the modal character of a people made by the literati. Mrs. Trollope offers an example with her cavalier characterization of our culture in *The Domestic Manners of the Americans.* But she is only one of many variously persuasive writers who spoke with commanding assurance on American society. Charles Dickens[22] was one of these—as was the more perceptive Alexis de Tocqueville, whose *Democracy in America*[23] has become a classic document in social history. And the tradition continues, even among those who get most exercised about the social determinism of the social scientist and his disposition, as they say, to "pigeonhole" people. Lawrence Durrell, for example, is only one of the latest among those who find a stable, culturally conditioned national character:

> Just as one particular vineyard will always give you a special wine with discernible characteristics so a Spain, an Italy, a Greece will always give you the same type of culture—will express itself through the human being just as it does through its wild flowers. We tend to see culture as a sort of historic pattern dictated by the human will, but for me this is no longer absolutely true.
>
> I don't believe the British character, for example, or the German has changed a jot since Tacitus first described it; and . . . if you want a bit of real, live Aristophanes, you have only to listen to the chaffering of the barrowmen and peddlers in the Athens Plaka. . . .[24]

There is stability in culture, a continuity in time linking past and future, and a pattern as between elements which damps out outrageous discrepancies. Culture tends to be conservative. Our trivial span of 70 years yields a false impression of change as we re-

Figure 3.2

Suggested new treatment of antithetical elements in our culture

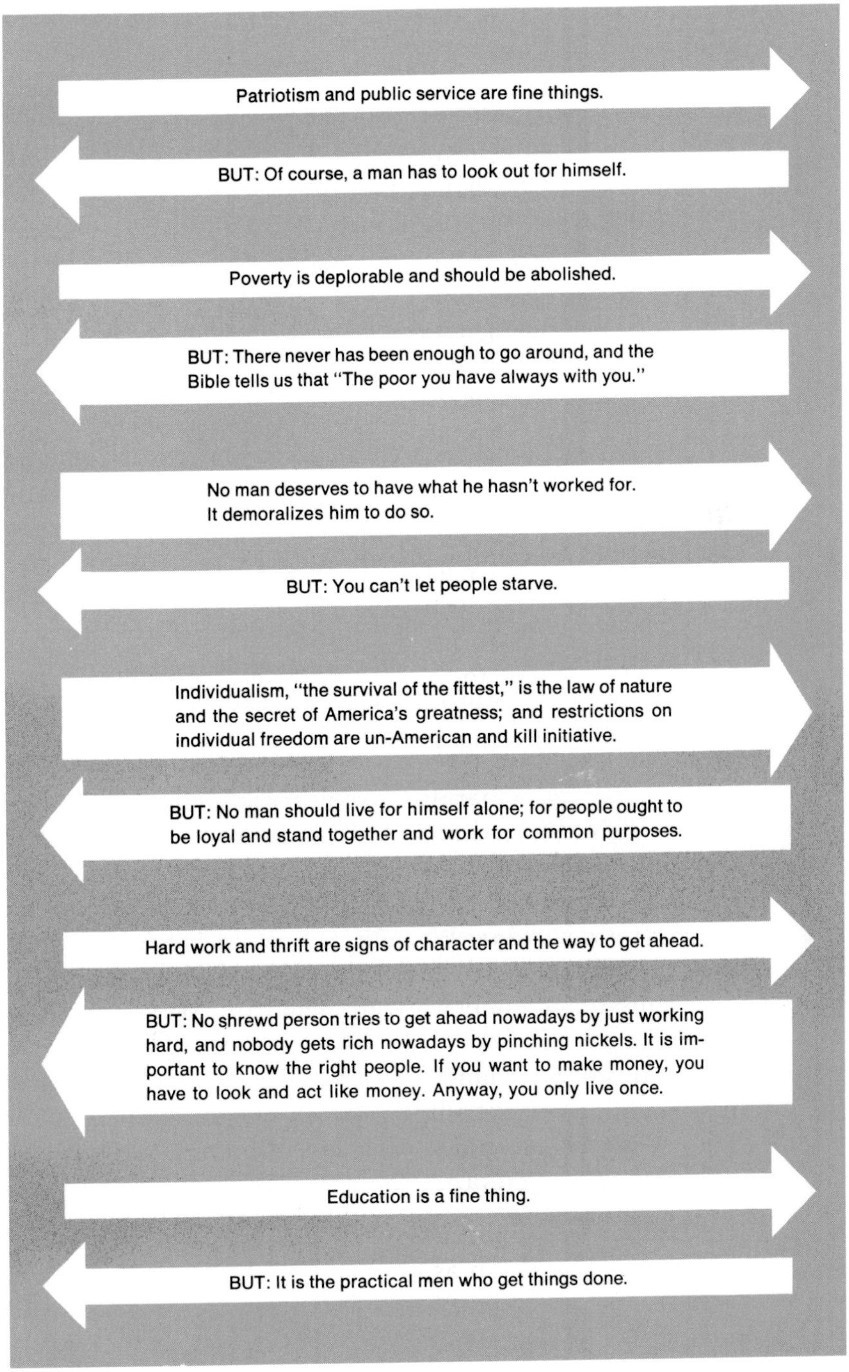

Patriotism and public service are fine things.

BUT: Of course, a man has to look out for himself.

Poverty is deplorable and should be abolished.

BUT: There never has been enough to go around, and the Bible tells us that "The poor you have always with you."

No man deserves to have what he hasn't worked for. It demoralizes him to do so.

BUT: You can't let people starve.

Individualism, "the survival of the fittest," is the law of nature and the secret of America's greatness; and restrictions on individual freedom are un-American and kill initiative.

BUT: No man should live for himself alone; for people ought to be loyal and stand together and work for common purposes.

Hard work and thrift are signs of character and the way to get ahead.

BUT: No shrewd person tries to get ahead nowadays by just working hard, and nobody gets rich nowadays by pinching nickels. It is important to know the right people. If you want to make money, you have to look and act like money. Anyway, you only live once.

Education is a fine thing.

BUT: It is the practical men who get things done.

capitulate, through the intervention of parents and teachers, eons of cultural development. And even though we deal with surface features having no exact prototype in past generations, the innovation rests, like the exposed part of an iceberg, on an enormous submerged portion. For,

> . . . ideas, no less than the living beings in whose minds they arise, must be begotten by parents not very unlike themselves, the most original still differing but slightly from the parents that have given rise to them. Life is like a fugue, everything must grow out of the subject and there must be nothing new.[25]

This continuity of culture was stressed by Durkheim—the way in which:

> Early generations are replaced by later ones, and meanwhile society remains with its own structure and its own particular character. . . . There is an identity between France of the middle ages and contemporary France that one cannot fail to recognize. And so while generations of individuals succeed one another, throughout this perpetual flux of particular personalities there is something that persists, society [culture] with its own mode of thought, its particular temperament. . . .*

The constancies of culture sometimes convey the impression of a supernatural force acting independently of persons. If we speak metaphorically about the "power" of culture, or say that culture "specifies" appropriate conduct for various roles, it is not to be taken as a new supernaturalism. Culture is revealed in the common conduct of men. Cultural specifications of desirable conduct are represented as norms of behavior. We introject common elements of culture, and these become central parts of our personalities. So it is that we have a core of common understandings enabling relationships between members of the group. Sharing a body of culturally provided meanings, we can act toward others so as to elicit predictable responses.

Of course, the meanings that we're talking about are not true

* See Original Texts, Note 3.2.

meanings in any absolute sense. The meaning is given, arbitrarily, in the culture and forcefully inculcated in each person who joins the group. And so friendship, or hostility, or the civic role, or boss-worker relationships are not defined in the same way here, as they are there, or now as they were then. It is also true that the subjective meanings may not be identical for the persons related. (This is implied, of course, when we say that people have had a misunderstanding.)

Nevertheless, there is no enduring group so casual about the transmission of its culture as to allow great variation in the meanings attached to important acts and objects. Custom in the cultural realm has its parallels in habits and norms, in the psychological and social realms, respectively. There is, of course, deviation. In wartime, a few men are conscientious objectors. Some students are "grinds" and others "goof off." But in mundane matters of life and especially where public sentiment is strong, deviation is negligible. Commonly held views and values give rise to similar behaviors under similar circumstances. We must infer widely shared standards for behavior (norms) that define the tolerable range of conduct.

Norms, then, are revealed in modal behavior and reflect elements of the culture commonly shared and internalized by members of the group. Such was the norm revealed by the production mode of 6,600 units among a group of workers observed by Roethlisberger and Dickson at a plant of the Western Electric Company in Cicero, Illinois.[26]

To produce more was to be a rate-buster; to produce less, a chiseler. There is, as it were, a golden mean which best fits the cultural prescriptions. This is characteristic of many dimensions of many behaviors. Take the dimension of goodness as defined by honesty. Somewhere in between a compulsive truthfulness and unreliable mendacity there seems to lie the approved norm in American society. Floyd Allport has investigated this tendency for behaviors to "peak" in their frequencies, so revealing norms of conduct characteristic of our culture.[27]

As a tool of inquiry

If a group, a structure of human relationships, is to survive, then newcomers must get culture, the culture peculiar to that group. So, after considering population input, we turned to culture, asking what the concept implied. We have seen that it points up the diversity of human ways, the flexibility of human nature. It means that conceptions of *what is* and *what ought to be* are systematically inculcated in those entering the group by persons charged with their training. It exists and is conveyed through a set of symbols. Isolated from competing cultural influences, we tend to become ethnocentric. Yet the isolation is never so complete, the coercion of tradition never so thorough, as to preclude variant—even antithetical—notions. Such cultural crosscurrents make for change. But despite the change, we can often discern certain patterns and continuities. These lend identity to a culture and boundaries to the group that carries it.

Thus the concept balloons to embrace many implications. It may seem muddily abstract. Can we walk it down the abstraction ladder to reach the realities of concrete behavior? If so, how do we do it? How do we get at culture? To answer these questions, it will be useful to come at them from three angles: (1) *dimensions* of analysis of culture; (2) the *content* of culture; and (3) some specific *techniques* of analysis as illustrations.

Dimensions of analysis of culture

Culture has been analyzed in several dimensions: in the *space* and *time* dimensions, in terms of the *generality* of culture traits, and in degree of *complexity.*

A culture area is a geographical region within which people commonly display distinctive traits. Such traits may be the use of obsidian blades or woodpecker scalps, the complex of traits associated with maize or the buffalo, a given dialect, the igloo house or the teepee. When plotting the distribution of such culture traits in space, we often find that boundaries are not clear-cut, a given trait simply becoming less and less characteristic until, finally, it fades away. The matter of plotting culture areas is complicated, too, since frequently a practice, apparently similar in two groups, may have different meanings.

Pre-Columbian culture areas have been charted for the United States and for considerable portions of the rest of the world. Nor have we dealt exclusively with preliterate peoples. In 1917, F. J. Galpin wrote his research bulletin, *The Social Anatomy of an Agricultural Community.*[28] In this study he tried to define the limits of an agricultural community, a culture area, drawing boundaries that embraced common activities: the area through which people subscribed to a given paper, used the same banking facilities, were drawn to central shopping areas, and the like. Although Wissler has suggested that there are only two clear-cut modern culture areas, that embracing oriental culture and that of Euro-American culture, it is clear that many smaller cultural areas are distinctive, such as rural French Quebec, or the Ozark and Appalachian regions of the United States. Bounding such areas yields some clues as to cultural diffusion in the past, the spread of traits from one group to another. It also provides a bench mark for the analysis of subsequent inputs affecting the indigenous culture. But more significant is the way in which area analysis sets the stage for discovering what traits fit together, for posing the problem of functional connections.

In the time dimension, we look for such things as significant seasonal celebrations and the temporal schedule of behaviors which memorialize central convictions and commitments of the group.[29] We can distinguish two sorts of ceremonies, although these categories are not exclusive, and I doubt that they are exhaustive.

There is the ceremony that *reaffirms* traditional beliefs and behaviors. Christmas, Veterans Day, Yom Kippur, Easter, Mother's and Father's Days, Memorial Day, Sunday and Sabbath services, funerals—these are principally occasions for affirming the virtues embedded in our traditions—and for recommitment to them. These are some of the institutional safeguards which assure that a man's mortality will not jeopardize the immortality of men.

There is a second sort of ceremony that *redefines* the person's role, revealing the culturally prescribed sequence of the life cycle. Such ceremonies occur at pivotal points in the life history: at confirmation; at graduation; when the Australian, the Hopi, the Zuni, or American joins his fraternity or his religious organization; at marriage; at childbirth. In some groups these stages are clearly defined, in others ambiguously. It has been suggested that in our society, adolescence is just such an ill-defined, never-never land, and that this ambiguity accounts for certain of the problems associated with adolescence. In any case, this culturally prescribed arrangement of the course of life provides a clear-cut distinction between past and future, between duties and privileges of the previous stage and those of the succeeding stage. "When I was a child I spake as a child, I understood as a child, I thought as a child; but when I became a man I put away childish things." Observing these rites of passage[30] we get clues as to the things deemed significant in a given group and the appropriate means for achieving them. Consider a high school graduation, the themes expressed in invocation and benediction, the statements of salutatorian and valedictorian, the main speaker's analysis of the crisis we confront and what must be done to preserve the things we esteem. Consider the mottoes chosen to represent the spirit of the group: *Ad Astra per Aspera, Ad Summa Contendimus,* and the like.

Linton has suggested that a relevant dimension in the analysis of culture is the generality of the trait. There are some traits which are *universals.* Everyone does it, thinks it, believes it. Certain of the clothing habits of men and women, respectively, come close to being universals within a given group. At a second level of generality there are *specialties.* People are sharply discriminated in terms of their special training and particular talents. This is reflected in the organization of highly specialized work roles. But specialties are also seen in different styles of life distinguishing categories of persons who would be incompetent to swap roles. At much expense and a world of trouble, M. Jourdain finds it quite impossible to become a "gentleman,"[31] and similarly, the provincial, middle-class, college-educated man finds it quite impossible to think, believe, or act in the role of a lower-class person. Again, there are *alternatives*—ways of thinking, believing, and acting which allow a wider range. One may do it this way, or he may do it that way. And finally, there are the *idiosyncracies* of personal behavior which are quite outside the culture pattern.

The commonest way of breaking down the concept of culture has been to see it in terms of level of *complexity:* traits, complexes, institutions, and themes. Traits refer to behavior focused on an object and the knowledge—both what is and what ought to be—involved in such behavior. The production and use of a football is a culture trait, characteristic of, but varying within, the Euro-American culture. It includes knowing that it is to be used chiefly in the autumn, in the context of team rivalry; conveys overtones of strength, virility, and associated prestige; involves techniques of handling, passing, kicking, and the like. Sumner referred to such specific customary acts and artifacts which can be discerned in a group as *folkways.*[32] They include all manner of customary behaviors, not for the most part mandatory, but traditionally handed down and carried out automatically, unreflectively: three meals a day, the use of cosmetics, cuffs on trousers and buttons on sleeves, applauding by clapping, shaking hands, the kiss to show affection, shaving, engagement and wedding rings, flowers and tombstones on graves, wearing ties, using the color black for adult funerals and white for children's, men removing hats in elevators, and the like.

Such elementary behaviors and their associated ideas pervade our lives. Indeed, "John Dewey has said in all seriousness that the part played by custom in shaping the behavior of the individual as over against any way in which he can affect traditional custom, is as the proportion of the total vocabulary of his mother tongue over against those words of his own baby talk that are taken into the vernacular of his family."[33] This view seems to render the individual impotent in the face of the folkways. But in reality, the extensive control of behavior through the folkways is fortunate, since they represent ready-made decisions with which we need not concern ourselves. While folkways are moderately binding, they are at the same time liberating. We would never get to bed—or, almost as disturbing, never get out of it—lacking those customary definitions and prescriptions which free us from solving every problem anew.

A second sort of culture trait is distinguished from the first in being charged with a sense of public welfare, moral rightness, and therefore personal necessity. Such a trait is called a *mos* (plural, *mores*), after Sumner's use of the term. It includes such traits as the belief that the adult male should work, saluting the flag, standing up for the national anthem, uncovering in the presence of the dead, the male ostensibly taking the lead in dating-courting conduct, an attitude of reverence in church, and the commitment to universal suffrage (in the United States).

We must be clear that such beliefs and behaviors thought to be right, good, and necessary, are likely to be so only within a given group. The sacred cow in India is a case in point, a creature ill-sustained on inadequate forage, which may not be used for its meat by undernourished people. The mores are not necessarily right or true from some transcendental and objective point of view. They may be objectively detrimental. But within the context of the culture, they are thought to be both necessary and desirable. From the standpoint of the group, the folkways and mores have this social effect: they identify the like-minded, right-thinking people, promote a sense of solidarity, and provide a basis for reciprocal support and for mutual protection against those beyond the pale.

The folkways and the mores do not stand alone, as isolated traits. Any given belief or behavior is intricately bound up with a whole network of knowledges, symbolized in act and artifact. We can use that football, mentioned above, to illustrate (Figure 3.3). It symbolizes knowledge of butchering and skinning, the chemistry of tanning hides, knowledge of valves and the metallurgical and manufacturing skills involved, knowledge of rubber extraction and fabrication—or knowledge of the chemistry of synthetic rubber. It symbolizes stadia, school spirit, ranking systems reflected in the standing of players among themselves from varsity through scrubs and between players and nonplayers. It involves professional and amateur gambling, the sports goods industry, the alumni association, musicians and cheerleaders—and schools and clinics for training them. It touches the administration and faculty of major universities as one of their largest budget items. It involves leagues of competing teams, bowl games, television, journalism, conceptions of education, recruitment for professional teams, and local townspeople whose businesses are affected by the gladiatorial display. It means rallies and bonfires; stirring speeches by players, coaches, deans, and miscellaneous dignitaries; cross-country travel and hotels; special food at training tables; and advertising through the mass media which report the games.

This partial enumeration suggests that the football (and other culture traits) can be seen as the focus of a whole complex of activities. And to this cluster of interconnected traits we give the name, *culture complex*. The maize complex, the football complex, the buffalo complex, the automotive complex refer to just such clusters. Their spread and their dominance give us more adequate understanding of the behavior of people in a given group.

For those functions deemed indispensable by members of the group, regular ways of behaving must be *institutionalized*. Institutions are standardized procedures for achieving culturally prescribed ends: the care, rearing, and indoctrination of the young, the propitiation of the Gods and the support of public morality, the production and allocation of wealth and power, the search for reliable knowledge, the care of physical, mental, and criminal dependents. Behavior in these realms is so vested with a public interest that societies carefully specify rights and duties investing the relationships in these social structures. Thus, if parental care is inadequate, the courts have the power of appointing a guardian and so breaking the parent-child relationship. If a merchant de-

Figure 3.3
Rules that underlie roles and relationships and their exemplification in clusters of conduct

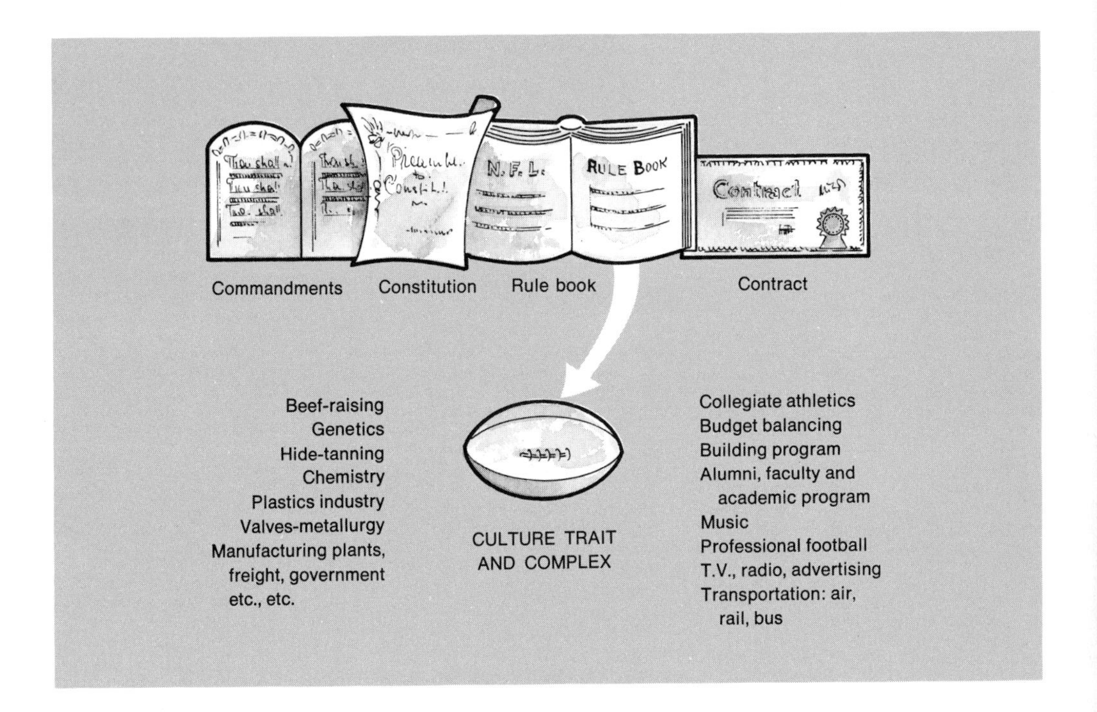

frauds his customers, his license may be revoked. Institutions, as I shall suggest in Part Two, are, in fact, the gyroscope of the social and cultural systems. Someone has suggested that they are "frozen answers to basic questions." The very word, *institutionalize,* carries this connotation of conservative stability. And since all enduring groups have beliefs and ways of life they cherish, arrangements must be made for conserving them in the face of changing personnel and changing circumstances. The analysis of institutional patterns will carry us close to the central characteristics of a culture.

Some investigators have tried to get at such core characteristics by crosscutting institutions and less formal behavior patterns in the search for some *theme* or motif assumed to thread its way through all aspects of group life. The Mundugamor, the Tchambuli, the Arapesh, the Zuni, the Kwakiutl, and the Dobu have been described in such terms.[34] And so indeed have the peoples of more complex cultures: the Americans, the British, the Germans, and the French. Because the problem is so broadly posed and the data so uncertain, this is a very hazardous undertaking. I shall mention some of the ways of attacking it in the discussion of techniques.

Content of culture

We have been thinking about *dimensions* of analysis of culture. But the dimensions of an object—length, breadth, height—are different from the thing itself (a table, for example). We may attempt to describe and understand a culture in terms of the space dimension, the time dimension, along the dimension of generality, or in terms of complexity (trait, complex, institution, theme). But what is the concrete thing we look at? What is the content in a study of culture? The answer is given in our definition. We look at the *acts and artifacts that symbolize the knowledge,* both existential and normative, which constitutes culture. We look at men's behavior and the products of that behavior. The anthropologist in the field lives with his group, maintaining a dawn-to-dusk surveillance over his subjects in an unobtrusive, participant-observer style. The sociologist may observe behavior through a one-way screen, recording conversations, coding gestures, and relating these to the problem dealt with and other relevant aspects of the situation. He may live in the neighborhood seeing, listening, working, playing—and recording—as Hollingshead did in "Elmtown," Whyte on Norton Street, and Liebow at "Tally's Corner."[35] That is to say, first of all, his data may derive from people's acts. Or the observations may have to do with the products of men's acts—the things they write, the themes they use, the nature of their heroes and villains, the records of the patent office, the Sears, Roebuck catalog, the federal budget, popular plays and novels, Holy Writ, the law as it bears on the whole intricate network of men's dealings with one another. What the relevant data are, and what concrete observations should be made, will obviously depend upon the problem posed.

Techniques of analysis

The techniques involved in getting at culture are, roughly, these: direct observation or analysis of others' observations. Direct observation is a very complicated business requiring both skill and wisdom. The categories of things to be observed must be set in the context of the problem and the problem in the context of relevant theory. The observer must be astute in picking up and recording both the objective act, the gestures and inflections, and, separated from this, the inferred subjective state of the actor. He must, if he is a participant observer, take care to observe the dual requirements of the role, identifying in a genuine way with his fellows in the situation, yet maintaining a degree of distance allowing him to appraise the behavior objectively. He must not allow himself to become all participant or all observer. He must keep in mind the requirements of analysis—the sorting and manipulating of the data—and so make his observations as to meet these requirements.

Indirect observation requires the selection of reliable, relevant, and representative observations made by others. It then demands careful manipulation of the data in order to derive general summarizing statements and statements revealing the interdependence of selected variables. Consider this example: McGranahan and Wayne compared American and German traits by analyzing the 45 most popular plays in each country for a given year.[36] Although theater audiences could not be taken as representing the populations of the two countries, the investigators assumed that they could be thought of as literate and influential. If plays are successful because they give forceful expression to the thoughts and feelings of their audiences, then such data as these might be expected to tap basic themes in German and American culture. Criteria were carefully specified for determining the most popular plays.

> It was found that the structure of nearly all dramas could be described in terms of the pattern of conflict, the interplay of opposing forces that underlay the plot; conflict between youthful lovers and parents, between honest folk and criminals, between revolutionary and reactionary political forces, between moral and immoral impulses within the individual . . . it was further found that these conflicts could be classified into six major categories called the "love" theme, the "morality" theme, the "idealism" theme, the "power" theme, the "career" theme, and the "outcast" theme.

Ninety summaries of these plays, with authors and titles deleted and settings disguised, were analyzed by nine judges. Their task

Table 3.1

	U.S.	Germany
Basic themes: distribution in percent*		
Love	60	31
Morality	36	9
Idealism	4	44
Power	2	33
Outcast	0	18
Career	11	9
Disagreement among judges	13	2
Level of action: coded for 45 plays (percent)		
Ideological	4	51
Personal	96	47
Disagreement among judges		2

* These percentages do not add to 100 percent because some plays were classified as having two or more themes.

was to classify plays by theme, by type of ending, and the like (Table 3.1).

We find the American plays focusing on love and morality, the German plays on idealism and power. Personal goals and their pursuit, celebrated in American plays "are frequently portrayed as the root obstacle in the German plays, the materialism against which the idealist must fight. . . . While the American plays carry the lesson that virtue [pays off], the lesson to be found in the German plays is that success in worldly conflicts is won through power and ruthlessness." Thus from men's artifacts (their plays, in this case) we can infer their views and values, their knowledge of what is and ought to be—i.e., elements of their culture.

Similarly, the mass media—newspapers, radio programs, television, magazines—provide data useful for identifying central themes and emphases in the culture. Such analyses may involve frequency counts of words, phrases, assertions pro and con, measures of intensity of statements, recurrent themes, and the like.

Many other techniques are available (some of them, like projective tests, fairly recently developed) for teasing out the judgments, beliefs, feelings, opinions, and characteristics of a people. With the development of opinion polling and, in recent years, the use of carefully drawn probability samples, we are accumulating a wealth of data bearing on prevailing and changing cultural themes.

In contemporary societies, much detailed information must be gathered for administrative purposes. The data in Figures 3.4, 3.5, and 3.6, for example, allow us to make some tentative inferences as to central and peripheral elements of our culture. These and

Figure 3.4

How we spent our money—personal consumption expenditures, United States, 1965

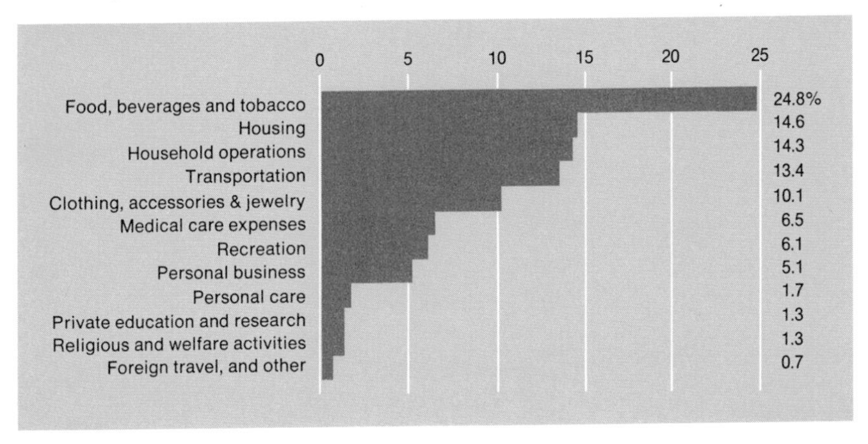

Figure 3.5

How we planned to spend our money—percent of total budget outlays by federal agency, 1969

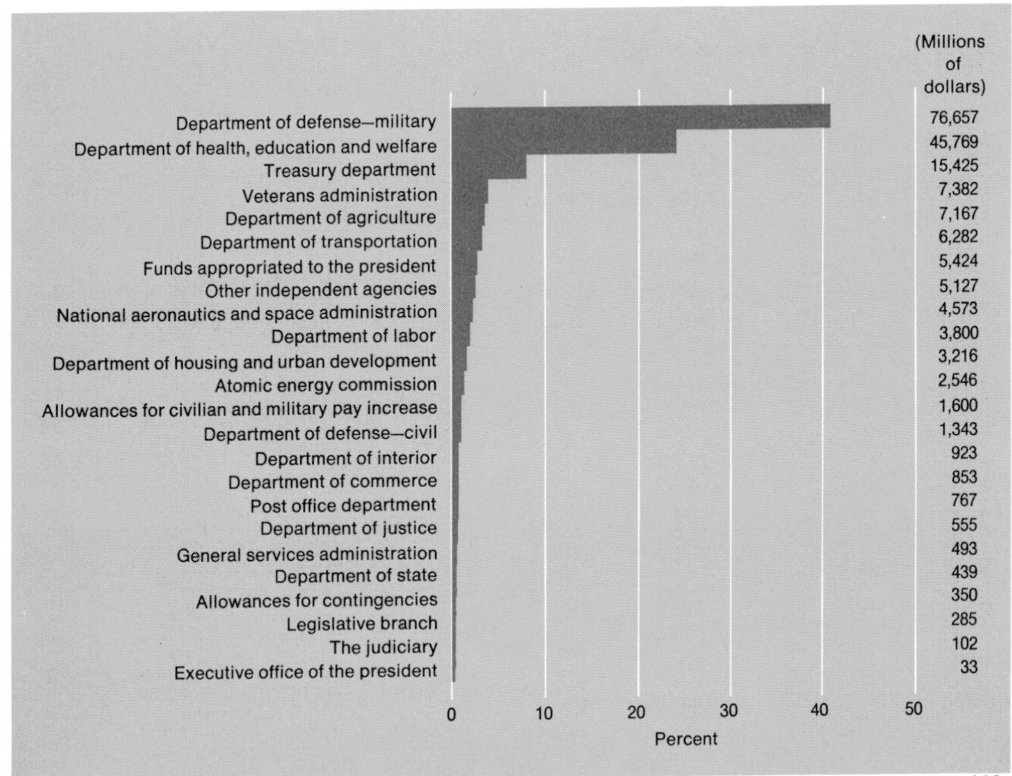

other data may provide useful clues as to the nature of a people culture.[4]

How we spend our money as consumers and as a nation, and how widely car ownership is distributed—these tell us something about our culture. From such data we can draw inferences about productivity in our society, about the level of technology, science and education, about fertility and mortality, about warmaking and the complexity of our government.

We can also use statistics to help answer the question: How accurate are our inferences? Consider this illustration.

Suppose that we're inclined to draw this inference: knowledge of what is and what ought to be in our society is such as to put blacks in a position subordinate to whites. Is this in fact an element of American culture? As we observe the way people live in Harlem or in Chicago's Black Belt our conviction is strengthened that this is indeed the case.

But surely there are deprived whites living in both urban and rural slums. Indeed, our earlier inference may be shaken when we discover that most of the poor (69 percent in 1964) are whites!† On the other hand, we know that whites make up about 90 percent of the population.‡ And we might suppose that they should appear among the poor with the same frequency (90 out of 100 times) that they appear in the general population—if, that is, no social, cultural, or genetic factors are at work to deprive blacks disproportionately. So we must ask ourselves whether the expected percent of whites among the poor (90 percent) is so different from the observed percent (69 percent) that we're led to see this as evidence of a culture trait: systematic subordination of blacks to whites. (Of course we can put the question the other way

* See the publications of the U.S. Bureau of the Census, the U.S. Office of Vital Statistics, and those of the Department of Health, Education, and Welfare, as well as the publications of insurance companies and trade associations; the United Nations Demographic Survey; the *Sociological Almanac for the United States* by Gendell and Zetterberg; and a host of other data collected by business, industry, and government at every level.

† A Social Security Administration study reported that, as of March, 1964, 10.7 million nonwhites were living below the poverty line and 23.9 million whites, for a total of 34.6 million poor. (Mollie Orshansky, "Who's Who among the Poor: A Demographic View of Poverty," *Social Security Bulletin*, July, 1965).

‡ Actually, the figure is closer to 89 percent (blacks were 11.1 percent in 1968), but I shall use the 90 percent figure as an easier one to deal with in our illustration.

§ See Aside on Methods Number 3: "Using the Normal Distribution of Sampling Errors to Check whether a Sample Finding Is Likely to Have Occurred by Chance," page 614.

Figure 3.6

Change in number of persons per car in the United States, 1900–1965

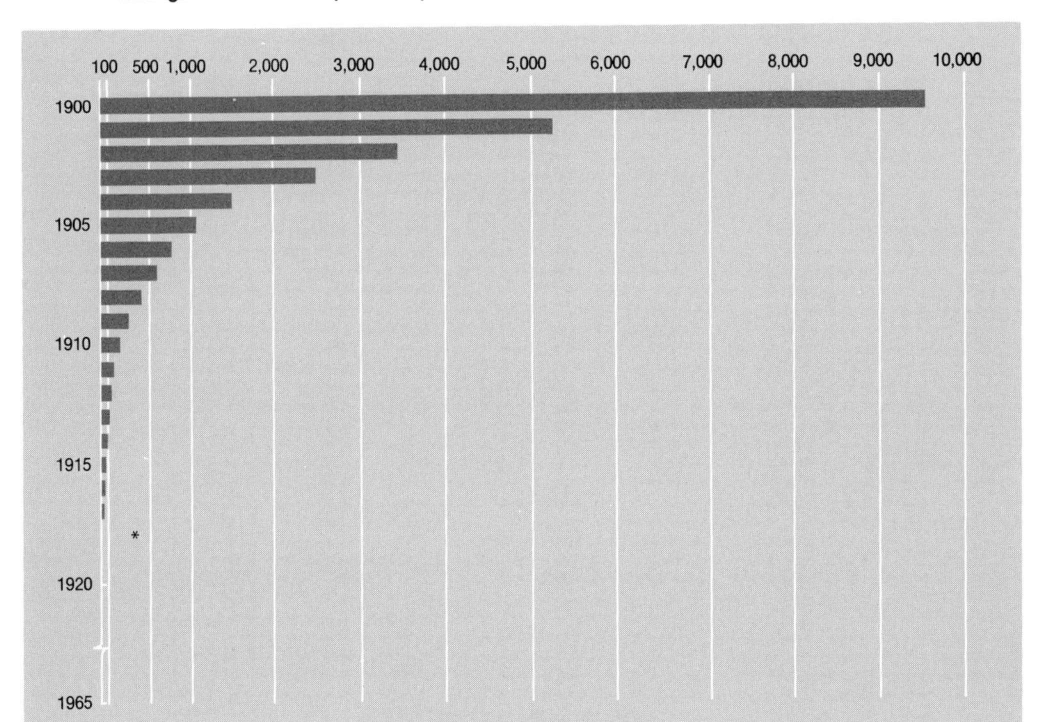

* From 1918 to 1965, number of persons per car ranges from 16.97 to 33—figures too small to represent accurately.

around. Is the expected percent of blacks among the poor—10 percent—so much less than the observed percent, that we see this as a clue to the culturally prescribed subordination of blacks?) If the statistical analysis of the difference between them shows that the two outcomes are so far apart as to be inconceivable on a chance basis, we may conclude that the difference is not accidental.§ It is attributable to some regular influence. And of course, we will see that influence in the culturally given prescriptions for black-white relationships.

There are, then, ways of using this important concept, culture. We can analyze it within a spatial or temporal framework, in terms of its generality or its complexity (as folkway, mos, complex, institution, or theme). We concentrate upon the particular content dictated by our problem: adages and aphorisms, literature, indexes of science, technology, or the state of medical knowledge—the group's *materia medica* or its infant mortality rate—kinship networks, religious conduct, juridical lore and processes. And there are available techniques which I have crudely classified as direct and indirect observation, while providing a few cursory examples.

* * * *

Groups are built—continuously rebuilt—to the extent that losses are replaced by newcomers who learn what is and what ought to be as defined in that group. Indeed, group survival requires infant and immigrant to learn to mesh their beliefs and behaviors with those of others in a system of relationships. Relationships imply reciprocal communication. Such communication presupposes shared understandings, enabling us to predict others' responses. These shared understandings constitute the core of culture which I have defined as socially shared and socially transmitted knowledge, symbolized in act and artifact. Transmitting culture to the newcomer is, therefore, a necessary condition for sustaining the human group: and special sectors of the culture for sustaining specialized subgroups—age and sex groups, occupational groups, fraternities, friendly cliques, government services, the pool hall gang, and the like.

The network of relationships which is a group is built upon a foundation of prefabricated cultural prescriptions. This is perhaps a plausible assertion. But taken alone it leaves unanswered two important questions. First, what is the process by which these prescriptions about appropriate conduct are built into the person so that he may take up the roles required by his relationships with others: How is culture transmitted? And second, what or who are the effective agents in this process? In the next chapter we turn to the first of these two questions, focusing especially on the socialization process and bringing to bear the support of reason and the evidence of experience.

References

TEXT

1. Ralph Linton, *The Study of Man* (New York: Appleton-Century, 1936).
2. This is the core of Max Weber's definition of a social relationship. A social relationship exists, he said, in ". . . the behavior of a plurality of actors in so far as, in its meaningful content, the action of each takes account of the other and is oriented in these terms. The social relationship thus consists entirely and exclusively in the . . . probability that there will be an anticipated course of action" (Max Weber, *The Theory of Social and Economic Organization,* trans. A. J. Henderson and Talcott Parsons [New York: Oxford University Press, 1947], p. 118).
3. Robert MacIver, *The Web of Government* (New York: Macmillan Co., 1948), p. 61.
4. These characteristics of a social system are sometimes hard to grasp in concrete situations, often because the connections between parts of the system are indirect and complex. Lincoln Steffens provides an illustration:

   "Why were these law-breakers so strong? And why was there such an opposition to the simple, superficial reforms of Dr. Parkhurst? [Why] the opposition of good, prominent citizens who had no apparent connection with the underworld? As Dr. Parkhurst forced such results as the voluntary closing of some saloons, he was hated more and more openly by people who one might expect to see approving his course: bankers, business men, and even other clergymen. There was something to find out about the organization of society. I asked my friends in Wall Street to justify their indignation at Parkhurst, but all they would say was that his crusade 'hurt business.' That was the first time I heard that expression. 'How can the closing of saloons hurt business in Wall Street?' I asked James B. Dill, who knew everything. He kicked my shin, hard, and when I exclaimed, he answered my question: 'Why does your mouth cry out when only your shin is hurt?' That was the answer . . ." (Lincoln Steffens, *The Autobiography of Lincoln Steffens* [New York: Harcourt, Brace & World, Inc., 1931], pp. 219, 220.)
5. Clyde Kluckhohn, *Mirror for Man* (New York: McGraw-Hill–Whittlesey, 1949), p. 17.
6. E. B. Tylor, *Primitive Culture* (New York: Henry Holt & Co., Inc., 1889).
7. Robert E. Park, "The Urban Community as a Spatial Pattern and a Moral Order," in E. W. Burgess (ed.), *The Urban Community* (Chicago: University of Chicago Press, 1926), p. 12.
8. From "You've Got to Be Carefully Taught." Copyright © 1949 by Richard Rodgers and Oscar Hammerstein, 2nd. Used by permission of the publisher, Williamson Music, Inc., New York, New York.
9. This and the two following quotations are from Stanley M. Garn, "Cultural Factors Affecting the Study of Human Biology," *Human Biology,* Vol. 26, No. 2 (May, 1954), by permission of the Wayne State University Press.
10. E. Sapir, "Language and Culture," *Encyclopedia of the Social Sciences* (New York: Macmillan Co., 1930), Vol. IX, pp. 155–68 (italics mine).
11. John Dewey, *Democracy and Education* (New York: Macmillan Co., 1921), p. 5.
12. See, or rather hear, Professor Walter Goldschmidt's useful recording for the National Association of Educational Broadcasters, entitled "A Word in Your Ear."
13. Horace Miner, "Body Ritual among the Nacirema," *American Anthropologist,* Vol. 58 (June, 1956), pp. 503–7.
14. This diversity is best documented in the Human Relations Area Files begun some years ago at Yale. Duplicates of this file are found at major universities throughout the country. They provide comparative data on hundreds of tribes around the globe, classified by type of behavior.
15. Samuel A. Stouffer, *Communism, Conformity and Civil Liberties* (New York: Doubleday & Co., 1955), pp. 60–62 *passim.*
16. Norvall D. Glenn and Jon P. Alston, "Rural-Urban Differences in Reported Attitudes and Behavior," *Southwestern Social Science Quarterly,* March, 1967, pp. 381–400.

17. Ralph Linton, "One Hundred Percent American," *The American Mercury*, Vol. 40 (April, 1939).
18. Robert Lynd, *Knowledge for What?* reprinted by permission of Princeton University Press, copyright 1939. All rights reserved.
19. Gunnar Myrdal, *An American Dilemma* (New York: Harper & Bros., 1944).
20. William Graham Sumner, *Folkways* (Boston: Ginn & Co., 1940); first published in 1906.
21. Ruth Benedict, *Patterns of Culture* (New York: New American Library—Mentor Books, 1953); first published in 1934.
22. See Una Pope-Hennessy, *Charles Dickens* (New York: Howell, Soskin, Publishers, Inc., 1946), especially chap. xii, "Sampling America."
23. Alexis de Tocqueville, *Democracy in America* (New York: Alfred A. Knopf, Inc., 1945).
24. Lawrence Durrell, "Landscape with Literary Figures," *New York Times Book Review*, June 12, 1960, Section 7, p. 1. Reprinted by permission of the author. © 1960 by The New York Times Company.
25. Samuel Butler, *The Way of All Flesh* (New York: Macmillan Co., 1925), p. 220.
26. F. J. Roethlisberger and W. J. Dickson, *Management and the Worker* (Cambridge, Mass.: Harvard University Press, 1940).
27. Floyd H. Allport, "The J-Curve Hypothesis of Non-Conforming Behavior," in G. E. Swanson, T. M. Newcomb, and E. L. Hartley (eds.), *Readings in Social Psychology* (2d ed.; New York: Henry Holt & Co., Inc., 1952), pp. 231–42.
28. F. J. Galpin, *The Social Anatomy of an Agricultural Community*, University of Wisconsin Agricultural Experiment Station Research Bulletin No. 34, 1915.
29. A dramatic example of the temporal structuring of culture is reported by Marcel Mauss in his *Essai sur les Variations Saissonières des Sociétés Eskimos.* He writes:

   "In summer, members of the group live in widely dispersed tents. In winter, they live in tightly clustered houses. While the tent contains only one family, the winter dwelling usually contains several. . . . While the summer provides an almost limitless field for hunting and fishing, in winter, on the contrary, the hunting area is greatly restricted. . . . Religion among the Eskimos goes through the same cycle as the rest of their social organization. There is, so to speak, a summer religion and a winter religion: the private domestic cult of summer and the general state of religious fervor in the winter.

   "But this contrast between style of summer and winter living is seen not only in rites, celebrations and religious ceremonies of all sorts. It has an equally telling impact on ideas, collective representations—in a word, on the whole mental life of the group. In certain tribes during a series of festivals we see everybody divide into two groups. In one are all those born in winter: in the other, those born in the summertime.

   "Thus the very pattern of life is classified, men and things bearing the mark of this cardinal contrast between the two seasons. Each season serves to define a whole species of beings and things. One might say that the conceptions of winter and summer are like two poles around which the whole Eskimo thought system gravitates." [See Original Texts, Note 3.]
30. The person who coined this phrase is often done the honor (so common has it become) of not being recognized as its author. See Arnold van Gennep, *The Rites of Passage* (Chicago: University of Chicago Press, 1960).
31. The reference is, of course, to the enterprising hero of Molière's *Bourgeois Gentilhomme.*
32. William Graham Sumner, *Folkways* (Boston: Ginn & Co., 1940).
33. Cited in Ruth Benedict, *Patterns of Culture* (Boston: Houghton Mifflin Co., 1961), p. 2.
34. *Ibid.;* also Reo Fortune, *Sorcerers of Dobu* (London: George Routledge & Sons, Ltd., 1932); Margaret Mead, *Sex and Temperament in Three Primitive Societies* (New York: New American Library—Mentor Books, 1950).
35. References are to August B. Hollingshead, *Elmtown's Youth* (New York: John Wiley & Sons, Inc., 1949); and Elliot Liebow, *Tally's Corner: A Study of Negro Streetcorner Men* (Boston: Little, Brown & Co., 1967).
36. Donald V. McGranahan and Ivor Wayne, "German and American Traits Reflected in Popular Drama," *Human Relations*, Vol. 1, pp. 429–55, *passim.*

FIGURES

3.1 (*a*) (*b*) A. B. Garrett, J. F. Haskins, and H. H. Sisler, *Essentials of Chemis-*

try (New York: Ginn and Co., 1951), p. 347; (*d*) Neal Gross, Ward S. Mason, and Alexander W. McEachern, *Explorations in Role Analysis* (New York: John Wiley & Sons, 1958), p. 53.

3.4 Bureau of the Census, *Pocket Data Book, U.S., 1967* (Washington, D.C.: USGPO, 1966) Table 228, p. 187.

3.5 Based on data from the Executive Office of the President, *Budget of the United States Government, 1969* (Washington, D.C.: USGPO, 1968), Table 4, p. 55.

3.6 Bureau of the Census, *Historical Statistics of the United States, 1789–1945,* and *Continuation to 1952* (Washington, D.C.: USGPO, 1949 and 1954), and *Pocket Data Book, U.S., 1967* (Washington, D.C.: USGPO, December 1966), Table 2, p. 35 and Table 373, p. 282.

chapter 4 **Process of cultural transmission: socialization**

. . . the eye sees not itself
But by reflection, by some other things.
Shakespeare, *Julius Caesar,* I, ii, 52

Genes don't convey culture. We are not automatically and inevitably human beings. Culture must be transmitted—caught and taught—if the group is to be built, if the organism is to be transmuted into human form. The process of transmitting culture, of transforming newcomers, is called socialization.

We shall be thinking chiefly about the child as newcomer to the human group. But the principles of the socialization process come into play whenever a person enters a new group. For there is always the problem of so shaping his behavior (in its covert as well as its overt aspects) that it meshes effectively with others' behavior. If this is to happen, the newcomer must learn the appropriate score—how he is expected to act toward all the objects of his particular world.

These expectations are conveyed in the symbols of speech (or writing, or gestures). As symbols, they make up an internal repertoire, stored in memory and representing both the person communicating and what he communicated, teacher and things taught. As symbols, or images, the other and his expectations of us become part of us. Since the reality of things consists in the images we have of them, we are able to deal with them at a distance. We are freed from the immediate world of tangible things which, were we to deal with them in their endless concrete detail, would make a "big, buzzing, booming confusion" of our lives.

But if we are freed from the concrete event, we are bound by the introjected meanings which become part of us. Learned in give and take with others, these are the meanings of those objects—physical, abstract and social—with which we must deal. In the category of social objects, the self is certainly the most significant. Indeed, we can think of the socialization process as one in which the person's identity is established. But one does not build his identity without identifiers, and in this process the meaning of *self* is gradually revealed through the responses of *others*. Knowledge of self and of others is the critical, dual outcome of the socialization process. This knowledge is indispensable not only because *A* and *B* (for example, child and parent) triangulate on *X* (the objects of life) and reveal their meaning but also because in this process the bonds of mutual agreement are established. Indeed, in many cases the nature of *X* may be less important than the fact that *A* and *B* agree on it (and perhaps erroneously). For in seeing things alike, in making common cause, group as well as personal identity is established. The limits of allegiance, rights, and duties are defined. The culturally framed knowledge of self, of other, and of the relationship between the two—this is the outcome.

From the person's perspective, socialization is the process of entering the human group—of being inducted, as MacIver put it, into the secrets of society. It is a process in which a number of minor miracles occur: sheer behavior is transformed into conduct, the individual as an organic unit becomes a person, self-aware and able to guide his conduct by the increasingly subtle cues that signal others' expectations.

From the social perspective, it is the process of rebuilding the group.

There are different stages in this process of socialization. We'll look briefly at what Mead, Piaget, and Freud have to say on this matter.

There are also differences in the way old-timers induct newcomers. On this point we'll review one piece of research that seeks an answer to the question: Does it make any difference whether the parent-child relationship is indulgent or demanding? Of course, the strongest differences are revealed in strongly contrasting cultures—say, that of the people of Alor (Indonesia), and our own urban, middle class.

Replenishing group losses by recruiting adults is a somewhat different matter. It leads us to consider the socialization of the immigrant (using Israel as our example) and, within our own society, later socialization in subgroups. Indeed, we pick up increments of our culture—specialties, in particular—throughout our lives. When we go to a new school, start to work (or change a field of work), join a new club, enlist in the armed services, enter upon marriage and parenthood, retire to join the oldsters on St. Petersburg's green benches—whenever we enter a new social context we are being further inducted into the secrets of society. We travel toward death through peopled time and space. The several legs of the trip are differentiated in part by our induction into various groups.

Transmitting culture to the child

Internalization of the other

The first entrance is by all odds the most dramatic and the most significant. The newcomer to the human group finds himself an alien in the hands of utter strangers. Both physically and mentally he is almost powerless. In some groups his impotence is underlined by the almost unqualified power of the father (*patria potestas*), including the right, sometimes exercised, of life and death over the infant. There is an infinite distance between his age (zero) and that of his parents (say, 25) in extent of knowledge. By the time he is 25 and they 50, he will have cut down his parents' lead considerably. (In some respects he will have outdistanced them.) But when he enters the human group, he is quite at the mercy of parents and siblings. They determine both what and when he shall eat and wear, when he shall sleep and wake, what he shall think and feel, how he shall express his thoughts and feelings (what language he shall speak and how he shall do it), what his political and religious commitments shall be, what sort of vocation he shall aspire to.[1]

Not that parents are ogres. They give what they have to give: their own limited knowledge, their prejudices and passions. There is no alternative to this giving of themselves; nor for the receiver is there any option. Neither can withhold the messages conveyed to the other. Before the age of six the personality of the child has been deeply marked by the introjected images provided chiefly by parents and siblings. These images (ideas, signs, impressions) conveyed by parental word and gesture are, in fact, the parent. For the reality of the other consists not in his corporeal self but in the symbolic messages he emits. In this sense we incorporate others—they become quite literally part of us. The Biblical statement, "Ye are severally one of another," reflects this conception as does the communion service. Indeed, we might say that the process of socialization is the process of becoming severally one of another, of fusion, a merging of self and other.

It would be strange if it were otherwise. For when we reflect on it, we find it hard to say with precision where the boundaries lie separating us as concrete individuals from the physical and the biological realms, to say nothing of the social. When are the air we breathe, the light and sound waves impinging on us—when are these us, and when non-us? Or the food we ingest and excrete—when is it us and when non-us? If there is some problem in asserting a clearly bounded identity here, how much more so is it to be expected in the realm of human interchange. Or if, as Locke contended,[2] a man's title to his product derives from the fact that it is a thing invested with his energy, his sense of craftsmanship and beauty—vested, in short, with elements of himself—how infinitely more so must the self be fused with its product when that "product" is a person as in the case of teacher-student, parent-child, employer-employee relationships? In human relationships, a theory of unqualified individualism is both spurious and dangerous.

There is, then, a kind of permeability of the human psyche by virtue of man's capacity to symbolize. Here the crucial significance of language is obvious. It provides the symbols from which the image of the other is formed. Symbols make light luggage. We can carry a great freight of them around with us. And since many of them represent the people with whom we deal, the person carrying them becomes a society in microcosm. Marcel Mauss says:

> Other people need not be there, physically, corporeally distinguishable from us; for we always carry with us and in us a number of clearly identifiable others.*

* See Original Texts, Note 4.1.

So it was that Charles Horton Cooley said, "a separate individual is an abstraction unknown to experience, and so likewise is a society when regarded as something apart from individuals."[3] Cooley's views are particularly germane to the problem of socialization, especially as he developed them in his *Human Nature and the Social Order*. His central theme is that the solid reality of social life consists in the images people have of one another. These images are built up through the process of symbolic interaction.

> So far as the study of immediate social relations is concerned, the personal idea is the real person. That is to say, it is in this alone that one man exists for another. . . . *The immediate social reality is the personal idea.* . . . Society, then, in its immediate aspect, is a relation among personal ideas.
>
> Thus the imaginary companionship which a child of three or four years so naïvely creates and expresses, is something elementary and almost omnipresent in the thought of a normal person . . . [for] we have no higher life that is really apart from other people. It is by imagining them that our personality is built up; to be without the power of imagining them is to be a low-grade idiot; and in the measure that a mind is lacking in this power it is degenerate. Apart from this mental society there is no wisdom, no power, justice, or right, no higher existence at all. The life of the mind is essentially a life of intercourse.[4]

Thus self and other are deeply and indivisibly bound together. This has special significance for the socialization process because it means that, willy-nilly, the child must incorporate, internalize his parents (and the others to whom he is regularly exposed). The ability to manipulate symbols which enables this internalization has interesting and ambivalent consequences. It means that the person is freed from bondage to the concrete reality and can deal with objects at a distance or in their absence. This is what we do when we turn things over in our memories, solve problems, reflect on certain matters. The power of a relationship may be felt even—sometimes especially felt—in the absence of the other.

But if we are emancipated from dependence on the immediate and tangible reality, we are not free to shake the symbols of it which we have internalized. "Even when we are quite alone," Darwin observed, "how often do we think with pleasure or pain of what others think of us—of their imagined approbation or disapprobation."[5] The very core of Freudian theory relates to these deeply buried images persisting in the subconscious. Even to deal, however unsatisfactorily, with a violent and tyrannical father, a child must come to "understand" him. In doing so, in making the father intelligible, he must bring that father within himself. Similarly, although it is not a good one, there is perhaps something to the syllogism of which the first two terms are: "Wars are made in the minds of men. The minds of men are made at mother's knee. Therefore. . . ." There is a terrifying power exerted by the elders —the internalized elders—in the socialization process. It is a long-lasting power by virtue of the symbolic character of human interaction.[6]

Physical, abstract, and social objects

The symbolic interpenetration of self and other, of parent and child in the socialization process, results in the transmission of knowledge of what is and what ought to be. The other who becomes part of us is a congeries of knowings, feelings, and believings which become ours as he becomes us. Put more abstractly, as *A* and *B* interact, culturally prescribed definitions of *X* emerge and become fixed. In this process we learn the significance of certain objects: of *physical objects*—cabbages and cornflakes, crucifixes and Cadillacs, TV and vitamins, pens and planes and pencils; of *social objects*—mother and father, playmate and preacher, teacher and employer, insider and outsider, the self (which is above all significant for us among social objects); and the behavioral significance of *abstract* words—justice, equality, Republican, Democratic, Socialist, Communist, playing square, being a "square," Catholic, Protestant, Jew, and so on.

It seems probable that these objects are crystallized for the person as the smooth, ongoing tenor of his life is interrupted, as action is impeded. A complete, unimpeded satisfaction of wants would tie us to the level of sensory perception. But some interference, some obstacle thrown in our path, creates the life of imagination, prompts us to isolate the object, to hold it in suspension, as it were, while possible alternatives are considered. For the young just entering a strange group, such blocking is a very familiar experience. The very nature of things is carved out of an intractable world in which the elders are constantly interposing obstacles. The objects of the world are not merely "out there," possessing some intrinsic character which will reveal itself when an independent mind is mature enough for the knowing. The objects of the world are gradually revealed to us as we act upon them and they upon us through the mediation of the elders. To know is to experience, selectively, those objects deemed relevant within a culture, and to interpret such experiences in terms dictated by the culture as mediated in the socialization process.

A television set, for example, is a physical object toward which we act, with which we have experiences. It represents a complicated set of knowings, both about what is and what ought to be. It is not available to all people. From the user's point of view, it involves learning some things about entertainment, business (advertising), and citizenship (campaign speeches). Some programs are "worthwhile" and others are not. There are times when one must yield in his preference for a given program to the desires of others and do the things he *ought* to do, such as study. Thus a physical object gains meaning as we experience it within a cultural frame under the tutelage of significant others. Even though physical objects might be thought to be essentially alike for all persons, this is so—if it is so—only within the realm of immediate sensory perception. As regards function, the object is different for different groups, and the person entering the group must learn the appropriate functions. The Christian cross is a physical object, but a very different one to the devout Christian than to the Jew whose family was killed by "Christians" in an anti-Semitic pogrom.

Especially with abstract objects such as communism, what is learned is learned not so much in direct physical contact with the sounds and sights of communist activity, but in interaction with others whose conception of, and attitudes toward, the object we internalize. Many of our most important attitudes are learned as we pick up others' attitudes, rather than in contact with the object of the attitude. This is especially true as the child acquires from his parents the attitudes deemed appropriate within the group he is entering.

The social object, a person, is a complicated problem for the newcomer because such objects are so complex. In the one case the object is male, in another female, each requiring different responses. The person may be husband or wife, cousin, uncle, aunt, brother, sister, grandparent, teacher, preacher, clerk, doctor, salesman, policeman. A great variety of roles must be identified, along with certain dimensions of the roles such as reliability, competence, intent, and the like. Things are further complicated since, with social objects, what we act toward is not the tangible object but rather the image which each of us has of another.* Indeed, the corporeal aspect of another may remain the same while the image changes. ("When I first met him, a year ago, I found him witty and entertaining; but having heard the same stories ten times over, an evening with him is a dismal prospect." Or consider the case of the Negro who has "passed" and then, somewhere along the line, is "unmasked.") Conversely, a person may change in physical appearance, yet still be seen and dealt with as before. It is, therefore, not the physical aspect but the image of the social object and its transmission that is the significant thing.

But the crucial social object about which the person must learn and toward which he must act is himself. The socialization process may be thought of as directed above all toward answering the question for the newcomer: "Who am I?" Even to pose the question of self-recognition implies something of the nature of the process: to recognize or identify the self implies the position of an outsider. It suggests that the subject must come to think, feel, and act toward himself as object. But the person does this only to the extent that he can stand in another's position, seeing and appraising himself through another's eyes. Thus the ability to take the role of the other and self-consciousness are twin-born. To "be" another and to be one's self are cognate matters. The self as a social object emerges as the images of other social objects emerge.[7]

Because this process of self-realization requires seeing one's self reflected in others' eyes, Cooley used the phrase, the "looking-glass self."

* This is perhaps too strong a statement, although the emphasis is right. There are times when we transform persons, social objects, into physical objects and treat them as such. In an army, in all large organizations where things are done "by the numbers," there is a tendency to treat people as things. And this may be appropriate, depending upon the group, its personnel and purposes. It might, for example, be very bad for the patient and for everyone involved in the healing processes if a person having an appendectomy were to be treated as a whole person, as anything but a case of appendicitis. Isidor Thorner casts light on the necessarily restricted role of the nurse and, which is the point here, the limited number of attributes of the patient which become relevant in this relationship. This lack of range and depth of attributes is characteristic of physical, in contrast to social, objects ("Nursing: The Functional Significance of an Institutional Pattern," *American Sociological Review*, Vol. 20 [October, 1955], pp. 531–38).

The converse is true, too: occasionally we treat physical objects as social objects. Walking through a dark room in the middle of the night, we bark our shins against a chair. Now we may act toward the chair as though it were a social object, reproaching it vigorously and even kicking it back "to teach it a lesson."

In a very large and interesting class of cases the social reference takes the form of a somewhat definite imagination of how one's self . . . appears in a particular mind, and the kind of self-feeling one has is determined by the attitude toward this, attributed to that other mind. A social self of this sort might be called the reflected or looking-glass self:

> Each to each a looking-glass
> Reflects the other that doth pass.

A self-idea of this sort seems to have three principal elements: the imagination of our appearance to the other person; the imagination of his judgment of that appearance; and some sort of self-feeling, such as pride or mortification.[8]

As we think in terms of the parent-child relationship in the socialization process, we can paraphrase Cooley's three elements of the self-idea in these questions: (1) How does the child imagine he appears to his mother and father? (2) How does he suppose they judge the picture they have of him? And (3) how does he react to the judgment of his appearance which he imputes to his parents? In its dissection this analysis makes the process much too rational, conscious, and calculated. Cooley means rather to suggest a constant interplay between personal images, as people deal with one another, and their evaluations of such images.[9] It is instructive to recall the etymology of the word, *person:* it comes from the Greek and originally meant *mask.* (We use the word in its literal significance on playbills, *dramatis personae.*) In this sense it conveys precisely the proper notion that becoming a person involves learning to wear the right masks at the right times, learning to define situations and enact the appropriate roles correctly. It also conveys the correct notion that underneath the mask there are other elements of the personality which must be understood if we are to grasp a person's motives, the meaning of his act, and his expectations of us.

But socialization involves not only agreement as to the nature of these three sorts of objects but also *the recognition that we are agreed.* In the process of learning to discriminate, identify, understand, and evaluate the objects with which our worlds are furnished, we learn to see them *as others see them.* We do not learn what these objects are in any immutable or absolute sense. We agree with others, first of all, because the powerful elders insist we do. But underlying the coercion of the elders is the unarticulated requirement of common cognition if we are to communicate—and hence, to live—and common values if we are to live in some degree of harmony. If this is a requisite for personal survival, it is also mandatory from the perspective of the group. A high degree of consensus is required if the person is to fulfill his role as a member of the group. It is the perception of consensus on matters deemed essential by the group that defines the person's allegiance and the group's boundaries. Those who agree with us are our kind.

This strain to see things as do our significant others is something which must appeal both to our own experience and our reason. For we deal with most of the objects of life in the company of others. We *triangulate* on objects: persons *A* and *B* oriented toward, concerned about, arguing over, collaborating with respect to an object, *X*. Thus:

1. I love my fiance (or Picasso's art, or the *Chicago Tribune,* or artichokes).
2. I love my parents.
3. Therefore my parents *must* (or should) share my passion for . . . .

Failure to identify and appraise *X* (a thing, an idea, another person) as do our friends, our employers, our fellow worshippers and fellow citizens—such failure would mean a failure in communication, a threat to relationships. We tend, then, to "see" alike and to associate with those who see as we do. We read papers expressing the "right" editorial views, switch off radio and television programs expressing the "wrong" sentiments. And especially in the socialization process, the child is constrained to view *X* in the same light as do his parents and his neighbors, people of the same community and the same communion. This may be easy to achieve since, not being exposed to alternatives, he simply and literally has no choice. Or the parents, aware of alternative views of an object, *X,* and inclined in one direction, may use their power to bring the child's views of *X* into line. But we should not overlook the tendency and the desire, from the child's side, to see the world as respected and powerful parents see it. All his rewards lie in this direction.

Even beyond childhood we are inclined to see things—war service or the C.O. position, pot, premarital chastity, longhairs and skinheads—as valued others do. And, to put it the other way around, the degree of acceptance and liking among people varies with the extent of consensus on significant objects or issues.

Achieving consensus on all these matters relating to life's essential objects is not a simple matter in our day. It takes much time, enormous expenditures, and the combined efforts of many people. Family, school, church, and government are prominently involved in the process of socialization, the first two being explicitly charged with it. Business participates in many ways. Also implicated are the Boy Scouts (and Girl), summer camps, the Catholic Youth Organization, the P.A.L. (Police Athletic League), 4–H Clubs, and a host of other agencies. The process, once narrowly defined, clearly focused, and fairly achieved by the early teens, now requires many more years.

To mention various agents of socialization must not mislead us. It is not a process wholly conscious and calculated. Outcomes are often unintended, produced by a cryptic mix of influences typically unidentified and unassessed: family size, sibling position, region, race, religion, parental prejudices, relatives and guests, class and crises—factors ad infinitum. In the process, attitudes and values are shaped, becoming, along with cognitions, the essential person. To challenge them is to affront the person: for his conceptions of what ought to be lie at the center of his being. Slowly, often imperceptibly, the newcomer picks up his culture.

Stages in the socialization process

I have said *imperceptibly* the individual becomes a person, behavior becomes conduct. Yet is is possible to establish some bench marks along the way, less arbitrary than Shakespeare's seven ages of man. Some of the more penetrating suggestions as to stages in the socialization process come from George Herbert Mead, from Jean Piaget, and from Sigmund Freud.*

Mead was curious about the development of the self-concept and the relationship between self and society.[10] We gain some understanding of these matters, he suggests, if we think of socialization as proceeding through three stages: an early stage of haphazard emulation, a play stage, and a game stage. The first stage, characteristic of the child under two or three years, is one in which he copies others' activities without understanding the mean-

* On the applied side, and with a strong biological orientation, we have the work by Ilg and Gesell at Yale. Many of the advisers to parents, Dr. Spock for example, detect certain stages in development which require differentiated behaviors and responses. For a comprehensive review of the socialization literature see David A. Goslin (ed.), *Handbook of Socialization Theory and Research* (Skokie, Ill.: Rand McNally & Co., 1969).

ing of the actions. This is an elementary step in learning to take the role of the other. He "reads" the paper—upside down. He paces the floor, hands behind back, "reflectively." He repairs a mirror, with a hammer. Such activities Mead conceives as a prelude to the stage when the child actually takes on different roles meaningfully. This is the play stage when he plays father or physician and in doing so, is able to act back toward his self. He looks upon himself as a patient when he assumes the doctor's role, as a child when he assumes the father's role.

This capacity of the subject for treating itself as object is sometimes revealed when the child refers to itself in the third person: not "I want water," but "Mary wants a glass of water," Mary being the speaker. Here in the play stage the *social* character of selfhood is clearly revealed. The child's conception of self conforms to the way he thinks it is conceived by others. The role is rehearsed to meet another's expectations. It is roughly correct to say, then, that the way in which a child conceives himself is conditioned by the roles which he takes; and that these roles are defined by others' treatment of him. This is the perception contained in Shaw's astute statement to the effect that the difference between a duchess and a flower girl lies not so much in the way they act as in the way they are treated.[11]

But if the child takes on various roles, he develops a series of discrete selves, wavering and perhaps inconsistent. It is in the third or game stage that Mead sees a more consistent self-conception emerging. He uses the word "game" to express the requirement faced by the child of reconciling diverse expectations and meeting common ones. Like a member of a team, he must develop a self-concept and a pattern of conduct consistent with the expectations of all other members. Instead of taking the role of *the* other, he must take the role of *all* others, the "generalized other" as Mead calls it. A given situation will elicit from every member of the group the response expected of a person in that role. Situation: man on first base, the hit goes between second and third. Solution: shortstop fields ball, throws to second baseman, who moves up to take the throw and sends it on to first for a double play. Every man on both teams—and the spectators, too—expects this behavior of any person (shortstop) in this situation. And so it is with any adequately socialized person who, for example, respects his parents, is loyal to his country, works conscientiously at his job, outwits a shrewd adversary, but is indulgent with children, women, and other dependents. That is to say, he takes the role and meets the expectations of the generalized other.

We have a generalized other when we internalize the shared prescriptions for conduct in commonly encountered situations.

Mead's third stage has something in common with the fourth and last stage which Piaget has distinguished in mastering the rules of the game. This is the stage which he calls that of the *codification of rules.* "Not only is every detail of procedure in the game fixed, but the actual code of rules to be observed is known to the whole society."[12] This clearly implies the sense of the generalized other: for a sense of the rules is an acknowledgment of common expectations.

Piaget and his Swiss group have been working for some 35 years in the attempt to unravel the mysteries of the socialization process. For some time his study, *The Moral Judgment of the Child,* has been known throughout the world as a pioneer effort in understanding this significant aspect of socialization. Morality is a matter of adherence to rules: and Piaget distinguishes four stages in the development of the child's conceptions of the rules of the game: first, a stage of erratic and ephemeral individualism, with strong motor activity; second, the egocentric stage (roughly, ages two to five), "combining imitation of others with a purely individual use of the examples received"; third, between ages seven and eight, a stage of incipient cooperation, with an agreement on rules which may last the length of a single game but do not exist independent of the particular game; and finally, fourth, the stage mentioned above in which there is a codification of rules known to all members of the group, thus conveying much the same notion as Mead's generalized other.

Piaget also distinguishes three stages in the child's growing awareness of the rules: first, a stage in which the rules do not have a mandatory quality, being taken as interesting examples rather than as obligatory realities; a second stage in which rules come to be seen as sacred, immutable, emanating from powerful adults and lasting forever; and a third stage in which a rule is looked upon as a law stemming from mutual consent, which should be respected but, also, which may be changed if the change is in accord with general sentiment.

For Freud, the socialization process was, at its core, the struggle to redirect primal impulses into culturally required and approved channels of conduct; for man is, first of all, an organism propelled by deep-rooted and preemptory drives.* To confront a constraining culture is to generate conflicts which may be resolved in a number of ways, among them by the use of psychic defense mechanisms: repression, sublimation, displacement, projection, and the like. As diffuse sexual and aggressive drives seek expression within the restrictive context of human society, determinate stages of the socialization process may be distinguished: infancy, latency, and puberty. Infancy covers the period up to about age five with satisfactions focused in the erotogenic zones—mouth, anus, and genitals—while culturally prescribed controls over feeding and elimination are imposed on the child. The second, or latency stage bridges, roughly, ages 6 to 12, a period during which the child's great dependence on and attachment to the mother is attenuated—that is to say, oedipal inclinations are masked and a sense of the rules of the game begins to crystallize (in Freudian terms the superego, or conscience, gains in strength). In the third, the puberty stage, starting at approximately age 13 the focus of gratification is on the genitals, and heterosexual impulses gain in strength, once again controlled and deflected by the constraining cultural context mediated by the elders.

Now Freud was disposed to view man as endowed with a quantum of energy which, if not allowed to flow directly toward its goal, would seek alternative or compensatory outlets. Like a child's balloon, if constricted at one point it would billow out elsewhere. On the whole, the more restrictive the cultural context and the more repressive the socialization process, the greater the likelihood that this psychic energy would flow out in aggressive and damaging fashion, both for the person concerned and for others. This being so, it becomes extremely important that the relationship between parent—particularly mother—and child be a supportive one, gentle and affectionate. Thus the child has secure anchorage during this turbulent business of becoming socialized.† In its popular and somewhat distorted version, this principle has often become a prescription of permissiveness.

* Freud (1856–1939) made significant contributions to sociology in his analysis of remote repercussions of mother-father-child relationships. The student who is unfamiliar with Freudian terminology and theory should consult such references as the following: Anna Freud, *The Ego and Mechanisms of Defence* (New York: International Universities Press, Inc., 1946); and Gordon S. Bloom, *Psychoanalytic Theories of Personality* (New York: McGraw-Hill Book Co., 1953).

† It is necessarily turbulent, in Freud's view, because the culture of whatever group born into is inevitably, often harshly, restrictive. Denying the gratification of libidinal impulses, the demands of the culture generate ill-suppressed hostilities, often deflected or sublimated in various ways.

Different patterns of socialization

Does leniency in socialization promote adjustment?

What we have been discussing, quite obviously, is different (although by no means contradictory) interpretations of the socialization process—various theories as to the way in which the child enters the human group. But theories—that the sun circles the earth, or that phlogiston is what turns metallic ore into metal—are made by fallible men. So it behooves us to turn to research (controlled observation) to test some of these notions about the socialization process. And examining a piece of concrete research will allow us to tie the idea of socialization to the field of sociology as we discussed it in the introductory chapter: the controlled observation and interpretation of different patterns of human relationships, their sources and consequences. Using Professor Sewell's study to which I alluded earlier,[13] consider these questions: (1) What are the "differing patterns of human relationships" that we are observing? (2) What interpretation is involved? (3) How is the observing done and in what sense is it controlled observation? (4) How is the problem formulated as an hypothesis? (5) How are the data manipulated in order to test the hypothesis? Take them seriatim.

What are the differing patterns? Although people in various roles share in the transmission of culture to the child—father as well as mother, siblings, relatives, friends, and neighbors—the early and elemental aspects of socialization fall chiefly within the mother's sphere. Sewell is investigating the significance of different training practices, such as breast versus bottle feeding, self-demand nursing schedules in contrast to a more rigid and regular schedule, the use or nonuse of punishment in toilet training, and the like. So we are dealing here with differing patterns of mother-child relationships, relationships that differ along the dimension of leniency-severity. Our interest, then, is focused on the behavior of four persons: two persons (mother and child) in each of two categories. In the one category the mother trains the child in a way we call rigid, or rigorous, or demanding. In the other group the mother behaves indulgently, permissively. We might put the contrasting relationships, schematically, in this way (Figure 4.1): R and R' represent the differing patterns of relationship built from the articulation of r_2 and r'_2 (children's roles) with r_1 and r'_1 (mothers' roles). The differing relationships (and let us remind ourselves that these are *inferred* from observed behavior), indul-

Figure 4.1

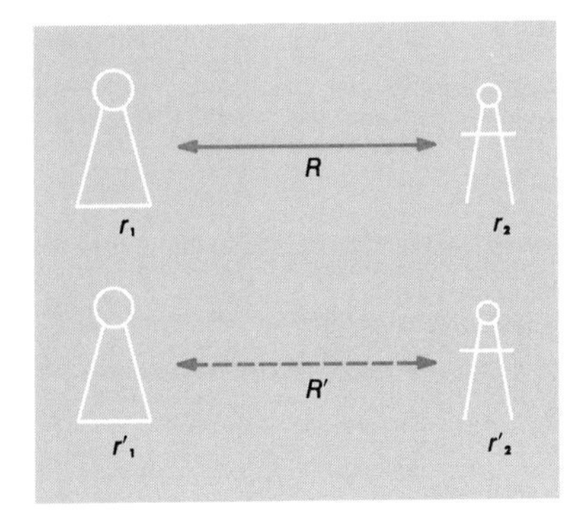

gent and demanding, are represented by broken and solid lines, respectively.

What is the interpretation involved here? The interpretation to be tested is built on the theory of socialization just mentioned. Psychoanalytic prescriptions derived from Freudian theory emphasize such things as breast feeding, frequent sucking periods, and casual and unforced toilet training. Karl Menninger, for example, asserts that every child should be guaranteed seven things:

1. He should have the opportunity for frequent sucking periods not limited in time, not artificially interrupted, and preferably at the mother's breast.
2. There should be no attempt to train the functions of excretion in accordance with adult standards until the child can sit alone securely, until he has acquired a primitive sign language by means of which he can make known his bodily need, and until he shows some autonomous inclination to learn. . . .
3. There must be a long and uninterrupted period of consistent and skillful "psychological mothering" by one individual. This brings about a biological and psychological symbiosis in which two organisms with essentially different needs profit mutually. . . .
4. He should have a father and a mother in harmonious relationship with one another to set a consistent pattern for his love development.
5. He should be spared reproaches, intimidations, threats, warnings, and punishments regarding physical manifestations of his sexuality. . . .

6. He should be accorded the dignity of a separate individual possessed of his own needs, rights, and feelings. . . .
7. In all communications with the child, truthfulness, honesty and sincerity on the part of the parents are unequivocally essential.[14]

Such plausible prescriptions as these have dominated our thinking, if not our practice, for some time. But persuasive as such reasoning may be, the sociologist insists on testing it. This is the only defense we have against the tendency to use a theory to justify our preconceptions. The psychoanalysts, of course, are not working exclusively in the realm of speculation. They have their clinical observations. But typically the client is an adult whose difficulties must, in terms of the theory, be traced back through time to origins in infancy. Sewell points out two dangers in this procedure which make testing mandatory: first, the reconstruction of infant experiences may be erroneous; and second, there is no way of knowing whether the psychoanalysts' clients differ from the rest of the population in the infant training they have undergone. That is to say, the psychoanalyst may be disposed to make his inferences on the basis of a distorted sample.

How is the observing done and in what sense is it controlled observation? First, Sewell must specify those behaviors of the mother which allow us to make the inference of an indulgent—or a demanding—mother-child relationship. His independent variable is some measure of degree of severity in child-training practices among mothers of Wisconsin farm children. Degree of severity is registered in manner and timing of nursing, weaning, bowel and bladder training, punishment for toilet accidents, sleep security (sleeping alone or with mother during the first year of life).

Highly trained interviewers obtained the information on these training practices from the mother. These practices were measured simply by dichotomizing them according to degree of severity. For example, weaning was abrupt or gradual, bowel training early or late, nursing by bottle or breast, and so on. The dependent variable, measures of adjustment presumed to depend upon severity or indulgence in child training, came from three major sources: parents, teachers, and personality or behavior inventories. There were measures on aggression, arguing, fighting, nail-biting, finger-sucking, stuttering, fears, eating troubles, crying, sleep disturbances, and so on—13 such component scores on the

Table 4.1

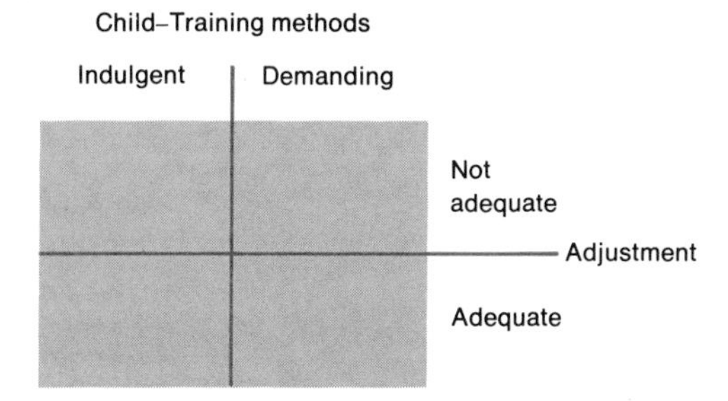

tests of general adjustment and measures on 26 types of behavior suggesting adequacy of adjustment.

Now we have two sets of observations: one set on child training practices and one on adjustment. Since both training and adjustment have two values (indulgent-demanding and adequate-inadequate), we can represent the way in which the findings will be summarized in a four-celled table such as Table 4.1. (Note in passing that when we dichotomize our data—when, for example, we take an array* of adjustment scores ranging, theoretically, from 100 to 0 and split the distribution so that half our subjects have higher scores than the other half—there are two outcomes from the point of view of accuracy. First, when we make an error in classification it will be a whopping one. It will not be a matter of being slightly, but completely wrong. Second, fewer errors in classification are likely to be made with only two categories in which to sort the data, since every additional category or division represents an additional problem in classification.)

Before we leave this matter of controlled observation, we must ask how Sewell can know that differences in adjustment (adequate and inadequate) are attributable to differences in socialization practices *rather than* to differences in parental income, occupation, race, and the like. As his report indicates, he tries to control other variables which might otherwise confound his hypothesis

* An array is simply a distribution of values—for example, students' test scores—arranged in some order (say, from highest to lowest). If for each score we note the number of students getting that score, we have a frequency distribution. See Aside on Methods, Number 4.

by eliminating them. That is to say, he eliminates all mother-child pairs except persons who are white, members of farm families, in Wisconsin, native born, with children between five and six years of age who are products of unbroken and never broken unions. Hence differences in race, or income, or occupation, or nativity, or marital status, or age of child *cannot* account for any differences in adjustment observed between children experiencing indulgent and those experiencing demanding child-training practices.

How is the hypothesis formulated? Now if the interpretation of the mother-child relationship in the socialization process is as Menninger describes it, then all of Sewell's cases should fall into the lower left and the upper right cells. Thus, we might state the hypothesis: the indicated measures of indulgent child training are positively related to specified measures of better adjustment. Or we might pose the logically prior hypothesis of *no relationship* between these child-training practices and these measures of adjustment. This is called a *null hypothesis* (H_0) and is commonly set up to serve as a target, as it were. If we can reject it, then an alternative hypothesis to account for the results is that hypothesis (H_1) derived from our theory which asserts a determinate relationship between the variables. If we cannot reject the null hypothesis, then we are probably badly off the track somewhere—anywhere—along the line between the original formulation of the problem and the statement of results.

How is the hypothesis tested? How are the data analyzed? In analyzing his data on 162 cases, Sewell uses a device called the Chi-square test (χ^2). This measure enables us to compare the distribution of cases actually observed with the distribution *which would obtain were there no relationship between the independent and the dependent variables.* As an illustration, assume that we have 100 mother-child pairs, 50 of them representing an indulgent relationship and 50 a rigid and demanding relationship. Suppose also that half of these pairs involve children who have made a satisfactory adjustment on such measures as Sewell used, the other half being children whose adjustment scores are low. Now if there is no relationship between extent of indulging-demanding on the one hand and adequacy of adjustment on the other, the distribution of cases (the frequencies we would expect) should look like that shown in Table 4.2.

The extent to which this is not true—the extent to which the frequencies of our actual observations (f_o) differ from the frequencies, above, which we would expect on the assumption of no

Table 4.2

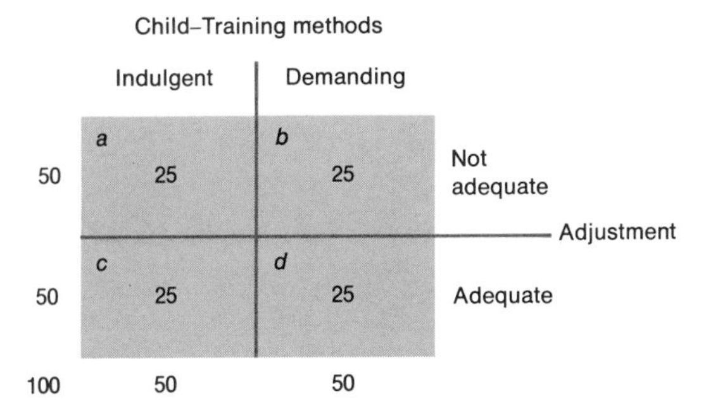

	Child–Training methods: Indulgent	Child–Training methods: Demanding	Adjustment
50	*a* 25	*b* 25	Not adequate
50	*c* 25	*d* 25	Adequate
100	50	50	

relationship (f_e = frequencies to be expected on this assumption)* —gives us some clue to the significance† of our findings. If the ($f_o - f_e$) values are large—if, that is, the distribution of observed frequencies is such that it could not reasonably be attributed to chance—then it is a nonchance, a systematic relationship which we have uncovered and which wants explaining. And, of course, since the observations are testing an hypothesis derived from a theory, in this case Freudian theories of socialization, we have that explanation ready at hand.

Having followed Professor Sewell so far, we have earned a right to his findings; and he the right to the last word.

> Of the 460 chi square tests, only 18 were significant at or beyond the .05 level. Of these, eleven were in the expected direction and seven were in the opposite direction from that expected on the basis of psychoanalytic writings. Such practices as breast feeding, gradual weaning, demand schedule, and easy and late induction to bowel and bladder training, which have been so much emphasized in the psychoanalytic

* See Aside on Methods Number 5: "Calculating Expected Frequencies to Compare with Observed Frequencies."

† When the investigator uses the word *significance* in this way it has a special meaning. The conjunction of two events—say, indulgent mother and happy child—would be statistically significant were their coincidence to be so frequent that it could not be deemed coincidental! But despite its statistical significance, a finding may not be important. Which is to say, significance and importance are two different matters. For example, there may be a statistically significant relationship between size of income and fondness for nonrepresentational art. But this might be thought relatively unimportant. On the other hand, to discover that there is no significant difference between freshmen and seniors in measures of knowledge would be a most important (and distressing) finding.

literature were almost barren in terms of relation to personality adjustment as measured in this study. . . .

Finally a word . . . about the limitations of this study. First, it must be admitted that the controls employed, although better than in most studies of this type, were very crude. . . . Second, the data on training experiences, although gathered and treated with care, may be inadequate for reasons cited or unknown. Third, the measures of personality employed in the study are far from perfect in relation to either their validity or their reliability. Consequently, the possibility remains that the results may be different when the children are tested at later periods in their development and with more satisfactory measures. But despite these and other limitations, the results of this study are unequivocal for the sample covered, and their generality must be affirmed or denied by means of better-designed and executed empirical studies, not by dialectic.

Contrasting patterns: Alorese and middle-class, urban Americans

These contrasts in socialization which we have been discussing (strict and lenient mothering) are fairly mild ones when we consider the intercultural range of practices. The mothers of Alor are quite indifferent to Dr. Menninger's good counsel. From the second week of life the Alorese youngster learns to do without its mother. (She goes back to the fields.) "Mothers, even when present, seem to provide only casual and disinterested care, and as the child grows older his lot continues to be one of neglect and rebuff."[15] The child is roughly, often precipitously weaned, incited to anger and jealousy (the mother may deliberately take another infant to feed), intimidated ("a boy often has . . . fingers and arrows poked into his distended abdomen. . . ."), frightened, threatened, punished and rewarded inconsistently, kept awake at night. It seems a reasonable inference that this child is being prepared for adult roles differing markedly from those of the middle-class American.

The contrast is brought home to us when we reflect on the rearing of the white, urban middle-class child in our society. Introduced to the world through the antiseptic ministrations of hospital personnel, he is nurtured in the Skinner box of an apartment or suburban home, permitted free expression at either end of his alimentary canal, checked by pediatrician, orthodontist, oculist,

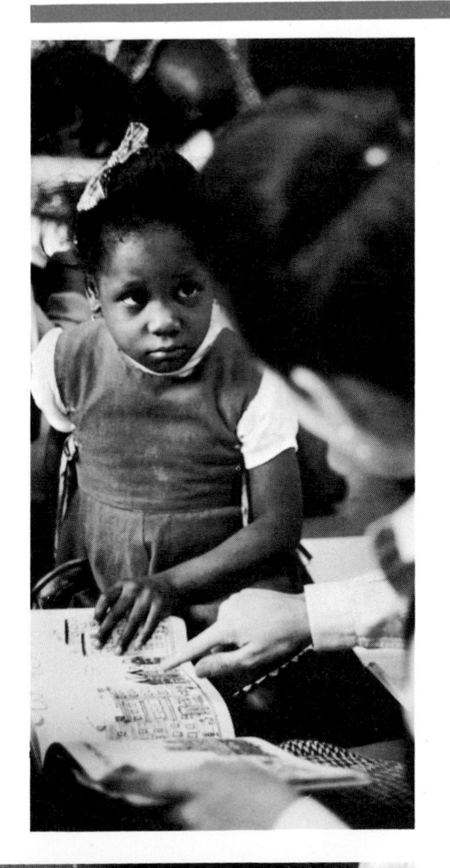

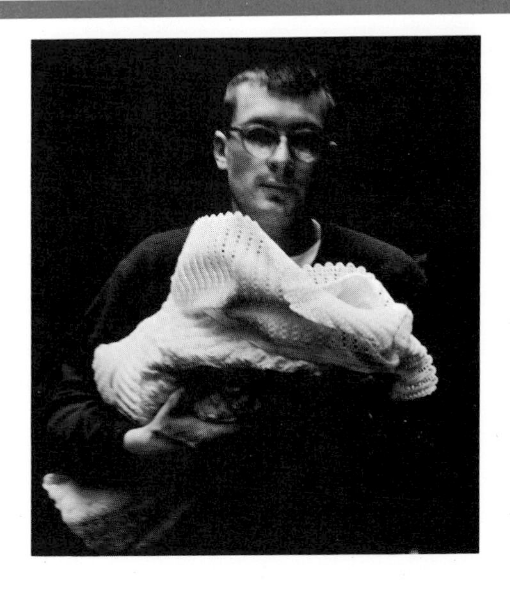

. . . The newcomer to the human group finds himself an alien in the hands of utter strangers.

The socialization process may be thought of as . . . answering the question for the newcomer: "Who am I?"

...Although people in various roles share in the transmission of culture to the child ... the early and elemental aspects of socialization fall chiefly within the mother's sphere.

...as in entering a prison group, effective socialization entails a severance ...of past ties....

...The newly inducted GI has a period ...during which his outside contacts are restricted.

and sometimes psychiatrist. His aggressions are amusedly indulged. He may be overfed, overclothed, and overchauffered. He is ritually celebrated on birthdates and other family occasions. And as privilege or penalty, he is funnelled through the long and costly school corridor to emerge, finally, after an education not always accurately described as "higher." No child of Alor, he.

Such differences in child rearing interest us for many reasons. Among other things, they are a chief source of personal uniqueness. With the exception of single-egg twins, each human individual is unique as a result of the independent segregation and assortment of genes received from his parents. But *with no exceptions whatsoever,* each child stands at the hub of a social context quite peculiar to himself and generating that particular constellation of attributes which distinguish him as a personality. (On the other hand, such personal uniquenesses will not be permitted to interfere with the inculcation of the general elements of culture, characterizing the group of which the mediators, parents and teachers, are members. He will have to know and follow the score, holding idiosyncratic interpretations to an insignificant minimum.)

Later socialization

But different ways of socialization are significant, for our purposes, from a social rather than an individual perspective. Different methods of rearing, training, and educating lead to different slots in a complex social structure. Beliefs and behaviors have consequences; and different ways of inducting the newcomer affect his destiny as a social creature, as a group member. Depending on his early socialization, he will have the inclination and the ability to enter subsequent groups. Depending on his early socialization, he will be acceptable or unacceptable to groups he enters later. For socialization is a continuous process, and the later stages are necessarily conditioned by aptitudes and attitudes learned earlier.

Socializing the immigrant

Consider joining a national group—immigration to the United States. To enter this group is clearly hard or easy depending upon the likenesses between the culture earlier inculcated and the culture of the new land (group). Command of the language, familiarity with the style of life, a generally high appraisal of things

American, ease the way into the new group. And these features derive from antecedent socialization. Emma Lazarus expressed a kindly sentiment, inscribed on the Statue of Liberty:

> . . . Give me your tired, your poor,
> Your huddled masses yearning to breathe free,
> The wretched refuse of your teeming shore.
> Send these, the homeless tempest-tossed to me,
> I lift my lamp beside the golden door.

But while we applaud such charitable sentiments Lazarus' invitation is misleading. For we are not typically hospitable to those regarded as "refuse." Every group is selective in its recruitment, including even the family, which controls both the quantity and the quality of its recruits. (The number of children is controlled and so, in the rearing, is the newcomer made "qualitatively" acceptable.) All groups select, indoctrinate (socialize), and eliminate the unfit and undesirable—each group, obviously, in terms of its own standards. The group which is the national society is no exception. With the nation as with other groups, those who seek and most readily gain admission are those congenially encultured. Thus in the United States, until 1966, of the 154,657 persons annually admittable, 96.8 percent were Europeans. Closer still to the culture of the group they were entering, 81.6 percent were from northern and western Europe. But the most significant figure is this: 70 percent of the total immigrant quota was assigned to three nations: the United Kingdom, Germany, and the Irish Free State. In general, the 40 million immigrants who have entered the United States were culturally qualified to enter the group—or the subgroup, in the case of Orientals and southeast European immigrants, many of them illiterate and destitute, who came to do the most menial labor. What they had to offer has been well articulated with what the group needed. One evidence of this is the similarity of curves representing business activity or, inversely, unemployment, and the curve representing flow of immigrants.

Doubtless the input into any organization never makes a perfect match with the requirements of the group. Where there is little self-selection, as in a drafted army or a state university, the problem of assimilation is acute. And so we have indoctrination programs, orientation programs, in-service training, Americanization schools, and the like.

But self-selection figures significantly in the immigration process. And immigration quotas are ostensibly designed to promote self-selection, so encouraging only those who are "best qualified" to join a new nationality group. Yet with all this, it is not easy to achieve the aim of bringing the newcomer to understand and participate in the life of the new group he has entered. We spend 15 to 20 years inducting the child into the first group he must enter. It is not surprising, then, that the later entrance into a different nationality group entails a host of problems, despite self-selection. Sometimes the immigrant wives remain resistantly immured at home. There are problems of recertification and requalification of professionals such as lawyers and physicians. Similarly with technicians, new and different standards may be required in their trades, compelling them to undergo adaptive training.

A dramatic illustration of the problem of assimilating diverse newcomers to the group is provided in the recent history of immigration to Israel, which in 1950 was about 80 percent foreign born. Prime Minister Ben Gurion declared:

> We shall bring into the country a nation of unusual character, spread all over the world, speaking many languages, influenced by many cultures, divided into various communities and sects. It is our duty to cast this differentiated and colourful people into the mould of a reformed nation. We have to uproot all the geographical, cultural, social and linguistic divisions which separate them and give them one language, one culture and one citizenship.[16]

The dimensions of this socialization problem are suggested by Figures 4.2 and 4.3.

In Israel's first 10 years (1948–58), her population almost tripled. The Law of Return, passed by the *Knesset* in July, 1950, granted to every Jew the right to immigrate to Israel, should he so choose. This open door policy brought over a million Jews from 70 different countries within 10 years. Fewer than 2 percent of the immigrants entering after 1948 had any agricultural experience. More than half lacked vocational or professional training of any kind. Most were poor. Included were children, the sick, and the aged. Many were illiterate. Few spoke Hebrew. They had to be woven, culturally, into the fabric of Israeli society.

Later socialization in subgroups

The great number of persons involved, their diversity and the rapid rate of their immigration, make Israel a forceful illustration of the problems and process of entering the group (later socialization). But it does not come as close to home for most people as

Figure 4.2
Origin of principal streams of Jewish immigrants to Israel and Palestine: 1919 to 1952

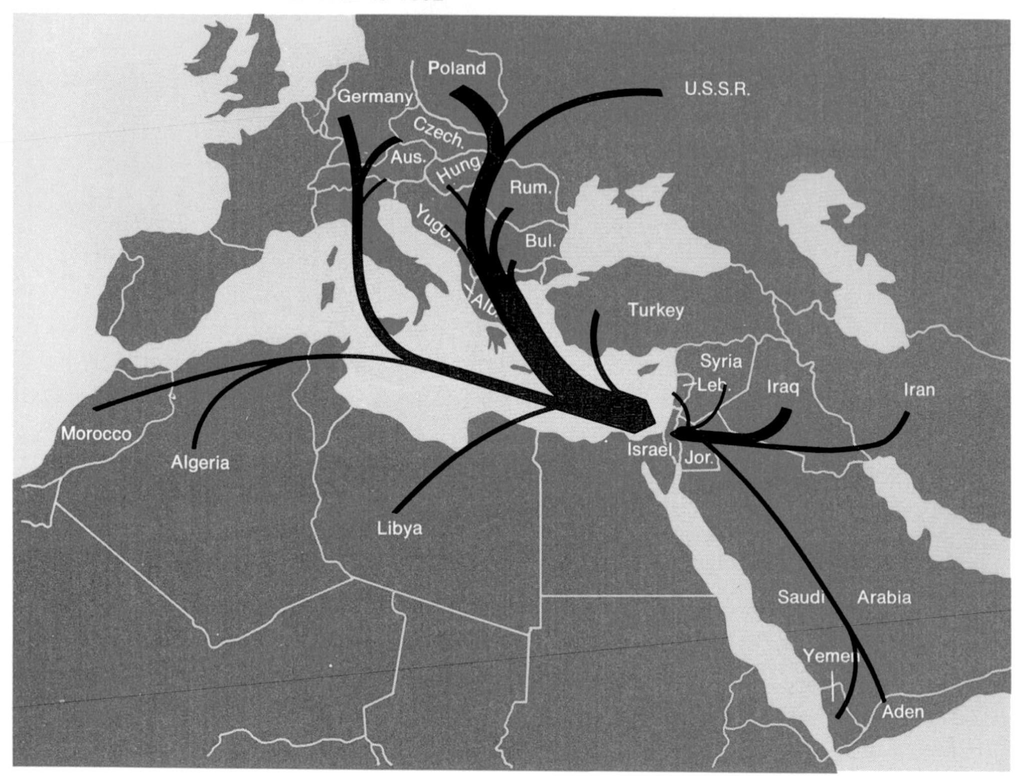

the more mundane matter of entering a new school group or joining a work group. In his study, "The Military Academy as an Assimilating Institution,"[17] Professor Dornbusch reveals some of the principal elements of socialization in a school group. As in the case of *The Nun's Story* or in the matter of entering a prison group, effective socialization depends on a rejection or a renunciation of the past and a commitment to the present.

The rejection of the past is accomplished in various ways. The "swab" at the Coast Guard Academy is effectively isolated from the past, since he is not allowed to leave the base; nor is he permitted to have dealings with noncadets. The use of uniforms (and sometimes standardized campus clothing achieves the same end) erases signs of differentials that might be linked to the past. They emphasize the common condition and common destiny of members of the group. Sometimes letters from home are forbidden.

Figure 4.3
Jewish population and Jewish immigration for Israel and Palestine: 1919–52

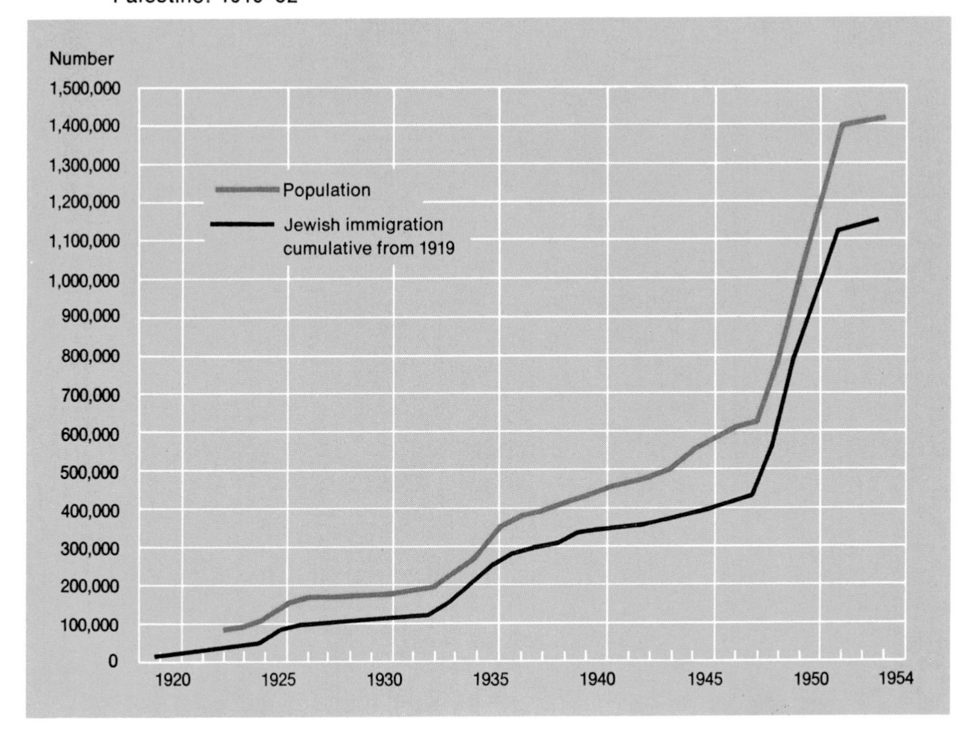

Sometimes receipt of money from outside sources is forbidden. This pattern of isolation is a common phase of the socialization process. (It is, of course, unnecessary with the infant, since there are no antecedent experiences except those of the intrauterine period to be extinguished.) The newly inducted inmate of a federal prison undergoes a period of quarantine for about a month. The newly inducted GI has a period of basic training during which his outside contacts are restricted. During her novitiate the nun may not be allowed to leave the convent, so cutting contact with family, friends, the past. Such severance from the past is certainly promoted by acquiring a language peculiar to the new group. Parents sometimes get a slight sense of this effect when their children return from school for the holidays.

The obverse side of the coin is commitment to the present, identification with the current group. Learning the language, the slang, the mystic symbols of the group helps to achieve this end. Isolation in the present situation is also achieved by an exhausting schedule, so absorbing time and energy that nostalgic retrospection is almost impossible. Camp counselors are aware of this device and put it to effective practice. Uniforms, badges, pins emphasize, not only the distinctiveness of the group, its separation from other groups, but the identity of those within the group. And here the only status differences are those relevant to the value system of the current group. Group solidarity, identification with it, is enhanced by common sharing and survival through bad experiences such as hazing.

Commitment to the group is enhanced where there is a clear-cut gradation of experiences with plenty of opportunity for imaginal role-rehearsal, in preparation for the next stage. One knows where he is going and the destination is desirable. Not only is it desirable, but however difficult of attainment, it is possible. Dealings—especially informal ones—with admired upperclassmen enhance both the desirability of achieving group goals and the probability of doing so. For the upperclassman is what the newcomer will become. The single-minded pursuit of the goal deemed desirable is made easier if there are such models available, especially models who can be put in dramatic focus. This is an important reason for celebrating our heroes. Lincoln, Churchill, Martin Luther King, and John F. Kennedy are persons not merely to venerate but to emulate. The exemplary nun referred to in *The Nun's Story* as *"la règle vivante"* performs this function for the novices.

In the service of this imaginal role-rehearsal ("anticipatory socialization"), rites of passage are useful. Confirmation, Bar Mitzvah, the driver's license, high school graduation, marriage—these ritual watersheds separate past from future, emphasizing the new role requirements and providing evidence of progress toward various goals.

Finally, we should note the importance, for the socialization process, of the rigorous weeding out of defectors and delinquents, the disenchanted, disabled or disaffected. The fewer the alternative views of the group, of its goals and procedures, the more effective the socialization process. Perhaps it is an enervating academic view that wholehearted commitment to anything is a function of ignorance. But as a principle in socialization, it is doubtless true that the newcomer becomes a loyal old-timer more readily when he is denied the luxury of skepticism.

Work groups are likely to be more rigorous in their recruitment and socialization of new members; for the calculus of profit provides a yardstick and exerts pressure for continuously improved selection and training. But always supplementing the selective re-

Table 4.3

Influence of family group on children's selection of occupation

Comparison of the distribution of occupations among fathers of American scientists and occupations of fathers in the population at large.

	Distribution of occupations	
Occupational categories	Percent of fathers of men listed in *American Men of Science*	Percent of fathers of men in general population
Professional	43.1	3.0
Commercial	35.7	34.1
Agricultural	21.2	41.1

cruitment practiced by the group is the self-selection practiced by those entering it. Neither sort of selection produces a perfect fit between the role to be filled and the aptitudes and attitudes of the newcomer. Indoctrination procedures are usually necessary. Nonetheless, the two selective processes work together to sort individuals into slots in the work-system in a way sufficiently effective to enable performance of a task and, indeed, to enable the recognition of occupational types. Henry Fielding, in 1742, seems to have thought the lawyer a recognizable type.

> I question not but several of my readers will know the lawyer in the stage-coach the moment they hear his voice. . . . I declare here once for all, I describe not men, but manners; not an individual, but a species.[18]

Later socialization necessarily builds on what happened before. There is much evidence that the family group which the person first enters has an emphatic influence on the occupational group which he later enters. Consider the data shown in Table 4.3.[19]

Similarly, Bernard Barber makes the point that there appears to be a connection between the person's religion, inculcated in early socialization, and the probability of his entering one of the scientific professions. Catholics in the United States—disregarding other relevant variables, such as class—are not proportionately represented among scientific workers in the United States.

> Father Cooper says he "would be loathe to have to defend the thesis that five percent or even three percent of the leadership in American science and scholarship is Catholic. Yet we

Catholics constitute something like twenty per cent of the total population."[20]

As for American Jews, we have no figures at all, but it is very probable that they are at least proportionately represented in science and learning, at least in the universities. This is what we might expect for two reasons. First, the Jewish values seem to favor learning and empirical rationality. And, second, there is an important relevant factor in the American social system. The Jews have been remarkably socially mobile in the U.S., and the free professions, including science, have been more open to them than large industry and many areas of business.[21]

That persons enter groups appropriate in terms of the attitudes and values they bring to them is supported by some evidence provided by Rosenberg. He questioned a group of students who planned to become businessmen, dividing them into two categories, "very conservative" and "not very conservative," depending on their responses to these four statements.

Democracy depends fundamentally on the existence of free business enterprise.

The "welfare state" tends to destroy individual initiative.

The laws governing labor unions today are not strict enough.

Labor unions in this country are doing a fine job.

Those who answered these four questions "yes," "yes," "yes," and "no," respectively, were called "very conservative," and those who answered any other way were called "not very conservative." The question raised is whether students' orientations on these matters will predict the occupational group they enter later. Rosenberg's data are shown in Table 4.4. Consider comparable data for medical students who were asked about what they expected to gain most satisfaction in their lives (Table 4.5). Rosenberg combined his teachers and businessmen in relating dominant value complex to the occupational group entered. Again, the data are revealing (Table 4.6). Thus groups replace their losses with those whose socialization has provided appropriate knowledge of what is and what ought to be. Through this process they've been equipped with variants on the cultural theme. So people are recruited —and select themselves —to join different groups, replacing departing members.

* * * *

Let us review, briefly. Given the raw material (population),

Table 4.4

Student attitudes as they affect persistence in training for business careers

	Orientation in 1950		
Career choice in 1952	Very conservative $N = 22$	Not very conservative $N = 56$	
Persisted in plans to enter business	73%	36%	$p < .01$
Changed occupational choice	27%	64%	

Table 4.5

Student attitudes as they affect persistence in training for careers in medicine

	Statement on main satisfaction in life in 1950		
Career choice in 1952	Career or occupation $N = 20$	Family relationships $N = 27$	
Still chose medicine	80%	33%	$p < .01$
Left medicine	20%	67%	

Table 4.6

Teachers' and businessmen's agreement with the dominant value orientation of their occupation as it affects persistence in pursuing their career plans

	Attitude in 1950		
Career choice in 1952	Agreeing with dominant value complex $N = 124$	Disagreeing with dominant value complex $N = 64$	
Remained in occupation	57%	27%	$p < .01$
Changed occupation	43%	73%	

groups are built and rebuilt through a process we call socialization. This process involves such an interpenetration of self and other that the other's expectations, expectations that reflect cultural prescriptions, become one's own. The process is a long and arduous one for the human child, and the stages of development have been charted in various ways. The interpretations of Mead, Piaget, and Freud provide useful insights.

To illustrate how a theory of early socialization might be tested by a sociologist, we reviewed Sewell's test of the hypothesis that indulgent rather than demanding infant training practices promote good adjustment in the child's subsequent relationships.

But as we noted, this first entry into the human group is only one of many. Some people migrate to new countries and enter new nationality groups. All of us enter school groups, since it is a legal requirement. And most of us enter work groups, worship groups, play groups, and a variety of other groups. In each case, adaptive or socializing processes are involved, and those subcultural emphases picked up in prior socialization influence the choice of and success in these groups later entered. (As Rosenberg's study illustrated, thing-oriented persons tend to give up their plans to become teachers; person-oriented students stay with it.)

In discussing culture in Chapter 2, we emphasized the social aspect of culture. Culture is learned and taught; there is a "student" and a "teacher." Much, no doubt, is unwittingly transmitted. But the proper induction of the newcomer is a matter of such import that no enduring group leaves it to chance. And so we look to the leverage applied by the group and the evidence for its coercive influence, attending especially to family and school as agents of cultural transmission.

References

TEXT

1. "From the moment of his birth the customs into which he is born shape [the individual's] experience and behavior. By the time he can talk, he is the little creature of his culture, and by the time he is grown and able to take part in its activities, its habits are his habits, its beliefs his beliefs, its impossibilities his impossibilities. Every child that is born into his group will share them with him, and no child born into one on the opposite side of the globe can ever achieve the thousandth part" (Ruth Benedict, *Patterns of Culture* [Boston: Houghton Mifflin Co., 1961], p. 2).
2. John Locke, *Second Essay on Civil Government* (New York: E. P. Dutton & Co., Inc., 1924), chap. v.
3. Charles Horton Cooley, *Human Nature and the Social Order* (New York: Charles Scribner's Sons, 1902), p. 84.
4. *Ibid.*, pp. 61, 62. Italics mine.
5. Charles Darwin, *The Descent of Man* (New York: Random House, n.d.), chap. iv.
6. If the foregoing conveys an onerous sense of social determination, it should be taken as an antidote to the delusive sense of self-determination that we pick up from various sources: sometimes an ignorance of history, or the religious and political values we imbibe (stressing unfettered individualism), or the vast cultural distance we traverse in a short life-span (giving the illusion of breathtaking speed and change). And of course there is the very real individuality based on the uniqueness of each person as a biological and social creation.

   As an antidote to this antidote, perhaps you will wish to read Dennis H. Wrong's article, "The Oversocialized Conception of Man in Modern Sociology," in the *American Sociological Review,* Vol. 26 (1961), pp. 183–93. The difficulty with this piece is that it overlooks the frequent situation of group demands for creativity, novelty, change, innovation. And it fails to stress the inevitable crossing of group boundaries when, in the encounter between different beliefs and behaviors, conflict and creativity emerge.

For a critique see Judith Blake and Kingsley Davis's chapter, "Norms, Values and Sanctions," in Robert E. L. Faris (ed.), *Handbook of Modern Sociology* (Skokie, Ill.: Rand McNally & Co., 1964).

7. This would suggest that insight (self-knowledge) and empathy (capacity for feeling in and with another and presumably understanding another) ought to go together. Indeed this is what R. F. Dymond found in her work on the conception of self (R. F. Dymond, A. S. Hughes, and J. L. Raabe, "Measurable Changes in Empathy with Age," *Journal of Consulting Psychology*, Vol. 16 [1952], pp. 202–6; also, C. R. Rogers and R. F. Dymond [eds.], *Psychotherapy and Personality Change* [Chicago: University of Chicago Press, 1954]).
8. Cooley, *op. cit.*, pp. 151, 152.
9. For an insightful development of this theme, see Erving Goffman, *The Presentation of Self in Everyday Life* (New York: Doubleday & Co., Anchor Books, 1959).
10. George Herbert Mead, *Mind, Self and Society* (Chicago: University of Chicago Press, 1934). See especially Part III, "The Self," pp. 135–226.
11. George Bernard Shaw, "Pygmalion," in *Four Plays* (New York: Modern Library, Inc., 1953).
12. Jean Piaget, *The Moral Judgment of the Child* (New York: Free Press of Glencoe, Inc., n.d.), pp. 16–18, *passim.*
13. William Sewell, "Infant Training and the Personality of the Child," *American Journal of Sociology*, Vol. 48 (September, 1952), pp. 150–59.

    If the reader is inclined to see the test of a Freudian position as a misguided detour into psychology and personality, he should reconsider Freud as a sociologist with a special interest in the family. Certainly the mother-father-child triangle, the family as mediator of a preexisting and coercive culture and personal adjustment defined in relational terms (how does the child manage his relationships with peers, parents, teachers?)—these are clearly social dimensions and sociological concerns.

    It is worth noting that, although Sewell's hypothesis is *not* supported, this finding is nonetheless worth having. For if we accept his translation of Freudian ideas into testable terms (of course, there may be some debate as to whether these were, indeed, St. Sigmund's convictions), and if we see the research as technically competent, then we are spared false belief and fruitless behavior.
14. From pp. 39–40 of *Love Against Hate* by Karl Menninger, copyright, 1942, by Karl Menninger and Jeanetta Lyle Menninger. Reprinted by permission of Harcourt, Brace & World, Inc.
15. Taken from Cora DuBois in Abram Kardiner, *Psychological Frontiers of Society* (New York: Columbia University Press, 1945), and quoted in T. M. Newcomb, *Social Psychology* (New York: Dryden Press, 1950), pp. 442, 443.
16. Joseph Shaked, "The Education of New Immigrant Workers in Israel," in *Some Studies in Education of Immigrants for Citizenship*, No. 16, UNESCO Educational Studies and Documents Series (Paris: UNESCO Workshops, 1955), p. 32
17. Sanford M. Dornbusch, "The Military Academy as an Assimilating Institution," *Social Forces*, Vol. 33, No. 4 (May, 1955).
18. Henry Fielding, *Joseph Andrews* (London: F. C. and J. Rivington, 1920).
19. These data are reprinted with permission of Free Press of Glencoe from *Science and the Social Order* by Bernard Barber, pp. 134, 135. Copyright 1952 by The Free Press, a corporation. The data came originally from *Science*, Volume 24 (1906), pp. 732–44.
20. Barber, *op. cit.*, p. 136. He is quoting J. M. Cooper, "Catholics and Scientific Research," *Commonweal*, Vol. XLII (1945), p. 147–49.
21. Morris Rosenberg, "Factors Influencing Change of Occupational Choice," reprinted with permission of Free Press of Glencoe from *The Language of Social Research* by Paul F. Lazarsfeld and Morris Rosenberg. Copyright 1955 by The Free Press, a corporation.

FIGURES

4.2 Norman Lawrence, *Israel: Jewish Population and Immigration*, International Population Statistics Reports, Series P–90, No. 2 (Washington, D.C.: USGPO, 1952), p. 20.

4.3 *Ibid*, p. 4.

chapter 5

Agent of cultural transmission: the group

. . . I did not in the least want to shoot him. I decided that I would watch him for a little while to make sure that he did not turn savage again, and then go home.
But at that moment I glanced round at the crowd that had followed me. . . . And suddenly I realized that I would have to shoot the elephant after all. The people expected it of me and I had got to do it; I could feel their two thousand wills pressing me forward, irresistibly. . . . Here was I, the white man with his gun, standing in front of the unarmed native crowd—seemingly the leading actor of the piece; but in reality I was only an absurd puppet pushed to and fro by the will of those yellow faces behind.
George Orwell, *Shooting an Elephant*

Up to this point we have been thinking about the *process* through which a group persists by replacing losses. We see this process in the rearing of the child to meet the requirements of his particular society. We see it in the indoctrination of the immigrant, culminating, from the legal standpoint, in naturalization and from a social standpoint, in assimilation. We see this process in the puberty rites marking the transition from youth to adult responsibilities, the induction of a student into college, into his fraternity, into the Armed Forces; and in the hiring and in-service training of the new employee.

This is the process by which, as Reuter once put it, "individuals are taught to function in the group in which *their wishes are created and realized.*"[1] It is the process through which one comes to prefer majority vote to concurring in a dictator's mandate (or vice versa). It is the process by which one becomes Methodist rather than Catholic, prefers roast beef to escargots, gefilte fish to roast pork, becomes a Republican rather than a Democrat. It leads one to read the underground newspapers and magazines and wear a beard rather than joining the clean-shaven philistines with *Harper's* and the *Atlantic.* It disposes one to enter the clan of lawyers rather than the ranks of the physical scientists, etc., etc.

Now we cannot understand how such preferences, capacities, attitudes, and judgments emerge except as we appreciate the extent to which others, in transmitting culture, exert enormous influence on us. And so we turn now to the *agency* of cultural transmission, the group, and to the evidence of its influence upon the person.

Such an influence we have implied in our characterization of the concept, culture. Culture is social, it is learned, it is inculcated. So much is this so, so imperative are the demands of others upon us to abide by the dictates of Amy Vanderbilt and the mandates of democratic beliefs, that we both anticipate and suffer penalties for nonconformity. The group, through its agents, shapes the person. There is no "natural" unfolding of the personality without human intervention. Men are made. Motherhood is revered, wherever it is understood, as the consummately creative role, the work of ultimate artistry. Parents and teachers, in their institutional workshops, are the rebuilders of groups through the making of persons. They wield a powerful influence, at once liberating and restrictive. Family and school liberate our potential as human beings while restricting it to those channels appropriate to the group. (For most mortals the potential is but partially realized, and it may, of course, be for ill as well as good.)

These are the matters, then, with which this chapter is concerned: the influence of the group, considered in the abstract; and, in the concrete, family and school as groups primarily responsible for making men and re-creating groups.

The influence of the group

One way of appreciating the influence of the group—of others—is to raise the question: What would happen if there were no others? Or, to put it more plausibly, if interaction with others is reduced, what happens?* There is a great body of evidence which bears in various ways on this question. The following paragraphs touch a few scattered pieces of this evidence.

As suggested by others' absence

The very absence of others, the effect of which we wish to investigate, makes it almost impossible to get reliable data. For this reason there has been much controversy over so-called "wolf children," feral creatures supposedly reared outside the human circle.[2] But Professor Kingsley Davis has given us one fairly well-documented case of extreme isolation from human contact: that of an illegitimate child kept in seclusion from the age of two and discovered at six and one-half years of age.[3] The mother was a deaf mute. Both she and the child spent most of their time together in a dark room shut off from the rest of the mother's family. Characteristics of the child, when discovered, that seem to stem from this isolation are these: a mental age test score (Stanford-Binet) of 19 months:† behavior like that of a child of six months, but more hostile and erratic; an initial diagnosis of deafness that, when shown to be wrong, was supplanted by a diagnosis of feeble-mindedness. But with intensive help, this youngster's I.Q. score trebled in a year and a half. Presently she reached what appeared to be a normal level.

This, it will be observed, is a before-and-after case. There is no carefully contrived control group of matched youngsters experiencing normal human contacts. But normal rearing is so clearly different in the matter of human intercourse and this child's recovery so dramatic, it seems legitimate to infer the deleterious consequences of isolation and to assert the presence of others as a necessary source of socialization.

Extreme but fortunately more transient cases of isolation are seen in recent laboratory work on the effects of sensory deprivation. Dr. John Lilly has reported on some relevant psychological

* The writers of fiction, like Kilroy, have already been here. Writing an introduction to two of Joseph Conrad's short pieces, Albert J. Guerard says: ". . . His is one of the greatest portraits in all fiction of *moral deterioration and reversion to savagery as a result of physical isolation*" (Introduction to Joseph Conrad, *Heart of Darkness* and *The Secret Sharer* [New York: Signet Books, 1957], p. 13).

† An intelligence test score is calculated by relating mental age, in months (given by the test score) to chronological age, in months; thus:

$$\frac{\text{Mental age}}{\text{Chronological age}} \times 100 = \text{Intelligence quotient.}$$

In this case the values are $\frac{19}{78} \times 100 = 20$.

outcomes when external stimuli are cut off.[4] The procedure is to suspend the subject in a tank of slowly flowing water kept at body temperature, face down, wearing only a head mask for breathing. An initial feeling of great comfort and relaxation gradually gives way to some curious effects. Lacking all sensory input, the subject finds his thoughts going around, becoming magnified, distorted. Anxiety mounts as he becomes increasingly disoriented. He may begin to suffer hallucinations.

Dr. Milton Meltzer draws upon his experiences as Chief Medical Officer at Alcatraz to make these observations on the effect of isolation from others:

> . . . the prison experience in general and solitary confinement in particular, threatens the inmate's integration by depriving him of stimuli and various sets of reaction patterns or things in the environment towards which he can orient himself and constantly *redefine himself in the service of knowing who he is.* As these are withdrawn he tends to regress towards an infantile ego state of split and paired good-bad objects. . . .
>
> To the degree that the basic state is achieved so is the man vulnerable to forceful indoctrination . . . at this point he is capable of massive incorporation, introjections and identifications.[5]

We might note, in passing, a deduction drawn from the theory of socialization discussed in the preceding chapter and bearing on this matter of personal disorganization under conditions of extreme isolation. If it is true that, in becoming a human being, we internalize the other—if by virtue of our capacity for symbolic interaction, the single person becomes a group in microcosm—then the more integrated the group, the greater its cohesiveness, the clearer its goals and the means for achieving them, the better integrated the person. The better integrated person should be better able to survive conditions of sensory deprivation, of isolation. He should be less readily "brainwashed," better able to maintain his personal integrity. Such a theory and such a prediction are consonant with the findings on mental illness among the Hutterites.[6] They are consonant with the observation that political prisoners had emphatically better survival rates than criminal prisoners among Danish inmates of a German concentration camp. Of the former, 13 percent died; of the latter, 30 percent. "The consciousness that one is not imprisoned because of an occasional transgression of the law for the sake of gain but that one suffers the misery and humiliation *for the sake of a common cause* seems to be a life-sustaining factor of unsuspected importance . . . the inner bond with the world outside the concentration camps is maintained."[7]

The absence of others means a failure to get culture. This means, in turn, a person of stunted growth, shortchanged on health and human attributes.

As suggested by others' presence

These examples point in a negative fashion to the power of the group. They stress the harmful outcomes of the *absence* of others.* Let us turn now to the significance of others' *presence,* the impact of the group upon the person.

Consider, first, how his group influences the way a person thinks. What problems are raised, how solutions are sought, the kind of evidence brought to bear, the extent of reliance upon the supernatural for solutions, what sorts of solutions are likely or tolerable —these are matters in which the person's thinking is emphatically under the influence of the group.

Professor Lucien Levy-Bruhl in a series of studies on the mentality of primitive peoples[8] commences with this assumption: Mental processes must be understood relative to the group in which they operate.

> Mental processes will vary as groups vary. This is especially brought home to us when we recognize that institutions, our very customs are, at bottom, only our common imagery, our ideas, so to speak, concretely registered.†

The basic point seems indisputable: both form and content of thought vary from group to group. For example, the problems

* Many other observations suggest the dehumanizing effects of isolation. For example, reports on U.S. prisoners of war in Korea highlight three important features of the process popularly called "brainwashing": isolation from the past, punishment in the present, and rewards held out for the future. The withholding and manipulation of mail, the prohibition of group meetings, playing men off against one another, and the segregation of men by race, nationality, and rank, together with the substitution of Chinese leaders—these isolating devices proved effective in severing familiar bonds, reducing the person to the naked impotence of an unsupported individual, and so preparing the way for indoctrination. "The most significant feature of Chinese prisoner camp control was the systematic destruction of the prisoners' formal and informal group structure" (Edgar H. Schein, discussing POW's in Korea. See *Symposium No. 4, Methods of Forceful Indoctrination: Observations and Interviews* [New York: Group for the Advancement of Psychiatry, July, 1957]).

† See Original Texts, Note 5.1.

central to primitive life are not ours, nor their modes of solution. Their omens, dreams, oracles, and ordeals, their divinatory practices aimed at revealing malevolent and invisible forces, the hidden, mystical source of the visible misfortune—these suggest, as M. Davy points out, that words like *accusation, judgment, innocence,* and *guilt* carry very different meanings for them than for us.

Consider now the matter of group influence upon the *content* of the person's thought, upon *what* rather than *how* he thinks. A study by Charters and Newcomb shows us how group identification can alter the content of thought, in this case, the orthodoxy of religious beliefs. The investigators varied level of awareness of their religious membership group for Catholics, Jews, and Protestants (chiefly Lutherans).[9] Catholic students—I report only on this category for simplicity's sake while noting in passing that the hypothesis was not supported for Jews and Protestants—were randomly divided into experimental and control groups. One control group, whose members were unaware that they were in the experiment, met in the auditorium along with other university students in the class. A second control group consisted wholly of Catholic students, but their awareness of this fact was not underlined as was the case with the experimental group. With the latter, their common faith was emphasized by the investigator as he requested their help in developing a questionnaire on religious beliefs. That is to say, a sharp awareness of their common group membership was aroused in the experimental group, in contrast to the treatment of the control groups where Ss (subjects) were simply asked to fill out a questionnaire (the same one, of course).

The responses of Catholics in the two control groups were very much alike despite the fact that in one control group Catholic students were part of an auditorium lecture group of 500, while the other control group comprised a separated group of students, all Catholic. But there were significant differences between the control groups and the experimental group (in which consciousness of group membership had been purposely aroused) on questionnaire items dealing with the Catholic faith, the church, on religion in general. Among members of the experimental group for whom "the potency of religious group membership was deliberately increased," responses "more closely approximated the orthodox Catholic position" than was the case with "control subjects whose awareness of membership was not increased."[10]

Now let us raise a related question: How does group membership affect a person's *perceptions?* In a classical experiment

Muzafer Sherif posed the problem: How are standards or guide-posts established for judging certain characteristics of physical objects? How does the person make a judgment in an utterly unstructured situation, when he is alone? How does he do it as a member of a group?[11] To create a situation in which points of reference were completely lacking, Sherif made use of the autokinetic phenomenon, the "false" perception of movement in a visual object seen in an unstructured field—i.e., outside any frame of reference. To achieve this effect, Sherif exposed his subjects to a pinpoint of light in a room completely dark. The results, when he was dealing with individual subjects, alone, Sherif summarized in these two sentences:

> When individuals repeatedly perceive movement which offers no objective basis for gauging the extent of movement, there develops within them, in the course of successive presentations [of the apparently moving pinpoint of light] a standard (norm or reference point). This subjectively established standard or norm serves as a reference point with which each successive experienced movement is compared and judged to be short, long, or medium—within the range peculiar to the subject.[12]

A second phase of Sherif's study raised the question: How are individual judgments (already having been formed as described above) influenced when in company with others each subject is asked again to judge the distance moved by the pinpoint of light. There were two subjects in each of eight groups, and three subjects in each of eight other groups. The findings are summarized in Sherif's conclusion:

> When the individual, in whom a range and a norm within that range are first developed in the individual situation, is put into a group situation, together with other individuals who also come into the situation with their own ranges and norms established in their own individual sessions, the ranges and norms tend to converge. But the convergence is not so close as when they first work in the group situation, having less opportunity to set up stable individual norms.[13]

Bearing on the same point—the influence of the group upon perception and judgment of certain dimensions of physical objects—is another important study, this one by Solomon Asch.[14] A central theme of his book, *Social Psychology*, is that "in society we

Table 5.1
Extent of yielding to group influence

Subjects	Estimates (matching of lines)				
		Correct		Pro-majority errors	
	Total Number	*N*	%	*N*	%
Experimental: minority of one v. unanimous majority (*N* = 31)	217	145	66.8	72	33.2
Control (*N* = 25)	175	162	92.6	13	7.4*

* The control group, of course, had no instructed majority to mislead the naïve subject.

become dependent on others for understanding, feeling and the extension of the sense of reality."[15] In a set of well-known experiments Asch raises the question: To what extent is the individual's judgment distorted under the influence of other group members' erroneous judgments? He asked his subjects to judge which of three lines on one card was the same length as a standard comparison line on a second card. Judgments were orally expressed, seriatim, by members of groups of seven to nine persons, one of whom was a naïve—i.e., uninstructed—subject, while the others had been told to make occasional, palpably wrong judgments. Thus the naïve subject was caught between two contradictory and irreconcilable forces: the evidence of his own senses and the unanimous testimony of a group of peers. The results of one phase of this study are given in the Table 5.1. To test the extent to which such findings depart from outcomes that might be expected if there were no relationship between group influence and accuracy of judgment, we can arrange the data in a four-celled table and apply the chi-square test as in Table 5.2 (see Chapter 4, pp. 138–39). Expected frequencies, on the assumption that the incidence of error would be as great in the one group as in the other, are given in parentheses.

Here we see, in Asch's subjects, a marked distortion of judgment conforming to the erroneous estimates of the majority. A third of all estimates made by the naïve subjects were errors identical with or in the direction of the distorted estimates of the majority. Those who yielded fell into three categories: those who "saw" wrongly, who judged wrongly, and who reported wrongly. One person apparently came to see lines unequally long as being of the same length. Most were ambivalent, knowing that their eyes saw one thing while their judgment told them, erroneously, that the majority must be right. The third category of subjects knew they saw a different line-matching solution than did the majority, felt their judgment was correct, but yielded "because of an overmastering need not to appear different from or inferior to others. . . ." Asch underlines one point that is worth repeating here.

> The distortions . . . in action, judgment, and, to some extent, perception were a consequence of pressures from the social sphere, not of tendencies whose source is in the individual himself. . . . The effects we have observed had their start in a prior contamination of the social field [that is, the majority in a group of Ss had been instructed to answer erroneously on some line-matching problems]—evidence of the profound difference, from the standpoint of the individual, between being in a group that possesses an adequate view and being in a group whose view is distorted.[16]

Of course, what we must realize is that in the significant groups in which most of us achieve our humanity—the family, school, work, and military and play groups—there is *always* "a prior contamination of the social field." Furthermore, if people's judgments are distorted under the influence of the group where the matter at issue is a fairly unambiguous one of physical perception, how much more might we expect to find people yielding to the prevailing sentiments of an already "contaminated social field" on matters of politics, race, religion, and morality!

The groups we belong to shape our conception of the good, as well as the true. Norms of behavior (stipulating conduct in the service of our values) emerge under group influence. And these norms, especially when they are central to group operations, are maintained within a fairly narrow range of tolerance. One of the best illustrations of the influence of the group in the establishment of such norms comes from the well-known study of the bank-wiring room (wiring for telephone relays) at the Hawthorne Works of the Western Electric Company in Chicago. Among these workers there was a clearly specified norm: 6,600 completed connections was a day's work. One maverick named Mueller was very fast in his work and tended to "overproduce." He said:

> Right now I'm turning out over 7,000 a day, around 7,040. The rest of the fellows kick because I do that. They want me to come down to around 6,600; but I don't see why I should.[17]

Table 5.2

Applying the chi-square test to Asch's data

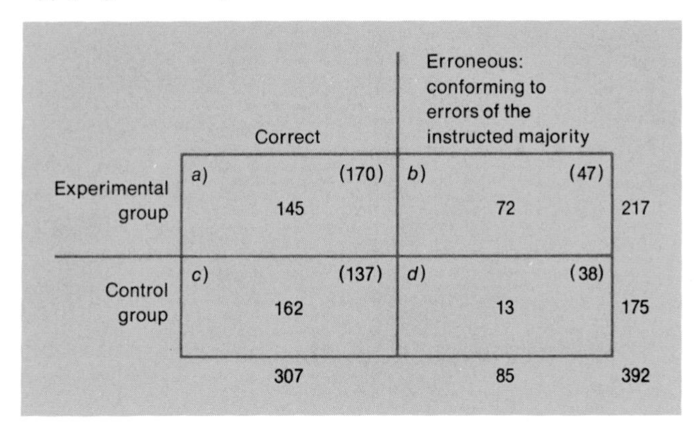

	Correct	Erroneous: conforming to errors of the instructed majority	
Experimental group	a) (170) 145	b) (47) 72	217
Control group	c) (137) 162	d) (38) 13	175
	307	85	392

Formula to be evaluated: $\chi^2 = \Sigma(f_o^2/f_e) - N$

Cell	f_o	f_e	f_o^2	f_o^2/f_e	
a)	145	170	21,025	124	
b)	72	47	5,184	110	Thus $\chi^2 = 430 - 392 = 38$ and,
c)	163	137	26,244	192	where degrees of freedom = 1 and
d)	13	38	169	4	$\chi^2 = 38$, $p < .001$.
				$\Sigma(f_o^2/f_e) = 430$	

Homans summarizes the norms of the group—norms imposed upon its members—in the following statements:

1. You should not turn out too much work. If you do, you are a "rate-buster."
2. You shouldn't turn out too little work. If you do, you're a "chiseler."
3. You shouldn't tell a supervisor anything that will react to the detriment of an associate. If you do you are a "squealer."
4. You should not attempt to maintain social distance or act officious. If you are an inspector, e.g., you should not act like one.
5. You should not be noisy, self-assertive, and anxious for leadership.[18]

While we can appeal to our own experience for confirmation of the group's influence upon behavior (consider, for example, the group-linked constraint we feel when, among a group of worshipers, we find it mandatory to mute our conversation), the influence of the group upon memory may not be so obvious. Yet consider these questions: *Why* do we remember what we do? *How* do we commemorate? *What* do we remember? What determines the accuracy with which we remember? As Maurice Halbwachs has suggested,[19] certainly the answers to these questions lead us to recognize the way in which the person's remembering is influenced by his group membership. Remembering is useful in preserving common values. As its etymology suggests, it *brings back to mind* acts and events we should guard against ("Remember the Maine," "Remember Pearl Harbor") and celebrates those deeds that we should emulate ("My only regret is that I have but one life to give for my country"). Our heroes and villains provide common memories, common points of reference for reaffirming our convictions and commitments. Professor Klapp says:

> While hero worship in America ranges from the adulation of entertainers and other celebrities to such diverse things as the celebration of legendary heroes, the decoration of military heroes, and the cult of saints, . . . it represents a generic process, . . . the tendency to select certain individuals as collective ideals, to accord them special status, and to surround them with behavior characterized as "hero worship."
>
> Hero worship in America expresses our characteristic values. Through the heroism of all societies, no doubt, run certain common threads: great achievement, heroism in war, martyrdom, and the like. The hero worship of American society reveals the run of our interests and consequently the fields in which heroes emerge.[20]

Amplifying his thesis in another study, Klapp suggests that the tribe's memorializing of its heroes, villains, and fools yields several significant outcomes. Such figures serve as simplified symbols dramatically pinpointing conceptions of good and evil. For the person, they provide "norms of self-judgment and roles for emulation or avoidance." They heighten the we-feeling, the solidarity of the group, perpetuating certain common values, nourishing and maintaining

> certain socially necessary sentiments—pride in great men, admiration of courage and self-sacrifice, hatred of vice, contempt for folly, a sense of national destiny, the historic continuity of a church militant . . . the memory of a great hero or anti-hero . . . is like an heirloom.[21]

Families have their own heirlooms and groups their own memorable events, which is why there are as many calendars as there are different groups, the division of time expressed sometimes in religious terms (as in Saints' days) or in business terms (market and exchange days).[22] One group can't use another's calendar. Its requirements are different; its memories are different.

I have been offering some suggestive evidence on the influence of the group upon the person. But to speak of the "group's influence," is to speak figuratively and ambiguously. The group is not animate, sensate, psychic as is the human actor. I mean more precisely certain characteristics or dimensions of the group—its size, its salience, its voting or preference structure (for example, size of the majority)—are clearly related to individual and aggregate characteristics of its members. This point will become clear in a final illustration. There are many other studies which provide supporting evidence; but Durkheim's classic study of suicide[23] will serve us especially well.* For aside from illustrating the influence of one aspect or dimension of the group, it will underline a point or two bearing on methods of inquiry.

The general problem posed is this: Why do people commit suicide? This is a very fuzzy formulation of the problem. We might reword it to emphasize our concern with differences: Why do some people commit suicide while others do not? But clearly, since we use the word *people,* we mean to seek some general explanation which applies to types or categories of persons. Thus we might rephrase the question this way: Why is it that suicide rates vary consistently as between different categories of persons? Let us be clear about this. It is not a question of explaining a given person's suicide, exploring that conjuncture of circumstances leading to the frame of mind prompting self-destruction. If we interpret suicide A as a result of a given motive, suicide B in terms of some other psychological quirk, we may conceivably provide two suggestive interpretations of two separate acts. But we have not enlightened ourselves as to the predisposing condition common to both—that is, we have achieved no insight as to the nature of suicide. If, on the other hand, our inquiry reveals that both A and B can be described as suffering some psychosis—we have restated the problem, not answered it. The question as reformu-

* Emile Durkheim, born in 1858 (the year after Comte died) is a central figure in the sociological tradition. His work stressed the unique nature of social phenomena, the unifying effect of the division of labor and the social nature of suicide, religion, and education, theretofore explained in psychological terms.

lated still awaits an answer: What then accounts for the quite predictable development of such psychoses which register themselves in a remarkably regular suicide rate? Durkheim's problem is to explain *suicide in general* as it characterizes a given group in contrast to other groups. And as he observes, there are indeed characteristic and quite stable suicide rates. "Each society," he notes, "is predisposed to contribute a definite quota of voluntary deaths."

But if we are to inquire into the causes of suicide, we had better know what we are talking about. A central requirement of controlled observation is an unambiguous definition of our central terms. This is not so simple as might appear. For example, we must decide whether to include under the heading of suicide only those acts where the intent was clear. Shall we take account of the means by which the act was accomplished? Does it make a difference whether the act was a positive one, carried out with some lethal weapon, or a negative one, as where death results from refusal to eat? Do we consider it a case of suicide when a person volunteers for a mortal mission, knowing full well that his death is foreordained? Durkheim considers these problems and concludes by defining suicide as "any death which is the direct or indirect result of a positive or negative act accomplished by the victim himself."[24]

The next step is to consider the common and current interpretations of such behavior. One such explanation likely to be offered by the alienists of Durkheim's day was simply that the suicide was psychopathic. Here Durkheim underlines the selective—and so, distorted—evidence with which the psychotherapist characteristically deals, and the importance of the negative case. "From the suicides they [the alienists, or psychotherapists] have known who were, of course, insane, no conclusion can be drawn as to those not observed who, moreover, are much more numerous."[25] This statement may be a bit obscure. At bottom is the issue of selective exposure and distorted sampling leading to false conclusions. Consider an analogy. A cardiac specialist concludes that people die of heart disease. (People who commit suicide are insane.) But the heart specialist underestimates the number of those who die from causes other than cardiac diseases. (The psychotherapist has no contact with those who are quite sane, yet nonetheless commit suicide.)

Durkheim checks further on this commonsense notion of a link between mental disorder and suicide. His data show insanity varying directly with suicide. But diagnoses of insanity are more frequent among urban dwellers. So it may be some feature of urban civilization, a third variable, that accounts both for high insanity and high suicide rates. He also finds rates of insanity higher among women than among men. Hence, if there were a relationship between insanity and suicide, we would predict higher suicide rates for women. But this is exactly contrary to the facts. Suicides are disproportionately male.

Furthermore, if we order the data on insanity by the three major religious faiths (the data are from European countries and provinces: Silesia, Mecklenburg, Bavaria, Prussia, and so on), we find that "insanity is evidently much more frequent among the Jews than among the other religious faiths. . . ," yet there is relatively little suicide among Jews. "In this case . . . suicide varies in inverse proportion to psychopathic states, rather than being consistent with them."[26] Further inquiry brings him to the conclusion that:

> . . . no psychopathic state bears a regular and indisputable relation to suicide. A society does not depend for its number of suicides on having more or fewer neuropaths or alcoholics. . . . Admittedly under similar circumstances, the degenerate is more apt to commit suicide than the well man; but he does not necessarily do so because of his condition. This potentiality of his becomes effective only through the action of other factors which we must discover.[27]

In similar fashion Durkheim disposes of other popular notions: that suicide is related to racial or ethnic characteristics, or that it is to be explained by what he calls "cosmic factors" (variations in temperature and the like), or simply by imitation.

Now he turns to the matter of social causes. Can we find something in the nature of the group, some attribute or dimension of the group, which helps us to understand those differing patterns of behavior registered in contrasting suicide rates? "We shall try," he says,

> . . . to determine the productive causes of suicide directly, without concerning ourselves with the forms they can assume in particular individuals. Disregarding the individual as such, his motives and his ideas, we shall seek directly the states of the various social environments (religious confessions, family, political society, occupational groups, etc.), in terms of which the variations of suicide occur. Only then returning to

the individual shall we study how these general causes become individualized so as to produce the homicidal results involved.[28]

Turning first to the data revealing a consistent and continuing difference between Catholic and Protestant suicide rates (emphatically higher for the latter), Durkheim writes:

> . . . both [Protestantism and Catholicism] prohibit suicide . . . penalize it morally . . . teach that a new life begins beyond the tomb where men are punished for their evil actions [and that] these prohibitions are of divine origin; they are represented not as the logical conclusions of correct reason, but God Himself is their authority.
>
> [Now the] essential difference between Catholicism and Protestantism is that the second permits free inquiry to a far greater degree than the first.
>
> All variation is abhorrent to Catholic thought. The Protestant is far more the author of his faith.
>
> We thus reach our first conclusion, that the proclivity of Protestantism for suicide must relate to the spirit of free inquiry that animates this religion. [Now] free inquiry develops only if its development becomes imperative, that is, if certain ideas and sentiments which have hitherto adequately guided conduct are found to have lost their efficacy. Then reflection intervenes to fill the gap that has appeared. . . . if it is correct to say that free inquiry once proclaimed, multiplies schisms, it must be added that it presupposes them and derives from them. So if Protestantism concedes a greater freedom to individual thought than Catholicism, it is because it has fewer common beliefs and practices.
>
> The more numerous the manners of action and thought of a religious character are, which are accordingly removed from free inquiry, the more the idea of God presents itself in all details of existence, and makes individual wills converge to one identical goal. Inversely, *the greater concessions a confessional group makes to individual judgment, the less it dominates lives, the less its cohesion and vitality.*[29]

This is a general statement, an interpretation, based on such observations as Durkheim could make with the data available to him. First, he observes higher suicide rates for Protestants than for Catholics. Then he develops this interpretation of the data:

Table 5.3
The connection between education and suicide rates*

Population†	Average percent of marriages with both partners literate	Suicide rate
Group I	39	41
Group II	15	32
Group III	6	15

* Education indexed by literacy and suicide rates is based on suicides per million inhabitants.

† Group I includes the population of Piedmont, Lombardy, Liguria, Rome, and Tuscany provinces; Group II includes Venice, Emilia, Umbria, Marches Campana, and Sardinia provinces; and Group III includes Sicily, Abruzzi, Apulia, Calabria, and Basilicata provinces.

high suicide rates are related to lack of consensus, to a high degree of individualism, to low group cohesion. Now a third step. He deduces an hypothesis as to the relationship between education and suicide: (1) Protestants, compared with Catholics, have higher suicide rates. (2) Liberated from clerical tradition, Protestants seek answers from secular sources and favor education. (3) Level of education should, therefore, be positively related to suicide rates.

> . . . if the progressive weakening of collective and customary prejudices produce a trend to suicide and if Protestantism derives thence its special predisposition to it, [then] (1) the desire for learning must be stronger among Protestants than among Catholics; (2), in so far as this denotes a weakening of common beliefs, it should vary with suicide, fairly generally.[30]

To test this prediction, Durkheim uses data on three clusters of Italian provinces, thus holding constant the factor of religion (all Catholics). The percent of marriages in which both husband and wife were literate provides him with an index of education. The data are shown in Table 5.3.

Since suicide rates vary with level of education achieved, and since in his day any extended education was almost a male monopoly, Durkheim suspects that the same factor underlies the difference in suicide rates between men and women.

He also finds a higher rate of suicide in times and groups that are politically unstable, in smaller in contrast to larger families, and among single persons in contrast to married.*

Now we are finally ready for Durkheim's conclusions. He has shown that family size is inversely related to suicide rates, that such rates are directly related to degree of political instability, that they vary directly with proportion of population which is Protestant, that there is a higher incidence of suicide among the single than among married persons.

> . . . this is due not to a special characteristic of each [of these spheres of life] but to a characteristic common to all. Religion does not owe its efficacy to the special nature of religious sentiments, since domestic and political societies both produce the same effects when strongly integrated. . . . It is not the specific nature of the domestic or political tie which can explain the immunity [from suicide] they confer, since religious society has the same advantage. The cause can only be found in a single quality possessed by all these social groups, though perhaps to varying degrees. The only quality satisfying this condition is that they are all strongly integrated social groups. So we reach the general conclusion: suicide varies inversely with the degree of integration of the social groups of which the individual forms a part.
>
> . . . The bond that unites [people] with the common cause attaches them to life and the lofty goal they envisage prevents their feeling personal troubles so deeply. There is, in short, in a cohesive and animated society a constant interchange of ideas and feelings from all to each and each to all, something like a mutual moral support, which instead of throwing the individual on his own resources, leads him to share in the collective energy and supports his own when exhausted.[31]

And so, according to Durkheim, as one dimension of the group varies (its integration or cohesiveness), the consequences are felt by the person and reflected in variations in the suicide rate.

We have been dealing with the general question: Whence the leverage, the power that accounts for the inculcation of the requisite culture, enabling the person to enter the group? And we have looked first at certain evidence of the group's influence considered

* See Aside on Methods: Number 6: "Control of Variables."

. . . The group, through its agents, shapes the person. . . . Parents and teachers . . . are the rebuilders of groups through the making of persons.

. . . Norms of behavior . . . emerge under group influence. And these norms . . . are maintained within a fairly narrow range of tolerance.

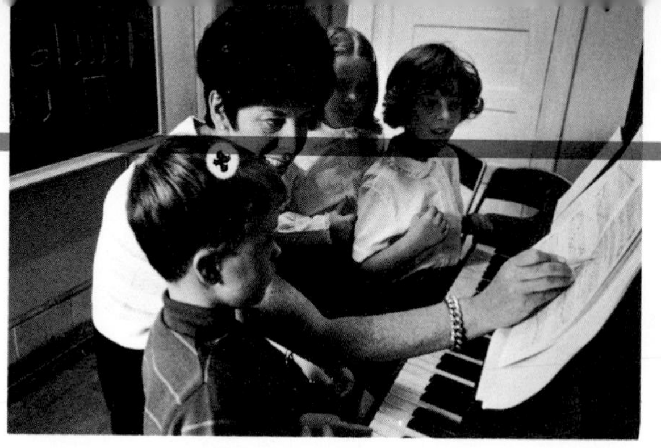

. . . Wherever there is systematic instruction in skills, knowledge, and attitudes, "teachers" are at work.

. . . public education has a social function: the survival of the group by guaranteeing the knowledge, skills, and values required to man its roles. . . . the stress (is) . . . on transmitting the group's culture, not on changing it.

in the abstract. The data indicate that the isolated individual never becomes a person, never achieves a self, never acquires culture, never learns the score, never becomes a human being in any intelligible sense of the word. On the other hand, the evidence points to the way the group conditions our thought processes: its salience affects our degree of conformity, it influences our opinions and political views, our perception of physical objects, our norms of behavior. It sets the framework for the person's thinking and remembering. And finally, Durkheim's work suggests that one dimension of the group, its cohesiveness,[32] affects even such an apparently idiosyncratic sort of behavior as suicide.

But let us turn now to specific groups, the two groups chiefly charged and consciously invested with the task of cultural transmission. These are the family and the school.

The family as agent of cultural transmission

Later, in Chapter 9, we shall look at family and education as part of the institutional structure, institutions moving the young toward adult independence. At this point I want only to point to certain features of family and school that endow these groups with power as agents of cultural transmission. For example, there is a tendency toward homogamy in marriage (spouses having like characteristics), with the result that the children are confronted with a powerful coalition. Again, while filial piety is not the dominant theme we find in old Chinese culture, respect for parents and an emotional identification with them reinforce the influence of the elders. Finally, there are certain traits imposed on the child willy-nilly by the fact of birth in a given family: religious identification, class position, expectations and aspirations, perhaps even political preferences.

Who marries whom? Influences making for partner homogamy and strength of parental influence

To the extent that marriages are homogamous, the probability of common premises, preferences, and prejudices is increased. To the extent that the partners do in fact share such common commitments, the child confronts an effective coalition. His not to reason why, his simply to comply—with the unanimous mandates of his world of powerful adults.

The evidence suggests that homogamy is common in American marriages.

> Like tends to marry like is the general rule: marriages do not ordinarily occur between persons of different race, creed, or ethnic origin, nor between those widely separated in age, job, education, or social class, nor even between those dissimilar in their somatic or psychosomatic defects.[33]

Law has promoted homogamy in marriage. Aside from health restrictions and minimum age laws, we have imposed restrictions on interracial marriage throughout most of our history. As late as 1965, white-Negro marriages were prohibited in 21 states. Other prohibitions were these: Caucasians and mongolians in nine states, whites and Malays in four states, whites and Indians in three states, Indians and Negroes in two states. "Although statistically the chances of marriages between Malays and Negroes would not seem to be great in Utah and Wyoming, those states [took] no chances and forbade them."[34]

In 1967, the Supreme Court unanimously ruled that states may not forbid marriage between whites and nonwhites. The Chief Justice wrote: "We have consistently denied the constitutionality of measures which restrict the rights of citizens on account of race. . . . The 14th Amendment requires that the freedom of choice to marry not be restricted by invidious racial discriminations."

But despite court permission, it is likely that birds of like feather will indeed flock together and, having met, will marry. Marriage, with few exceptions, is contingent on meeting. And so we may ask: What part does propinquity play in mate selection? About 40 years ago, studying the court records of 5,000 Philadelphia marriages, Bossard found that over half the partners had lived within a mile of one another.[35] And while we are doubtless more mobile today, it is still true that propinquity affects choice of marriage partner. In 1966, 87 percent of the 1.4 million brides were residents of the state where they married. (Grooms were only a bit more mobile: 82 percent of them lived in the state where they married.)[36] Probably most lived closer than these gross data would suggest. People living near one another tend to resemble one another—in backgrounds, values, attitudes, life style—more than they resemble "outsiders." Thus propinquity increases the trait-homogamy of the partners. And so the impact of each in the socialization process is reinforced.

One might suppose that the richer or better educated would cut a wider swath in their spouse-hunting activities. But even if they are not quite so restricted to a given area, travel more, have distant summer places, go away to college, nonetheless they tend to go to the same sorts of places—meet, marry, and make homogamous unions.

Familial duty and sentiment

The power of the parents over the child derives not only from homogamy of traits, a homogamy required by law, resulting from propinquity or from a preference for the comfortably familiar. It stems, too, from the notions of filial piety which still obtain, though doubtless in attenuated fashion. The relationship between child and socializing agent is suffused with emotion. What might otherwise be an intolerable dictatorship is often tempered with tenderness. And so the newcomer emulates his parents, the group's agents of socialization, not only because he is powerless to do otherwise, not only because, being similar in many traits, they present him with a single, reinforced set of expectations, but also because they are "worthy" and loved models. As the physician is for the medical student, as the older nun is *la règle vivante* ("a living rule book") for the novice, so the mother is for the daughter, the father for the son.

Thus familial duty and sentiment reinforce the effects of homogamy making for parental power. Indeed, at the risk of offending sacred sentiments attaching to home and mother, I would suggest that becoming a member of the human group is a process much resembling brainwashing. The family setting provides the conditions for a totalitarian government. The child is close to state zero, inexperienced, relatively impotent, an easy target for indoctrination. The parents are omniscient and omnipotent. They are gods and dictators. They have available to them most of the conditions that have made brainwashing and reindoctrination an effective totalitarian technique. Indeed, parents have the advantage of not having to extinguish the experience of decades before commencing indoctrination.

And so the child is scolded, spanked, shamed, humiliated, embarrassed, nurtured, fed, encouraged, praised, taught. Typically he is isolated, although not necessarily by design, from counter influences—at least during the preschool years. His mentors and his parents are likely to have moved in the same circles, have had similar education, similar background within the same social class; and their continued intercourse will be unwittingly selective, barring contact for their children with most of the spectrum of human attributes available in their culture. His indoctrination involves onerous repetition of the party line. And unlike academic learning, which consciously eschews one of the most effective of all the levers for learning, the child's indoctrination within the family is heavily laden with emotion.

Ascribed traits and attitudes transmitted from forebears to progeny

Aside from conscious parental indoctrination, the child acquires certain familial attributes willy-nilly. Nativity, place of residence, parental income, father's occupation, religion, education—these are family traits and automatically become those of the newcomer.

Thus Herbert Hyman in his review of what we know about the political socialization of the child can say that intergenerational political preferences "are so similar that one can conclude that social differentiations in voting preference [and above all in party preference] are almost complete at the pre-adult level."[37]

We know that favorable attitudes toward labor, toward unions, and "collectivism" are characteristic of lower-class, rather than upper-class, persons. And the children of the poorer classes reflect this orientation, being more favorably disposed toward unions than their middle- and upper-class counterparts.[38]

Professor Hyman reviews past studies of extent of agreement between parents and children on attitude toward war and its likelihood, view of the New Deal, attitude toward Communist and Fascist positions, ethnocentrism, liberalism, conservatism, the U.S.S.R., and party preferences. A few inquiries report no great similarity between parents' and children's views. But about three fourths of the studies do report finding marked agreement between political views of the two generations.

But the moderate size of the correlations between attitudes of father and son suggest that parents are not the only agents transmitting political preferences and other views. Indeed, in one early study of similarities between the moral code of children and five socializing agents, the correlation (r) between parents and children was only .55;* that is, variance in parental views accounted for something around 30 percent of the variance in children's views (although this influence was greater than that of any other of the agents studied: friends, club leaders, school, and Sunday school teachers).[39] The relative impact of other agents of socialization seems to increase through time. For example, the school's influence increases in two senses. Political and other attitudes have been shown to change with additional years of schooling. And the average number of years of schooling achieved has increased over the years. (It was on this basis that Samuel Stouffer, having found greater concern for civil liberties among the better educated, and an increasing proportion of the population achieving higher levels of education, predicted an increased concern to preserve our Bill of Rights and to tolerate various sorts of deviants.)[40] It is to this matter of the school's influence that we now turn, seeing it, after the family, as the principal agent for transmitting culture.

The school as the group's agent of cultural transmission

Formal education is the most powerful of the tools consciously and consistently used to bring the influence of the group to bear upon the person.† The teacher is delegated by the group to inculcate those elements of culture necessary for satisfactory group membership. Like parents, teachers are vested with a public responsibility. Like parents, they share in the task of "fabricating" human beings. And to some extent they are able to work, like parents, upon relatively malleable material—upon persons much of whose behavior has not yet been irreversibly channeled.

* We run across the Pearsonian *r*, or the product moment correlation coefficient, so frequently in the social sciences, it is worth stopping briefly to illustrate its meaning. See Aside on Methods: Number 7: "The Pearsonian Correlation Coefficient," p. 625.

† This is a strong statement. But recall that law requires every normal person to submit to this influence, a mandatory exposure to indoctrination which is true of no other human association save the family and the state. Consider, also, the way in which this influence is standardized (again, by law) in contrast to the broadly varying influences of different families. I speak here only of the United States, obviously. In other societies, newcomers to the group may be inducted—i.e., educated—chiefly through other agencies.

The function of public education

Education is the means by which the group models persons to fit its requirements. (This is not, of course, the common view of education; and I shall point out presently why I think the common view illusory and this view correct.) Formal education consists in sets of standardized roles defined in law—federal, state, and local—in custom, and in the credos of professional organizations. We think ordinarily of such roles as those associated with the public schools, colleges, academies, and universities: teachers, professors, students, principals, superintendents, presidents, regents, and the like. But, of course, it is not true that education only occurs where, as in Western societies, it is separately institutionalized.

> . . . everyone . . . has for teachers both the form of government under which he lives, and his friends and his mistresses, and the people about him, and the books he reads and, finally, chance, that is to say an infinite number of events whose connection and causes we are unable, through ignorance, to perceive.[41]

Priest and parent and peers have educational roles; and so do fellow workers, actors, employers, and grandparents. Wherever there is systematic instruction in skills, knowledge, and attitudes, "teachers" are at work. Learning the multiplication table or Shamanistic secrets, the notions of fair play or the arts of mendacity, pressure chipping of flint or metallurgy, people are learning and being taught.

But in complex societies, education is not left to the chance influence of informal teaching. Educational roles are institutionalized to insure a "proper" human being who embodies the core elements of the cultural heritage. Durkheim says:

> That is the task of education, and thus we see it in all its greatness. Education does not restrict itself to developing the individual in accordance with his [genetic] nature, teasing out those hidden capacities that lie there, dormant, asking only to be revealed. *It creates a new being.**

Durkheim has perfectly expressed this view that education is the instrument of the group to induct succeeding generations into

* See Original Texts, Note 5.2.

their appropriate roles in the group. "Education, far from having as its unique or principal object the individual and his interests, is above all the means by which society perpetually recreates the conditions of its very existence."[42] But professional educators and public spokesmen take a contrary position. Education, they say, is the process of developing as far as possible the particular potential of the individual. This conventional view of education is excessively individualistic. It masks the social—and coercive—character of public education. With a virtuous concern for the individual, it disguises the narrow limits within which the group allows variation in what is taught. For public education has a social function: the survival of the group by guaranteeing the knowledge, skills, and values required to man its roles. Thus we should expect the stress to be on transmitting the group's culture, not on changing it.

Winston Churchill once declared that he did not become Prime Minister of England to preside over the dissolution of the British empire. So it is with our Boards of Education in the United States. They do not see themselves as having been elected to promote change in the community through novelties in education purchased with tax dollars. Their task is to see that education preserves the community. For this reason public education is and must be essentially a conservative force, the "means by which [the group] perpetually recreates the conditions of its very existence." It is precisely because education is an instrument for perpetuating the conditions of the group's existence that a small minority of students have struck our universities in past years.

We should not be surprised, therefore, if students inclined toward, or teachers disposed to encourage, independent thought are regarded as subversive; for quite literally that is what they are. Even at the university level, the public school can encourage innovation with impunity only in those realms—for example, engineering—where the material consequences are more of the same (bigger and better) and where the social consequences are remote and obscure.

Through education, then, we induct persons into the group in ways that respond to the needs of the group. In a nation in which it is possible for a Secretary of Defense to say: "What is good for General Motors is good for the United States," it is to be expected that "driver education" will have an important part in the curriculum.[43] In an increasingly complex society, the proliferation of courses will reflect the specialized needs of the group.

The increased emphasis in recent years upon language, mathematics, and the physical sciences is, again, a response through education to the need felt by various groups in the United States for strengthening the nation vis-à-vis the U.S.S.R. Similarly, formal education serves the needs of the group in undeveloped rural areas by reducing its demands on the child—a shortened school year, the common withdrawals during planting and harvesting seasons, a disregard for the letter of the school law.

It follows, clearly, that what is appropriate education for one group will not be appropriate in another. The educational patterns of one society cannot be successfully imposed on another having a different pattern of beliefs and behaviors. This is why, as Kingsley Davis points out, the attempt to transplant British education in India was necessarily such a thumping failure. "The Western model collides with two great realities in Hindu life—*ruralism* and *caste*."[44]

We have often seen free public education as the instrument par excellence of a democracy. That is to say, form of government and type of education are seen as necessarily connected. Thus we assert that if the suffrage extends to all citizens, it is imperative to provide universal, "free" education. (Democratic revolutionaries have agreed with Danton: *"Next to bread, education is the first need of the people."*) The assumptions of our form of government require that education provide that equality of opportunity which guarantees both personal fulfillment and the disclosure of socially useful *in*equalities. To an indeterminate extent this has been true. Much of the imagery of education has made it, from the person's perspective, a social escalator, the proper instrument for improving one's standing. This has probably led us to underemphasize the extent to which education responds to differentials in the group, tending in general to reproduce them. Especially have we overlooked the extent to which other socializing agencies, such as the family, have already set the conditions of knowledge and aspiration that qualify the school's influence.

* * * *

Human groups, we have noted, are constantly rebuilt—losses replenished—through an input of newcomers who acquire culture as they are socialized by the elders and old-timers. This cultural transmission is a social process. In the absence of others, the process is aborted. In the presence of others, the self is shaped: what and how we think, and feel, what we perceive and what we remember. Even the apparently individual matter of suicide is seen to be an outcome of social factors—for Durkheim, degree of social cohesion.

In complex human groups, transmission of culture becomes a matter chiefly for family and school as agents of the group. The impact of the family is increased by monogamy in marriage, by conceptions of familial duty, by the sentiment that strengthens family ties, and by the fact that young are tagged with family attributes: religion, family income, political preference, and the like.

Finally, we can see education as a process geared to group survival. Differences in education reflect group differences—the need to transmit different elements from the repertoire of cultural possibilities. The nature of education, then, differs between groups and for different sorts of persons within a given group.

There is no escaping the influence of the groups in which we acquire selves and assimilate the central elements of our culture. The result is twofold. The group is regularly recreated as the newcomer achieves his identity. It is to this matter of the person as product that we turn in the next chapter.

References

TEXT

1. E. B. Reuter, *Handbook of Sociology* (New York: Dryden Press, 1946). Italics mine.
2. See, for example, the article by William F. Ogburn, "The Wolf Boy of Agra," *American Journal of Sociology,* Vol. 64, No. 5 (March, 1959).
3. Kingsley Davis, "Extreme Social Isolation of a Child," *American Journal of Sociology,* Vol. 45 (January, 1940), pp. 554–65; and "Final Note on a Case of Extreme Isolation," *American Journal of Sociology,* Vol. 52, No. 5 (March, 1947), pp. 432–37.
4. John C. Lilly, "Effects of Physical Restraint and of Reduction of Ordinary Levels of Physical Stimuli on Intact, Healthy Persons," (New York: Group for the Advancement of Psychiatry, 1956), *Symposium No. 2,* pp. 13–20. See also reports of his testimony before a congressional committee, *New York Times,* April 15, 1956.
5. Milton Meltzer, "Factors Used to Increase the Susceptibility of Individuals to Forceful Indoctrination: Observation and Experiments" (New York: Group for the Advancement of Psychiatry, December, 1956), *Symposium No. 3,* p. 103 .
6. Joseph Eaton, "Controlled Acculturation: A Survival Technique of the Hutterites," *American Sociological Review,* Vol. 17, pp. 331–40.
7. See H. B. M. Murphy, *Flight and Resettlement* (Paris: UNESCO, 1955), p. 38. The quotation is from Hedwig Larsen, H. Hoffmeyer *et al.,* "Famine Disease in German Concentration Camps," *Act. Neur. et Psychiat.* Scand. supp. 83, 1952. Italics mine.
8. Mental Functions in *Primitive Societies* (1910), *Primitive Mentality* (1922), and *The Soul of the Primitive* (1927).
9. W. W. Charters, Jr., and Theodore M. Newcomb, "Some Attitudinal Effects of Experimentally Increased Salience of a Membership Group," in Maccoby, Newcomb and Hartley (eds.), *Readings in Social Psychology* (New York: Henry Holt & Co., Inc., 1958), p. 276.

10. *Ibid.*, p. 278.
11. Muzafer Sherif, "Group Influence upon the Formation of Norms and Attitudes," in Newcomb, Hartley *et al.*, *Readings in Social Psychology* (New York: Henry Holt & Co., Inc., 1947), pp. 77–90. See also Muzafer Sherif, *The Psychology of Social Norms* (New York: Harper & Bros., 1936), and "An Experiment Approach to the Study of Attitudes," *Sociometry*, Vol. 1 (1937), pp. 90–98.
12. Sherif, "Group Influence upon the Formation of Norms and Attitudes," *op. cit.*, p. 80.
13. Ibid., p. 83.
14. Solomon E. Asch, *Social Psychology* (Englewood Cliffs, N.J.: Prentice-Hall, Inc., 1952), chap. xvi, "Group Forces in the Modification and Distortion of Judgments," pp. 450–501.
15. *Ibid.*, p. 450.
16. *Ibid.*, p. 495.
17. George Homans, *The Human Group* (New York: Harcourt, Brace & World, Inc., 1950), p. 123. Homans' quotation is from F. J. Roethlisberger and W. J. Dickson, *Management and the Worker* (Cambridge, Mass.: Harvard University Press, 1939), p. 417.
18. Homans, *op. cit.*, p. 79.
19. Maurice Halbwachs, "Mémoire et Société," *Année sociologique*, Vol. I (Third Series, 1940), republished as *La Mémoire Collective* (Paris: Presses Universitaires de France, 1950).
20. Orrin E. Klapp, "Hero Worship in America," *American Sociological Review*, Vol. 19, No. 1 (February, 1949), pp. 53, 62.
21. Orrin E. Klapp, "Heroes, Villains and Fools as Agents of Social Control," *American Sociological Review*, Vol. 19, No. 1 (February, 1954), p. 62.
22. Halbwachs, *op. cit.*, p. 120.
23. Emile Durkheim, *Suicide*, trans. John A. Spaulding and George Simpson (New York: Free Press of Glencoe, Inc., 1951).
24. *Ibid.*, p. 42.
25. *Ibid.*, p. 62. Compare this with Professor Sewell's criticism of psychoanalytic theory as the basis for prescribing child-training practices (see chap. iv). We should remember that *Suicide* was first published in 1897 and that theory and practice in psychotherapy were then embryonic. So, also, was sociology. Statistics were undeveloped, Durkheim's data were poor, and many of his measures were simple *ad hoc* inventions. But with these precautions, the main points should be kept in mind: (1) Durkheim reveals the influence of the group—more accurately, one of its dimensions, degree of cohesiveness—as it affects what common sense erroneously sees as an altogether idiosyncratic, personal act. (2) The strategy of his inquiry (in contrast to the tactics) offers a good example of controlled observation.
26. *Ibid.*, p. 72.
27. *Ibid.*, p. 81. Let me enter several reservations here. First, the archaic use of such a term as *degenerate* should remind us that, in 1897, psychology, to say nothing of sociology, was little developed. Second, there is a danger of concluding prematurely that psychic states have nothing to do with suicide. But we must remember that Durkheim was dealing with *rates* for areas (regions, nations) and categories of persons (Protestants, Catholics, Jews). He was *not* dealing with the convergence of two or more traits in a single person, as a psychologist would. The latter would raise the question: What constellation of personality traits in this person accounts for an inward turning of aggression resulting in suicide? Durkheim would ask: What are the attributes of groups, registered in certain rates, that vary concomitantly with suicide rates? Thus psychologists and sociologists address themselves to different questions. Third, it should be noted, as C. S. Robinson does in an important study, "Ecological Correlations and Behavior of Individuals," that measures based on aggregates—proportions, ratios, and the like—give very different results from those relating individuals' attributes. Robinson demonstrates that "there need be no correspondence between the individual correlation and the [correlation of aggregate measures]." Indeed, it is possible for the direction of the relationship to be *reversed!* (*American Sociological Review*, Vol. 15, No. 3 [June, 1950], p. 354.)
28. *Ibid.*, p. 151.
29. *Ibid.*, pp. 157–59, *passim.*
30. *Ibid*, p. 162.
31. *Ibid.*, pp. 208–10, *passim.*
32. In a study of 228 work groups where degree of cohesiveness was also the independent variable, Seashore found measures of anxiety inversely related to group cohesiveness. In productivity there was less intragroup but more intergroup variation among high cohesive

groups (Stanley E. Seashore, *Group Cohesiveness in the Industrial Work Group* [Ann Arbor, Mich.: Survey Research Center, Institute for Social Research, 1954]).

In an effort to build on and transcend the work of Durkheim, Ronald W. Maris studied 2,153 suicides—the officially recorded ones—in Cook County, Illinois. His general conclusion was that suicide varies inversely with the extent to which the person is bound into a network of interpersonal dependencies. These impose a degree of external constraint. See his *Social Forces in Urban Suicide* (Homewood, Ill.: Dorsey Press, 1969).

33. John Sirjamaki, *The American Family in the Twentieth Century* (Cambridge: Harvard University Press, 1953), p. 66.
34. George Eaton Simpson and J. Milton Yinger, *Racial and Cultural Minorities* (New York: Harper & Row, Publishers, 1965), pp. 375, 376.
35. James H. S. Bossard, "Residential Propinquity as a Factor in Marriage Selection," *American Journal of Sociology,* Vol. 38 (September, 1932), pp. 219–24.
36. Public Health Service, National Center for Health Statistics, U.S. Department of Health, Education and Welfare, *Vital Statistics of the United States: 1966,* Vol. III, "Marriage and Divorce" (Washington, D.C.: U.S. Government Printing Office, 1969), calculated from Table 1–33.
37. Herbert Hyman, *Political Socialization* (New York: Free Press of Glencoe, Inc., 1959), p. 36.
38. *Ibid.*, p. 39.
39. H. Hartshorne, M. May, and F. Shuttleworth, *Studies in the Nature of Character, III* (New York: Macmillan Co., 1930), p. 98.
40. Samuel A. Stouffer, *Communism, Conformity and Civil Liberties* (New York: Doubleday & Co., Inc., 1955), p. 92.
41. Claude Adrien Helvetius, *de l'Esprit* (Paris, 1758), discours iii, chap. i.
42. Émile Durkheim, *Éducation et sociologie* (Paris: Librairie Felix Alcon, 1922), p. 123. See also Professor Sorokin's similar statement. The school is "primarily a testing, selecting and distributing agency . . . allocating people to the niches necessary to perform their social function" (*Social Mobility* [New York: Harper & Bros., 1927], p. 188).
43. *The New York Times* reports that "High Schools in U.S. Trained 1,338,346 to Drive in 1958–59."

"As a result of a 'marked advance' in their programs, Delaware, New Jersey, N. Carolina, Utah, and the District of Columbia received Progress Awards in the 12th annual evaluation by the Association of Casualty and Surety Companies . . . insurance companies give discounts ranging as high as 10% from the extra premiums charged to 'unmarried male drivers under 25 years' if a youth has successfully completed such a program. The insurance reports showed that 63% of the 21,000 public high schools in the country offered some kind of driver training to 67.7% of the eligible students . . . the insurance group said that 'the revolt against frills in the secondary school curriculum' had not forced a reduction in driver training—an implied criticism of New York City [where] complete driver training is offered only in 6 vocational schools, largely because members of the school administration feel that such training in academic high schools is unnecessary and difficult to give (*New York Times,* October 5, 1959)."

44. Kingsley Davis, *The Population of India and Pakistan* (Princeton, N.J.: Princeton University Press, 1931), p. 159.

TABLES

5.1 Solomon E. Asch, *Social Psychology* (Englewood Cliffs, N.J.: Prentice-Hall, Inc., 1952), p. 450.

5.1 Émile Durkheim, *Suicide,* trans. John A. Spaulding and George Simpson (New York: Free Press of Glencoe, Inc., 1951).

chapter 6 Product of cultural transmission: the person and the group

Human dignity is a matter of social permission.
Peter L. Berger

Through the flashback technique in novels (or in films or psychoanalysis) we discover features of a man's social ancestry that shape his present life and foreshadow the future. In this chapter we look in two directions: back to the social influences that progressively fix* his adult roles, and thus define the person (Figure 6.1); and forward to the social structure (Part Two) continuously being rebuilt as roles vacated are refilled.

For a fourth to a third of his life, the newcomer to the human

* The word *fix* perhaps conveys an unintended finality and immutability. I mean to suggest, rather, a progressively narrowed range of options and alternatives (as antecedent experience conditions the future) or, more positively, an increasingly specific definition of appropriate roles, worked out by the person in collaboration with others sharing his "life space." This is the idea conveyed in Figure 6.1 sounding this chapter's theme.

Figure 6.1
The trip from birth to death through peopled space and time: the shaping of role and status

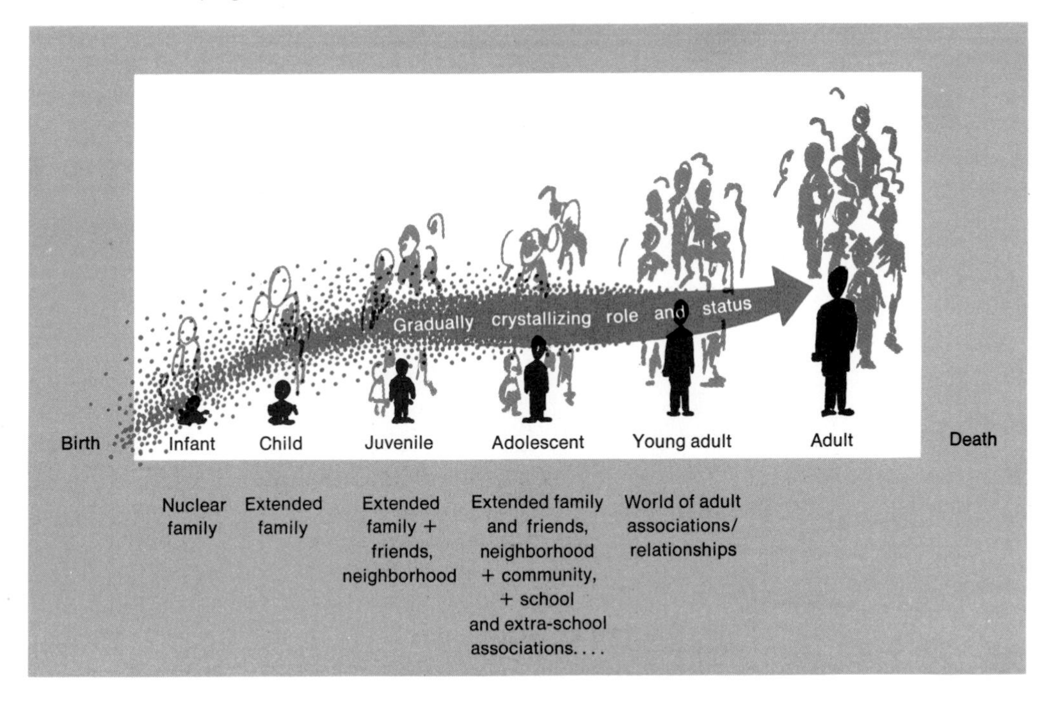

group is tutored in its ways. Failures and successes are defined by punishments and rewards. The usual outcome is a person rehearsed to take his part in a number of plays. The male is ready for dual roles as husband and father in the domestic drama. In the work theater he is fellow worker to some, subordinate and superordinate to others. In religion, politics, and play he has been understudy to the elders, anticipating his time on stage. Rehearsals have been scheduled over a long period in the parental family, in school and neighborhood. The first two are the chief formal socializing agencies. But also crucial are the informal rehearsals with one's peers, the local neighborhood gang. Family, school, and gang collaborate in working through the script that we call culture. In these early and elementary social circles—at least by the time he has completed formal schooling—continuous exposure to a limited and reinforcing set of influences has led the understudy to some command of his part in the play, his roles, and the conditions for playing them.

In this process, absence is as significant as presence, omission as commission. The entrant's influences are unintentionally limited to the themes of his culture as interpreted in his group. Ruth Benedict makes the point of selective limitation when she writes:

> It is in cultural life as it is in speech; selection is the prime necessity. The numbers of sounds that can be produced by our vocal cords and our oral and nasal cavities are practically unlimited. . . .
>
> In culture, too, we must imagine a great arc on which are ranged the possible interests provided either by the human age-cycle or by the environment or by man's various activities. A culture that capitalized even a considerable proportion of these would be as unintelligible as a language that used all the clicks, all the glottal stops, all the labials, dentals, sibilants and gutturals from voiceless to voiced, from oral to nasal. Its identity as a culture depends upon the *selection of some segments of this arc.* Every human society everywhere has made such selection in its cultural institutions.[1]

The exclusion of other influences is carried further in regional and local enclaves with their variations on the theme. Because of what he is not, as well as what he *is* taught, the person becomes an accepted member of the group, crystallizing with ever greater precision the roles required in support of the relationships of which the group is built.

But the theatrical use of the word, role, is not enough to convey the meaning of the concept. And so we shall attend to its social meaning. Then we shall ask several questions. First, what are the general types of influence that come to play on the person, working toward the crystallization of his roles? Second, what are the sources of variation and stability in role performance? Third, what different aspects or dimensions of roles are stressed in different sorts of groups? And finally, what about those situations in which the demands of one role are at odds with those of another? What does it mean for the group? For the person?

The meaning of the concept, role

Let us be clear about what we mean by this term, *role;* for it is a critical, elemental concept in sociology. A role is a regular way of acting, expected of all persons occupying a given position in the social order as they deal with specified categories of others. Thus, the parental role consists in behavior expected of an adult confronting his/her children. (The role includes indirect, as well as direct confrontations as, for example, when the parent consults the physician, or the teacher, or the policeman *about* this child.) The employer role stipulates conduct appropriate in relationships with employees. The role of the communicant is that appropriate to the person when confronting his God, a priest, or fellow communicants—and so on across the spectrum of life's activities. In short, a role is the culturally specified behavior for dealing with classes of social objects.

Each of us has a number of roles, not always compatible, associated with various positions (statuses) in the structure of the group. Through time these roles—familial, work, religious, civic—become defined in more precise detail. We can identify three sorts of influences at work to shape the person's roles and status and so to build the group.

Types of influence that shape role and status

We can see the process of building the human group through socialization as one in which the newcomer is first identified by categories shared with major sectors of the population—age, sex, race. With time, his identity is narrowed and specified, as classification in additional categories, and membership in additional groups, give him a particular configuration of attributes shared by fewer people. Successive experiences define life chances and aptitudes, channel interests, and specify the prospects—thus fixing the positions and roles that define the person.

To help tidy up our thinking on this matter, consider three sorts of categories and groups that contribute to the crystallizing of role.[2] There are, first, the socially significant biological traits. Second, there are various categories with which the person's family is identified. Third, there are the groups in which the person, as a separate individual, is directly implicated. The outcome, the precipitate, is seen in a long roster of personality variables. The following outline puts these influences more explicitly.

1. Biological attributes having social meaning because certain expectations as to belief and behavior are typically, or stereotypically, linked with them: sex, age, race.

2. Social characteristics stemming from the categories describing the parental family: occupation, class, religion. . . .
3. Personal characteristics stemming from his particular family and the groups in which the person participates: his job, his educational achievement, his income, his views and values.

These influences make a sort of developmental scale in which the value for a given variable implicates a cluster of antecedent variables. Thus the groups with which the person voluntarily affiliates are conditioned by antecedent categories describing his family, and these, in turn—as in the case of parental occupation or class—are conditioned and implicated in the categories of sex, age, and race.

This classification follows several sequences. It follows the time sequence of personal development: biological identity, social identity (conferred by the family), and personal identity. It also follows a sequence from very general to quite specific influences—from broad categories to the particular combination of group memberships that shape roles and confer personal identity. (Almost everyone is male or female, and each person shares this attribute with about half the population. But considerably fewer than half the population are existentialists, Seventh Day Adventists, or Presbyterians.)

There are other sequences implicit in this classification of role-shaping influences. The classification moves, roughly, from ascribed to acquired or achieved attributes. Conferred at birth, ascribed attributes are typically dealt with as discrete distributions—male-female, white-black). But moving through time, the person becomes a more refined creation, with attributes whose measures fall in continuous distributions—measures of knowledge or problem-solving ability, position on a scale measuring religious behavior or belief, political or aesthetic preferences, income and the like.

Yet another sequence involved here is the one we follow in identifying another person. It is a sequence in assessing the probability of another's responses, a sequence in the building of relationships. For do we not, in coming to know another, typically gain initial impressions from such gross externalities as sex, race, age, language, or accent? And do we not tend then to discover other categories to which the person may be assigned on the basis of his occupation or his place of residence? And only later, having "cased the joint" as it were, do we know the more particular and personal details enabling us, if we are so disposed, to establish the reciprocal interchange, between now-established roles, that makes a human relationship.

Socially relevant biological traits: race, age, sex

The categories with external visibility, the socially significant biological traits, are early and crucial in their role-shaping influence. Anyone with normal hearing, sight, and sensitivity cannot fail to have some faint appreciation of the significance of race in shaping roles. For 11 out of every 100 people in the United States, there is throughout their lives no role, no relationship, untouched by the fact of race. (The same can be said of the white 90 percent of the population although, obviously, they are not so keenly aware of the benefaction conferred by the accident of birth, coupled with prevailing racial stereotypes.)

Age—and I shall mention only race, age, and sex in this discussion of the biological hooks for role prescription—age is a universal criterion for assigning expectation-sets. Clearly, different roles must be assigned to dependent young and old, and independent middle age. Dependence and independence are in part biological facts of the life cycle. But *how* the roles are defined is a cultural matter, varying widely from group to group. Consider that age category for which we have coined the maudlin euphemism, "senior citizen."

The definition of old age as a state and as a role varies greatly. In the United States we have a legal definition of old age: 65 is a common age of retirement and full social security benefits commence at this time. But

> . . . among the Bontoc Igorot in the Philippines a woman reaches "her prime" at 23, while at 30 she is "getting old," before 45 she "is old," and by 50, if she is so fortunate as to live that long, she is a mass of wrinkles from foot to forehead.[3]

In his analysis of the role of the aged, Leo Simmons studied 71 tribes scattered around the globe: 16 in North America, 10 in Central and South America, 14 in Africa, 3 in Europe, 16 in Asia, and 12 in Oceania and Australia.[4] A few of his findings help us to grasp the complexity and variation in the role definitions attached to age —in this case, old age.

The control of property rights by older people varies with the type of economy and with the form of family organization. Aged women tend to enjoy control over property more in groups gaining their living from collecting, or hunting or fishing, and where the family organization is matrilocal or matrilineal, whereas aged men consistently control property to a greater degree in farming and herding groups and where family organization is patriarchal. With a shift from gathering economies toward herding and agriculture, there is a decline in communal sharing of food and a tendency for preplanned and organized help for the needy aged. The aged are often accorded respect, sometimes bordering on reverence (they are often the custodians of sacred lore). But this seldom continues when the oldster becomes a senile dependent.

Respect for aged women appears to be linked with elemental economic forms and with matriarchal family systems, but men seem to command more respect in stable social orders whose economies turn on herding or agriculture. The oldsters often become men Fridays to vigorous younger ones, making themselves as useful as they can (although in magic and sorcery they may retain control). Diviners are likely to be senior citizens. So also are sacrificial victims. For in the event of disaster, an older rather than a younger person is likely to be found responsible, or so it is among the Xosa. There are a few cases of cannibalism where, under pressure of adversity, the older persons may be served up. More common, apparently, is the practice, as among the Chippewa, of an exit from this vale of tears agreed on by the aged person and his kinfolk, and effected by the latter.

Dealing as he does with 71 widely distributed groups, Simmons is able to tease out of the data (by means of a coefficient of association)* some suggestions as to uniformities in the role of the aged. But we notice also in his data the frequent need to discrimi-

* See Aside on Methods; Number 8: "A Simple Coefficient of Association between Variables."

† The term *status* refers to those labels we use to tell where a person stands, relative to others, in the social structure. (The word is borrowed directly from the Latin, meaning circumstance, condition, or state.) For example, in the category sex, we have male and female. Similarly as to employment: employed and unemployed; or for race: Caucasoid, Negroid, Mongoloid; or for marital status: single, married, widowed, divorced; or for location in the labor force: unskilled, semiskilled, skilled, clerical, and so on. Such *position* labels connote the complex expectation-sets we call roles, typically the more institutionalized roles. (Some use the words *position* and *status* interchangeably.)

The exclusive status attached to sex is illustrated in an old German saying: Women are for "Kirchen, Kuchen and Kindern." (A woman's place is at church, in the kitchen, and with children.)

Table 6.1
Estimated accuracy of role-taking in same- and opposite-sex roles, in situations oriented toward male and female roles

	Sex of role-taker (1)	Sex role taken (2)	Sex orientation of the situation (3)	Mean score on accuracy of performance (4)
Playing same-sex roles	m	m	f	3.50
	f	f	m	3.13
	m	m	m	2.88
	f	f	f	2.50
Opposite-sex role-playing	m	f	m	2.50
	f	m	f	2.25
	m	f	f	2.00
	f	m	m	1.88

nate between old men and old women. Sex makes a difference in role prescriptions far beyond the point of its reproductive significance.

One gets the impression from Simmons' data that where eminence does not depend upon demonstrable achievement but rather upon occult powers in controlling the mysteries of the universe, distinction (rather than extinction) may characterize the role of the aged. The aged are, he says, the "guardians of life's emergencies, the custodians of (esoteric) knowledge, and the directors of ceremonies and pastimes . . . they have been the chief conservators of the status quo. And finally, after death, they have become supernatural agents. . . ."[5]

Some intimation of the significance of sex in role definition is suggested by an experiment in role-taking in which James C. Brown tested the notion that ". . . there exists a partial disjunction between the cultural worlds of males and females, in contemporary American society, which gulf is greater than that between any other such pair of status-categories." For sex is an exclusive status† and "more durable, more pervasive and more universal than any other."[6] Race and age may approximate the visibility of sex, but they lack the legibility of clothing, coiffure, and distinctive naming.

To test the disjunction between sex roles, Brown had eight boys and eight girls role-play 64 performances. Certain of the results are summarized in Table 6.1. Two of these performances were oriented toward the male role (a blowout on an automobile trip and being insulted in a rough neighborhood), and two oriented toward female roles (a meeting of a girls' sewing club and a Ladies' Aid meeting). Two boys and two girls performed in each situation, in half of them playing their own sex roles and, in the other half, performing just as he/she would behave in the opposite sex role. Persons of the sex whose role was being taken rated the performance of the role-taker on a 4-point scale as to accuracy of performance: poor, fair, good, and excellent (1,2,3, and 4, respectively).

There are problems with this study: the accuracy-of-performance rating by the young subjects, the inadequacy of the sample for the population to which generalizations are extended, the effect of previous trials on subsequent role-playing. But these things can be said for this population. (1) Sex roles *are* emphatically discriminated. (2) The interaction of three factors—those situational factors heading the first three columns of Table 6.1—accounts for 60 percent of the variance in accuracy of role performance. (3) There are individual differences in role-taking skill and perceptiveness, but the joint effect of these psychological variables is less than that of just two (among many) situational, or social, variables. (4) The problem, as usual, is more complicated than at first appeared. Two examples: the male role was most readily perceived in female-oriented situations and the female role in male situations, and males were slightly more skillful perceivers of others than females.

Race, age, and sex are critical pivots for role definition in our society. Their relevance for sociological inquiry is forcefully suggested in a set of tentative propositions about age and sex roles offered by Leonard S. Cottrell, Jr.

1. The degree of adjustment to roles which a society assigns to its age-sex categories varies directly with the clarity with which such roles are defined.
   i. The degree of clarity is determined by the proportion of the social situations in which the individual is called on to act for which there are explicit definitions of the reciprocal behavior expected.
   ii. Clarity of definition of role is reduced by:
      (1) Discrepancies between what is given verbally and what is demonstrated in practice.
      (2) Contacts among members of subculture groups which have different roles for the same age-sex categories.

(3) Inconsistency in the response and expectations exhibited to the individual by members of his social world.

2. The degree of adjustment to specified age-sex roles varies directly with the consistency with which others in the individual's life situations exhibit to him the response called for by his role.
3. When a society assigns or permits more than one role to a given age-sex category, the degree of adjustment to the roles varies directly with the compatibility of the roles.
4. When incompatible roles belong to a given age-sex category, the degree of adjustment varies directly with the extent to which means exist for minimizing the overlap of situations calling for incompatible roles.
5. The degree of adjustment varies indirectly with the discrepancy between the abilities of the individual and those required in the roles of a given age-sex category.
6. The degree of adjustment to the roles of specified age-sex categories varies directly with the extent to which the role permits the individual to realize the dominant goals set by his sub-cultural group.
7. When the role represents an excess of deprivation or frustration of dominant goal satisfactions, adjustment varies directly with:
   i. The extent to which the frustrating role is defined as a path to another role which promises the desired gratifications, and/or
   ii. The accessibility of substitute gratifications.

(The remaining propositions have to do with adjustment to future roles.)

8. The degree of adjustment to a future role varies directly with the degree of clarity with which the future role is defined.
9. The degree of adjustment to a future role varies directly with the amount of opportunity for:
   i. Emotionally intimate contact which allows identification with persons functioning in the role.
   ii. Imaginal or incipient rehearsal in the future role.
   iii. Practice in the role through play or other similar activity.

10. The degree of adjustment to a future role varies directly with the degree of importance attached to and the definiteness of the transitional procedures used by the society in designating the change in role.
11. The degree of adjustment to a future role varies directly with the completeness of the shift in the responses and expectations exhibited by the society to the individual in his new role.
12. Adjustment to more mature roles is aided rather than handicapped by occasional sanctioned regressions to less demanding roles.[7]

These propositions might apply with equal force to other roles. But since age and sex refer to universal statuses, they have their widest possible bearing here.

Traits ascribed to the person through his family of orientation

Let us turn from these socially relevant biological traits to the second category of characteristics shaping men's roles. These are attributes of the parental family ascribed to the person. He is born to a family of a given faith, a certain occupation, a certain social class. As we shall see in Chapter 8, the cluster of familial attributes telescoped in the term *class* entails a wealth of role-shaping influences, influences on husband-wife roles, parental roles, work roles, roles as citizen, communicant, and student.

On a scale of extent of influence, we might say that the role-shaping factors in our first category, biological traits such as age and sex, offer least option or range. Less rigid, less prescriptive are the role-forming influences that stem from the ascribed characteristics of the parental family, such as class. Most opportunity for individuation, for personal role creation, comes from membership in groups outside the family: school, camp, travel, guests and visitors from different backgrounds, and the like. In a way, the building of a role-set defining a unique personality is a matter of progressive emancipation from restrictions of the first two categories of role conditioners. But, of course, it also means, once the choices are made, a narrowing or fixing or crystallizing of roles. This is, indeed, what makes the person discernible.

*. . . Family, school,
and gang
collaborate
in working through
the script
that we call
culture.*

*. . . A role is
a regular way
of acting,
expected of
all persons
occupying
a given
position in
the social order. . . .*

. . . The role includes indirect . . . confrontations as, for example, when the parent consults . . . the teacher . . . about *this child.*

. . . variations between roles—differences related to differing group requirements. . . . the nurse-patient relationship depends for its maintenance on certain characteristics of the nurse's role.

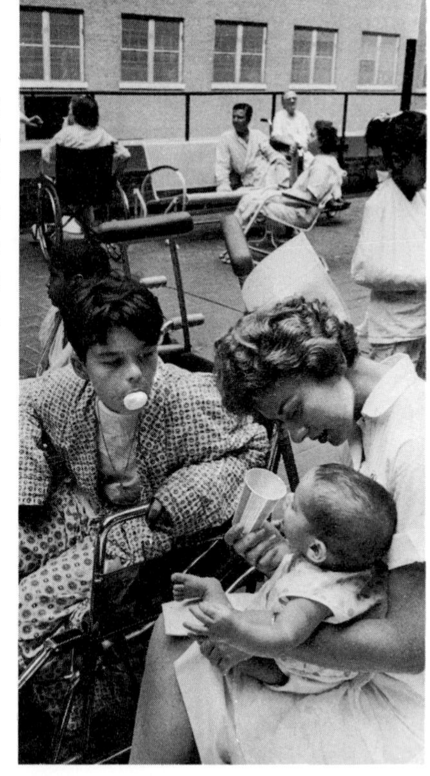

. . . personal predisposition and group needs converge in the fixing of role and status.

Traits achieved through group participation

For our third category of role influences, those groups in which the person participates directly, as an individual, and achievement in which shapes the role to be played, the school provides a good example. To illustrate the influence of education in shaping the civic role and, beyond that, to show something of the dynamics of the role-fixing process, let's look at an intriguing study by Theodore Newcomb. In his *Personality and Social Change*[8] he shows how one aspect of the civic role, the attitudes supporting civic behavior, are formed in the course of a college career. About 30 years later, in another study of the same population, he asks: Have these attitudes conditioning the civic role persisted? And if so, what accounts for their persistence?

These are important questions, since the learning and fixing of a role implies the persistence of attitudes supporting performance in that role. To the first question posed above—and let me put it more generally: Do attitudes tend to persist?—the answer is yes. To the second question as to the mechanisms promoting persistence, we might offer the following set of propositions:

1. Attitudes are shaped in an intricate dialectic between self and other. They only emerge, that is to say, out of a social context. Thus:
   1.1 Personality can be seen as the subjective aspect of culture.
   1.2 Outside of a social context, attitudes toward objects would not be formed.
   1.3 Personal integrity, or unity, or balance is some function of the unity and integrity of the person's sociocultural setting.
2. His attitudes once shaped, the person tends to associate with others whose attitudes are compatible with his. He seeks a social context, not always consciously, whose effect is to support and reinforce his attitudes. This means that:
   2.1 When we are successful in joining compatible groups (finding a congenial husband or wife, a school setting, a work or religious group responding to our views, interests and abilities), "an *intra*personal state of balance comes to correspond with [a state of] interpersonal" balance.[9]
   2.2 When we find ourselves out of harmony with others, we seek to achieve intra- and interpersonal balance through inducing changes in the relationship.
   ". . . an imbalanced state, under conditions of continued interaction, is likely to be an unstable one simply because,

when it is discovered, it arouses *intra*personal imbalance on the part of one or more interactors, and this state arouses forces toward change."[10]

2.3 We may achieve balance, psychically and socially, so arriving at relatively stable role definitions, by various devices: avoiding incompatible attitudes held by others (restricting communication with them, developing hostility toward them), by persuading others to our attitudes, by changing our own attitudes in accord with others', or by changing the situation. This often means changing our affiliations—i.e., entering new and different groups.

The persistence of attitudes and the fixing of roles through selection of appropriate (reinforcing) environments—social environments, and specifically in this case, husbands—is well illustrated by Newcomb's two studies of Bennington College women, once in the 1930's and again in the 1960's. His original data show a clear and regular change in the direction of "political and economic progressivism" (PEP) on the part of many Bennington women during their college careers in the 1930's. Thus attitudes were shaped. The question, then, is whether they persisted, and if so—our second question—what the mechanism of persistence was. One of Newcomb's findings, represented in Figure 6.2, speaks to the first question. The data tells us that, by knowing their PEP scores in the late 1930's, one could predict remarkably well these Bennington College graduates' presidential preferences in 1960! Thus, were you to predict that those in the least conservative quartile (on their PEP scores in the 1930's) would all vote for Kennedy in 1960, you would incur only a 9 percent error. Or in predicting that those in the most conservative quartile would all vote for Nixon, one would be right in two thirds of the cases. Attitudes did persist.

Now for our second question: What was the mechanism? If, as suggested above, attitudes persist through the conscious or unwitting selection of attitude-reinforcing environments, we must look at those with whom these women associated to see if, in fact, they selected others supporting such attitudes as those reflected in their PEP scores. Above all, one might ask, what sorts of husbands did they select? Newcomb found that the husbands, despite the disproportionate share of them from Ivy League schools and from wealthy and conservative backgrounds, were *less* conservative than their backgrounds would indicate.

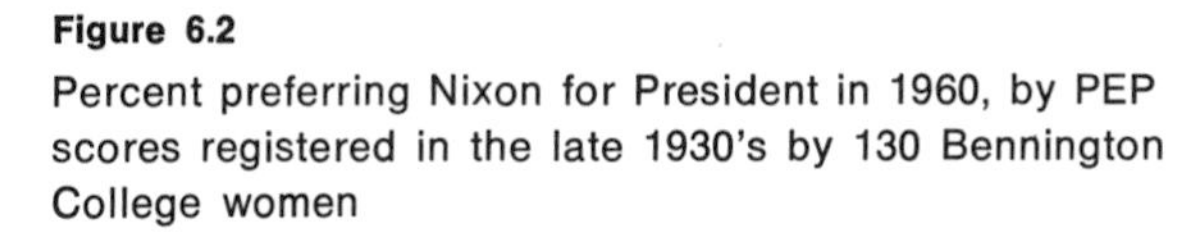
Figure 6.2
Percent preferring Nixon for President in 1960, by PEP scores registered in the late 1930's by 130 Bennington College women

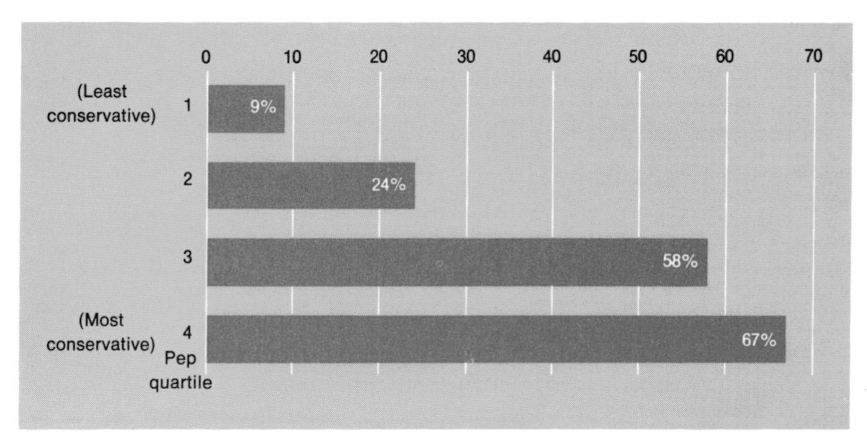

Our Bennington graduates of the late 1930's found their husbands in the kinds of places where their families expected them to be found, but they selected somewhat atypical members of these "proper" populations of eligibles; they tended not to have conservative attitudes that were then typical of these populations.[11]

Thus we get some notion of the funneling process through which a person's role becomes fixed: initial attitude formation under the tutelage of parents, peers, and pedagogues, the selection (often unwitting) of reinforcing social environments and the avoidance or conversion of those presenting incompatible attitudes, a firmer fixing of attitudes and the roles in which they're implicated, and so on around the circle.

Sources of variation and stability in role performance

Behavior in a given role has two sources. One is the unique ancestry of the incumbent, a set of social influences, diverse and unduplicated, converging in the person. The other consists in commonly held conceptions of performance appropriate to a given position. Thus the incumbent of a given role—student, for example—is the focus of (1) a set of expectations common to most members of the group, and (2) a set of predispositions peculiar to him and stemming from his unique social ancestry. Differences in role performance result from discrepancies between the two, between social exposures peculiar to the person and those common to most members of the group.

The positions into which people are sorted are usually those in which public and personal definitions of the role are reasonably compatible. But seldom, if ever, does the person's social ancestry provide a perfect preparation for the roles he will carry as an adult. As he enters a new school, a new job, achieves a new position in the company, joins the church, allies himself with wife, he undergoes supplementary socialization, in-service training, as it were. This is simply an extension of his social ancestry, effecting a more adequate fit between the expectations characterizing a new position and the trained capacities brought to it.

Variations in role performance are due not only to differences in the social ancestry of incumbents; they also stem from the existing set of group affiliations peculiar to each person. Even within a single group, others' expectations are not uniform, either as to behaviors expected or as to the rigidity with which the incumbent is expected to adhere to these behaviors, and these alone. Uniformity and rigidity of expectations vary from group to group and from role to role. A great range of behavior is accepted among those called "parents," but a more restricted range is expected of those called "teachers."

But I should not convey the notion of endless variation in role performance. The contrary is the case. Roles refer to behavior in publicly recognized positions or "slots" in the social order. They endure through time, being successively filled by one incumbent after another. That they are publicly recognized implies that the expectations establishing norms of conduct are general and to a degree coercive. Indeed, the expectations are often stated in the law.

Role, then, is a distinctly social concept rooted in the requirements of the social order. It does not refer to the psychological idiosyncracies of the incumbents. It is accurate to say that most of the difference in behavior of persons in different roles is due to the roles, not to the particular personalities of the incumbents. Conversely, the similarity of behavior of persons in the same role is a function of the socially sanctioned demands of the role, not the coincidental similarity of incumbents' personalities.

Indeed, there is some folk wisdom in the view of the disgruntled citizen who says it makes no difference which candidate one votes for. Yet if, to a degree, he is right, it is for the wrong reason. In his view, both candidates will act alike because they are equally unreliable, if not corrupt. But if their behavior is so very much alike, it is rather because each is the focus of essentially the same set of expectations. It is true that as one mounts toward the apex of a power pyramid—toward bank president, university president, U.S. President—two different incumbents will surround themselves with different advisers and, therefore, different sets of expectations. Yet the numbers subtended by such social pyramids are greater the higher one goes, and the greater, therefore, is the pressure to meet the common demands of the dependent many. Napoleon's statement was perceptive: "I am their leader; therefore I must follow them." Furthermore, it is toward the peak of the pyramid that persons in leadership roles confront others who incorporate the demands and expectations of *their* followers. Nixon, like Johnson, confronts Castro, Mao, and Brezhnev, Vietnam, black demands and student revolts, the governors of Mississippi, Alabama, and 48 other states, the American Legion, the NAM and AMA. Whether I mention the name of a man, a nation, or a voluntary association, a persisting point of view, an enduring interest is implied. It is an interest and a point of view corporately held, outlasting the membership or lifetime of an individual. No matter who the incumbent of a peak position, he confronts a set of pressures very like those his predecessor dealt with and those his successor will encounter.

In this view, then, we see the conduct of the person largely defined by his position in the group. So faithfully do normal persons reflect the expectations defining their roles that if we wish to know a stranger, we spar with him initially until we have discovered the groups and categories he's identified with: black or white, old or young, male or female, doctor, lawyer, beggarman, thief. . . . These give us clues to the roles he will take—which is to say, the kind of person he is.

The shaping of roles through group requirements

Let's turn now from variations in performance of a given role to variations between roles—differences related to differing group requirements. Restaurants, legal firms, department stores and colleges, churches, fraternities, and political parties stipulate the role requirements thought desirable for performance as waitress, lawyer, salesman and teacher, priest, "brother," and Republican, respectively. Such role prescriptions doubtless develop from the trial and error of daily experience, an experience later codified in job descriptions by product- and profit-minded employers. But more sophisticated notions of the role requirements for meeting organizational goals come from sociological theory.

Parsons has suggested that groups vary in the role patterns required to meet their objectives. For example, take a very simple, two-person group, nurse and patient. They are a part of that set of relationships we call a hospital. Now, *how is a person's role fixed by her work with such a group?* How is the role patterned so as to maintain the dyadic subsystem of nurse-and-patient, and to achieve the goal of the patient's health? Isidor Thorner raises these questions and, in offering an answer, uses a set of concepts proffered by Parsons for analyzing the various ways in which roles are patterned to meet social system requirements.[12] Let us look at Thorner's suggestive analysis of role requirements imposed by the nature of nurse-patient relationships.

The situation is a common one, nurse and patient constituting an elementary social system with roles geared to the restoration of health. The objective reflects an almost unqualified value, health. The predicament is a delicate one, with the patient helpless and vulnerable, yielding himself to bodily intrusions not ordinarily tolerated. Now what are the concepts that help us understand how, in this situation, the nurse's role is necessarily patterned?

The first of these concepts, describing the orientation of nurse to patient is *universalism*. This means that the nurse sees the patient, not as a unique person, but as a case—not in terms of his particular and unduplicated constellation of attributes, but as, say, an appendectomy, in room 38. He is treated as a member of a category all of whom have similar symptoms, similar diagnoses. similar treatment and prognoses. Now in the treatment of the sick we confront problems of cause and effect. Given a set of symptoms, we infer a cause and manipulate matters so as to produce health. Diagnosis means that we identify the disease and classify the patient as belonging *with all other patients having the same symptoms*. Hence we treat him precisely as we would any other person suffering appendicitis. If the nurse regards her charge as a member of a class, *patient*, and subclass, *appendix case*, we describe the orientation as universalistic. This is quite in contrast to treating him as a particular person. If the nurse finds the patient distinctively handsome, buoyant, humorous, and wealthy, we're on the way to a *particularistic* performance. (So, also, when he begins to respond to the nurse, not as a member of the class, nurse, but as an attractive woman, the patient is about to move out of the patient role and become a suitor.) Thus behavior directed toward a particular, unduplicated other supersedes behavior directed to a member of a general category. (The significant question is whether this defeats the manifest purpose of the relationship, which is healing.)

In general terms, when group objectives stress matters of the head—diagnosis or analysis, classifying, generalizing in order to predict and promote certain outcomes—we have a *universalistic* standard for role performance. If, on the other hand, the stress is on the heart, as with a couple in love or in a family group, the role performance is guided by characteristics of the other shared with no one else. The orientation of each to the other is *particularistic.* In business, or in science, universalistic standards will guide role performance. But when we act toward another in a certain way because he is a friend, or a kinsman, or a neighbor—then particularistic standards are at work.[13]

To return to Thorner's discussion of the nurse's role, a second requirement is that it be oriented toward the *performance* of the patient. She is not, supposedly, concerned with *who* he is, but with *what he does:* changes in temperature, pulse beat, a relapse, recovery. The nurse's role is contingent upon and varies with the performance of her charge as he makes the transition from patient to person. The emphasis is upon *achieved* states of the patient, not upon *ascribed qualities.*

> Achievement-oriented roles are those which place the accent on the performances of the incumbent, ascribed roles, on his qualities or attributes independently of specific expected performances. . . . [In the former case] the expectation is that the actor is committed to the achievement of certain goals or expressive performances and that expectations are oriented to his "effectiveness" or "success" in achieving them. . . .
>
> On the other hand . . . all objects have attributes, they not only *do* this or that, but they *are* such and such. They have attributes of sex, age, intelligence, physical characteristics, statuses in relational systems. . . . The focus of orientation

then may be what the object *is* in this sense, e.g., that he is ego's father, that he is a physician, or that he is over six feet tall.[14]

A third aspect of role performance is the range of situations encompassed by a relationship. This what Parsons calls the *specicity-diffuseness* dimension. In the case of the nurse, she is both entitled and obliged to restrict the scope of her relationship to the patient, as patient.

> The nurse, like the mother in relation to the infant, caters to the patient's needs and, therefore, presents the most convenient "object of cathexis" on whom he may discharge his craving for response as well as aggressive impulses. This is the situation which predisposes the patient to the transference phenomenon ("falling in love" with the nurse) and provides not only the condition for willing conformance to the nurse's authority, but also the opportunity for exploiting the patient's vulnerability. In this complex situation the interests of all . . . must be safeguarded so that therapeutic measures may be undertaken with maximum effectiveness. . . .
>
> Hence it is a functional prerequisite [of the nurse's role] that all concerned take for granted that the exclusive focus of interest is not the unique person, but the patient. . . . The mutuality of privileges and obligations is *functionally specific* in that it only applies while the nurse is on duty and insofar as the patient is defined as such.[15]

The division of labor in modern work groups tends to emphasize this functional specificity of role. On the other hand, in the child's relationship to its mother, an extremely broad and diffuse range of expectations is regarded as legitimate.

Finally, in Thorner's analysis, the nurse's role is one of affective neutrality. Contrived expressions of personal concern—"And how are we feeling this morning?"—should not be construed as violations of this norm. The significance of affective neutrality in the nurse's role may be better appreciated by considering its opposite, especially, say, in the case where the nurse marries her patient. To this suggestion, Thorner reports his respondents reacting with something bordering on revulsion. Commenting on this, he says:

> Marrying a patient is disapproved because it implies that the nurse has taken advantage of the patient's vulnerability and placed the gratification of private interest and emotional

> expression above professional obligation and loyalty. It is *prima facie* evidence to the profession . . . that discrimination has occurred among patients [contrary to universalistic expectations], that affective neutrality has broken down, and finally, that segregation of emotional relationships (other than what is therapeutically indicated) to the private sphere, outside working hours has failed.[16]

Thus the nurse-patient relationship depends for its maintenance on certain characteristics of the nurse's role. Through recruitment, training, and the reinforcement of standards through professional organizations, the role requirements of this position become fixed in the incumbent we call nurse.* These requirements of the nurse's role are, in summary: affective neutrality and functional specificity as attitudinal variables, and universalism and performance as standards for assessing, and responding to, the patient's demands upon the nurse.

We've looked at the development of standards for role performance from two perspectives. The person, socialized in certain beliefs and behaviors, joins groups that reinforce his role definitions. (So it was with the Bennington girls.) On the other hand, from the perspective of the group—say, an occupational group like that of nurses—we can discover dimensions of role performance that are mandatory if the group's goals are to be achieved. In both cases, the role-shaping influences at work fall under the third category outlined on pages 187–88.

Inconsistent roles, from perspective of person and group

> . . . we may practically say that [the person] has as many different social selves as there are distinct *groups* of persons about whose opinion he cares. He generally shows a different side of himself to each of these different groups. Many a

* We must suppose that characteristics of the role are more readily fixed in the novice when others consistently provide a common professional model. And this consistency among the novice's models is in part a function of the systematic dismissal of the maladapted. This implies assessing performance and shearing off the lower end of the performance scale.

Note that the requirements reside in the position, or status, regardless of who the incumbent happens to be.

> youth who is demure enough before his parents and teachers, swears and swaggers like a pirate among his "tough" young friends. We do not show ourselves to our children as to our club companions, to our customers as to the laborers we employ, to our own masters and employers as to our intimate friends.[17]

In the roles that are their elemental units, social structures built by men lack the rigidity of physical structures. Within limits, definitions of roles and performances in them vary. Beyond this, as the quotation suggests, there may be stress between roles incompatibly defined.

Role incompatibility cuts two ways, affecting the integrity of both person and group. Thus the study of role compatibility opens two significant lines of inquiry: (1) effects on the person of counterdemanding roles as a result of his membership in groups having different rules of the game and inconsistent expectations, and (2) effects on the integration of the group of role-sets differing in degree of compatibility.

Every person has several significant group affiliations simultaneously (and a set of expectations defining his role in each): a family, a church, a job, a few congenial others with whom he enjoys his leisure. "He is determined, socially, in the sense that [such] groups intersect in his person by virtue of his affiliation with them."[18]

This situation can be graphically expressed as in Figure 6.3.

Membership in two or more groups need not always entail role incompatibility. Yet, in a complex social order, this may often be the case. We recognize it in the phrase, "conflict of interest," as when a government official has some affiliation with a company which could profit from a connection in government. Some roles are especially susceptible to incompatible expectations. The foreman may find that management's and workers' expectations of him are in conflict. Like the foreman, the noncommissioned officer may be caught in the middle. The noncom

> . . . had the role of agent of the command and in case the orders from above conflicted with what his men thought was right and necessary, he was expected by his superiors to carry out the orders. But he also was an enlisted man, sharing enlisted men's attitudes, often hostile attitudes, toward the commissioned ranks . . . the system of informal controls was

Figure 6.3

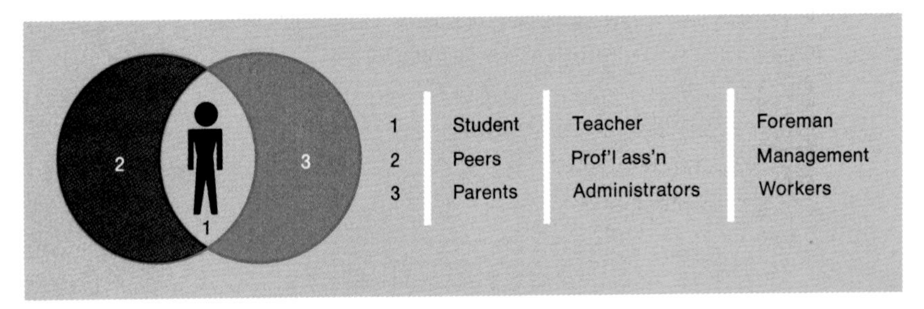

> such as to reward him for siding with the men in a conflict situation and punish him if he did not . . . on the other hand, open and flagrant disobedience by him of an order from above could not be tolerated by the command.[19]

Let us look at the study from which this quotation is taken as an example of inquiry into conflicting roles. Our standpoint is that of a person confronted by expectations to some degree irreconcilable.

One hundred and ninety-six Harvard and Radcliffe students were asked how they would act, and which action fellow students and authorities would approve if, while proctoring an examination, they found (1) a fellow student cheating, and (2) a roommate and close friend cheating. Respondents were offered five solutions, or action choices, ranging from harsh to lenient, as follows:

A. Take away his notes and exam book, dismiss him, and report him for cheating.
B. Take away his notes, let him finish the exam, but report him for cheating.
C. If he can be led to withdraw from the exam on some excuse, do *not* report him for cheating; otherwise report him.
D. Take away his notes, but let him finish the exam, and *not* report him for cheating.
E. Act as if nothing had happened and *not* report him for cheating.

Discrepancies in expectations are graphically represented in Figure 6.4. We may infer that some students would be torn when, in a situation like this, they sense incompatible expectations. This was true in 28 percent of the cases. For these people, "the range of acts approved by the authorities did not overlap in any way with the range of acts approved by the students. For them, simultaneous conformity to both was impossible."[20]

For another, small group of respondents (11 percent of the total), there was no problem at all. For them the range of approved acts was identical for the authorities and the students.

Most (61 percent) perceived a difference in the expectations of authorities and students but were able to find at least one action, one solution, that would be approved by both. Perhaps it is just such compromises that are most commonly invented to resolve the problem of incompatible rules, roles, and relationships that most members of complex societies sometimes confront.

Now consider the matter from the perspective of the group. Insofar as people have similar life experiences—which means, in large measure, having the same set of group affiliations, or common constellations of positions (statuses)—we might expect role incompatibility to be minimized, social integration enhanced. Put the other way around, measures of *mal*integration should be inversely related to the extent to which members of a group share in common a cluster of statuses with the relatively institutionalized roles that define them.*

Furthermore, it seems reasonable to assume that, in the process of adjusting to a social and biophysical environment, compatible sets of statuses/roles sort themselves out, the flagrantly incompatible elements in these clusters being discarded. This is what Professors Gibbs and Martin argue when they say:

> . . . that the actual occupancy of statuses in a society reflects the degree of compatibility among statuses. If two statuses have conflicting roles, thereby making them incompatible statuses when occupied simultaneously, it is assumed that these two statuses would be less frequently occupied simultaneously than would two statuses with roles that do not conflict.[21]

If this seems plausible, we need to ask: What are the mechanisms for eliminating incompatible roles and statuses? Gibbs and

* See William J. Goode, "A Theory of Role Strain," *American Sociological Review*, Vol. 25, No. 4 (August, 1960), p. 485, footnote 7, where he says: "I distinguish role and status on the basis only of 'degree of institutionalization': all role relations are somewhat institutionalized, but statuses are more fully institutionalized." This is the sense in which I am using the concept, status: a position in the social structure whose associated role is relatively institutionalized.

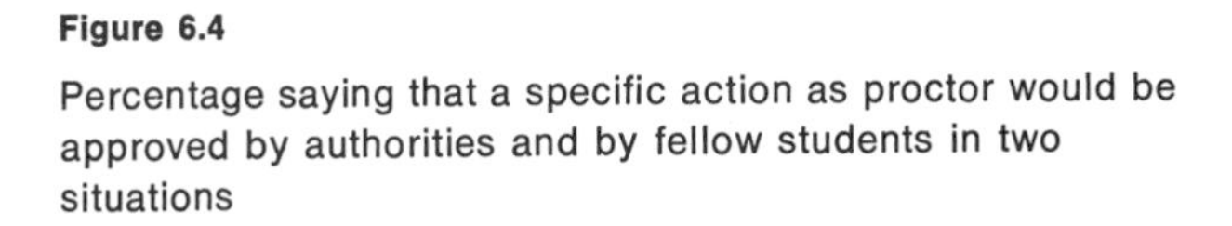

Figure 6.4

Percentage saying that a specific action as proctor would be approved by authorities and by fellow students in two situations

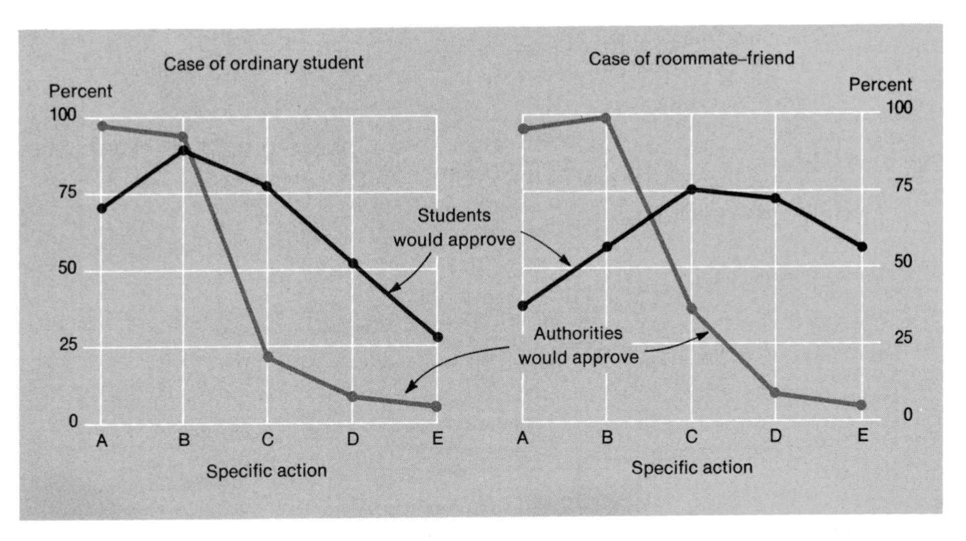

Martin mention three: social taboos on simultaneous incumbency, personal dissatisfaction, and personal incapacity. Social disapproval varies, depending on the role-pair we're considering. Woman and physician make a more congenial pair of statuses in the U.S.S.R. than in the United States, as do woman and street cleaner. Woman and engineer are a socially incompatible role- and status-pair in our society. Male and nurse are attributes joined only at risk of social disparagement. The small-town teacher moonlighting as grocery clerk might find himself under pressure to relinquish one or the other of these two roles. Taking as cue the large percentage of divorced bartenders, Gibbs and Martin suggest that, here, the "demands of an occupational status may create dissatisfaction with a particular marital status."[22] Finally, there is the matter of incapacity. Old age may not go with the status "profitably employed."

If, as these investigators argue, role or status compatibility is reflected in the frequency with which certain clusters of statuses and roles appear in a population, then it might be argued that the commoner such clusters, the greater the group's integration. Conversely, the less such clusters cohere in a population, the lower the group's integration and the higher such indices of *mal*integration as suicide. And this is the hypothesis proposed by Gibbs and Martin: the greater a measure of status integration (i.e., the more frequently clusters of statuses and roles cohere in a population), the lower the suicide rates.* The underlying theoretical argument goes like this:

Postulate 1
The suicide rate of a population varies inversely with the stability and durability of the social relationships within the population.

Postulate 2
The stability and durability of social relationships within a population vary directly with the extent to which individuals in that population conform to the patterned and socially sanctioned demands and expectations placed upon them by others.

Postulate 3
The extent to which individuals in a population conform to the patterned and socially sanctioned demands and expectations placed upon them by others varies inversely with the extent to which individuals in that population are confronted with role conflicts.

Postulate 4
The extent to which individuals in a population are confronted with role conflicts varies directly with the extent to which individuals occupy incompatible statuses in that population.

Postulate 5
The extent to which individuals occupy incompatible statuses in a population varies inversely with the degree of status integration in that population.[23]

* We are on the way, as we shall see, to a test of Émile Durkheim's most general and most important proposition in his classic work, *Suicide*. He writes, "So we reach the general conclusion: suicide varies inversely with the degree of integration of the social groups of which the individual forms a part." Refer to page 165 ff. (Trans. John A. Spaulding and George Simpson [New York: Free Press of Glencoe, Inc., 1951], p. 209.

Table 6.2

Extent of coherence between marital status and selected status configurations in two hypothetical societies

Marital status	All occupied status configurations (clusters*)				
	Cluster 1: R_1, A_1, Re_1, O_1, S_1, P_1	Cluster 2: R_2, A_2, Re_2, O_2, S_2, P_2	Cluster 3: R_1, A_3, Re_3, O_3, S_1, P_1	Cluster 4: R_1, A_4, Re_1, O_4, S_1, P_3	Cluster 5: R_2, A_5, Re_3, O_5, S_2, P_2
Marital integration at a maximum (1.0)					
Single	.00	.00	.00	1.00	.00
Married	.00	1.00	.00	.00	1.00
Widowed	1.00	.00	.00	.00	.00
Divorced	.00	.00	1.00	.00	.00
ΣX	1.00	1.00	1.00	1.00	1.00
Measure of status integration ΣX^2	1.0000	1.0000	1.0000	1.0000	1.0000
Proportion (P) of population in this cluster	.0700	.4300	.0300	.1500	.3200
$\Sigma[P(\Sigma X^2)]$†	.07	+ .43	+ .03	+ .15	+ .32 = 1.00
Marital integration less than maximum (.54)					
Single	.15	.05	.00	.35	.05
Married	.05	.75	.05	.25	.90
Widowed	.60	.15	.25	.20	.00
Divorced	.20	.05	.70	.20	.00
ΣX	1.00	1.00	1.00	1.00	1.00
Measure of status integration ΣX^2	.4250	.5900	.5550	.2650	.8150
Proportion (P) of population in this cluster	.1435	.3825	.0870	.1970	.1900
$\Sigma[P(\Sigma X^2)]$†	.06	+ .23	+ .05	+ .05	+ .15 = .54

* Key: R = Race; A = Age; Re = Religion; O = Occupation; S = Sex; P = Parental status; Subscripts = Statuses within categories

† Measure of status integration weighted by proportion of population occupying that status configuration.

From the above postulates there follows the major theorem: *The suicide rate of a population varies inversely with the degree of status integration in that population.*

What is needed now is a measure of status integration, the extent to which, given one status—for example, marital status: widowed—other statuses cohere with it. Gibbs and Martin provide two hypothetical sets of data and show (Table 6.2) how they may be handled to get three measures of status integration: one yielding intergroup comparisons, a second yielding intercluster comparisons, and a third providing intracluster comparisons. These will become clear after we examine the data and look at some findings.

You will notice that ΣX^2, as a measure of common status and role configurations, varies from 1.00 down toward .00. The minimal value is approached as the number of statuses in a category increase and the spread among them is greater. To take the first column of the first part of Table 6.2, all members of the group who are widowed *share the same* age, religious, racial, occupational, sex, and parental statuses. Now if each of these clusters, or status configurations, is weighted by the proportion (P) of the total population in each, and if, then, we sum them, we get the case of complete status integration and a value of 1.00. If, on the other hand, different clusters of statuses do not cohere—if each marital status is not linked with a distinct combination of age, sex, race, religious, and occupational statuses—then the measure of status integration declines. This is the case in the lower part of Table 6.2 where the measure of status integration drops to .54.

Before leaving this matter of role compatibility measured through an index of status integration, it will be interesting to report Gibbs and Martin's preliminary findings. First, there is the matter of comparisons between societies. Using their hypothetical second society with a status integration measure of .54, their prediction is that any society having greater measured status integration will have a lower suicide rate, any society with a lower value on this index will have a higher suicide rate. At the time of this study, they had no data on genuine societies, but tried the measure on 30 states "for which the necessary data were available for a measure of the integration of occupation, with age, sex and color in 1950."[24] The coefficient of correlation (See Aside on Methods, Number 7) between this measure of status integration (independent variable) and suicide rates (dependent variable), for 30 states, was −.57.

Now a second way of testing the link between measures of status integration and suicide rates is to make intercluster comparisons. For if the argument and the hypothesis presented on pages 210–11 are correct, the value of ΣX^2 should vary inversely with suicide rates. Thus, in the second part of Table 6.2, the highest suicide rate should be found for persons exhibiting the configuration of statuses represented in cluster 4, for which the value of ΣX^2 is .2650. (And the lowest suicide rate should be found among persons in cluster 5, where the value of ΣX^2 is high, .8150). Now, taking six race-sex combinations, Gibbs and Martin studied their coherence with each of 11 occupational statuses. Then, rank-ordering the suicide rates and the measures of status integration, they got the results shown in Table 6.3.) To relate this test to the

Table 6.3

Occupation integration and mean annual suicide rates per 100,000 U.S. population

Race-sex status configuration	Occupational integration (1950)		Suicide (1949–51)	
	Measure	Rank	Rate	Rank
Negro female	.2473	1	1.5	6
White female	.1828	2	5.3	5
Other female	.1416	4	5.9	4
Negro male	.1588	3	6.1	3
White male	.1295	5	18.5	2
Other male	.1243	6	21.3	1

Table 6.4

Male suicide rates

Marital status	Percent of males aged 60–64 (1950)	Average annual suicide rate (1949–51)
Married	.793	36.2
Widowed	.096	64.7
Single	.086	76.4
Divorced	.025	111.1
	1.000	

presentation in Table 6.2, the 11 occupational statuses would be in the left-hand stub, the race-sex status configurations, or clusters, heading the columns. The measures reported are the ΣX^2 values.) The rank-order correlation coefficient (rho) for these data gives a value of –.94, corresponding to $p < .01$. These data clearly support the hypothesis: the more occupational status coheres with race and sex statuses, the lower the suicide rates.

Finally, we can make intracluster comparisons, in this case a comparison of suicide rates for persons falling in various status configurations *within* a cluster. For example, in the lower part of Table 6.2 first column, the predicted rank order of suicide rates from low to high would be: widowed, divorced, single, and married. (Remember that the data in this table are fictitious.) Now Gibbs and Martin actually did this for U.S. males, aged 60–64 in 1950, for four marital statuses. Their findings are shown in Table 6.4. Again, these data support the notion that when statuses within a group cohere—when roles are compatible and status integration is high —measures of malintegration, such as suicide, are low. Gibbs and Martin stress the exploratory nature of this initial study, the lack of adequate data, and the oversimplified index of integration. In a subsequent test using Ceylonese data and relating measures of marital integration, by sex and ethnic status, to suicide rates, these sociologists get qualified confirmation of the earlier findings. ("Out of 18 rho's computed, 14 were in the predicted direction.")[25] This later study has special interest as it detects isomorphisms—similar forms and relationships—among people whose cultures differ markedly.

But lest we be bemused and deflected by the illustration, let us recall the central point. Role incompatibility has consequences both for the person and for the group. From the person's perspective, Stouffer's study illustrates the dilemma of a study official (proctor) straddling two sets of incompatible expectations. His position is sometimes awkward because two roles "intersect in his person, faculty and student." Other positions—for example, noncom and foreman—may be similarly subject to counterdemanding roles.

From the perspective of the group, we have seen how roles and statuses vary in their coherence. Such variations in cohesiveness, or integration, may be expected to entail predictable outcomes. One such outcome appears to be an inverse relationship between suicide and status integration.

* * * *

Now a cursory backward glance before we move on to consider structures that sustain human groups. In Part One we dwelt on the continuous building of the group as newcomers learn the cultural score through the socialization process and the offices of peers and elders. Over time, and at some pains, a social alchemy works to transform an organism of near-infinite potential into a person with the particular skills, knowledge, attitudes, and values appropriate to the roles he must play. In this constraining-liberating process, the product of a genetic encounter with uncertain outcomes, a callow, asexual, illiterate, uncommitted organism becomes a mature man (or woman), variously adept in symbolic manipulation (of the King's English, or Mandarin or Hindi), dedicated to Judeo-Christian (or Buddhist, or Moslem) ideals, and to secular salvation through the Republican party (or Democratic, or Labor, or Socialist, or Communist). The renewal of the group depends on his becoming a person; his becoming a person depends on his implication in the group.

We've been thinking about the way groups are built as infants

Figure 6–5*a* **Figure 6–5*b***

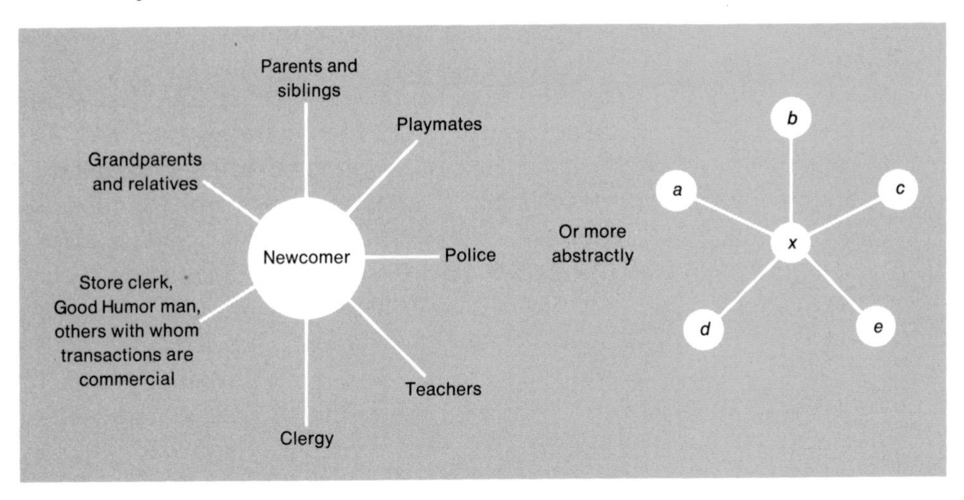

Figure 6–5c

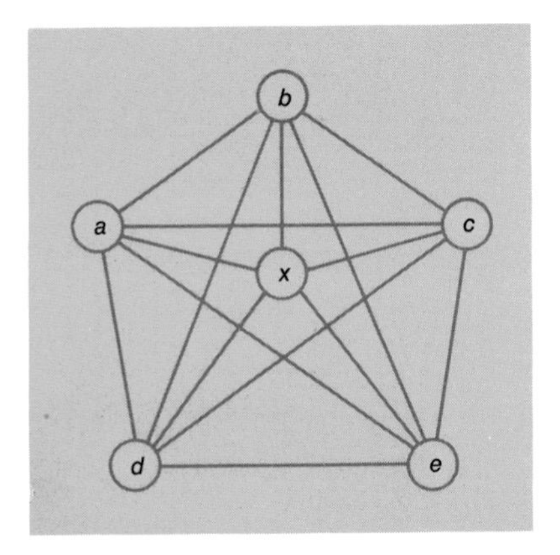

and migrants replenish losses. Our focus in Part One has been largely on the newcomer who acquires his humanity as he acquires his culture, through fruitful transactions with others (*a,b,c,d,* and *e* in Figure 6.5*b*).

The gradual fixing of role and status is a process contingent on many things. The shaping of self, and its roles, hinges on such factors as race, sex, and age—biological attributes given crucial definition in the group's culture. It also depends on the attributes ascribed to the person by virtue of his parents' position. And it depends, finally, on personal choice and achievement.

Roles are fixed, as we have seen, because attitudes early inculcated are reinforced through selective exposure, largely unwitting, to those whose views and values are like our own. Our choice of newspapers, television shows, friends, and spouses tends to be restrictive—as we doubtless think, discriminatingly so. But beyond this, roles are fixed through organizational requirements. And so, as we saw (using the hospital and the nurse for illustration) role characteristics are shaped to the means and goals of the group. (In the fixing of the nurse's role, she is trained in standards that are *universalistic* and oriented to the patient's *performance*, developing attitudes toward her charges that are *emotionally neutral* and *specific* to the healing task.) Thus personal predisposition and group needs converge in the fixing of role and status.

But to assume a simple, easy convergence from a broad and ambiguous set of possibilities at birth to a sharply focused adult personality would be to oversimplify, and so distort, the case. Multiple group memberships open the possibility of incompatible roles with dual outcomes: a challenge to the integrity of the person and to the integrity of the group. We have offered empirical examples in Stouffer's study of conflicting social norms, and that by Gibbs and Martin on correlates of status integration.

In Part Two our attention shifts from the *articulation of roles that comprise a relationship* to the *articulation of relationships that comprise* the group. We might illustrate the shift by contrasting Figure 6.5*b* with Figure 6.5*c*. Now we have a closed, a bounded system of relationships, direct and indirect, that constitutes a group. Now the concepts of culture and socialization are not our prime focus, but rather the idea of social structure (Chapters 7 through 11).

There is, in the social edifice, an intricate but discernible arrangement of parts. Because the parts interlock like the roots of a plant, they are fairly hard to uproot—i.e., to change. And having a degree of endurance, the outlines of a pattern, or structure, emerge. For example, we can see the group's values reflected in a layer-cake structure of rewards: power, privilege, and prestige. We can see the structure of authority, the division of labor, the distribution of income in the organizational chart of a corporation. And we can see social structure, again, in those arrangements institutionalized to perform the tasks without which a group could not sustain itself.

These are the matters we shall explore in Part Two, commencing with an overall view of the meaning and dimensions of social structure.

References

TEXT

1. Ruth Benedict, *Patterns of Culture* (Boston: Houghton Mifflin Co., 1961), pp. 21, 22.
2. I am relying in the following few paragraphs on the argument set forth in Theodore M. Newcomb and E. K. Wilson (eds.), *The Study of College Peer Groups: Problems and Prospects for Research,* chap. iii, "The Entering Student: Attributes and Change Agents" (Chicago: Aldine Publishing Co., 1966).
3. Leo W. Simmons, *The Role of the Aged in Primitive Society* (New Haven: Yale University Press, 1945), p. 17.
4. *Ibid.,* pp. 6–10.
5. *Ibid.,* p. 176.
6. James C. Brown, "An Experiment in Role-Taking," *American Sociological Review,* Vol. 17, No. 5 (October, 1952), p. 588.
7. Leonard S. Cottrell, Jr., "Individual Adjustment to Age and Sex Roles," *American Sociological Review,* Vol. 7, No. 5 (October, 1942), pp. 618–19.

   See, also, in the same issue of the *Review,* Ralph Linton on "Age and Sex Categories," and Talcott Parsons, "Age and Sex in the Social Structure of the United States."

   A later issue of the *Review* carried seven articles on age and sex roles, Vol. 29, No. 4 (August, 1964).
8. Theodore M. Newcomb, *Personality and Social Change* (New York: Dryden Press, 1957). This study on the political posture of Bennington students was carried out between 1935 and 1939, the report being first published in 1943.
9. Theodore M. Newcomb, "Persistence and Regression of Changed Attitudes: Long-Range Studies," *Journal of Social Issues,* Vol. 19, No. 4 (October, 1963), p. 12.
10. *Ibid.,* p. 12.
11. *Ibid.,* p. 9.
12. Isidor Thorner, "Nursing: Functional Significance of an Institutional Pattern," *American Sociological Review,* published by The American Sociological Association, Vol. 20, No. 5 (October, 1955).
13. Talcott Parsons, *The Social System* (New York: Free Press of Glencoe, Inc., 1951), p. 62.
14. *Ibid.,* p. 64.
15. Thorner, *op. cit.,* p. 532.
16. *Ibid.,* p. 533.
17. William James, *The Philosophy of William James* (New York: Random House, Modern Library ed., n.d.), pp. 128–29. On the matters of discrepant roles see also Erving Gottman, *The Presentation of Self in Everyday Life* (New York: Doubleday & Co., Inc., 1967), ch. iv., pp. 141–66.
18. Georg Simmel, *Conflict and The Web of Group-Affiliations,* trans. Kurt H. Wolff and Reinhard Bendix (New York: Free Press of Glencoe, Inc., 1955), p. 150.
19. Samuel A. Stouffer, "An Analysis of Conflicting Social Norms," *American Sociological Review,* Vol. 14, No. 6 (December, 1949), p. 707.
20. *Ibid.,* p. 716.
21. Jack P. Gibbs and Walter T. Martin, "A Theory of Status Integration and Its Relationship to Suicide," *American Sociological Review,* Vol. 23, No. 2 (April, 1958), p. 142.
22. *Ibid.,* p. 142.
23. *Ibid.,* p. 143. Here the investigators drop to a footnote worth repeating. "An alternative theorem making use of the concept of role conflict can be stated: The suicide rate of a population varies directly with the degree of role conflict in that population. [But] . . . no quantitative measure of the amount of role conflict in a society or popula-

tion has been developed. Consequently such a proposition remains untestable."

24. *Ibid.*, p. 146.
25. Jack P. Gibbs and Walter T. Martin, "Status Integration and Suicide in Ceylon," *American Journal of Sociology*, Vol. 64, No. 6 (May, 1959), p. 590.

TABLES

6.1 Adapted from a summary in James C. Brown, "An Experiment in Role-Taking," *American Sociological Review*, Vol. 17, No. 5 (October, 1952), p. 592.

6.2 Jack P. Gibbs and Walter T. Martin, "A Theory of Status Integration and Its Relationship to Suicide," *American Sociological Review*, Vol. 27, No. 2 (April, 1958).

6.3 *Ibid.*, p. 146.

6.4 *Ibid.*, p. 147.

FIGURES

6.2 Based on data from Theodore M. Newcomb, "Persistence and Regression of Changed Attitudes: Long-Range Studies," *Journal of Social Issues*, Vol. 19, No. 4 (October, 1963), Table 1, p. 7.

6.4 Samuel A. Stouffer, "An Analysis of Conflicting Social Norms," *American Sociological Review*, Vol. 14, No. 6 (December, 1949), p. 711.

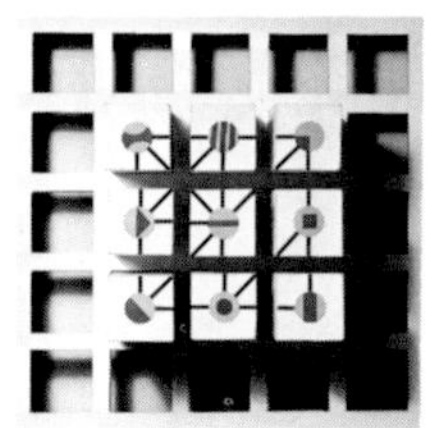

part two

Sustaining the group

The design stresses structure—a discernible arrangement of social parts. Roles, defined by the ordinary rules of life (the cutout squares) are bound together in a system of relationships. The purposely exaggerated symmetry and stability of this design belie ever present flux and change. Yet these do not destroy social structures: they reshape them.

chapter 7 **The social edifice: structures of human relationships**

The social edifice: structures of human relationships

If you wave a sparkler rapidly back and forth you get the impression of an arc of light inscribed in the air. So, too, as people repeatedly deal with one another, their patterned interactions create a sense of line and structure inscribed in the social matrix.

Form or structure in the human group emerges as people daily deal with one another in ways culturally prescribed. These prescriptions promote the repetition of expected conduct in various roles. Thus the channels that guide conduct are deepened and relationships defined. We identify a friendship, for example, when we repeatedly observe two persons doing things together, helping one another, sharing the bitter and the sweet. Such actions are the rules of friendship. Repeated observation of the behavior allows us to infer the relationship. The theme design for Part Two points (a bit too rigidly) to the way roles, represented on the cube faces, are shaped by the cultural stipulations (the cutout squares in the base), defining relationships which, as they are repeated, reveal a social structure.

The word *structure* means an arrangement of *differentiated* parts. The body is made up of a remarkable collection of unlike parts, all linked together in a discernible structure. "The head bone's connected to the neck bone. The neck bone's connected to the shoulder bone. The shoulder bone's connected to the back bone. Now hear the word of the Lord." A social structure, too, consists in unlike elements, each performing in a somewhat different way. When we speak of an age-sex structure we mean, for example, that a male, 20 years old, will act differently toward others—and they to him—than will people in other age-sex categories. His repeated performance in his role as a 20-year-old male reinforces relationships that mark off one sector of the social structure.

The frequency with which we use the word *structure*—kinship structure, power structure, authority structure, age-sex structure, race and ethnic structure, class structure, institutional structure —suggests the many perspectives from which we may view the social structure. For example, the composition of a population reveals the demographic structure of society. Or, looking at the spatial distribution of men and their activities, we see the structure of a community as would the human ecologist. Examining a specific organization, we may see a structure of tasks that pattern men's dealings with one another. From a fourth perspective, we can see a layer-cake structure in human groups to the extent that different categories of persons have more and less of those things valued by group members—wealth, skills, education, and the like. Again, social structure is revealed in the institutionalized patterns of behavior that repeat themselves daily, weekly, year in, year out. It is through these recurrent behaviors that family and school have an identity. So, likewise, with groups that work and worship and live together: we know them by the discernible structure whose building blocks are habitual relationships.

Let's review briefly these several perspectives on the social order.

Demographic structure

The age-sex structure was shown by population pyramids in Chapter 2. Such graphic representations of age and sex differences in a group become socially significant as they point to commonly ex-

Figure 7.1

Nationality structure, United States

Percent of white population foreign born plus native born with one or both parents foreign born.

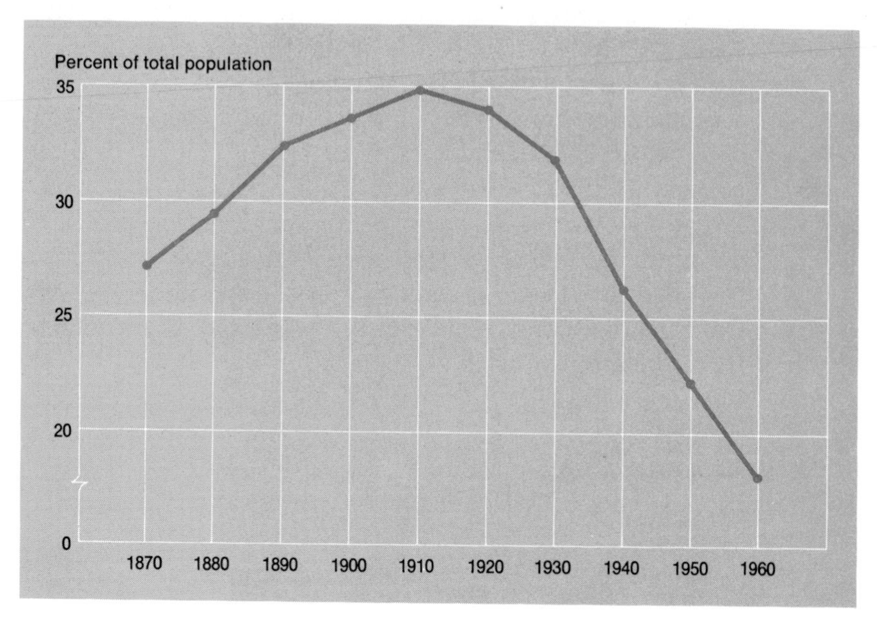

pected differences in role performance*—and the relationships built as the roles are linked. Similarly the nationality and race composition of American society (Figures 7.1 and 7.2) provide clues to the way different backgrounds and prevailing stereotypes may result in productive or clashing conceptions of appropriate role performance. Or we can look at the structure of the labor force (Figure 7.3), or the distribution of rewards (Figure 7.4). From such data we can infer the distribution of tasks characterizing a society, the relative rank of types of work roles, and the rewards and power accorded them. Hence we know something about the relationships between the incumbents of these various roles.

* To take an interesting example, we find in an Israeli kibbutz age-graded peer groups: the infant house, the toddler's house at age 1, another house for the kindergartener, a dormitory for those in grades 1 to 6 and another house for those in grades 7 to 12. (See Melford Spiro, *Children of the Kibbutz* [New York: Schocken Books, Inc., 1965].)

Figure 7.2
Racial structure, United States
(Negro population)

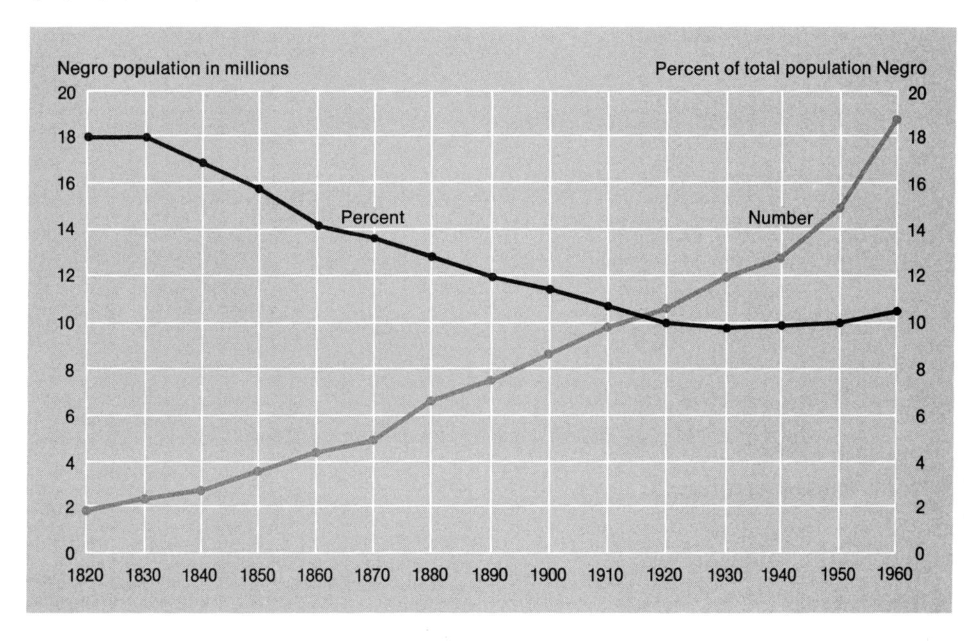

Figure 7.3
Occupational structure and median income, United States, 1967
(by occupation of family head)

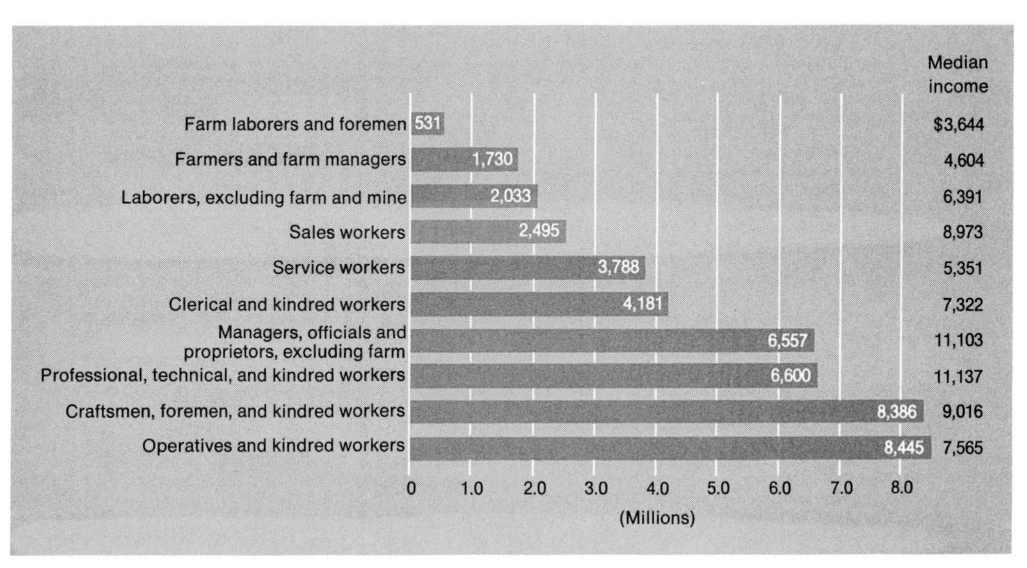

Figure 7.4
Income structure for U.S. families, 1967
(by color of head of household)

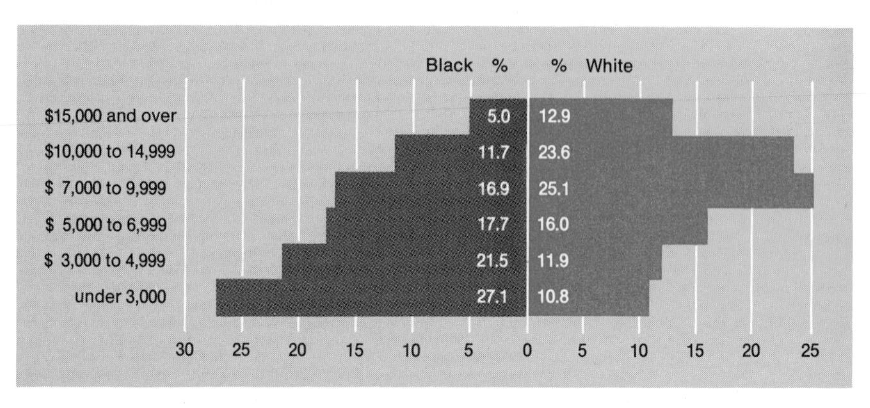

Ecological structure

There is a patterning of human relationships revealed in space and time. Ways in which men think and act are not randomly distributed in space. In our cities we find a central business district (how can this be explained?), suburbs and slums, garment districts and vice areas, theater districts and ghettos, and Harlems and secondhand car districts. Human communities take on form and structure, not under the aegis of city plan commissions but as a result of competitive processes, largely unplanned and unwitting. From the plant and animal ecologists, the sociologist borrows the term *symbiosis* to convey the notion of unplanned interdependence. It describes a social structure arising from the interlocking of complementary differences. The young couple on a date proceed with the unwitting collaboration of the state highway commission, the legislators who appropriate funds, and the automobile and petroleum industries, under the protection of insurance companies. Should they attend a movie, another host of unknown others becomes implicated. Durkheim used the words "organic solidarity" to describe the way in which differentiated activities—especially the division of labor—bind us into one another's destinies.

Neither the unwitting character of such relationships nor the biological analogy should be overdrawn. With man, sentiment, tradition, and preference enter in to modify a strictly anonymous competition that better describes the world of plants and animals.

Man has a culture, a body of knowledge symbolized in act and artifact, and including especially knowledge of what *ought* to be. (He can, for example, establish restrictive housing covenants that alter the distribution of population from what it would be were impersonal competition the sole determinant.)

Yet, underlying the conscious pursuit of preferred ways, we see in human populations an impersonal adaptation to environment. The result is a discernible structure of relationships in time and space.

The temporal structure of human relationships

Consider some garden variety examples of the temporal patterning of relationships. The whole urban network of transport and communication is contrived to enable the encounter of the right persons at (as we hope) the right time. (Transport, indeed, might be subsumed under communication, since it is a principal device for achieving face-to-face communication among members of the group.) This temporal structuring controls encounters, conditions the intersection of experience, strengthens or attenuates relationships. Student and teacher, priest and communicant, official and citizen, husband and wife, worker and boss—all the relationships implied by these role labels are sustained by the Illinois Central or Penn Central (with government assistance), by TWA and Greyhound, by subway or metro, by highways and sidewalks that convey A to B's side, enabling each to meet the reciprocal expectations that define the relationship.

Time is significant as a frame for human relationships in many ways. Cultural accretion depends on it. Different generations step into the cultural stream at different time points, complicating parent-child relationships. Every culture has its calendar, a temporal map locating significant, recurrent events. "No people," Professor Hughes notes, "has for long lived without some established group ways which turn with the sun."[1] And with persons as with a people: private calendars are created to mark off times of personal significance: before and after the sit-in, or the game with State, or the time of first encounter, or of parting.

Temporal intervals bound statuses. After periods of time, infants become children, children adolescents, and adolescents adults. At 62, adults become the aged by fiat (when they are eligible for social security). After a certain length of time in role a worker gains seniority, the captain his majority, the recruit his

PFC stripe. Time symbolizes the strength and demands of a relationship, as suggested in the pledge "'til death do us part."

Finally, the cycle of seasons may define a cycle in human relationships, as Mauss points out in his classic essay on "Seasonal Variations in Eskimo Societies."* In this work he describes structural changes in the social order that are linked with the seasonal dispersion and concentration of Eskimo groups. Contrasting patterns of summer and winter life are shaped by the ways of the animals they hunt. And so, Mauss points out, there emerges a cyclical rhythm in their religious and familial life, in their moral and judicial patterns.

In the summer, settlements are sparse, in winter dense and clustered. From summer to winter their shelter shifts from tents to houses. A summer dwelling houses a single family, while in wintertime as many as six to nine families live in a single dwelling. And so Mauss sees here a genuinely symbiotic phenomenon. As the game concentrate or disperse, according to the season, there is a concomitant expansion and contraction of the social structure.

This is reflected in religious practices. These are minimal in summer, limited to domestic rites: rituals of birth and death and the observance of certain proscriptions. But the winter is a time of continuous religious excitement. It is then that myths and tales are transmitted from one generation to another. The slightest event requires the more or less serious intervention of magicians. In sum, one can see the whole of the winter life as a sort of extended religious festival.

The contrast between summer and winter life, Mauss goes on to say, extends to ideas: people's birth dates, summer or winter, serve to classify them. "Each season serves to define a whole order of beings and things." Laws affecting family relationships and property follow the same temporal cycle.

> Eskimo social life undergoes, then, a sort of regular rhythm. It is not the same at different seasons of the year. Now if this curious alternation is most clearly seen among the Eskimos it is not peculiar to or exclusive with them. Social life is not sustained at the same level throughout the year but rather goes through regular and successive phases of increasing and decreasing intensity, of rest and activity, of expenditure of energy and restoration.[2]

* See Reference 2, page 248.

The spatial structure of human relationships

"The Urban Community As A Spatial Pattern and a Moral Order," is the title of an essay by an American sociologist, Robert E. Park.[3] It suggests the reason for our interest in the spatial structure of people's traits and activities. Other things equal, spatial propinquity → social propinquity → an articulation of interdependent roles → psychic propinquity: common attitudes and values that identify and bound the group. A common habitat enables frequency of interaction; frequency of interaction is associated with people's attractiveness and accommodation to one another; and common conceptions of a range of objects are developed and reinforced. This yields what Durkheim called "moral density," a consistency of viewpoint regularly reinforced through recurrent contacts and enhancing group solidarity.

Let us assume that physical and social distance are positively related—that one's friends and familiars are commonly those who are close enough, physically, to associate with frequently. Now the more frequent the interaction between two persons, A and B, and the more attractive B is for A, the more accurate is A in assessing B's view of some object, X (for example, another person). This means that A's expectations of B's behavior are likely to be fulfilled. A expects B to act in a given way. He does so. A's image of B is reinforced. The relationship is predictable, which is to say, stable. To recall Weber's definition of a social relationship, there is a high probability that, in the meaningful content of such a relationship, an anticipated course of action will ensue. And conversely, the evidence indicates that accuracy in estimating others' behavior and belief *declines* with reduced frequency of interaction and attractiveness. Thus, as to a person with whom I deal infrequently, my expectations of his conduct are much more likely to be wrong. My anticipations are more often unfulfilled, my "predictions" unrealized. He does not behave as he "should," and this is unsettling. Such erratic behavior arouses uncertainty and distrust. We are disposed to call such an other irresponsible. Hence we are inclined to have as little as possible to do with him, resulting in future estimates of him and his conduct that may then be more inaccurate than ever.

Consider the extent of agreement between those who are "close" and those who are not so "close" to one another. Bear in mind the question at issue: What is the connection between spatial propinquity and social/psychic closeness? Table 7.1 has to do with the extent of agreement between friends and nonfriends as to a char-

Table 7.1

Spatial, social, and psychic propinquity revealed in extent of agreement in assessing the attractiveness of others

Extent of agreement as to attractiveness of other house members*		Percent of assessments falling at indicated level of agreement among: Member and two best friends (closeness)	Member and two fellow residents least attractive to him (distance)
.75 and over	High	47	0
.74–.50	↑	38	29
.49–.25		15	15
.24–.00	↓	0	18
.00	Low	0	38
Total		100	100

* Rho values. See Aside on Methods: Number 9 "Measuring Degree of Association between Two Sets of Rank-Ordered Observations."

acteristic (degree of attractiveness) of 17 other persons living in a student residence. These data suggest that people who often deal with one another are likely to be friendly and to see the world through like lenses. A primary predisposing factor is physical propinquity, location in shared space. Thus the spatial, the social, and the moral order are likely to be coterminous, the first setting the conditions of frequency of interaction, hence conditioning the strength of the social bond and the extent to which the significant objects of life carry similar values.

Conversely, the spatial segregation of differentiated modes of life—of differing social patterns—tends to draw boundary lines between groups. Physical barriers, reinforced by cultural barriers (which themselves encourage the retention of physical barriers, as when anti-Negro prejudice promotes segregated communities), sustain a relationship of organism to habitat that *maximizes access and encounter among the like-minded,* minimizes association with others. We might call this the mechanism of differential exposure, or selective isolation. We see it operating in our choice of newspapers and editorial policies, in the choice of certain radio and TV programs and rejection of others. Throughout our lives we erect these belief- and behavior-protecting ramparts, the Berlin Walls that maintain our identity and protect our predispositions within a favored group having, often, a specific *locus.* The effect is to produce a constancy of character persisting through time and lending a distinctive identity to particular quarters. When we use names like Wall Street, or LaSalle Street, Harlem or the Black Belt,

Figure 7.5

Generalizations of internal structure of cities

The concentric zone theory is a generalization for all cities. The arrangement of the sectors in the sector theory varies from city to city. The diagram for multiple nuclei represents one possible pattern among innumerable variations.

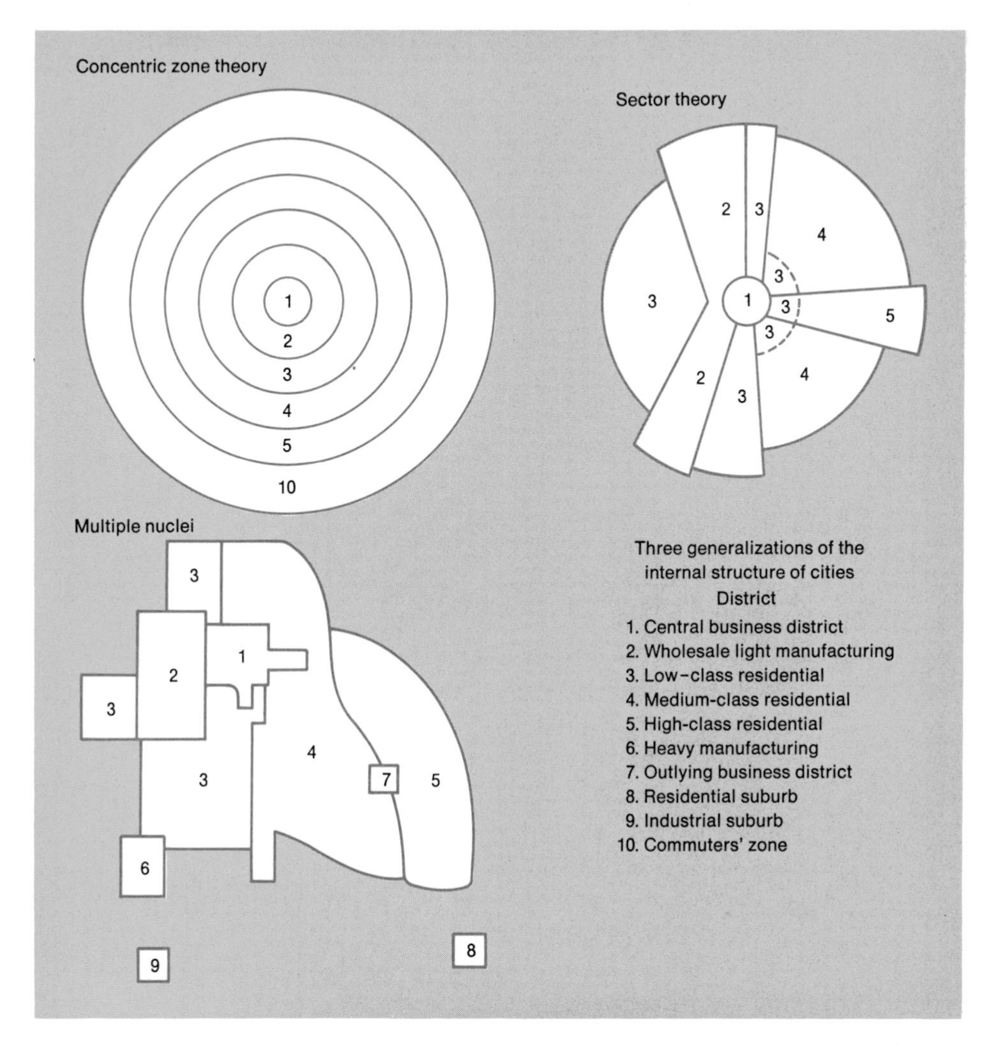

Brooklyn or Brookline, Nob Hill or Little Italy, the Bowery, the Village, the garment, fur, and theater districts, we refer to such spatially defined areas that retain their character (persist in the structure of relationships) through time despite continuous changes in population.

Various graphic models have been used to represent these natural areas, so-called because the social structure they create is unplanned. Three such models are represented in Figure 7.5.

But however the models may differ, these things are agreed:

1. A determinate, nonrandom pattern of settlement, land use, of social and psychic characteristics emerges.
2. The marketplace, the downtown shopping area, or retail business district is consistently at a central location, a point of maximum accessibility.
3. Adjacent to an expanding central business district and along rail, river, and shore lines are areas of deteriorated housing, cutrate commercial outfits, rescue missions, and wholesale and storage facilities.
4. Single-family housing, more costly and in better repair, tends to be at the outer reaches of the corporate area, with apartment houses, dual or duplex housing, and tenements at points successively nearer the center—nearer commercial and industrial uses.
5. The relative status of various ethnic groups is registered in their differing capacity to compete for preferred residential areas.
6. The growth of human settlements tends to be from the original, central settlement outwards, with population and supporting institutions pressing toward the peripheries.
7. Where movement or transiency is greatest and where, in consequence, relationships are unstable, a social order is ill defined and ill sustained.
8. In deteriorated residential districts, which are alone available to poor migrants and minorities low in status, having slight opportunity to achieve the goals of middle-class America as described and diffused through the mass media—in such districts the social order tends to be integrated through deviant norms, and rates of illegal and aberrant activities are high.
9. Increases in number of persons in a human settlement entail increased diversity of belief and behavior leading to the substitution of formal (governmental) controls for the informal controls of custom and tradition.
10. This spatial patterning of people and their behaviors develops as men accommodate through competitive processes to their environment.

Illustrations of the spatial patterning of social traits are seen in the following figures. The first, Figure 7.6, tells us that, in Detroit, the better educated live outside, the less well educated inside, the city.

Figure 7.6

Percent of males, 25 years of age and older, in Detroit metropolitan area, by level of educational achievement, 1960

The data show that between 1940 and 1960 the percent of all males 25 years of age or older, living in Detroit—the city itself—dropped 22.7 percent. But among those having least education the decline was only 7.2 percent, whereas for those with most education the drop was 34.1 percent.

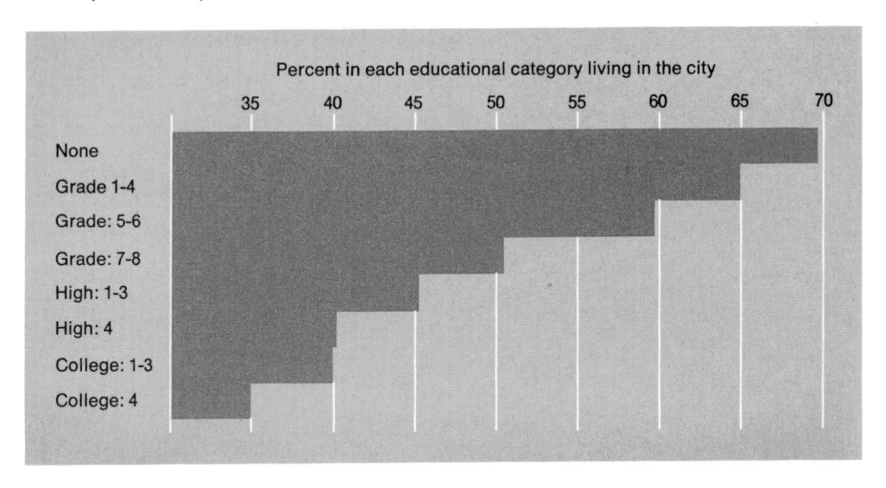

Two final examples are taken from early studies of the link between spatial and social structure. In Figure 7.7 we see a remarkably smooth gradient of delinquency rates, declining with distance from the city until, approaching Calumet City, South Chicago, and Gary, they rise again. In Figure 7.8, again we see a gradient—this time in religious identification. The picture for Protestants is almost the reverse: high in rural and suburban fringes and declining as one moves toward the central city.

Organizational structure

Generic characteristics

Complex societies like ours are made up of organizations. And the individual organization has, of course, its own social structure.

Figure 7.7

Delinquency rates in representative mile-square areas in Chicago, 1927

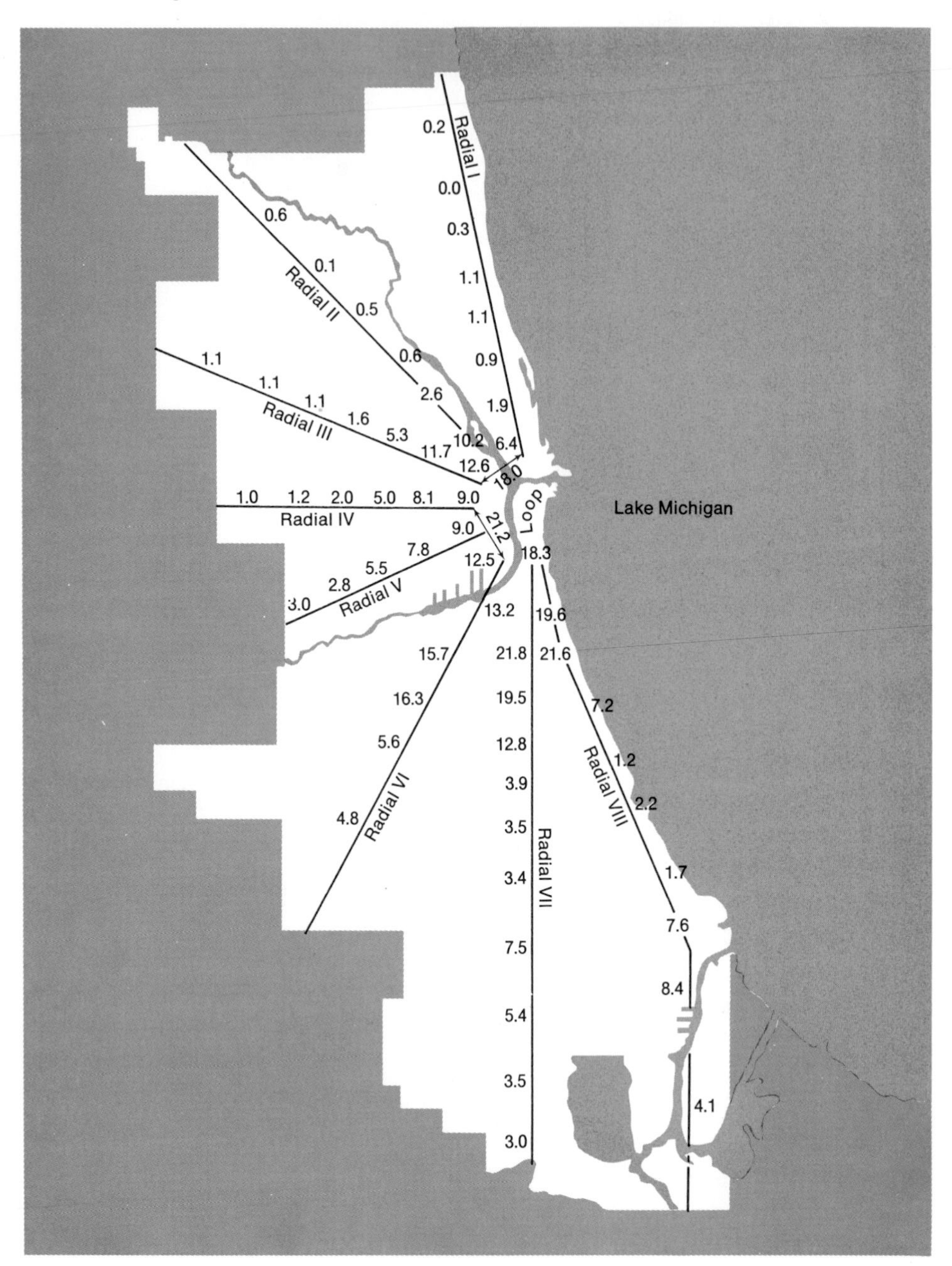

Figure 7.8
Proportion of Jews in total church membership, Chicago and counties of the region, 1936

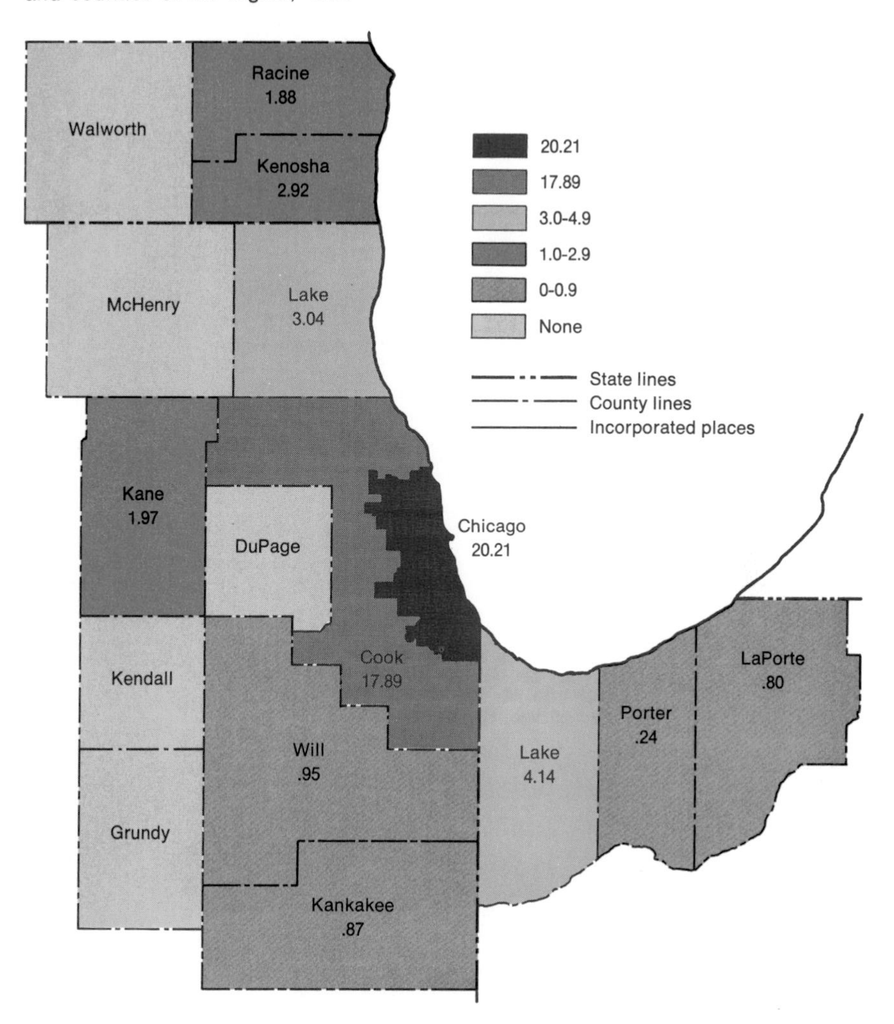

In all organizations there is a vertical arrangement of elements—positions or offices having varying degrees of authority, responsibility, and rewards. We also find a horizontal arrangement representing a division of labor and the coordination of differentiated roles. There is a third common feature, some transformation of raw material by the organization: the patient is cured, the house is built, the student learns, people's minds are changed, cars are produced, enemies killed.

. . . Human communities take on form and structure . . . largely unplanned and unwitting.

. . . An enormous range in size is apparent from primary group . . . one "characterized by intimate face-to-face association . . ." to the large and far-flung bureaucratic organization. . . .

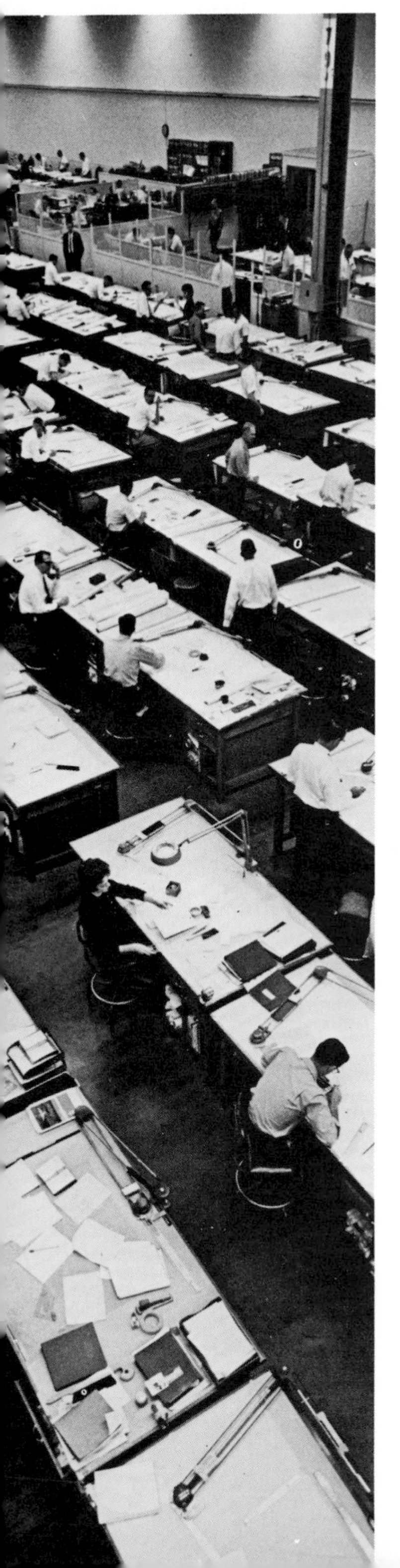

. . . we see . . . persons
who stand
on about the same rung
of the ladder
of socially valued traits.

But the variations on the common themes are innumerable. An enormous range in size is apparent from primary group (an elementary social structure) to bureaucracy. Cooley, who coined the term, defined a *primary group* as one "characterized by intimate face-to-face association and cooperation"; its special significance stems from the fact that such elementary organizations—family, play groups, neighborhood groups—"are fundamental in forming the social nature and ideals of the individual."[4] An example of a primary group is the neighborhood gang studied some years ago by William F. Whyte.[5] A group of boys met regularly at a particular corner. Out of their recurrent interaction a group structure emerged: leader, lieutenants, followers. One of their favorite activities was bowling. Whyte found that there was a marked positive correlation between bowling scores and rank in the group. This was not merely because winners become leaders. It also turned out that leaders are winners—i.e., they create optimum conditions for safeguarding their standing in the group. The followers, too, applied sanctions to sustain theirs, and their leader's, relative standing in this street corner society. Even in such a small, informal primary group we find a social structure. Orders and favors go down the ranks, compliance goes up. The leader initiates action, unifies the group, and deals with outsiders on behalf of the group.

In a recent study, Elliot Liebow tells us of a much more loosely organized street corner group of Negro men whose society condemned them to failure in all the usual relationships of life—relationships with friends, wives, lovers, children, and employers.[6] But even the loose and ephemeral structure of such a group provided the means of temporarily transforming defeat into a degree of self-respect.

Contrast such simple social structures with the Radio Corporation of America, which has 120,000 employees, 12,000 different sorts of products and services, for lease or sale in 120 nations and territories (gross sales of more than $3 billion in 1968). Products include television—sets and stations (NBC)—tape recorders, radios, phonographs, computers, electronic typesetters, weather satellites, instruments for space exploration, radar devices, educational hardware (computer-assisted instruction), publishing (Random House), electronic installations maintained for the government both here and abroad, and international telegraph service.

(RCA also owns Hertz car rental company.) In such an organization the communication network is vastly complex, division of labor is refined, and levels of organization multiply.

Or, using technology as a clue, consider the complexity of a civic organization. When a New Yorker turns on the faucet, lights the gas stove, flips a light switch, or uses the phone, he is but vaguely aware of the enormous infrastructure that supports these commonplace actions: over 6,000 miles of pipe which carry, every day, 1.2 billion gallons of water; nearly 8,000 miles of gas mains; more than 70,000 miles of electric cable.[7] The faucet, gas stove, light switch, and phone are the small, visible part of a technical iceberg. Similarly, in a complex organization the web of relationships each of us can see is a very small part of the organizational iceberg.

But size and complexity do not exhaust the dimensions describing organizational differences. Organizations change through time and vary in space. Some groups, such as *ad hoc* committees, have a single, specific objective. When this end is achieved, the group disbands. On the other hand, we immortalize some groups by institutionalizing them. The patterns of relationships that we see in the family, in government, in religion, and in the economy persist over long periods of time.

Some interesting aspects of organizational structure only reveal themselves through time. Thus Professor Thompson tells us that the distribution of *authority* and the distribution of *ability* within organizations has changed over the years. Once they were essentially the same. But through time there has been an increasing gap between the structure of authority (the power to decide and to implement decisions) and the structure of ability. To take a familiar instance, top authority in a university quite commonly resides in men who are ignorant of the specialties of those who serve on their faculties.

In the past, organizations were essentially hierarchical in form with authority flowing from top to bottom. Roles were allocated, not on the basis of highly demanding specialties, but on the basis of inherited position, or power, or demonstrable superiority in certain essential tasks.

But on this vertical pattern there has been grafted a lateral sort of organization. It is based on the interlocking of highly differentiated specialties. The historical drift of organizational structure might be represented, then, by a change from a pyramidal devolution of power and expertise, to a diamond-shaped structure, constantly broadening in the lateral dimension as shown in Figure 7.9.

Speaking to this point, a specialist in organizational analysis says:

> . . . modern bureaucracy attempts to fit specialization into the old hierarchical framework. The fitting is more and more difficult. There is a growing gap between the right to decide, which is authority, and the power to do, which is specialized ability. This gap is growing because technological change, with resulting increase in specialization, occurs at a faster rate than the change in cultural definitions of [the authority structure]. This situation produces tensions and strains the willingness to co-operate. Much bureaucratic behavior can be understood as a reaction to those tensions. In short, the most symptomatic characteristic of modern bureaucracy is the growing imbalance between ability and authority.[8]

The spatial dimension of organizations may be seen in two ways: certain group structures may be repeated throughout the reaches of society, or a single organization may be national or international in its scope. PTA's, restaurants, and schools are examples of the first: whether in Maine, Texas, or Oregon, roles and relationships are arranged in familiar structures. The large and farflung bureaucratic organization exemplifies the second sort of spatial reach—General Motors, the Department of Defense. There is a tendency for organizational boundaries to spread. Effective communication networks make this possible. Expansion occurs sometimes for economic reasons—the search for resources and markets. It may also come about as people are increasingly aware that their destinies are tied to others'. Thus, in the fall of 1968, an organization was formed in Holland to enable people to express their views about the candidates for President of the United States! So to join the American people in discussion of their candidates is almost unprecedented, for elections are regarded as exclusively internal, domestic matters. But these Netherlanders did not see it as a matter touching Americans alone. Their leader was reported in *The New York Times* as saying:

> The American electorate is one and one-half percent of the world population. It is unacceptable that one and one-half percent of the world population decides who shall be the most powerful man in the world, who decides for us in matters of war and peace, racial relations and the fight against

Figure 7.9

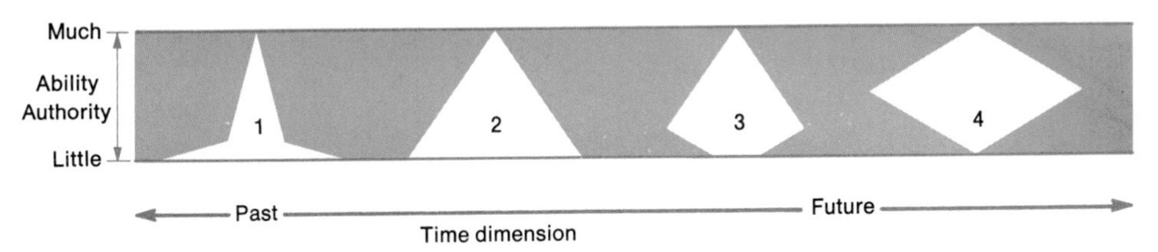

Notes:

1 is meant to represent a quasi-religious structure of authority. The leader has quite remarkable powers (mana) and commensurate authority. Most subordinates are equally far from the heights of power. Such leadership has been called "charismatic," (the noun is *charisma*) to describe a person supernaturally endowed and so commanding the unqualified allegiance of his followers. For example, we read that Chinese pilots, discarding the old Russian training methods and relying instead, on the thoughts of Mao Tse-tung, have greatly shortened the training period and vastly increased their combat efficiency. The *Times* reports them as saying: "With Mao Tse-tung's thoughts in our minds, we can tell exactly where we are heading, even in clouds or dense fog" (*New York Times*, dateline January 14, 1967).

2 is the conventional pyramid pattern of organization based, not on mana, but on breeding—either in the biological or social sense. Ability and power increase as one moves toward the apex.

3 and 4 represent an erosion of extremes of authority and ability. Few are as distinctively wise or ignorant, gifted or incompetent, as was once the case. There will be tension, then, to adjust the authority structure to the revised ability structure.

> poverty. The United States President meddles in our affairs. We should meddle in his.[9]

Organizational structure has been analyzed from many other angles. Some organizations can be differentiated according to the way members are brought to comply with group goals and the means of achieving them. Do they gain compliance through coercion, or chiefly through *quid pro quo* exchanges, or because members share ideas and commitments in common?[10] Some organizations may be characterized by type of authority employed. For example, Gouldner speaks of two types of bureaucracy, punishment-centered and representative bureaucracy.[11] The social structure of still other organizations differ depending on material processed—things, persons, or ideas—and on the goals of the transformation. U.S. Steel is organized to transform ore into metal for profit. A school is organized to process people, changing them as knowledge, skills, and appreciation are developed. A number of scientists set up a research organization to solve problems and extend knowledge. The social structure of the group should change, then, depending on whether we are making steel, educating children, or doing scientific research.

Some sociologists have found patterns of social organization clearly linked to technology. Consider the scheme in Table 7.2 in which the chief variables are (1) frequency with which problems are encountered in transforming raw materials (whether things, people or ideas) and (2) the availability of regular procedures of analysis to solve these problems.[12]

These variations in technology might be expected to influence the nature of the task and, hence, the definition of roles and the nature of relationships. For example, in type 2 (Table 7.2), both supervisors and technicians will have a good deal of discretion and considerable autonomy in making decisions at their respective levels. Yet all involved will be constrained to consult with others on likely solutions to novel problems. And to evaluate their solutions, they will seek feedback on the outcomes of these solutions. Persons and subgroups will be highly interdependent. The organization itself will be flexible, with several power centers. But type 3 will be formal, with highly centralized planning and authority, generally opposite in its structure to type 2.

Perhaps sociologists have most often viewed organizations as natural social systems, generating many informal networks of relationship that have little or no obvious bearing on the formal structure rationally contrived to turn out a given product. In the rational model, the arrangement of roles is influenced by: (1) the view of organization as a means, an instrument of production, (2) an elaborate set of rules specifying appropriate role performance in some detail, (3) carefully developed and regularly assessed procedures thought to promote production, (4) impersonality in role assignment, in evaluation of performance, and in rewarding and punishing. But looking at the unofficial groupings in an organization one is likely to see a rather different structure, one that vastly complicates the formal table of organization. Agreements are tacit, association is spontaneous, or at least little planned, relationships are personal, and rather than serving some external purpose, the end may be in the relationship itself.

Thus if we study a college community we find a social structure that includes subgroups not formally organized to promote the product and serving ends that may be quite different from those of the organization. A chief end of college and university life is the transmission and generation of ideas. But some informal groupings may be only ritually—or less—concerned about the life of the intellect. As the instrument for cultivating ideas, the college itself is obviously central. Yet some students may feel little identification with the college, while for others it is a focal point of identity. Crosscutting these two variables, Clark and Trow find

Table 7.2
Differentiating organizations on the basis of technological problems

	Problems in transforming raw materials		
Type	Number	Regular procedures for solving available	Technology and examples
1	Many	Yes	Engineering (heavy machinery)
2	Many	No	Nonroutine (aerospace)
3	Few	Yes	Routine (steel production)
4	Few	No	Craft industry (glass)

Table 7.3

	Involved with ideas: Much	Involved with ideas: Little
Identify with their college: Much	Academic (1)	Collegiate (2)
Identify with their college: Little	Nonconformist (3)	Vocational (4)

four sorts of student groups and four student subcultures (Table 7.3).[13]

Words describing these several subgroups and subcultures are these (but see the Clark and Trow work cited for fuller characterization):

1. Identification with intellectual concerns as represented in the work of the serious academic faculty members.
2. ". . . a world of football, fraternities and sororities, dates, cars, drinking and campus fun."
3. the nonconformist, offbeat, independent, intellectual, radical, alienated, bohemian. . . .
4. ". . . college is largely off-the-job training, an organization of courses and credits leading to a diploma and a better job than they could otherwise command."

Obviously, the four-celled table should not suggest a campus community divided neatly into four quarters. Nor is it meant that these are cleanly separated categories. But it does suggest that informal groups emerge which may develop ends and means quite different from those of the organization that embraces them. Only one of the four (cell 1) aligns perfectly with formal purpose and program. Thus, to study the organizational structure in those terms alone would be to miss important elements of a campus community.

* * * *

Social structure may be revealed, as we have seen, from demographic, ecological, and organizational perspectives. Organizational structures have many dimensions: size, complexity, differences emerging through time and space. Their social structure may vary depending on means of gaining compliance from subordinates. Differences in technology—different means of processing their raw materials—may entail differences in social structure. And, as we have noted, there are informal, more or less spontaneously generated elements in organizations that multiply its structural elements far beyond those indicated in formal tables of organization.

Now, finally, let us note two more perspectives from which we can descry the social structure of a group: class, and institutional structures. (We shan't dwell long on these, since they are matters for succeeding chapters in Part Two.)

Class structure

It is a fact of social life that some men stand higher (or lower) than others. I say "social life" because standing is always relative to others' positions on some scale representing conduct valued by group members: power, skill, goodness, authority, command over material things, wisdom, courage, and the like. Einstein, Martin Luther King, Jacqueline Onassis, Pope Paul, an Eagle Scout, Clint Murchison, a Phi Beta Kappa, the person winning a Nobel prize, or the soldier awarded the Medal of Honor—these people all have more of something valued by group members.

We rank people across many walks of life and sometimes do it in highly refined detail. For example, in 1962 Congress set minimum and maximum salaries for physicians, dentists, and nurses employed by the Veterans' Administration (Public Law 87–793, October 11, 1962). Ranks and incomes are shown in Table 7.4.

Or consider the data in Table 7.5 showing average income by education and race in 1966. From such data we can reasonably infer that education is valued, that fine distinctions in occupational level are differently rewarded, that nonwhites are less re-

Table 7.4

U.S. Veterans' Administration salary schedule for physicians, dentists, and nurses

Grade	Physicians and dentists		Nurses	
	Minimum	Maximum	Minimum	Maximum
Director	$16,000	$19,000		
Assistant director			$12,845	$16,245
Executive	15,250	18,750		
Chief	14,565	18,405	11,150	14,070
Senior	12,845	16,245	9,475	11,995
Intermediate	11,150	14,070	8,045	10,165
Full grade	9,475	11,995	6,675	8,700
Associate	8,045	10,165	5,820	7,575
Junior			5,035	6,565

Table 7.5

Educational attainment and mean earnings of male year-round, full-time workers 14 years old and over*

Years of school completed		White			Nonwhite		
		Number with earnings† (32,424)	Percent distri-bution	Mean earnings ($7,724)	Number with earnings† (3,041)	Percent distri-bution	Mean earnings ($4,700)
Elementary:	8 years or less	$ 6,585	20.3	$ 5,433	$1,201	39.5	$3,751
High school:	1 to 3 years	5,697	17.6	6,722	682	22.4	4,644
	4 years	11,232	34.6	7,481	762	25.1	5,230
College:	1 to 3 years	3,896	12.0	8,770	209	6.9	5,879
	4 years	3,016	9.3	11,010	101	3.3	6,972
	5 years or more	1,998	6.2	12,495	86	2.8	8,129

* For 1966 (number of persons as of March, 1967).
† Numbers in thousands.

warded than whites even when sex and level of education are held constant and, conceivably, that there is some discrimination against women in the labor force. (For example, in the salary schedule in Table 7.4, there is no grade of "Director" or "Executive" in the schedule for nurses.)

Thus we see in human groups—organizations, communities, societies—a layer-cake structure, a hierarchy of statuses and roles whose incumbents are unequal in their possession of valued traits. The traits themselves are not the same from group to group. But inequality itself is ubiquitous—and celebrated. Indeed, if all men had in equal degree whatever traits were honored, there would be nothing to honor. Our values depend on distinctions. People exemplifying such values in greater degree than others are commonly rewarded, whether in cash, kudos, or clout—i.e., wealth, prestige, and power.

The way we rank people is a clue to the values of a society (and the rules of conduct implied by those values: if saintliness, then lead a life of self-denial and service to others; if wealth, then get enough education to sharpen native wit in climbing the business ladder). Likewise, the bases on which rank is accorded tell us something about the group. If one's standing is largely a family matter, transmitted from the past, we are dealing with a conservative society in which relationships are guided by traditional rules. If, on the other hand, standing is largely a matter of personal achievement, then we have a group more fluid and changing.

Viewing social structure from this perspective, we see categories of persons who stand on about the same rung of the ladder of socially valued traits. And the sociologist asks, as we shall in the next chapter, what those rungs stand for, how people reach them, and to what extent people move up and down.

Institutional structure

If the study of class gives us a layer-cake view of social structure, to study institutions is to look at the pillars that support the social edifice. For we institutionalize those social patterns that seem essential to sustain our values. For example, children must be protected, nourished, and reared. Again, means must be found to collaborate both in the complicated business of producing things and in exchanging the product of one man's work for another's. Also, rules must be worked out to free people from fraud and force. In the incessant effort to meet such needs, we institutionalize certain social mechanisms. Indeed, this is what institutionalization implies: devising, typically in trial-and-error fashion, familial, economic, political, and other systems that for a time, and more or less well, help us realize our values. We have an example of this process in the relatively recent problem of elderly dependents. Placing a high value on life and its extension, and having an increased proportion of persons in the old-age category, prompted us to institutionalize ways of caring for the aged—hence such devices as social security.

Institutions, then, are fairly enduring social patterns in support of societal values and, therefore, personal needs. In the last three chapters of Part Two, we shall have a closer look at the institutional structure.

* * * *

From five perspectives—demographic, ecological, organizational, class, and institutional—we can see structures of human relationships. But these separate viewpoints may fix our attention on the blocks of social structure, so missing the mortar that binds them together. What is it that lends unity and cohesion to the whole? Sociologists think of several factors that affect the integrity of social structures. One of these, cultural integration, is the extent to which group members subscribe to common values and beliefs. A second, normative integration, is the extent to which role performance is the same for any incumbent of a given social position. Normative integration, then, will depend on the level of cultural integration. Both of these will depend on the frequency with which people of like mind deal with one another, reinforcing common beliefs and behaviors. Landecker has called this "communicative integration": the extent to which "communicative contacts permeate a group."[14] Finally, there is the unity that stems from the meshing of differentiated parts exemplified, particularly, in the division of labor. Functional integration, as it has been called, stresses the interdependence of roles and relationships in human groups—especially complex ones.

To illustrate *types of integration:* A widely shared belief in the intrinsic rightness of work conscientiously and completely performed (*cultural*), reinforced by dealings with others who share this conviction (*communicative*), is reflected in standards of performance in work roles (*normative*), yielding products that are used in other enterprises and rewards—wages and salaries—that go to support of dependents, contributions to the church, taxes in support of schools and the military, and others (*functional*). Such are the ways in which elements of the social structure are bound together—integrated.

But integration is a matter of degree. And so, therefore, are group cohesiveness and group identity. Functional integration may tie us tightly to those with whom we vigorously disagree. A lack of integration is revealed in the bumper stickers reading: "Love America or leave it." Opposition to the war in Vietnam offends those who follow the Decatur principle: "My country, may she ever be right, but right or wrong, my country." When shared values no longer hold, relationships (in this case, citizen-citizen relationships) are threatened, become unpredictable, and herald instability and change in the social order.

In discussing social structure, we should beware lest the physical analogy convey a false impression of rigidity and immutability. Social life is fluid. It emerges through the transactions that unique individuals have with one another.

Yet it would be equally—even more—erroneous to see social life as utterly mercurial. Groups do have forms and boundaries, and structural elements. That a structure does in fact exist gains credibility as we see how, knowing their position in that structure, we can predict the way people feel, think, and act.

Evidence of this predictability is offered in the following chapter as we examine the class structure and its correlates.

References

TEXT

1. Everett Hughes, *Men and Their Work* (New York: Free Press, 1958), p. 13.
2. Marcel Mauss, "Essai sur les variations saisonnieres des sociétiés eskimos: étude de morphologie sociale," *l'Année sociologique,* Vol. 9 (1904–5), pp. 39–132, *passim.*
3. Ernest W. Burgess (ed.), *The Urban Community* (Chicago: University of Chicago Press, 1925). The essay is reprinted in Ralph H. Turner (ed.), *Robert E. Park on Social Control and Collective Behavior* (Chicago: University of Chicago Press—Phoenix paperback, 1967).
4. Charles Horton Cooley, *Social Organization* (New York: Charles Scribner's Sons, 1929), p. 23.
5. William F. Whyte, *Street Corner Society* (Chicago: University of Chicago Press, 1943).
6. Elliot Liebow, *Tally's Corner: A Study of Negro Streetcorner Man* (Boston: Little, Brown & Co., 1967).
7. Reported in *The New York Times* for December 19, 1968, p. 49.
8. Victor A. Thompson, *Modern Organization* (New York: Alfred A. Knopf, Inc., 1961, p. 6).
9. Tuesday, October 15, 1968.
10. See Amitai Etzioni, *A Comparative Analysis of Complex Organizations* (New York: Free Press, 1961).
11. Alvin Gouldner, *Patterns of Industrial Bureaucracy* (New York: Free Press, 1954).
12. The scheme here is adapted from Charles Perrow's article, "A Framework for the Comparative Analysis of Organizations," *American Sociological Review,* Vol. 32, No. 2 (April, 1967).
13. Burton R. Clark and Martin Trow, "The Organizational Context," chap. ii in Theodore M. Newcomb and Everett K. Wilson (eds.), *College Peer Groups* (Chicago: Aldine Publishing Co., 1966 copyright © by National Opinion Research Center), pp. 20–24.
14. Werner Landecker, "Types of Integration and their Measurement," *American Journal of Sociology,* Vol. 61 (January, 1951), p. 336.

TABLES

7.1 Adapted from Theodore M. Newcomb, *The Acquaintance Process* (New York: Holt, Rinehart & Winston, Inc., 1961), pp. 99–102, *passim.*

7.5 Bureau of the Census, "Current Population Reports: Consumer Income," Series P–60, No. 58 (Washington, D.C.: U.S. Government Printing Office, April 4, 1969), Table F, p. 6.

FIGURES

7.1 Bureau of the Census, *Historical Statistics of the United States, 1789–1957; Continuation to 1962 and Revisions* (Washington, D.C.: U.S. Government Printing Office, 1965), Series A20, A52, A53, A56 and A57, pp. 8 and 9 and 1, respectively.

7.2 *Ibid.,* Series A59 and A65, pp. 9 and 1, respectively.

7.3 Adapted from Bureau of the Census, "Household Income in 1967 by Selected Characteristics of the Head," *Current Population Reports,* Series P–60, No. 57

(Washington, D.C.: U.S. Government Printing Office, 1968), Table 2, p. 3.

7.4 Bureau of the Census, "Income in 1967 of Families in the United States," *Current Population Reports,* Series P–60, No. 59 (Washington, D.C.: U.S. Government Printing Office, 1969), Table 2, p. 22.

7.5 Chauncey D. Harris and Edward L. Ullman, "The Nature of Cities," in Paul K. Hatt and Albert J. Reiss, Jr. (eds.), *Cities and Society* (New York: Free Press, 1957). © 1951, 1957 by The Free Press; reprinted with permission.

7.6 Leo F. Schnore, "Urban Structure and Suburban Selectivity," *Demography,* Vol. 1 (1964), Table 3, p. 168.

7.7 Clifford R. Shaw *et al., Delinquency Areas* (Chicago: University of Chicago Press, 1942), p. 69. © by the University of Chicago; used by permission.

7.8 Bureau of the Census, based on data supplied in a special prepublication compilation by the Census of Religious Bodies.

chapter 8 Social Structure: stratification

She thinks that even up in heaven
Her class lies late and snores,
While poor black cherubs rise at seven
To do celestial chores.
Countee Cullen, *Epitaph: A Lady I Know*

The sole equality on earth is death.
Philip James Bailey, *A Country Town*

Men make distinctions between better and worse: they have values. Those who have most of the good—however "good" is defined—stand higher. *Stratification* means the hierarchical ordering of social positions (and the roles associated with these positions) along the scale of a group's values. Different locations in the stratification system (classes) always point to inequalities in the possession of things valued by the group: virtue, wealth, wisdom, virility, grace, valor, skill, saintliness.

We prefer, for example, more pay to less pay and higher rank to lower. This is well reflected in the highly stratified realm of the military. (See Figure 8.1.) In the distribution of rewards and punishments in our society, we have preferred white to black. Thus the more highly valued jobs—as professionals, technical workers, managers, and officials—have gone mainly to whites: in 1962, among male employed persons, 27.6 percent of whites, 8.2

Figure 8.1

Monthly base pay by rank for U.S. military personnel having 10 to 12 years of service

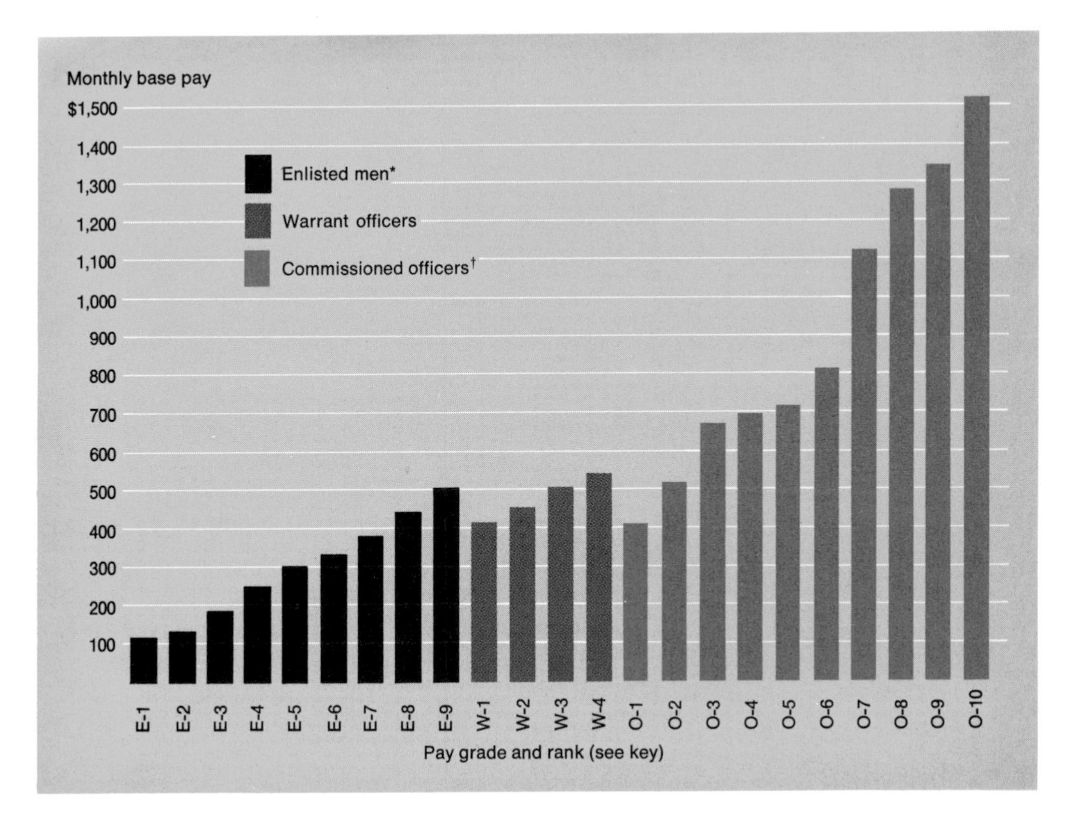

* Grade	Army	Air Force	Marine	Navy & Coast Guard
E-9	Sergeant Major	Chief Master Sergeant	Sergeant Major—Master Gunnery Sgt.	Master Chief Petty Officer
E-8	First Sergeant—Master Sergeant	Senior Master Sergeant	First Sergeant—Master Sergeant	Senior Chief Petty Officer
E-7	Sergeant 1st Class—Spec. 7	Master Sergeant	Gunnery Sergeant	Chief Petty Officer
E-6	Staff Sergeant—Spec. 6	Technical Sergeant	Staff Sergeant	Petty Officer 1st Class
E-5	Sergeant—Spec. 5	Staff Sergeant	Sergeant	Petty Officer 2d Class
E-4	Corporal—Spec. 4	Airman First Class	Corporal	Petty Officer 3d Class
E-3	Private First Class	Airman Second Class	Lance Corporal	Seaman
E-2	Private	Airman Third Class	Private First Class	Seaman Apprentice
E-1	Private	Airman Basic	Private	Seaman Recruit

† Grade	Army, Air Force, and Marine Corps	Navy & Coast Guard
0-10	General	Admiral
0-9	Lt. General	Vice Admiral
0-8	Major General	Rear Admiral
0-7	Brig. General	Rear Admiral
0-6	Colonel	Captain
0-5	Lt. Colonel	Commander
0-4	Major	Lt. Commander
0-3	Captain	Lieutenant
0-2	First Lieutenant	Lieutenant (j.g.)
0-1	Second Lieutenant	Ensign

percent of blacks where in these preferred occupations.[1] Similarly, South Carolina rewarded whiteness by assigning 160 out of 161 draft board positions to whites in 1967.* Valuing high income, public service, and social prestige, Americans quite consistently rate Supreme Court Justices and physicians at the top of the occupational pyramid, college professors over ministers and these, in turn and in descending order, over bankers, public school teachers, novelists, reporters, mail carriers, garage mechanics, and restaurant cooks. We value virtue and assign the first citizens of the City of God high standing in the City of Man. (See Table 8.1.) We value education: those having more of it get higher incomes. The data in Table 8.2 are typical of findings on parallel inequalities in education and income.[2]

Thus we differentiate status and role along the scale of group values. It follows, then, that relationships are similarly differentiated. Roles characteristic of a given class (parental roles, work roles, the roles of communicant, or citizen) build into characteristic class-linked types of relationships. We have much evidence as to how parent-child relationships differ by class. Middle-class children are exposed to influences quite different from those affecting their lower-class counterparts.[3] They are more often controlled through reasoning, an inculcated sense of guilt, or the threat of withholding love. The working-class parent more readily resorts to physical punishment. Among middle-class parents, punishment hinges on the child's intent, while the lower-class parent fixes on the tangible outcomes of misbehavior. Kohn's work shows marked differences between these two classes in the values that guide parental behavior.[3] Thus research reveals rather different parent-child relationships, by class.

If roles and relationships differ by class, so too, we would expect, would the standards guiding behavior and belief. Thus the sociologist studying social stratification reveals an otherwise invisible structure of rules, roles, and relationships.

Explaining the class structure

To describe is not to explain. How do we account for the existence of classes? Why is it that the garbage man (or sanitary en-

* See Aside on Methods, Number 10, page 636.

Table 8.1

Variations, by historical periods, in number and percentage of saints in three class categories*

Historical period, centuries	Upper		Middle		Lower		Total	
	N	%	*N*	%	*N*	%	*N*	%
1st–5th	574	67	225	26	57	7	856	100
6th–10th	724	95	30	4	6	1	760	100
11th–15th	488	83	76	13	24	4	588	100
16th–20th	159	55	96	33	35	12	290	100
Total	1,945	78	427	17	122	5	2,494	100

* Saints were assigned to the upper class if they were landed nobility; to the middle class if they had been merchants, industrialists, professionals, or free farmers; and to the lower class if they were manual workers. The investigators report that assignments to middle and lower class were sometimes problematic. But they could determine quite surely whether a saint belonged in the upper class. (As the data indicate, 78 percent of the 2,494 saints did come from upper-class backgrounds.)

Some of the George's data for upper- and middle-class categories are in error: there are five fewer in the upper class and five more in the middle class. But this difference is too slight to affect the percentage distribution.

Table 8.2

Median 1968 U.S. income by level of education achieved by family heads and related individuals aged 25 or older

Level of education	Median income
Elementary school:	
Fewer than eight years	$ 5,172
Eight years	6,874
High school:	
One to three years	8,182
Four years	9,520
College:	
One to three years	10,864
Four years	13,110
Five years or more	14,135

gineer) is less rewarded than the physician? The former comes sooner to productive labor and makes a social contribution. And despite the fact that he lacks the privilege of extensive education, he promotes the health and welfare of his community engaging, as he does, in preventive medicine. Why, then, his lower standing?

Various theories have been proposed, none of them entirely satisfactory. One argument has it that classes arise when the more

. . . Why, then,
his
lower standing?

. . . Through the family
we get . . . reputation
and position
. . . race, sex,
and nationality. . . .

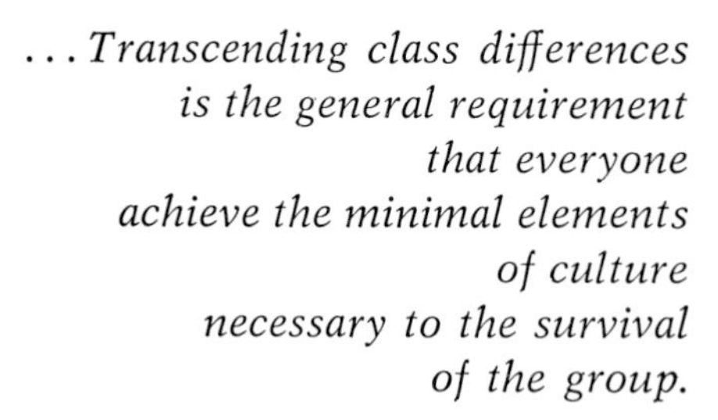

. . . Transcending class differences
is the general requirement
that everyone
achieve the minimal elements
of culture
necessary to the survival
of the group.

*. . . class conditions our pleasures.
Simply to enumerate a variety of sports
suggests the likelihood of class distinctions . . . .*

*. . . class conditions,
but it does not
irrevocably determine.
There is a good deal
of individual mobility.*

powerful require the powerless to do society's dirty work. Thus conquerors subordinate the vanquished, masters rule the slaves. Myths are elaborated to legitimate the preferred position of the masters. The slave's position is then said to be his natural state, stemming from his primitive, childlike traits, his limited intellect, his elemental emotions. From this it follows that the institutions of the privileged would be wasted on the inferior ones. Hence, not being exposed to civilizing influences, deprivation and backwardness are perpetuated, giving substance to alleged inferiority.

At certain times and places this explanation may help us understand the grosser sorts of stratification (forceful domination and submission). One thinks of slaves in American society and the policy of apartheid in South Africa. But one thinks, too, of the emphasis in American society, on assimilating the immigrant, and the great stress on fighting to the top, no matter how humble one's origins. On the whole, this explanation doesn't help much in understanding the enormously complicated hierarchy of positions that characterize the class system in our society. And it depends too much on the conscious calculations and conspiratorial shrewdness of an elite to fit the traditional deprecation of class in American society.

Another argument follows this line: Social relationships necessitate norms that guide conduct in predictable (and desirable) ways. But people differ in their biological and social ancestry. Hence they will fulfill these norms in differing degree. When they perform as prescribed (or overperform) they are rewarded; oth-
Others may be derided as spinelessly lazy or irresponsible.) And
erwise they are punished. (The hardworking man gains approval.
since meeting (or failing to meet) these expectations moves people toward positions of advantage (or disadvantage), the positions themselves are invested with unequal prestige or power or pay. (Medical education is stiff, weeding out those unable to perform. Hence being an M.D. means being able to meet peoples' expectations of performance in accordance with professional norms.)[4]

This theory tells us something about the inevitability of unequal rewards. But this is no revelation. All our observations confirm the ubiquity of inequality. The problem is not so much to explain its inevitability as to understand why it takes such various forms. Under what conditions are class strata few and simple? Or numerous and complex? Why do we sometimes find stress on biological breeding? Or on social breeding? Or on personal achievement quite regardless of background?

Another theory, proposed by Davis and Moore,[5] does try to explain the forms that stratification takes: who gets more of whatever is valued, and why. Their argument runs something like this: To sustain a human group requires that a number of tasks be done. These tasks differ in their importance to the group, in their desirability (as indicated by commonly shared values), and in their difficulty, including the training required for their performance. Now if certain tasks are especially important, people must be induced to do them despite their difficulty and the investment of time, energy, and money needed to train for them. This is accomplished by boosting the rewards, material and psychic. Thus there comes to be a hierarchy of unequally rewarded positions.

A chief difficulty in explaining something that is universally found is this: there is no way of determining what would happen in its absence. We are reduced to after-the-fact reasoning. Here we say: since everywhere we find medicine men, they must be functionally important in their societies. Therefore they will be highly rewarded. But we have no way of demonstrating that their social function is the *source* of high rewards. For we can't test whether, in the absence of such functions (or their being carried out some other way) the stratification system would change.

In any case, the pressing research question is this: How do stratification systems differ, and how can we explain the differences?

Different bases of stratification: ascription and achievement

A person's standing depends both on who he *is* and what he *does*.

> As a member of a family the young person's relationship with others is defined by who he is instead of what he can do. As he moves out from under the family umbrella, his peer group serves as a transitional setting. In it he moves from particularistic toward universalistic role prescriptions, from roles based upon ascription to those increasingly defined by demonstrated achievement.[6]

The family is the important source of those ascribed traits that have some influence on class standing. Indeed, a social class has been defined as "a large group of families [which] are approximately equal to each other and clearly differentiated from other families. . . ."[7] Through the family we get our initial standing: it confers its own reputation and position, endows us with race, sex, and nationality and probably with religious preferences. Such class-linked family influences launch the young on differing social trajectories (Recall our definition of the field). This is crudely represented in Figure 8.2.

The criterion at work here, conditioning one's class standing and so, in turn, affecting future relationships, is that of *ascription*. The person's standing is ascribed, and in good measure his several roles prescribed, by the accident of birth. Speaking of religion, a trait immediately conferred by our parents, Cleveland Amory writes:

> Boston is 2,350,000 people [but] Boston society according to the Boston Social Register is 8,000 people. Yet to the Proper Bostonian this volume which admits only one Jewish man and, in a city now 70 percent Catholic . . . less than a dozen Catholic families, is impossibly large.[8]

Nor is standing ascribed only on the basis of one's immediate family position. A *New York Times* obituary reports the death of a woman of modest achievement. (She studied at a school for girls in Illinois and at a business college in Iowa.) But she had forebears who fought in the French and Indian War, the Revolution, and the War of 1812. On these grounds she gained membership in the Daughters of Founders and Patriots, the Daughters of Colonial Wars, the Society of Colonial Dames, the Colonial Daughters of the Seventeenth Century, the Daughters of 1812, the Order of the Crown, the Order of Lafayette, the Mary Washington Memorial Association, the Daughters of American Colonists, the National Society of Patriotic Women of America, and the Daughters of the American Revolution, which she served as president. Other affiliations, not necessarily stemming from standing ascribed to her on the basis of ancestor performance, were: the National Society of New England Women, the American Red Cross, the Greenwich Women's Club, the Colony Club of Detroit, the National Arts Club, the Women's National Republican Club of New York, and the American Women's Club in London.[9]

The criterion of ascription runs counter to the stress on equality of opportunity and demonstrated achievement—elements stressed in a democratic creed. "The citizen in a democratical government," wrote Ferguson, "cannot conceive [as do the European nobility] how a man that is born free should be inferior to another, who does not excell him in parts, integrity, or in service

Figure 8.2

Differing antecedent relationships have differing consequences

The class structure represented is what A. B. Hollingshead found in Elmtown. But the particular division into classes is irrelevant for the point made here.

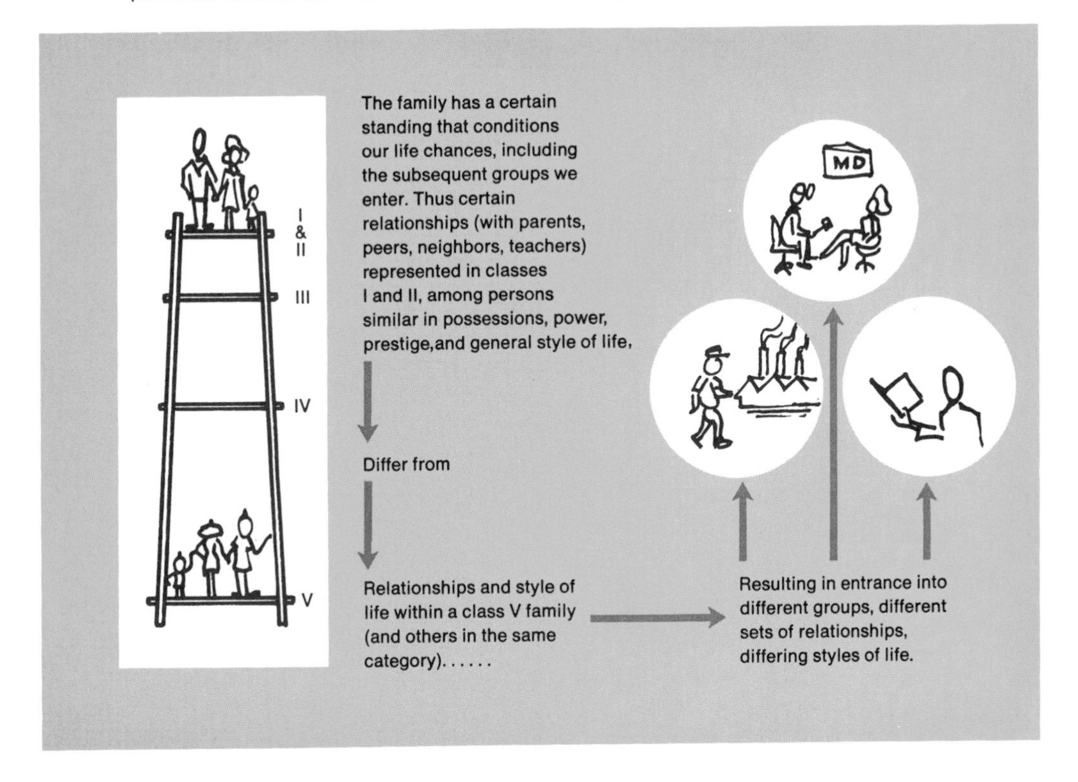

performed to his country."[10] Yet, even in a "democratical" country such as ours, standing may be ascribed on the basis of traits irrelevant to performance. Our inheritance practices put blood ties over achievement. Standing, higher or lower, is ascribed on the basis of race. And it is hard to divest the names of the Cabots, the Lowells, and the Lodges of a certain celestial aura quite independent of demonstrable achievement.

I & II
III
IV
V
The family has a certain standing that conditions our life chances, including the subsequent groups we enter. Thus certain relationships (with parents, peers, neighbors, teachers) represented in classes I and II, among persons similar in possessions, power, prestige,and general style of life,
Differ from
Relationships and style of life within a class V family (and others in the same category)......
Resulting in entrance into different groups, different sets of relationships, differing styles of life.
MD

Thus ascribed traits—father's occupation, a WASP*-ish background, forebears who were colonial warriors, belonging to minority ethnic groups—condition our destinies. This is what Max Weber had in mind when he defined class as a category of persons

* White, Anglo-Saxon Protestant.

having similar life chances.* When people's life chances are immutably set by the accident of birth—when whom one marries, works with, eats, plays, and worships with is predetermined by the position of the family of orientation—we have a caste system.

> O let us love our occupations
> Bless the squire and his relations
> Live upon our daily rations
> And always know our proper station.[11]

> The rich man in his castle,
> The poor man at his gate,
> God made them, high or lowly
> And order'd their estate.[12]

Caste, to rely on Weber again, is the fixing and legitimation of social distance by a religious principle. It is prescribed by God and nature that the son's pattern of roles and relationships shall parallel the father's. Such a situation, only remotely approximated in most societies (as, for example, in white-black relationships in the United States) may be thought of as the limiting case. In actuality, the traits affecting the person's destiny are a complex amalgam, including those *taught* as well as those caught (ascribed to him as a member of a given family).

Traits taught, or learned, imply achievement, a second criterion of standing. If ascribed traits refer to the past, the person's achieved traits point to the present and to the characteristics required by the position. A given occupation, for example, will require certain skills and knowledge. It may require the person to

* For Weber, class was based on wealth. What he says is this: A class consists in a category of persons having a ". . . typical chance for a supply of goods, external living conditions, and personal life experiences, in so far as this chance is determined by the amount and kind of power. . . to dispose of goods or skills for the sake of income in a given economic order." Or, again, "We may speak of a 'class' when (1) a number of people have in common a specific causal component of their life chances, in so far as (2) this component is represented exclusively by economic interests in the possession of goods and opportunities for income, and (3) is represented under the conditions of the commodity or labor markets" (H. H. Gerth and C. Wright Mills, *From Max Weber: Essays in Sociology* [New York: Oxford University Press, Inc., 1946], p. 181).

† This is not to imply that the standing accorded a position is immutably fixed by impersonal law. Position incumbents do band together—the AMA, trade unions, and others—to enhance their standing and increase their rewards. Science and technology change the reward structure: the airlines pilot outstrips the railroad engineer, while the TV repairman may reap more rewards than the teacher.

make decisions and exercise authority. It will reward the incumbent with a certain income and a degree of prestige. These are attached to the position. For example, we know that there is marked agreement among Americans on the relative prestige of occupations. This is true despite differences among the people ranking occupations—differences in sex, age, education, and occupation. So it would seem that the position itself accounts for the prestige rather than characteristics ascribed to the incumbent.†

But ascription and achievement are not independent determinants of class standing. For ascription interacts with achievement. What is caught (parental position and opportunities conferred by family membership) affects what is taught and learned, that is to say, achieved. Some children of the "rich, the wellborn, and the able" may have the motivation and knowledge, the skills and values (for example, dedication to public service) to merit through achievement the high standing ascribed to them through their families. Differences in ascribed status make for differences in achievement. And conversely, what is taught (achieved through the person's own efforts) may modify or supersede what is caught (ascribed to him through his family's standing), so distinguishing the person's position and prospects from those of his parental family. In the United States, personal achievement through education is for some an important way of altering the social trajectory implicit in the family's position. Education may modify the impact of ascription in three ways: by responding to the unique set and sequence of experiences endowing each person with his individuality, by inculcating cultural universals that mute class-linked differences, and by teaching/training in a great range of specialties. Consider the second and third points.

While much of what is taught varies by class, the elementary aspects of culture are transmitted to all. For some, learning has to do with achieving capabilities universally required of all members of the group. Certain common learnings—among us, the three R's, a general morality, the common meanings of a common citizenship—must be achieved by all to be identified as citizens of the United States. Transcending class differences is the general requirement that everyone achieve the minimal elements of culture necessary to the survival of the group. Such common learnings tend to mute or mask class differentials.

But beyond these common achievements there is, in a complex society like ours, an extraordinary specialization in subgroups, chiefly occupational ones. Doctors, lawyers, merchantmen, chiefs, rich men, poor men, beggarmen, thieves—these are but the faintest intimation of the range of our more than 20,000 occupational specialties.* The achievement of these specialized learnings works against ascriptive classifications, making for social mobility and altering class lines.

So class standing depends both on what is caught and what is taught, on ascription and achievement. And since not all sorts and degrees of achievement are equally valued in any human society, the rewards conferred will vary. They vary, too, along the road to some terminal role. Typically, membership in one group requiring less achievement and conferring slighter rewards is prerequisite to membership in another involving more achievement and greater rewards. In scouting we have the tenderfoot, the second-class scout, first-class, star, life, and eagle scouts. In the United States civil service we have ratings from G–1 to G–14, with power, responsibility, and income differentiated accordingly. In academic ranks we have student assistants, instructors, and assistant, associate, and full professors. As we have seen, there is a lengthy hierarchy in military occupations. Battle and campaign ribbons, the Congressional Medal of Honor, decals on fuselage of plane or prow of ship also symbolize a sort of collective rank and achievement. In business there are chairmen of the board, directors of the corporation, presidents, vice presidents, staff officers, plant managers, superintendents, and so on down the ladder, with rewards ostensibly geared to demonstrated achievement. So also in the church, from postulant to mother superior, from parish priest to Pope. In each case, we have the hierarchical ordering of roles along the yardstick of some scale of values, with a corresponding differentiation in possessions, power, prestige, privilege, and duties.

The conservatism of class

Several aspects of American society tend to qualify clear and sharp class lines: the number of discernible levels, alternate paths to success, the numerous ways in which persons are ranked, the common training of group members in the "universals," the

* See the *Dictionary of Occupational Titles*. 3d ed. (Department of Labor, USGPO, 1965).

education of specialists, technological innovation, and a changing occupational structure. Given motivation, education, and persistent industry, class position need not follow automatically from that of the parental family. But these attributes, despite the Horatio Alger ethos, are not readily given. It is probably accurate to say that the tendency in a social order, even one so rapidly changing as ours, is a conservative one. If parents provide the model for the child, if class characteristics are mediated through family and school, if "childhood shows the man, as morning shows the day," then the social order is sustained. And on the whole there does seem an inertia in social systems making such recapitulation the rule rather than the exception.

Of course, I do not mean that a given generation impresses, in intricate detail, its mold upon its successor: that the son of a Methodist, Republican plumber invariably echoes his father's religious and political sentiments while fitting and repairing pipes. But the data do indicate that a higher than expected number of professionals are drawn from the ranks of professionals; that the plumber's son is likely to have less expectation of, aspiration for, and access to, the preparation necessary to become a professional. The tendency toward intergenerational recapitulation stems from an early differentiation of life chances in the context of family, friends, neighborhood, and school. The fortunes, like "the sins of the father, are to be laid upon the children." For example, Natalie Rogoff's research shows how roles emptied of the fathers tend to be refilled by the sons.

> One of the recurrent findings in . . . research on occupational mobility is that sons are more likely to enter their father's occupation than to enter any other single occupation. This is upheld, without exception, by the data in this study. . . . Stability is always greater than average mobility into or out of an occupation. However, there are variations in these measures from one occupation to another.[13]

Some correlates of class

Class implies a set of influences, a circle of exposures commonly experienced by a category of persons. Within a given class we find people with whom we can talk intelligibly, who live in similar houses, read similar magazines, enjoy the same sorts of music, have similar educations, similar occupations, similar aspirations. Since most of us are class-bound provincials, we are often not aware of the impact of class.

One task of the sociologist is to assess this impact: the connection between class and fertility, class and longevity, class and sexual behavior, class and child-rearing patterns, class and religious conduct, class and the extent, types, and treatment of mental illness—in short, class and style of life. Class has been a good predictor of behavior and belief because it captures a complex cluster of variables that create

> different basic conditions of life at different levels of the social order. Members of different social classes, by virtue of enjoying (or suffering) different conditions of life, come to see the world differently—to develop different conceptions of social reality, different . . . hopes and fears, different conceptions of the desirable.[14]

Methods of measuring the independent variable

In teasing out the correlates of class, a necessary first step is to get measures on the independent variable—i.e., to assign respondents accurately to a class position. This has been done in various ways. We shall review four of these methods.

First, there is the method of self-rating in which the person is asked to classify himself as being, for example, in the upper, middle, lower, or working class. While such subjective ratings may correlate with other variables, the method suffers certain defects. Respondents may not be willing or able to place themselves accurately. Responses vary, too, depending on the words used to describe class positions. For example, persons who might otherwise classify themselves as middle or upper class will sometimes shift to "worker" when it is offered as an option.

A second method uses several dimensions in an effort to get an objective index of a family's position. In an early study of stratification in Newburyport, Massachusetts,[15] Warner rated his families on four seven-point scales: occupational standing, source of income (whether from inheritance, earned, from profits and fees, from salary, wages, private or public relief), type of house, and area lived in. Greatest weight was given occupation: its scale score was weighted by a factor of four. Scores on source of income and type of house lived in were multiplied by three. The area-lived-in score was doubled. The sum of these weighted scores provided a measure of a family's class standing.*

A third method works with the reputation a family has among others in the community. This was the method employed by Hollingshead in his study, *Elmtown's Youth.*[16] From a careful analysis of lengthy interviews with 50 persons, Hollingshead was able to sort out the criteria people used to rate other families in the community. In the interviews his respondents mentioned specific families by name. Eventually, then, he was able to identify 20 families on whose relative standing there was high agreement. Then he used these families' names as points along a scale—points to help his judges as they tried to assign other families to their correct class positions. Each family was rated by seven or more judges, resident in the community for at least 20 years and not having close relatives in the study. This measure of the independent variable allowed Hollingshead to predict from family class position a host of adolescent behaviors: vocational aspirations, school grades, drop-out rates, dating patterns, leisure-time activities, and the like.

A fourth method employs a single objective measure as an index of class standing: education, income, or occupation. A good example is the National Opinion Research Center's study of the prestige accorded 90 occupations by a national sample of respondents. Each person falling in the sample rated each occupation on a five-point scale depending on his appraisal of the occupation as having excellent, good, average, below average, or poor standing. These five ratings were arbitrarily assigned scores of 100, 80, 60, 40, and 20. The average of all the ratings assigned a given occupation was the measure of its relative standing. As a matter of interest, Table 8.3 reproduces the first occupation and every third thereafter from the list of 90 occupations, along with the prestige score and rank.

A satisfactory measure of the independent variable should be a stable one, not changing much through time and, preferably, working as well in other places as it does in American society. These are two characteristics of the NORC scale of occupational prestige. The first research was done in 1947. A replication in 1963 made it possible to assess the stability of this measure. The agree-

* For example, top ratings might go to a physician, independently wealthy, living in a large, well-furnished town house in the most desirable (as a real estate agent would see it) part of town. Scoring and weighting these correlates of class gives us: 7×4 (occupation) $+ 7 \times 3$ (source of income) $+ 7 \times 3$ (type of house), and 7×2 (area lived in) for a total of 84. Thoreau, living at Walden Pond, would have rated $1 \times 4 + 1 \times 3 + 1 \times 3 + 1 \times 2$ for a total of 12.

ment was almost perfect as measured by a correlation of .99 between the 1947 and 1963 ratings.

Furthermore, as Table 8.4 shows, the measure is quite stable from country to country. (One might enter some reservations: the study designs of the six surveys were not altogether comparable, and some of the studies were not based on national samples. Even so, the strength of the relationships suggests strong agreement across different societies and cultures on the relative rank of occupations.) The extent of agreement on occupational prestige is weakest between the U.S.S.R. and Japan. (Only 54 percent of the variance is explained by a correlation of .74.) On the other hand, there is almost complete agreement between the Great Britain and New Zealand samples, Great Britain and Germany, and the United States and New Zealand. It's fair to assume that we have, in occupational prestige, a useful, transnational index of class.

Dependent variables: the correlates

Having some measure of class standing, the sociologist can move on to test some hypotheses asserting a relationship between class and a host of dependent variables. Much work has been done on stratification, and I shall offer here only a few illustrations that suggest the range of social life affected by class: race and position in the labor force, demographic variables (longevity, fertility, and mortality), style of life (distribution of expenditures, places where people live, choice of spouses and friends, and social and spatial barriers between classes), and class-linked behaviors and beliefs (mental health, aesthetic preferences, and desires, aspirations, and pleasures).

Class and race

In the United States, aside from sex, that attribute (with the ascribed and often fictitious traits associated with it) most firmly fixing destiny, values, and style of life, is race. Figure 8.3 provides a graphic description of the relation between class and a castelike racial division (white and Negro).

The first figure might be taken to represent something close to the pre–Civil War class and caste structure in the United States with the most privileged Negro yet more deprived than the lowest-class white. Stage 3 (*c*) shows the caste-line axis having been ro-

Table 8.3

Occupational prestige scale—1963

Occupation	Prestige score	Rank
U.S. Supreme Court Justice	94	1.0
Scientist	92	3.5*
Cabinet member in the federal government	90	8.0
Chemist	89	11.0
Dentist	88	14.0
Psychologist	87	17.5
Mayor of a large city	87	17.5
Civil engineer	86	21.5
Biologist	85	24.5
Captain in the regular army	82	27.5
Owner of a factory that employs about 100 people	80	31.5
Musician in a symphony orchestra	78	34.5
Official of an international labor union	77	37.0
County agricultural agent	76	39.0
Farm owner and operator	74	44.0
Newspaper columnist	73	46.0
Radio announcer	70	49.5
Insurance agent	69	51.5
A local official of a labor union	67	54.5
Traveling salesman for a wholesale concern	66	57.0
Playground director	63	62.5
Owner-operator of a lunch stand	63	62.5
Truck driver	59	67.0
Milk route man	56	70.0
Restaurant cook	55	72.5
Dockworker	50	77.5
Coal miner	50	77.5
Farmhand	48	83.0
Clothes presser in a laundry	45	85.0
Garbage collector	39	88.0

* Some rankings end in .5 results from two or more occupations being given the same prestige score by the national sample of respondents. Thus prestige scores of 94, 93, 93, and 92 might be ranked 1, 2.5, 2.5, and 4 (rather than 1, 2, 3, and 4).

Table 8.4

Correlations between prestige scores assigned to comparable occupations in six national studies

	U.S.S.R.	Japan	Great Britain	New Zealand	United States	Germany
U.S.S.R.		.74	.83	.83	.90	.90
Japan			.92	.91	.93	.93
Great Britain				.97	.94	.97
New Zealand					.97	.96
United States						.96
Average correlation	.84	.89	.93	.93	.94	.94

Figure 8.3

Class and castelike racial divisions

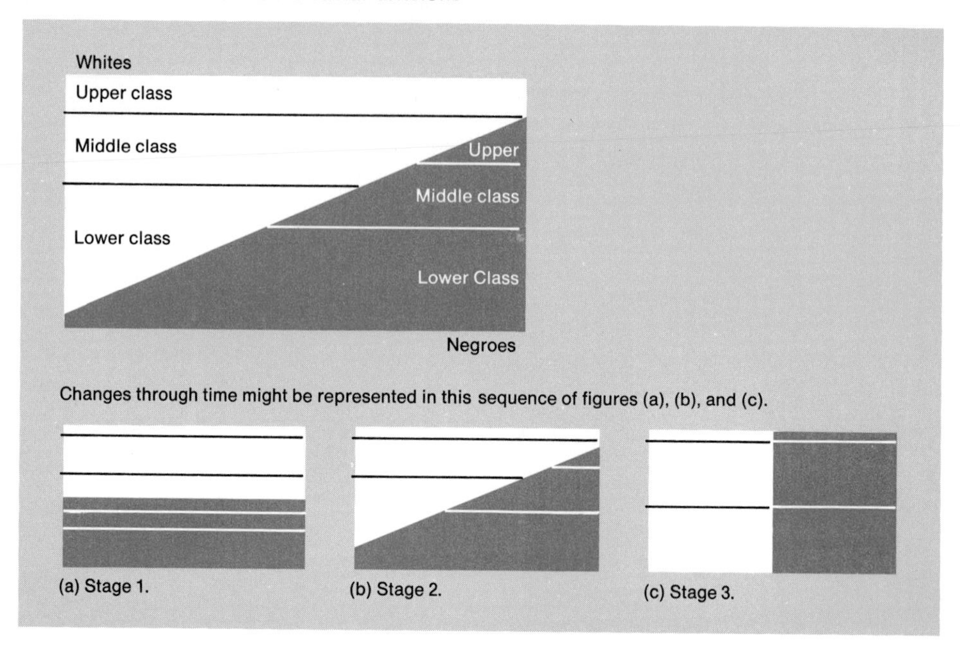

tated to a vertical position with property, prestige, and power equitably distributed between two separate but equal categories. This is the "apartheid" solution advocated by the nationalist descendants of the Boers in South Africa. This is an incongruous solution since, as Kahl points out, if members of two groups are in fact thought of as equal, nobody would bother to keep them apart. It is the solution rejected as spurious in the 1954 Supreme Court decision on segregation in the schools.

In our social order the tendency through time has been to diminish the significance of race as a criterion of status and opportunity. The democratic ethos, the findings of sociologists,* and

*I do not mean to suggest that there are no differences between race-labeled categories. We know that sickle-celled anemia is linked with Negroid attributes. But the differences of social significance—such as ability to perform in various work roles—appear to have social and cultural, not biological roots. Such differences may therefore be eliminated by social and cultural changes. A psychologist, Arthur Jensen, has interpreted the data relating race to I.Q. scores as meaning that genetic barriers may prevent us from completely closing the gap between measures of Negroid and Caucasian intelligence ("How Much Can We Boost I.Q. and Scholastic Achievement?" *Harvard Educational Review,* Vol. 39, No. 1 [Winter, 1969]). He tries, of course, to take account of the social dispossession that lowers Negro scores. Sociologists would take the position that race- and class-linked deprivation is so pervasive that, until these factors can be eliminated, it seems premature to attribute differences in achievement to race.

Figure 8.4

Percent distribution of employed whites and nonwhites by occupation group, United States, 1965*

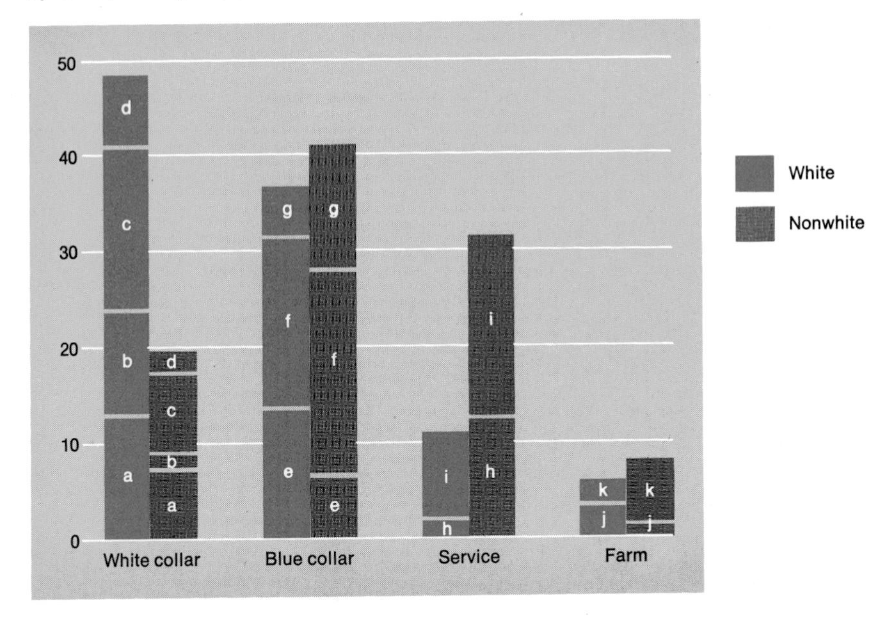

a—Professional and technical workers.
b—Managers, officials, and proprietors.
c—Clerical workers.
d—Sales workers.
e—Craftsmen and foremen.
f—Operatives.
g—Nonfarm laborers.
h—Private household workers.
i—Other service workers.
j—Farmers and managers.
k—Farm laborers and foremen.

* Percents sum to 100 for each race category.

the requirements of a competitive, instrumentally oriented culture shift the emphasis away from ascription and toward achievement as the criterion of status.

To the extent that this is so, we might expect opportunities for Negroes to multiply among the more rewarding occupations. To a modest degree this has happened in recent years. But, as Figure 8.4 shows, whites are skewed toward the more prestigeful, white-collar occupations, blacks toward the less rewarding ones.

Class and demographic variables

Demographic variables—longevity, fertility, mortality—correlate with class. Again using race as an index of social status, we find that at almost every age Negroes have fewer years yet to live than

Table 8.5

Differences between whites and nonwhites in years of life remaining at selected ages, by sex: United States, 1964

Age	Average number of years of life remaining					
	Males			Females		
	White	Nonwhite	Difference	White	Nonwhite	Difference
0	67.7	61.1	6.6	74.6	67.2	7.4
5	64.6	59.5	5.1	71.3	65.1	6.2
15	54.9	49.9	5.0	61.5	55.4	6.1
25	45.6	40.9	4.7	51.8	45.9	5.9
45	27.4	24.7	2.7	32.9	28.7	4.2
65	13.0	12.8	0.2	16.3	15.6	0.7
75	8.1	9.8	−1.7	9.6	11.1	1.5

whites (Table 8.5). At birth, a white infant can expect about seven more years of life than a Negro baby. For whites, the difference in longevity between top and bottom classes was about 10 years in 1920. By 1940, this length-of-life advantage for persons in the upper class had been cut to eight years.[17] As to fertility, for some decades there has been an inverse relationship between indices of class—occupational level, extent of education, size of income—and family size. In general, this still holds: but it is a weaker relationship than has obtained in the past.

Class and life styles

People differ, of course, by level of education achieved, and this may be used as an index of social status. Size of income is a clear-cut correlate of educational achievement, as Figures 8.5 and 8.6 vividly demonstrate. (These data were collected in March, 1967, from a national probability sample of some 52,000 households.)

Education, occupation, and income are linked variables. Since they represent such central spheres of life, we would expect them to have pervasive influences on life style. And so it is: differing life styles connected with class are revealed in many ways. The way a person spends his money may well indicate where his heart lies and what his head dictates. It seems reasonable to assume that his budget discloses conceptions of need, and of customary behavior, offering a clue to style of living. "The budget of an individual or family," says Warner, "is in part a symbol system, or a set of collective representations that expresses the social value of a per-

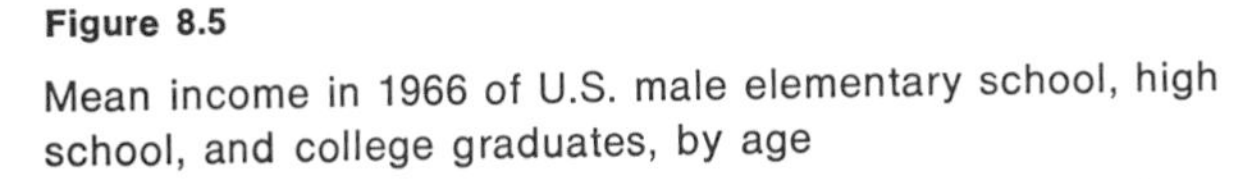

Figure 8.5

Mean income in 1966 of U.S. male elementary school, high school, and college graduates, by age

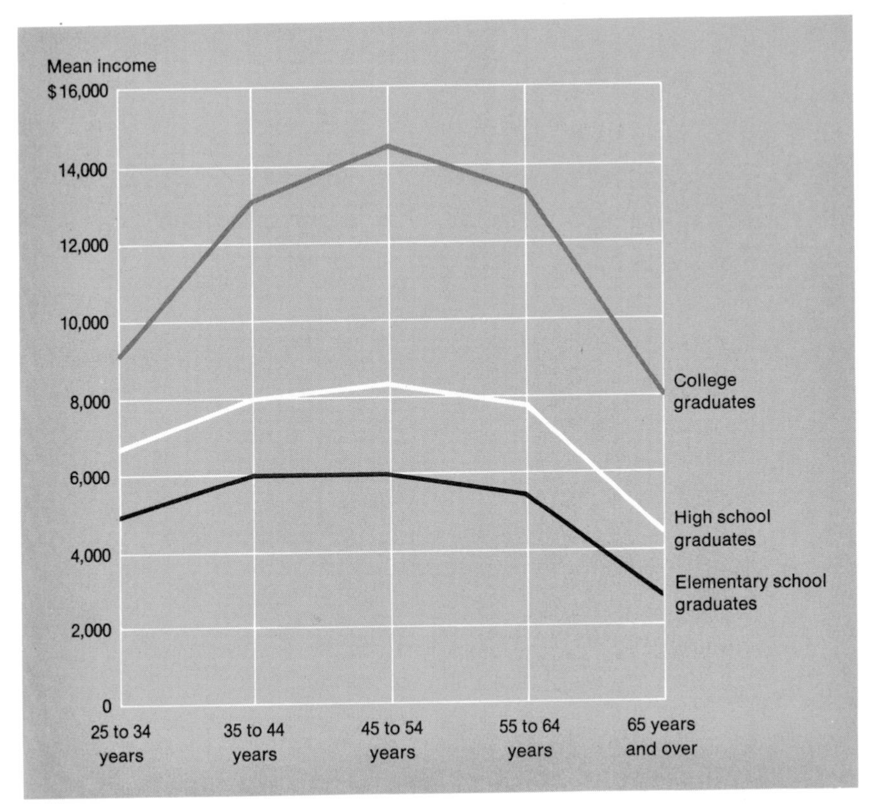

son's membership in a group life."[18] Warner's findings point up the necessary preoccupation of the lower-lower's with matters of the body;* the focus of the upper-upper's on matters moral, civic, intellectual, and interpersonal; the concern of the lower-upper's with the furniture of life—houses, cars, and boats—and with club memberships that provide useful symbols of election and foster

* George Orwell provides grim details of the necessary preoccupation of the poor with matters of sheer bodily sustenance in his *Down and Out in Paris and London* (London: Secker & Warburg, 1960). Orwell is writing of those whom Warner would call the lower-lowers. Warner elaborates the familiar trichotomy of class categories (upper, middle, and lower), subdividing each into three classes: hence the ninefold set of categories. These are: upper-upper, middle-upper, and lower-upper; upper-middle, middle-middle, and lower-middle; upper-lower, middle-lower, and lower-lower. (These labels have prompted the irreverent reference to their users as the dental plate school of stratification.) Of course, the investigator may not find, in a given community, families that fit all of these categories.

Figure 8.6

Estimated lifetime income for U.S. males 25 years and older by level of education achieved

Based on income and life expectancy experience of 1966 and 1956.

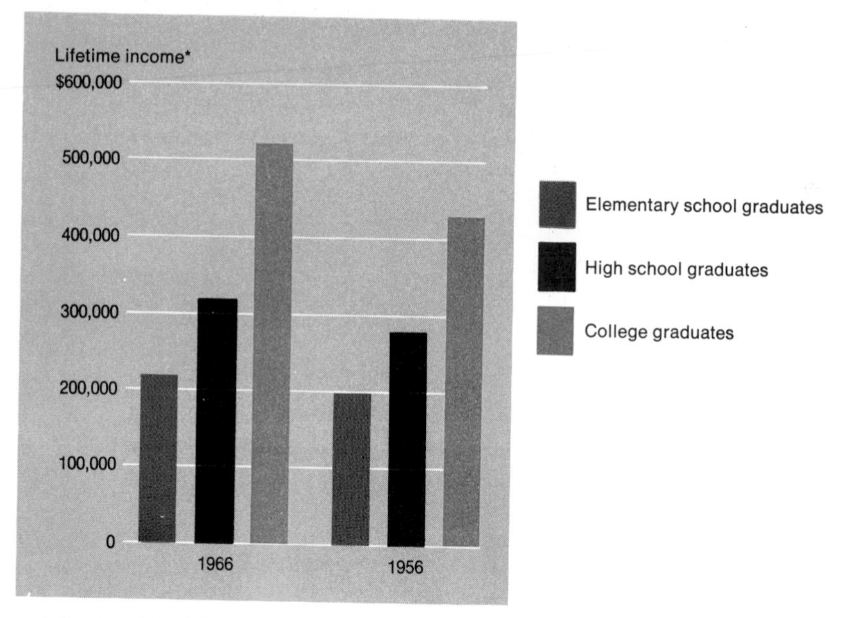

* Constant 1966 dollars.

profitable opportunities. The prominence of vacation travel and sporting equipment among Yankee City's lower-upper's might be interpreted as the necessary cost of a taut and stressful life oriented toward peak achievement.

Style of life is registered spatially. There is an interplay between attributes of people and their habitat. The rich and the wellborn commute from Long Island to the city by private launch, while those less able to buy distance live closer in and use conventional commuting techniques. Styles of life, then, come to be reflected in differing locations, differing habitats. These patterns are not randomly distributed in space. As a result, the person is exposed, not to the spectrum of cultural possibilities, but to those peculiar to his district, his zone, his neighborhood. And so to revert to the classic study by Warner, we have the Merrimac River serving to mark the least desirable neighborhood, the down-by-the-tracks area in Newburyport; and Hill street, at a higher elevation, is reserved for those of more elevated status. (The relation between physical and social altitude is an interesting question. Clearly the

Figure 8.7

Residential configuration of Yankee City: the ecology of life styles

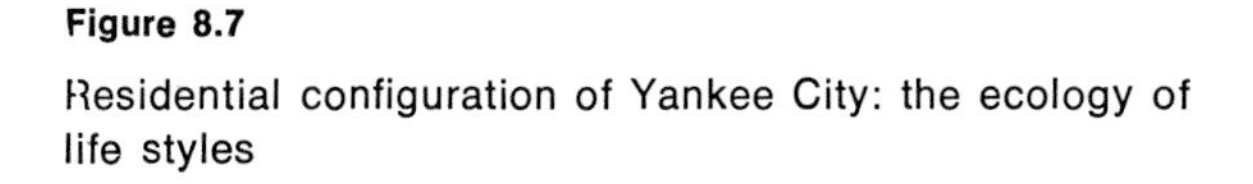

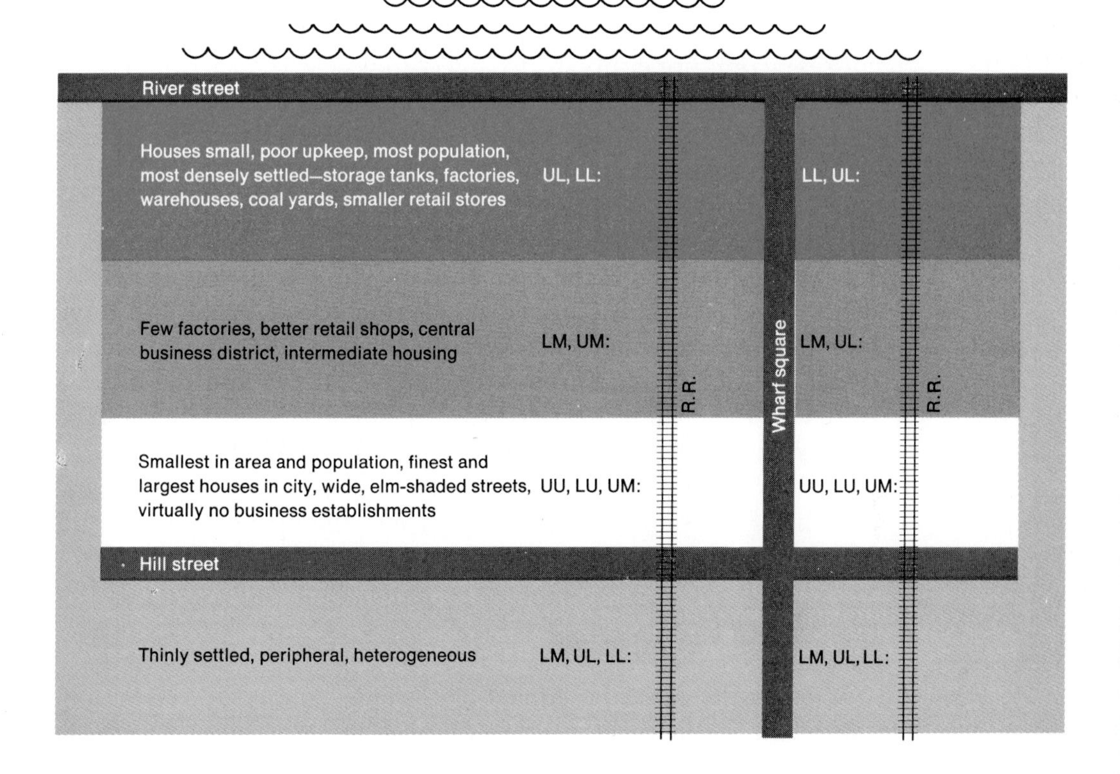

relationship is inverse for James West's subjects in Plainville.* On the other hand, casual observation would suggest that in cities, distance from industrial sites and transportation routes would prompt those able to bear the costs to seek the altitudes of urban America's Nob Hills.)

Figure 8.7 gives us some impression of the ecology of class, the geography of life styles. Table 8.6 offers supporting data. What concerns us here is the way in which these sequestered subcommunities provide a seedbed for different ways of life.

* James West, *Plainville, U.S.A.* (New York: Columbia University Press, 1945; a Columbia Paperback edition was published in 1961). In this community the good—and more costly—farmland lies low, along the river. The poorer families are higher, literally, although lower in standing, occupying the less desirable land. Clearly, neither vertical nor horizontal distance stands alone in reflecting class position. Land use is determined sometimes—perhaps too seldom—by planning commissions. Land zoned for particular uses modifies the distribution of residences—as do the now illegal restrictive covenants.

Class touches life patterns in innumerable ways. For example, there is a tendency for marriage to be intraclass.* This may be enforced by law where race (Negroes, Indians) reinforces other class attributes. Warner found that class was linked with the age at which people in Yankee City entered marriage. For the six classes from upper-upper to lower-lower, the median ages of marriage were 28, 27, 26, 25, 24, and 23.[19]

Modes of life are shaped and reinforced not only by the class of the family entered at birth and by intraclass marriage, but also by social and spatial barriers between classes.† Thus interaction comes to be predominantly intraclass. Stratification studies show repeatedly that this is the case. In their study of 199 male respondents, aged 30–49, in Cambridge, Massachusetts, Kahl and Davis found close correspondence between respondents' status (occupational prestige as measured on the NORC scale) and the average status of their three best friends.[20] Hollingshead's data on Elmtown show a strong tendency for clique relationships to be intraclass.[21] Warner found Yankee City cliques were formed with persons of the same or adjacent classes,[22] the intraclass-only tendency being strongest at the top and bottom of the class hierarchy.

Class-linked behaviors and beliefs

This being the case, the impact of class on the person tends to be consistent and persistent—affecting his attitudes, values, expectations, and aspirations. We saw in Chapter 5 some evidence of the power wielded by his associates over the person's views and values. We would predict, therefore, as a result of the channeled interaction associated with class position, a series of class-linked behaviors and beliefs. Consider as illustrations such subtle and

* The generality of this pattern is suggested by Levi-Strauss when he writes that ". . . each [Bororo] clan is subdivided into three groups: upper, middle, and lower. One regulation takes precedence over all others: that an 'upper' should marry another 'upper,' a 'middle' another 'middle,' and a 'lower' another 'lower.' Despite, that is to say, all the appearances of institutionalized brotherhood, the Bororo village is made up in the last analysis of three groups, each of which always marries within its own numbers" (Claude levi-Strauss, *Tristes Tropiques* [Paris: Librairie Plon, 1955], p. 230).

† Social barriers are erected and sustained through adverse stereotypes. People on the wrong side of the tracks, down by the canal (Elmtown), or down by the river (the "Riverbrookers," Yankee City) are those with whom the "right" people prefer not to associate, at least beyond the requirements of commercial transactions. "Riverbrookers," Warner writes, "were contemptuously referred to by all, their sexual morals were considered low, and their behavior was usually looked upon as ludicrous and uncouth. . . depreciatory stories were told despite the fact that it was easily verifiable that they were no

Table 8.6

Relationship between class and area lived in: Elmtown

Among other things this table tells us that all members of Classes 1 and 2 live in the preferred sections of Elmtown. They share these areas with 80 percent of the Class 3's, 18 percent of the Class 4's, and 2 percent of the Class 5's.

Area lived in	Classes 1 and 2	Class 3	Class 4	Class 5	Totals
"The 400" / Old Residential / West End	28 (8.1)	85 (30.9)	41 (64.5)	4 (54.7)	158
Down by the Mill / Mill Addition / Down by the Canal	0 (15.0)	20 (57.8)	158 (120.4)	117 (102.1)	295
North of the Tracks / Below the Canal	0 (4.9)	3 (19.4)	26 (40.2)	70 (34.2)	99
Totals	28	108	225	191	552

Note: Figures in parentheses are the frequencies that might be expected were there no relationship between class and place of residence. If the reader wishes to assess the significance of the difference between these and the observed frequencies, he can apply the χ^2 test discussed and illustrated in Aside on Methods, Number 5.

diverse concomitants of class as mental health, aesthetic preference, aspirations, and the use of leisure.

If psychic attributes are socially conditioned and if class is a significant social variable, then indices of mental health should vary with class position. If we take as an index of class the income and prestige associated with various occupations,‡ we find an inverse relationship with a number of psychotic conditions. In 1949, Professor Clark summarized his findings on white male first admissions for psychoses, admissions between 1922 and 1934, in

more true of Riverbrookers than they were of other classes. . . The low behavior was attributed to the Riverbrooker . . . *because* of his low social position" (W. Lloyd Warner (ed.), *Yankee City* [New Haven, Conn.: Yale University Press, 1963], p. 39).

This points to the probability that class may cause an unfavorable reputation as well as—or rather than—an unfavorable reputation causing lowered class status. But the point here is that such barrier-creating stereotypes reduce interclass, and intensify intraclass communication.

‡ Kahl and Davis report that occupation makes the best scale for "a measure of the over-all complex of class behavior" (Joseph A. Kahl, *The American Class Structure* [New York: Rinehart & Co., 1957], p. 46). But it is also true that a number of other variables are effective indicators of class standing. It's worth noting, also, that social change may render an index of class more, or less, adequate. For example, extension of education may make level of education achieved a useless index between 1st and 12th grades. Since everyone does it, there will be no variance and no variable.

Table 8.7

Income and prestige of 17 occupational categories related to various psychosis rates for white male first admissions

Type of psychosis	Occupational factor	
	Income	Prestige
Schizophrenia (all types)	−.71	−.81
Manic-depressive	−.02	−.01
Alcoholic psychoses	−.78	−.92
General paralysis	−.75	−.73
Senile psychoses and psychoses with arteriosclerosis	−.57	−.50
All psychoses	−.75	−.83

the Chicago area, as shown in Table 8.7. Similar findings came from a study of the diagnosis and treatment of persons under psychiatric care, either with a psychiatrist, a psychiatric clinic, or a mental hospital in the New Haven area. Figure 8.8 confirms and extends these findings. The complex linkage between class, a pattern of living, the ailments accompanying it, and their expression is suggested in this statement by the investigators:

> Psychosomatic reactions . . . are related inversely to class. The class IV's and the class V's somatize their complaints to a greater extent than class I, II and III patients. On the other hand, obsessive-compulsives are concentrated in classes I and II. The gradient for hysterical patients runs in the opposite direction; in this illness there is an extreme concentration in class V.[23]

Differing aesthetic preferences—although there are fewer data available—reflect differences in life patterns varying by class. The presence and kind of books on the shelves, pictures on the walls, magazines, newspapers and journals, flower arrangements, objets d'art, music and musical instruments—these may be conceived as instructive indexes of class-conditioned styles of life. One test of the link between class and musical preference was made by Professor Karl Schuessler. With the exception of popular music, he found strong associations between socioeconomic background and preference for various sorts of music: classical, jazz, hillbilly, and popular.

> These findings may be tentatively interpreted as follows: socioeconomic position operates to channelize experiences in such a way that a given individual tends to form a favorable attitude toward certain kinds of music, and music training

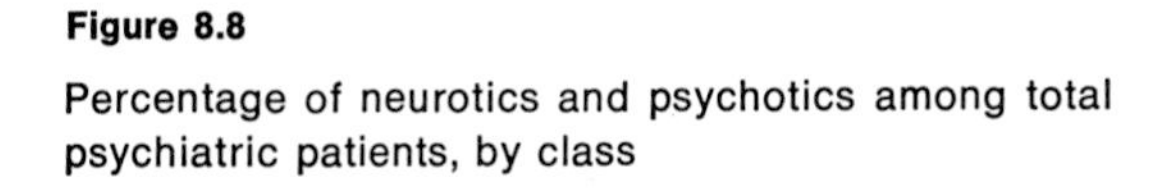

Figure 8.8

Percentage of neurotics and psychotics among total psychiatric patients, by class

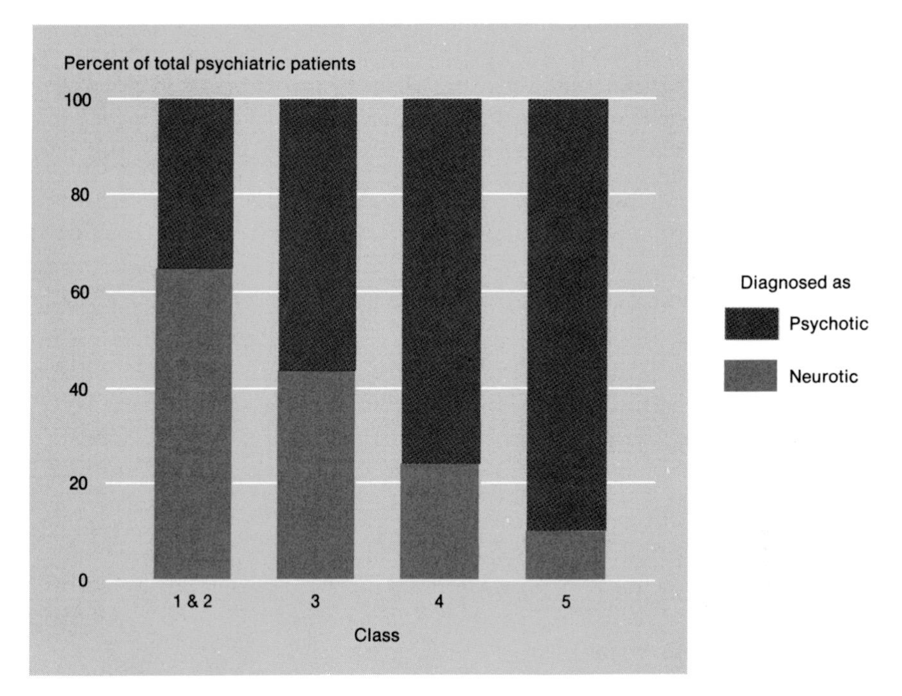

* But obviously the link between class and mental illness is extremely complex. See, for example, the work of Bruce and Barbara Dohrenwend, *Social Status and Psychological Disorder* (New York: Wiley, 1969).

> . . . has a pronounced influence on musical taste. Likewise, familiarity affects musical taste, and socioeconomic position may cause an individual to be *regularly exposed to some kinds of music and remain virtually isolated from other kinds.*[24]

Class differences correlate, too, with people's desires, aspirations, and pleasures. Figure 8.9 shows us how the vocational aspirations of 735 youth of high school age were linked to class position. Note the sharp relationship of the family's class position to professional aspirations. The apparent relationship between class and plans to go into farming may be misleading. Four of

Figure 8.9

The vocational aims of 735 Elmtown youth

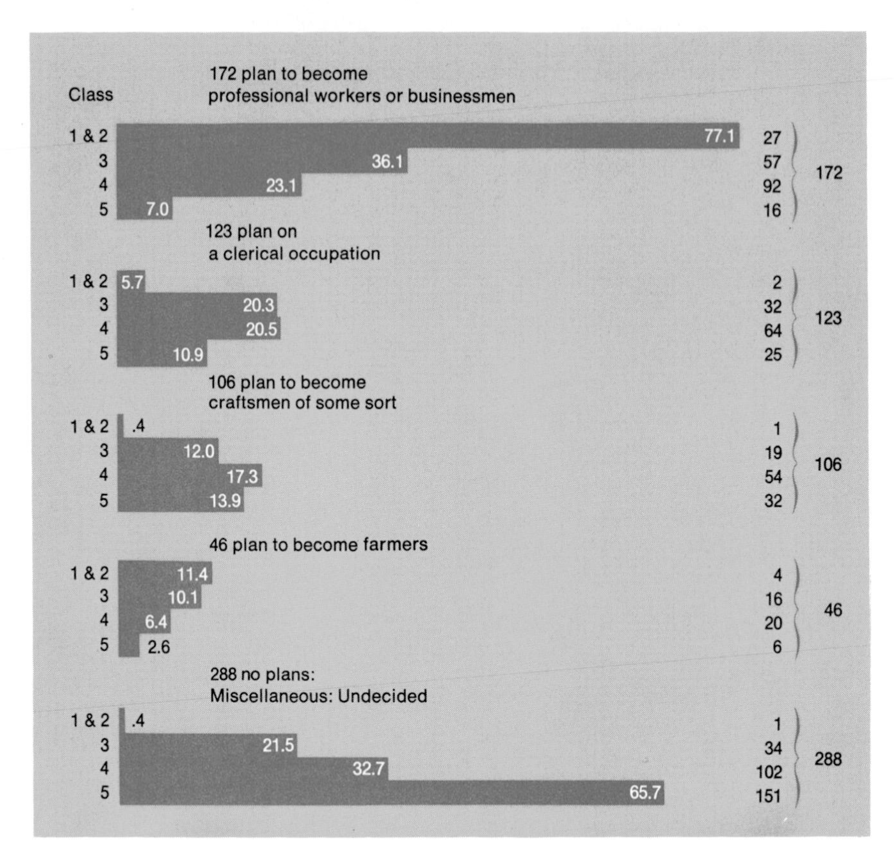

these 46 young people come from class 1 and class 2 families. They may very well mean by this that they plan to manage family-owned farms operated by tenants. At the bottom of Figure 8.9, the emphatic relationship between class and indecision should be noted. A plausible interpretation might be that young people in classes 4 and 5 are caught in a dilemma; the pressure to echo appropriate middle-class aspirations, on the one hand, and the felt unreality of such aspirations on the other. To respond as undecided is, then, a way out.

Figure 8.10 also takes people's desires and aspirations as the dependent variable. For each of four indices of class standing, we find that those having least, aspire least (insofar as recommending a college education is a clue to level of aspiration).

Figure 8.10

Percent of a national sample of respondents (NORC) deeming college education desirable in order for a young man to get along in the world, by four indices of class.

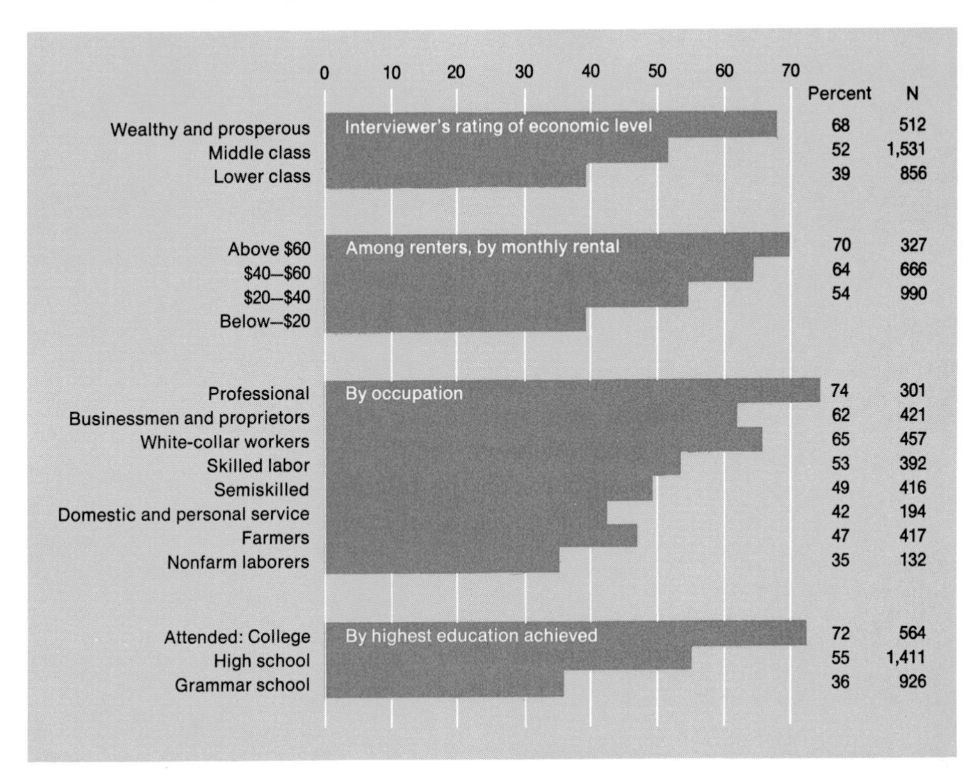

> Implicitly, these findings demonstrate that the individual in lowly position sets his strivings and expectancies for success in the light of the established social hierarchy of groups and a belief in differential opportunities within the hierarchy.[25]

These data are the more telling since, when dealing with such an unexceptionally virtuous matter as education, variance in response is reduced. (When the desire for a college education becomes a commonplace piety, expressions of impiety might be expected only infrequently. And, of course, if one of our variables doesn't vary, there can be no connection between them—in this case between class and belief in the need for a college education.) But however great the agreement on college education, there is a consistent positive relationship between class standing and the desirability of college. This relationship holds when age and sex are controlled.

As a final example, class conditions our pleasures. Simply to enumerate a variety of sports suggests the likelihood of class distinctions: horse racing (instructively called the sport of kings), yachting, polo, squash, lacrosse, tennis, golf, boxing, baseball, and football. Sometimes distinctions are very finely drawn. In hawking (we are back in 12th-century England):

> . . . many kinds of birds of prey were used; in later years, legislation was to reserve their use to different ranks of men according to the esteem in which they were held. The great jerfalcons of Greenland, Iceland and Norway were reserved for royalty. The more common peregrin was, under the same statute, deemed appropriate for earls, the goshawk for the yeoman, the sparrow-hawk for priests. Merlins were allotted to knights, being between the falcons and hawks in size and power.[26]

Coming closer to the present, a study of a sample of families in Cuyahoga County, Ohio, found that upper-middle-class persons rely more on libraries, home diversions, and lecture-study groups than do those from other classes. People in the two lowest classes use parks and playgrounds, commercial entertainment, and church occasions more than other classes in their leisure time.[27]

Mobility, stability and change in the class structure

In human groups that are growing and changing, class lines are not immutable. Individuals alter their class positions. And the boundaries between strata may change. In winding up our discussion of class structure, let's consider both social mobility and structural change.

Mobility

In our society getting on means moving up. A central element in our culture is the value placed on improving one's position—through increased income, a job entailing more authority, an access of prestige. Social mobility is a long-standing problem for sociologists. How much mobility is there? What's the balance between upward and downward mobility? Is there more, or less, mobility now than there once was? Is the apparent mobility spurious? Is it simply a matter of movement, turnover in a fairly stable class structure? Let's back up a moment to attack this last question.

People stand at different points on the ladders of wealth, prestige, and power. If we want to know where they stand, we have to know where others stand. Suppose you are startled to see that one of the rungs of the ladder your father is standing on is cracked. "Which one?" he asks. "Fourth from the top," you say. The number tells him where (what level) relative to others, the cracked rung is. Social phenomena are always relational, and class standing is a relative matter. Thus, even though people's situations improve (or worsen), their standing may remain what it was.

Think about a stable society. Here we have a situation in which positions vacated through death and retirement and mobility (up and down) are regularly filled by others. While we see individual movement, the whole structure retains its general character.

Or we can conceive of the whole structure moving up (or down) while the elements within it retain their relative positions. If three people stand on a ladder and each moves up (or down) one rung, their positions relative to one another remain exactly the same.

Along the income dimension, this is what happened in the opulent 1960's. Real income for Americans in 1966 (i.e., what dollars could buy) was about four times greater than it was in 1900. "Americans own more than 60 million automobiles; 95 percent of American households own at least one television set . . . and over 60 percent of American families own their homes."[28] But the relative standing of certain categories remains almost unchanged. Consider nonwhite (chiefly Negro) families. We see but slight change in the ratio of nonwhite to white median income at eight recent time points:[29] 1947, .51; 1953, .56; 1957, .54; 1964, .56; 1966, .60; 1967, .59; 1968, .60; and 1969, .61.

Or consider the poor who, according to the definition of poverty developed by the Social Security Administration, declined from about 40 million in 1960 to 26 million in 1967. But while there are fewer poor, due to rising income levels, the relative standing of people (using income as an index) has remained virtually unchanged.

There is a difference, then, in a reduction of poverty that results from everyone moving up a rung, and a reduction that results from a redistribution of wealth—for example, top and bottom moving to a middle rung. The first entails mobility but no change in social structure. The second means both mobility *and* a change in the class structure.

To investigate social mobility we have to compare statuses (both in the sense of position and of standing) at two points in time. So there are two problems: what to use for an index of position and standing, and how to get two or more time points between which people's positions may have changed.

Income, occupation, and education are the most commonly used indexes. In different ways they represent the three scales proposed by Max Weber: class, status, and power. The study we shall look at uses occupational position which, while it "does not encompass all aspects of the concept of class, . . . is probably the best single indicator of it. . . ."[30] Occupation is not a perfect indication of standing. Some people not employed may yet have high standing. Others in high-ranking occupations may, because of other characteristics, rank low. But on the whole, occupation and occupational mobility are reasonably well related to social standing and social mobility.

Table 8.8 gives us some data on occupational change in a generation's time, a father-son sort of contrast. For simplicity's sake I have omitted two categories: farm occupations (a mixed bag) and persons not in the experienced civilian labor force. Their addition would bring the row totals up to 100 percent.

As you look along the main diagonals, several things become clear. First, there is a striking degree of mobility suggested by the data, both upward and downward. Second, most mobility is downward among Negroes, upward among whites. For example, 9.7 + 19.4 + 53.0 is the extent of downward mobility among Negroes whose fathers were in higher white-collar occupations, a total of 82.1 percent. (The figure would be up to 7.5 percent higher had I not omitted farm occupations and those not in the labor force.) Comparable figures for Negroes whose fathers were in the lower-white-collar and higher-manual categories are 75.1 and 64.1 percent, respectively. Contrast this with downward mobility among whites in the first three occupational categories: 38.7, 28.1, and 24.0 percent. (Again, these are slight understatements because of the two categories I've dropped from the table.) There is upward mobility among Negroes in the three lower occupational categories: 14.5, 15.6, and 26.5 percent, respectively. But the comparable figures for whites are much higher: 45.1, 39.9, and 55.3 percent. It follows, third, that the inheritance of class position is not the iron-clad rule, although it prevails in the categories with most members. The lower manual is the only category for which it holds for Ne-

Table 8.8

Mobility from father's occupation to 1962 occupation of civilian men 25 to 64 years

Father's occupation by race	Respondents' occupation, 1962*				Total	
	Higher white collar	Lower white collar	Higher manual	Lower manual	Percent	Number (000)
Negro						
Higher white collar	10.4	*9.7*	*19.4*	*53.0*	92.5	134
Lower white collar	**14.5**	9.1	*6.0*	*69.1*	98.7	55
Higher manual	**8.8**	**6.8**	11.2	*64.1*	90.9	251
Lower manual	**8.0**	**7.0**	**11.5**	63.2	89.7	973
White						
Higher white collar	54.3	*15.3*	*11.5*	*11.9*	93.0	5,836
Lower white collar	**45.1**	18.3	*13.5*	*14.6*	91.5	2,652
Higher manual	**28.1**	**11.8**	27.9	*24.0*	91.8	6,512
Lower Manual	**21.3**	**11.5**	**22.5**	36.0	91.3	8,798

Note: Italic numbers represent percent of those who are downwardly mobile, nonitalic numbers represent nonmobile, and boldface numbers represent upwardly mobile.

* These are combinations of census major occupation groups. *Higher white collar:* professional and kindred workers, and managers, officials, and proprietors, except farm. *Lower white collar:* sales, clerical, and kindred workers. *Higher manual:* craftsmen, foremen, and kindred workers. *Lower manual:* operatives and kindred workers, service workers, and laborers, except farm.

groes (although this is by far the largest one). For whites it holds chiefly for top and bottom, again the categories including most people.

Combining whites (nearly 90 percent of our population) and Negroes in a more detailed analysis of occupational changes in a generation (17 occupational categories are used) Blau and Duncan conclude:

> First, occupational inheritance is in all cases greater than expected on the assumption [that son's occupation is independent of father's. This was especially so among the self-employed: farmers, proprietors, and independent professionals.] . . . Second, social mobility is nevertheless pervasive. . . . Third, upward mobility . . . is more prevalent than downward mobility . . . and short-distance movements occur more often than long-distance ones.[31]

Blau and Duncan pursue their inquiry by asking: What factors, in addition to father's occupation, account for variance in sons' occupations? For actually, the correlation between fathers' and sons' occupational ratings is only about .4, meaning that one can account for only 16 percent of the variance in the sons' occupations by referring to variance in fathers' occupations.*

A simplified version of their model of influences and connections would look like Table 8.9.

As the diagram indicates, the influence of family background seems to fade through time. Perhaps it would be more accurate to say that familial influences are mediated through experiences intervening between social origin and destination.

One of the signal contributions made in this study is the determination of the part played by each of several variables in contributing to occupational position (and with it, social standing). Figure 8.11 indicates the significance of the person's own educational experience and the relatively lighter influence of a variety of background factors.

A class structure will be stable when, as persons move up or down or out, there is a fairly smooth succession on the various rungs (positions, roles) of the social ladder. We have assumed that downward mobility is often a matter of misfortune, of incapacities associated with age, and the like; and that upward mobility is stimulated by the value placed in our society on upward striving.

But there are other sources of social mobility. There are different routes to success, different scales for measuring achievement, and circumstance may change the relative values attached to them. For example, with the attack on Pearl Harbor standing in the military hierarchy became a significant measure of success. At one point in time, a society will celebrate its priests and theologians, at another its philosophers, yet again its scientists and captains of industry. Electronics, chemical industries, space exploration—these developments respond to social needs, reflect social values. Since they entail a rearrangement of parts, they imply structural changes, shifts in the labor force. And since prestige, income, and power are altered, such changes imply a rearrangement of rungs in the social ladder.

Status consistency, stability and change

To speak of "the" social ladder is misleading. For as I have indicated, there are several ladders or scales, and people have standings on each of them: occupation, income, level of education

* Refer to Aside on Methods: Number 7.

Table 8.9

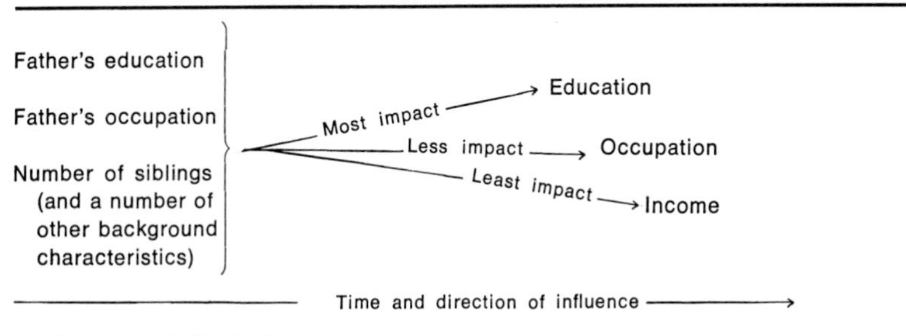

* Largely ascriptive factors
† Achievement factors

Figure 8.11

Sources of variation in occupational achievement, for men 20–64 years old in experienced civilian labor force: March, 1962

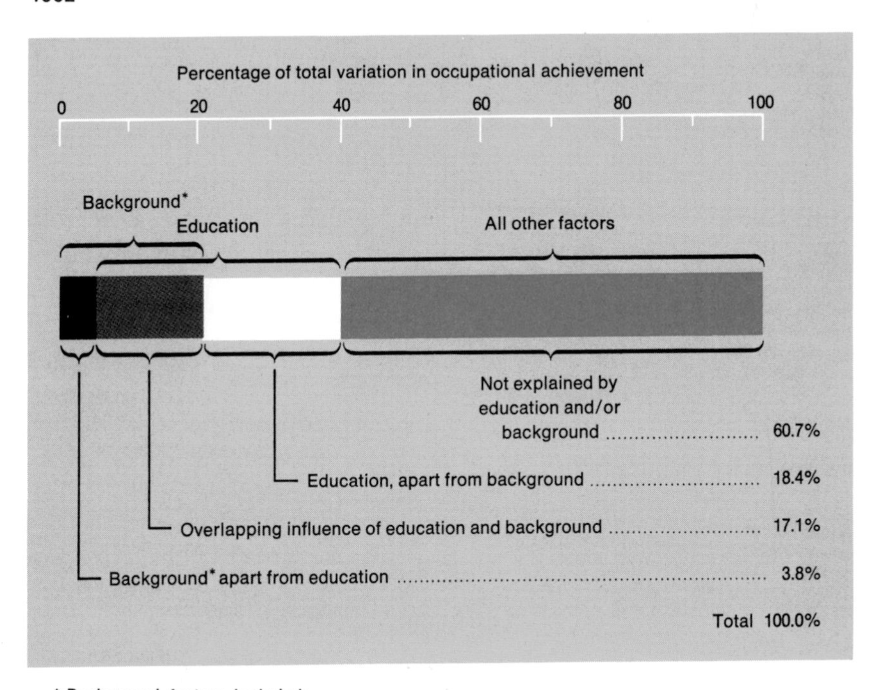

* Background factors included:
Family head's occupation.
Family head's education.
Number of siblings and sibling position.
Nativity.
Color.
Region of birth and region of residence.

achieved, ethnic status, and the like. Part of the mobility traditionally characterizing our society has come from a discrepancy between ascribed standing on one scale (Irish Catholic, Nisei) and achieved standing aspired to on another scale (political power, wealth). We can think of the WASP who is a renowned physician practicing on Park Avenue as having high status across a number of ranking scales: wealth, occupation, ethnicity, and so on. Or we can think of a very poor, unemployed Harlem Negro, a migrant from the rural South, as having low status across a number of ranking scales. On the other hand, we think of the distinguished Negro physician, or Supreme Court Justice, who is high on one scale (occupation) and low in terms of prevailing American values on another scale (race or ethnicity). Here we have inconsistent standings. In the first two illustrations, standing, or class, has *crystallized.*

This is the term used by Lenski in one of the first empirical studies of the significance of status consistency.* Working with a probability sample ($N = 749$) of the Detroit metropolitan area, Lenski tested the hypothesis that "individuals characterized by a low degree of status crystallization differ significantly in their political attitudes and behavior from individuals characterized by a high degree of status crystallization, when status differences in the vertical dimension are controlled."[32] The argument for this, as stated in a later study, goes as follows:

> . . . status inconsistency is a source of stress for individuals, especially when the inconsistencies are substantial, since the individual prefers to think of himself in terms of his higher status or statuses while others have a tendency to treat him in terms of the lower. The resulting conflict between expectations and experiences is bound to be disturbing, and . . . one common pattern of response is to react against the social

* Unfortunately the word *status* has been used in two senses, and both of them come into play here. In one usage, status means position in the social structure. Thus if one asks: What do you do? you answer: doctor, lawyer, beggarman, thief (giving *position* in the occupational structure). Or if you ask: What is her marital status? you mean: Which among several marital *positions* characterize her? Is she married? Widowed? Divorced? Single? A second usage means standing or *rank* relative to others. "Status crystallization," combining both usages, can be taken to mean the extent to which rank is consistent across a number of statuses—in Lenski's study, positions in the occupational, educational, income, and ethnic structures.

† Lenski's reasoning in support of this measure of status crystallization will give you some sense of the sociologist at work. He writes:

> The use of squared deviations from the mean rather than simple devia-

order, which is thought to be responsible, by supporting a political party advocating change.[33]

Lenski's first job was to get measures of status on each of four ranking scales. We can think of these four scales as thermometers, one each for income, education, occupation, and ethnic standing. But clearly they are not, like thermometers, measuring the same thing. Hence the problem of commensurability. Lenski solved this by ranging respondents' scores from high to low, converting these distributions into cumulative frequencies, and then calculating scores for a person depending on his position in the cumulative distribution. For example, 29 respondents had incomes of $10,000 or more per year, while 95.3 percent got less. These top incomes were received by the top 4.7 percent. Taking the midpoint of this range, 95.4 to 100.0, the score for people falling in this top-income category was, then, $95.4 + 0.5(4.6) = 95.4 + 2.3 = 97.7$ or, rounded off, 98. So it was that each respondent was scored on each of the four scales.

The second task was geting a measure of crystallization, the measure of extent of sameness or consistency among these four scores. The measure contrived was this: the square root of the sum of the four squared deviations from their respective means, subtracted from 100—i.e., $100 - \sqrt{\Sigma(\bar{X} - X)^2}$. Thus, where the second term, the measure of deviation = 0, the crystallization score would be 100, and the greater the value of the deviation measure the lower the crystallization score.†

Now we come to the central questions. (1) Does behavior (such as voting or expression of political preference) vary with degree of status crystallization? (2) Do high and low status crystallization predict to differing political behavior even when members of these two categories have similar incomes and educations, similar mean occupational and ethnic scores? (Here again is the need for controlled observation. To attribute some influence to degree of

tions was employed to emphasize the effect of larger deviations and to minimize the effect of smaller deviations. This was considered desirable since the techniques employed in quantifying positions (or intervals) in the several hierarchies were sufficiently crude so that no great importance could be attached to small deviations.

The technique of subtracting the resulting figure from one hundred was employed so that respondents whose status was highly crystallized would have numerically higher crystallization scores than those whose status was poorly crystallized. This was done solely to avoid semantic difficulties. (Gerhard E. Lenski; "Status Crystallization: A Non-Vertical Dimension of Social Status," *American Sociological Review,* Vol. 19 [August, 1954], p. 408, n. 14.)

status crystallization, we must control by eliminating other variables known to influence political preference.) (3) For given scores on status crystallization, does it make any difference *which* ranking scales a person is high or low on? Whether, for example, occupation is high, education low, or vice versa?

The answer to the first question is given in Figure 8.12 relating voting behavior (1948, 1950) and voting preference (1952) to degree of status crystallization. This last, the independent variable, was simply dichotomized, high crystallization being defined as scores of 53 or more and low crystallization as those of 52 or less. As the figure shows, occupying discrepant statuses in four ranking systems (lack of status crystallization) does appear to be related to political preference.

Now consider the second question. High and low crystallization categories not only differed in degree of status consistency; they also differed on mean scores on all four status scales. For example, the high status crystallization category also was high on income and occupational status. Hence one might conclude that it was these characteristics, rather than status consistency, that accounted for Republican preferences.

To eliminate these confounding variables Lenski dropped 26 cases with the highest incomes from the high crystallization category and 8 respondents with the lowest incomes in the low crystallization category. This eliminated the income and occupation differences. In fact, the low crystallization category was now a bit higher on these variables, thus stacking the cards against the hypothesis that low status crystallization would be related to Democratic political preference.

With these controls in effect, political differences between the two categories were reduced. But still respondents in the low crystallization category preferred the Democratic party and its candidates, and took more liberal positions on three issues: government health insurance, price controls, and a general extension of government powers.

The third question, you will recall, was whether, among those having low crystallization, it made any difference what the pattern of discrepant statuses was. Analysis of the data enables two tentative conclusions. The tendency for Democratic party preference and political liberalism to be linked with low status crystallization persists despite variations in the pattern of status inconsistencies. But, secondly, certain patterns of low status crystallization yield more liberal responses than others. For example, where income is high and occupation is low, only 4.8 percent of a subsample were

Figure 8.12

Percent of voters favoring the Democratic party, by degree of status crystallization

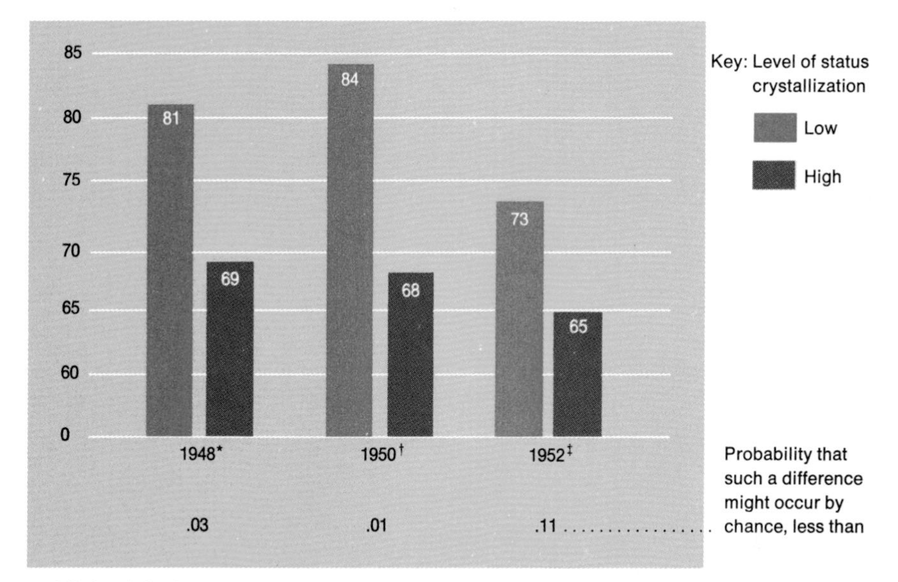

* Voting behavior
† Voting behavior
‡ Expression of party preference

strongly liberal in their responses. But in the reverse situation, occupation high and income low, 29.4 percent gave strong liberal responses.

Lenski concludes his study of this dimension of social status with the following statement. Note that it offers us an important clue in assessing the stability of a social order (or conversely, its vulnerability to change).

> Conceivably a society with a relatively large proportion of persons whose status is poorly crystallized is a society which is in an unstable condition. In brief, under such conditions *the social system itself generates its own pressures for change.*[34]

* * * *

Class gives us a telling perspective on the structure of society. Values commonly held but unequally achieved (or inherited) lead to inequalities in wealth, prestige, and power. And with these inequalities there are linked marked differences in life chances and life styles. In its extremest form, caste, the future is quite completely foreshadowed at birth.

In our society, class conditions, but does not irrevocably determine. There is a good deal of individual mobility. And there is a lesser mobility stemming from changes in the social structure itself.

Mobility is no doubt increased from both sources in an urban industrial society. For here we find high value placed on the rational determination of more effective means to achieve our ends. The tendency is then to disparage ascribed status and to place the emphasis on demonstrated achievement.* As with the Negro in professional sports, this may increase mobility, although it need not necessarily alter the class structure.

On this point you should note the distinction between individual and social phenomena. A social structure may remain fairly stable despite—indeed, because of—much individual movement. For example, in an intergenerational study by Glass, for any status of the father, half or more of the sons fell in a different occupational category.[35] Most were mobile. Yet the distribution of sons across seven occupational statuses was almost precisely the same as that of the fathers. There was much individual shifting, but virtually no change in social structure. Reviewing research on occupational prestige from 1925 to 1963, Hodge, Siegel, and Rossi make the same observation, and cite René Dubos who says:

> Universal instability of constituents seems to be compatible with a stability and even monotony of organized life.
>
> Such is the picture one gleans of occupational structures. . . . Between 1947 and 1963 we are fully aware that many *individual* changes in occupation were under way as men advanced in their career lines, retired or entered the labor force. Yet, despite the turnover of incumbents, occupational morphology, at least insofar as prestige is concerned, remained remarkably stable.[36]

* Consider, for example, Du Pont's advertising by-line: "Better things for better living, through chemistry." Or an earlier version of this do-it-better, means-oriented theme: "If a man has good corn, or wood, or boards, or pigs to sell, or can make better chairs or knives, crucibles or church organs than anybody else, you will find a broad, hard-beaten road to his house, though it be in the woods" (Ralph Waldo Emerson, *Journals*, Vol. 8 [June 27, 1839], pp. 528–29). We see an interesting reversal of values among some young people who are revolted at the ever-striving, means-oriented pattern of adult life, a pattern which, they would contend, obscures the ends of life. Different values emerge, then, which dictate minimal employment, doing one's own thing, and living in harmony and love with others.

Finally, as we have seen, when standing differs across several ranking scales, some impulse toward change is triggered—certainly for the individual and possibly, as we value achieved over ascribed statuses, for the class structure itself.

Now we turn in the next three chapters to a different perspective on social structure: relationships that we institutionalize in support of social necessities.

References

TEXT

1. U.S. Department of Labor, *The Economic Situation of Negroes in the United States* (Bulletin S–3, rev. 1962 [Washington, D.C.: U.S. Department of Commerce, Bureau of the Census, 1962]), pp. 6, 7.
2. Bureau of the Census, "Income in 1968," *Current Population Reports,* Series P–60 (Washington, D.C.: United States Government Printing Office, 1969), Table 22, p. 51.
3. See, for example, Urie Bronfenbrenner, "Socialization and Social Class through Space and Time," in Eleanor E. Maccoby, Theodore M. Newcomb, and Eugene L. Hartley (eds.), *Readings in Social Psychology* (New York: Henry Holt & Co., Inc., 1958); Melvin Kohn, "Social Class and Parent-Child Relationships," *American Journal of Sociology,* Vol. 68, No. 4 (January, 1963); and especially, Kohn's *Class and Conformity* (Homewood, Ill.: Dorsey Press, 1969), chap. ii and pp. 104–5.
4. R. Dahrendorf, *On the Sources of Inequalities Among Men* (Tubingen, 1961). The illustrations are mine, not Dahrendorf's, and I hope they do justice to his argument.
5. Kingsley Davis and Wilbert Moore, "Some Principles of Stratification," *American Sociological Review,* Vol. 10 (1945), pp. 242–49.
6. See S. N. Eisenstadt, *From Generation to Generation* (New York: Free Press, 1966). See pp. 288–94, *passim.*
7. Joseph A. Kahl, *The American Class Structure* (New York: Rinehart & Co., 1957), p. 12.
8. Cleveland Amory, "The Proper Bostonians," *Harper's Magazine,* September, 1947, p. 201.
9. Reported in *The New York Times,* April 21, 1959.
10. Adam Ferguson, *Principles of Moral and Political Science* (Edinburg, 1792), Vol. I, pp. 244 *et seq.* An 18th-century social theorist of some distinction, Ferguson, along with Adam Smith, David Hume and others is identified as a member of the Scottish school of moral philosophers.
11. Charles Dickens, *The Chimes,* second quarter.
12. Mrs. C. F. Alexander, "All Things Bright and Beautiful." These lines in the *Church Hymnal for the Christian Year* were to have been excised, according to a *New York Times* news article. The Church of England, seeking to "keep up with the times," wishes to eliminate lines "thought to smack of feudalism. A committee headed by the Vicar of Christchurch, Orpington, Kent, is carrying out the revisions" (*The New York Times,* September 20, 1963).
13. Natalie Rogoff, "Recent Trends in Urban Occupational Mobility." Reprinted with permision of The Free Press, from *Cities and Society* by Paul K. Hatt and Albert J. Reiss, Jr., (eds.). Copyright 1951, 1957 by The Free Press, a corporation.
14. Melvin Kohn, "Social Class and Parent-Child Relationships," *American Journal of Sociology,* Vol. 68, No. 4 (January, 1963), p. 471.
15. See W. Lloyd Warner (ed.), *Yankee City* (New Haven, Conn.: Yale University Press, 1963). This is an abridged edition of the original five-volume study carried out between 1930 and 1935.
16. A. B. Hollingshead, *Elmtown's Youth*

(New York: John Wiley & Sons, Inc., 1949).

17. Albert Mayer and Philip Hauser, "Class Differentials in Expectation of Life at Birth," in Reinhard Bendix and Seymour M. Lipset (eds.), *Class, Status and Power* (New York: Free Press, 1953).
18. Warner (ed.), *op. cit.*, p. 93.
19. *Ibid.*, p. 61. I have rounded Warner's data, given to two decimal points, to the nearest year. For example, his figure for median age at marriage for the upper-uppers is 27.90.
20. Joseph A. Kahl and James A. Davis, "A Comparison of Indexes of Socio-Economic Status," *American Sociological Review*, Vol. 20 (June, 1955), reported in Kahl, *op. cit.*, pp. 137, 138.
21. A. B. Hollingshead, *Elmtown's Youth* (New York: John Wiley & Sons, Inc., 1949), p. 214.
22. W. Lloyd Warner, *The Social Life of a Modern Community* (Vol. I in the Yankee City Series [New Haven, Conn.: Yale University Press, 1941]), p. 354.
23. A. B. Hollingshead and Frederick C. Redlich, *Social Class and Mental Illness: A Community Study* (New York: John Wiley & Sons, Inc., 1958), p. 226.
24. Karl F. Schuessler, "Social Backgrounds and Musical Taste," *American Sociological Review*, Vol. 13, No. 3 (June, 1948), p. 333 (italics mine).
25. Herbert H. Hyman, "The Value Systems of Different Classes," in Bendix and Lipset, *op. cit.*, p. 438.
26. Richard Barber, *Henry Plantagenet* (New York: Roy Publishers, Inc., 1964), pp. 58, 59.
27. Clyde R. White, "Social Class Differences in the Uses of Leisure," *American Journal of Sociology*, Vol. 61, No. 2 (September, 1955), p. 145.
28. Department of Health, Education, and Welfare, *Toward a Social Report* (Washington, D.C.: U.S. Government Printing Office, 1969), p. 42.
29. *Ibid.*, p. 44. Taken from Ida C. Merriam, "Welfare and Its Measurement," in Eleanor H. Sheldon and Wilbert E. Moore (eds.), *Indicators of Social Change* (New York: Russell Sage Foundation, 1968), and from "Selected Characteristics of Persons and Families: March, 1970," *Current Population Reports*, Series P–20, No. 204 (Washington, D.C.: United States Government Printing Office, 1970), Table 2, p. 4.
30. Peter M. Blau and Otis Dudley Duncan, *The American Occupational Structure* (New York: John Wiley & Sons, Inc., 1967), p. 6.
31. *Ibid.*, p. 36.
32. Gerhard E. Lenski, "Status Crystallization: A Non-Vertical Dimension of Social Status," *American Sociological Review*, Vol. 19 (August, 1954), pp. 405–6.
33. ———., "Status Inconsistency and the Vote: A Four Nation Test," *American Sociological Review*, Vol. 32, No. 2 (April, 1967), p. 298.
34. *Ibid.*, p. 412.
35. D. V. Glass (ed.), *Social Mobility in Britain* (London: George Routledge & Sons, Ltd., 1954).
36. Robert W. Hodge, Paul M. Siegel, and Peter H. Rossi, "Occupational Prestige in the United States, 1925–1963," *American Journal of Sociology*, Vol. 70, No. 3 (November, 1964), p. 302. The first sentence is quoted from René Dubos, *The Dreams of Reason: Science and Utopias* (New York: Columbia University Press, 1961), p. 124.

TABLES

8.1 Katherine and Charles H. George, "Roman Catholic Sainthood and Social Status: A Statistical and Analytical Study," *Journal of Religion*, Vol. 5 (1953–55), pp. 85–98. Their source was Alban Butler, *Lives of the Saints*, ed. and supplemented by Herbert Thurston, *et al.* (12 vols., 1926–1938, with a supplementary volume, 1949).

8.3 Selected occupational rankings from Robert W. Hodge, Paul M. Siegel, and Peter H. Rossi, "Occupational Prestige in the United States, 1925–63," *American Journal of Sociology*, Vol. 70 (November, 1964), Table 1, pp. 290–92.

8.4 Alex Inkeles and Peter H. Rossi, "National Comparisons of Occupational Prestige," *American Journal of Sociology*, Vol. 61 (1956), p. 332.

8.5 U.S. Department of Health, Education, and Welfare, *Toward a Social Report* (Washington, D.C.: U.S. Government Printing Office, 1969), Table 3, p. 6.

8.6 A. B. Hollingshead, *Elmtown's Youth* (New York: John Wiley & Sons, Inc., 1949). Adapted from Appendix Table IX, p. 462.

8.7 Robert E. Clark, "Psychoses, Income, and Occupational Prestige," *American Journal of Sociology*, March, 1949.

8.8 U.S. Department of Health, Education, and Welfare, *op. cit.*, Table 4, p. 24.

FIGURES

8.1 Department of Defense, High School

News Service Report" (Great Lakes, Ill., September, 1967), p. 23.

8.3 Allison Davis, Burleigh B. Gardner, and Mary R. Gardner, *Deep South: A Social-Anthropological Study of Caste and Class* (Chicago: University of Chicago Press, 1941), p. 10. Copyright 1941 by the University of Chicago.

8.4 Bureau of Labor Statistics, Department of Labor, "The Negroes in the United States: Their Economic and Social Situation" (Bulletin No. 1511 [Washington, D.C.: U.S. Government Printing Office, June, 1966]), Table IIB–1, p. 107.

8.5 Bureau of the Census, "Annual Mean Income, Lifetime Income, and Educational Attainment of Men in the United States for Selected Years, 1956–1966," *Current Population Reports,* Series P–60, No. 56 (Washington, D.C.: U.S. Government Printing Office, 1968), Fig. 2, p. 4.

8.6 *Ibid.,* cover Figure.

8.7 Adapted from Warner (ed.), *Yankee City,* p. 364.

8.8 August B. Hollingshead and Frederick C. Redlich, *Social Class and Mental Illness: A Community Study* (New York: John Wiley & Sons, Inc., 1958), p. 223.

8.9 Hollingshead, *op. cit.* Adapted from Table XIX, Appendix, p. 469.

8.10 Adapted from Herbert Hyman, "The Value Systems of Different Classes: A Social Psychological Contribution to the Analysis of Stratification," in Reinhard Bendix and Seymour Martin Lipset (eds.), *Class, Status and Power: A Reader in Social Stratification* (New York: Free Press, 1953), Table 1, chap. iv. Copyright 1953 by The Free Press; reprinted with permission of The Free Press.

8.11 P. M. Blau and O. D. Duncan, *The American Occupational Structure* (New York: John Wiley & Sons, Inc., 1967), Appendix H. *op. cit.,* p. 23.

8.12 Gerhard E. Lenski, "Status Crystallization: A Non-Vertical Dimension of Social Status," *American Sociological Review,* Vol. 19 (August, 1954), Table 2, p. 408.

chapter 9 Social structure: institutions of induction

The vilest abortionist is he who attempts to mould a child's character.
George Bernard Shaw, "Maxims for Revolutionists"

Education does not limit itself to developing the individual in accordance with his original nature, teasing out the hidden potential that lies there, only waiting to be revealed. It creates a new being. That is education's mission. And in that we see its greatness."
Emile Durkheim, *Éducation et sociologie*

The continuous supply of adequately socialized replacements for those dying, or otherwise departing,* requires a social mechanism. Such a mechanism we find in family and school, institutionalized agents of socialization that we discussed briefly in Chapter 5. The family as an institution is a system of rules generally shared—and of roles locally exhibited—in homes throughout the country. Look down from the air on any American community: converging arteries of traffic, tall buildings at the core, warehouses and light manufacturing plants, apartment houses, duplex and single-family dwellings stretching out, mile upon mile to suburbia. In each of

* In the category of "otherwise departing," I include persons who leave their usual roles: the imprisoned, those hospitalized or chronically ill, people retiring and so moving out of the labor force, and out-migrants.

these homes we find a similar set of roles, varying somewhat by class but within a given range of tolerance and supported by common understandings. Characteristic of institutionalized patterns, these roles and rules are so routinized that they are duplicated in other communities throughout the land.

A Glance at the internal structure of the family

Each family can be seen as a social micro system, a "unity of interacting personalities" as Burgess called it. And each of these micro systems meshes with the external social order, the macro system, performing functions required for its survival. Thus we have two perspectives for looking at this institution: its internal structure and its linkage with the larger social order. Let's look first at some of the ideas and research bearing on the internal structure of the family. In Figure 9.1 the numbers represent the sequence in which we will consider the interlocking set of relationships that constitutes the nuclear family. In each case, we will consider one aspect of the relationship that varies, either as independent or dependent variable.

Relationships

Parent-child relationships

A recurrent finding of sociological research is the way in which one attribute of the parents, class position, varies with or predicts to the patterns of child rearing. Our data have to do, chiefly, with middle- and lower-class parents. (Material on the upper class is most meager.) The lower-class American inherits a cultural tradition that stipulates a parental role peculiar to his condition. Accustomed to dealing with things, under supervision, he stresses obedient response to orders, being neat and clean, and pleasing one's superiors, parents, and other adults. The middle-class parent deals with the child in a way that has been called "developmental."[1] Accustomed to more self-directed work with ideas, symbols, and human relationships, this parent emphasizes inner states in the growth of his child: curiosity, happiness, sharing, and cooperation, eagerness to learn, confidence in parents, and the development of self-control. Professor Bronfenbrenner, summarizing 25 years of studies of parent-child relationships (up to 1958) says:

> Over the entire . . . period studied, parent-child relationships in the middle-class are consistently reported as more acceptant and equalitarian, while those in the working class are oriented toward maintaining order and obedience.[2]

These contrasts, by class, can be summarized as in Table 9.1. It is based on a perceptive essay by Melvin Kohn[3] in which he suggests that differences, by class, in child-rearing patterns cannot be explained simply by invoking differences in education. He argues persuasively that knowing is supported by valuing, that middle- and lower-class parental values stem from and reinforce quite different life conditions that have their reflection in different modes of child rearing. "The interpretive model in essence, is: social class → conditions of life → values → behavior."[4]

Husband-wife relationships

Consider, now, the husband-wife relationship (relationship number 2 in Figure 9.1) and the role of each. Some investigators have thought that husband and wife roles have changed through time, shifting from fairly fixed institutional forms toward an equalitarian and often transient companionship, transforming the family into a voluntary association.[5] Certainly the change from a rural-agrarian past to an urban-industrial present cannot fail to have penetrated every aspect of American life. If Alexis de Tocqueville's observations were correct, there is a marked contrast between the position of women and the role of wife in the United States today and the situation as he saw it in 1840.

> In no country has such constant care been taken as in America to trace two clearly distinct lines of action for the two sexes and to make them keep pace one with the other, but in two pathways that are always different. American women never manage the outward concerns of the family or conduct a business or take part in political life; nor are they, on the other hand, ever compelled to perform the rough labor of the fields or to make any of those laborious efforts which demand the exertion of physical strength. No families are so poor as to form an exception to this rule. If, on the one hand, an American woman cannot escape from the quiet cir-

Figure 9.1

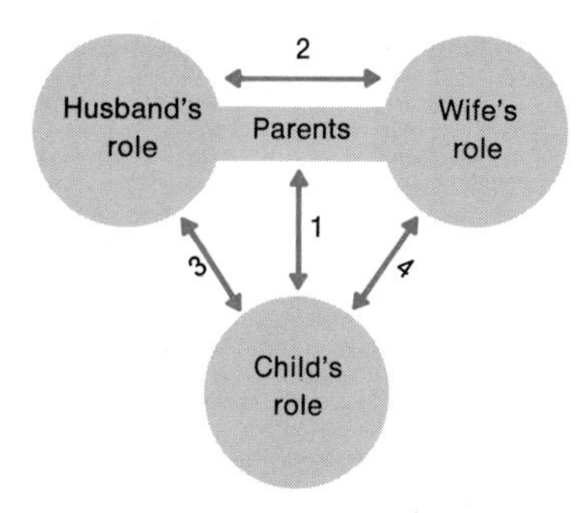

Table 9.1
Contrasts, by class, in child-rearing patterns

Class	Characteristics of parental occupations	General orientation of parents	Want children to be	Stress upon	Source of control
Working and lower middle	Dealing with things under supervision, getting ahead dependent on a collective orientation	Traditional	Neat, clean obedient, respectful, please adults	Overt acts	External proscriptions and punishment stemming from the immediate consequences of an act
Middle	Working with ideas, symbols, relationships . . . self-directed, getting ahead dependent on one's own achievements	Developmental	Happy, sharing, cooperative, curious, eager learners, loving, self-controlled	Inner states	Self-direction and punishment stemming from the intent of the act

cle of domestic employments, she is never forced, on the other, to go beyond it. Hence it is that the women of America, who often exhibit a masculine strength of understanding and a manly energy, generally preserve great delicacy of personal appearance and always retain the manners of women although they sometimes show that they have the hearts and minds of men.

Nor have the Americans ever supposed that one consequence of democratic principles is the subversion of marital power or the confusion of the natural authorities in families. They hold that every association must have a head in order to accomplish its object, and that the natural head of the con-

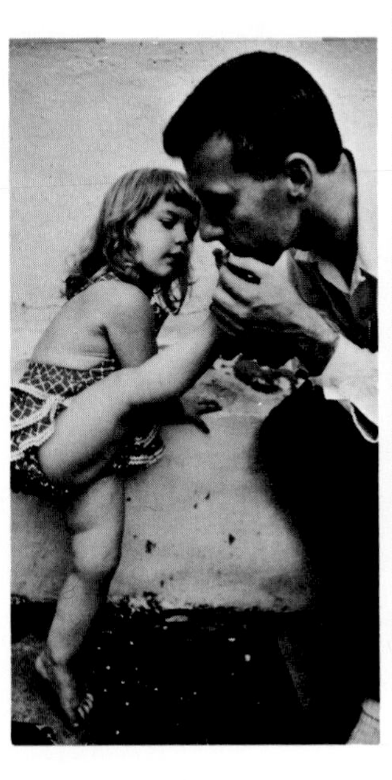

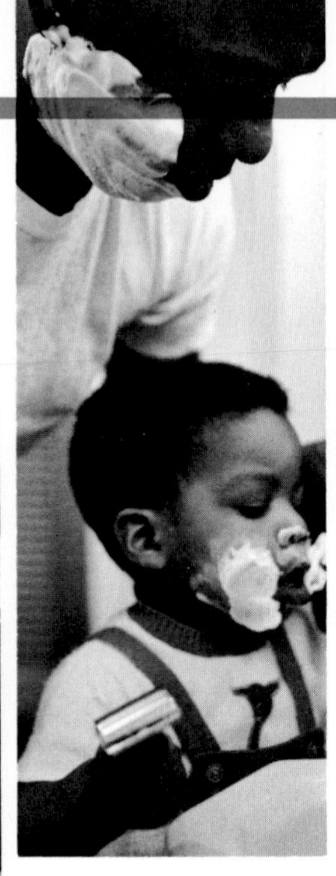

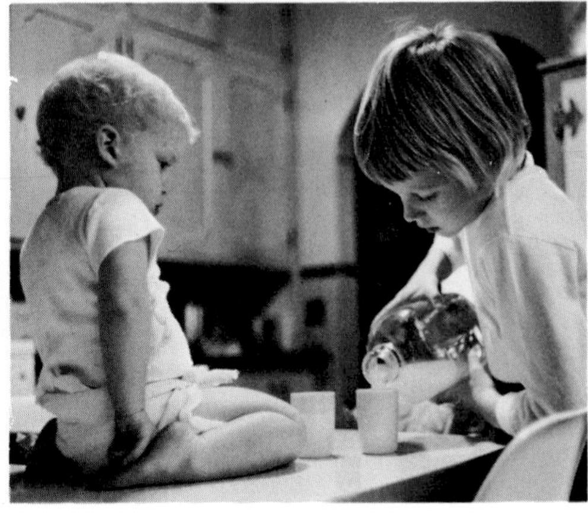

. . . the structure of the family viewed as a micro system. We can see . . . a structure of relationships . . . father-son, father-daughter, and brother-sister.

. . . the more complex the society, the more education displaces the family as training ground for adult roles.

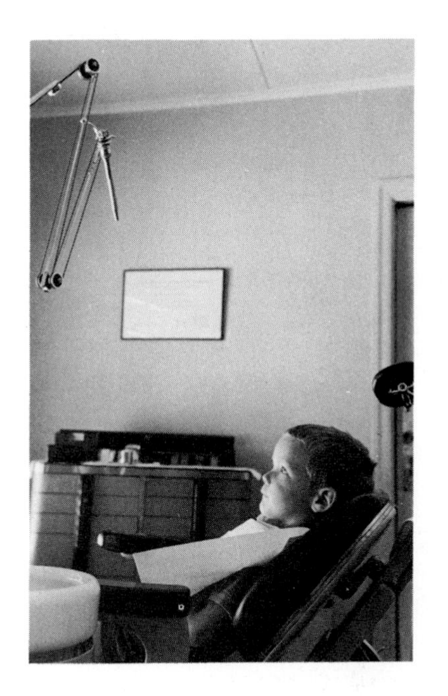

. . . education. . . . patrols the entrance gates to occupations. One doesn't become a doctor or a nurse . . . dentist, lawyer, engineer—without passing educational hurdles.

. . . in settings we institutionalize as educational, there are teachers other than those officially so designated. We can also be sure that there are social settings outside the school, in which important learnings are regularly achieved.

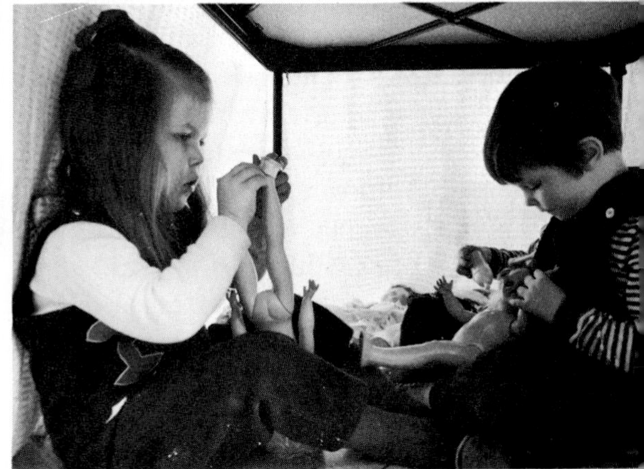

jugal association is man. They do not therefore deny him the right of directing his partner, and they maintain that in the smaller association of husband and wife as well as in the great social community the object of democracy is to regulate and legalize the powers that are necessary, and not to subvert all power.

This opinion is not peculiar to one sex and contested by the other; I never observed that the women of America consider conjugal authority as an unfortunate usurpation of their rights, or that they thought themselves degraded by submitting to it. . . .

Thus the Americans do not think that man and woman have either the duty or the right to perform the same offices, but they show an equal regard for both their respective parts; and though their lot is different, they consider both of them as being of equal value.[6]

But a sharply defined division of labor in the husband-wife relationship is not peculiar to our society. In many others we also find the wife typically cast in the nurturant role, the main source of warmth and sentiment. The husband, on the other hand, is identified as the task-oriented person, breadwinner and defender. Parsons and Bales use the words *expressive* and *instrumental* to denote these functions in the family (or any other) group.[7]

Eighty years after de Tocqueville wrote, both because of the changing nature of our labor force and as a result of women's seeking equality in the economic sphere, there was established in the U.S. Department of Labor a Women's Bureau to formulate "standards and policies for promoting the welfare of wage-earning women, improving their working conditions and advancing their opportunities for profitable employment." In the same year (1920) we passed an amendment to the Constitution of the United States, Article XIX, which reads: "The right of citizens of the United States to vote shall not be denied or abridged by the United States or by any state on account of sex." Recent legislation would remove special protections and reassert equal rights, the double-edged result of barring double standards. Clearly it has not been possible, in the years since de Tocqueville, to keep the American woman in her place!*

But to think of the husband-wife relationship as shifting through time from husband-dominant to equalitarian is, doubtless, to project contemporary middle-class standards and to oversimplify matters. There are other possibilities: the wife-dominant re-

Table 9.2
Distribution of power in the husband-wife relationship

	Percent
Equalitarian (or "autonomic" relationships as Straus calls them)	40
Husband-dominant	25
Conflicting (both seeking to dominate)	23
Wife-dominant	12
	100

lationship or one in which each dominates as he can, thus creating conflict.

Looking at this dimension of the husband-wife relationship, Straus found the distribution among the four sorts of marital dominance (287 families in a Wisconsin county in 1959) shown in Table 9.2.[8]

Since a relationship doesn't stand alone, one can ask what difference it makes—in this case, to the sons in these families—whether the spouse relationship is husband- or wife-dominant, equalitarian or conflicting. Straus answers that the nature of the husband-wife relationship affects the way essential family functions are performed. And the way these are carried out affects, in turn, performance in the son's role. We could put it schematically as shown in Table 9.3.

Straus's findings suggest, if inconclusively, that the wife-dominant family is associated with tense and rejecting sons, the equali-

* The phrase, "keeping (someone) in his place" suggests the possible parallel between women and Negroes as minority groups—minorities, not in a numerical sense but as being subject to adverse stereotypes that limit life chances. One might raise the question whether there is a sequence of liberation for women, as appears to be the case for Negroes. I have mentioned, above, the American woman's penetration of the world of work, a process of slow but gradual assertion of equality in the economic sphere: and the 19th Amendment to the Constitution asserting equality in political sphere. It is suggestive to compare the sequence of *women's liberation* with the order of demands by Negroes for full citizenship. (The following rank order of demands by Negroes is the same as the order of willingness on the part of whites to make concessions.)

1. Equal opportunity in the economic sphere.
2. Equality in justice and in political activities.
3. Equality in public services—restaurants, hotels, stores, bars, transportation.
4. Equality in the social sphere: clubs, voluntary associations, unions.
5. Intermarriage.

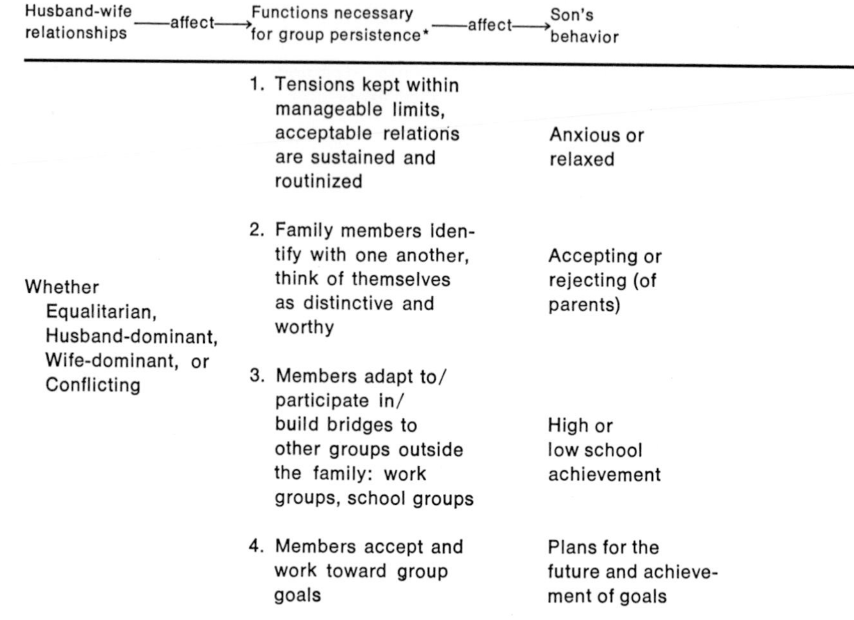

Table 9.3

Husband-wife relationships —affect→	Functions necessary for group persistence* —affect→	Son's behavior
Whether Equalitarian, Husband-dominant, Wife-dominant, or Conflicting	1. Tensions kept within manageable limits, acceptable relations are sustained and routinized	Anxious or relaxed
	2. Family members identify with one another, think of themselves as distinctive and worthy	Accepting or rejecting (of parents)
	3. Members adapt to/ participate in/ build bridges to other groups outside the family: work groups, school groups	High or low school achievement
	4. Members accept and work toward group goals	Plans for the future and achievement of goals

* These paraphrase the four functions suggested as indispensable for any enduring group by Talcott Parsons.

tarian relationship with relatively relaxed and parent-accepting sons, and that the husband-dominant family falls between the other two. But the conflicting relationship yielded no clear correlates in sons' behavior. Nor did hypotheses about sons' school achievement or tendency to strive toward future goals seem to be related to the nature of the spouse relationship, as measured.

Such findings are obviously tentative. Some of Straus's categories were very small. (He had only 12 percent of 287 cases in the wife-dominant category to begin with.) The failure to predict from spouse-relationship to school achievement or to the sons' drive toward future goals doesn't ring true. One is persuaded that the husband-wife relationship must have some outcomes, for the children, in attitudes toward the future and in achievement in extrafamilial groups. Perhaps the logic of the underlying theory is defective, or the measuring instruments, or the modes of analysis. Any, or all, of these is always possible in the detective work of sociological research.

In her study, *The Unemployed Man and His Family,* Mirra Komarovsky explores a related problem, the effect of unemployment

Table 9.4
Some types of nuclear family role structure emerging from differences in power structure and patterns of decision making

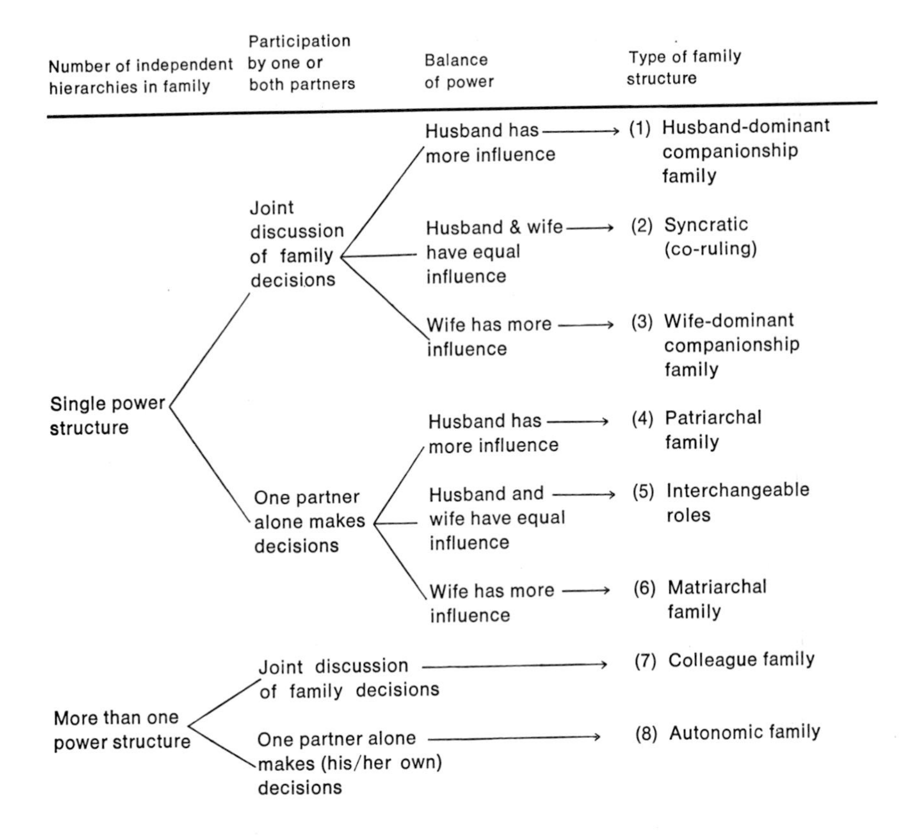

Number of independent hierarchies in family	Participation by one or both partners	Balance of power	Type of family structure
Single power structure	Joint discussion of family decisions	Husband has more influence	(1) Husband-dominant companionship family
		Husband & wife have equal influence	(2) Syncratic (co-ruling)
		Wife has more influence	(3) Wife-dominant companionship family
	One partner alone makes decisions	Husband has more influence	(4) Patriarchal family
		Husband and wife have equal influence	(5) Interchangeable roles
		Wife has more influence	(6) Matriarchal family
More than one power structure	Joint discussion of family decisions		(7) Colleague family
	One partner alone makes (his/her own) decisions		(8) Autonomic family

on the authority of husband and father (relationships numbers 2 and 3 in Figure 9.1). She found that in about 1 out of 5 of her 58 families the husband's influence declined. This occurred chiefly in families (8 out of 12 of them) where acceptance of the husband's authority had been simply out of fear, or was the necessary price for bed and board. Deterioration of the husband's authority occurred least where the authority was grounded in love and respect or where the wife was something of a traditionalist, accepting the dominance in the husband's role as natural, to be taken for granted.

Analyzing various dimensions of the husband-wife relationship reveals how complex such a deceptively simple structure as the nuclear family is. Elaborating on the power-dominance theme, Zelditch generates eight types of nuclear family structure (Table 9.4). Power means control over decisions. Among these perhaps the most crucial are those touching the children. In the following section we'll consider one such culturally patterned decision affecting the mother's influence over the child.

Mother-child relationships

Let's turn now to arrow number 4, the mother-child relationship in Figure 9.1. I should like to call your attention to an intriguing piece of research carried out by Whiting, Kluckhohn, and Anthony.[9] Why, these investigators asked, do we find initiation rites for young men—emphatic, dramatic, sometimes sanguinary—in some groups while such ceremonies are lacking in others? What is the social function served by initiation rites? Under what conditions is this social function necessary? Or unnecessary? As they worked out their interpretation of this observed difference in patterns of behavior* their theoretical statement took the following form. Where boys are particularly dependent upon mothers and hostile toward fathers, then some sort of initiation rites are necessary to:

1. Put a final stop to [the boy's] wish to return to his mother's arms and lap.
2. Prevent an open revolt against his father who has displaced him from his mother's bed.
3. Ensure identification with the adult males of the society.

The general hypothesis that follows is this: a protracted period of intimacy and dependence of male children upon their mothers will be associated with dramatic and sometimes violent initiation rites at puberty. Contrariwise, in societies not emphasizing dependence of male infants upon mothers and where the father exercises considerable authority, such initiation rites will be missing or extremely mild.

What we need, then, are measures on two variables: (1) some index of the male infant's intimacy with and dependence on the

* Let me remind you again of our definition of the field. In the Komarovsky study, the Straus study, and in the one we are now treating by Whiting *et al.*, we are dealing with controlled observations and interpretations of differing patterns of human relationships: their sources and/or consequences.

mother (the independent variable) and (2) some measure, for the dependent variable, of the existence and extent of initiation rites at puberty. For the latter the investigators use the simplest of nominal scales: the trait is either present or absent. For the independent variable, measures of son-mother intimacy and dependence, they ask whether the infant sleeps with the mother to the exclusion of the father, for at least a year ("long") or less ("short"); and whether, following the birth of the child, there is a taboo on sexual intercourse for at least a year ("long") or less ("short"). Thus, using these two measures on the independent variable (postpartum sex taboo and exclusive mother-son sleeping arrangements), there are four possible combinations: long-long and short-short, or long-short and short-long. The hypothesis predicts that the long-long combination, a lengthy period of postpartum sex taboo and of mother-son sleeping, will be associated with puberty initiation rites of some severity. Contrariwise, the short-short combination should be associated with an absence of initiation rites at puberty. Either of the other combinations should lie in between, in presence or absence of such rites. The findings are presented in Table 9.5. The data are from 55 tribes selected for their geographic distribution, diversity of cultures, and because the data on puberty rites were adequate.

The analysis of these data suggests that the social function of puberty rites, for the male, may be to overcome the influence of a tight mother-son relationship, establishing the youth in the role appropriate to adult males.

We can see the direction of the relationship—and the support of the hypothesis—more clearly if we collapse the table and convert the data into percentages. (See Table 9.6. Can you see how the circled cells in the table indicate the direction of relationship?)

Research is full of pitfalls. This is about the same as saying that rigorous thinking, the solution of difficult problems, is a hard and hazardous undertaking. Having arrived at tentative interpretations, it is always necessary to assess sources of error (as these investigators do), couching one's conclusions in terms less pretentious than fundamental laws of nature. Thus we must recognize that the data from the Human Relations Area Files are uneven in accuracy and wealth of detail; and that coding such data always involves the chance of error—as does every step in research procedure. (The HRAF, developed over the years at Yale, is an extensive and intricately coded collection of data, from anthropologists' and others' reports, on more than 250 tribes and societies

Table 9.5

Relationship between a year or more of both exclusive mother-son sleeping arrangements and postpartum sex taboo, and the occurrence of initiation ceremonies at puberty

Customs in infancy		Customs at adolescent initiation ceremonies	
Exclusive mother-son sleeping arrangements	Postpartum sex taboo	Absent	Present*
Long	Long	Ganda Khalapur Rajput Nyakusa Tepoztlan Trobriander Yapese	Azande(hgs) Camayura(hs) Chagga(hgs) Cheyenne(ht) Chiricahua(ht) Dahomean(hgs) Fijian(gs) Jivaro(ht) Kwoma(hgs) Lesu(gs) Nuer(hs) Samoans(g) Tiv(hgs)
Long	Short	Ashanti Malaita Siriono	Cabaga(ht)
Short	Long	Araucanian Pilaga Pondo Tallensi	Kwakiutl(s) Ojibwa(t) Ooldea(hgs)
Short	Short	Alorese Balinese Druz Egypt (Silwa) Eskimo (Copper) French Igorot (Bontoc) Japanese (Suye Mura) Koryak (Maritime) Lakher Lamba Lapps Lepcha Maori Mixtecans Navaho Ontong Javanese Papago Serbs Tanala (Menabe) Trukese U.S. (Homestead) Yagua	Hopi(hs) Timbira(hst)

* Letters in parentheses indicate certain characteristics of the ceremony: *h* = painful hazing, *g* = genital operations, *s* = seclusion from women, and *t* = tests of manliness.

Table 9.6
The relationship between mother-son intimacy dependency and the presence or absence of adolescent initiation rites

	Adolescent initiation rites					
	Absent		Present		Totals	
Mother-son intimacy and dependency	*N*	%	*N*	%	*N*	%
Maximum	6	32	13	(68)	19	100
Intermediate	7	64	4	36	11	100
Minimum	23	(92)	2	8	25	100
N =	36		19		55	

$\chi^2 = 69.5 - 55 = 14.5$ $d/f = 2$, and $p < .001$

around the world.) On the other hand, an excess of caution may deny us the occasional insights of a brave, imaginative sortie.*

It is just such a sortie that Whiting *et al.* make in concluding their study—one worth our consideration. For it reveals the power of an idea when, supported by empirical research in one setting, it can be extended to other groups and cognate behaviors.

Where, in our society, the investigators ask, do we find virtually ritualized violence among adolescent males? The answer: this occurs, if anywhere, among delinquent juveniles with their gangs, their rumbles, their rebellious defiance of authority, their assertion of independence, their anxious demonstration of virility. This isn't true, clearly, of all juveniles, just as it is not true that all tribes have initiation ceremonies for adolescent males. A critical distinction between the delinquent and the nondelinquent may

* There is reason in research for the self-conscious stalking of vagrant ideas. Without forsaking the hard-headed aspects of research, one feels the appeal of Professor Jerome Bruner's statement when he prefaces a paper of his with the statement: "There is bound to be foolishness in such a preliminary exercise. But in the interest of clarity and *to render the foolishness more discernible* I [speak boldly] so that each theorem can stand on its own bottom. There is a minimum of qualification, for any proposition can be made to seem reasonable if enough qualifications are attached. *Better to be flat-footed and wrong than guardedly indeterminate.*" (Jerome S. Bruner, "Theorems for a Theory of Instruction," dittoed, n.d.; a working paper produced for the President's Committee on Education. Italics mine.) This is a statement from a position of strength and security. Unhappily for the development of any science, we are often so insecure in the face of research uncertainties that we hide behind the precision of the trivial and the obscurity of infinite qualifications. Needless to say the errors of undisciplined fantasy are equally damaging for effective inquiry.

well be that the former must rip himself, metaphorically speaking, from an enveloping female world, asserting himself as an adult and finding his role as a male. And so the investigators suggest that

> . . . insofar as there has been an increase in juvenile delinquency in our society, it should be accompanied by an increase in the exclusiveness of mother-child relationships and/or a decrease in the authority of the father. It is not unreasonable [to suppose] that industrialization and urbanization has done just this.
>
> [If so] . . . then it can be countered either by decreasing the exclusiveness of the early mother-child relationship, increasing the authority of the father during childhood, or instituting a formal means of coping with adolescent boys functionally equivalent to those described in this paper [i.e., puberty rites, avuncular residence, moving to a "men's house," etc.][10]

Let's pursue this point a little further, paying attention to the contrast in American society between relationships 3 and 4 (see Figure 9.1). Parsons and Bales have stressed the fact that, for the boy, the socialization process requires readjustments not demanded of the girl. We get some intimation of the argument from Figure 9.2.

During the socialization process in such a micro system the male child has the problem of straightening out sex-linked roles affecting six relationships: F–M, M–D, S–D, F–S, M–S, and F–D. He must also learn three aspects of his identity: *generational* (which he shares with D); *familial* (embracing both sexes and both generations); and *sexual* (shared with F only). But in contrast with D, the son must at some point disengage himself from M, shifting his identification to F.

> Then we can say that the boy has to undergo at this stage a *double* "emancipation." In common with his sister he has to recognize that, in a sense not previously so important, he must not pretend to adulthood, he is unequivocally a child. But as differentiated from her, he must substitute a new identification with an unfamiliar and in a very important sense threatening object, the father, at the expense of his previous solidarity with his mother. He must renounce his previous dependency in a more radical sense. The girl, on the other hand, though she must internalize the father as object does

Figure 9.2
Basis of sex-role identification in the nuclear family*

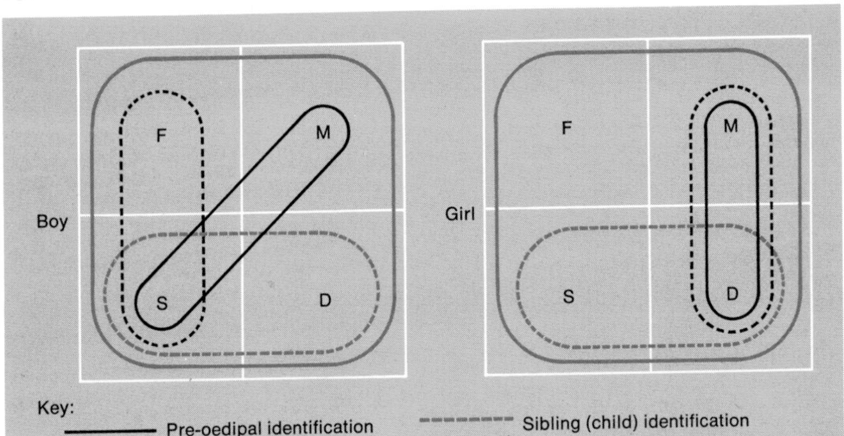

* F—father; M—mother; S—son; D—daughter.

> so only in his role as instrumental leader of the family as a system, not in the dual role which includes sex-role-model as well . . . the boy must proceed farther and more radically on the path away from expressive primacy toward instrumental primacy. He is, therefore, subjected to greater strain.[11]

I have been offering some illustrations of problems touching the structure of the family viewed as a micro system. We can see this unity of interacting personalities as a structure of relationships: husband-wife, parent-child, mother-son and mother-daughter, father-son, father-daughter, and brother-sister. The parent-child relationship has been shown to vary in significant ways by class. Describing four ways in which power may be allocated in the husband-wife relationship, Straus points to possible consequences in the son's behavior. Parsons brings up problems peculiar to mother-son, father-son relationships. These—together with the cross-cultural study of mother-son intimacy and dependence, and its outcomes—highlight the significance of analyzing family structure. For out of these structural variations (different patterns of mother-father-child relationships) flow very different consequences as each generation is inducted into a world prefabricated from the most distant past.

Roles

Wife and mother roles

Now let us shift our perspective from the double-headed arrows representing relationships (Figure 9.1) to the roles that are joined in these relationships. Sociologists have long been interested in those changes in the woman's role that have altered the network of familial relationships. With radically new means of producing, packaging, distributing, preserving, and preparing foods, technologically refined means of cleaning and maintaining a household, and the reduction in land to be maintained, the woman has more leisure, as a housewife. In addition, with increased use of contraception, making children more nearly a matter of choice than chance, she has the opportunity for greater investment of self, per child, as well as the option of a wider range of activities.* She exercises this option increasingly in the political and economic spheres. (M. de Tocqueville would scarcely recognize the modern American middle-class wife.) Women serve as senators and congresswomen. They preside over such businesses as Lord and Taylor's. They work in factories and business establishments. They own a tremendous amount in securities, controlling (*de jure*, if not *de facto*) major segments of business and industry—this, in part, by virtue of their longevity. Their increased participation in the world of work is suggested in Table 9.7.

A study made by the Women's Bureau of the Department of Labor in 1966 found that among women graduating from college in 1957, 85 percent had been married, 66 percent were mothers, and 51 percent were in the labor force. Of those not married (the widowed, divorced, single, or separated) 94 percent were employed. Among those still married, 41 percent were working.

As both cause and consequence, average educational achievement of women has increased, and in extrafamilial roles as in the

* In 1955 Freedman *et al.* drew a probability sample of the approximately 17 million wives in the United States, aged 18 to 39 inclusive. In interviews with 2,713 wives it was found that 70% of all couples and 83% of all fecund couples practiced contraception of some sort. (Recall that probability sampling allows us to bracket these figures *within predictable limits of sampling error.*) Percent using contraceptive techniques varies by wife's age and husband's occupation. The proportion of contraceptive users declines, in general, with occupational status. By four age categories between 18 and 39, the percent of users for all couples is 68% (youngest wives), 73%, 73% and 65% (oldest wives). For fecund couples the figures are 71%, 84%, 90% and 90%. (Ronald Freedman, Pascal K. Whelpton, and Arthur A. Campbell, *Family Planning, Sterility, and Population Growth* (New York: McGraw-Hill Book Co., 1959), pp. 10, 11, 133.

Table 9.7
Percent of all U.S. married women who are working and all U.S. working women who are married

Year	Percent of married women working	Percent of working women married
1890	4.5	13.9
1900	5.8	15.4
1910	10.8	24.7
1920	9.0	23.0
1930	11.5	28.9
1940	16.7	36.4
1950	24.4	52.1
1960	31.4	59.9
1968	38.3	63.4

marriage relationship itself, they move toward equality in option and action.

Husband and father roles

In sketching changes in the woman's role, I have by implication noted changes in the role of husband and father. No longer is he the exclusive incumbent of work and civic roles. In American society there has been a steady decline in the importance of extractive industry (mining, fishing, forestry, agriculture), so reducing the realm of economic activity in which men had a monopoly. In the shift of our labor force from thing-manipulation to symbol-manipulation with an emphasis on psychic rather than physical strength, the male no longer has exclusive access to decision-making roles in politics and business. He no longer enjoys an unchallenged position as thinker-creator.

While the woman has been invading these spheres, the man has come to share in the hitherto motherly monopolies. Not only the increased career activity of woman but also certain views from psychology have led to a redefinition of the father's role. Especially in middle-class families, expressions of paternal care and affection are seen as necessary to the unfolding personality of the child. The father's involvement with the child may commence with clinics for expectant parents, ranging through participation at childbirth to occasional attendance at PTA meetings.

But on the whole, with the separation of workplace from home place, and especially in the middle class, the commuting pattern has reduced the amount of father-child contact in many families leading to a not uncommon matricentric pattern. This, of course, is what Figure 9.2 suggests: an early orientation toward mother (and, in elementary school, toward female teachers) creating the greater probability of radical disjunctures in the socialization of the male child.

The child's role

Such disjunctures (to turn to the child) are discussed in a perceptive analysis by Ruth Benedict.[12] The child's independence may not, in our society, be gradually achieved by small and easy increments. The shift to a heterosexual phase of development may be sudden, especially for the only child, or for the child having siblings of one sex only. Or, emerging from the protection of the small nuclear family, the child may be hit suddenly and shockingly with a world of duplicity and violence.

We have lengthened the period of the child's dependence by withdrawing youth, increasingly, from the labor market. While the exploitation of children has decreased, it may be that the sense of adult self-sufficiency and responsible contribution to the family group has declined, concomitantly. It's probable that household and family duties of children are fewer than formerly. Along with this, there has been an extension of the period of formal education. And at the other end we have thrust education toward the point of birth with cooperative baby pools, prenursery schools, and nursery and kindergarten arrangements.* For some time, average family size has declined (although the postwar years show some recovery and a sort of convergence on a typical family size). These trends are recorded in the Figure 9.3.

The small nuclear family means, of course, a decline in number of siblings and increased dependence for peer relationships on outside associations. This may augur a decline in intimacy and perhaps in understanding between parents and children as they are separated through the interposition of external agencies—school, youth groups, and commercial and other sorts of recreation. Or,

* If one thinks of American society as a three-layer cake, top and bottom being the dependent aged and the dependent young, it is clear that these two sectors are expanding, as a proportion of the total, while the independent middle sector is contracting. The support of more, at a higher standard of living, by fewer is a luxury that could be indulged only in a society marked by high achievement in science and technology, with all that this may imply: a rational and ingeniously exploitative posture vis-à-vis the biological and physical—and probably the social—world, new sources of power to replace human brawn, a high proportion of the labor force in service occupations, and the like.

Figure 9.3
Average number of births by ages 45–49

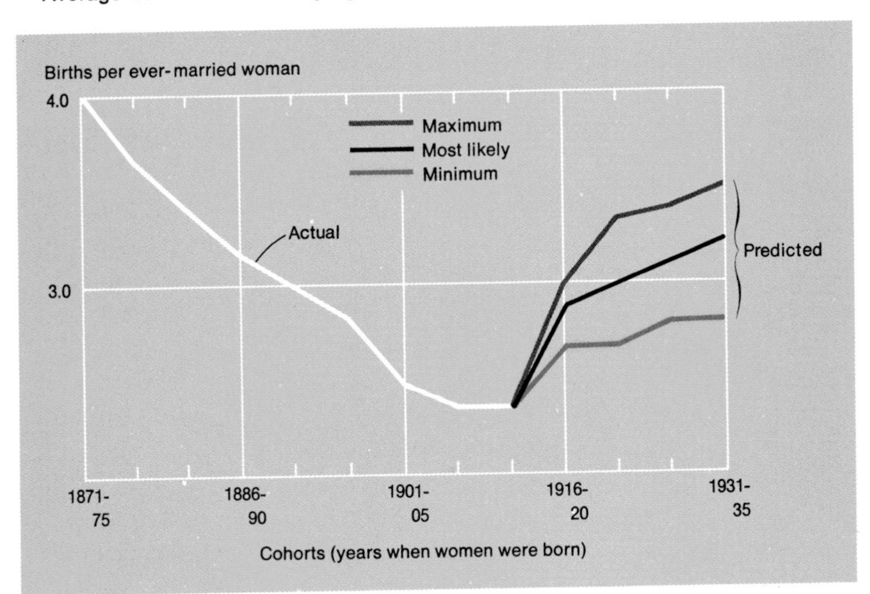

as seems to me a likelier interpretation, social arrangements are being contrived to meet the requirements of independence training formerly met within the household-as-a-farming-enterprise. But since such training may now occur in several contexts, young people may find themselves at the intersection of inconsistent, if not incompatible expectations—those of peers, parents, teachers, police, coreligionists, *et al.*

Formation and dissolution of families in the United States

Let's turn, now, to some general features of the family in American society taken as a whole, beginning with data on its formation and dissolution, followed by some examples of the way institutional characteristics interlock (family and religion, work patterns and family patterns).

Americans tend to be a much married, early married, and remarried people. Our marriage rates are higher than those of most Western European societies. Over a period of years the percent of the population over age 15 that is married has increased quite consistently. This may be due to the declining significance of economic barriers to marriage. It is doubtless due in part to the ability to control births, adapting family size to circumstance. It's conceivable that the marriage rate is related to ease of divorce in somewhat the same way as birth rates and death rates are connected. (See Figure 9.4.) We can think of an institutionalized relationship, such as marriage, being regularly broken by death, divorce, and separation, and regularly replenished by newly married couples. Some of this is simply an internal shifting of spouses: our divorce rates are high and most divorced persons remarry.

Sociologists have turned up some answers to the question: Why do some couples break up and others do not? Research indicates that people in homogamous marriages (persons sharing background traits in common) are less vulnerable to divorce than those of unlike attributes. Among the latter, there are two types: where the wife marries down (hypogamous) and where the wife marries up (hypergamous). The former is more likely than the latter to end in divorce.

Childless couples are more likely to divorce than those having children, but this correlation is probably a result of the short duration of marriage prior to divorce. (Highest divorce rates are in the first five years of marriage, particularly in the second year.)

Dissolution of marriage is highest among poor, Negro urban families. (We get a vivid sense of family disruption in this category from Elliot Liebow's *Tally's Corner.*) High divorce rates are also associated with urban residence, early marriage, a short period of courtship and engagement, unhappy parental marriages, disapproval of friends and relatives, and unlike backgrounds. In general, the higher ranking the occupation, the lower the divorce rates for couples in that category (Table 9.8).

Since early marriage is connected with a higher probability of divorce, the declining median age at first marriage may have something to do with increased divorce rates in the United States. Age at first marriage declined sharply after the beginning of World War II. (See Figure 9.5.) By 1968, median ages at first marriage were about 21 and 23 for bride and groom, respectively.

Families are formed, in our society, in accordance with values and preferences embedded in our culture. Parents and children constitute the usual family unit. This is the nuclear family. Along with neolocal residence (new location: the newly married couple sets up an independent household), this excludes spouses' parents, children's grandparents. Social security and various insurance devices have made the elders dependent no longer on their children but on the state and other agencies. Three-generation households are becoming rather rare in the United States.

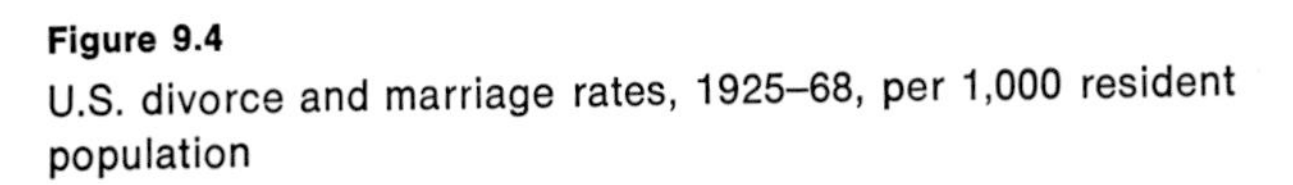

Figure 9.4
U.S. divorce and marriage rates, 1925–68, per 1,000 resident population

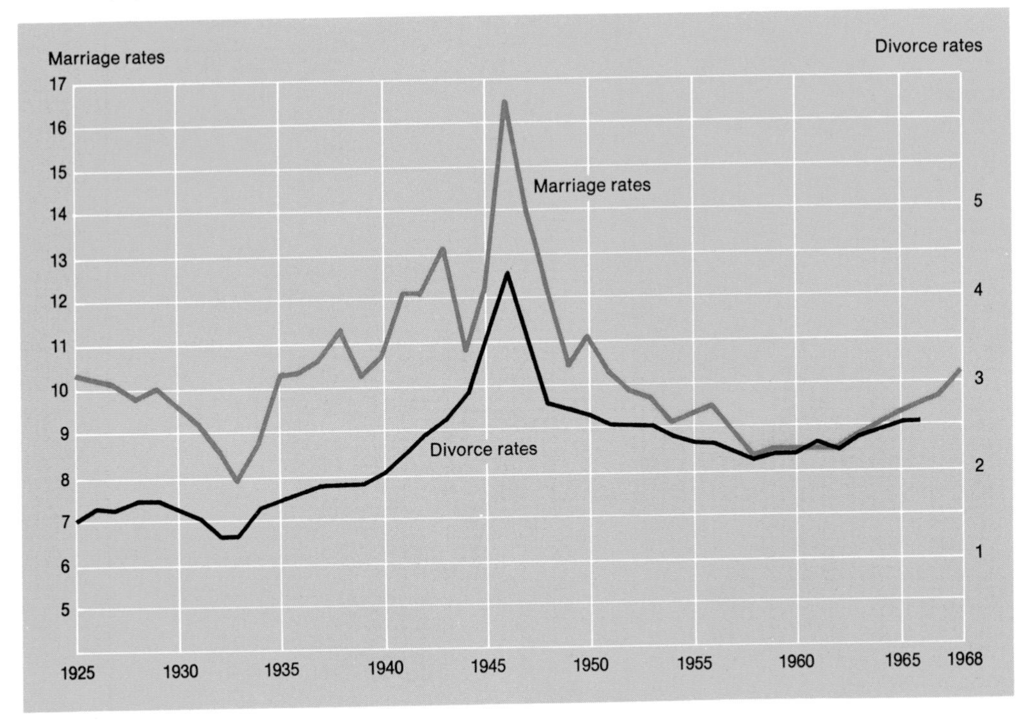

Table 9.8
Index of proneness to divorce, by occupation, Detroit, 1948

Occupation	Index
Professional and proprietary	67.7
Clerical, sales, service	83.2
Skilled, foremen	74.1
Semiskilled, operatives	126.1
Unskilled	179.7

Our sort of family is formed because it is the social mechanism instituted to achieve certain ends. In the United States it is the sole legitimate agency for sexual access, for reproducing children and conferring their identity, and for providing initial adaptation to requirements of the larger society. It is also typically an economic unit—not, as was once the common case, for production, but for consumption.

Figure 9.5
Median age at first marriage in United States

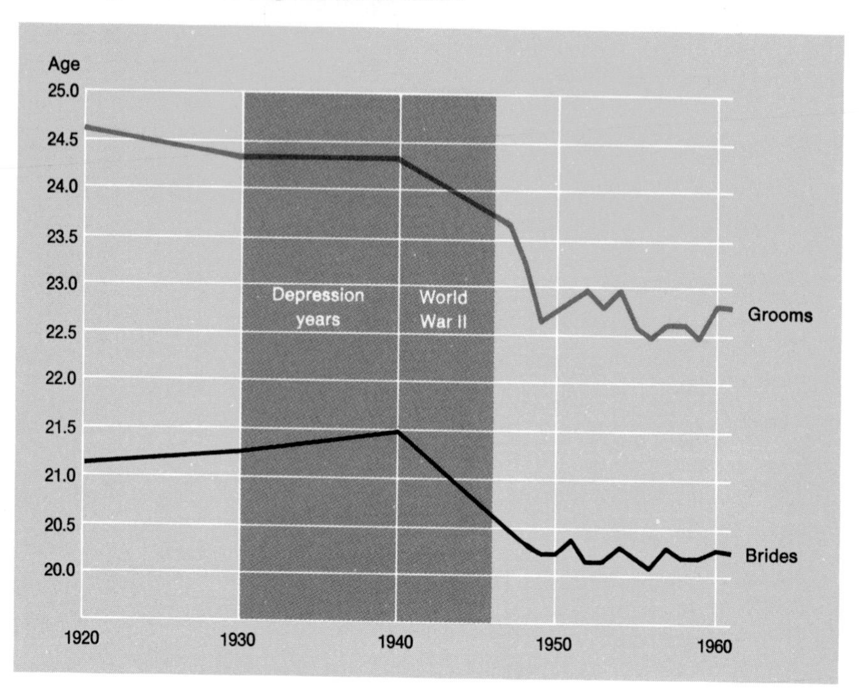

Links between institutions: family and religion, family and work relationships

There is no statement more basic to an understanding of the social order than that which asserts the interconnectedness of social things. So it is with the major institutions that form an interdigitating framework for the social order. Family, school, church, government, and work, while by no means perfectly orchestrated tend, nonetheless, to play in the same key and to resolve dissonances in favor of a common theme. To put it a different way, variations in one institutional theme are likely to be connected with variations in another.

Family and religion

Take as one example of interinstitutional connections the way in which dissolution of the family by divorce is linked with religious affiliation. Table 9.9 presents relevant data from three studies while

Table 9.9

Percent of marriages of mixed and nonmixed religious faiths ending in divorce or separation*

Religious categories	Landis study in Michigan (N = 4,108)		Bell study in Maryland (N = 13,528)	Weeks study in Washington (N = 6,548)
	N	%		
Both Catholic	573	4.4	6.4	3.8
Both Jewish	96	5.2	4.6	—
Both Protestant	2,794	6.0	6.8	10.0
Mixed, Catholic-Protestant	192	14.1	15.2	17.4
Both none	39	17.9	16.7	23.9
Protestant changed to Catholic	56	10.7		
Catholic changed to Protestant	57	10.6		
Protestant father–Catholic mother	90	6.7		
Catholic father–Protestant mother	102	20.6		
Father none–Mother Catholic	41	9.8		
Father none–Mother Protestant	84	19.0		

* Enter, here, a methodological caveat. First, the terms Catholic, Protestant, and Jewish are spongy ones: Protestant denominations vary widely, and some "Protestants" may in fact be atheists or agnostics, certainly noncommunicants. The same problem applies to Catholics and Jews. Thus, to an unknown extent, the high divorce rates for interfaith marriages may reflect *absence* of, rather than *difference* in, religious commitments. For some suggestive evidence on this point, see Lee B. Burchinal and Loren E. Chancellor, "Survival Rates among Religiously Homogamous and Interreligious Marriages," *Social Forces,* Vol. 41, No. 4 (May, 1963), pp. 353–62. Furthermore, we should note that while these data suggest a connection between two institutional spheres, family and church, divorce, like other aspects of family life, is touched by factors not controlled here: income, number of children, length of marriage, urban or rural residence, type of occupation, and the like.

Figure 9.6 is a graphic summary of the Landis study of the families of 4,108 Michigan State College students.*

Family and work

Take another illustration of interinstitutional linkages, in this case the connection between family relationships and work relationships. It would seem reasonable that, both as a result of self-

* We should remind ourselves that a correlation is not a statement of cause and effect. If *inter*faith marriages are more vulnerable to divorce than *intra*faith marriages (but note the high rates for nonfaith marriages), it may well be that the same factors prompting an interfaith marriage may be the underlying reason for the divorce—say, antitraditionalism, or independence, or rebellion. In any case, see Lee B. Burchinal and Loren E. Chancellor, "Survival Rates among Religiously Homogamous and Interreligious Marriages," in *Social Forces,* Vol. 41, No. 4 (May, 1963), pp. 353–62 and Glenn Vernon, "Interfaith Marriage," in R. D. Knudten (ed.), *The Sociology of Religion* (New York: Appleton Century, 1968), pp. 459–64.

recruitment and employment policies, persons in quite different work settings might differ in personality and typical behaviors; and that such differences might be registered in familial (and other) relationships. Thus one might expect William H. Whyte's "organization man" in his anonymous gray flannel suit, an adaptive, accommodating, radar-responding, other-directed sort of person* to train his children in similar fashion. On the other hand, the self-employed, or the person covering a variety of tasks in an entrepreneurial setting, might be expected to display a paternal pattern emphasizing drive, discipline, and self-reliance.

Some such notions as these stimulated research to discover whether there was a difference in parental behaviors between families whose fathers worked in bureaucratic settings and those whose fathers were entrepreneurs. The implicit assumption that a change in style of working from the entrepreneurial to the bureaucratic organization has been paralleled by a change in parent-child relationships accounts for the title of this work, *The Changing American Parent*.[13]

Entrepreneurial families were defined as those in which the husband was (1) self-employed, or (2) gained at least half of his income from fees, profits, or commissions, or (3) was employed by a small organization (having at most two levels of supervision), or (4) was farm born or (5) was foreign born. All other families were classified as "bureaucratic." In these families

> husbands work for someone else in organizations with three or more supervisory levels. Their income is primarily in the form of wages or salary. They are not taking entrepreneurial risks. Nor do most of them have entrepreneurial opportunities.[14]

This is a good illustration of a common methodological problem. We have here two quite abstract ideas, entrepreneurial and bureaucratic—ideas that must be cast in operational terms if we are to test the hypothesis. It is seldom a simple matter to contrive valid indexes of such terms. And we find Swanson and Miller shifting from characteristics of work setting to those of birthplace in their operational definition of "entrepreneurial."

Five hundred and eighty-two mothers having children under age

* The last two terms are Professor David Riesman's. For a provocative study of the changing American character see his *The Lonely Crowd* (New Haven, Conn.: Yale University Press, 1961).

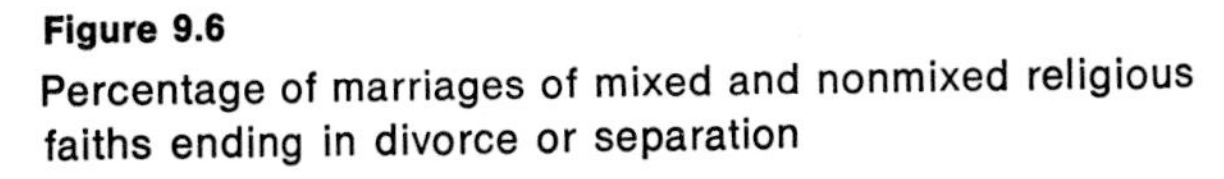

Figure 9.6
Percentage of marriages of mixed and nonmixed religious faiths ending in divorce or separation

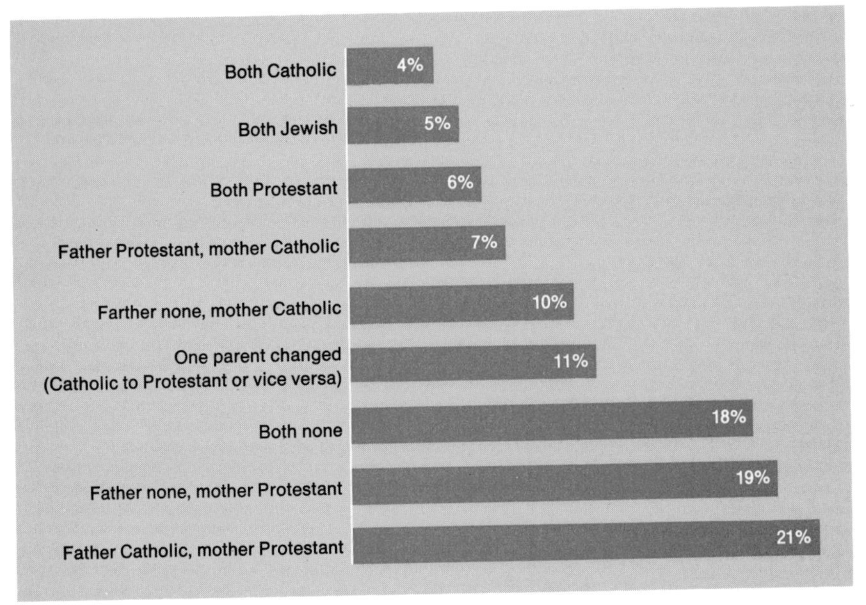

19 were interviewed in an area probability sample of Detroit. After eliminating Negroes, families with adopted children or stepchildren, and those in which husband and wife were not living together, the sample numbered 479 families. Some of the investigators' findings are as follows.

Bearing on the development of strong self-control, entrepreneurial mothers were more likely than bureaucratic mothers to pay no attention, or delayed attention to the baby's crying, to feed the baby on a schedule, to begin urinary training before the baby was 11 months old, and to use symbolic punishments. For the development of an active and independent approach to the world, mothers from the entrepreneurial families were more likely than their bureaucratic counterparts to: use harsh means to prevent the child from sucking parts of its body, to deny that the child touched its sex organs, to approve leaving the child at home with a competent woman while the mother shopped or visited, to feel that a child should be on his own as soon as possible to solve his own problems, and to feel that only males should perform activities traditionally associated with their sex.

On a number of other beliefs and behaviors, there were no statistically significant differences between the entrepreneurial and bureaucratic families. (I have reported only those on which the probability of the observed difference occurring by chance was less than .05.) Complex as the problem is and tenuous as are certain of the findings, we are left with the conviction that there is an important connection between work relationships and parent-child relationships. There is, furthermore, the likelihood that both sets of relationships have changed over time. One has the sense of a moving equilibrium—an equilibrium always imperfectly achieved, of course.

* * * *

We have looked at the family as a micro system, a structure of relationships. With four persons—mother, father, daughter and son—we have six relationships. We might represent such a micro system, schematically, as in Figure 9.7. For certain of these relationships I have illustrated the sociologist's approach: the significance of different permutations of power in the husband-wife relationships, the variations of parent-child relationships by class, and the significance, for achieving the role of adult male, of variations in the dependency dimension of the mother-child relationship.

In a discussion of the roles that comprise these relationships, we see three changes that herald significant shifts in family structure: the extension of women's roles to realms hitherto exclusively men's, the redefinition of the man's role, with a reduction in his monopolies and some blurring of sex-linked roles, and, finally, the problem of the child's—expecially the son's—role with an extended period of dependency and the difficulty, in a feminine world, of achieving the role of adult, independent male.

Over the years the size of the family has declined, then recovered a bit, with some evidence of an emerging modal family of just over three children. While marriage rates have gone up, so have rates of divorce and separation. The nuclear and neolocal family, typical in American society, has aspects of transiency and an air of convenient companionship to an extent probably not true in past centuries. And this is what we should expect for two reasons: (1) change in other sectors of the social order—in the accumulation of knowledge, in scientific discoveries and technological development, in the economy, in religion and government—have been great and rapid, and (2) since elements of the social order are interdependent, change in one sector exerts leverage for adaptive change in other sectors.

The connectedness of institutions has been illustrated in two ways. Family and church are linked, as is evidenced in the relation-

Figure 9.7

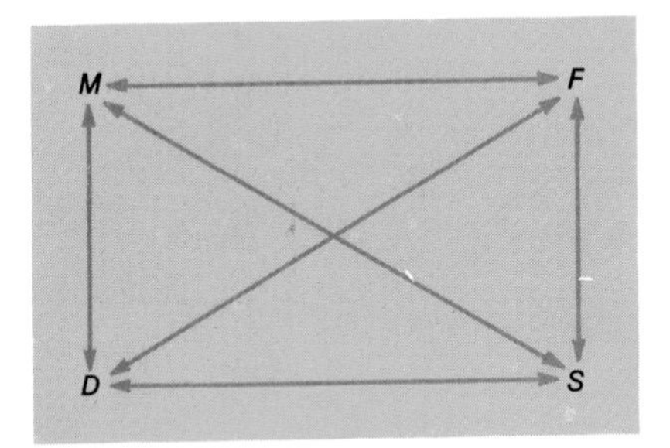

ship between divorce rates and religious affiliation. (I skirt the obvious: the sacraments celebrating birth and death and christening, or the effect of the church on contraceptive practices.) Finally, there is the probable connection between relationships at work and those in the bosom of the family, a connection that Miller and Swanson tried to test when they suggested that work relationships in entrepreneurial and bureaucratic settings had their parallels in parent-child relationships.*

Education as an inducting institution

> 'Tis education forms the common mind:
> Just as the twig is bent the tree's inclined
> Alexander Pope, *Moral Essays,* Epistle I, line 149

Twig bending, in complex societies like ours, is institutionalized on a massive scale. In four or five years, the 3.5 million infants born in 1968 (minus a few deaths) will be entering nursery schools and kindergartens. For those who finish high school, 20 percent of their life-span will be spent in the protective custody of schools. For four-year college graduates, the figure is 26 percent; for those spending another four years in graduate school, it's just under a third of the life-span.

* In offering "illustrations" and using words like "finally," I may inadvertently have suggested a representative reporting of research on the family or, worse still, an exhaustive coverage of sociological inquiries into this institution. To put it mildly this is not the case: first, due to my ignorance of this field; and second, because to cover the sociology of the family would require many volumes. For current research see the indexes of the *American Sociological Review, Sociological Abstracts,* the *American Journal of Sociology,* the *American Journal of Orthopsychiatry,* and Harold T. Christensen, *Handbook of Marriage and the Family* (Skokie, Ill.: Rand McNally & Co., 1964).

Taking our total population at 200 million, persons whose energies are invested primarily in formal education constitute about 29 percent of the whole. Table 9.10 shows how these 59 million people distribute themselves through four roles.

We have been rapidly increasing our investments, both public and private, in education. The figure in 1964 was about $39 billion for public and private schools at all levels. As Figure 9.8 shows, that was better than 6 percent of the gross national product. Just 21 years earlier, it was under 2 percent.

To these investments should be added some 4 to 5 billions, annually, from private enterprise. In recent years business has been taking up education as an interesting and profitable sideline. The market for teaching devices runs to something around $800 million a year—this for slide and overhead projectors, motion picture cameras, language laboratory equipment, and the like. New developments, such as computer-assisted instruction and the talking typewriter, may be expected to enlarge profits from educational hardware.

How account for this great preoccupation with formal education? First, socialization is an essential social function. Second, the more complex the society, the more education displaces the family as training ground for adult roles. Third, the more complex the society, the more—and the more diverse—the educational channels leading to occupational, civic, and other roles. Thus the institutionalizing of education guarantees a regular input of the knowledge, skills, attitudes, and values necessary to sustain the group. As an example—and the most obvious, the preparation for work—there is a substantial association between school performance and the prestige ranking of occupations chosen by students. (For 21 occupations, the rank-order correlation coefficient between mean high school grade and the prestige score of occupations chosen by students was .78.)[15]

In the rest of this chapter I want to suggest answers to three questions: (1) What is the social function of education? (2) What sorts of evidence do we have that our schools perform this function? (3) What do we know about what is taught, by whom, and how?*

* Is it unnecessary (as one might hope) to remind ourselves that here as elsewhere the discussion fixes on what is—not on what might be or ought to be?

Table 9.10
Investment in induction
Numbers of persons involved in formal education in 1965–66 (000's omitted).

	Students		Teachers	Administrators	Board members et al.
	Public	Private			
Elementary school	31,200	5,400	22,045	112.4	
Secondary school	12,000	1,300			
College and university	4,000	2,000	466	53.9	
Total	55,900		2,511	166.3	656

Figure 9.8
Percent of gross national product invested in U.S. education
Alaska and Hawaii included for 1959 and 1964 data

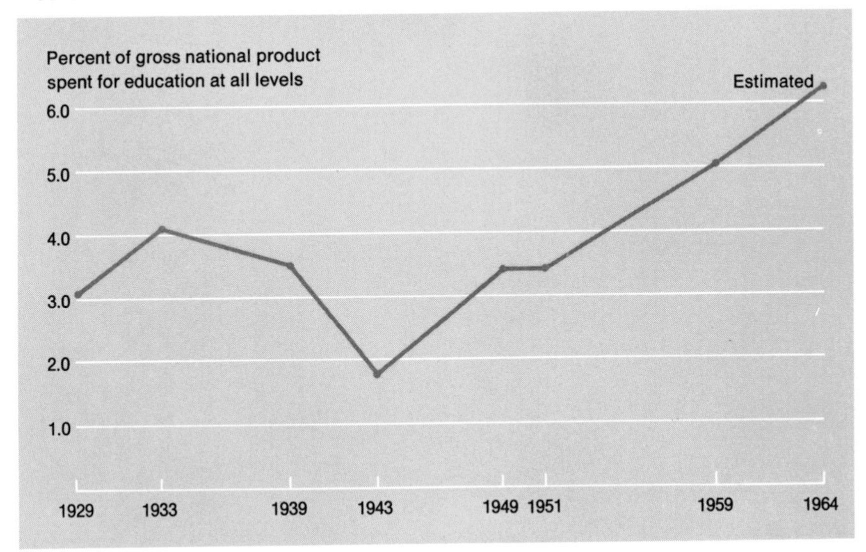

The social function of education

Education is the chief means of resolving a paradox: the fact of the group's immortality despite the continual loss of its constituent parts. Our nation, your town, the A&P, your church, the Republican party—these groups persist over decades, generations, and longer. They persist despite withdrawal, death, and defection of citizens, residents, workers, communicants, and members. To sustain such groups is to sustain a pattern of relationships for, and in which, we must be trained.

And this is the social function of public education. Through sundry educational devices the newcomer is inducted into the secrets of society, taught the tribal lore so that he may take up his part in the complex orchestration of roles. The beliefs and behaviors that we institutionalize under the label, "education," are aimed at recruiting, developing, and sorting out the talents, attitudes, and values appropriate to the continuous fulfillment of the roles requisite for group survival.

Education involves three processes essential to any enduring organization: selective recruitment, indoctrination (or orientation, or in-service training), and separation of the maladapted. Failure in any one of these processes implies, to that degree, the transformation of the group. Although it is by no means totally effective, education provides social insurance against such threats to the existing social structure. It recruits selectively. The children of professional parents it recruits early, keeps late. The children of subsistence farmers it recruits late, dismisses early. During the high school years, education recruits some for further training, allowing others to drop out. It sorts some into the college preparatory curriculum, some into the general curriculum, and others into the commerical curriculum. It recruits some for the High School of Music and Arts, some for the Bronx High School of Science, others for Harlem Vocational. Thus through the educational process the group recruits and sorts its human input into the "right" preparatory experiences. It then transmits those elements of the culture deemed by powerful elders to be indispensable for the general welfare. And throughout the process it sorts and separates the maladapted, the misfits.

As the necessary means of group survival, public education is an intrinsically conservative process, guaranteeing the future by recreating the past. The young newcomer is always the vulnerable one, confronting a prefabricated, ongoing organization. Teachers are the agents for creating a socially prescribed product. Of course, what is prescribed will change through time as conditions of the social order change.

In our times there are three sorts of roles for which persons must be educated if the group is to survive: specialists' roles, coordinating roles, and group-binding (integrating, or civic) roles. A society as complex as ours obviously requires specialized training. For technical training, from plumber and printer to engineer and physicist, society fixes highly specific systems of induction.

But beyond trained specialists, our society requires, quite as much, training for the coordinating roles that bridge the specialties. This is the more necessary since, although strangers to most of our fellow Americans, each of us is implicated in their lives. In this intricate network every man's activities become vested with a public interest. Legal, clerical, and sales work are prime examples of this essential, intermediating function.

Finally, and especially because of its complexity, a modern society requires of its members a certain minimum of skills, knowledge, and allegiances that are shared in common. These enable minimal communication, provide an identity, and legitimize the demands of the group upon the person (as in the case of taxation and military service). For establishing personal and group identity, the school is asked to inculcate commitment to our common cause.

Three conditions of our social order prompt expansion and proliferation in education: complexity, affluence, and danger. In the United States, public education responded to the challenge of Sputnik with greater emphasis on mathematics, foreign language, and the technical training deemed necessary to achieve parity in power. The complexity of our social order is reflected and reinforced by our complex educational structure shown schematically in Figure 9.9. Our affluence is reflected in the vast amounts we are able to spend for education, public and private, and in the increased proportion of our population achieving higher levels of education.

In Western societies, organized or official education has come to involve ever more people, ever more subjects over longer time spans. An increasing proportion of our population is going beyond high school. The number of 18- to 21-year-olds was about the same in 1960 as in 1939. But in 1939 only 14 percent of them were in college, whereas the figure for 1961 was 38 percent.[16] To keep them there we spent about $6.23 billion.

"Keeping them there" suggests a latent function of education: the withholding from the labor market of a large segment of our population that could not possibly be absorbed in our highly mechanized, automated economy. As John Updike's fey teacher put it: "School is where you go between when your parents can't take you and industry can't take you."[17]

The great expansion of education in the United States, both training for and withholding from the labor market, is a response to the requirements of social survival. The social function of education, as Durkheim put it, is to arouse and to develop in the child a certain number of physical, intellectual and moral states which are demanded of him both by the political society as a whole and the special milieu for which he is specifically destined.[18]

Thus the ostensible task is to man the social order. A latent function is to keep the unemployable young profitably occupied, or at least to prevent that work which the devil is alleged to have for idle hands.

Evidence that schools perform a social function

Many sociological studies attest the way education reflects and reinforces the social structure. Theodore Parsons studied a central California community in which people of northwest European ancestry (Anglos) regarded those of Mexican origin as dirty, immoral, irresponsible, and unintelligent. On special occasions at the Catholic church, Mexicans were allowed to sit or stand in the back. They were not accepted at the other two churches. They were employed in the lower ranks of the labor force and were relatively powerless in political affairs. The school reflected this division in the community. In a dual tracking system, the Mexicans were in the slow group, the Anglos in the other. At graduation, the Mexicans marched in last and sat on the back of the platform. Explaining why she had asked an Anglo child to lead five Mexican youngsters out of the classroom, a teacher said: "His father owns one of the big farms in the area and . . . one day he will have to know how to handle the Mexicans." Anglo children were also called on to help Mexican children recite in class, again reflecting their relative positions.[19]

Poor children of limited background may find little that is meaningful in a school curriculum geared to a white-collar, middle-class world. When the gap is great between present school requirements and future work possibilities, we might expect the student to "cop out," or to rebel in one way or another. This is what Stinchcombe found in his study, *Rebellion in a High School.* The effect is to close off opportunities, increasing the probability that poor sons will follow in poor father's footsteps. Thus education may reinforce the class structure.

Hollingshead reports similar findings in his study of youth in *Elmtown.* The lower the class of the high school student's family, the (1) higher the drop-out rate, (2) lower the vocational aspira-

Figure 9.9

Percent of population 17 years old graduating from high school shown against a background of the complex U.S. education structure

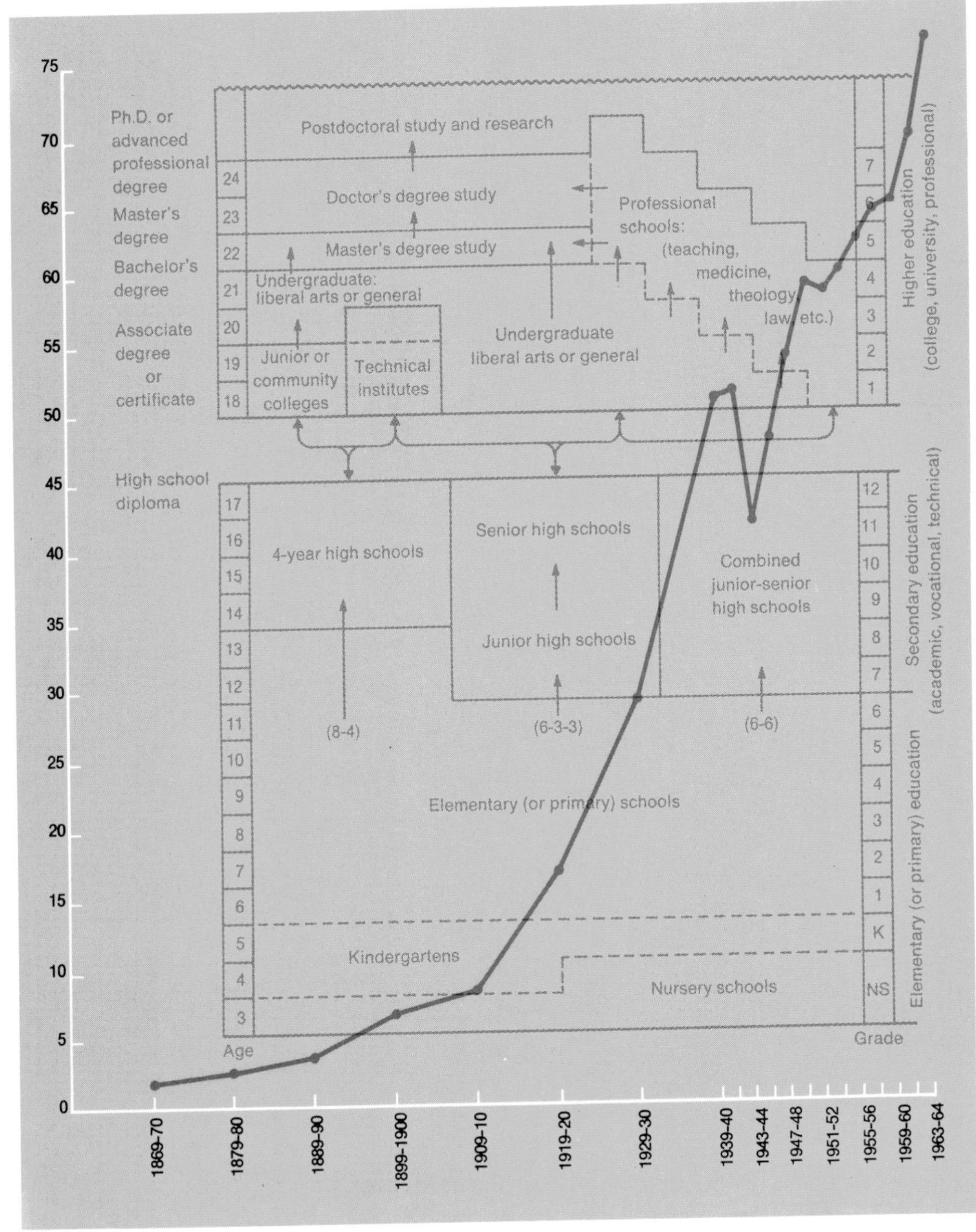

tion, (3) lower the proportion planning on college, (4) lower the course grades and the higher the number of failures, (5) higher the proportion in commercial and vocational curricula, (6) lower the education of the parents, (7) lower the intelligence test scores, and (8) greater the number of recorded discipline problems.

Such research data on the way an educational system reinforces the class structure of the group may lead to misconceptions. Like all facts, these do not speak for themselves. They require interpretation. How does it happen that the group assures its survival through the use of the institution of education, a prime effect being to train the children in parental roles? Perhaps the American nurtured on the Horatio Alger ideal and devoted to individual self-determination will resist this ultraconservative and static picture of the group endlessly perpetuating itself at the expense of individual differences, initiative, imagination, and change. To the extent that it is true, we might be disposed to think that middle-class teachers, a group Willard Waller once described as comprising unmarriageable women and unsalable men, are the witless stooges of dominant upper-class interests, favoring the children of the masters in their painful concern to please the powers and advance their own interests. This interpretation of the facts might be called the conspiratorial theory. Or it might be suggested that, since marriage and mating are selective matters, the rich and the wellborn are also the able. Thus genetic differentials parallel class lines and are reflected in differing levels of achievement. This we might call the *Drosophila* theory or the fruit fly fiction. More plausible than either the genetic gambit or the conspiratorial theory is a third interpretation, one that asserts: Class differences in educability stem from family differences in stimulation, training, and motivation. The home of the lower-class child is no launching pad for upper-class orbiting. (Here again we see the interlocking of major social institutions.)

A person's social past has a momentum that carries into the future. This is not merely because the past was the seedbed of his knowledge, hopes, and values. It is also because others' acts toward him are guided by meanings attached to that background. On these meanings, expectations of future performance are based. There is some evidence that a teacher's expectations may influence, in subtle and unintended ways, the achievement of her charges.

What meanings might a teacher attach to backgrounds suggested by words like "poor," or "Negro," or "Puerto Rican," or "Mexican-American?" Or to "wealthy family," or "good academic

Figure 9.10

		Before (pretests)	Experimental treatment	After (retests)
Experimental	One fifth of the students, kindergarten through 5th grade, randomly chosen	All children tested in May 1964, using Flanagan tests of general ability	Sept. 1964 report to teachers that certain students (experimental group) are academic "spurters"	Retests at appropriate levels, 4 months after start of school, at end of 1964-65 year and again in May, 1966 (all children)
Control	All the rest of the students,		No mention of students falling in the control group	

background?" Is it possible that performance in the teacher's role changes depending on the differing background traits she finds—or thinks exist—among her students? And if she does adapt her behavior, how does she do it? And what are the outcomes?

Robert Rosenthal did a study in which each of 12 psychology students was given five rats to teach to run a maze. Although the animals were quite alike, half the students were told that their rats had been bred for brightness in running a maze. The other half were informed that their rats suffered genetic limitations, making them poor maze-runners. Reports from the "teachers" who thought they had well-bred rats revealed that they had been more gentle with their rats than the slow-group "teachers"—had handled them more and saw them as pleasant, bright, and likable creatures. From the beginning, these "high-potential" rats outperformed the others.

This is the self-fulfilling prophecy at work. Expecting certain outcomes, one acts (not always consciously) in ways that bring the expected to pass. Might the same principle be at work in human relationships—for example, teacher-student?

In a later study, Rosenthal and Jacobson attacked this question.[20] The design of the research can be represented as in Figure 9.10.

While both groups of students showed gains, those from whom better performance was expected (the randomly chosen "spurters") outperformed members of the control group. This was especially so for the first and second graders at the end of the first year, and for the fifth graders at the end of the second year.

Notice how slight and subtle the experimental treatment was. Teachers were very casually told ("By the way, in case you're interested . . .") that they had, in each case, about five youngsters who had shown on the pretest—the "before" situation—that they were spurters. This apparently was all it took for the teachers to find them more promising, more attractive, and better adjusted. That they also gained markedly more than control group children was not, it seems, due to the teacher spending more time with them.

> . . . the explanation we are seeking lies in a subtler feature of the interaction of the teacher and her pupils. Her tone of voice, facial expression, touch and posture may be the means by which—probably quite unwittingly—she communicates her expectations to the pupils. Such communication might help the child by changing his conception of himself, his anticipation of his own behavior, his motivation or his cognitive skills.*

Expectations stem from experience. Experience is past behavior. Customary behavior in the past is a way of saying "tradition." Public education reflects tradition in the structure of relationships set up to teach and learn. (In January, 1970, the Mississippi House of Representatives debated and declined to repeal a state law forbidding the teaching of evolution in the state's schools.) And teachers, too, reveal in their teaching, expectations growing out of their pasts.† As the Rosenthal experiment suggests, this is likely to work to the advantage of ordinary, white middle-class students (thus reinforcing the traditional), and to the disadvantage of others of whom not much is expected. So there are forces at work that make education a past-conserving institution.

But, of course, there is change in our society—much of it—and

* If expectations fulfilled appear to be gratifying, what of expectations not fulfilled? The investigators found that when, among control group students, performance was *higher than expected* (especially among slow-track children, of whom expectations were low), "The more they gained, the more unfavorably they were rated" by their teachers. "Evidently it is likely to be difficult for a slow-track child, even if his [test scores] are rising, to be seen by his teacher as well adjusted and as a potentially successful student." (Robert Rosenthal and Lenore Jacobson "Teacher Expectations for the Disadvantaged," *Scientific American*, Vol. 281, No. 4 [April, 1968], pp. 19–23.)

† Of course, this is not peculiar to teachers. Few of us can transcend by much the experiences of our past or, for that matter, fully realize the potential seeded in that past.

there is upward mobility. And education is the main social mechanism for advancing in standing. (This you'll recall from our discussion of intergenerational mobility in Chapter 7.) Educational opportunity and differential fertility work hand in hand to the extent that upper- and middle-class persons fail to reproduce themselves. As a result of such class differences in fertility, the schools must draw from the lower strata, train in the necessary skills, values, and attitudes, and send into higher-class positions perhaps a dozen out of every hundred. Furthermore, persons moving down and out of positions of power and privilege must be replaced by others, trained out of lower-class backgrounds and moved up in the group structure. Thus, for some persons, the school does act as a social escalator while simultaneously preserving the structure.

Other changes in urban, industrialized societies have strongly affected the social function of education. An enormously productive technology had required two adaptive changes on the part of education: (1) absorbing displaced or unneeded manpower and (2) extending the period of education for technically demanding roles.

Neither needed nor wanted on farm or in factory, young people spend more time in school and are increasingly isolated from adult influence, other than that of their teachers. At the same time they are much more exposed to the influence of their peers. What the sociologist finds emerging, then, is an adolescent subculture with its own values and beliefs, its esoteric language and distinctive behavior. Insofar as the characteristics of the adolescent subculture are eccentric to the mainstream of the group's life, the school performs an important protective function. It acts as custodian until such time as its charges can be absorbed with impunity by the group. But if we emphasize, not the latent function of custodianship but the manifest function of staffing the social order with the best talent available, then the emergence of an adolescent culture, isolated from adult life, may work against achieving this objective.

Some of the evidence shows that the mediocre rather than the talented student is rewarded in our public schools. Grades of "A," Professor Coleman found, go to students of exceptional ability *only where* the student population itself honors academic achievement.[21] Where the life of the intellect is not esteemed in the student subculture—and this seems often to be the case—students with high grade records are those of mediocre aptitude, the "squares" unable to achieve in activities honored by their peers.

These activities are interscholastic athletics and social life. The abler students, sensitive to the sources of reward in the private world of the adolescent subculture, seek the plaudits of their peers in athletics and social popularity. Ability is not exploited when peers deride, or fail to recognize it. In Professor Coleman's study of 10 high schools, the

> . . . high performers, those who received good grades [were not] the boys whose ability was greatest but a more mediocre few. Thus the "intellectuals" of such a society . . . will not, in fact, be those with most intellectual ability. . . . In every school, without exception, the boys named as best athletes were named more often—on the average over twice as often—as members of the leading crowd than were those named as best students.[22]

Nor did the girls in Coleman's 10 high schools wish to be remembered as brilliant students. Among them to an even greater extent than among the boys, the person named as "best student" had few friends and was not found in the leading crowd. "In all cases, the leading crowd [pulled] away from the brilliant-student ideal."[23]

If technology sends young people back to teachers and peers, education in turn adapts to changes in the labor force induced by technology. As dealing with things demands less manpower (extractive industry: farming, forestry, fishing, mining) and dealing with people and symbols requires more workers, the schools produce service workers and symbol manipulators. The importance of words (and numbers) is suggested by the decline of illiteracy in the United States (Figure 9.11). And by a concomitant 240 percent increase in white-collar workers between 1900 and 1960.

Not only does education adapt to the condition of the labor force. At the behest of professions, accrediting associations, and state licensing departments, it patrols the entrance gates to occupations. One doesn't become a doctor or a nurse, an architect, sociologist, chemist, dentist, lawyer, engineer—without passing educational hurdles.

Finally, education performs a preeminently social function as it links with institutions of government. Education reinforces a democratic polity if, as we assume, a literate and participating electorate is necessary to democracy. A final set of data suggests that, if widespread participation is required for democratic government, then literacy (education), too, must be widespread. (See Figure 9.12.)

Figure 9.11
Illiteracy in the United States*

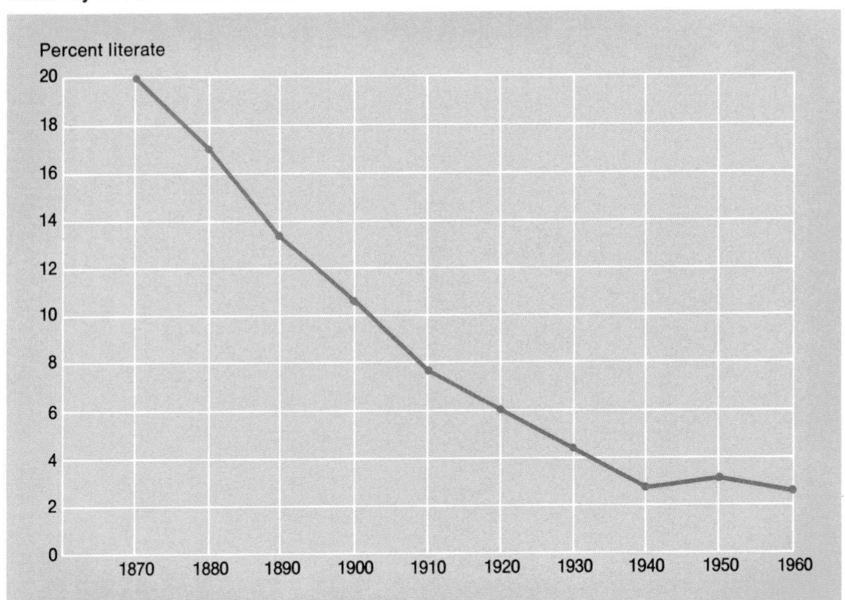

* Illiteracy is defined as the inability to read and write a simple message either in English or any other language.

Who teaches what? And how?

Learning and teaching are not confined to persons officially designated as teachers and students. This is one of the chief contributions of anthropologists, whose cross-cultural studies show that the same or similar functions—teaching, for example—may be carried out by different agents and in different ways. We are remarkably ignorant about the changes stemming from allegedly educational experiences and from experiences not recognized as educational. We can be sure that in settings we institutionalize as educational, there are teachers other than those officially so designated. We can also be sure that there are social settings outside the school in which important learnings are regularly achieved.

Toward the end of Chapter 5 the overindividualized, overpsychologized view of education is discussed. This view overlooks the social—the group-preserving—function of education. Thus there may be a disenchanting gap between educational ideology (develop the unique capacities of each individual to the limit of his potential) and educational product.

Beyond this, such a view is likely to overlook or minimize the social levers of learning. The "theory and practice of education remains focused on individuals; teachers exhort individuals to concentrate their energies in scholarly directions, while the community of adolescents [responding to the conditions of their group] diverts these energies into other channels."[24]

Teaching and learning are social matters. And the relationship between teacher and learner is always affected by the total constellation of relationships in which each is implicated. The effectiveness of learning depends not only on teacher and student but on the relationship with parents (the motivation and background they provide); with employer, present or prospective, whose requirements lend relevance to the learning process; and with administrators, the board of education, and many others. Education if it is to be understood, must be seen as an orchestration of social influences.

A social perspective on education has long been available in the work of anthropologists. Nowhere is the connection between education and other aspects of the social order more apparent than in their studies. They have often reported, for example, the way many Indian groups eschew corporal punishment. Lowie has written that "there is almost a direct ratio between rudeness of culture and gentleness with children."[25] This we understand when we link disciplinary procedures with the methods used to induct youth into the status of adulthood: tests of strength, fortitude, endurance, suffering. The pain of corporal punishment cannot be used as an educational device when the group places a premium upon ability to withstand it, to suffer without flinching, to invite pain, to accept it not as demeaning, or as an index of reproach and disapproval, but as proper for the worthy. Nor are we likely to understand high school courses in driver training without some appreciation of the part played in American society by General Motors and automobile insurance companies. We cannot fully understand the teaching, disciplinarian relationship of the mother's brother to his nephew, anthropologists point out, except as we see how it links with, supports, the culturally defined relationship between parents and child. Nor shall we understand the peculiar characteristics of our educational system except as we take into account the peculiarities of our husband-wife and parent-child relationships along with other social phenomena.

Figure 9.12

Relation between illiteracy (as an index of educational level) and percent of eligible voters voting in presidential election*

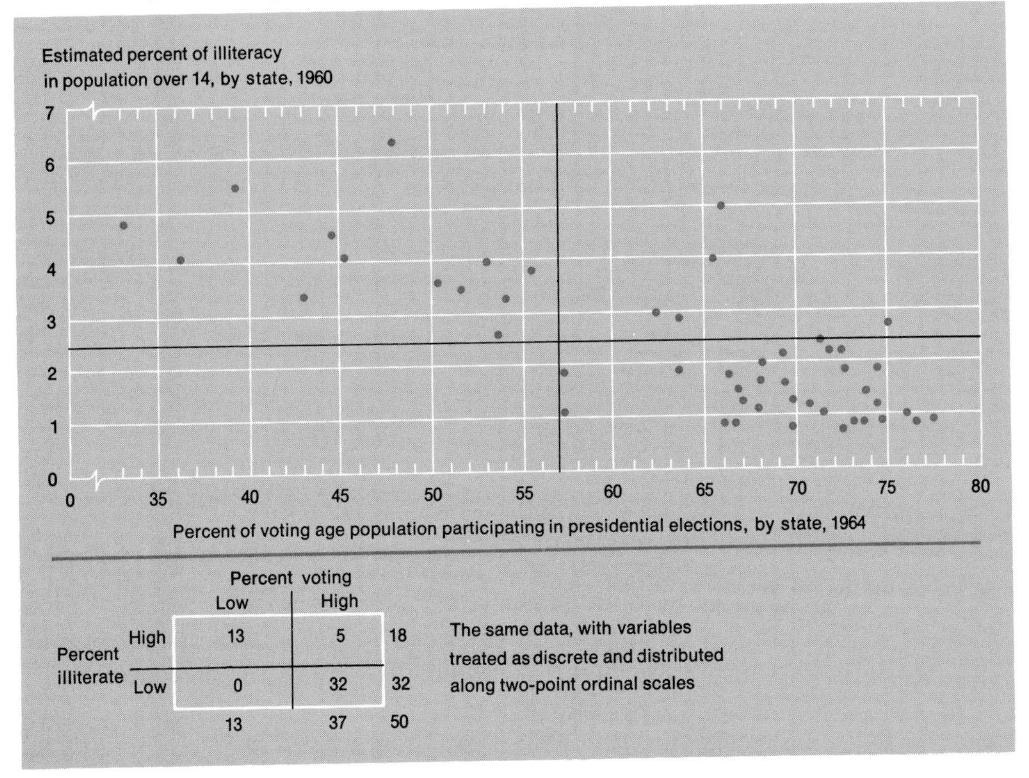

		Percent voting: Low	Percent voting: High	
Percent illiterate	High	13	5	18
	Low	0	32	32
		13	37	50

* Each dot represents one of the 50 states.

A second thing that anthropology clearly demonstrates is what I have stressed above: teaching occurs in vastly varying situations, under the auspices of many different teachers. Public ridicule, praise from the elders, punishment by the gods, hunting and warring exercises, derisive songs sung publicly by the best girl of a cowardly youth, instruction from his mother's uncle for the young boy, the pedagogical use of men's societies, brotherhoods, and so on. . . . Nowhere is the preeminently social function of education better illustrated than in the monographs of anthropologists.

* * * *

In this chapter we have focused on the two institutions which, above all others, fit newcomers to roles vacated by those departing.

We looked first at the internal structure of the family, its institutionalized relationships and their constituent roles. Then we sketched some gross characteristics of the changing American family, moving on, finally, to consider the ties between family and other institutions (see the summary on page 320).

Turning then to the institution of education, we stressed its social functions. This emphasis led us to pose problems rather different from those which, under the influence of psychology, we have posed in the past. Let us summarize briefly the notions that derive from this position.

To underline the point: the function of education is preeminently a social one. It is the principal means of promoting group survival. Since the group consists in a structure of relationships, these relationships and their constituent roles (not their incumbents) must be preserved. Education has the task of continuously filling these roles by training new incumbents.

There is a strong tendency for son to replace father in the latter's roles. But such a simple, conservative pattern of intergenerational repetition is not completely possible: in part because of differing fertility rates between classes; in part because of the downward mobility of some, vacating roles that must be filled by the upwardly mobile; and in part because of new developments that create new roles for which the son's simple recapitulation of the father's role would be inadequate.

In a rapidly changing society such as ours, much of the old manpower has been rendered superfluous. Thus the school takes on a custodial function. In addition, new roles, new specialties require extended training. Both influences sweep an increasing proportion of our youth into the schools where they are held incommunicado, as it were, out of contact with the adult world. In this setting, values emerge that sometimes make intellectual achievement a third and last choice for those of mediocre aptitude while the able, sensitive as we all are to the approval of our peers, find that approval in social and athletic prowess.

Thus we see the institutionalizing of educational processes as essential in maintaining the group. For a raw input of unsocialized creatures must be transmuted, becoming human beings with those skills and attitudes necessary to staff that role structure peculiar to a given group. The social function of education is an adaptive one, primarily.

School and work are closely connected. So we shall turn now to consider economy and welfare, social arangements that we institute to allocate scarce goods and services.

References

TEXT

1. Evelyn Millis Duval, "Conceptions of Parenthood," *American Journal of Sociology*, Vol. 52 (November, 1946), pp. 193–203.
2. Urie Bronfenbrenner, "Socialization and Social Class through Time and Space," in Eleanor E. Maccoby, Theodore M. Newcomb, and Eugene L. Hartley (eds.), *Readings in Social Psychology* (New York: Holt, Rinehart & Winston, Inc., 1958).
3. Melvin L. Kohn, "Social Class and Parent-Child Relationships: An Interpretation" *American Journal of Sociology*, Vol. 68, No. 4 (January, 1963), pp. 471–80. See also in this connection Martha Ericson, "Child-rearing and Social Status," *American Journal of Sociology*, Vol. 52, No. 3 (November, 1946), pp. 190–92. In this comparison of middle- and lower-class child-rearing practices she reports the middle-class parents as being more demanding, starting toilet training practices earlier, supervising more closely the child's activities, placing more emphasis on early responsiveness and on individual achievement. Her middle-class children were taken off the bottle earlier (fewer were breast-fed), three times as many as among the lower-class children were thumb-suckers. Middle-class youngsters were expected to be back in the house earlier at night. They start later going alone to movies at night. They are expected to prepare themselves for some profession. In general, she found them more achievement oriented and anxious.
4. Kohn, *op. cit.*, p. 480.
5. Ernest W. Burgess and Harvey J. Locke, *The Family: From Institution to Companionship* (New York: American Book Co., 1953).
6. Alexis de Tocqueville, *Democracy in America* (New York: Alfred A. Knopf, Inc., 1946), Vol. II, pp. 212–14.
7. Talcott Parsons and Robert F. Bales, *Family, Socialization, and Interaction Process* (New York: Free Press, 1955).
8. Murray A. Straus, "Conjugal Power Structure and Adolescent Personality," *Marriage and Family Living*, Vol., 24, No. 1 (February, 1962), pp. 17–25.
9. John W. M. Whiting, Richard Kluckhohn, and Albert Anthony, "The Function of Male Initiation Ceremonies at Puberty," in Eleanor E. Maccoby, Theodore M. Newcomb and Eugene L. Hartley, *Readings in Social Psychology* (New York: Holt, Rinehart & Winston, Inc., 1958), pp. 359–70.
10. *Ibid.*, p. 370.
11. Talcott Parsons and Robert F. Bales, in collaboration with James Olds, Morris Zelditch, Jr., and Philip E. Slater, *Family, Socialization and Interaction Process* (New York: Free Press, 1955), pp. 98, 99. Used by permission of The Macmillan Company.
12. Ruth Benedict, "Continuities and Discontinuities in Cultural Conditioning," *Psychiatry*, May, 1939.
13. Daniel R. Miller and Guy E. Swanson, *The Changing American Parent* (New York: John Wiley & Sons, Inc., 1958).
14. *Ibid.*, pp. 68–71, 78.
15. See Charles E. Werts, "Career Choice Patterns," *Sociology of Education*, Vol. 40, No. 4 (Fall, 1967), Table 1, p. 353. For 21 of these occupations, prestige scores were available from the NORC study. See Robert W. Hodge, Paul M. Siegel, and Peter H. Rossi, "Occupational Prestige in the United States,

1925–63," *American Journal of Sociology*, Vol. 70, No. 3 (November, 1964), Table 1, pp. 290–92. Thus for 21 occupations chosen by students, we had two scores: prestige score and students' grade performance. The analysis shows that the prestige accorded an occupation is quite closely related to the school performance of young people planning to enter that occupation.
16. Martin Trow, "The Democratization of Higher Education in America," *European Journal of Sociology*, Vol. 3, No. 2 (1962), p. 231.
17. John Updike, *The Centaur* (New York: Alfred A. Knopf, Inc., 1963). The whole statement goes like this: "The Founding Fathers . . . in their wisdom decided that children were an unnatural strain on parents. So they provided jails called schools, equipped with tortures called an education. School is where you go between when your parents can't take you and industry can't take you. I am a paid keeper of Society's unusables—the lame, the halt, the insane and the ignorant. The only incentive I can give you kid, to behave yourself, is this: if you don't buckle down and learn something, you'll be as dumb as I am, and you'll have to teach school to earn a living."
18. Emile Durkheim, *Education and Sociology*, trans. Sherwood Fox (New York: Free Press, 1956), p. 71.
19. Theodore W. Parsons, Ph.D. dissertation, Stanford University.
20. Robert Rosenthal and Lenore F. Jacobson, "Teacher Expectations for the Disadvantaged," *Scientific American*, Vol. 281, No. 4 (April, 1968), pp. 19–23.
21. James S. Coleman, "The Adolescent Subculture and Academic Achievement," *American Journal of Sociology*, Vol. 65, No. 4 (January, 1960), p. 337, *passim*. See also Coleman's *The Adolescent Society* (New York: Free Press, 1961).
22. *Ibid.*
23. *Ibid.*
24. Coleman, *op. cit.*, p. 338.
25. Lowie's statement is cited by George A. Pettitt in his *Primitive Education in North America* (Berkeley and Los Angeles: University of California Press, 1946), p. 6.

TABLES

9.4 Morris Zelditch, Jr., "Family, Marriage and Kinship," in Robert E. L. Faris (ed.), *Handbook of Modern Sociology* (Skokie, Ill.: Rand McNally & Co., 1964), Figure 4, p. 700.
9.5 John W. M. Whiting, Richard Kluckhohn, and Albert Anthony, "The Function of Male Initiation Ceremonies at Puberty," in Eleanor E. Maccoby, Theodore M. Newcomb and Eugene L. Hartley (eds.), *Readings in Social Psychology* (New York: Holt, Rinehard & Winston, Inc., 1958).
9.6 Bureau of the Census, *Historical Statistics of the United States* (Washington, D.C.: U.S. Government Printing Office, 1949), Series D 1–10, p. 63; *Statistical Abstracts*, 1950, Tables 207 and 27, pp. 172 and 21, respectively; *Statistical Abstracts*, 1963, Tables 299 and 31, pp. 229 and 36, respectively; and *Statistical Abstracts*, 1969, Tables 318 and 319, p. 220.
9.8 William J. Goode, *After Divorce* (New York: © The Free Press, a Corporation, 1956, reprinted with permission of The Macmillan Company), p. 47.
9.9 Judson T. Landis, "Marriages of Mixed and Non-Mixed Religious Faith," *American Sociological Review*, Vol. 14, No. 3 (June, 1949), p. 403.
9.10 *Annual Report of the United States Commission on Education* (Washington, D.C.: U.S. Government Printing Office, 1967).

FIGURES

9.2 Talcott Parsons and Robert F. Bales, in collaboration with James Olds, Morris Zelditch, Jr., and Philip E. Slater, *Family, Socialization and Interaction Process* (New York: Free Press, 1955), p. 99. Used by permission of The Macmillan Company.
9.3 Ronald Freedman, Pascal K. Whelpton, and Arthur A. Campbell, *Family Planning, Sterility, and Population Growth* (New York: McGraw-Hill Book Co., 1959), p. 227.
9.4 U.S. Department of Health, Education, and Welfare, Public Health Service, *Marriage Statistics Analysis U.S. 1962* (Washington, D.C.: U.S. Government Printing Office, 1962), Table 1, p. 2; and *Statistical Abstracts* (1969), Table 2, p. 47.
9.5 Data from Gunnar Boalt, *Family and Marriage* (New York: David McKay Co., Inc., 1965), Table 8, p. 66.
9.6 Landis, *op. cit.*, p. 403.
9.8 U.S. Department of Health, Education, and Welfare, Office of Education, *Biennial Survey of Education in the United States; Statistics of State School Systems; Financial Statistics of Institutions*

of Higher Education; unpublished data, U.S. Department of Commerce, Office of Business Economics, *Survey of Current Business,* July, 1958, July, 1964, and April, 1965; and U.S. Department of Health, Education, and Welfare, Office of Education, *Digest of Educational Statistics* (Washington, D.C.: U.S. Government Printing Office, 1965), p. 136.

9.9 U.S. Department of Health, Education and Welfare, *Digest of Educational Statistics,* Office of Education (Washington, D.C.: U.S. Government Printing Office, 1965), Table 37.

9.11 U.S. Department of Health, Education, and Welfare, Department of Education, "Illiteracy in the Population: United States, 1870 to 1960," *Digest of Educational Statistics* (Washington, D.C.: U.S. Government Printing Office, 1965), Table 103, p. 130.

9.12 U.S. Department of Health, Education and Welfare, *American Education,* Vol. II, No. 9 (Washington, D.C.: U.S. Government Printing Office, October, 1966), pp. 8, 9.

chapter 10 **Social structure: institutions to allocate scarce goods**

Institutions are supporting pillars of a social structure. They fix the means for achieving culturally prescribed values through the building of appropriate relationships. But whatever the culture, there is always the requirement of preparing the young for adult roles. And among adult roles, that of worker is central.

Work roles are linked in intricate ways to form the organizations—businesses, industries, professions, services—that, taken together, form the economy. From the sociologist's perspective, the economy is a social arrangement through which men produce and allocate things needed and desired. Pay, when it reflects the prestige commonly accorded a man's work, is a tacit statement of the person's social worth.

But a person may be worthy, even though he isn't "worth" an income. A child is given food, clothing, and shelter even though he doesn't earn them. Pay distributed to workers has a secondary distribution through the family in support of spouses, dependent young, and old.

Yet there are those whose needs cannot be met directly from work earnings, or secondarily, through family sources. Here welfare steps in for a tertiary distribution of work's yield: money flows from earned income, through taxes or philanthropy, to welfare agencies, thence to the needy. When 26 percent of New York City's enormous 1969 budget went to welfare services, it demonstrated that "to each according to his need" has become a significant criterion for allocating wealth.

The claims of the needy neighbor and the claims of kinship cannot be honored except as men see work as necessary. If man does not live by bread alone, foods and fibers are something more than optional luxuries. And while we may envy the lilies of the field that toil not, neither do they spin, sinful descendants of Eve and Adam are not so automatically provided for. The old Persian poet is enjoying fantasies when he describes that idyllic situation with:

> A Book of Verses underneath the Bough,
> A Jug of Wine, a Loaf of Bread—and Thou
> Beside me singing in the Wilderness—

For, as all workers of the world would unite in pointing out, bread, wine and all valued things (goods and services for which demand exceeds free supply) are nurtured in the soilbed of sorrowing toil. Few can indulge an offhand attitude toward work. Given the scarcity of valued things and the lack of any instinctive guides for their production and consumption, we can avoid force and fraud, only by instituting behaviors in the world of work. Thus as human institutions, the social arrangements of men at work become targets of sociological inquiry.

Work as a social arrangement

Let's be clear what the sociology of work is about. Work—and the discipline of economics—is so often associated with the production, exchange, and consumption of *things* that we overlook social dimensions. But culture penetrates the world of work as it does all other spheres of life. Thus attitudes toward work, toward unions, aspirations to get ahead, responses to various incentives—these are cultural products varying by class, race, religion, and other social characteristics. They inform the differing patterns of relationships that we observe among work crews, between labor and management, production and maintenance workers, salesmen and customers, government and industry representatives. Work is a social enterprise. We sometimes err in our preoccupation with man-machine and machine-product relationships. Perhaps it is this fix upon the material product that has led to a misunderstanding of the best-known theorist of work relations.

For simply to link Marx with materialism is seriously to misconstrue his thesis.* Certainly the production, distribution, and consumption of things (and services, as well) he saw as fundamental. And so do we. But the requirement of foods and fibers is to be taken for granted as a universal imperative. (There is no variance, here, and with no variance, no variables, and no problem; for there are no differences to explain.) Things, material things, were not, actually, the focus of Marx's inquiry, but the *mode of social organization* in producing and distributing things. He was pointing to the way in which relationships between employer and employee, owner, manager, and worker, bourgeoisie and proletariat were patterned, and the way this patterning changed through history from periods of oriental despotism to European feudalism, the latter superseded by bourgeois capitalism and ultimately (and he thought inevitably) to be supplanted by socialism. One mode of organizing the relations of production gives way to another under the stress between positions that come to be seen as illegitimately differentiated by power and ownership of property. When workers become aware of their "alienation from the means of production," viewing themselves as a class wrongfully deprived, they will supplant the masters, initiating new relations of production. And since these relations of production constitute the real foundation of the social order, a necessary corollary must be a transformation in family, education, science, religion, polity—all other sectors of the social order that resonate to shifts in economic organization.

On many counts, Marxist theory is inadequate from the viewpoint of historian, economist, and sociologist. The fantasy of a

* Contributions of Karl Marx (1818–1883) to sociology lie in the fields of institutional structure (links between ways of organizing production and other institutional spheres), stratification, and social change. Driven by a strong moral concern, he attacked adventitious inequality, showing the historical necessity for its abolition. (See C. Wright Mills, *The Marxists*, New York: Dell Publishing Co., 1962, pp. 30–96.)

classless society is possible only on the basis of a simplistic theory of stratification quite at odds with sociologists' findings. Marx's staging of history, with its emphasis on the disenchantment of an urban proletariat, does not accord with time and circumstance in the revolutions of Russia and China. Critically underestimated is the possibility of releasing a head of revolutionary steam through evolutionary devices. Such devices are social inventions, softening the impact of chance adversity. Often legal and thus universalistic in their prescriptions, they may guarantee equality of opportunity (as through public education), rewards increasingly based on achievement (rather than on traits stemming from the accident of birth and ascribed to family, race, sex, or class), and protection against hazards to health and wealth (Old-Age, Survivors, and Disability Insurance, minimum wage laws, Medicare). If these social innovations are, as some aver, "creeping socialism," they do not seem to constitute the revolutionary socialism that must, in Marxist strategy, be occasioned by the obdurate resistance of a favored few to the legitimate claims of the many. It is hard to imagine the First Lady echoing Marie Antoinette's "Let them eat cake."

Nonetheless, Marx makes three contributions of critical significance to sociology. He brings home to us the fact that men's conceptions of the good, the true, and the beautiful (and the productions embodying these conceptions) are unintelligible apart from the social context from which they emerge. This is the fundamental insight still but partially plumbed in the field of the sociology of knowledge. Second, he frees us from a simplistic theory of social change—one that still seems to prevail. Despite the sometimes sinister connotations of Marxism, his was not a conspiratorial theory of history and social change. Immanent in the social order he saw quite impersonal, change-inducing forces. Individual actors there were, of course. But for the most part they were prisoners of their positions in the social structure, largely unaware of their roles in the social drama. And third, he shifts our perspective on the economy, taking a distinctly sociological position. For he sees it as a set of human relationships defined by the distribution—maldistribution, as he saw it—of responsibilities, rights, and rewards. The emphasis, then, is not so much on indexes of production, or the GNP (gross national product), or on discount rates, taxation, or the distribution of *things,* but on the *structure of relationships* in production, as such relationships entail or are represented by, such strictly economic variables as the foregoing.

Questions a sociologist might ask

So we are looking, now, at an extremely complicated *social* arrangement, the relationships of production, distribution, and consumption. It is an adaptive arrangement made by people with others, most of these being unknown, to exchange the product of brawn and brain. This exchange, symbolized in money, enables families, persons, groups to achieve some of their goals. In institutionalizing patterns of work we are offering an answer to the question: How can we garner, process, and allocate the things from soil and sea, the wisdom and skills from human hands and minds, that we need to satisfy our wants? Like other institutionalized answers, the organization of work consists in a generally shared set of *rules* (explicit and implicit, legal and customary) exemplified locally (in stores, factories, and offices) in a set of *roles* and *relationships:* boss-worker, lawyer or social worker–client, physician-patient, teacher-student, producer-wholesaler. . . . In studying the institutionalization of work patterns, the sociologist is likely to ask such questions as these:

1. How do men regard work (and leisure)? Has work an intrinsic virtue or is it to be viewed as a regrettably necesssary means to desirable ends?
2. What views about the nature of man underlie the authority structure of the workplace, the incentive system of rewards and punishments?
3. How are beliefs supporting work behavior buttressed or challenged in religion and other institutional spheres?
4. What is the standing of a given occupation in the status hierarchy of American society? Has it changed? And if so, how and why?
5. What is the occupational structure of a society? What are the chief occupational categories and how have they changed through time?
6. How are people recruited into these different occupations? How are the roles appropriate to each occupation created and sustained? What are the devices by which apprentices and novices are trained to conform to the life style of their type of work?
7. How do beliefs and behaviors in the world of work articulate with those of other institutions? What, for example, are the occupational functions of an educational system? Why does education, in our society, tend to displace other criteria for vocational placement? What are the effects of working condi-

tions, rewards, and habits upon the institution of the family? How are the occupational positions of women and children determined?

8. To what extent are occupations passed on from father to son? How much movement up the occupational ladder is there? Is there more or less rigidity in the occupational structure than there has been in the past?
9. What occupational characteristics—or, more generally, what social conditions—are linked with the development of labor unions and professional societies?
10. How do occupational groups vary in political attitudes, life expectancy, interests, measures of intelligence, insanity rates, reading tastes, family size, and standards of conduct? How do we explain them? What consequences do these differences have for the community?
11. What are the characteristics of the work situation? How do they vary from occupation to occupation? What are the social factors affecting productivity, absenteeism, morale, the cohesiveness of work groups?
12. What accounts for workers' resistance—or easy adaptation—to changes in the work situation?[1]

Three universal features of work

We can ask questions such as these about the organization of work in any society, for work has certain universal features. First, preferences are always represented in the things men strive for. And these commonly desired ends go beyond material things. Men work to serve others, to gain power over others, to enhance their social standing. Second, men typically collaborate through a prescribed structure of artfully interlocking roles. (This is the feature of work that makes for functional integration. Durkheim called it "organic solidarity" in his study of *The Division of Labor.*) Finally, there are the myths surrounding work patterns, justifying one system over others—for example, capitalism over the welfare state, or socialism.

Putting these ideas more generally, in all groups we find:

1. *Understandings as to necessary and desirable goods.* (Note that these are not necessarily "good" goods. Perhaps the sugar in soft drinks contributes to active careers in caries for the dental profession. Cyclamates in diet foods may have an effect on genes. Thalidomide was doubtless an effective tranquilizer, but pregnant women using it ran the risk of delivering monstrosities. And

cigarettes, some evidence suggests however far they "travel the smoke" and no matter what's "counting up front," may nonetheless be contributing to the development of lung cancer.)

2. *A prescribed way of mobilizing social energy,* of organizing effort in order to get these goods. These are the patterns of relationship reflected in the organizational chart of a business or industry, relations between union steward, workers, and management, between government and company representatives, and the like. (There are unofficial behaviors and informal relationships not formally prescribed.)

3. And finally, *a set of beliefs, myths, symbols, and rules that describe, prescribe, and justify our goods as goals,* and the means of seeking these goals. All people, that is to say, define what is good, prescribe ways of getting these goods, and develop descriptive and normative statements about the ends and means of work. There are valued goods, roles (and relationships) for getting them, and rules for the roles. As we would expect, work roles and the rules guiding them will differ from group to group through time and space.

Cultural perspectives on work

People's words and deeds tell us what they know and believe. Some things they say and do reveal their orientation toward work. Let's consider first the rules of work. (I am using "rule" as a shorthand term for attitudes and standards that guide men's conduct at work. We will then turn to roles and relationships, the organization of men at work—point 2, above.)

Conceptions of work

There are various conceptions of work. One view sees work as necessary, but scarcely sufficient for achieving the important ends of life. For some—and this may be part of the distinction between Weber's Protestant ethic and traditional Catholicism—the terrestrial stint is mere prologue to celestial bliss. When the heavenly future is so certain, ulcerous striving for kudos and cash in the here and now becomes an ill-advised if not immoral displacement of time and talent. For, during the brief span of years allotted one on earth, the important thing is convivial amity with one's fellows, while paying one's decent respects to God.

This is the antithesis of the attitude toward work expressed by "Boss" Kettering when he wrote:

> I often tell my people that I don't want any fellow who has a job working for me; what I want is a fellow whom a job has. I want the job to get the fellow and not the fellow to get the job. And I want that job to get hold of this young man so hard that no matter where he is the job has got him for keeps. I want that job to have him in its clutches when he goes to bed at night, and in the morning I want that same job to be sitting on the foot of his bed telling him it's time to get up and go to work. And when a job gets a fellow that way, he's sure to amount to something.[2]

Such contrasting conceptions of what ought to be in the orientation toward work may have serious outcomes. So it was that after World War II, when the United States was heavily committed to reviving the economies of war-devastated allies, our government wished to stimulate the rationalization of French business and industry. This meant increased production, at lower unit cost, for distribution to a greater market. But as David Landes points out, French business had been typically a matter of family enterprise, geared to local markets and providing a modest but adequate living for a kin group.[3] Exhortations to expand, to boost production, to extend the market fell on quite indifferent ears.

One view of work, then, sees it as a good in itself and holds that the person should be by work possessed. A second view makes work a worldly necessity in the trip toward otherworldly rewards. There is perhaps a third view of work found in some phases of finance capitalism. Work becomes a somewhat speculative enterprise, intriguingly touched by chance elements. The worker's role is that of the speculator operating through our great exchanges. In this role the worker is indifferent to the goods produced and sold, indifferent to satisfactions intrinsic to the making and using of things. The work role of the speculator simply revolves about a change in price. And however the element of chance is reduced by the shrewdness of the "inside dopester," anticipating change in price is a kind of guessing game.

Three views of work—it's intrinsically virtuous, or an aspect of life secondary to social rewards and salvation, or a speculative game—do not exhaust the possibilities. (One thinks, additionally of the view of work attributed to the legendary Hippy: a refusal to take a job in a computerized, dehumanized, bureaucratic work machine, in the service of a system of questionable morality at the price of one's calling—i.e., doing one's thing.) But these various viewpoints do suggest significantly differing cultural perspectives on work, viewpoints that concern the sociologist as they influence the structure of work relationships.

Attitudes toward work; toward distribution of goods and property

Embedded in the culture we also find differing attitudes toward types of work (and workers), differing conceptions of property and rights in it, and differing assumptions about man's nature and what incentives prompt him to produce.

Under frontier conditions and where extractive industry dominates the economy, occupations requiring brawn may take precedence over brain-exploiting occupations, manipulation of things over manipulation of symbols. Men confined to the bowels of the social ship will, like Eugene O'Neill's stokers in *The Hairy Ape,* glorify their role as being heart and guts of the enterprise. Among the gypsum miners studied by Alvin Gouldner, there was an air of death-defying, Dionysian daring and an independence that marked them off emphatically from the pedestrian factory workers on the surface. Type of work valued is likely to vary with level of social and cultural development.

That aspect of culture that we call technology will qualify attitudes toward work and its performance. With industry in an embryonic stage of development, there was a premium on unskilled labor, and the employment of children was widely approved. Even today where subsistence agriculture still obtains, the school year is cut short: children fill out the labor force at planting time and harvest. Thus the conditions under which it is proper to perform certain work are culturally differentiated in time and space. The admirable Crichton was top dog when, his English master and the family he served having been shipwrecked, he was the only person with the technical skills needed for survival.[4] But when the family was rescued and returned to England, Crichton resumed his erstwhile role as a gentleman's gentleman. Furthermore, he did so not only without regret or recrimination but with pride in his position as butler and valet, an attitude toward such work that would doubtless be uncommon in the United States.

The Japanese are skilled in industrial technology, but their traditions dictate a mode of organizing men at work that contrasts sharply with ours.

> Japanese workers are hired for life. They are practically never fired. Promotions go largely by seniority even at mana-

> gerial levels. The incompetent executive moves up with advancing years to positions with titles appropriate to his age—even when this means devising types of duties that will keep him from interfering with the progress of the firm. The pay of workers bears no relation to their productivity. The pay envelope is the sum of a complex set of factors, in which length of service and number of dependents figure prominently. All management decisions are made on a group basis—at least nominally. If an individual were credited with a certain decision that turned out to be unwise, then the individual would lose face. To spare management people from such humiliation, to all appearances the group as a whole shares responsibility in all decisions.[5]

Overall contrasts in the culture of work are represented in the abstract labels that we apply to economies: a domestic economy, capitalism, state capitalism, socialism. (See Table 10.1.)

Values, views, and rules vary, too, on the matter of distributing goods. For an interesting contrast, taken from anthropological literature, let us go with Margaret Mead to visit the Arapesh, in northern New Guinea. They grow yams.

> The fortunate man who thinks he has a large surplus [of yams] will consult his elders, or they themselves may tell him that his supply is sufficient. He then . . . gives a large feast [an *abullu*] to which most of the locality come, and members of adjacent and related hamlets. . . . He has the honor of having given the *abullu* . . . and his gardening luck has increased the food supply of the community. Although this is always phrased positively—that a man is "permitted" to make an *abullu*—it is actually an effective measure against any man's accumulating wealth disproportionate to the wealth accumulated by others.
>
> If there is meat on his smoking rack over the fire, it is either meat which was killed by another . . . and has been given to him, in which case he and his family may eat it; or, it is meat which he himself has killed and which he is smoking to give away to someone else, for to eat one's own kill, even though it be only a small bird, is a crime to which only the morally—which usually means in Arapesh, mentally—deficient will stoop. If the house in which he is living is nominally his, it will have been constructed, in part at least, from the posts and planks of other people's houses, which have been dismantled or temporarily deserted, and from which he

has borrowed timber. He will not cut his rafters to fit his house, if they are too long, because they may be needed later for someone else's house which is of a different shape or size.[6]

But exotic New Guinea is not the only example of variant views on the distribution of goods. The doctrines of the communist countries (with differences among themselves: the U.S.S.R., China, Yugoslavia), producers' and consumers' cooperatives President Nixon's proposal for a guaranteed annual minimum family income of $2,500, the kibbutzim of the Israelis, the utopian communes of some American youth—these suggest the range of views on distributing the goods of life.

So, also, do we find a great range of beliefs about property, its ownership and control. It is common for some sorts of property to be communally held, while other sorts are privately owned. But the types so owned, and the balance between public and private ownership vary broadly from group to group and time to time. The proportion of goods communally owned in the United States has increased markedly over the years. U.S. citizens own in common power-producing and flood control installations like TVA; thousands of miles of public highway; vast values in military installations, planes and ships and weapons; great resources in public parks and state and national forests; enormous reserves of grain and the storage facilities for it; and schools and post offices and other government facilities in almost every community in the nation. Yet our ratio of private to public ownership is rather high, especially when compared with, say, the Hutterites or the Coronation Gulf Eskimos about whom Stefansson writes.

Natural resources and raw materials were owned in common but made articles were privately owned. The blubber of a seal that was needed for light and heat, or lean or fat [meat] that were needed for meals, belonged no more to the man who secured them than to anyone else. . . . A meal that had been cooked was in a sense private property; but it was open to everyone under the laws of hospitality . . . it was very bad form to start a meal in any village without at the least sending a youngster outdoors to shout at the top of his voice that the family were about to dine.[7]

Beliefs about work incentives

Of all the cultural prescriptions touching the world of work, none embodies more fundamental assumptions about the nature of

Table 10.1

Examples of overall ways of organizing man at work: domestic, capitalist, and socialist economies

Type of economy	Unit of economic organization	Prime objective	Principal means of coordinating decisions about allocation of goods and services	Owned by	Operated by
Domestic	Households	Satisfaction of a variety of familial needs/wants	Face-to-face product and service exchange within households and, at market, where agreements to exchange are consummated, between households	Family, or its representative	Head of family and its members
Capitalist	The privately owned firm or business enterprise	Money profit, "discounted for risk"*	Symbolic exchanges (paper transactions) in the market: Wall Street, LaSalle Street, Chicago grain exchange, etc.	Individual owner(s) or shareholders	Owners, self-employed executives, hired managers
State Capitalism	The publicly owned firm or business enterprise: Renault car manufacturing company in France, etc.	Money profit	Symbolic exchanges in the market (paper transactions as is the case with private capitalism)	The state	State-appointed managers and their employees: Canadian National Railways, etc.
Socialism	The public service: postal service, etc.	Satisfaction of community needs/wants	State planning agencies via official regulations, taxation, prescription of quotas, subsidies . . .	The state, or subsidiary public agencies	The state, or provincial governments, public service corporations, collectives, unions, cooperative associations

* An important secondary objective is safety, or the desire to minimize risk, Oscar Lang points out. Hence the primary aim of money profit is qualified by this secondary objective.

man, about "what makes Sammy run," than those bearing on incentives. In reporting on his Eskimos, Stefansson implies that the only incentive necessary was the pressure of others' expectations. Thus he writes:

> I never knew even one who didn't try his best, although there were, of course, the same differences of energy and apti-

> tude which we find among ourselves. If there had been a shirker, he would have received the same food; but even in a circle of punctilious courtesy he would have felt that he was not being fed gladly. It is the nearest thing to impossible, when you know how primitive society works . . . to conceive of anyone with that combination of indolence and strength of character which would make it possible for a well man to remain long a burden on the community . . . those who were selfish lost standing. Those who were altruistic rose in the public esteem.[8]

The common assumption in Euro-American capitalism seems to be that the carrot and the goad are required to stimulate mulish man to productive effort. The carrot is promotion and increases in pay. The goad is the threat of unemployment, demotion, reduced income and, ultimately, starvation. This view has a long ancestry.

If it is true that a man will not work without rewards and punishments externally imposed, then certain ought's are, by implication, stipulated in the employer-employee relationship. The former *should* induce production through the prospects of promotions and raises. He *should* spur production through the threat of unemployment. Bendix describes how an emerging class of entrepreneurs and managers found such ideological support with the unfolding of the Industrial Revolution.[9] A rising social class, a middle class of merchants and industrialists, was pitted against the landed aristocracy. They celebrated the promise of technology. They capitalized on a high birthrate and traditional conceptions of husband-wife and parent-child relationships to employ women and children under what we would regard as incredibly bad conditions. They were persuaded that the relationship between employer and worker was necessarily and properly that of the deserving rich to the undeserving poor, of able to incompetent, of benevolent to needy, and that the appropriate and necessary incentive was the threat—the impersonal threat, to be sure—of destitution, even death.

This is probably the dominant view of work incentives in our society today. And so we are astonished to find workers casual about cutting work, cavalier about punctuality, careless despite the prospect of losing a job. Allison Davis gives us an example of a Negro factory worker in Chicago, perhaps representing a sizable category of American workers.

> . . . born in Mississippi, Ruth's parents were unskilled workers, . . . at the very bottom of the economic hierarchy.

> The family came to Chicago in 1935. For a long time, they were unable to secure either work or relief. Both then, and later when the father was given a job as an unskilled laborer on WPA, Ruth, her four sisters and brother, and her parents lived in the large cellar of an old tenement on the South Side. The cellar had been divided into nine rooms, one for each family. There was no kitchen, only an open corner at the back of the cellar, with a small gas stove and a faucet. The nine families shared this corner as their "kitchen." They shared their small stocks of furniture, their bedclothes, and their wearing apparel. Most important of all, they shared their food and even their money. When a family was both out of work and off relief, the other families put their money and food into a communal "pot," in which the destitute family shared. *This is a hard system to beat, for those who believe in the effectiveness of economic intimidation in making good workers.* When workers can survive at this level, and still have the social support and approval of their friends, they can scarcely be threatened or starved into better work habits.[10]

We might add that, if deprivation doesn't work, neither, for the poorest category of worker, is the reward of upward mobility an incentive. For such rewards may not be genuine possibilities; they may provide no more incentive than in the case of a small Negro boy whose teacher held out to her pupils the possibility that one of them might become president of the United States. As the story goes, the Negro youngster whispered to a white classmate: "I'll sell you my chance for a quarter."

Note, finally, a small lesson that can be learned from these cursory comments on incentives. The vulgar proposition about human relationships (a man works under threat of punishment and/or promise of reward) is typically too gross, disregarding *conditions under which it fails to hold true.* Water boils at 212° Fahrenheit *only* at sea level—i.e., only under specified conditions. The volume of a gas is an inverse function of pressure *only* at specified temperatures. The punishment-reward theory of incentives applies *only* when such incentives are relevant and meaningful for a given category of workers. And the evidence suggests that relevance and meaning vary widely. Some people are moved to embrace a life of poverty and celibacy. Others are strongly motivated to pile up property in the here and now where moth and rust corrupt. Others may, like the Kwakiutl, accumulate goods, not for their apparent uses, but to gain status by destroying them in rivalry with other goods-destroyers. Incentives may change as we grow older—as with Willie Lohman (*Death of a Salesman*) who discovered belatedly that he couldn't take it with him. And different generations may listen to different drummers. Culture permits and prescribes wondrously variant conduct, at work as in other spheres of life.

Values apparently underlying the organization of men at work

From such observations we can infer general values that guide the arrangement of men's work relationships. In societies like ours, where science and technology enable marked mastery of the environment, such convictions and commitments as the following seem reasonable inferences:

1. Man stands above all things and beings and so is justified in shaping them to gratify his ever increasing needs. Not only does he rule ocean, earth, and firmament: he rules himself. Assimilating human nature to other realms of nature, he believes it both possible and good to shape his destiny more precisely to desired ends. Levels of productivity and quality control apply to human as well as to nonhuman resources.
2. It is good "to strive, to seek, to gain and not to yield." We do not value the vegetable whose destiny is written in its genes. "The fault lies, not in our stars but in ourselves, that we are underlings." Our laurels go to the man who, despite limitations of birth and breeding, yet achieves the bigger and the better. We value demonstrable achievement.
3. Thus it is good to look forward, not backward. We have, as Professor Lynd once put it, a "tilt toward the future." And this faith (and beyond faith, hope, and beyond hope, confidence) is in a future not so far distant—not in some Beulah land of serene bliss, but in rewards to be realized, at least in part, within a man's lifetime.
4. To fix on the near rather than the distant future is to be concerned with proximate rather than ultimate ends, and with concrete ways of achieving them. Since proximate goals (for example, getting a good grade) are but means to more distant ends (high grade point average, Phi Beta Kappa, a flying start on one's career), we become, in fact, means oriented, instrumentally oriented. Thus we value improved techniques. ("Let a man

but build a better mousetrap and the world will beat a path to his door.")

5. A stress on achievement, a future orientation and an instrumental one, suggest as corollary the value placed on calculating reason, on knowledge that can be relied on to achieve our ends. There is implied some priority of head over heart, some control of impulse and feelings in the service of efficient realization of our goals. Self-discipline, conscientious commitment to work, a degree of austerity, hardheadedness, and a deprecation of sentiment—these characteristics come to be valued in the world of work.
6. Finally, degree of achievement is certified through verifiable measures of action and product. Professors may be bypassed for promotion because they fail "to produce," i.e., to write books and articles. In industry, men making time and motion studies set norms of production, providing yardsticks for measuring work performance. What is relevant is a man's performance and the product attesting that performance. Good intentions, facile justifications, simply won't do. Eliza Doolittle speaks the put-up-or-shut-up language of the world of work when she cries, "Show me!"

Work relationships in bureaucratic structures

Belief in man's supremacy in nature, and its justifiability, a stress on achievement, the reshaping of his world, a tilt toward the future, an emphasis on the constant improvement of means, control of impulse, an emphasis on action, performance, productivity—such cultural themes inform the world of work. These values (as is the case with all values) are realized in social structures. Today, in our society, there is a typical social structure, a pattern through which relationships at work are ordered. We call it *bureaucracy.*

The meaning of bureaucracy

Let's be clear about three things. First, sociologists use the term for descriptive and analytical purposes, *not* in a derogatory sense. The word commonly carries connotations of timeserving, made possible by the anonymity of the worker in the vast reaches of bumbling mass enterprise. "Red tape" is the familiar epithet used to describe bureaucratic operations. Bureaucracy is accused of being inefficient and costly, hamstringing enterprise by a thousand trivial regulations, just as the Lilliputians restrained Gulliver. But such allegations are no more than allegations until subjected to empirical test. It is hard to imagine jet planes or social security checks issuing from organizations that could not be described as bureaucratic. Whether more could be produced, more cheaply, through a different pattern of organization must be determined by test, not epithet.

Second, as the sociologist uses the word, "bureaucratic" is not an adjective applied exclusively to government.* Bureaucracy is found in private as well as public works. Indeed, wherever we have great numbers of persons, a complex social order with diverse needs to be met and capacities to be exploited, a money economy, an elaborate technology, and a well-developed system of contract law, bureaucratic forms of work organization are invariably found. This mode of organizing men at work is an outgrowth of social conditions, not a straitjacket deliberately imposed by the rulers.

Finally, we should be aware that to sketch features of bureaucratic organization is to outline a structure of relationships never corresponding, in detail, to any actual enterprise. Just such a distilled formulation of this concept is found in the work of Max Weber. We will turn soon to an elaboration of this concept as background for discussing an empirical study of bureaucracy in a factory producing gypsum products.

For several reasons it seems desirable to focus on this way of organizing men's efforts at work.† First, bureaucracy is significant because it's so general: while its purest exemplification is seen in the organization of work, we find it also in religion, in education —wherever the rational linking of many men's efforts is necessary. Second, it mirrors modern life. Although bureaucratic organization is not new—the organization of government in ancient China provides an excellent example—it is more fully elaborated in our time and place, and especially in the realm of work, than else-

* See Gian Carlo Menotti's musical drama, *The Consul*, a tragedy which turns on the human costs of bureaucracy and the police state.

† There are, of course, other illustrations of the sociology of work that might be offered: inquiries into different levels of morale or cohesion in work groups, their sources and consequences, or the structure of unofficial relationships among workers, or the connections between beliefs and behaviors at work and those in other institutional spheres (family, religion, government), or effects on productivity of changes in relationship among workers, and between workers and supervisors or management, or effects of different leadership styles, and the like. But here, as elsewhere in this approach to sociology, we cannot cover the waterfront.

where, or in the past. (Consider A.T.&T. which, in 1967, had 650,-800 people on its payroll and over $35 billion in assets.)[11] Third, since bureaucracy refers directly to a structure of statuses and interlocking roles, studies turning on this concept are at the core of sociology.

Characteristics of bureaucratic organization

Now let's get to the meat of the matter: What are the features that distinguish bureaucracies, at least in degree, from other work settings? For a definition, let us call bureaucracy a hierarchical form of social organization rationally geared to the achievement of precisely specified objectives by means of a division of labor based on demonstrated competence. This form of organization, Weber writes,

> . . . offers above all the optimum possibility for carrying through the principle of specializing administrative functions according to purely objective considerations. Individual performances are allocated to functionaries who have specialized training and who by constant practice learn more and more. The objective discharge of business primarily means a discharge of business according to calculable rules and without regard for persons.[12]

This is a beginning. Now let us consider in more detail the characteristics of bureaucratic organization.

1. There is a finely refined differentiation of roles, a clear-cut division of interlocking activities regarded as duties inherent in a given position: eighth grade teacher, tech. sergeant, gaffer (the master craftsman in producing glassware), anaesthetist, first clarinet . . . *ad infinitum.*
2. These roles are dealt with *as roles,* quite regardless of who is performing in them.
3. Recruitment for these roles is on the basis of demonstrated capacity. Enter the personnel man. One may be appointed by a superior or assigned his role on the basis of a qualifying examination. Such roles are not filled by election, or by popularity contests.
4. There is a meticulous specification of these roles through job descriptions and rules that state, in terms as clear as may be,

expectations defining the worker's relationship to a remote and anonymous management as well as to fellow workers and immediate supervisor.

Such rules allow workers to accept demands made of them without implying a "personal submission to the supervisor that would betray their self-image as 'any man's equal.' "[13]

The rules permit the supervisor to assess work performed without invoking any debatable claims as to his personal superiority.

They also offer a basis for measures of work, measures which can, in turn, justify rewards (in pay and promotion) and punishments (docking the worker's wages or otherwise penalizing him).

Furthermore, they preclude the need for reissuing instructions in each particular case. It is the worker's responsibility to read and know the rules. *Caveat vendor laboris!*

5. Rules are written, not oral, emphasizing their impersonality and promoting continuity despite the fact that successive incumbents may be drawn from quite heterogeneous backgrounds. (The emphasis on writing and the whole clerical-recording apparatus of modern business enterprise is to be contrasted with oral transmission in simpler societies.)
6. There is an increased emphasis on evaluation, preferably a quantified assessment making comparisons possible. This includes accounting procedures, time-motion studies, the careful selection and continuous appraisal of the workers who are the instruments of production, and a check on the quantity and quality of their output.
7. Planning and control are carried out through a chain of command, a strictly ordered system of subordination and superordination following the distribution of authority.
8. Impersonality: This characteristic has been implied, above, in the emphasis on demonstrable achievement and the treatment of work roles without regard to particular incumbents. It means, also, that loyalty is to the organization, not the person. Sentiment affecting personal ties is appropriate only as it supports production, promotes organizational objectives. The realm of the family and all matters strictly idiosyncratic are to be separated from the realm of work.
9. Coordinating roles become increasingly important—those roles in which the task is to articulate others' activities.
10. The worker progresses through the hierarchy of authority and rewards on the basis of sharpened skills and capacities.

A research example: sorts and sources of bureaucratic rules and roles

Such characteristics as these make up the commonly accepted portrait of bureaucratic organization. But it remains to be seen when and if they apply in concrete cases. A three-year study by Professor Gouldner and his students helps us refine and amplify this pattern of work organization.[14] His study hinges on a shift toward bureaucratic rules and roles attending the replacement of a plant manager in a factory and mine of the General Gypsum Company. Data come from three sources: (1) 174 interviews, 132 of these constituting a sample so stratified as to take into account workers' seniority, rank, and department, (2) direct observations in plant and mine (one of the research team was employed in the mine), and (3) documentary material including company correspondence, memoranda and reports, arbitrators' decisions, and newspaper clippings.

The plant was located just outside a small community of some 700 souls, a farm-based, tradition-oriented community whose people emphasized friendly relationships; the importance of the family unit; interest in baseball, the volunteer fire department, and hunting; thrift, personal dignity, and equality among men, whatever their formal standing. They were reported as loyal to insiders, somewhat suspicious of outsiders, pro-Nordic and anti-Semitic. Community influentials were heads of old farm families and professionals such as ministers and physicians.

These local and traditional values were reflected in the gypsum factory and mine. Interview data tell us that before the advent of the new manager, rules were few and leniently enforced. There was little checking up. Workers seldom felt pushed. Their obligations to superiors were limited to the immediate and obvious technical requirements of the job. Nobody, one respondent said, was fired. A worker always got a second chance. It was quite usual for a worker to help himself to company equipment and materials. While asserting a sense of personal equality with anyone, workers yet applauded a solicitous posture on the part of the plant manager and his lieutenants, who not only tolerated minor deviations but acted in unrequired ways to care for the workers. Close family and community ties were reflected in the plant, where many workers were neighbors, friends, and relatives.

Thus, before the arrival of a new plant manager, we find rules and roles somewhat at odds with the picture I have drawn of bureaucratic forms. Instead of precisely measured performance in a narrowly defined work role against standards impersonally administered and held to for all incumbents of that role—instead of this we find relationships emphatically tinctured by sentiment, roles diffusely and fuzzily defined, and such ascriptive qualities as kinship stressed. Two social spheres are fused here, that of home and community on the one hand and that of workplace on the other. Workers' descriptions of the plant under the old manager as being "like a family" confirm this analysis. And that is what they meant, in part, by referring to management as "lenient."

> "Leniency" is a judgment rendered by workers when supervisors temper the performance of their managerial roles by taking into account obligations that would be *relevant in other relationships.* Thus when workers lauded management for allowing the injured to do [physically undemanding] work in the sample room, or permitting workers to use Company material and tools for personal use, or giving those who violate managerial expectations a "second chance," they were employing criteria legitimately applicable to the relations among *friends* and *neighbors,* rather than in a *business* and *industrial* context.[15]

When the plant manager died, his successor felt an obligation, out of gratitude for his appointment (and in accordance with orders), to revise easygoing, haphazard methods, increase efficiency, and boost production. Symbolic of the change was the contrast between old and new personnel managers. The old personnel man was demoted and "a college educated, authority conscious, rule-oriented individual was substituted for an informal, 'lenient' man who had little taste for paper work," and preferred to hire farm boys whose qualifications he picked up through the local grapevine.[16] We see here the confrontation of two schemes: the rational, efficiency-enhancing values of bureaucratic organization versus the traditional indulgency pattern previously pervading the plant.

Stepping into others' shoes is seldom easy, and in this case the new manager stood at the point where these two forms of work organization collided. He faced problems common to all successors. He inherited commitments made by his predecessor. These had to be honored or defaulted, either course being hazardous. He took with him the expectations of some friends that they would profit from his elevation. He inherited old lieutenants, not readily discarded, whose loyalties might lie with the predecessor and whose position enabled them to make things tough for the successor. And he inherited workers who tended to idealize the past and disparage the present. (In this case, "old Doug," the former manager, was remembered as having faith in his men, being on intimate and friendly terms with them, and acting as an equal. He was sincere, not feigning that folksiness that Merton has called "pseudo-gemeinschaft." He was a man who made his own decisions without everlastingly deferring until he could consult the main office.)

In this situation, bureaucratic rules became a personal and an organizational defense. They helped to deflect antagonism from the new manager (who merely mediated the rules) to the front office where they originated. The hierarchical organization of bureaucracy lowered the visibility of top echelons, blurring targets of antagonism. Strategic replacements in middle management created a cadre of the loyal and obligated, eliminated some dissidents while generating enough anxiety among others to prompt them to try, at least superficially, to stay in line.

Such an increase in bureaucratization is probably a function of frequent managerial shifts. In this plant, Gouldner reports that average tenure for six managers was four years. The more frequent the shift of incumbents, the more necessary, for group stability, that rules and roles remain unchanged. Gouldner puts it this way:

> . . . Bureaucratization is . . . functional to a group subjected to an institutionally compelled high rate of succession while, in turn, a high rate of succession operates as a selecting mechanism, sifting out or disposing to bureaucratic modes of organization.[17]

And so the old rules were tightened, new rules made, and both enforced with dispassionate vigor.

This was easier among the factory workers, on the surface, than among the miners, underground. These latter were a spontaneous, profane, equalitarian, friendly, tough, hardworking, and cohesive group. (Miners were proud of the quantity and quality of their work—although absenteeism was high. Surface workers were seen as goldbrickers.) Instances of reveling and rebelling were regarded as the natural concomitants of dangerous work. The extension of bureaucratic rules was not, then, a marked success among the miners. Among them, supervisors found the no-absenteeism rule unworkable.

But distinctions are seen not only between the two work settings (surface and mine) but between types of rules—distinctions as to who initiates them, whose values are supported and whose violated by them, how violations of the rules are explained, and how they affect the standing of workers and management. Such distinctions led Gouldner to conclude that the conception of a single type of bureaucracy is an oversimplification. His observations in the gypsum plant suggest three types: (1) mock bureaucracy (as when management and workers tacitly agree to disregard a rule like the "No Smoking" one—except when the insurance inspector is around); (2) representative bureaucracy (as when management and workers cooperate in drawing up safety rules); and (3) punishment-centered bureaucracy, as in management's reprisals for unexcused absences or workers using grievance procedures against management.

Now in summary, let's list a few tentative propositions that emerge from this research on the structure of work roles in a gypsum factory and mine.

First, bureaucratic rules are set up and enforced when relationships break down. As we say when things go awry, "There oughta be a law." The sort of rule invoked depends on A's interpretation of B's failure to meet expectations. When this failure is thought to be due to technical inadequacy (carelessness or ignorance, as in the case of violating safety rules), the "response will take the form of developing a 'representative bureaucracy,' but when it is deemed a matter of intentional defaulting (insubordination), the organization of work moves toward a 'punishment-centered bureaucracy.' "[18]

Bureaucratic rules are instituted when they are thought to be correct both as to what *is* and what *ought* to be in a given circumstance—when they are seen as technically correct and morally right. But when they are so defined depends, among other things, on the conditions of work. Danger is one such condition that may affect bureaucratic rules: such rules were relaxed for the gypsum miners, allowing absenteeism and drinking to a degree not tolerable in the factory. To do otherwise would have been technically incorrect, since such rules were virtually unenforceable. And a rule whose violation cannot be punished is not only a useless rule: it contaminates responses to other rules. It would have been morally incorrect since it was assumed that the hazards of mining required such Dionysian safety valves.

Worker resistance to bureaucratic rules depends on the solidarity of the work group and on the degree to which such rules and roles threaten or enhance the standing of workers and management. (Both of these variables come into play, as we shall see, in resistance to changes in work roles among operators in a pajama factory.) Resistance also depends on the compatibility of bureaucratic rules with workers' beliefs. On all these counts Gouldner's miners were a "tight little island," a unified group with particular beliefs and behaviors, making the application of bureaucratic rules impractical.

Such work rules have consequences, some of which Gouldner's research helps us see. Being public and general, bureaucratic rules take the curse out of supervision by making both boss and worker subject to the same requirements. Thus the dignity of the subordinate is safeguarded. "Impersonal and general rules serve in part to obscure the existence of power disparities which are not legitimate in terms of the group's norms"[19]—in this case, equalitarian norms. Being definitive and relatively unambiguous, they may be thought to have been worked out with more deliberation than off-the-cuff orders. Seeming, then, less capricious or arbitrary, they may elicit less resistance, be more likely to win compliance. Obviously, they reduce the number of orders that need be given, thus the number of interactions between superior and subordinate in which the former will exhibit his authority. The control such rules exert is remote, from above and beyond. This is advantageous especially where immediate supervision is impossible. Again, where rules are public and general, sanctions for their violation became legitimate, otherwise not.

> . . . By and large, aggression and punishments directed toward in-group members are not preferred patterns of behavior in our culture and require especially unambiguous justification. Bureaucratic rules are thereby particularly functional in a context in which reliance upon the in-group has been shaken.[20]

Such rules also provide a base line for exceptions and favors, so supporting worker morale. As Gouldner put it: "Formal rules gave supervisors something with which they could 'bargain' in order to secure informal cooperation from workers."[21]

Bureaucratic rules engender apathy in two ways. They define minimum expectations and a level at which, therefore, workers are likely to perform. And such rules "permit 'activity' without 'participation'; they enable an employee to work without being emotionally committed to it."[22]

Finally, bureaucratic rules may reduce tension in the work group when they stipulate and clarify the chain of command and communication; support and legitimate reciprocal expectations; apply to all members of a category, bridging different belief and

. . . work relationships . . . provide,
in a fairly orderly way,
for producing goods
and services
and for distributing
the fruits of these efforts.

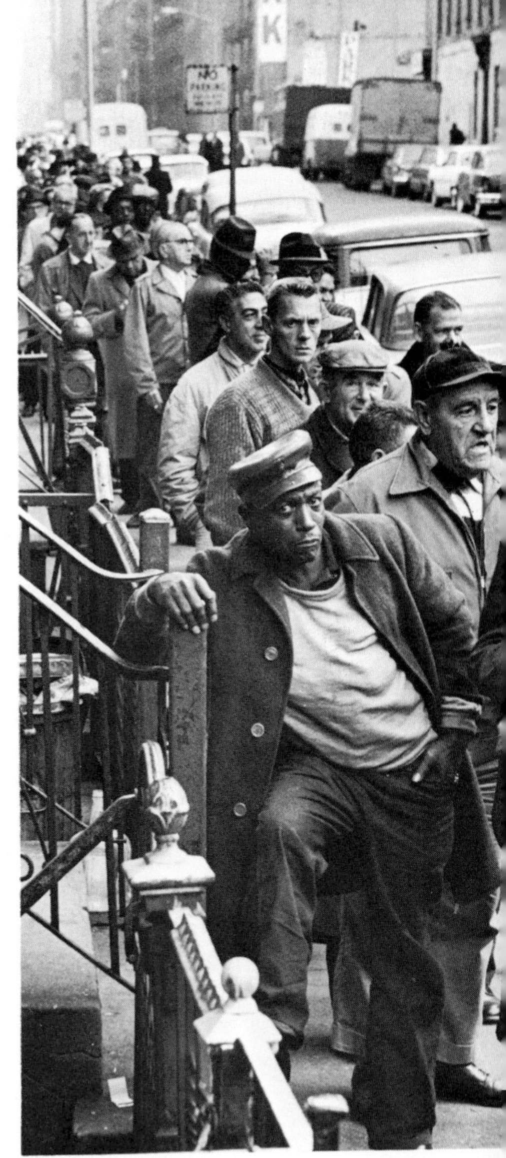

. . . But some roles preclude work. . . .
And for others, although they work,
the rewards are too meager
to support a standard of living
deemed decent by group members.
. . . all human groups
work out some means
of redistributing wealth. . . .

value systems; hold unofficial dealings to a tolerable minimum; and support the need for close supervision. "Bureaucratic rules do not eliminate the need for close supervision but, instead, primarily function to reduce the tensions created by it."[23] The sequence, as Gouldner puts it, is this: low motivation and inadequate performance in the work role lead to close supervision, creating tensions which are mitigated if not resolved through the development of rules that reinforce a low level of performance and lack of commitment to the job.

These are the suggested functions of bureaucratic rules that emerge from one piece of research on the social structure of a work group. Let us turn, now, from the matter of rules to that of roles—work roles and some dimensions for their analysis.

Work roles

Dimensions of bureaucratic work roles

From our discussion of bureaucracy we might infer certain distinctive features of contemporary work roles. For example, in a mass society with intricate division of labor one might expect job descriptions to be specific and detailed. Otherwise, casual and varying performances might affect too many others adversely. Thus, on a scale measuring the precision (or fuzziness) of job descriptions, we would expect bureaucratic work roles to be clearly and specifically stipulated, rather than fuzzily or diffusely.

Similarly, we would expect the emphasis to be on achievement, rather than ascription: what a person can do rather than who he is. Productive efficiency is the goal. Only traits that promote or impair productivity are relevant.

A related emphasis, then, would be the expectation of action, and reaction, defined by the role, not the particular incumbent. This is Parsons' universalistic criterion: *all* clients, students, soldiers, customers, teachers, regardless of name, or ancestry, or unique background—all are expected to act in the same way in like situations. Expectations are universalistic, not particularistic.

Finally, large work organizations with many small specialties, stressing ever greater productive efficiency and assessing achievement with profit-minded precision, will tend to suppress sentiment and elevate the cool, calculating intellect. Hence the emphasis in work roles on affective neutrality, rather than affectivity.

If we think of these dimensions of role performance as ranging between two poles (Figure 10.1), the tendency in large, modern

Figure 10.1

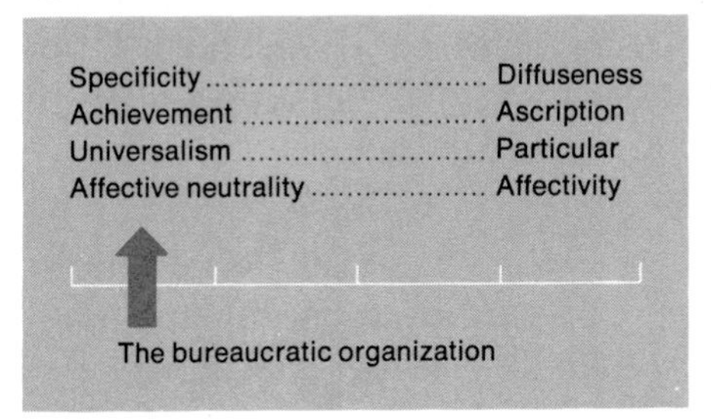

work organizations is to define roles closer to the left than the right-hand end of the scale.

Changes in labor and leisure

Work roles are conditioned, in the large, by broad cultural currents that modify men's wants and capabilities. Underlying the great shift from work in extractive industry (agriculture, mining, forestry, fishing) is the upward sweep of technology and invention, the stress on science that enables an elaborate technology, and the commitment to education that promotes science. Differently put, changes in our knowledge of what is and what ought to be exert influences reflected in the changed structure of the labor force.

Through the centuries, modal occupational roles have changed more dramatically than we time-anchored children of one age can readily imagine. From hunting and gathering economies, man's work shifted to pastoral activity, herding, and then to cultivation of the soil. Agricultural activities became increasingly complex and mechanized while commercial and industrial occupations took over ever larger sectors of the labor force. Now we are in a time when electronic communication, servomechanisms, and control systems displace old work roles and an increasing proportion of the labor force devotes itself to research, development, education, the professions, and sundry services. The changed distribution of occupational roles is indicated in Figure 10.2.

During the first 60 years of this century, clerical workers increased, as a percent of the labor force, by about 11 percent, professional and technical workers by 8 percent. There was a 7 percent increase in operatives and 4 percent in service workers, while managers, officials, and proprietors increased their share of the labor force by 3 percent.

On the other hand, farmers and farm managers declined as a percent of the labor force by 16 percent, and farm laborers and foremen were down by 15 percent. Other laborers became 7 percent less of the labor force, and private household workers dropped by 3 percent.[24]

During these 60 years, the category, "professional, technical and kindred workers" increased sevenfold, the number of lawyers just about doubled, and physicians fell 25 percent short of doubling. But scientists increased 23-fold. And there, certainly, is a commentary on the character of American society.

Such shifts in the labor force imply a parallel change in schooling, for occupation and education are tightly linked institutional spheres. This is attested by the fact that as one goes down the occupational scale in income and prestige, level of education attained declines accordingly.

Productivity has increased with an increase in education and a shift toward white-collar occupations. It is also commonly assumed that productivity of labor and increase of leisure are linked —and that, indeed, we face the awesome prospect of more free time than we know how to use. But the evidence suggests that the threat of leisure may be exaggerated.

There is no question that some people have more leisure, and some more than they wish. Wilensky writes (I am leaning heavily on his work): "There is a kind of forced withdrawal from work among three categories: (1) the involuntarily retired, (2) the intermittently unemployed, and (3) the chronically unemployed—all growing segments of the population."[25] The first category is the oldsters. Other sectors of the population enjoying, or suffering, enforced leisure are the foreign born, Negroes, and the young.

It is clear, too, that if we use the 19th century as our base point for comparison, hours of work have declined from horrendous highs to what we now deem reasonable. In the century from 1850 to 1950, "we moved from a 70- or 72-hour workweek down to a 40-hour week—a 12-hour-day, six-day week to an 8-hour-day, five-day week."[26] But if we are less historically parochial we find that, based on estimates of annual and lifetime leisure, "the skilled urban worker has now achieved the position of his *13th century* counterpart, whose long work-day, seasonally varied, was offset by many holidays, rest periods, and long vacations; annual hours of work now, as then, remain in the range 1900–2500."[27] Wilensky comments on the work role of women, and of "pace-setting elites":

On balance, the female "work week" may be as long as it was

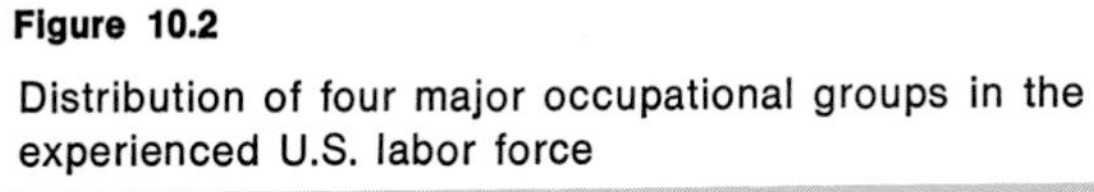

Figure 10.2

Distribution of four major occupational groups in the experienced U.S. labor force

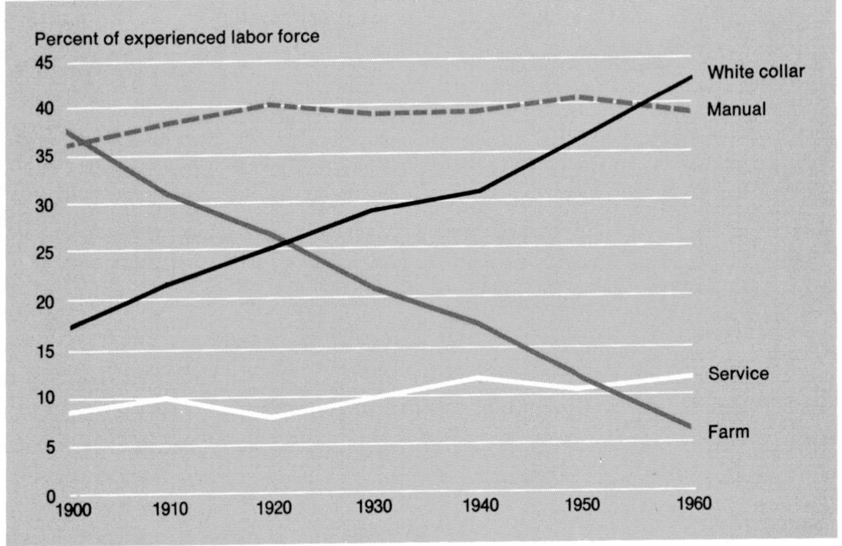

a century ago . . . for women in all the rich countries, both opportunity and motivation to work run high. . . . It seems plain that emancipation, while it has released women for the labor market, has not to an equal extent released them from housewifery. Studies of the weekly round of women report a range of averages of 50 to 80 hours a week in housework, child care, and paid labor. If a woman takes a job today, she has to figure on adding her work week to a forty- or fifty-hour "homemaking" minimum [this especially at the two peak periods of extra-household work for women, ages 20–24 and over age 40].

People in the upper strata have in fact lost out [in lifetime leisure]. Even though their work lives are shorter and their vacations longer than those of lower strata, they work many hours, week after week—sometimes reaching a truly startling lifetime total."[28]

Wilensky estimates that workers in the long-hours category will increase, in their proportion of the male labor force, from 20.5 percent in 1950 to 26.9 percent in 1970.

Our society, apparently, is one in which voluntary leisure is not, nor does it threaten to become, such an oppressive burden as we are sometimes led to think. But enforced leisure is another matter. Its uneven distribution can readily be seen as a practical as well as a research problem. For here "an old paradox becomes more prominent: those whose productivity is highest will work longer hours partly to support the forced leisure of men rendered obsolete by the activities of long-hour men."[29]

In a study from which most of the foregoing data were drawn, one based on a probability sample of six professional groups and a cross section of the "middle mass" in the Detroit area, Wilensky found that 10 percent of his 1,156 respondents were "moonlighters," holding more than one job. This worker had the following distinctive characteristics: an erratic work history, blocked mobility, a sense of being worse off than others he compared himself to, and, in addition, two crucial traits. The moonlighter was caught in a life-cycle squeeze, at that point in his career when support of dependents exerted most pressure and the gap between wants and resources was greatest. He also worked on a peculiar schedule, or a schedule that was more under his own control than is commonly the case.

Study of time devoted to work, leisure, and changes in the proportion of each is a problem in accurate description for the sociologist. (So is the content of the leisure, the *way* members of the group spend their time.) Even as a descriptive problem it is not simple, since patterns of labor and leisure vary widely among different categories: age, sex, race, nativity, class, occupation, region, religion, and the like. Such differences may lead to intriguing questions. For example, Wilensky raises the question whether long hours are to entrepreneurial Jews what moonlighting is to ambitious Catholics. And there is the problem raised by Weber (which we will consider in the next chapter): How are different orientations toward work connected with religious affiliation?

Another aspect of the work role—and the last we shall consider in this cursory introduction to the sociology of work—bears on the matter of incentives: inducements and resistances to work. An empirical study of resistance to change in the work role will provide a concrete example of research in this field.

Rewards and resistances

Perhaps a few are induced to work from a sense of obligation. It has become almost a standard statement for some high-ranking government officials to say, in resigning, that continued government service is a sacrifice they can no longer impose on their families. They have been working, presumably, out of a sense of civic obligation which, in hours and income, conflicts with another obligation to take up work roles less demanding in time and more rewarding in income. For a favored few, avocation and vocation are identical: the content of the work is rewarding in itself. (Teachers sometimes ruefully console themselves that their psychic income compensates for the limited largesse of the tax-minded citizenry. But for most, wages and salaries are a major inducement to perform in the work role.)

Income is some index, however crude, of what we do to and for others. Represented in cash, it is an enormously flexible symbolic medium for establishing and defining certain relationships in the service of satisfying our wants. Its use, following unimagined channels as it leaves the spender's hands, binds together great numbers of people unknown to one another. The rarity and value of each person's contribution to others is registered—not always in terms of stable or "correct" standards, equitably applied—in the distribution of income. For the United States this distribution (1967) is shown in Figure 10.3.

Some shift in the distribution of work rewards is indicated by the data in Figure 10.4, a change probably stemming from the leverage of organized labor and from legislation setting minimum wages, providing income for the retired, and, in general, using the tool of taxation to redistribute the national income.

Of course, people get returns other than income from their work: standing, power and authority, the satisfaction of craftsmanship and problem solving, helping others. Certainly, ever since the classic study at the Hawthorne plant of Western Electric in Chicago, no informed person could conceive of wages as the sole significant reward for the worker, especially in his day-to-day operations. (In this study unanticipated responses of workers—production up regardless of whether working conditions were bettered or worsened—led research workers to this conclusion: It was not the physical but the social conditions of work that were crucial. When workers were intrigued, involved, participating in a common project, management got productivity not otherwise forthcoming.)[30]

A research example: rewards in work (and resistances to it)

An illuminating study of rewards in, and resistances to, work is that by Lester Coch and John R. P. French, Jr.[31] Work roles studied

Figure 10.3

Distribution of total aggregate incomes ($449.5 billion) among all U.S. families (49.8 million) in 1967

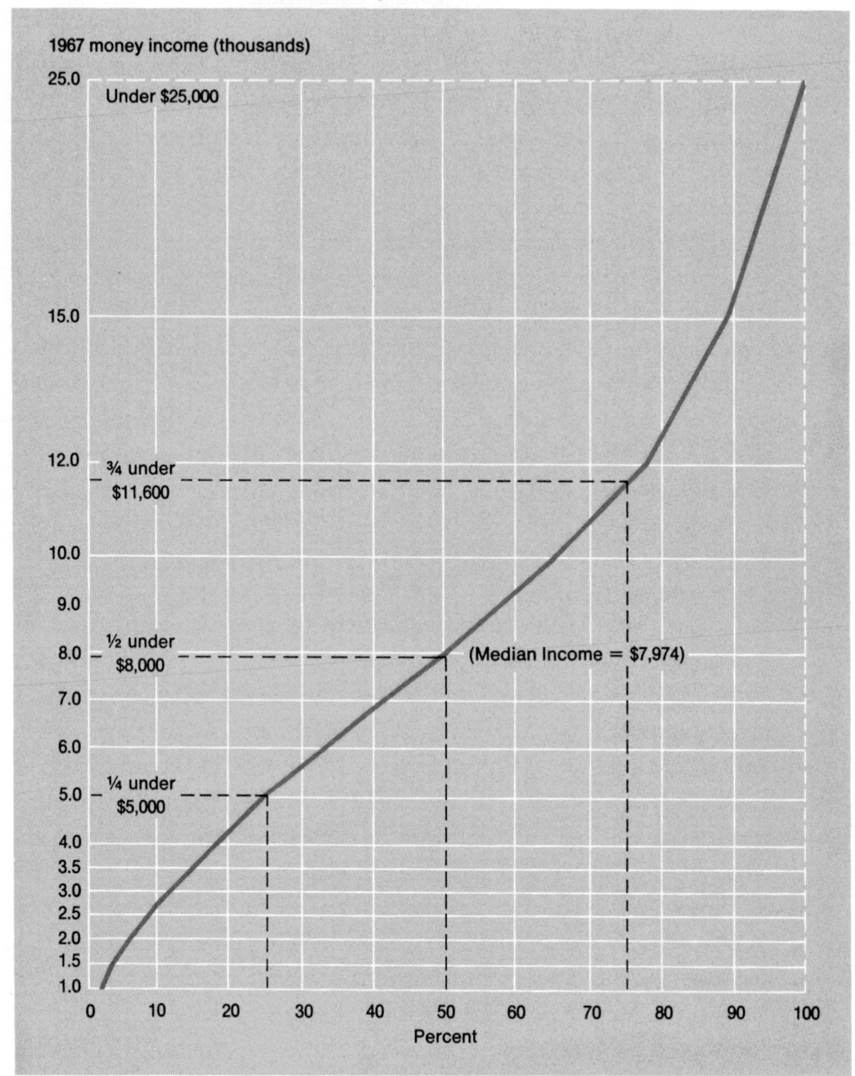

were those of employees in a Virginia pajama factory, about 600 of them, of whom 500 were women operators. Workers' average age was 23, and average number of years of schooling was eight.

Let's look at this research in some detail, for it helps us answer more adequately, and see more clearly, the complexity of the question: What induces us to work? Furthermore, it sharpens our ap-

Figure 10.4

Number of U.S. families receiving specified income*

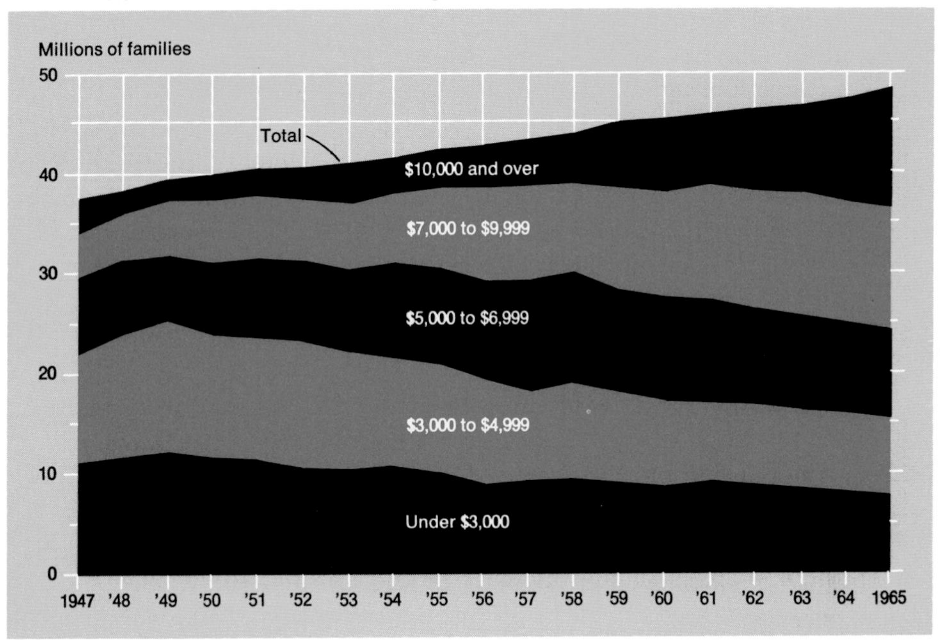

* In constant 1965 dollars.

preciation of the social ends and means of work, the significance of group membership that we discussed in Chapter 5. Finally, it is a first-rate example of the fruitful interplay of deductive and inductive, theoretical and empirical, aspects of inquiry.

The investigators were trying to learn what accounts for resistance to—or conversely, for ease or flexibility in adapting to—changes in the work role. Such changes are common in competitive enterprises, especially those affected by a high rate of innovation. (The automobile industry with its annual transformations is a good example.) As in many work settings, adaptation to such changes can be measured by changes in productivity—in the case of our pajama makers, before and after modifications in their work roles.

After a change in the pattern of work, the transfers (those whose work roles were altered) had to give up some familiar ways of behaving and learn new ones. While the drop in productivity entailed by transfer was compensated for so that, on the average, workers did not suffer a drop in income, Coch and French observed what we might call the Sysiphus effect. (Sysiphus was condemned by the gods to strive eternally to push, up a great hill, a gigantic boulder that incessantly rolled down.) A worker strove to push her production up to the standard level of 60 units an hour and then, her work role altered, level of production rolled back on her again. The changed work role, with its new problems apparently induced a sense of failure, feelings of frustration, and lowered aspiration. These, in turn, were reflected in expressions of resentment and aggression toward management, higher rates of absenteeism and turnover (quitting). Among 198 operators whose work roles had not been changed in 34 weeks, mean rate of turnover was 4.5 percent per month. Among 85 who had been transferred within this period, mean turnover rate was 12 percent per month.

In a first try at explaining resistance to change in work roles, the investigators put it this way: Resistance to such change stems from frustration. The extent of frustration is a function of the relative strength of two forces, one toward, the other away from, achievement of given production norms. The upward force depends in part on the difficulty of the job and the worker's skill. The downward or restraining force increases as number of units produced asymptotically approaches some limit. "Other things equal, the faster an operator is sewing the more difficult it is to increase her speed by a given amount."[32] If either of these forces is weak, frustration will be low, and "the strength of frustration is a function of the weaker of these two opposing forces, provided that the weaker force is stronger than a certain minimum necessary to produce frustration."

Now such a formulation fits the facts about learning and relearning of work roles. It would lead us to predict just such learning curves as those in Figure 10.5. But it does not help us understand why workers transferred, in contrast to those not transferred, are unwilling to learn. That it is a matter of willingness—more precisely, of motivation—and not skills seems indicated, since skilled and unskilled operators had comparable recovery rates after modification of their work routines.

The investigators were led, then, to look for some other factor accounting for resistance to change (and, by implication, the rewards experienced in nonchange). They write that strong, group-anchored sentiments seemed to generate, on the one hand, negative attitudes toward management while, on the other hand, "changed groups with high we-feeling and positive cooperative attitudes [were those with the] best relearners." The influence of such group standards is suggested in the record of one worker

Figure 10.5

A comparison of the learning curve for new, inexperienced employees with the relearning curve for transfers who eventually recover to standard production

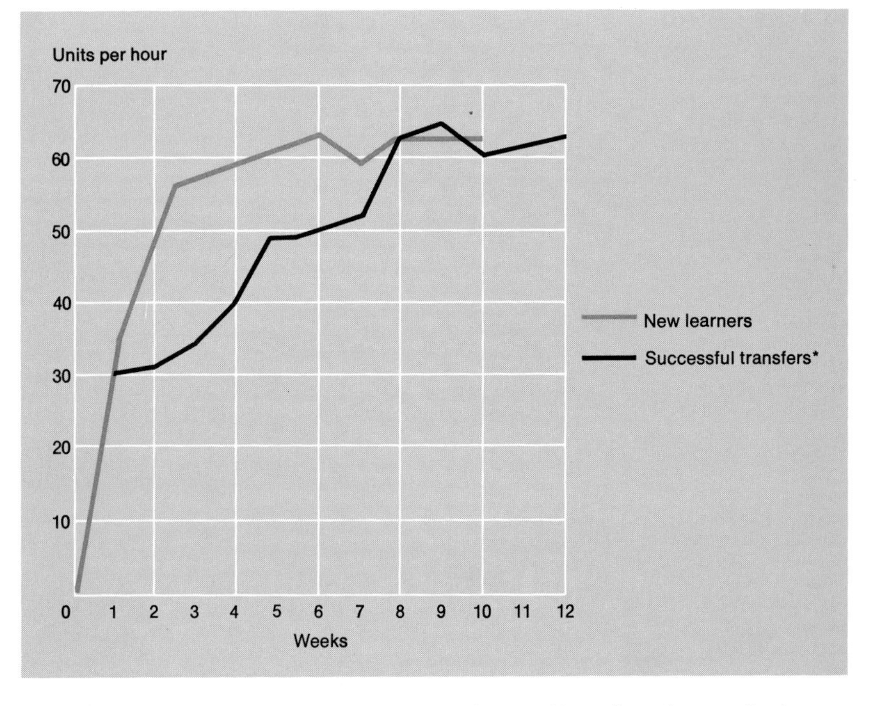

***** Refers only to those whose work role was changed, who neither quit nor became chronic substandard operators.

over a period of 40 days, the first 20 days as a member of a group with an apparent unofficial production norm of about 50 units (10 units below standard), and the last 20 days as a single worker. Figure 10.6 presents this worker's record.

Such evidence justifies the inference that group dimensions may help account for the limiting of production on the part of transferred workers. For while *individual* reactions to change (see Figure 10.5) may be understood as resulting from an interplay between two forces working for and against productivity, consistent differences between *groups* of workers in resistance to change appear to derive from characteristics of the groups themselves. Thus it seemed that "the most appropriate methods for overcoming resistance to change would be group methods." The dimension chosen as the independent variable in the experiment was the *level of group participation* in determining the change in work

Figure 10.6

Resistance as a group effect

Production record of one employee as member of a work group and as a single worker.

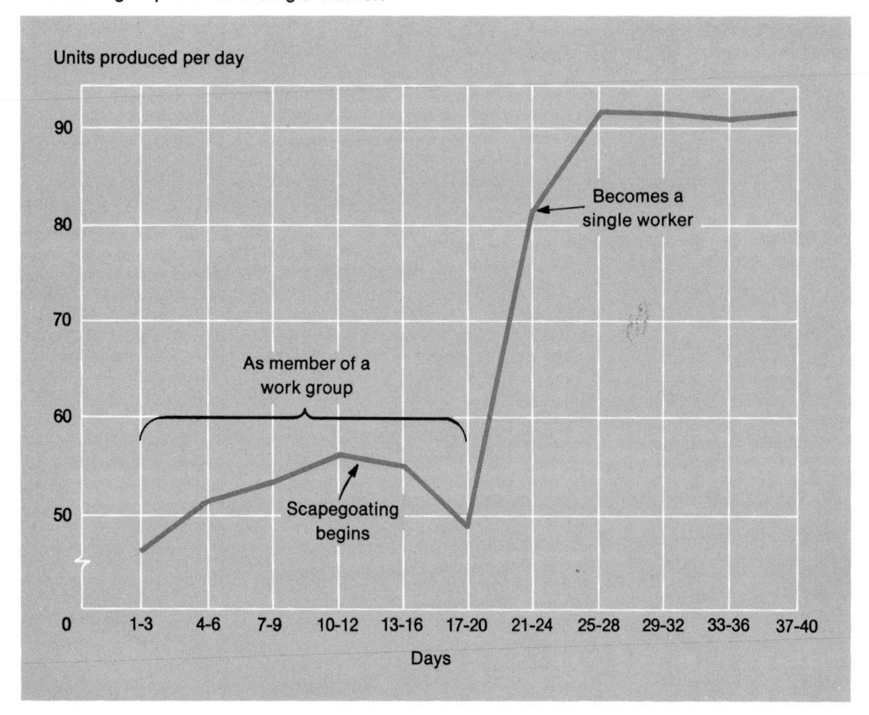

roles. The dependent variable was level of production and speed of recovery to prechange levels.

For the control group of hand pressers, the change in work routines was made in the usual fashion, management determining the need, production department designing the change, and time study people setting the new piece rate. The record of these hand pressers then served as base point for assessing the significance of the experimental treatment. This treatment was of two sorts, both requiring worker participation in effecting a change in work pattern. The first (experimental group 1) included a presentation of the problem to all workers whose routine was to be changed, their designation of members of their group to be trained in the new pattern, and, finally, a retraining of all members of the group by their representatives who had learned the new techniques.

Experimental groups 2 and 3 raised the level of participation in these decisions by making all the operators direct participants in

Table 10.2

Summary scheme of the Coch and French experiment in "overcoming resistance to change"

	Experimental group 1 ($N = 13$)	Experimental group 2 ($N = 8$) and experimental group 3 ($N = 7$)*	Control group
Treatment	Production problem presented, discussed and worker *representatives* participate in designing changes in work role, learn new processes, then transmit to whole group at a second meeting	Same as for group 1, except group 2 and group 3 are smaller groups, and all operators participate in designing changes in work roles	No change in way of altering work routines. Production department changes work role, sets new piece rate, explains change, and new process is initiated (usual procedure)
Outcomes	Good relearning, at end of 14 days an average of 61 units/hour (60 being norm set), cooperative, got on well with same supervisor as in control group, no quits in first 40 days, one act of aggression against supervisor	Recovered faster than group 1, achieved efficiency ratings 14 percent above prechange level, worked well with supervisors, no acts of aggression, no quits in first 40 days	Little improvement, hostile, aggressive responses against supervisor, methods engineer, deliberate restriction of production, grievances filed, 17 percent quit in first 40 days

* Matched with respect to: previously established effeciency ratings; degree of change in work role; and extent of cohesiveness observed in group.

the whole process of change. The plan of the experiment is summarized in Table 10.2, and the results are given in Figure 10.7.

The control group in this first experiment was given the full participation treatment two and a half months later. The dramatic results of this second experiment are recorded in Figure 10.8.

The investigators tot up their findings in this paragraph:

> The first experiment showed that the rate of recovery is directly proportional to the amount of participation, and that the rates of turnover and aggression are inversely proportional to the amount of that participation. The second experiment demonstrated more conclusively that the results obtained depended on the experimental treatment rather than on personality factors like skill or aggressiveness, for identical individuals yielded markedly different results in the control treatment as contrasted with the total participation treatment.

Figure 10.7

The effects of participation through representation and of total participation on recovery after an easy transfer

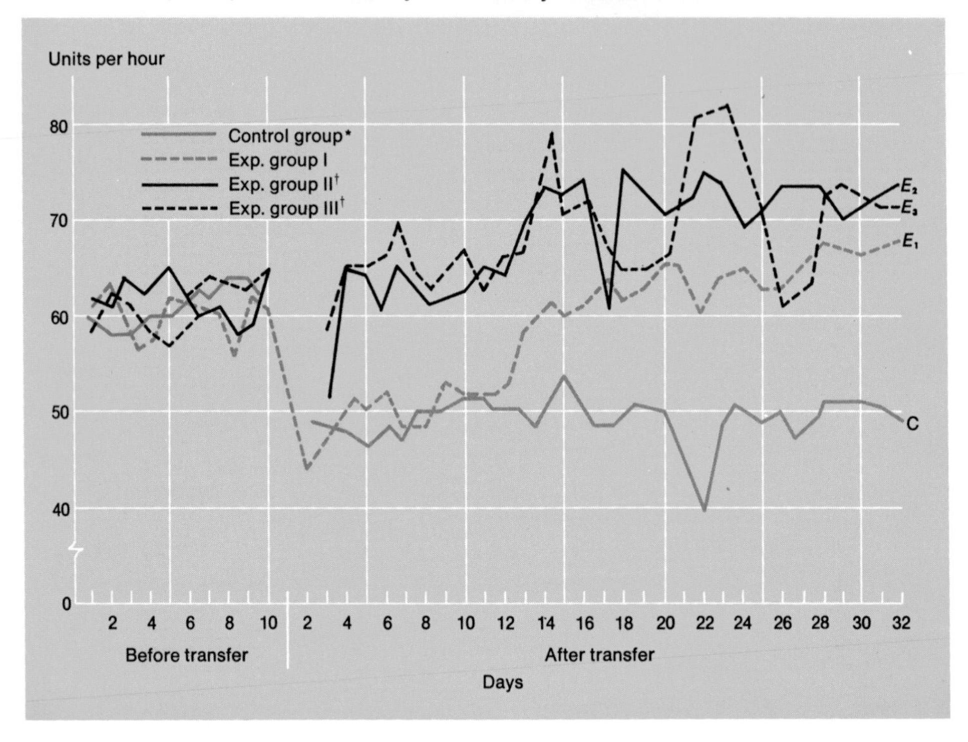

* Participation through representation
† Total participation

After summarizing their findings, Coch and French look back, as good research people always do, to review and revise the theoretical position from which they started. They comment on the remarkable constancy of production levels over hundreds of individuals and groups in this factory. They suggest that where we find a situation like this, approximating a stable state in a work system, it is reasonable to infer roughly equivalent forces of opposite sign (+ and −), counterbalancing one another. This steady state was represented among the pajama factory workers by the standard production level of just over 60 units per hour achieved by all the groups (E_1, E_2, E_3, and C) just prior to their transfer. For the control group, while production requirements remained the same (60 units per hour), the transfer entailed an increase in job diffi-

Figure 10.8

Levels of productivity for workers in the control group

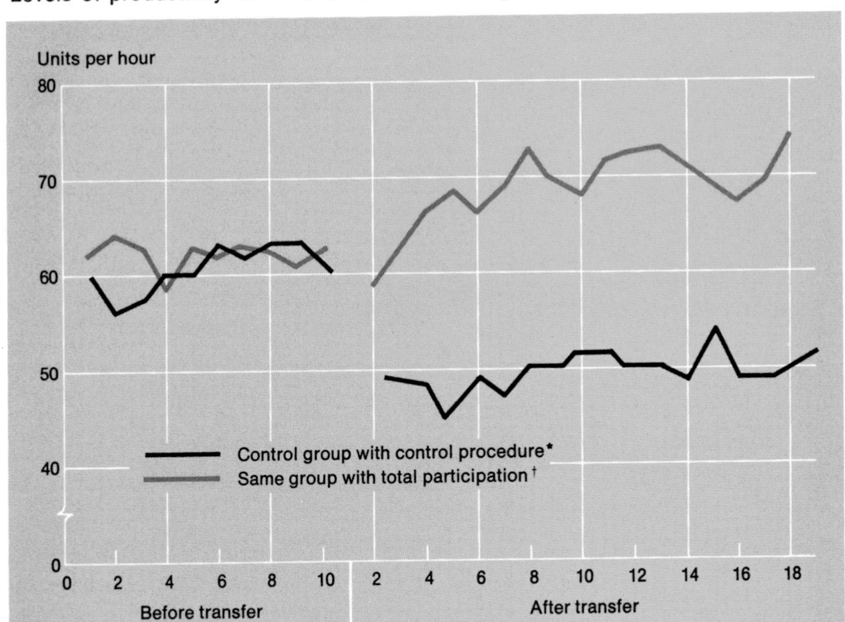

* As controls in the first experiment
† Two and a half months later, when given the total participation treatment.

culty confronted by workers less skilled in the new task than they had been in the old, familiar work roles. Thus the wish for a more comfortable situation (strain avoidance) should increase, depressing levels of production *unless* some countervailing force were to overcome this inclination toward strain avoidance. Coch and French describe level of strain avoidance this way.

$$\text{Strain avoidance} = \frac{(\text{Job difficulty}) \times (\text{Stipulated production level})}{\text{Skill of operator}}$$

Overcoming strain avoidance—resistance to change—apparently depended on the worker's relationship to the change agent. For the control group the change agent was management, an adversary. One result was the setting of a group standard restricting production to 50 units per hour. There was little variation around this production mean: indeed, the standard deviation for number of units produced was lower for this group than for the other three. This points to the kind of group influence represented in Figure 10.6.

But the change-inducing agent in the experimental situations was the worker himself, and his fellow workers, in addition to representatives of management. As Coch and French put it, "A force induced by a friend may be accepted in such a way that it acts more like an own force." The range and depth of a friend's characteristics that we internalize, as we deal repeatedly with him, are much greater than those of an enemy. A friend, that is to say, carves out a greater sector of the self. Among friends, then, changes induced by others can be identified as one's own changes. This is precisely what is revealed in phrases used by members of the experimental groups. They spoke of the new job as "our job," and the new piece rates as "our rates." Thus a dyadic, adversary relationship between workers and management was transformed into a triadic relationship in which workers and representatives of management triangulated on a common problem of production.

Welfare

We institutionalize work relationships to provide, in a fairly orderly way, for producing goods and services and for distributing the fruits of these efforts. But some roles preclude work in the ordinary sense: dependent children, mothers, the aged, the sick and infirm. And for others, although they work, the rewards are too meager to support a standard of living deemed decent by group members.

Changing perspectives on "unearned" rewards

So all human groups work out some means of redistributing wealth, the means depending on commonly held conceptions of the sources of sickness and poverty. Poverty and illness have been seen as God's judgment, either penalty or blessing, and in any case, providing opportunity for the well-to-do to exercise compassion. As recently as 1937 the Archbishop of Lima, Peru, is reported to have said: "Poverty is the most certain road to eternal felicity. Only the state which succeeds in making the poor appreciate the spiritual treasures of poverty can solve its social problems."[33] With these views, welfare activities will be largely a matter of religiously motivated charity. There will be no conviction about the need to eliminate poverty.*

Another cleric, Thomas Malthus, saw poverty as the inevitable result of irreconcilable biological drives. The only solution—and an unlikely one, he thought—was moral restraint.

For some 19th-century communists, the interests of the bourgeoisie led inexorably to the impoverishment of the proletariat. The solution, then, was a revolution to establish a classless society in which each would contribute according to his ability and each would receive according to his need.

In our society we seem to be of two minds. Some think the fate of the poor—16.7 million whites and 7.6 million nonwhites in 1969—is simply the result of irresponsible sloth. The proper social policy, therefore, is to let the poor suffer the penalty for indolence. But a second view increasingly prevails. It sees most of the poor and dependent as disadvantaged for reasons beyond their control: the child, as O'Neill puts it in one of his plays, "was diseased at birth, stricken with a hereditary ill that only the most vital men are able to shake off. I mean poverty—the most deadly and prevalent of all diseases."[34] Or indigent old age, or protracted and costly sickness, or subjection on account of race, or the deprivation of an isolated Appalachian hinterland—matters beyond the person's control may be the source of poverty. Being social rather than personal defects, a social cure is indicated. This view was reinforced by the experience of depression in the 1930's. Then, as though by some malign but impersonal force, industrious and prospering people, were suddenly made paupers.

It deprivation is social, if needs are not fully met, either through the rewards of work or through a secondary distribution as wage earners support dependent kin, and if this situation is chronic, then some sort of institutional safety net must be contrived. (It *must*, that is, if people favor equality of opportunity, deplore limitations imposed by the accident of birth, and seek the fullest use of manpower.) Finally, if these are social matters, and if society changes, then definitions of deprivation will change. In our society the definition of poverty has shifted. Once based on sub-

* In the following I am identifying welfare activities as those aimed at reducing poverty and its effects. This is because our interest is in the organization of work and, by extension, in social arrangements for those who do not or cannot work. This is far from the whole of welfare work. As institutionalized in our society, welfare activities include help for the mentally and emotionally disturbed, recreational activities for youth, educational services for those deprived of adequate training, adoption services, and innumerable others.

sistence needs it is increasingly described in terms of relative deprivation.*

We get some idea of the institutionalization of welfare from the data on public welfare expenditures in Table 10.3.

Among American communities, New York City is probably the best example of the institutionalization of welfare. In 1968–69, about a fourth of the city's budget—more than $1.5 billion—was spent to provide welfare, Medicaid, and similar services for nearly 800,000 people on the city's public assistance rolls, 80 percent of them Negroes and Puerto Ricans.[35]

These data refer only to public programs. To them we must add —take 1966 as an example—$13.6 billion in private philanthropy.

Whom do we depreciate? Characteristics of the poor

I have suggested that we can regard income as a sort of tracer in human affairs, an index of one dimension of human relationships. If wages and salaries indicate what one man means to others, then by looking at the rich and poor we can infer the traits that are valued and depreciated in our society.

The range of rewards is greater than Figure 10.3 (page 372) indicates. Nearly 98 percent of our population receives annual incomes under $25,000. But *Fortune* magazine reports that we have two billionaires, six persons whose net worth is at least half a billion, and more than 100 others who fall in the over-$100 million category.[36] At the other end of the scale are the poor—8 percent of white families and 33 percent of nonwhite families in 1968.[37] What are their characteristics?

First the poor are poorly educated. They are, therefore, poorly prepared to advance their interests economically or defend their interests politically. The data in Figure 10.9 show the link between education and income. Greater rewards go to the better educated. And the figure also shows, as we would expect, that the rewards go to the white. At every level of education, median nonwhite

* If you will try your hand at saying, in concrete terms, what "poor" means, you will find it a tough task. One soon discovers that it depends—on a wide variety of things, sometimes including very subtle psychic states. In 1969, the poverty line for a nonfarm family of four persons was $3,743 annually—by a U.S. government definition of "poor." The official definition starts with the cost of a nutritionally adequate diet. For families of three or more persons, the poverty line is set at three times the cost of this minimum diet, this figure then being adjusted depending on age of family members, place of residence, sex of family head, changes in the Consumer Price Index, and the like.

Table 10.3

Estimated U.S. social welfare expenditures under public programs for fiscal year 1967–68

Welfare program	Amount (in millions)	Percent of total	Per capita cost
Social insurance: includes old-age, survivors', disability and health insurance, railroad unemployment, retirement and disability insurance, general unemployment insurance, workmen's compensation, etc.	$ 42,851	38	$210
Public aid: to aged, blind, permanently and totally disabled, work relief, Job Corps, food stamp program, etc.	11,135	10	55
Health and medical programs: hospital and medical care, civilian and military, maternal and child health programs, medical research, school health programs, etc.	8,037	7.6	40
Veterans programs: pensions and compensation, health and medical, education, life insurance, welfare, etc.	7,324	6	36
Education	38,782	35	191
Housing	415	0.4	—
Other social welfare: vocational rehabilitation, institutional care, school meals, special OEO program, etc.	3,855	3	19
Totals	$112,399	100	$551

family income is markedly lower than that for whites. Median Negro family income was 61 percent that of whites in 1969. A comparison of white and nonwhite income distribution in 1968 is given in Figure 10.10.

The poor, then, are disproportionately nonwhite (chiefly Negro) and ill-educated. Third, the poor fall disproportionately into certain occupational categories. Among males working full time in 1966, the percent of low earners was 4.7 for those in white-collar occupations, 7.3 for blue-collar workers, 15.8 among service workers, and for farm workers, 47.2 percent.[38]

As in the case of limited education, occupations low in prestige and income tie into the race variable, and both of these with poverty. Nonwhites, as we see in Figure 10.11, are underrepresented in white collar occupations, especially professional, technical and managerial. They are overrepresented in manual labor, among service workers and (especially women) in private household work.

Figure 10.9

Median U.S. income by educational level achieved for white and Negro heads of families over 25, 1968

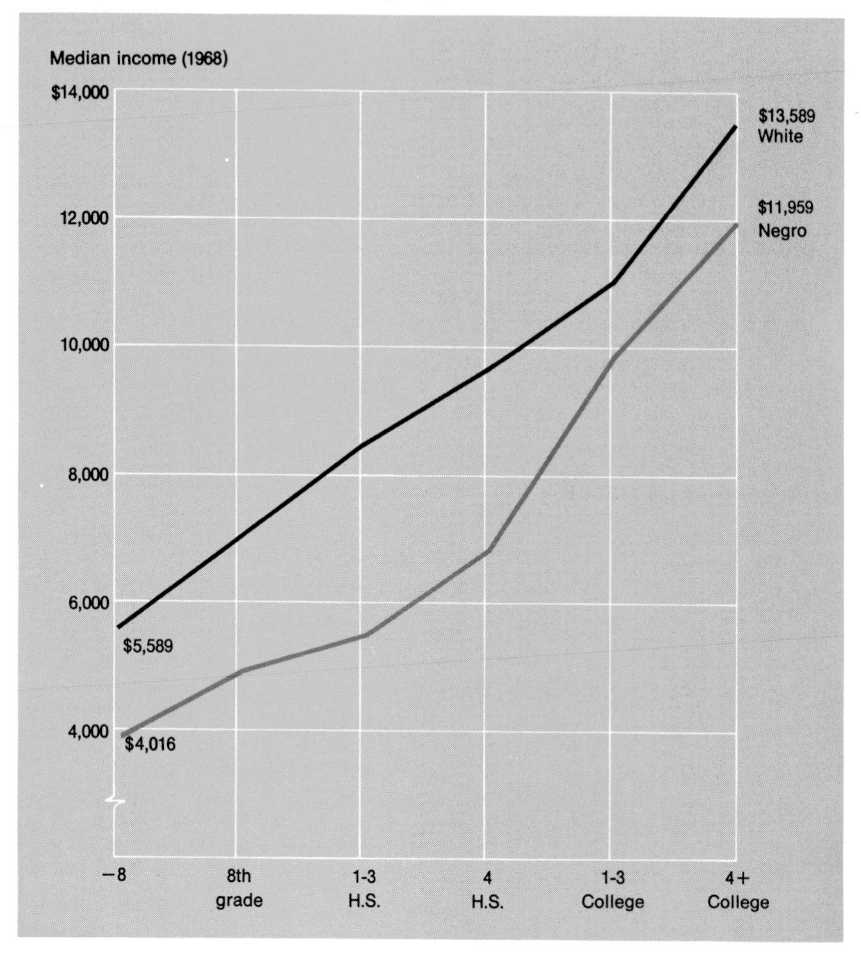

Unemployment, of course, links with poverty. And race, age, and place of residence are linked with unemployment. In the central cities of our 20 largest metropolitan areas, the unemployment rate in 1967 was 3.7 for all whites and 11.5 for white persons 16 to 19 years of age. Comparable figures for nonwhites were 7.6 and 31.6. Except for nonwhite youth, unemployment rates were slightly lower in the urban fringes.

Regional differences in poverty are sharpened by the fact that over half of U.S. Negroes live in the South. Of course poor whites

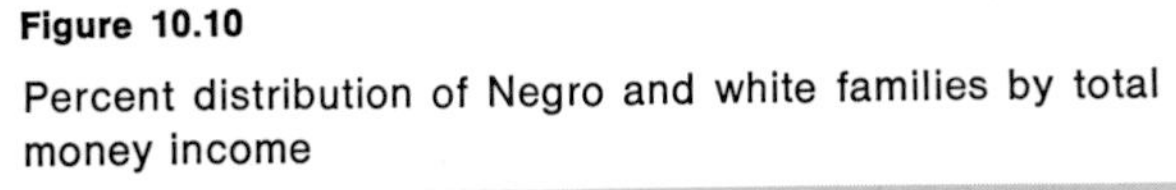

Figure 10.10

Percent distribution of Negro and white families by total money income

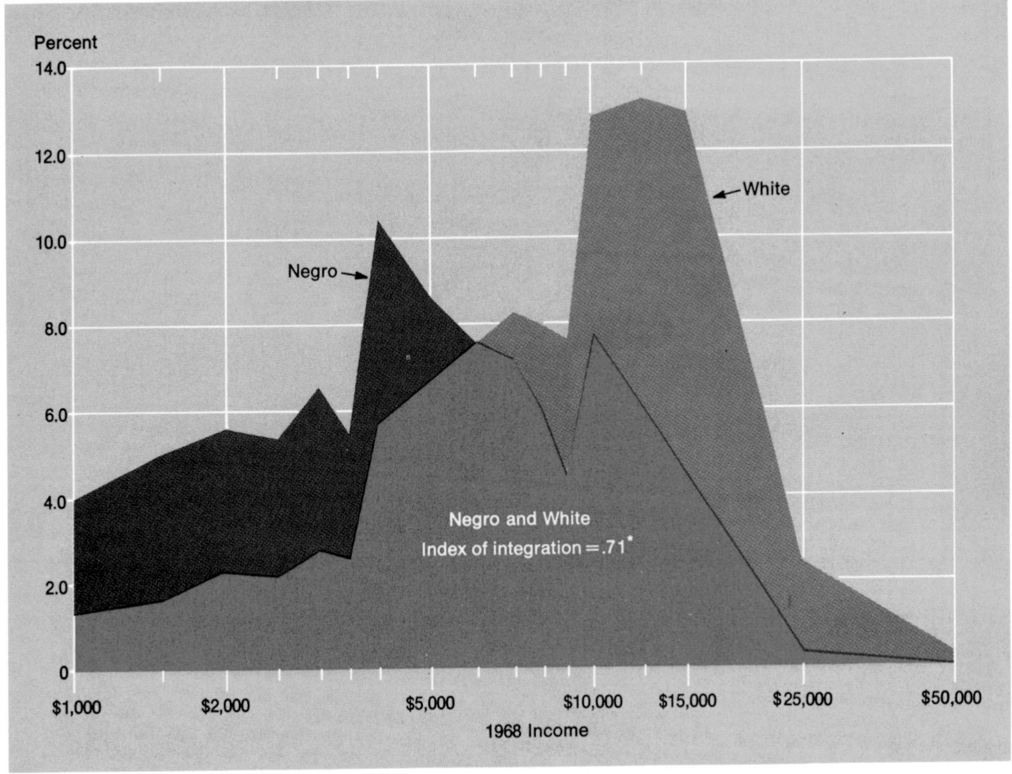

* The index of integration is 1 minus an index of differentiation. The index of differentiation is computed by summing, for each income category, the difference between percent of Negroes and percent of whites receiving that income. (The + or − sign is disregarded.) For Negro and white families in the United States in 1968, the index of differentiation was .29. Thus the degree of overlap (the index of integration) was 1 − .29 or .71.

contribute, too, to the heavy incidence of poverty in this region.

Two final variables discriminate the poor, age and sex of head of family. The poor are young and old. In 1966, "Family heads below age 25 and those age 55 and over accounted for nearly half of all low earners, although they represented only one-fourth of all workers."[39] And families headed by females consistently register a higher incidence of poverty. (See Figure 10.12.)

In sum, then, the poor are disproportionately found among the young and old, in the South and in northern urban ghettos (blacks and Puerto Ricans, in particular), among those with little education, in families with female heads (husbands and fathers often being missing), and among service, manual, and farm workers.

Figure 10.11

Distribution of nonwhites and whites in the 1966 U.S. labor force, by occupation

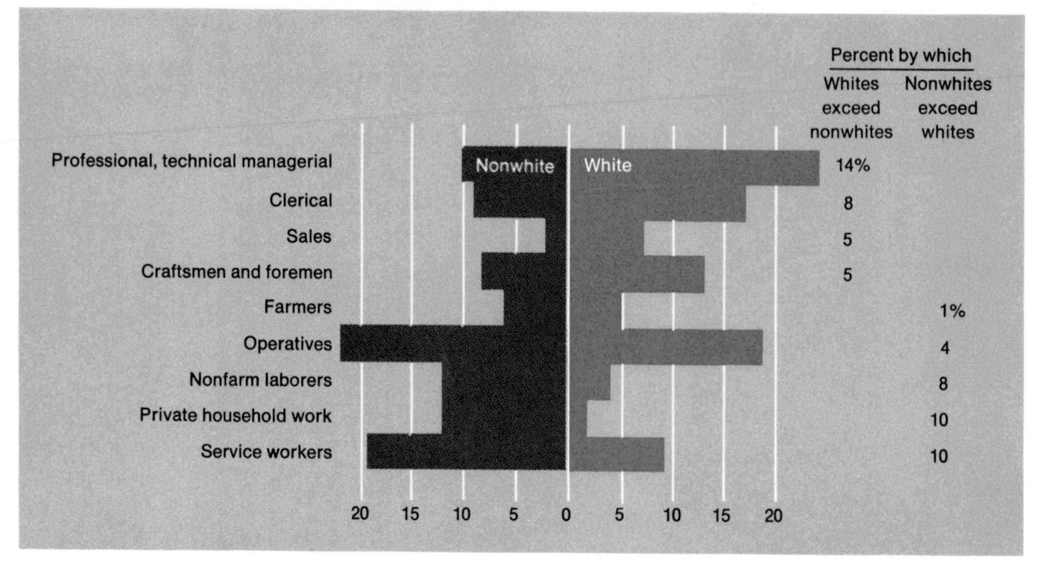

* Base for these percentages is 7,968,000 for nonwhites and 66,097,000 for whites.

These are categories with the least valued roles who stand as subordinates in their relationships with others.

Because we know that role and status are socially conditioned and because we believe that the person should not be penalized (or rewarded) for social circumstances beyond his control, we institutionalize the safety net of compensatory welfare services.

But what compensatory social device best serves is a much debated issue. Some still think that "the deserving poor" is a phrase whose terms are contradictory. Some would insist on a test of merit (adequate) and means (inadequate) as a condition of aid. Some would prefer work and service programs. Others favor direct cash aid. In the past, welfare programs were built on cash benefits: veterans' pensions, aid to the blind and disabled, old age assistance, social security, aid to families with dependent children. Later programs offered goods and services: the food stamp program, VISTA, Headstart, the Job Corps, Community Action programs, Medicaid and the like. Currently there is a disposition to revert to direct cash aid with a minimum guaranteed anual income. In 1970 there went to Congress an administration proposal

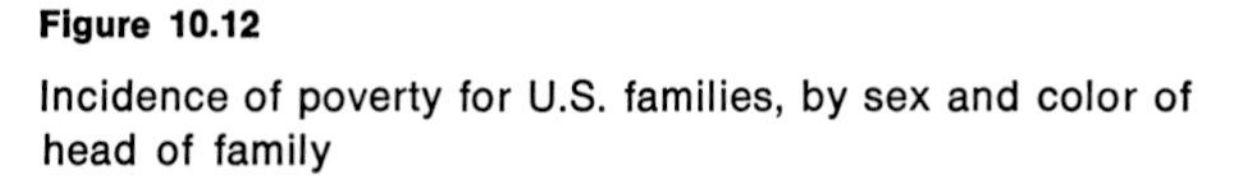

Figure 10.12
Incidence of poverty for U.S. families, by sex and color of head of family

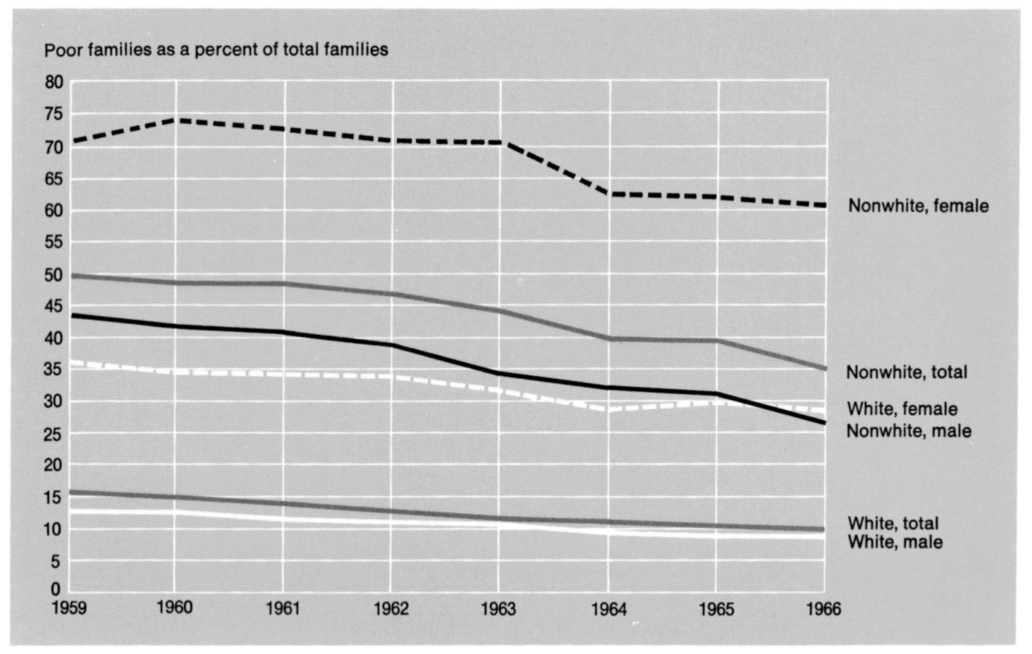

that would provide a base income of $1,600 in cash plus $894 in food stamps for a family of four.

Whatever the proposal, American society has no present means for achieving the goal of a compensatory redistribution of income to offset inequality of opportunity.

* * * *

We have seen how the rules governing production, distribution, and consumption of valued goods and services vary widely, depending on the cultural context. We have seen, too, that the world of work may—must if it is to be fully apprehended—be viewed as a structure of relationship geared to the achievement of omnipresent needs. Thus we see the bureaucratic organization of great enterprises that typify our times both as a set of rules (values and the standards for achieving them) and as an intricate set of relationships.

It was Max Weber who gave impetus to the study of bureaucratic social structures. But it is doubtful that his formulation will stand without revision. One sequel to his work we have seen in Gouldner's research. Around the problem of succession in a managerial role, Gouldner explores the functions of bureaucratic rules, discriminates elements of the social structure of work, and asks: What behaviors and beliefs have what effects on what parts of the structure, under what conditions? In the process he proposes three variations on the bureaucratic theme: mock, representative, and punishment-centered bureaucracies.

When we break down relationships into their constituent roles, we look more microscopically at the social structure of work. There are many dimensions of roles which, depending on the problem, are appropriate for inquiry. Parsons suggests certain dimensions, abstract categories for the study of work (and other) roles. At a more concrete level, we have taken as an illustration the dimension of degree of participation in decision making as an aspect of the worker's role that had great significance for a group of women operators in a garment factory.

Finally, some way of safeguarding the welfare of persons outside the labor force is invariably institutionalized. Workers get their pay directly. Beyond this, obligations of kinship require a secondary distribution of the rewards of work. Still there remain those suffering special disabilities, placing them outside the distribution network of rewards. Because of their relationships with others, many are poor: blacks, the isolated and therefore ignorant, the young and old. And because of their poverty, they are in a subordinate role in relationships with others. For these, a significant sector of American society, a tertiary distribution is arranged through welfare institutions.

In exploring the institutional structure we have seen how rules and roles instituted in one sphere condition those in others. (Home and school prepare for work and welfare. Father's work role may be linked with modes of child rearing. Community and family relationships spill over into the work setting of the gypsum factory.) Work and family are not hermetically sealed and separated social spheres. Nor are economy and polity, or work and religion. This is nowhere clearer than in the connections between economy and polity. Indeed, men govern in work settings and work at governing. An economist, Arthur F. Burns speaks of the interplay between these institutions:

> More than 12 million individuals are now working directly for government—Federal, state, or local. [This is nearly one in five persons in the civilian labor force.] Many others work in private firms that produce exclusively or mainly for the

> government. The prices charged by these enterprises are not set in free markets. They are commonly arranged by negotiation among experts, and they are sometimes determined years after the product has been delivered. The government controls the prices charged by railroads, airlines, pipelines, light and power companies, and even many motor carriers. It dominates the price-making process in agriculture. It controls the supply of petroleum by setting quotas on production and imports. It influences the supply of many other products by tariffs, subsidies, and its own stockpiling. It fixes minimum wages and intervenes in the collective-bargaining process. It fixes the price of gold and thus controls the foreign exchanges. It sets a ceiling on some interest rates, insures many private loans, and even engages in direct lending. It compels people to save for their old age and other contingencies on a collective principle. It uses the tax laws to encourage home ownership, good health, and philanthropy. It regulates the free market itself by stern anti-trust laws. And it uses its vast powers over the supply of money, the cost and availability of credit, the level of taxes, and the rate and direction of its own expenditures, to promote a high level of over-all production and employment.[40]

So, too, with economy and religion: parallel beliefs and behaviors link these institutions, as we shall see.

Just as it was an easy step from home and school to work, so it is an easy transition from economic institutions to those which celebrate shared values and reconcile competing claims to them. We move, now, from the relationships of men at work to those of men under the authority of God and law.

References

TEXT

1. These questions are largely adapted and paraphrased from Theodore Caplow, *The Sociology of Work* (Minneapolis: University of Minnesota Press, 1954). See also William Foote Whyte, *Men at Work* (Homewood, Ill.: Dorsey Press, 1961), p. 5.
2. Whyte, *op. cit.*, p. 58; taken from *Coronet* (September, 1959), p. 72.
3. David S. Landes, "French Business and the Businessman: A Social and Cultural Analysis," chap. xix, in Edward M. Earle (ed.), *Modern France* (Princeton, N.J.: Princeton University Press, 1951), pp. 334–53.
4. The reference is to James M. Barrie's play, *The Admirable Crichton.*
5. Whyte, *op. cit.*, p. 66. Whyte is sum-

marizing material from a study by James Abegglen, *The Japanese Factory* (New York: Free Press, 1958).
6. Margaret Mead, "The Arapesh of New Guinea," in *Cooperation and Competition among Primitive Peoples*, ed., Margaret Mead (2d ed.; Boston: Beacon Press, 1961), pp. 29–31, *passim.*
7. Vilhjalmur Stefansson, "Vilhjalmur Stefansson," in Clifton Fadiman (ed.), *I Believe* (New York: Simon & Schuster, Inc., 1939), pp. 266, 267, *passim.*
8. *Ibid.*, p. 267.
9. Reinhard Bendix, *Work and Authority in Industry: Ideologies of Management in the Course of Industrialization* (New York and Evanston: Harper & Row, Publishers, 1963).
10. Allison Davis, "The Motivation of the Underprivileged Worker," in William Foote Whyte (ed.), *Industry and Society* (New York: McGraw-Hill Book Co., 1946), p. 95. See also, on the matter of motivation and incentive, William Foote Whyte, *Money and Motivation* (New York: Harper & Bros., 1955).

    A bit later in the chapter from which I've quoted, Davis helps us appreciate the ties between institutions: family, work, and school. He writes: "To the underprivileged adolescent, the words and the goals of his teacher—those words and goals to which middle-class adolescents react with respect and hard striving—mean very little. For the words of the teacher are not connected with the acts of training in his home, with the actual rewards in school, or with actual steps in moving toward a career." (Davis, *op. cit.*, p. 99.)
11. See "The Top of the Top," *Fortune*, Vol. 85, No. 7 (June 15, 1967), p. 194.
12. Max Weber, *From Max Weber: Essays in Sociology*, trans. Hans Gerth and C. Wright Mills (New York: Oxford University Press, Inc., 1946), p. 215.
13. See Peter Blau, *The Dynamics of Bureaucracy* (Chicago: University of Chicago Press, 1955).
14. Alvin Gouldner, *Patterns of Industrial Bureaucracy* (New York: Free Press, 1954).
15. Reprinted with permission of the Free Press from *Patterns of Industrial Bureaucracy* by Alvin Gouldner, p. 55. Copyright 1954 by The Free Press, a corporation. First italics mine.
16. *Ibid.*, p. 63.
17. *Ibid.*, p. 97.
18. Gouldner, *op. cit.*, p. 233.
19. *Ibid.*, p. 165.
20. *Ibid.*, p. 172.
21. *Ibid.*, p. 173.
22. *Ibid.*, p. 176.
23. *Ibid.*, p. 177.
24. Calculated from data in Donald J. Bogue, *The Population of the United States* (New York: Free Press, 1959), p. 475.
25. Harold L. Wilensky, "Varieties of Work Experience," in Henry Borow (ed.), *Man in a World at Work* (Boston: Houghton Mifflin Co., 1964), p. 131.
26. ———, "The Uneven Distribution of Leisure: The Impact of Economic Growth on 'Free Time,'" *Social Problems*, Vol. 9, No. 1 (Summer, 1961), p. 130.
27. ———, "Varieties of Work Experience," p. 130.
28. *Ibid.;* the two quotations are from pp. 131 and 130, respectively.
29. *Ibid.*, p. 133.
30. See Elton Mayo, *The Human Problems of an Industrial Civilization* (New York: Macmillan Co., 1933), and F. J. Roethlisberger and W. J. Dickson, *Management and the Worker* (Cambridge, Mass.: Harvard University Press, 1939).
31. Lester Coch and John R. P. French, Jr., "Overcoming Resistance to Change," *Human Relations*, Vol. I (1948).
32. *Ibid.* All following citations are from Coch and French, pp. 517–529.
33. *New York Times*, July 14, 1969.
34. Eugene O'Neill, *Fog.*
35. Figures come from a *New York Times* editorial, January 6, 1968.
36. May, 1968 issue of *Fortune.*
37. U.S. Bureau of the Census, *Current Population Reports*, "Revision in Poverty Statistics, 1959 to 1968," Series P–23, No. 28 (Washington, D.C.: U.S. Government Printing Office, Aug. 12, 1969), Table D, p. 7.
38. ———, *Current Population Reports*, "Consumer Income," Series P–60, No. 58 (Washington, D.C.: U.S. Government Printing Office, April 4, 1969), Table D, p. 5.
39. ———, *Current Population Reports*, "Year-round Workers with Low Earnings in 1966," Series P–60, No. 58 (Washington, D.C.: U.S. Government Printing Office, April 4, 1969), p. 2.
40. Arthur F. Burns, "Of Growth and Gain," a review of Adolf A. Berle's book, *The American Economic Republic* (New York: Harcourt, Brace & World, Inc., 1963), published in *The Reporter*, Vol. 29, No. 4 (September 12, 1963), p. 52. Copyright 1963 by the Reporter Magazine Company.

TABLES

10.1 Oscar Lange, "What Is Economics?" *Review of Economic Studies,* Vol. 12, No. 1 (London: London School of Economics, 1945–46), pp. 19–32, *passim.*

10.3 Bureau of the Census, *Statistical Abstract of the United States: 1969* (Washington, D.C.: United States Government Printing Office, 1969), adapted from Tables 401, 402, 403, pp. 274–76.

FIGURES

10.2 Bureau of the Census publications, quoted by Philip M. Hauser in "Labor Force," in *Handbook of Modern Sociology,* ed. Robert E. L. Faris (Skokie, Ill.: Rand McNally & Co., 1964), Table 11, p. 183.

10.3 Based on data from Bureau of the Census, "Income in 1967 of Families in the United States," *Current Population Reports,* Series P–60, No. 59 (Washington, D.C.: U.S. Government Printing Office, 1969).

10.4 ———, "Consumer Income," *Current Population Reports,* Series P–60, No. 51 (Washington, D.C.: U.S. Government Printing Office, January 12, 1967).

10.5 Lester Coch and John R. P. French, Jr., "Overcoming Resistance to Change," *Human Relations,* Vol. 1 (1948), p. 514.

10.7 *Ibid.,* p. 522.

10.8. *Ibid.,* p. 523.

10.9 Bureau of the Census, "Income in 1968 of Families and Persons in the United States," *Current Population Reports,* Series P–60, No. 63 (Washington, D.C.: U.S. Government Printing Office, 1969), based on data in Table 22, pp. 54 and 56.

10.10 Bureau of the Census, "measures of overlap of income distributions of white and Negro families in the United States," Technical Paper 22 (Washington, D.C.: U.S. Government Printing Office, 1970), p. 5.

10.11 Based on data from Bureau of the Census, "Social and Economic Conditions of Negroes in the United States," *Current Population Reports,* Series P–23, No. 24 (Washington, D.C.: U.S. Government Printing Office, October, 1967), p. 39.

10.12. Bureau of the Census, "The Extent of Poverty in the United States: 1959 to 1966," *Current Population Reports,* Series P–20, No. 54 (Washington, D.C.: U.S. Government Printing Office, 1968), cover.

chapter 11 Social structure: institutions legitimating relationships

The Bible is for the Government of the People,
by the People, and for the People.
General Prologue, Wycliffe translation of the Bible, 1384.

It may seem strange to bracket religion and polity—especially since, in American society, we make much of the separation of church and state. Yet, as the Prologue to the Wycliffe Bible intimates, these two institutions have basic features in common.

In some form, each is found in all human groups. Each is a pillar of the social structure as represented in our theme design. Each is universal in its demands on group members. Both celebrate values shared in common by communicants and citizens. Each promulgates rules that both restrict and liberate as men deal with one another. Both institutions are rooted in the fundamental nature of human relationships. Each generates social unity *and* social strain, change and disruption. Each penetrates other realms of social life, connects with other institutions. (Discovering the nature and extent of these connections is, as we shall see, a central interest of the sociologist.) These are the matters to which we now turn.

The generality of religion and polity

> You may find communities without walls; without letters, without kings; without money, with no need of coinage, without acquaintance with theaters or gymnasia; but a community without holy rite, without a God, that uses not prayer, without sacrifice to win good or avert evil—no man ever saw or ever will see.[1]

> Society is indeed a contract. . . . It is a partnership in all science; in all art; a partnership in every virtue, and in all perfection. As the ends of such a partnership cannot be obtained in many generations, it becomes a partnership between those who are living, those who are dead and those who are to be born.[2]

Men's institutions hang on a framework of rules. Church and government are two institutions whose end products are rules and their enforcement.* The rules we call creeds and codes and laws.

These we find everywhere. But they are universal in two other senses. Within a given group they apply to everyone. No American citizen can escape the responsibilities of citizenship. Even civic apathy carries its consequences for the indifferent citizen. No member of a Euro-American society can escape the Judeo-Christian tradition with its Mosaic code, the Golden Rule, and the Sermon on the Mount. Furthermore, as Burke says in the quotation above, the universal impact of these institutions stretches through time: the roots of the rules are in the past and they have a momentum—or inertia—that extends their influence to our children and theirs.

Law makes explicit those sets of expectations that constitute the citizen role. The relationships of citizen to citizen, governor to governed are thus defined. A special network of relationships en-

*Institutions may become ends in themselves, their rituals thoughtlessly performed in accordance with custom. But institutions grow and take root as *means:* to grow strong children, to promote the exchange of needed and desired things, to resolve conflicting claims, to achieve salvation. The rules articulated by church and state are institutional products (ends). But obviously they are *means* for achieving culturally prescribed values.

ables and enforces the meeting of these expectations. Taken as a whole, we call this network government: the lawmakers, the executives who carry out the law, the police and courts who enforce the law. In our society the lawmaking process aggregates individual preferences, registered in voting, transforming them into an integral characteristic of the group. When a majority has declared itself, the resulting decision applies equally to every citizen.* And through the power funneling from the whole group to its representative agents, failure to live up to expectations is punished. Through the agency of government, we try to resolve matters in dispute and achieve a common commitment despite inevitable differences.

The group-sustaining, socially integrative character of government under law is readily apparent. It is an integrative institution insofar as it underwrites reciprocal expectations. In our society it provides a means of so aggregating preferences that the will of a majority can be known. Expressed in law, this will states, and certifies as legitimate, the expectations that define the civic role. Government exacts fulfillment of these expectations by all who call themselves citizens. The civic role is universal, as is its embodiment in some system of rule.

As to religion, the findings of the anthropologists tend to support Plutarch on the universality of religious institutions. Even in the Soviet Union, officially inhospitable to religion, official anti-religious spokesmen are reported as being "bewildered by the resistance of the . . . remnants of the Russian Orthodox Church and the growth of an underground church among those who, deprived of regular church and priests, are practicing religious rites in secret."[3]

In the United States we are likely to underestimate the social

* Of course, this is an oversimplification. Some decisions require a simple plurality, some a two-thirds vote, and so on. It is true, too, that a recalcitrant minority sometimes flouts the law of the land. But the very phrase, "law of the land," implies the integral, nonexcepting nature of a legislative decision. And the arguments supporting the nonconformity of rebellious dissidents—the states' rights arguments of those opposing civil rights legislation, for example—are couched in terms of "the American tradition" of a federal government reserving rights of self-determination to the states. That is to say, a single, group tradition, a general social value, is invoked.

† This is the percent of the nation's population over age 14 who, when asked in a sample survey by the Bureau of the Census what their religion was, identified themselves with some faith. It is doubtless an overestimate of genuine religious commitment, by any definition. Yet the figure is so large, representing 119 million persons, that any credible reduction of it would still leave an impressive part of our population with clear religious identity and participation.

significance of religion, both because the communicant's role is voluntary as the civic role is not and because material successes through science may have obscured concerns for spiritual welfare. Western societies have been spectacularly successful in adapting to—indeed, recreating—their environments (perhaps more successful with the biophysical environment than the social milieu). This very technical proficiency may have led to a preoccupation with means and to increased ambiguity as to the ends of life. The weakening of tradition as the nuclear family supplants the extended family, the American emphasis on the bigger and better, the slant toward the future—in general, pride in past conquests and confidence that we control the future—these characteristics of our culture may lead us to underestimate the significance of religion.

But no sociologist can offhandedly dismiss an institution with which, apparently, 96 percent of the adult population identify themselves.† It is true that identification is not affiliation, to say nothing of participation. Yet restricting ourselves to membership, we still get something around 60 percent of the population who are members of some church group, perhaps 60 percent of them Protestants, a third Catholics, and 5 percent Jews.[4] A very large part of the U.S. population believes in some way in God, in the efficacy of prayer, in the Bible as the divinely inspired word of God, and in some version of heaven and hell. In any case, it is clear that religious belief and behavior are prominent parts of our social order and that the function of religion in that order must be investigated by the sociologist. Its universality in space and its persistence through time suggest that religion must be seen as playing an important part in social life. There is something to Durkheim's statement when he writes that

> . . . it is an essential postulate of sociology that a human institution cannot rest [solely] upon an error and a lie without which it could not exist. If it were not founded in the nature of things, it would have encountered in the facts a resistance over which it could never have triumphed.[5]

The meaning and sources of these institutions

Definitions

Definitions are legion—perhaps usefully so, as they highlight different features of the matter under study. Our stress is on the rule-making, rule-enforcing functions of church and state—this because of the social bonds formed as people adhere to common conceptions of what is right. Their daily relationships reflect and reinforce these conceptions. Thus we can see the polity as that sector of the social order in which, through official agencies, rules are promulgated that bind citizens together in a network of reciprocal rights and duties. And we can also see in Durkheim's definition of religion its group-sustaining influence: "a unified system of beliefs and practices relative to sacred things, binding together those who adhere to these beliefs and practices in a single moral community."[6]

The social roots of religious and political behavior

We deceive ourselves if we think of human institutions as carefully contrived social patterns. They are, rather, slowly growing developments shaped over centuries by the changing social milieu. To discover the roots of religious institutions, we should consider two social imperatives: (1) the absolute requirement, for human relationships, of dependable—i.e., predictable—responses, and (2) the need to solve the recurrent problems of human life.

Dependability in human relationships

The requirement of dependable performance in role, and therefore, stability in human relationships is a moral one. For *basic aspects of morality*—its "oughtness," its impersonality, its generality, the stress on personal responsibility, the significance of the intent or spirit of the act—these *are also requisites of a social order.* The near universality of religion may be derived from these requisites for sustaining a social structure. Through holy writ and rite, religious institutions reinforce social patterns. Rewards are promised for observance, punishment for infractions, of the moral code—infractions, that is to say, of the rules that legitimate the expectations that define the roles that make for stable human relationships.

Consider the mandatory element in the moral and the social. A social relationship is something which, by its very nature, involves the dependence of one person on another and a high probability that, given an action by one, the other will respond with a predictable reaction. To describe one aspect of this interplay between persons we use adjectives like "responsible" and "dependable." If someone agrees to meet you at a given time, he does so. If he contracts to do a job, he comes on time and performs his work conscientiously. If he says he will sell you this sort of article, he does in fact do so, and the article is as he claims it to be. Sometimes we use the stronger word *honesty* to describe the trust that can be placed in another to react as he is expected to. Of course, we are sometimes disappointed, not to say disillusioned—which is to say that performance is not always what it *should* be. Human conduct, in contrast to sheer behavior, carries connotations of better and worse, and the better is, of course, the preferred. In matters of any import, the preferred becomes mandatory. Performance in any significant role is informed with an "oughtness." Because of the common "oughtness" of our expectations, there is some leverage to guarantee that what ought to be, will be: that expectations will be met. And to meet expectations is to meet the prime requirement for sustaining a human relationship.

The stipulations for correct conduct are not aimed at any person. Religious sanctions for correct conduct apply equally to all communicants. Similarly with human relationships: they are defined by role, not by incumbent. They are impersonal in the sense that the overarching rule prescribes the role. Core elements of role prescriptions, like religious prescriptions, have this characteristic: they are *impersonally* mandatory.

But while the rule is impersonal, responsibility is personal. Each person is accountable to others, and to the law (which represents others). A parallel responsibility is to his gods who are typically and necessarily personalized conceptions. For men have always found it hard to conceive the inconceivable. Their closest approximation has been a god whose attributes are extensions, superior extensions, of the human. Man must create his gods in his own image. They are superhuman, of course, but in the same attributes that humans have: in power, benevolence, wrath, compassion, control.

> We Tibetans have a saying, "Gods, devils and men are alike in actions and thoughts," i.e., the same things will anger them and the same things will please them, and they will act accordingly."[7]

The extension to the gods of human attributes entails two consequences. We can understand the divine impulse; and we experience fear or guilt in our transgression. The link of child to father is profoundly personal. An omniscient Father knows the communicant deeply and intimately. With the faculty of penetrating innermost thoughts comes a power, more terrible than that of the earthly father, to reward and punish. And this personal responsibility to a celestial Father is paralleled by responsibility to one's fellows: for a common father implies a sibling relationship with fraternal obligations. Thus impersonality in the rule, personal responsibility in the role,* contribute to the dependability of human relationships.

The impersonality of the rule, or its suprapersonal character implies a third characteristic of religion and an element essential for the social order: reciprocity in human relationships. Given the role, any and all incumbents are expected to behave in a given way. If A responds to B in the appropriate way under conditions X, he may legitimately expect the same response from B *et al.* under similar circumstances. Anyone struck by disaster has certain legitimate expectations for help from his fellows; and he in turn must reciprocate when others are hurt.

As citizens having a common nationality, we have certain minimal expectations that we reciprocate—willingness to be taxed for others' children's education and they for ours; to respect others' property, and they ours; to abide by a majority decision, even when we are in the minority; to serve the common cause in war and peace, so serving fellow citizens as they serve us. The moral equality among children of God supports this generality of reciprocal expectations and obligations wherever an enduring system of relationships is built. It promotes consistency through time (behavior in the role tomorrow will be quite as it was yesterday) and space (within the group these people, here, will fulfill role expectations just about as those people do, there). Reciprocal obligations thus impose general requirements for performance on all roles within a given category: husbands and wives, employers and employees, students and teachers, citizens, rulers and ruled, *et al.* Both law and religion restrict the range of idiosyncratic conduct, channeling role performance in accord with legitimate expectations.

* Responsibility implies identification of the actor so that he may be held responsible. In this connection we may think of the name with which the child is christened, typically in church, as a sort of label on the package. It enables others to know whether the contents of this package are as specified, as expected. For the rest of his life, the person's name, the label of the product, stands linked with performances enabling others to reward him for successes, punish him for failures. This is why wearing masks at the Mardi Gras and costume balls is associated with liberation from the customary moral restraints and specified relationships of daily life. For some sort of identity is essential for pegging responsibility, for assuring the meeting of expectations. Conversely, anonymity is associated with amorality. This is in part why the transient, the migrant, the stranger whose

This may well suggest that to do unto others as you would have them do unto you is not merely a prescription. It is a description. It is an implicit proposition as to the conditions for maintaining stability in the human group. And it probably applies to hostile as well as to friendly relationships. To carry on the conflict successfully, it is necessary somehow to cut the other fellow down to one's own size, or else to inflate one's self to the adversary's size, responding in kind.†

Consider, finally, one more feature shared in common by the moral and the social, the spirit imputed to the person as he acts toward another. A social relationship exists, as Max Weber puts it, in ". . . the behavior of a plurality of actors in so far as, *in its meaningful content,* the action of each takes account of the other and is oriented in these terms."[8] Human relationships always involve the meaning or the intent of the actor. So also does moral conduct imply "good" or worthy intent. A few years ago the Under Secretary of Defense resigned when it was disclosed that his wife's company had garnered profits from big government contracts. His resignation was thought necessary because, however much he had kept to the letter of the law, he had neglected the *spirit* of the law, a spirit expected to inform the relationship of public servant to citizen. Human relationships always involve the spirit, the intent, the subjective aspect. We do not respond exclusively to the objective or external conditions of human behavior. We impute motives. All manner of cues are provided to reveal to the other what our intent, what our internal state is.

The fact that our symbols are not always exact makes it all the more necessary to code out of others' behaviors the meaning or intent of those behaviors. And it is also an aspect of morality that we are concerned with what a person means by what he says and does. If we are constrained to make judgments on the basis of crude externalities of conduct, it is because we have poor cues or poor instruments for getting at motives or intent. Often the sever-

identity is not established, may feel freer to act unresponsibly, and why others are disposed to view him with suspicion. (See in this connection Everett K. Wilson, "Mobility and the Maverick," *Antioch Review*, Vol. 17, No. 1 [March, 1957]). This is one reason why legislation has been passed against the hooded Ku Klux Klan whose members, in their anonymity, can flout conventional norms, fracture the law with impunity.

† It's instructive to note that our conception of good—i.e., morally correct—sportsmanship involves some element of this reciprocity. We match fighters and wrestlers by weight, put people into age classes, give one player a handicap in order to balance the relationship. Even in hunting, there are mandates of good sportsmanship tending in the direction of reciprocity. One must give the prey a fighting chance.

ity of punishment hangs on whether the offending behavior was intentional. Goodness is to some extent a matter of motive rather than of performance. Indeed, to treat a person simply as an object, dealing only with the externalities of behavior is to suggest not only an inhuman or a nonhuman relationship: it may be deemed immoral. We do not treat a person from an impoverished background, ill-educated and guided by values different from our own, as evil if his behavior is not animated by, say, malice or vindictiveness. Or if we are constrained to deal with persons who at first put us off, with time we may find them tolerable, if not genuinely likable. In such cases, we have gotten beneath the surface of conduct and discovered something about the motive or intent of the behavior.

Thus we see the roots of religion in the nature of human relationships, since these relationships are defined by dimensions intrinsically moral: the oughtness of reciprocal expectations, the impersonality or suprapersonality of the rules that govern roles, the acknowledgment that in like situations the rules apply to any and all members of the faith. The moral code represents a sector of the culture generally shared by all members of the group. Each properly socialized member comes to feel a personal responsibility for fulfilling expectations of God and group. Indeed, these expectations may be identical. And so there comes to be ". . . one body, and one Spirit . . . One God and Father of all, who is above all, and through all, and in you all."* It was this sense of generally shared, obligatory rules guiding and constraining the conduct of group members that led Durkheim to see people's gods as social creations incorporating, symbolically, the highest values of the group. Finally in sustaining a moral code, religious doctrine typically stresses another dimension critical in human relationships, the meaning or intent of the actor.

We could make an almost identical statement about the social roots of government. For the control of human relationships rep-

* This statement is from Paul's letter to the Ephesians, 4:4 and 6. This is not to overlook the fact that one group's gods may be another group's devils, that within a society there may be two or more social orders, incompatible or antithetical. These statements bear on relationships *within* a group of believers.

† This has nothing to do with the "law and order" that has become a battle cry of the political right. That cry simply means "my law and my order" and a suppression of dissent. MacIver's statement applies to all communities—of thieves, saints, or car salesmen—none of which can exist without a code of conduct to which its members generally adhere.

resented in government responds to the same fundamental need in human life. "Without law there is no order,† and without order men are lost, not knowing where they go, not knowing what they do."[9] As with other institutional rules, the rules of family, school, church, and work, law promotes that predictability in others' responses without which we would dwell in a world gone mad. And to say as much suggests that law, in a general sense, is already implicit in customary behavior, in the mores, and in the family which long preceded the formal instituting of governing roles. In the family (which MacIver refers to as the "seedbed of government"), we find a host of rules governing eligibility for marriage (endogamous and exogamous regulations), incest, premarital and extramarital relationships, division of labor between sexes and generations, control over property, descent of property, and title to and distribution of the fruits of labor. All such rules promote predictable interchange among men. In defining duties and rights of the citizen role, law enables people, even those otherwise unknown to one another, to build necessary relationships in support of common, civic interests.

As in the case of religion, government provides rules that assure a certain dependability in men's relationships with one another. The law prescribes and proscribes, as do the creeds and codes of religion. The most visible sign of the law is neither legislator nor judge, but the cop on the beat, a formidable figure invested with the power of arrest, and worse. Having in mind this symbol of legitimized constraints on man's conduct, it may seem odd to think of authority, both religious and political, as a social mechanism for enhancing freedom. Let us consider this matter.

Freedom through the restraints of rules

Dependability is linked with freedom, and freedom with restraints. A related source of political (and religious) organization lies in the paradox that men liberate themselves by imposing restraints. (Someone has written perceptively that freedom is the space formed by bounding walls.) Why must we accept the restraints of religious and political rules? And how can such limitations be conceived as liberating?

To impose the common requirements of citizenship becomes necessary because people differ. The citizen role consists in a set of rights and duties vis-à-vis fellow citizens. But rights and duties are not self-evident, self-defining, or similarly perceived. People differ—genetically, socially, culturally. And because they differ, the inculcation of common commitments is necessary: to vote, to abide by majority decision, to serve on juries and in other offices, in time of peril to defend the country, to resolve differences according to the legal rules of the game.

The social source of differences lies in the infinitely various permutations of social influence that converge in each personality. Differing social sets generate differing views, values, and conduct. This is an inevitable source of sometimes abrasive differences; for no two persons confront or respond to the same set of others, the same constellation of kinfolk, friends, siblings, and strangers. Differences—inadequacies, if you like—in the socialization process threaten the pattern of universal expectations that bind together all those called citizen. Similarly, as a result of social mobility, one may find both disposition and talents at odds with those of his new group. Such social differences may well generate incompatible claims, claims that might be socially disruptive but for the requirements built into the citizen role and enforced by government. So also with variant cultural themes typifying different religious, racial, regional, and nativity groups. Conflicting claims are accommodated or reconciled under law by ruling on the limits within which differences must be tolerated and beyond which corrective penalties are invoked.

The notion of government stemming from conflicting claims is implicit in Rousseau's thought. At the beginning of his argument he declares: "Man is born free; and everywhere he is in chains."[10] There comes a time in man's history when, perhaps due to the pressure of population upon available resources—or at least to rival claims for scarce resources—aspirations, satisfactions, even survival are threatened. Under these conditions an agreement, a "social contract" is made in the service of survival, each person surrendering some aspect of his personal will to the general will. This latter becomes sovereign, and each citizen becomes subservient to that will.

The elemental function of government, then (as Hobbes said) is to protect life, if not to promote liberty and happiness, when men who are relatively equal make incompatible claims on limited resources. In fact, Hobbes explains the origins of the institution of government by starting with the assumption of the equality of men.

> Nature hath made men so equall, in the faculties of body, and mind; as that though there bee found one man sometimes manifestly stronger in body, or of quicker mind than another; yet when all is reckoned together the difference between man and man is not so considerable as that one man can thereupon claim to himself any benefit to which another may not pretend, as well as he. . . .[11]

And since men are not remarkably different in body, mind, and moral stature, differing views and values confronting scarce resources lead to the war of each against all. In a state of nature, without government, man lived under conditions where his life was poor, solitary, nasty, brutish, and short. He was constrained, therefore, to contrive a compact with his fellows, agreeing to elevate one as governor.

There are several difficulties with these classical views of the sources of the institution of government. Note three of them: the imputation of rational contrivance, the implication that government is a sort of superfluous afterthought and the notion of reluctant surrender to the necessary but evil restraints of law.

Quite aside from the fact that these notions on government's origin cannot be tested, for lack of data, they probably attribute a spurious rationality to man. One is not persuaded that this institution—or any other—grew out of an antique brainstorming session. Rather, the likelihood is that it developed like Topsy, bit by arduous and mistaken bit.

A second difficulty, as MacIver put it, is that

> . . . by presenting government as something that supervenes in human society, something merely accessory to it, or something that actually perverts it, [such doctrines] misinterpret the service and minimize the necessity of government.[12]

A third error in these views of government might be called the fall-of-man notion. As the children of our colonial forebears intoned from their primers: "In Adam's fall / we sin-ned all." And so, cast out of an idyllic, ungoverned Garden, we became trapped in civilization. Thus, Rousseau sees the ordering of relationships under law as enslavement. (*L'homme est né libre, et partout il est dans les fers.*") To be free is to emancipate one's self *from* the restraints of government. The emphasis on freedom *from* disregards the need for social constraints if one is to be free *to* achieve one's ends. For such freedom is always contingent on collaboration with others. There is no such thing as a "free *individual.*" A person's freedom is always related to his role and status vis-à-vis others. Freedom has this ambivalent aspect: to be free to achieve one's ends implies agreement on and adherence to reciprocal obligations. Freedom to love, to learn, to earn, to play, to worship—indeed, to live—depends on enforceable agreements with others. Freedom necessarily involves commonly accepted limitations. Only under such restrictions can one have confidence that given means will lead to desired ends.

> Freedom may be defined in terms of the probability that specific groups or individuals can formulate their ends of conduct and initiate a course of action with a minimum degree of constraint from other persons and with a high degree of predictability of the consequences within the institutional and associational structure of the community.[13]

Government, then, is not mere restraint. It extends the range of choice, opens up options hitherto closed, and frees men to seek legitimate objectives by guaranteeing the order that is necessary if they are to reach their goals.

Thus a likely source of rule-making institutions lies in the freedom they confer as political (or religious) power is used to impose restraints. Neither too much nor too little power, however. Too much means regimentation, too little, anarchy—both being conditions under which people are not free to pursue their goals. A plausible link between concentration of power (one dimension of the governor-governed relationship) and extent of individual freedom is suggested in Figure 11.1.

Rule-making institutions have their sources in the dependability required of human relationships. Dependability, in turn, entails the restraints imposed by rules. But rules are also facilitating. They help us get where we want to go. Since achieving any significant goal is inevitably problematic, and since rules are facilitating, religion and polity can be seen as institutionalized means of problem solving. Let's consider the sorts of problems for which they offer solutions.

Religion and polity as two modes of problem-solving

We use political and religious institutions in at least three ways to help us resolve life's mundane problems. We invoke the aid of supernatural powers. We rely on moral codes to settle prob-

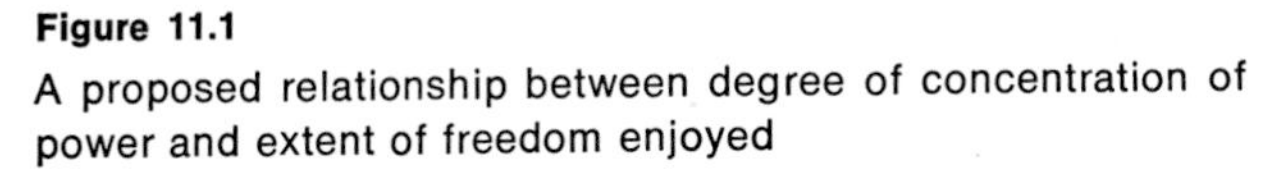

Figure 11.1
A proposed relationship between degree of concentration of power and extent of freedom enjoyed

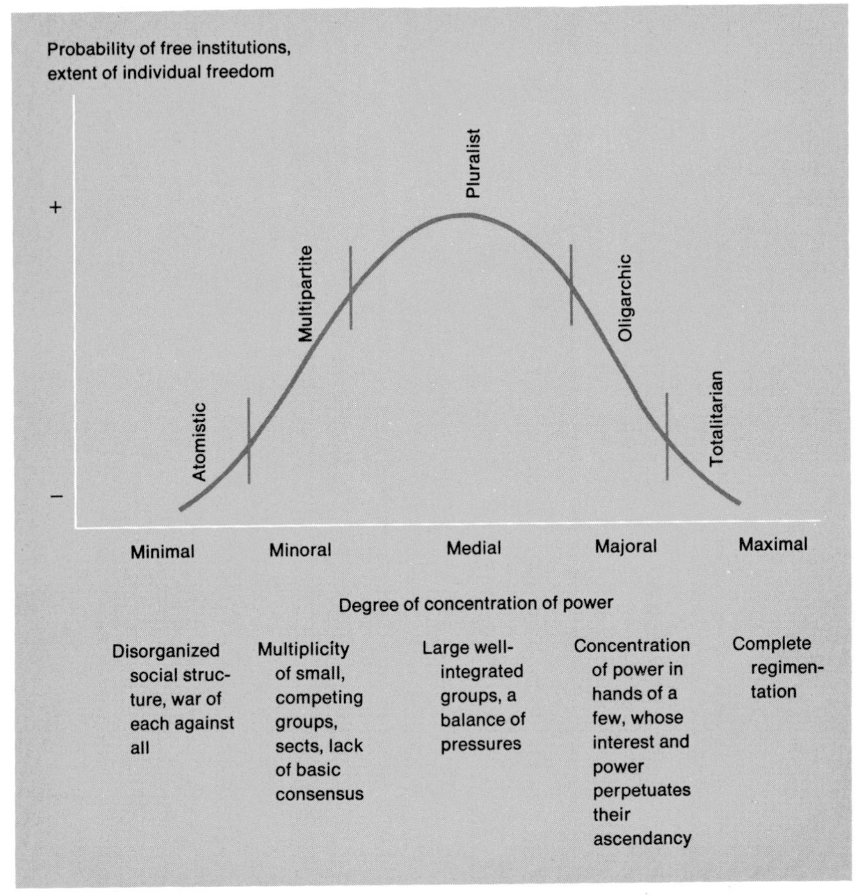

lems of conflicting interests and inclinations. And we refer to law and leadership for the legitimate resolution of personal and social problems (if these are, in fact, distinct).

Despite technically impressive excursions to Moon and Mars, our ignorance is at least equally impressive. A child of six, living close to the edge of mystery (a realm over which his elders have long since drawn the curtain of resigned agnosticism) will pose questions that nonplus the sage. And so, when an agnostic position is unacceptable, we develop supernatural explanations. In this sense religion provides a cognitive safety net helping us "know" the otherwise unknowable. We find an illustration in Malinowski's discussion of science, magic, and religion among the Trobrianders. These people, Malinowski reports, have

> . . . a whole system of principles of sailing, embodied in a complex and rich terminology, traditionally handed on and obeyed as rationally and consistently as is modern science by modern sailors. . . .
>
> But even with all their systematic knowledge, methodically applied, they are still at the mercy of powerful and incalculable tides, sudden gales during the monsoon season and unknown reefs. And here comes in their magic, performed over the canoe during its construction, carried out at the beginning and in the course of expeditions and resorted to in moments of real danger. . . .
>
> . . . While in the villages on the inner lagoon fishing is done in an easy and absolutely reliable manner by the method of poisoning, yielding abundant results without danger and uncertainty, there are on the shores of the open sea dangerous modes of fishing and also certain types in which the yield greatly varies according to whether shoals of fish appear beforehand or not. It is most significant that in the lagoon fishing, where man can rely completely upon his knowledge and skill, magic does not exist, while in the open-sea fishing, full of danger and uncertainty, there is extensive magical ritual to secure safety and good results.

A four-celled table suggests the nature of the implied relationship between religious behavior and anxiety-inducing problems (Table 11.1). (With Spencer and Malinowski, anxiety gives rise to rites for manipulating or propitiating the gods. But Durkheim and Radcliffe-Brown would reverse the relationship: the psychological state stems from the institutionalized behaviors, from religious rites).

What is implied, here, are two ways of "knowing." Although the two modes can be found in any society, often incongruously interlaced, it is useful to separate them to clarify our analysis. The one may be thought of as belief and commitment, myth and dogma bearing on the mysterious and ultimate problems of our worlds, especially touching those crises over which our control is minimal. The other may be viewed as belief and practice, theory

Table 11.1

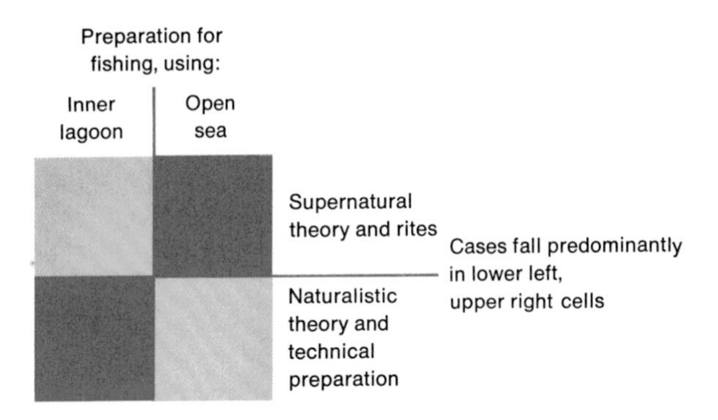

and its application, in realms increasingly susceptible to man's control.

Through supernaturalistic theory and doctrine, groups provide their members means of meeting recurrent problems for which their science and technology are inadequate. Through common conceptions of right conduct, of modes of propitiation and supplication, they can avert evil, allay anxiety, win through to the good. Since his spirits are projections of himself into the realm of the unknown, man's understanding of, and adjustment to, the universe is made easier—or if not easier, at least credible. For he modifies his environment, controls his condition by the same sorts of conduct through which he tries to modify his relationships with other men. Thus his relationship to God is an idealized reflection of his bond to fellow communicants. The two relationships are governed by similar imperatives. As a consequence, religion performs a crucial function as a system of social control. Customary conduct fits into the scheme of the universe. For anthropomorphic projections of divinity must include the valued specifications of conduct. God in turn exemplifies and demands such conduct.

A naturalistic world view, on the other hand, seeks solutions not by invoking the beneficent intervention of a third, omnipotent party, but by attempting to induce environmental changes directly. Such efforts are guided by verifiable observations and procedures. They are based on several assumptions, such as: (1) no event is uncaused, (2) given the same outcome on two or more occasions, the same causes are at work, (3) an idea, a proposition, may be regarded as true only when it can be walked down the abstraction ladder, tested, and confirmed empirically.

The naturalistic view, the scientific orientation toward the world, has led to remarkable achievements in the physical, biological, social, and psychological spheres. These achievements have fed on themselves, swelling the yield in technology, reducing our vulnerability in the face of the unknown. But it is not clear that such advances have contributed equally in the moral sphere: in promoting justice, happiness, goodness, or freedom. (Perhaps a case might be made that advances in goodness or increases in freedom depend on discriminating among various options, and that knowledge multiplies the options and refines powers of discrimination.) In any event, moral issues persist, as do the ultimate questions of origin, destiny, and the meaning of life. Such questions, scientifically unanswerable, remain in the realm of religion.

Religion speaks to a second range of problems, those bearing on everyday problems of morality. (So does the law. Lying, stealing, killing are not only morally offensive: they are legally actionable.) From Sinai and Calvary (in our society) come the rules for ideal relationships among men. From the Mosaic code through the New Testament, holy writ touches problems of marital relationships, filial and neighborly obligations, aggressive behavior, and the emotions that compromise human relationships: envy, avarice, pride, and the like. Through church and state, rewards and punishments are held out for abiding by, or departing from, the approved guidelines for conduct. And through their functionaries, rules are adapted to the contingencies of daily life.

In discussing the roots of these rule-making institutions, I have implied that dependability in human relationships, the disposition to extend freedom of choice, and the need for guidelines in problem solving are human conditions that *cause* some such social arrangements. These are assumptions, of course, and not, with the evidence at hand, demonstrable. But the argument appeals to reason, especially when we ask what would happen in the absence of such institutions. (Our answer must be, I think, that some comparable arrangements would be institutionalized to perform the same functions.)

Indeed, it might be better to think of dependability, freedom, and the facilitation of problem solving as functions—largely unplanned outcomes of religion and government—rather than attributing them to basic human needs. If we do ask about the functions of religion and the polity, we can classify social outcomes under two broad headings: their group-binding (integrative) and socially disruptive (disintegrative) functions.

The social functions of religion and polity

Integrative (group-binding) functions

Religion

Religion is group-binding to the extent that it penetrates all spheres of life, rendering act consistent with act, thought with thought, and act with thought.

> God is concerned with the whole of men's lives: on at least this one point all the churches agree. He is not merely the Lord of the Sabbath, but is equally concerned with men's activities the other six days of the week: their work, their play, their politics, their family life.[15]

Cutting across many spheres of life and offering solace and solutions in physical, mental, and emotional crises, religion contributes to the stability of the social order. The scale on which, in our society, religion meshes with other sectors of social life, is seldom understood. Churches in the United States are active in education, child welfare, treatment and prevention of crime and delinquency, recreation, care of the aged, the placement of unemployed, medical care, political action, radio and television broadcasting, and a wide range of social service activities. American churches spend millions annually on welfare and philanthropic activities. From the perspective of the social order, such services may be viewed as providing a safety net. For the disruptive, even explosive potential of a sense of unjust deprivation can be curbed through the welfare activities, the institutionalized "caring" of the church. When Marx spoke of religion as the "opiate of the people" he was referring to myth and dogma precluding a proper, active interest in one's own welfare and in redressing the wrongs of a maldistribution of wealth. The Marxist notion has been translated in terms both psychological (the tranquilizing influence of religion) and conspiratorial (the calculated suppression of the masses through superstitions or resignation religiously induced). In reality, the welfare functions of religion are social and have tended, in the United States at any rate, to promote evolutionary rather than revolutionary change. The church's welfare activities have sometimes served as bellwether models for programs instituted later through legislation.

The universality of religious prescriptions promotes integration.

Religion performs a group-maintaining function not only because it cuts across a broad range of men's mundane activities but also because it establishes standards equally applicable to all believers, the high as well as the lowly. Through it we get a statement of the cultural universals. It is only because of an indignant sense of the universality of sacred principles that the pirate could reply to Alexander, as Augustine reports:

> . . . for elegant and excellent was that pirate's answer to the great Macedonian Alexander, who had taken him: the king asking him how he durst molest the seas so, he replied with a free spirit, "How darest thou molest the whole world? But because I do it with a little ship only, I am called a thief: thou, doing it with a great navy, art called an emperor."[16]

George Bernard Shaw expresses the same sense of a betrayal of common standards: If a thief

> . . . snatches a loaf of bread from the baker's counter [he] is promptly run into gaol. Another man snatches bread from the tables of hundreds of widows and orphans and simple credulous souls who do not know the ways of company promoters; and, as likely as not, he is run into Parliament.[17]

The prescriptions of the group's religion bind together all members with universal imperatives.

The integrating effect of religion as it exerts pressure to match profession with practice. The universality of religious prescriptions—in our society, the almost all-embracing sweep of the Judeo-Christian faith—makes it possible to exert pressure to match profession with practice. When practices are out of line (as they must be, inevitably falling short of religious counsels of perfection) and when such deviation is harmful to some group, its members can appeal to the violated universals. The church then becomes an instrument of justice, sometimes interpreting and applying God's law before the courts apply man's law to redefine and rectify human relationships.

This has a special meaning for members of minority groups. With black Americans, a common faith has provided a moral bridge into the white community. The church has often been the threshold to communication, hence to community: first, in identifying a company of the dispossessed and, later, in identifying a larger moral community embracing blacks and whites. It was,

Frazier suggests, the single agency through which such identity, such social cohesion could be wrought.

> The adventitious gatherings in which tribeless men and women without even the bones of kinship could find an ephemeral solidarity became regular meetings for religious services and a new bond of cohesion was established in the New World. Not only was a new bond with their fellow slaves established but as they joined in the religious services of their white masters their moral isolation in the white world began to break down.[18]

Thus the church can be regarded as a first force, an opening wedge in the drive toward equity, toward enhancing normative integration. But with such a depressed and dispossessed minority as the American Negro, integration required first of all a lifting of the level of life to the point where something approaching a peer relationship with majority members could emerge. Just as upstream traffic on river or canal is impossible until the water in the lock is raised to a higher level, so full equity in black-white relationships depended on a lift in the Negro's life conditions. The church has sometimes served as such a lock in the stream of American society, not merely providing an emotional safety valve but generating collateral institutions to raise the level of life. The church was the source of organizations for economic cooperation, not only for buying and building churches, but for insurance companies and other forms of mutual assistance. It was through the internal organization of the church that the Negro's political impulses expressed themselves, a connection symbolized by the Reverend-Representative Adam Clayton Powell. The church was critical in the development of educational opportunities for the Negro. And after generations of inching toward equity, it was through the church and its leaders (from an Indian Hindu–Christian pacifist to Martin Luther King) that the nonviolent civil rights movement made the breakthrough, initiating what has been called the revolution in race relations.

Social integration through the identity of group and God. Religion is socially integrating, again, in the sense that gods are local, the unqualified Good is the God as defined within a given culture and by a given tribe. *Gott mit uns* reveals the common possessive posture of a nation toward its god. Official state doctrine invariably assumes that Providence is peculiarly receptive to its claims upon Him. National anthems disclose this conviction.

These sometimes go beyond mere supplication and take on the tone of injunctions not to forget His contractual obligations to the tribal cause. A verse of the national anthem not often sung by Englishmen (the tune is the same as our "My Country 'tis of Thee") goes this way:

> O lord our God, arise
> Scatter our enemies
> And make them fall.
> Confound their politics,
> Frustrate their knavish tricks,
> On thee our hopes we fix,
> God save us all.

This comes close to Durkheim's central thesis in a stimulating (and controversial) book entitled *The Elementary Forms of the Religious Life.*[19] For Durkheim, God must be seen as the more or less ambiguous symbol of the unqualified good (as group members conceive it). Notions of good and evil take on a transcendental character as they are commonly shared and reflected in the group's gods. And the persistence of moral and theological conceptions is not to be explained as due to God and His control over human affairs, but to men's creation of God, and of the church that institutionalizes the values they attribute to Him. Religion, then, is a social artifact—an artifact in the sense of creation, but not artificial; for it is an institution both natural to man and necessary for sustaining that continuing collective enterprise that is a society.

Polity

Legal prescriptions also apply universally to group members. No citizen is exempt from civic obligations. None is barred from the privileges of citizenship. (Denying the vote to the Negro, discrimination in hiring by union and employer, the refusal of a publicly franchised restaurant to serve all the public—these and many others practices fly in the face of legal norms.)

The law, too, penetrates most social spheres, setting limits to the range of permissible behavior in family life, the world of work, education, and even religion—as, for example, when it threatens the tax-exempt status of certain church income. In a complex society where every man's activities are vested with a public interest

—in a society preeminently characterized by functional integration—the meshing of diverse skills and needs seems to require an extension of the governmental function. Burn's statement (pages 388–89) points unmistakably to this development in our society.

As with religion, political institutions provide for celebrating exemplary conduct (the Medal of Honor winner, the dedicated public servant), incidentally defining the better and the worse performance in the civic role and urging realization of the ideal.

Finally, the sovereignty of the state comes close to the sovereignty of God as the focus of allegiance and the source of ultimate secular power. If, in Durkheim's view God is the group ideal (in our case, the state), then as the ultimate arbiter and locus of ultimate power, the group is God.

Social function of punishment. The integrative functions of government are probably least understood when we think of courts, police, and punishment. We probably see these branches of government as operating to reduce aberrant behavior, bringing the deviant into line. If they confine the range of conduct within tolerable limits, as a thermostat restricts heat variation around the desired point, then we may view such agencies as sustaining the prevailing values and the system of relationships embodying them, that is, the group.

While this may be true, it is a partial truth that obscures the mechanism by which it occurs. Indeed, if we think of punishment simply as a device to deter wrongdoers, it would be hard to persuade ourselves that various penalties, however swift, sure, and severe, have ever done much to discourage the criminal or reduce rates of recidivism. (In some statistical time series, crime rates vary *directly* with investment in law enforcement, and with frequency and severity of punishment.)*

If punishment, then, does not so obviously serve its ostensible function of deterrence, what is its use? What is the social function of police and courts and the punishment they mete out? An answer to this question has been given that points to the law-abiding rather than the lawbreaker, to the offended rather than the of-

* Punishment may, in fact, deter, but we lack means for demonstrating it; for we cannot answer the question: What would happen in the absence of punishment? Law officers, not surprisingly, are disposed to think that in the absence of their increasingly costly efforts, crime would be still higher. Of course, this whole question is too broadly posed, here. Controlled observation would require us to deal with specific types of offenses under specific conditions.

fender. This is an answer that has appealed to sociologists, at least since Durkheim made the distinction between the *cause* of a pattern of behavior and the *function* it may serve. (Ostensibly, we institute police, courts, and punishment *because* they will deter from criminal activity. But the function served by such a pattern may be something else.) Here is Durkheim's argument.[20]

The primary function of punishment is not to prevent recurrent offenses. If to some extent it achieves this end, it does so simply as a matter of guaranteeing overt and superficial propriety. It is a police procedure, in the narrow sense of the word, and in no sense a means of altering conviction and conduct. Nor is punishment a way of expunging the evil deed by a counteroffense that nullifies the former. This, Durkheim suggests, is as though a physician, in order to heal a diseased arm, began by amputating the other. *The essential function of punishment is to offer the occasion for reaffirming the group's values,* for a recommitment to conduct challenged by defections and delinquencies. He writes:

> This is the . . . moral evil caused by [illegal behavior]. It shatters . . . faith in the authority of . . . law.
>
> . . . punishment is only the palpable symbol through which an inner state is represented: it is a notation, a language through which either the general social conscience or that of the [authorities] expresses the feeling inspired by the deviant behavior.
>
> Punishment does not give discipline its authority; but it prevents discipline from losing its authority. . . . Severity of treatment is justified only to the extent that it is necessary to make disapproval of the act utterly unequivocal.

Perhaps the social function of punishment is especially visible when, as in the case of confession, it is self-imposed. The ex-Communist Whittaker Chambers, offering an accounting in his book *Witness,* is a case in point. Beyond the punishment it exacts, such a public and voluntary confession of wrongdoing provides a dramatic affirmation of the forces of good over evil, of right beliefs and behaviors over wrong ones—that is, of ours over theirs. It is, of course, a means of bringing the once-deviant person, now purged and chastened, back into the fold. Confession strengthens the hand of authority. Not only have official representatives of the group induced a confession, thus attesting their vigilance and technical competence; in addition, they have in the confession an inverted manual for conformist behavior. This social function of the self-imposed punishment of confession is seen in the Inquisition, in the witch trials of England and America, and in the breast-beating *mea culpas* of trials of "deviationists" in the U.S.S.R. Hausknecht sums things up for us:

> Any deviant individual, whether he is an ordinary thief or a political nonconformist, severely damages the fabric of the social order. Those charged with maintaining order must not only prevent further damage but must also repair the damage already done. *Confession is a unique means for making the inevitable existence of nonconformist behavior a means for strengthening the tendencies toward conformity.*[21]

Rules commonly accepted channel conduct within bounds tolerable to the group. And the punishments linked to the rules offer opportunities for regular reaffirmation of shared values. Indeed, one may ask whether values could be sustained without periodic challenges. But the rules of law mean more than this. For like the rules guiding conduct in other institutional spheres, they enhance freedom. They enable men to move more certainly toward chosen goals, provided, of course, that these goals fall within the range permitted by the common commitments of group members. Thus the paradox of law: simultaneously restricting and freeing.

Disintegrative functions of religion and polity

Religion

These rule-making institutions promote group unity as they celebrate standards that apply across the range of life's activities, as they impose these standards equally on all believers, as they stress some correspondence between practice and profession, as punishment for deviation stimulates general recommitment to group standards and, finally, as group gods define limits of allegiance.

Incompatible Gods, convictions and commitments. But to use the plural (to speak of gods) and to say that they define the limits of allegiance is to suggest the potential divisiveness, or disintegrative effect of religion. For intragroup harmony is related to intergroup antipathy. If religion tightens the drawstrings of the group, it also accentuates the differences (and if the differences are religiously founded they may be intolerable differences) between the one group and others. If God promotes unity, gods often generate conflict. If it is true that the church has opened doors for a suppressed minority, so also has it barred and bolted them. For our southern God, and the South African God, faithfully reflecting group values, have generally validated segregation and white supremacy. The Holy Inquisition, the treatment of the Huguenots, the Mormons, the Quakers, Dachau and Buchenwald, St. Bartholomew's Day, Salem's witches, Marcus Aurelius' treatment of the minority sect called Christians—these bring to mind the intergroup divisiveness that feeds on religious absolutes that parallel group sovereignty.* The church has often accepted St. Augustine's view: "When error prevails it is right to invoke liberty of conscience, but when on the contrary truth predominates, it is proper to use coercion."

Criticisms of the social order. Religion, furthermore, has a disruptive mission as it stands in judgment on the moral failures of the establishment. If religion serves social unity by pressing practice toward profession it is, at the same time, stressing the gap between the two and urging that people accept the costs of radical changes in the social order. The costs of Christianity would be considerable, for example, were white church members suddenly to transform their behavior toward blacks, or toward institutionalized warmaking, or toward the poor. (One interesting underestimate of the cost can be seen in the demand of the National Black Economic Development Conference. Under the leadership of James Forman these blacks rendered a bill of $500 million to the churches of white Christians and Jews. The charge of "fifteen dollars per nigger" was levied as reparation to Negroes in the United States, not so much for willful complicity in their exploitation as for failure to meet the mandates of religion in criticizing and correcting defects in the social order.)

In Latin America, liberal or leftist priests have been exerting pressure for social and political reforms. Churchmen in Paraguay and Brazil are goads and gadflies to officialdom. *The New York Times* reports that in Recife, Brazil, churches "are regularly sprayed with machine-gun fire and daubed with slogans condemning alleged Communist infiltration into the church."[22] A young priest, seen as radically critical of the government (he was also a professor of sociology) was killed, his body hung from a tree on the university campus in Recife.

* In the winter of 1969, police arrested eight members of a right-wing Bible study group. They were suspected of 31 bombings and acts of terrorism directed against liberal and left-wing organizations.

An example of the condemnation of the establishment can be seen in a new litany introduced at the Minneapolis convention of the United Presbyterian church in May, 1968. Six parts of the litany—it consisted of 10 supplications—were these.

> Forgive us for pretending to care for the poor, when we do not like poor people and do not want them in our homes.
>
> Forgive us when we deplore violence in our cities if we live in suburbs, where lawns are clipped and churches are large, or in green villages where there are too many steeples.
>
> Forgive us for cheering legislators who promise low taxes, but deny homes and schools and help to those in need; for self-righteousness that blames the poor for their poverty or the oppressed for their oppression.
>
> Forgive us for bypassing political duties; for condemning civil disobedience when we will not obey You; for reducing Your holy law to average virtue, by trying to be no better or worse than most men.
>
> Forgive us for frantic buying and selling; for advertising the unnecessary and coveting the extravagant, and calling it good business when it is not good for you.
>
> Forgive us for turning our churches into private clubs; for loving familiar hymns and religious feelings more than we love You; for pasting stained glass on eyes and ears to shut out the cry of the hungry and the hurt of the world.[23]

Accommodation of conventional religion to the social order. As this litany suggests, religion itself may be part of the establishment. Together with our denominational pluralism, this qualifies the challenge (and the disruptive function) of religion.

For example, a distinguished theologian condemned the union of political and religious forces in the Nixon administration as compromising religiously based criticism of official policy and practice. He warned against that "combination of religious sanctity and political power [which] represents a heady mixture for status quo conservatism."[24]

Even among black Americans, religion may have a moderating effect on demands for civil rights. Figure 11.2 suggests that conventional religiousness is inversely related to militancy in seeking equity in civil rights.

Denominational pluralism. In a complex society like ours with its great variety of subgroups we should, of course, expect to find differing, and potentially disruptive, religious commitments. To

Figure 11.2

Relationship between degree of religiousness and measures of militancy among Negroes*

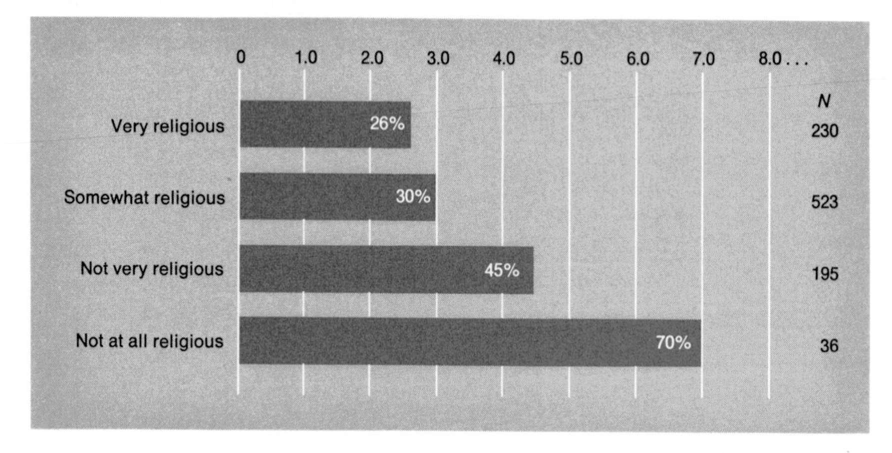

* In measuring the independent variable: "Those scored as 'very religious' attended church at least once a week, felt that religion was extremely important to them, and had no doubts about the existence of God and the devil. For progressively lower values of the index, frequency of church attendance, the importance of religion and acceptance of the belief items decline consistently until for those scored 'not at all religious,' church is rarely if ever attended, religion is not considered personally important and the belief items are rejected."

In measuring the dependent variable: "This index was made up of a number of dimensions of racial protest such as impatience over the speed of integration, opposition to discrimination in public facilities and the sale of property, perception of barriers to Negro advancement, support of civil rights demonstrations, and expressed willingness to take part in a demonstration. Those giving the militant response to five or more of the questions are considered militant, those giving such a response to three or four of the questions, moderate, and fewer than three conservative."

speak of Protestant, Catholic, and Jew is to understate the diversity of religion in American society. For religious divisions are much more numerous than this trichotomy would suggest. And other divisions may be more significant, as to doctrine and practice. Thus, for example, Professors Glock and Stark ask: "Is there an American Protestantism?" and the answer, as Table 11.2 suggests, is no. Belief in the existence of God varies from 99 percent among southern Baptists to 41 percent among Congregationalists, with Catholics closer to American and Missouri Lutherans, Presbyterians, American Baptists, and Disciples of Christ than they are to fundamentalist sects and southern Baptists. Similarly, the belief in the virgin birth of Christ is more common among three Protestant groups than it is among Catholics.

Table 11.2
Placement in rank order and percent of members holding specified religious beliefs*

Full statement of belief	Range of first- and last-ranked denomination: First	Last
(1) I know God really exists and I have no doubts about it.	99%	31%
(2) Jesus is the Divine Son of God and I have no doubts about it.	99	40
(3) Jesus was born of a virgin ("completely true" response checked).	99	21
(4) There is a life beyond death ("completely true" response checked).	97	36
(5) The devil actually exists ("completely true" response checked).	92	6
(6) A child is born into the world already guilty of sin ("completely true" response checked).	86	2
(7) Belief in Jesus Christ as Saviour is absolutely necessary (for salvation).	97	38
(8) Doing good for others is absolutely necessary (for salvation).	64	29
(9) Being of the Jewish religion definitely prevents salvation.	31	1

Religious groups†	N	Rank order of percent affirming these beliefs‡ (1)	(2)	(3)	(4)	(5)	(6)	(7)	(8)	(9)
Congregationalists	151	11.0	11.0	11.0	11.0	11.0	11.0	11.0	3.0	11.0
Methodists	415	10.0	10.0	10.0	10.0	10.0	9.0	10.0	4.5	9.5
Episcopalians	416	9.0	9.0	9.0	9.0	9.0	8.0	9.0	6.0	8.0
Disciples of Christ	50	6.0	6.5	7.0	8.0	8.0	10.0	4.5	1.0	6.0
Presbyterians	495	7.0	8.0	8.0	7.0	7.0	7.0	7.0	7.0	7.0
American Lutherans	208	8.0	6.5	6.0	6.0	5.5	3.0	6.0	8.0	4.5
American Baptists	141	5.0	5.0	5.0	5.0	5.5	6.0	4.5	9.0	4.5
Missouri Lutherans	116	3.5	3.0	3.0	3.0	3.0	1.0	1.5	10.0	1.0
Southern Baptists	79	1.0	1.0	1.0	1.0	1.0	5.0	1.5	11.0	2.0
Sects	255	2.0	2.0	2.0	2.0	2.0	4.0	3.0	2.0	3.0
Catholics	545	3.5	4.0	4.0	4.0	4.0	2.0	8.0	4.5	9.5

* Key questions from this study, put to a national sample, yielded parallel results.
† In four metropolitan counties in northern California, 1964.
‡ Refers to full statement of belief as numbered above.

It is a fair guess that religion is not more divisive than it is in the United States precisely because of its diversity. Differences, as these data suggest, follow continuous rather than discrete distributions, thus blunting the sharp edges of conflict, the black-and-white conflict of good versus evil, right versus wrong. The formal divisions between Protestant, Catholic, and Jew are often spurious, since there is much overlapping of beliefs and behavior. Significant religious divisions sometimes fall along other lines. It is likely, too, that a strong secular orientation masks, if it does not displace, religious commitments, so reducing their *dis*integrative potential.

Polity

The sovereignty of God and the ultimate authority of Holy Writ are echoed in the state. Political allegiance is exclusive. And while, as with religion, this contributes to integration within the group, it deepens the gulf between groups.

Even within groups, of course, there is typically latitude for political disagreement. Indeed, we can think of political arrangements as means of institutionalizing the expression and resolution of differences.

Professor Lipset points to the paradox that a stable democracy is impossible in the absence of mechanisms for revealing cleavage —as well as consensus.[26] But how the cleavages are made and revealed matters a great deal. The cleavages revealed in voting studies can threaten a democratic political system when they coincide precisely with class, race, religion, or region.* But when the social order is such as to permit or encourage political preference to cut across such categorical lines, common goals can be achieved by evolutionary rather than revolutionary means. Not all poor Catholics vote the Democratic ticket, nor do all wealthy Protestants plump for Republicans. Furthermore, a political party drawing some of its support from people whose *other affiliations* bind them to members of the opposition is under some

* Studies of political preference as registered in voting or survey responses, linked with such independent variables as class, race, religious affiliation, region, age, sex, rural or urban residence, occupation, and income—these appear to be the commonest subjects of inquiry for the sociologist.

A probability sample of four census tracts in San Francisco showed the relationship between class (respondent's own identification) and political affiliation:

	Percent Republican	Percent Democratic	*N*
Working class	25	75	241
Middle class	63	37	254
Total	44	56	495

The same study disclosed this connection between occupational situs (clusters of related occupations covering about the same range of statuses) and political affiliation, holding constant subjective class identification.

	Middle class Republican	Middle class Democratic	*N*
Commerce	72%	28%	108
Finance and records	66	34	64
Manufacturing	56	44	34
Building and maintenance	42	58	48
Total	63	37	254

pressure to make prudent concessions to selected views and values of that opposition.

> . . . considered from this perspective, the Tory worker or the middle-class socialist are not merely deviants from class patterns, but basic requirements for the maintenance of the [English] political system. A stable democracy requires a situation in which all the major political parties include supporters from many segments of the population. . . . [In the United States] the fact that Republicans have nominated Negroes and Jews even though most members of these groups in recent years have voted Democratic has undoubtedly had an important unifying effect and reduced the chance that party division along racial or religious lines could become permanent.[27]

Thus, important consequences flow from social pluralism, where there are many permutations on patterns of group affiliation, including party membership. From the person's perspective, this may mean pulls in different, sometimes opposing, directions. Lazarsfeld, Berelson, and Gaudet have analyzed the effects of such crosspressures on political behavior in their study, *The People's Choice.*[28] One such effect is a delay in the decision whether and how to vote (see Table 11.3). Thus, under crosspressures, unconditional party loyalty is less likely.† Rigid allegiances are challenged. A degree of independence and shifting is introduced. Hence voting becomes something more than a pro forma affair.

From the perspective of the social order, these interweaving

	Working class Republican	Working class Democratic	*N*
Commerce	54%	46%	24
Finance and records	36	64	25
Manufacturing	26	74	53
Building and maintenance	20	80	139
Total	25	75	241

(These data are from the study by R. J. Murphy and R. T. Morris, "Occupational Situs, Subjective Class Identification, and Political Affiliation," *American Sociological Review,* Vol. 26, No. 3 [June, 1961], p. 390. See also H. Eulau, S. J. Eldersveld, and M. Janowitz, *Political Behavior* [New York: Free Press, 1956], Sections III, IV and V.)

† See Aside on Methods, Number 11: "The Problem of the Chemist in His Own Test Tube—Controlling Interviewer Effect," p. 641.

cross- and counterpressures dilute extreme or radical positions, compromise revolutionary ardor, discourage convulsive change, permitting, rather, a more deliberate rate of change. To put it differently, the crosscutting of membership groups, while not precluding change, yet provides a sort of social gyroscope, slowing the rate of change but probably not affecting its direction.

Examples of sociological research on religious and political behavior

Religion and Capitalism

To assert and enforce standards of conduct through these rule-making institutions is to sustain a social order. But it would be naïve to envision priests and legislators consciously contriving the regulations required to maintain extant social arrangements. Nor should we think of religion and polity as the controlling institutions which, because they codify and enforce rules touching other social spheres, are therefore sole source and foundation of the social order.

On the contrary, the connection between these and other institutions is complex, in an overall sense unplanned, and for the sociologist, problematic. For Marx, as we have seen, it was not ideas, or values, or the rules to achieve them that were fundamental. The controlling institution was the economy, relationships instituted to produce and allocate goods. Religion was derivative, a superstructure built on social arrangements to achieve material needs.

Classic study by Max Weber

It is this link between two core institutions that Max Weber investigates in his study of *The Protestant Ethic and the Spirit of Capitalism.* Weber* sees capitalism, "the most fateful force in modern life," as the ultimate in rationality. (Rationality is that way of thinking that questions traditional answers and seeks

* In the century and a half preceding 1950 three men stand out as contributing most to sociology: Marx, Durkheim, and Max Weber (1864–1920). As a meticulous

scholar, Weber did much to refine and clarify the conceptual tools of the trade. He did work in the sociology of economic and political organization, the sociology of art and of urbanism, and in the sociology of religion, as suggested here.

Table 11.3
The relationship between cross-pressures* and delay in deciding how to vote, by level of interest

Time of vote decision	Voters with no, or one cross-pressure (%)		Voters with two or more cross-pressures (%)	
	Great interest	Less interest	Great interest	Less interest
September–November	7	21	21	33
June–August	20	29	35	41
May	73	50	44	26
	100	100	100	100
N =	92	117	34	94

* "Cross-pressures" refer to categories or groups pulling the person in different directions. For example, persons both rich and Protestant or poor and Catholic belong to categories known to vote, in disproportionate numbers, for Republican and Democratic candidates, respectively. Thus a poor Protestant or a rich Catholic was judged to be subject to cross-pressure. In addition, the following were seen as inducing cross-pressures: (1) family politically divided, (2) the person's vote in the previous election differed from his present inclination, (3) actual social standing differed from the person's perceived, or self-defined standing, (4) his stress on the importance of business or governmental experience for a candidate was inconsistent with his party preference, and (5) he senses a trend toward the other party.

the demonstrably most efficient means to achieve unambiguously stated ends.) Rationality penetrates the whole of modern life: not only the marketplace, or science and technology, but political life, the arts, education, even the family and the church. Indeed if we ask: What are the prerequisites for the emergence of modern capitalism? Weber points out a necessary change in the home: the separation of business from the household, of the family budget from the financing of the enterprise. This is, in effect, a separation of the domain of the heart from that of the head, a distinction between the realm of warm sentimentality and that of cool calculation.

Capitalism also entails the rational organization of manpower drawn from a freely moving labor force. Labor becomes, then, a market commodity dealt with quite independently of ascribed traits. Furthermore, there must be some means, as in bookkeeping, for rational calculation of the outcomes of social action, measures that enable the continual improvement of means to maximize output. But above all Weber contended (virtually inverting the Marxist thesis), there must be some spirit or ethos that justifies and requires the behaviors institutionalized in a capitalist economy. "The question of the motive forces in the expansion of modern capitalism," Weber writes, "is not in the first instance a question of the origin of the capital sums which were available for capitalist uses, but, above all of the development of the *spirit of capitalism.*"[29] What are the elements of this spirit?*

Central to the spirit of capitalism is an attitude toward work expressed in the word *vocation,* a calling. Work is not a necessary evil, not something merely to be tolerated, but a good in itself, an ethical imperative. We get the flavor of this orientation toward work in a Christian hymn whose injunction is "Work, For the Night is Coming." One of its stanzas goes:

> Work, for the night is coming. Work through the sunny noon.
> Fill brightest hours with labor. Rest comes sure and soon.
> Give every flying minute, something to keep in store.
> Work, for the night is coming, when man works no more.

Work represents a necessary investment of God-given talents. Success provides at least a faint intimation of Providential approval.

A related element is the emphasis on production, rather than consumption. The investment of self in work is for the greater glory of God, not for self-gratification. Acquisition is not regarded as evil—quite the contrary—provided it leads to a reinvestment for more effective exploitation of resources and an increase in productivity. It is the man who fails to multiply the talents his lord has given him who is called wicked and slothful. This stress on productivity has as its corollary a degree of self-denial, of moderation in personal life, of rigorous self-discipline. And so it is that legend links names like that of Rockefeller, Sr., with the frugality, even abstemiousness, that is reflected in the homilies of Benjamin Franklin.

If work is a duty and a discipline, if the emphasis is on multiplying the yield, there follows another element of the spirit of capitalism, the celebration of shrewdness, ingenuity, and inventiveness in devising more efficient means. This is one aspect of the rationalism that, for Weber, was the distinctive motif of modern society. Opposed to a traditionalism that revered established means, it encouraged a reorganization of men's relationships at work, and of work processes. It demanded meticulous accounting procedures. In the service of production and profit it would define roles with precision, treating incumbents impersonally.

* See Aside on Methods, Number 12: "Causal Explanations in Sociology," p. 643.

If such views and values are core aspects of the spirit of capitalism, where do they come from? Surely, Weber argues, it is not wages alone, the material rewards or penalties of the system that prompt the capitalist worker to perform as though his task were an absolute end in itself. This seems especially clear when we observe that profits are not used primarily to yield personal, material pleasures. Furthermore, such a way of acting and thinking must have institutional support. These are shared ways of believing and behaving, and they "had to originate somewhere, and not in isolated individuals alone, but as a way of life common to whole groups of men."[30] This way of life and the dictates supporting it Weber finds in certain of the Protestant sects.

The Protestant's propensity for trade and commerce had often been observed. "Even the Spaniards knew that heresy [i.e., the Calvinism of the Dutch] promoted trade."[31] And Weber cites Montesquieu's statement about the English (written 150 years before), that they "had progressed the farthest of all peoples of the world in three important things: in piety, in commerce, and in freedom."[32] He also cites Offenbacher, who said: "The Protestant prefers to eat well, the Catholic to sleep undisturbed."[33] The statement reflects Offenbacher's findings: marked secular ambition among the Protestants in contrast to the Catholics, and outstanding achievements not only in the realm of business but also in the civil service, in academic life, in science, and in the professions.

Thus we have a suggested link between two sets of values and two modes of conduct. There is "the ethic of a religious belief and the spirit of an economic system, the cure of souls and the balancing of accounts."[34] And the former is seen as a necessary, though not sufficient, cause of the latter emphatically qualifying a Marxist position that would make the mode of economic production the fundament of the social order with religion, "the opiate of the people," altogether secondary and dependent upon it. But what, precisely, was this ethic, this creedal catalyst, that enabled a radical reordering of the relationships of men at work?

The appropriate ethic, the *Weltanschauung* that is a necessary precondition for the development of modern capitalism, is discovered in the ascetic branches of Protestantism. Among these it is best exemplified in Calvinism, Weber contends. For in Calvinism we find a statement of spiritual imperatives that might well serve as a handbook for the "Compleat Capitalist." Here is the spirit of vocation, of stewardship, of work as a good in itself, and the approval of acquisition—not for self-indulgence, but for the elaboration of more effective means of production.

> This rationalization of conduct within this world, but for the sake of the world beyond, was the consequence of the concept of calling of ascetic Protestantism.
>
> . . . Christian asceticism, at first fleeing from the world into solitude, had already ruled the world which it had renounced from the monastery and through the church. . . . Now it strode into the market-place of life, slammed the door of the monastery behind it, and undertook to penetrate just that daily routine of life with its methodicalness, to fashion it into a life *in* the world, but neither *of* nor *for* this world.[35]

Above all, there was in the doctrine of Calvinism the belief in predestination, the notion that an omniscient and omnipotent God had marked a man from birth for salvation or damnation. Such a terrifying belief, one might suppose, would lead to resignation, apathy—to anything but an unremitting labor whose fruits were not to be translated into personal pleasures. But the case was quite otherwise, Weber argues, and this for two reasons. There was, first, the awful anxiety about one's destiny compelling him, despite the fact that man's miserable achievements could not move the majesty of God's judgment, to seek through achievement whatever slight assurance he might get of Providential blessing. And second, there was the doctrinal injunction to have faith in God's beneficence. Indeed, it was

> . . . held to be an absolute duty to consider oneself chosen, and to combat all doubts as temptations of the devil, since lack of self-confidence is the result of insufficient faith, hence of imperfect grace. . . .
>
> . . . in order to attain that self-confidence, intense worldly activity is recommended as the most suitable means. It and it alone disperses religious doubts and gives the certainty of grace.[36]

Thus with the Protestant reformation and especially in Calvinism we see spiritual elements promoting capitalism. (Lutheranism, to say nothing of Catholicism, were still tradition-bound, emphasizing salvation through faith rather than good works, adequate performance in one's proper place rather than an improvement of position, celestial rewards rather than terrestial demonstration of God's approval.) Such elements include, as we have seen: dedication to incessant labor as a good in itself, as-

Figure 11.3
The research design implicit in Weber's study of capitalism and the Protestant ethic

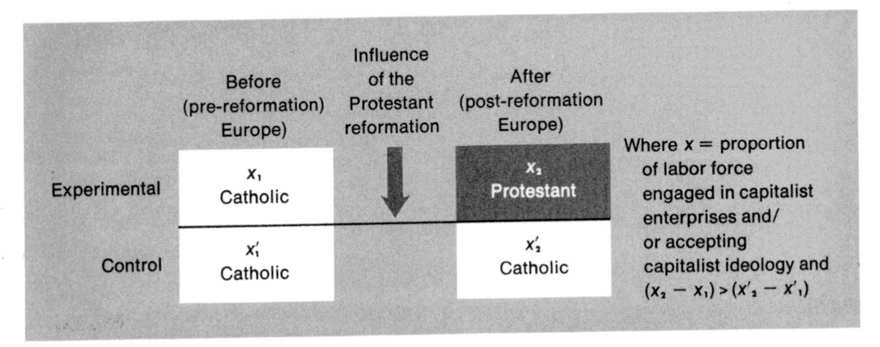

ceticism, a faith that one is among the chosen and that labor's fruits give evidence of it, the individualism of a personal fate Providentially assigned and to be confirmed through personal effort, the endlessness of acquisition and the constant effort to improve the means to increased productivity.

We can summarize Weber's argument, schematically, in the simple model of research design, as in Figure 11.3. Weber is asking the question often posed by historians—and indeed by ourselves in everyday life: What would have happened if . . . ? If things had been other than they were, if my decision had been different, if I had acted otherwise? The answer to such questions requires us to set up something comparable to a control situation, precisely to tell us what would have happened in the absence of an alleged causal influence.

The control situation, for Weber, consists in Catholic Europe, whose population remained uncommitted to the new doctrine, the supposed cause, necessary but not sufficient for the emergence of modern capitalism. In the context of his more general inquiries in the sociology of religion, the control situation may be thought of as those patterns of economic organization and conduct seen in the Orient, especially in China. For here if anywhere, Weber argues, we might reasonably expect to see the structure of relationships we call capitalism emerge. For the Chinese were not hedged about with religious prohibitions, the taking of interest was legitimate, and a hardheaded domestic economy was certainly aimed at maximizing the produce of soil and sea. Nor was there any nonsense about self-denial: the Chinese did not rule out the "genial life of the senses." Yet, despite such predisposing characteristics, capitalism did not flower in China. Why? Because of the absence of a Protestant ethic. Thus through retrospective historical analysis we answer the question: What would have happened if . . . ? In effect, we contrive an ex post facto or retrospective study design.

But perhaps this is a little too easy—or so some scholars have alleged in a running controversy through the years. Richard Tawney in his *Religion and the Rise of Capitalism* suggests that we had better not lean too hard on the Protestant-ethic interpretation until we have taken account of such significant and plausibly capitalism-promoting factors as the voyages of discovery in the 16th and 17th centuries, the expansion of commerce, the tradition-challenging contact of countries and cultures. Furthermore, the difference between Protestantism and Catholicism may stem not so much from the compatibility of the former as from the incompatibility of the latter with the capitalist posture.

Perhaps, as Luethy suggests, it was not so much the Reformation as the counter-Reformation, an "appalling break . . . in the cultural history of Europe . . . the shadow cast by Inquisition and heresy trials across the lands . . ."[37] that accounts for the decline in power, wealth, and intellectual and artistic life among Catholics, and the concomitant significance of Protestantism.

Again, some evidence suggests that the contrast between areas commercially, industrially, and financially active and those not so, corresponding to Protestant and Catholic dominance, repectively, were that way *before* the Reformation. And this in turn suggests another interpretation—one that the sociologist must always have in mind when he observes a connection between two variables. The necessary question is this: Does some third factor underly or explain both of these? Conceivably, the Protestant ethic itself, along with the spirit of capitalism is to be explained by some underlying characteristic.

So we will take Weber's interpretation with some reservations. But we must not do him the injustice of naïvely misconstruing his argument. He was exploring what he regarded as *a necessary,* not *the sufficient* cause for the emergence of capitalism. He was sensitive to the requirements of research strategy. Beyond the study of economic behavior before and after the advent of Protestantism he tried, through reference to Catholic Europe and non-Christian Asia, to answer the question: What would have happened in the absence of the Protestant ethic? In developing the notion of the ideal type he offers a tool to help us deepen our understanding of social phenomena. Perhaps above all we should heed the implicit allegation of this study: no significant social structure persists without supporting doctrine and creed. And this applies to the instrumentally oriented institutions of polity and economy, as well as to the expressively oriented institutions of kingroups and religious groups.

An empirical follow-up: Gerhard Lenski

There is another way of checking Weber's ideas. Beyond asking what variables he has left uncontrolled, or what other factors might readily be thought to have contributed to the development of modern capitalism—beyond these questions we can ask: Does the Weberian thesis help us to predict to concrete situations? Do Protestants, as Weber's thesis would predict, advance farther in the world of work than Catholics? Do they, more actively than Catholics, seek work that offers advancement? Do they, to a greater degree than Catholics, value work for its own sake? Do they reject, more than Catholics, the collective, security-providing rewards of unionism? Are Protestants self-employed (suggesting the entrepreneurial, capitalistic spirit) to a greater degree than Catholics? Are they persuaded, more so than Catholics, that ability (rather than family connections) yields rewards and that workingmen's sons do in fact have a good chance to advance in our system? Do Protestants, more than Catholics, think that God favors attempts to get ahead? Does installment buying—not paying, immediately, for what one gets—run more against the grain for Protestant than Catholic? Does greater devoutness characterizing family background mean, for Protestants, an orientation more rational, competitive, individualistic, and striving and for Catholics, less of such an orientation? An empirical study by Professor Gerhard Lenski offers answers to such questions as these, enabling us to check some of Weber's ideas.

Lenski's study of religious behavior in Detroit, based on a probability sample* of 750 families or dwelling units, succeeded in completing interviews with 87 percent of the sample. Among

* It is *only* with some variety of probability sampling that the investigator can calculate, adequately, an estimate of sampling error. To put it differently, it is only on the basis of probability theory that one can know the likelihood that his sample represents the whole—the population, or universe of elements sampled. A fundamental difference between science and nonscience lies in this: in a scientific undertaking strenuous efforts are made not merely to eliminate sources of error but *to estimate the extent of the error* that invariably creeps in from various sources.

the 8 percent refusing to grant interviews a disproportionate number were over age 60, so that Lenski cautions us that "conclusions based on the responses of older people are slightly less reliable than those based on younger and middle-aged persons."[38] By religious affiliation or identification, the Detroit population breakdown is shown in Table 11.4.[39] Comparable data for the United States (adults, age 14 and over) estimate Protestants (both Negro and white), Catholics, and Jews as 66, 26, and 3 percent of the population, respectively.

The dependent variables whose relation to religious belief and behavior was to be tested included measures of various aspects of family life and political and economic behavior. The focus, then, is on interinstitutional connections: religion on the one hand, the family, polity, and economy on the other. If a social order must be understood as a system, then characteristic conduct in one sector must affect and be affected by conduct in another sector. "It is this *systemic* view of society which distinguishes the sociological view of political and economic behavior from that of the more narrowly circumscribed disciplines of political science and economics."[40]

Weber's thesis, of course, has to do with the connection between behaviors institutionalized through church and marketplace. Let us turn now to some of Lenski's findings that bear on this alleged connection. Certain very general findings about the relation between income and occupation on the one hand (summarized as class) and religious affiliation on the other are given in Table 11.5.

The data show clearly the economically preferred position of Jews in Detroit. But the figures of special interest to us are the 19 and 12 percent of upper-middle-class white Protestants and Catholics, respectively. For a sample size of better than 200 in each case, a difference as great as 7 percentage points, and in the predicted direction (Protestants economically better off than Catholics) would be due to sampling error fewer than 1 in 10 times.

This begins to answer our first question: Do Protestants advance farther in the world of work than do Catholics? All of Lenski's data lead him to conclude that "White Protestant men rise farther in the class system than Catholics." He reports that "Catholics wound up in the lower half of the working class more often than Protestants three out of four times."[41]

If Weber's thesis is right, Protestants should get ahead in our economy to a greater extent than Catholics. To test this, Lenski compares fathers' and sons' standings on the occupational ladder. Table 11.6 summarizes his data, showing the greater upward mo-

Table 11.4

	Percent
White Protestants	41
White Catholics	35
Negro Protestants	15
Jews	4
Other and none	5

Table 11.5

Percent of respondents in various classes, by socioreligious groups, Detroit, 1958

Socioreligious group	Upper-middle*	Lower-middle†	Upper-working‡	Lower-working§	Total	*N*¶
Jews	43	30	9	17	99	23
White Protestants	19	25	31	25	100	259
White Catholics	12	27	35	25	99	220
Negro Protestants	2	10	19	69	100	94

* Upper middle-class respondents are those in families in which the family head was a businessman, a professional man, a clerk, or a salesman, and himself had an income of $8,000 or more in 1957.

† Lower middle-class are those in families in which the family head was in an occupation similar to the upper middle-class respondents but earned less than $8,000 in 1957.

‡ Upper working-class respondents are those in families in which the head was a manual worker or service worker who himself earned at least $5,000 in 1957.

§ Lower working-class are those in families in which the family head was in an occupation similar to the upper working-class respondents but earned less than $5,000 in 1957.

¶ The income of the family head was not reported in 28 cases, and hence the *N*'s shown here are slightly lower than the total *N*'s for each of these groups.

Table 11.6

Percent difference in Protestant and Catholic father-to-son mobility, by number of steps

	One step	Percent	Two steps	Percent	Three steps	Percent
Protestant upward	LM to UM	+10	UW to UM	− 1	LW to UM	+10
mobility exceeds	UW to LM	+ 3	LW to LM	− 4		
Catholic mobility	LW to UW	− 3				
Catholic downward	UM to LM	+ 2	UM to LW	+ 3	UM to LW	+12
mobility exceeds	LM to UW	− 3	LM to LW	+21		
Protestant mobility	UW to LW	+11				

LM = Lower middle
UM = Upper middle
UW = Upper working
LW = Lower working

bility of Protestants, the greater downward mobility of Catholics.

The relatively greater upward mobility of Protestants reflects underlying attitudes that differentiate Protestant from Catholic. For example, respondents were presented with five criteria for estimating the desirability of a job. These were: (1) high income, (2) no danger of being fired, (3) short working hours, (4) chances of advancement, and (5) the seeming importance of the work and the feeling of accomplishment it yields. Although differences were slight, the fourth criterion was picked most frequently by Jews, next by white Protestants, followed by Catholics and, last, black Protestants.

Likewise, in their attitudes toward work, white Protestants registered an orientation more in accord with Weber's Protestant ethic than did Catholics (see Table 11.7).

Again, we can check on Protestant-Catholic differences in attitude toward work by asking how respondents feel about labor unions. For the union posture opposes values embodied in the Protestant ethic. The unions stress security and aspire to prosperity for the masses rather than exceptional rewards stemming from personal prowess and conscientious commitment to work as a good in itself. Lenski reports that slightly over a fourth of the male workers in the lower-middle class in Detroit are union members. White Catholics in the lower-middle class are far more likely to become union members (38 percent) than are white Protestants (15 percent). Data on attendance at meetings and level of interest in their unions add confirmation.

Lenski's data also indicate that Protestants are more likely to believe that people of humble origins have a chance to rise through their own efforts and that ability is more important than family connections in getting ahead.

Now it might be argued that these are not, in fact, faith-linked differences in commitment to the get-ahead, Horatio Alger doctrines. One might suspect that the success, and expectation of it, on the part of white Protestants simply reflects ethnic dominance in the American social order and the relatively unfavorable position of Catholics and Negroes. That is to say, it is a phenomenon of prejudice and ethnocentrism rather than one of religion. But Lenski points out that despite the clearly depressed situation of the Negro, differences between black Protestants and white Catholics on these attitudes toward work are negligible.

> . . . Similarly, if attitudes were merely reflections of objective conditions in the job market, we would expect Jews to be

Table 11.7
Male Detroiters' attitudes toward work by socioreligious group, in percent

Socioreligious group	Attitude toward work*					Positive minus negative
	Positive	Neutral	Negative	Total	*N*	
Jews	43	50	8	100	12	34
White Protestants	30	50	21	101	111	9
Negro Protestants	24	54	22	100	41	2
White Catholics	23	57	21	101	106	2

* "Positive" means valuing work for its own sake or for the intrinsic rewards it provides. "Neutral" refers to a response that favors work, but for its extrinsic rewards, or because it's more acceptable than the alternative (not to work would be boring). "Negative" classifies a response indicating the person would be glad to give up work if he could. Percentages do not add to 100 due to rounding.

more pessimistic than Catholics. Yet neither of these relationships was found. Jews have much more confidence in ability than Catholics, and Catholics have little more than Negro Protestants. These findings indicate that such attitudes are partly independent of the extent of objective discrimination against groups. Whatever their origin, lack of confidence in ability and in chances for upward mobility almost certainly inhibit many Catholic youths who might otherwise rise in the system.[42]

Not only do Protestants believe, disproportionately, that effort pays off. They believe that God favors efforts to get ahead. Sixty percent of the white Protestants, followed by Jews (58 percent), white Catholics (55 percent), and black Protestants (33 percent) took this position.[43]

The juxtaposition of Jews and white Protestants in positions contrasting with those of Catholics and black Protestants is a consistent matter in Lenski's data. The last two repeatedly take positions that are less individualistic (or more collectivistic), more security oriented, less striving and competitive. The first two take positions roughly consonant with the Protestant ethic as Weber described it.

But to assert is not to demonstrate. To describe differences between socioreligious groups—even such consistent ones as these—is not to explain them. To describe such differences between groups is not to tell us whether religion accounts for these differences or whether the differences observed alter religious beliefs and behavior. In an attempt to determine whether religious orientations, or religious devoutness, do in fact have an influence on behavior in the sphere of work, Lenski argues:

> If the churches do contribute to these differences between socioreligious groups, we should expect that the greater the degree to which white Protestants are involved in their churches, the more likely they will be to display the individualistic, competitive, rationalistic patterns of thought and action identified with the Protestant Ethic and with the middle class. Similarly, we would expect that the more Catholics and Negro Protestants are involved in their churches, the more they will display the collectivistic, security-oriented, anti-entrepreneurial working-class patterns of thought and action. If, however, the churches are irrelevant and have no effect on economic behavior and attitudes, we would expect to find no noticeable differences between those members of a given group who attend their church regularly, and those who do not, when other relevant factors are controlled.[44]

We might argue further that, if religion has the hypothesized effect, the devoutness of the parents, being antecedent in time to the movement of their children in occupational and class status, would lead to upward mobility for white Protestants and Jews and would have little or no effect for white Catholics or black Protestants. Because Lenski's *N* for Jews is small and because black Protestants are virtually nonmobile because of race, thus blocking out the effect of religion, let us consider only white Protestants and Catholics. Ordering Lenski's data in Table 11.8 we get some indication that "the relationship of the individual white Protestant to his church *antedates* upward mobility."[45] Chi-square tests of the existence of a relationship between devoutness of

* If one were disposed to find simple solutions in human affairs a succession of inquiries into the link between religion and work would disabuse him of this fiction. Do Protestants, as Weber's theory states and Lenski's findings suggest, have a stronger drive to achieve than Catholics? The opposite was found in a national sample of 1,620 respondents. Drive-to-achieve also varied by income, region lived in, and age. (See Joseph Veroff, Sheila Field and Gerald Gurin, "Achievement motivation and Religious Background," *American Sociological Review*, 27:2, April, 1962.)

Marvin Bressler and Charles Westoff argued that, if Catholicism has its alleged effect on worldly striving, then varying exposure to its practices and doctrine should result in different attitudes and practices in the realm of work. So they set up two hypotheses for testing. In contrast to the influence of a solely secular education on Catholics, education in Cath-

Table 11.8
Percent of white Protestants and Catholics of working-class background who moved, and did not move, to middle-class status*

	Protestants			Catholics		
Parents' devoutness	Upwardly mobile	Not upwardly mobile	*N*	Upwardly mobile	Not upwardly mobile	*N*
Devout working-class or farm parents	51%	49%	43	31%	69%	84
Nondevout working class or farm parents	31%	69%	102	39%	61%	38

* For definitions of "working-class," see page 431. A respondent's parents were classified as devout if "(a) the respondent reported attending worship services every week and if he further stated that *both* his mother and father were at least as religious as he, or (*b*) if the respondent reported that he attended worship services less than once a week but at least once a month, and that *both* of his parents were *more* religious than he."

parents and mobility of children yielded a $p < .001$ for Protestants and $p > .99$ for Catholics.

Thus we see that empirical tests tend to confirm the notion that religious commitments have a significant bearing on the system of relationships we call capitalism. Concluding this part of his study Lenski writes:[46]

> With considerable regularity the Jews and white Protestants have identified themselves with the individualistic, competitive patterns of thought and action . . . historically associated with the Protestant Ethic or its secular counterpart, the spirit of capitalism . . . both faiths currently develop in their adherents attitudes, values, beliefs and behavior patterns which are in keeping with the spirit of capitalism to a greater degree than those developed by Catholicism.*

olic schools will be negatively related to: (1) values impelling the person to seek worldly success and (2) measures of actual economic success. Both hypotheses were refuted. (See their study, "Catholic Education, Economic Values and Achievement," *American Journal of Sociology,* LXIX:3, November, 1963.)

Uncontrolled variables and the increased penetration of secular values may wash out the relationship between religious affiliation and orientation to work. Otherwise it is hard to account for Greeley's findings that Catholics and non-Catholics in higher education are pretty much alike. Some of his data show Jews, more than either Catholics or Protestants behaving in accordance with Weber's Protestant ethic. (See Andrew M. Greeley, "Religion and Academic Career Plans," *American Journal of Sociology,* 72:6, May, 1967.)

All of this, starting with Weber's seminal essay, provides a good illustration of the continuing process of sociological inquiry.

Correlates of democracy, the locus of power, and the tolerance of deviants

Correlates of democracy

For Americans there is one question of special interest when we think about the link between the polity and other institutional spheres. What are the social conditions that promote or hinder the development of democratic modes of government? Lipset says:

> Perhaps the most common generalization linking political systems to other aspects of society has been that democracy is related to the state of economic development. The more well-to-do a nation, the greater the chances that it will sustain democracy. From Aristotle down to the present, men have argued that only in a wealthy society in which relatively few citizens lived at the level of real poverty could there be a situation in which the mass of the population intelligently participate in politics and develop the self-restraint necessary to avoid succumbing to the appeals of irresponsible demagogues. A society divided between a large impoverished mass and a small favored elite results either in oligarchy (dictatorial rule of the small upper stratum) or in tyranny (popular based dictatorship). To give these two political forms modern labels, tyranny's face today is communism or Peronism; while oligarchy appears in the traditionalist dictatorships found in parts of Latin America, Thailand, Spain, or Portugal.
>
> To test this hypothesis concretely, I have used various indices of economic development—wealth, industrialization, urbanization, and education [selected aspects of the social order used as independent variables]—and computed averages (means) for the countries which have been classified as more or less democratic in the Anglo-Saxon world and Europe, and in Latin America.[47]

Lipset's classification of nations by degree of stable democracy is listed in Table 11.9,[48] and the results of his inquiry, testing whether such a connection existed (between stable democratic forms and the diffusion of wealth and knowledge), and the strength of that connection, are given in Table 11.10.

These findings lend support to the notion that there are specific features of the social order significantly linked to form of government. Certain demographic features (concentration of population

Table 11.9

Classification by degree of stable democracy

European and English-speaking nations		Latin-American nations	
I Stable democracies	II Unstable democracies and dictatorships	III Unstable democracies and dictatorships	IV Stable dictatorships
Australia	Albania	Argentina	Bolivia
Belgium	Austria	Brazil	Cuba
Canada	Bulgaria	Chile	Dominican Republic
Denmark	Czechoslovakia	Colombia	Ecuador
Ireland	Finland	Costa Rica	El Salvador
Luxembourg	France	Mexico	Guatemala
Netherlands	Germany	Uruguay	Haiti
New Zealand	Greece		Honduras
Norway	Hungary		Nicaragua
Sweden	Iceland		Panama
Switzerland	Italy		Peru
United Kingdom	Poland		Venezuela
United States	Portugal		
	Rumania		
	Spain		
	U.S.S.R.		
	Yugoslavia		

Table 11.10

Comparisons of nations in four categories*

	Category of nation†			
Indexes of	I	II	III	IV
Wealth (in U.S. dollars)				
Per capita income	$695	$308	$171	$119
Persons per motor vehicle	17	143	99	274
Thousands persons per doctor	.86	1.4	2.1	4.4
Telephones per 1,000 persons	205	58	25	10
Radios per 1,000 persons	350	160	85	43
Newspapers copies per 1,000 persons	341	167	102	43
Urbanization				
Percent of population in cities over 20,000	43	24	28	17
Percent of population in cities over 100,000	28	16	22	12
Percent of population in metropolitan areas	38	23	26	15
Industrialization				
Percent of males in agriculture	21	41	52	67
Per capita energy consumed	3.6	1.4	.6	.25
Education				
Percent literate	96	85	74	46
Primary education enrollment	134	121	101	72
Postprimary education enrollment	44	22	13	8
Higher education enrollment	4.2	3.5	2.0	1.3

* All figures shown are means.

† See Table 11.9 for nations listed in each category.

in urban centers, itself a function of education and technological sophistication), and certain institutional characteristics (marked economic development, elaborate technology, high level of literacy and of education) appear to be buttresses for a stable democratic system.

We might note in passing that such findings have practical implications. This is as true of the sociologist's work as that of chemist or psychologist or economist. Should further research confirm these findings, certain principles seem to be suggested as guides for our foreign policy vis-a-vis the uncommitted nations.

The locus of power

Our discussion of the polity may have suggested that the sociologist is poaching on the field of political science. But if we take my definition of sociology in which the content of inquiry is differing patterns of human relationships, and if we recognize power as a crucial dimension of human relationships, then it is inevitable that sociology must inquire into matters political. Nor will we protest when political scientists such as Robert Dahl define their field in a way that embraces ours. Political science studies political systems, and a political system, Dahl writes, "Is any persistent pattern of human relationships that involves, to a significant extent, power, rule, or authority."[49] "Significant," here, is a spongy term, but one might suppose that family, work, worship—all major institutional arrangements—"involve to a significant extent power, rule, or authority." In any case, problems are public property, and the power aspect of roles and relationships is a dimension that the sociologist cannot disregard. Let us consider a couple of studies touching the locus of power, and challenges from right and left.

No system of authority, and least of all a democratic one, effectively controls the sources of the differences that produce the deviant. Movements that mobilize deviants and challenge existing power relationships concern the sociologist; for their study instructs us about conditions of social stability and change. (Lipset argues that while we have been much intrigued with such transient, extremist movements, we badly need to understand more about the factors that, in a democracy, operate to resist or curtail extremism. And, of course, one such factor, the crosscutting of group affiliations, we have already considered.)

About these movements of the left and right (the Birch Society, the Communists, the KKK), the sociologist asks questions such as these: What are their social roots, the social conditions generat-

Figure 11.4
Interlocking control among 11 far-right organizations
Fifty percent or more of the top figures play similar roles in the indicated groups.

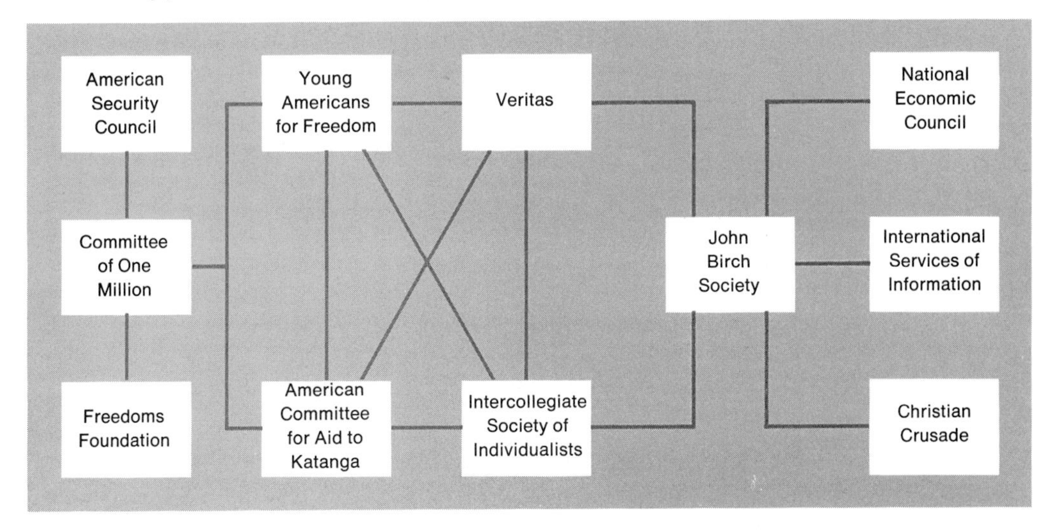

ing fears, protests, hopes, and commitments of their members? What sort of person do they recruit? What sectors of society do they come from? How do we account for their rise and fall, their failures and successes? To what extent are they grass roots? How is the protest given form and force?

A summary of one such study is provided in Figure 11.4. The general problem underlying this research was the extent to which far-right movements were grass roots. A corollary query was whether there existed, and to what degree, a central nucleus to gather and shape protest. The figure presents certain organizations on the far (political) right, 50 percent of whose "celebrities" (trustees, directors, sponsors) played similar roles in two or more organizations. Thus, more than half of the top people in the John Birch Society bridge into five other organizations: Christian Crusade, the National Economic Council, International Services of Information, Veritas, and the Intercollegiate Society of Individualists. This interlocking organizational control is also found in reform and philanthropic groups, in industry and business. Such analyses provide cues to the locus of power and the source of decisions. The investigators in this study conclude, reasonably enough, that while a diffuse anxiety and resentment must be available to be mobilized, such a nucleus as that represented in this interlocking, rightist elite is also necessary to lend form and substance to an otherwise amorphous protest.

Where power resides, either in the establishment or among those opposed to it, is not easy to discern. Men in power are often in the wings, not on center stage. In Yankee City and Jonesville (studied by Warner and his associates) and in Regional City where Floyd Hunter did his research on community power structure,* late-coming professionals tended to be out in front, while men of long, local lineage and wealth exerted, indirectly, disproportionately great influence on community decisions.[50] Table 11.11 shows that, in Regional City, few of the policy-making leaders were spotlighted by their official positions. Four out of 40 were in government positions. But over half were in business and industry. Six out of 40 were in the professions, all of them lawyers save one. Frequently, these men were directors of one another's corporations and belonged, many of them, to the same clubs. Decisions of some significance were often made informally, on ostensibly social occasions.

Hunter does us the service of underscoring the informal, and generally invisible, elements in a community power structure. But to think of a fixed structure is, in any complex community, to oversimplify matters. We can say that a person has power if he can so mobilize "influence resources" that, when he initiates or supports a proposal it wins, and when he opposes it, it loses. But is power so constant? Or does it shift, depending on the issue? Are issues alike, as to their valence or significance? Fluoridation? A school bond issue? A city income tax? Are they commensurable? (Does a loss on the sewer issue precisely counterbalance a win on the appointment of a favored candidate to a post in the Treasurer's office?) Shall we estimate power without reckoning a person's

* Hunter's study has stimulated interest, criticism and further attempts to uncover community power structures. We might note some of the methodological problems posed by this sort of research. How shall we discover where in a community the power to influence others resides? Hunter was not so ingenuous as to assume that official position was an unerring indicator of power. He used presumably knowledgeable judges who came to agree in their selection of the 40 persons most influential in the spheres of business, government, civic associations, and "society" activities. This is the power-by-reputation technique. Unfortunately, people's knowledge may be inadequate and their judgments distorted. A third method is to estimate power by frequency of participation in decision making. But this rests on the hazardous assumption that participation equals power. A fourth method, used by Professor Dahl to estimate influence, was to score, for different sorts of decisions over a period of time, the frequency of successful initiation of, or opposition to a proposal (see Robert A. Dahl, *Who Governs?* [New Haven, Conn: Yale University Press, 1961]).

Table 11.11

Policy-making leaders in Regional City

Type of occupation	Name of leader	Name of organizational affiliation	Position
Banking, Finance, Insurance	Hardy	Investment Company of Old State	President
	Mines	Producer's Investments	President
	Schmidt	First Bank	President
	Simpson	Second Bank	Vice-President
	Spade	Growers Bank	President
	Tarbell	Commercial Bank	Executive Vice-President
	Trable	Regional City Life	President
Commercial	Aiken	Livestock Company	Chairman, Board
	Black	Realty Company of Regional City	President
	Delbert	Allied Utilities	President
	Dunham	Regional Gas Heat Company	General Manager
	Graves	Refrigeration, Incorporated	President
	Parker	Mercantile Company	Executive Manager
	Parks	Paper Box Company	Chairman, Board
	Smith	Cotton Cloth Company	Manager
	C. Stokes	Oil Pipe Line Company	President
	Webster	Regional City Publishing Company	Managing Editor
	Williams	Mercantile Company	Chairman, Board
Government	Barner	City Government	Mayor
	Gordon	City Schools	Superintendent
	Rake	County Schools	Superintendent
	Worth	County Government	Treasurer
Labor	Gregory	Local Union	President
	Stone	Local Union	President
Leisure	Fairly	None	Social Leader
	Howe	None	Social Leader
	Mills	None	Social Leader
	Moore	None	Social Leader
	Stevens	None	Social Leader
Manufacture and Industry	Farris	Steel Spool Company	Chairman, Board
	Homer	Homer Chemical Company	Chairman, Board
	Spear	Homer Chemical Company	President
	E. Stokes	Stokes Gear Company	Chairman, Board
	Treat	Southern Yarn Company	President
Professional*	Farmer	Law Firm	Attorney
	Gould	Law Firm	Attorney
	Latham	Private Office	Dentist
	Moster	Law Firm	Attorney
	Street	Law Firm	Attorney
	Tidwell	Law Firm	Attorney

* Attorneys' affiliations not given. Without exception they are corporation lawyers.

We the People

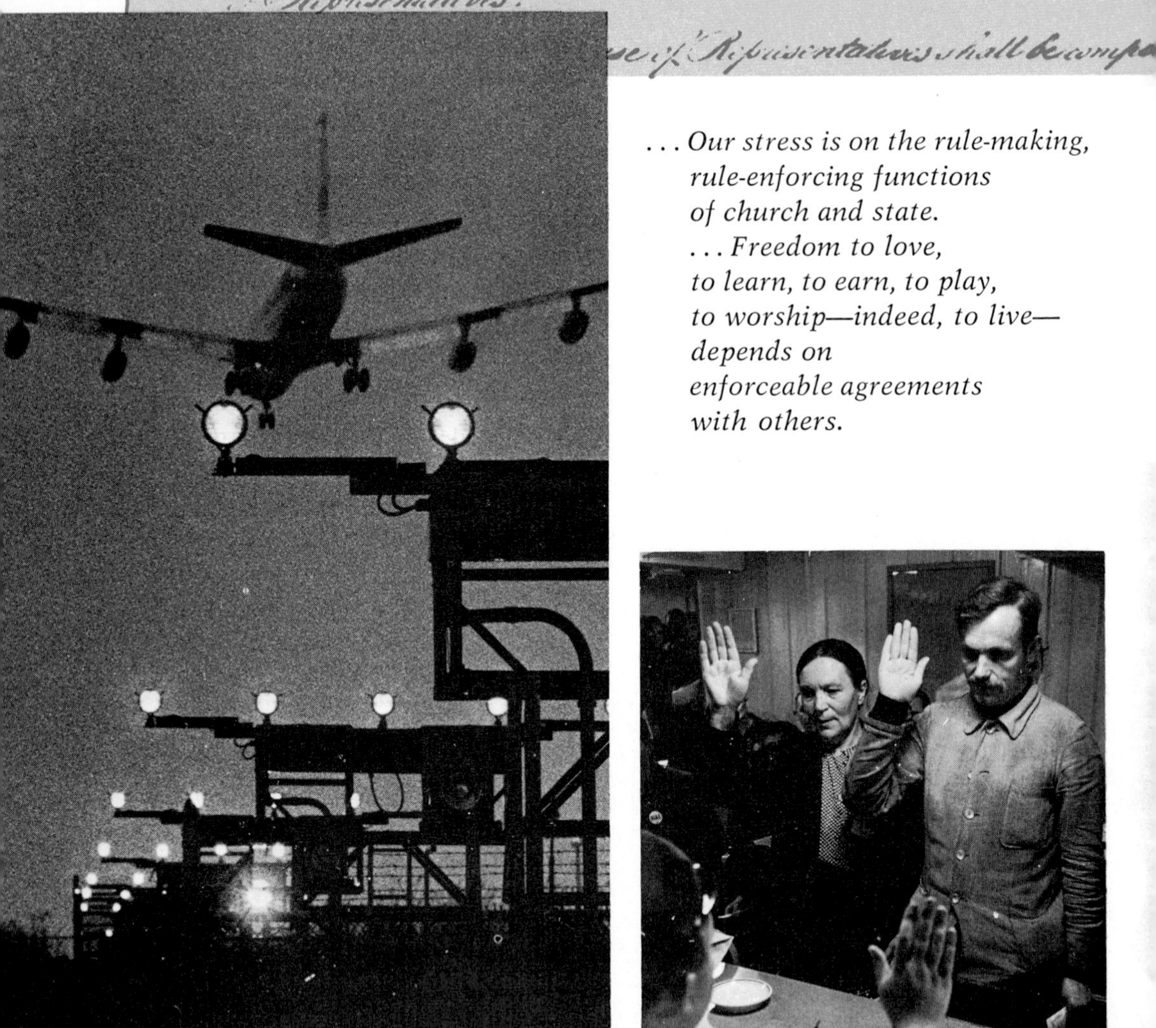

. . . Our stress is on the rule-making,
rule-enforcing functions
of church and state.
. . . Freedom to love,
to learn, to earn, to play,
to worship—indeed, to live—
depends on
enforceable agreements
with others.

NOMY *The ten commandments.*

12 Keep the ſabbath-day to ſanctify it, as the
ORD thy God hath commanded thee.

13 [i] Six days thou ſhalt labour, and do all thy
ork:

14 But the ſeventh day *is* the [k] ſabbath of the
ORD thy God: *in it* thou ſhalt not do any work
ou, nor thy ſon, nor thy daughter, nor thy
an-ſervant, nor thy maid-ſervant, nor thine ox

. . . no significant social structure persists without supporting doctrine and creed.

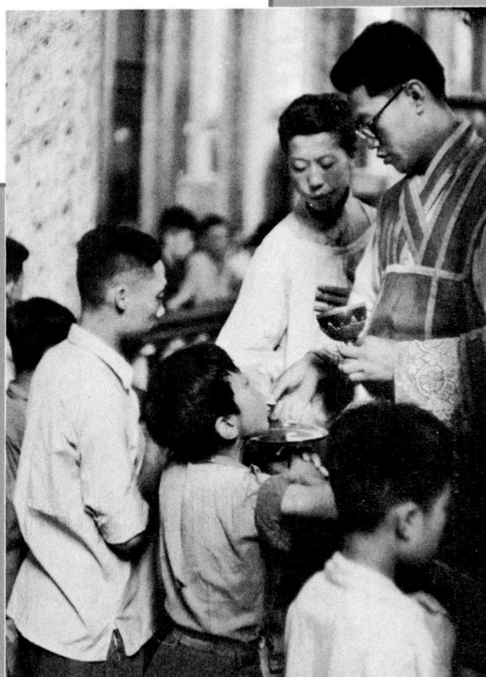

tas multo tem-
nus deus tuus
ſeparauit moy-
iordanem ad o-
confugiat ad
proximū ſuū
ante vnū et al-
aliquā urbium
ſolitudine que
te tribu ruben:
que eſt in tribu

A Scout Is **Obedient**

He obeys his parents, Scoutmaster, patrol leader, and all other duly constituted authorities.

A Scout Is **Cheerful**

He smiles whenever he can. His obedience to orders is prompt and cheery. He never shirks nor grumbles at hardships.

level of interest in a given outcome? Such are the thorny questions that must be faced by the sociologist studying community power structures.

Tolerance of deviants

To speak of power is to imply resistance that must be overcome. To speak of rules is to imply their violation. We would not institute a system of rules with their concomitant sanctions were there not a fair probability that, upon occasion, they would be violated. Thus the set of roles and relationships defining a group is preserved only through *constrained* adherence to the rules. But whatever the power vested in the authorities, this constraint is always imperfect, roughly as imperfect as the ratio of punishment to prevention. And so if deviance (due largely to cultivated human differences)[51] is to be expected, any enduring social system, like an organic system, has to be geared to ward off attack. If assaults on the system are fairly regular and actuarially predictable, then standing defenses can be established (the apparatus of law enforcement). But sometimes the threats are ambiguous, or unanticipated, or both. Under these circumstances, alarm spreads and members of the group may respond awkwardly, thrashing out in ways that violate their own cherished values.

There is always the problem, then, of the degree of threat generated by different sorts of deviation. And there is the more refined question as to whether different subgroups or categories of society react differently to such a threat. The First Amendment to our Constitution sustains a high level of tolerance for deviant views. ("Congress shall make no law respecting an establishment of religion, or prohibiting the free exercise thereof; or abridging the freedom of speech or of the press; or the right of the people peaceably to assembly, and to petition the Government for a redress of grievances.") But what is written on paper may differ from what is inscribed in men's hearts and minds. And it is a question of interest to the sociologist what degree of tolerance for deviant behavior does in fact characterize the group, and subgroups within it.

This is the problem posed by one sociologist, Samuel Stouffer, in a study entitled *Communism, Conformity, and Civil Liberties.*[52] A discussion of this research will not only tell us something about tolerance of deviant beliefs and behavior; it will also acquaint us with a careful piece of empirical research having some novel features.

Table 11.12
Scheme for classifying three levels of tolerance of nonconformity

15 interview items arranged in sets of 3, from those indicating most tolerance to those showing least	Patterns of response indicating tolerance of nonconformity (giving 2, or 3 tolerant responses in five to no sets)*	Classifying consistent patterns of response in 3 levels of tolerance of nonconformity (on a three-point ordinal scale)
5th set	+ + + + +	Relatively more tolerant (scoring + on 5 or 4 sets of interview items)
4th set	+ + + +	
3rd set	+ + +	In-between (scoring + on 3, or 2 sets)
2nd set	+ +	
1st set	+ Not giving 2 or 3 tolerant responses in any set	Relatively less tolerant (scoring + on 1, or 0 sets)

* + scored as tolerant.

The dependent variable in this study is a measure of degree of tolerance of nonconformity along an ordinal scale. (Nonconformity in this case means communism, socialism, or atheism.) There were three points along this scale called "relatively more tolerant," "in-between," and "relatively less tolerant." Stouffer was able to classify his respondents in these categories by the method described schematically in Table 11.12.*

To make matters more concrete, let's reproduce the three interview items in the fifth set. They were these (response scored as tolerant is indicated in boldface type):

> Now, I should like to ask you some questions about a man who admits he is a Communist. [Interviewer is addressing respondent.]
>
> (*a*) Suppose this admitted Communist wants to make a speech in your community. Should he be allowed to speak, or not?
>
> ______**Yes**
> ______No
> ______Don't know

* The preceding 12 items were similarly grouped in clusters of three questions each and scored in the same way. See Aside on Methods, Number 13: "The Guttman or Cornell Scale," p. 645.

(*b*) Suppose he wrote a book which is in your public library. Somebody in your community suggests the book should be removed from the library. Would you favor removing it, or not?

______Favor
______**Don't favor**
______Don't know

(*c*) Suppose this admitted Communist is a radio singer. Should he be fired, or not?

______Should be fired
______**Should not be fired**
______Don't know

Other items, in the four other sets of three questions each, dealt with antireligionists (atheists, for example), socialists, and persons whose loyalty had been questioned before a congressional investigating committee.

(A similar scale was developed for a second dependent variable, extent of perception of threat of communism within the United States.)

Now the problem was to discover how adult citizens responded to the threat of nonconforming views and values and, if various subgroups of citizens differed in their responses, how they did so. To answer these questions *two* national probability samples of adult, U.S. citizens were drawn, independently, by two research agencies. These were the National Opinion Research Center (NORC) and the American Institute of Public Opinion (AIPO). This is a unique aspect of the study, for such a parallel but independent gathering of data had not hitherto been done nor, to my knowledge has it been done since. It allows an item-by-item comparison of the findings of two agencies, operating independently. (The data from NORC and AIPO are quite alike, often identical.) A combination of the two samples gave Stouffer data gotten by 537 competent interviewers on 4,933 cases.

Another sample was drawn, this of community leaders in those cities of 10,000 to 150,000, falling in the sample. Leaders were defined as persons in these roles:

> . . . the mayor, the president of the Chamber of Commerce, the chairman of the Community Chest, the president of a . . . large labor-union local in the city, the chairmen of the Republican and Democratic county central committees, the commander of the largest American Legion post in the city, the regent of the D.A.R., the president of the local Women's club,

> the chairmen of the school board and the library board, the president of the bar association, the publisher of the locally owned newspaper of largest circulation.[53]

Let me summarize certain central findings of this study by asking the reader to estimate which, in the paired categories that follow, tend to be more tolerant of the sort of nonconformity represented in atheism, communism and socialism.*

> Community leaders, or the rank and file of the national cross section?
> Younger people or older people?
> The better, or the less well educated?
> People living in the larger cities, or in smaller places?
> Northerners, or Southerners?
> Men, or women?
> Non–church attenders or regular church attenders?
> Those viewing the internal communist threat as slight, or those seeing it as relatively great?

In each case, the first category is that of the more tolerant as classified (through use of the Guttman scale) in the scheme that I have just described. (Graphic illustrations of two sets of findings are shown in Figures 11.5 and 11.6).

Before leaving this study of leader and citizen response to deviant patterns (the tolerance dimension of civic relationships), let me add three comments.

First, this is a bare-bones, unqualified report of some of Stouffer's findings. It scarcely represents the care and clarity with which the investigator handles his data. The two-variable relationships listed above—for example, level of tolerance related to leadership-followership—neglects other variables that Stouffer holds constant in making his analysis. (You will note in Figure 11.6 that he relates age of respondent to level of tolerance while holding education constant, and relates tolerance and level of education achieved while controlling age.) Furthermore, as the sociologist must do, Stouffer takes pains to point to sources of error. Sampling is one such source, but one well handled in this study. Slight changes in wording and inflection of voice on the part of interviewers may introduce error. Again, error may be

* But, of course, you should consult the book itself to note variations in percentages for various items dealing with free speech, books in public libraries, the right to teach, and the like.

Figure 11.5

A comparison of community leaders* with a national cross section of adult U.S. population on level of tolerance of nonconforming views (communist, socialist, and atheist)

	Less tolerant	In-between	More tolerant	
	Percentage distribution of scale scores			
All cases				
Selected community leaders	5	29	66	1500
Cross-section in same cities as leaders	18	50	32	897
National cross-section, rural and urban	19	50	31	4933
By each survey agency				
Selected community leaders — AIPO Sample	5	30	65	742
Selected community leaders — NORC Sample	5	29	66	758
Cross-section in same cities as leaders — AIPO Sample	18	52	30	409
Cross-section in same cities as leaders — NORC Sample	18	47	35	488
National cross-section, rural and urban — AIPO Sample	20	50	30	2483
National cross-section, rural and urban — NORC Sample	19	50	31	2450

* For the definition of "community leader" see pages 446–47, and for the method of developing the measure of level of tolerance, see Aside on Methods, Number 13: "The Guttmann or Cornell Scale."

introduced when a sizable part of the sample is not interviewed, persons who may differ in some consistent fashion from those who do respond. In this study, 84 percent of the sample interviews were completed. What of the other 16 percent? Stouffer turns his attention to these people: those not at home, despite five visits by the interviewer; people too sick to be interviewed; those cases where the respondent could not speak English (or the interviewer's second language, if he had one); those who refused to be interviewed (7 percent); and those (another 1 percent) who broke off the interview for one reason or another. A careful analysis of nonrespondents' demographic and other characteristics, so far as these could be gotten, led Stouffer to conclude that the loss of these respondents did not distort the findings.

Second, such findings do not speak for themselves. There is the matter of interpretation. Stouffer suggests, for example, that these observations may "reflect the operation of a factor which may be essential to tolerance; namely, that of contact with people with disturbing and unpopular ideas." Another observation of interest:

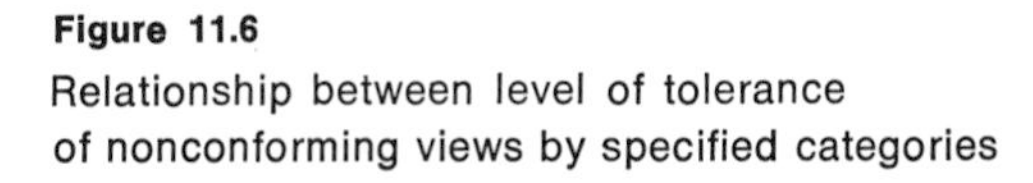

Figure 11.6
Relationship between level of tolerance of nonconforming views by specified categories

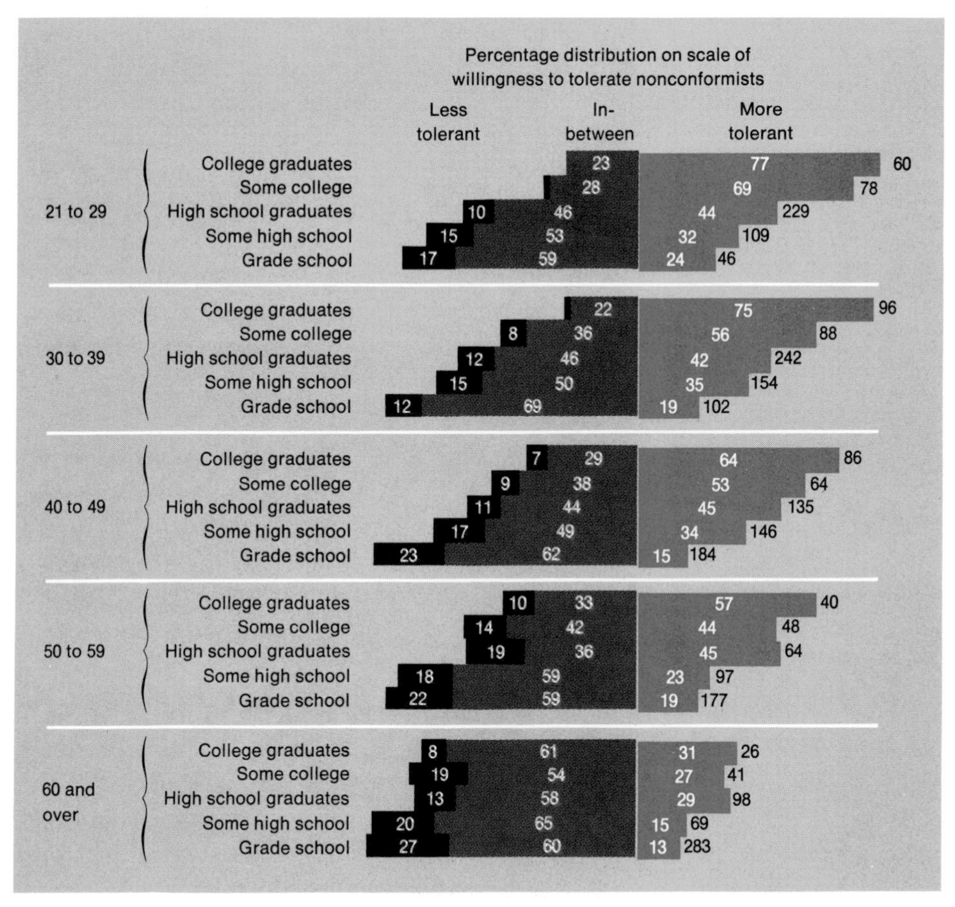

since level of education is positively related to the "relatively great tolerance" score, and since average level of education is moving up, it seems reasonable to predict that expression of unpopular views may be more tolerated in future than it has been in the past. It would be well to read the book, obviously, for further interpretations of the findings.

But let's not miss the point, fail to see the forest for the trees. Communism, socialism, and atheism do have some intrinsic interest, and Stouffer's methodology does help acquaint us with the field. But our concerns are more general: democratic process, the Bill of Rights, legitimate authority, and challenges to them. We noted the challenge to the establishment by such rightist groups as those studied by Stewart and Smith (see Figure 11.4). But this is not unique. The gauntlet is thrown down from left as well as right—and from intermediate points between these extremes. So, also, do criminal and other aberrant behaviors challenge group stability. But in our society certain challenges to authority—those touching belief and expression, in particular—are protected in law. This generates an interplay of challenge and response. And there are aways the questions: How much challenge is tolerable? Which categories of citizens are more tolerant of such deviations, which least? What sorts of challenges are there, and how do they differ in gravity?

The problem is complex, for deviation has ambivalent effects. If not too novel and if the rate of incidence is fairly steady, deviation may enhance social stability by providing the occasion, through trial and punishment, of reaffirming group values and authorized means for achieving them. (In this light, the courtroom is a secular church.)* Like other systems, a group develops certain values and the norms of conduct that embody them. So also there emerges a range of behavior to "right" and "left" of norms, a range commonly felt to be tolerable. What this range is, by type of deviation, for differing social categories is a problem of marked interest for the political sociologist.

* * * *

These institutions, as we have seen, span the range of men's relationships. Religion, even if its injunctions go unheeded six days of the week, yet leaves its trace in guilt and anxiety. Even the atheist profits from the moral code sustained through the church. Like his more conforming fellows, he, too, requires a fairly predictable social world in order to achieve his goals.

Law cuts across all spheres of life, perhaps increasingly so. Among other actions taken on June 12, 1967, the Supreme Court handed down rulings affecting prices of bedding and bicycles, upheld a contempt-of-court conviction of Martin Luther King and seven other Negro leaders, ruled that a suspect has a right to have his lawyer present at a police lineup, held that an employer violated the law in withholding vacation benefits from striking workers, declared unconstitutional Virginia's laws forbidding white-Negro marriages, and ruled that a New York law allowing police to trespass on private property to plant hidden microphones was unconstitutional.

* And the trial, as someone has said, is the Passion Play of secular society.

Figure 11.7

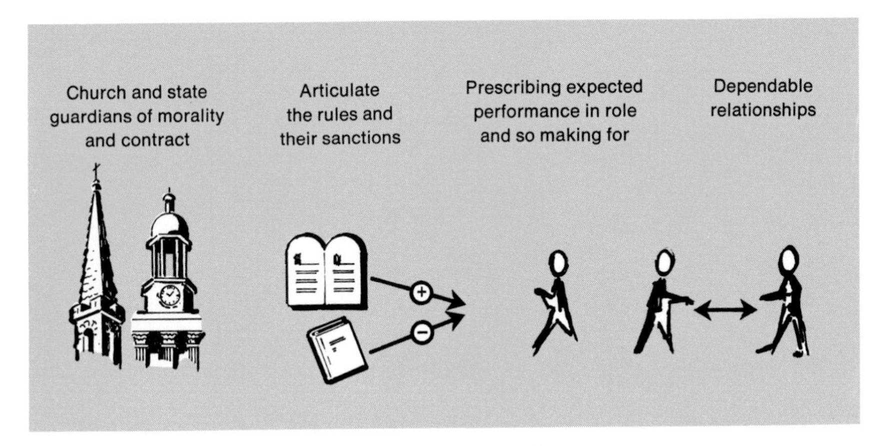

Religion and government both make rules that are binding on all communicants and all citizens. Indeed, religious mandates may go beyond this, asserting precepts that apply to all men, everywhere. And insofar as our government makes international agreements, some rules transcend group boundaries.

Universal and impersonal, the rules of church and state assert the rights and duties of all members of the group. Both specify what must, what ought to be, exerting pressure to bring practice into line with creed.

And each asserts claims to exclusive loyalties.

The significant result is a group-binding effect, on the one hand, and, especially as between groups—different faiths and nations—a divisive effect. Religion has its integrative effect in Northern Ireland, and drives wedges between Protestant and Catholic. Biafrans were drawn together in hunger and hurt, while the gulf between them and Nigeria deepened. Political and religious rites have much in common, as do political and religious wars.

Human organization implies government, government entails rules, and rules make for that dependability without which a human relationship is impossible. We could put it schematically as in Figure 11.7.

But no set of rules can embrace the diversity of men's backgrounds, interests, and aspirations. Nor can today's guidelines for conduct, save at the most abstract level, meet the unforeseen contingencies of tomorrow. The integrity of a social system is always imperfect. Just as physical structures decay, are remodeled or demolished, so too with social structures.

In Part Three we turn to this matter of social change.

References

TEXT

1. Plutarch (A.D., 46–120).
2. Edmund Burke, *Reflections on the Revolution in France* (New York: Rinehart & Co., 1959), p. 117.
3. Reported in *The New York Times,* March 7, 1966, p. 1.
4. See, for various estimates, Will Herberg, *Protestant, Catholic, Jew* (Garden City, N.Y.: Doubleday & Co., Inc., 1955) and Benson Landis, *The Yearbook of American Churches* (New York: National Council of Churches of Christ in the U.S.A., 1964).
5. Emile Durkheim, *The Elementary Forms of the Religious Life,* trans. Joseph Ward Swain (New York: Free Press, 1947), p. 2.
6. *Ibid.,* p 47.
7. C. A. Bell, *The People of Tibet* (Oxford: Clarendon Press, 1928), p. 72.
8. Max Weber, *The Theory of Social and Economic Organization,* trans. A. J. Henderson and Talcott Parsons (New York: Oxford University Press, Inc., 1947), p. 118.
9. Robert MacIver, *The Web of Government* (New York: Macmillan Co., 1948), p. 61.
10. Jean Jacques Rousseau, *Le Contrat social ou principes du droit politique* (Paris: Pourrat Freres, 1838), p. 26.

    In a brief introduction Rousseau justifies his writing on matters political. It is precisely his amateur standing that qualifies him, he argues. He goes on to say: "Were I a prince or a legislator I'd not waste time talking about what ought to be done. I'd put up or shut up!" (*"Je le ferois, ou je me tarois."*)

    Then comes the famous statement, *"L'homme est né libre, et partout il est dans les fers."*

    In Rousseau's *Emile, ou de l'éduca tion,* an important discussion of learning and teaching, we find a similar, startling opener when he writes: "From heavenly hands, all things are good. But in man's hands, all benefactions are corrupted." The original goes: *"Tout est bien sortant des mains de l'auteur des choses, tout dégénere entre les mains de l'homme."* (Paris: Ernest Flammarion, n.d.), Vol. I, p. 9.
11. Thomas Hobbes, *Leviathan* (New York: E. P. Dutton & Co., Inc., 1931), p. 63).
12. Robert MacIver, *The Web of Government* (New York: Macmillan Co., 1948), p. 31.
13. Gerard DeGré, "Freedom and Social Structure," *American Sociological Review,* Vol. 11, No. 5 (October, 1946), p. 530.
14. Bronislaw Malinowski, *Magic, Science and Religion* (Garden City, N.Y.: Doubleday & Co., Inc.—Anchor Books, 1954), pp. 30, 31. Reprinted by permission of George Braziller, Inc.
15. Gerhard Lenski, *The Religious Factor* (Garden City, N.Y.: Doubleday & Co., Inc., 1961), p. 1.
16. St. Augustine, *De Civitate Dei.*
17. George Bernard Shaw, "Imprisonment," *The Prefaces* (London, England: Constable & Co., Ltd., 1934), chap. xi, p. 302.
18. Reprinted by permission of Schocken Books, Inc., from *The Negro Church in America* by E. Franklin Frazier (New York: Schocken Books, Inc., 1963), pp. 82, 83.
19. Emile Durkheim, *The Elementary Forms of the Religious Life,* trans. Joseph Ward Swain (New York: Free Press, 1947). For a judicious appraisal of this important work see Imogen Seger, *Durkheim and His Critics on the Sociology of Religion* (New York: Columbia University Bureau of Applied Social Research, September, 1957).
20. The following, including the quotations from Durkheim, is paraphrased from Emile Durkheim, *Moral Education,* trans. E. K. Wilson and Herman Schnurer (New York: Free Press, 1961), editor's introduction, p. xxvii.
21. Murray Hausknecht, "Confession and Return," *Antioch Review,* Vol. 14, No. 1 (March, 1954), p. 79.
22. Report of July 14, 1969.
23. This litany was written by the Rev. Dr. David G. Buttrick of Pittsburgh Theological Seminary. The Presbyterian assembly was reported in *The New York Times* for May 17, 1968.
24. Reinhold Niebuhr, "The King's Chapel and The King's Court," *Christianity and Crisis,* Vol. XXIX, No. 14 (August 4, 1969).
25. Charles Y. Glock and Rodney Stark, "Is There An American Protestantism?" *Trans-action,* Vol. 3, No. 1 (November/December, 1965). The population sampled consisted of church members in four metropolitan counties in northern

California. Key questions from this study, put to a national sample, yielded similar results.

26. Seymour Martin Lipset, *Political Man: The Social Bases of Politics* (Garden City, N.Y.: Doubleday & Co., 1960), chap. i, "The Sociology of Politics," See also his chapter, "Political Sociology," in Robert K. Merton, Leonard Broom, and Leonard Cottrell (eds.), *Sociology Today* (New York: Basic Books, Inc., Publishers, 1959).
27. Lipset, *op. cit.*, p. 31. Copyright © 1960 by Seymour Martin Lipset. Reprinted by permission of Doubleday & Co., Inc.
28. Paul F. Lazarsfeld, Bernard Berelson, and Hazel Gaudet, *The People's Choice* (New York: Columbia University Press, 1948).
29. Max Weber, *The Protestant Ethic and the Spirit of Capitalism,* trans. Talcott Parsons (New York: Charles Scribner's Sons, 1952), p. 68.
30. Weber, *The Protestant Ethic and the Spirit of Capitalism,* p. 55.
31. *Ibid.*, p. 43.
32. Cited from Montesquieu, *Esprit des Lois,* Book XX, chap. vii in Weber, *The Protestant Ethic and the Spirit of Capitalism,* p. 45.
33. *Ibid.*, p. 41, and taken from Martin Offenbacher, *Konfession und soziale Schichtung: eine Studie über die wirtschaftliche Lage der Katholiken und Protestanten in Baden* (Tübingen and Leipzig, 1901), p. 58. The title of Offenbacher's work may be translated: *Religious Affiliation and Social Stratification: A Study of the Economic Role of Catholics and Protestants in Baden.*

    Weber's thesis, briefly reported here, has stimulated a running controversy over the years. While I note in passing some exceptions that have been taken to his argument, it is left largely uncontested in order to lay it, in uncluttered fashion, next to some empirical tests of it made by Professor Lenski. But the student should know that a number of scholars express serious reservations. Kurt Samuelsson, for example, finds no support for the Weberian thesis and raises serious question about Offenbacher's data and Weber's use of them. He throws serious doubt on the alleged greater propensity of Protestants for schooling. (Protestants in Baden apparently lived to a greater extent than Catholics in districts where advanced schools were available.) Samuelsson also finds Offenbacher's data on differentials in wealth both unreliable and misinterpreted. See Kurt Samuelsson, *Religion and Economic Action,* trans. E. Geoffrey French (Stockholm: Scandinavian University Books, 1961).
34. Luethy adds a useful note: "The establishment of relationships between remote concepts is among the favourite games of the human mind, and perhaps one of its most fruitful, for it reveals surprising links and opens new perspectives—but also one of the most dangerous and seductively misleading ones" (Herbert Luethy, "Once Again: Calvinism and Capitalism," *Encounter,* Vol. 22, No. 1 [January, 1964], p. 26).
35. Weber, *The Protestant Ethic and the Spirit of Capitalism, op. cit.*, p. 154.
36. *Ibid.*, pp. 111–12.
37. Luethy, *op. cit.*, p. 31.
38. From *The Religious Factor* by Gerhard Lenski. Copyright © 1961, 1963, by Doubleday & Company, Inc. Reprinted by permission of the publisher. The statement cited is from the revised edition, 1963, p. 17.
39. *Ibid.*, p. 21.
40. Lenski, *op. cit.*, 1961 ed., p. 24.
41. *Ibid.*, p. 77.
42. *Ibid.*, p. 94, 95.
43. *Ibid.*, p. 95.
44. *Ibid.*, p. 103.
45. Lenski, *op. cit.*, 1963 ed., p. 117.
46. Lenski, *op. cit.*, 1961 ed., p. 101.
47. Lipset, *op. cit.*, pp. 48–59, *passim.*
48. Professor Lipset settled on his classification of nations as follows. "The main criteria used to define European democracies are the uninterrupted continuation of political democracy since World War I and the absence over the past twenty-five years of a major political movement opposed to the democratic rules of the game. [This means] that no totalitarian movement, either fascist or communist received 20 per cent of the vote during this time. The somewhat less stringent criterion for Latin America is whether a given country has had a history of more or less free elections for most of the post–World War I period. Where in Europe we look for stable democracies, in South America we look for countries which have not had fairly constant dictatorial rule" (Lipset, *op. cit.*, p. 48).
49. Robert A. Dahl, *Modern Political Analysis* (Englewood Cliffs, N.J.: Prentice-Hall, Inc., 1963). It seems to me significant that this book, defining the

political scientist's object of inquiry as almost coterminous with the field of sociology, should be called *Modern* political analysis. See Heinz Eulau, *The Behavioral Persuasion* (New York: Random House, Inc., 1963).

50. Reference here is to the study of W. Lloyd Warner, J. O. Low, Paul S. Lunt, and Leo Srole, *Yankee City* edited and abridged in the Yale University Press edition of 1963; to W. Lloyd Warner and associates, *Democracy in Jonesville* (New York: Harper & Bros., 1949); and to Floyd Hunter, *Community Power Structure* (Chapel Hill: University of North Carolina Press, 1953).
51. The *cultivated* character of deviant behavior is stressed by a sociologist who pioneered in the subfield of criminology, Edwin H. Sutherland. Presenting a theory of the process by which a person comes to engage in systematic criminal behavior he writes (in part): "Criminal behavior is *learned* . . . in [differential association and] interaction with other persons . . . [and the learning] includes (*a*) techniques of committing the crime, which are sometimes very complicated, sometimes very simple; (*b*) the specific direction of motives, drives, rationalizations, and attitudes" (Edwin H. Sutherland, *Principles of Criminology* [4th ed.; Philadelphia: J. B. Lippincott Co., 1947], p. 6).
52. Samuel A. Stouffer, *Communism, Conformity, and Civil Liberties* (Garden City, N.Y.: Doubleday & Co., Inc., 1955). Copyright © 1955 by Samuel A. Stouffer.
53. *Ibid.*, p. 125.

TABLES

11.2 Based on data in Charles Y. Glock and Rodney Stark, "Is There An American Protestantism?" *Trans-action*, Vol. 3, No. 1 (November/December, 1965), pp. 9, 11, 13.

11.3 Paul F. Lazarsfeld, Bernard Berelson, and Hazel Gaudet, *The People's Choice* (New York: Columbia University Press, 1948). Adapted from Chart 22, p. 63. Also see pp. 59–60 *passim*.

11.5 Gerhard Lenski, *The Religious Factor* (Garden City, N.Y.: Doubleday & Co., Inc., 1961), p. 80.

11.7 *Ibid.*, p. 85.

11.8 *Ibid.*, p. 104 n.

11.10 Adapted from Seymour Martin Lipset, *Political Man: The Social Bases of Politics* (Garden City, N.Y.: Doubleday & Co., Inc., 1960), Table 11, p. 51–54. Copyright © 1960 by Semour Martin Lipset; reprinted by permission of Doubleday & Co., Inc.

11.11 Floyd Hunter, *Community Power Structure* (Chapel Hill: University of North Carolina Press, 1953), p. 76.

11.12 Samuel A. Stouffer, *Communism, Conformity, and Civil Liberties* (Garden City, N.Y.: Doubleday & Co., Inc., 1955). Copyright © 1955 by Samuel A. Stouffer; reprinted by permission of Doubleday & Co., Inc.

FIGURES

11.1 Adapted from Gerard DeGré, "Freedom and Social Structure," *American Sociological Review*, Vol. 11, No. 5 (October, 1946), p. 534.

11.2 Gary Marx, "Religion: Opiate or Inspiration of Civil Rights Militancy among Negroes?" *American Sociological Review*, Vol. 31, No. 1 (February, 1967), pp. 67–69.

11.4 Douglas K. Stewart and Ted C. Smith, "Celebrity Structure of the Far Right," *Western Political Quarterly*, Vol. 18, No. 2 (June, 1964), p. 353.

11.5 Stouffer, *op. cit.*, p. 51.

11.6 *Ibid.*, p. 93.

part three

Changing the group

The social order is constantly transformed. Its boundaries are permeable, susceptible to new influences. Thus roles (again, the cubes in our design) are redefined and rearranged, so forming new structures of relationships.

12. *Social change: protest and deviance*
13. *Social change, unplanned: the subtle drift from past to future*
14. *Social change, planned*

chapter 12 **Social change: protest and deviance**

Me seemes the world is runne quite out of square,
From the first point of his appointed sourse,
And being once amisse grows daily wourse and wourse.
Edmund Spenser, *The Faerie Queene*

To maintain a system of relationships, extreme aberrations must be prevented. But how much deviation is tolerable will depend on a number of conditions. (Let's define deviant behavior as that which violates the rules, whether legal or embedded in the mores, and the roles and relationships they govern.)* In times of crisis, the range of tolerance contracts. The slightest deviation may be interpreted as defection or treason. A revolutionary movement, a society at war, embattled religious sects confronting theological metaphor and the mammonism of the unsaved—these are conditions for tightening codes and conduct. On the other hand, with

* In this discussion deviation is not to be construed as bad or good. It carries the statistical implication of the unusual: belief and behavior that departs from the mode.

security and opulence, a wider range of beliefs and behaviors becomes tolerable.

Deviance as a social matter

A tolerable range of deviance

Paradoxically, too little as well as too much deviation can threaten a human group. For without some aberrant behavior we could not know the what or why of customary conduct. Without blacks or grays, we have but a foggy conception of white. Without treason or political indifference or cynicism, we have an incomplete sense of patriotic commitment. Deviant behavior provides the occasion for reaffirming—sometimes redefining—shared ideals. In doing this it marks the boundaries of the group, for groups are known by the standards they keep. Thus:

> Deviant forms of behavior, by marking the outer edges of group life, give the inner structure its special character and thus supply the framework within which the people of the group develop an orderly sense of their own cultural identity. Perhaps this is what Aldous Huxley had in mind when he wrote: "Now tidiness is undeniably good—but a good of which it is easily possible to have too much and at too high a price . . . The good life can only be lived in a society in which tidiness is preached and practised, but not too fanatically, and where efficiency is always haloed, as it were, by a tolerated margin of mess."[1]

Both ends of a scale may mark deviant conduct: tidiness and messiness, saints as well as sinners. Indeed, an excess of goodness could prove most disruptive. For very large numbers of people depend for their livelihood on a sustained level of deviant conduct —for example, the whole apparatus for defining, detecting, prosecuting, and punishing illegal behavior.

Thus the problem for human groups is to restrict deviant conduct within tolerable limits. There are illuminating parallels in thermal systems and in the physiology of the human body. A thermostat is a control device which limits the fluctuations of temperature in the system. When temperature exceeds a given point, the heat source is cut off. When the mercury drops below a given level, the heat cuts in. So, also, with organic systems adjusting to shock, injury, and disease.[2]

Deviance is socially created behavior

Deviant behavior is created behavior, and this in three senses. It is created as a result of distinctive socialization. (Adult models, neighborhood peers, pot hucksters *et al.*, may collaborate in producing the deviant.) It is created, or sustained when the way we treat deviants perpetuates or increases its incidence. (Prisons, hospitals, and detention homes may serve as informal classrooms, effectively teaching values, attitudes, and skills for a deviant career.) It is created by definitions conferred by the group's rule-making agencies. (A given behavior is not intrinsically deviant. It becomes "far out" only as measured from the bench mark of common sentiments and rules.)

Since deviance is a social creation, it follows that one group's deviation may be another's conformity—or at least that the conception of deviation is peculiar to social time and place. And not only the type, but the volume of such behavior may be geared to social conditions. For example, increase in group size means, as we have seen, something like an exponential increase in number of relationships. If these relationships, more numerous and complex, are to be woven into the fabric of society, the number of rules will multiply. And if rules multiply, so, very likely, will their violation.

Thus we would predict that: (1) both type and volume of deviant behavior would depend on social characteristics that vary from time to time and group to group, and (2) for a given society over a limited period of time (social conditions remaining much the same) type and volume would be stable, or normal.

A quota of deviance as a group characteristic

It was some such assumption as this that led Erikson to ask: Is there a quantum of deviant behavior that is normal for a given society?* And does the rate remain fairly stable even though type of

* Erikson builds on Durkheim, who suggests that every society, at a given time, has a quota of suicide appropriate to the social conditions then obtaining. And in distinguishing between what is pathological and what is normal in the social order, Durkheim insists that the pathological is *not* the existence of illegal or far-out conduct, but marked changes in their rates. See his *Suicide* (New York: Free Press, 1951—original publication in 1897), *passim,* and *The Rules of Sociological Method* for the distinction between the normal and the pathological. (Chicago: University of Chicago Press, 1938—original publication in 1895).

† Those who apprehend the divine, not by adhering to moral law as interpreted by church authorities, but directly through the gospel and the gift of grace. Erikson deals with the case of Anne Hutchison, sentenced to banishment.

Figure 12.1
Massachusetts Bay Colony conviction and offender rates*

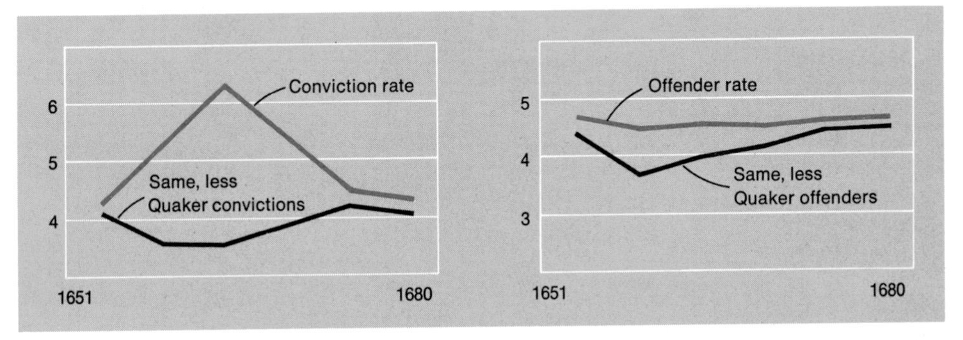

* Per 100 population

deviation varies?[3] The group he studied was the Puritans of Massachusetts Bay Colony, 1650–80. Deviation here was a matter of three successive crime waves, the offenders being antinomians,† Quakers, and witches. Offenses on which Erikson gathered data were these: crimes against the church, contempt of authority, fornication, disturbing the peace, and crimes against property or persons. Two slightly inconsistent sets of findings are represented in Figure 12.1.

Conviction rates vary. Offender rates are stable. The answer to the question, Does rate of deviant behavior remain fairly constant in a stable social context? seems to depend on whether we are talking about violations or the violator. If we fix on the act, then these data don't support the stability-of-deviance-rate notion. If we fix on the deviant role, they do.

Erikson argues that the deviant role, not the conviction rate is the significant factor in understanding the connection between the group and violation of its rules. For the threat to the group doesn't vary as the conviction rate might suggest. This is so because single-time offenders are in fact popularly assumed to be multiple offenders. Thus the statistical record is an artifact not reflecting social reality. "Most offenders who commit discrete acts of deviation are *treated as if* they were habitual offenders—so that, for example, one will describe a person imprisoned for a single act of larcency as 'a thief' on the apparent assumption that this is his livelihood, or at least his inner bent."[4] Thus the single offender is bracketed with multiple offenders as a chronic threat to the social order. Furthermore, "the bulk of people who can be reasonably described as deviant are censured for behavior which *is* persistent and habitual—alcoholics, mental patients, homosexuals, drug users, prostitutes, members of strange religious groupings, and the rest—people who cannot be described in terms of frequency of offending because public attitudes do not lend themselves to that kind of accounting."[5] The significant variable is not offenses, or convictions, but offenders. The actor and the role are what count in assessing stability and change potential. And on this point the findings are clear:

> [The] offender rate . . . changed very little during the thirty-year period for which we have adequate records, suggesting that an almost fixed proportion of the populace was engaged in deviant activity before the Quakers made their abrupt appearance in the colony, during the time they were in full swing, and after they had retired from the field altogether. A crime wave lashed across Essex County which almost doubled the number of offenses handled by the local court, yet the size of the deviant population itself did not increase to any appreciable degree.[6]

Stable deviance rates were sustained among the Puritans despite the fact that type of offense shifted—antinomians, Quakers, witches—new crimes displacing the older ones.

> Whether we look for the source of this displacement in the motives of the people involved, in the ever shifting definitions of deviance itself, or in some complex equation having to do with the density of deviant behavior in given units of social space, we are dealing with the notion that *deviation in society may take the form of a distinct "quota."*[7]

Thus we are driven to conclude that deviance is a built-in attribute of the social order, more to be viewed as a reflection than as a cause of social change. On the other hand, when deviant rates rise or fall, either steadily or precipitously, we are prompted to seek the social changes that account for them. (Such changes are suggested in Figure 12.2 in which three distinct phases of the curve correspond to the Depression years, World War II, and the postwar period. The sharp changes lead us to suspect that we are not dealing here with a society as stable as that of the Massachusetts Bay Colony between 1650 and 1680.)

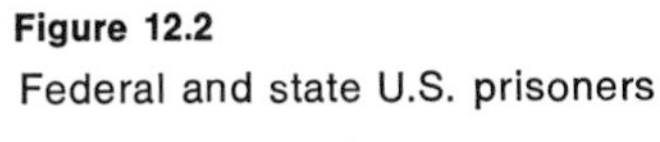

Figure 12.2
Federal and state U.S. prisoners

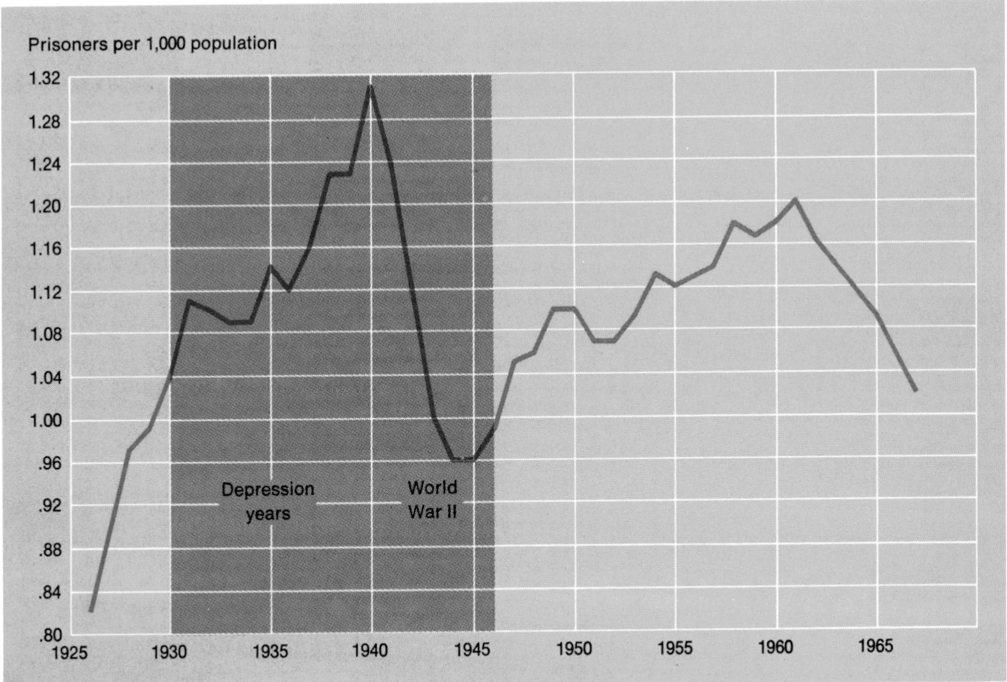

So we have two questions to put. What are the sources of ordinary—i.e., controlled or contained—deviance? And what sorts of social factors might account for extraordinary deviance?

Sources and controls of deviance

The rule of honor among thieves is not optional: it's a necessity growing out of their position in the social order. Every social group—neighborhood gangs, religious orders, Haight-Ashbury hippies, business organizations—imposes rules that define the tolerable range of members' conduct. This is inevitable because people differ, yet must follow standard role prescriptions. They differ for individual, social, and cultural reasons.

As individuals, genetic differences and drives for gratification could, unless channeled, disrupt accustomed relationships. As a social creation, each person emerges from a unique constellation of social influences, generating individual differences that, again, have a disruptive potential. Societal conditions, too, may make for deviance and problems of control. A wealthy society like ours can absorb the costs of deviance to an extent that poorer groups could not. Apparently we can afford to support some 200,000 persons in state and federal prisons, absorb the impact of 357.9 thousand crimes against the person and 2.4 million crimes against property (1965),[8] while spending 4.2 billion dollars for public law enforcement and criminal justice to combat crimes estimated to cost us about 2.5 percent of our gross national product.

Likewise, aspects of culture may affect the incidence of deviance. In American culture a stress on individualism ("doing your own thing") and a tradition of political and religious rebellion, with their Constitutional protections, may encourage a degree of nonconformity that threatens customary relationships. Or elements in our culture perceived as hypocritical—professing the ideal of peace and making war, stressing national self-determination yet intervening economically and militarily, celebrating equality of opportunity which is in fact denied to blacks, poor whites, and other minority groups—such contradictions may stimulate deviance.

With such a variety of change-inducing influences at work, how does it happen that deviation is as effectively controlled as it is? There are three means open to a group, organization, or society for controlling deviant behavior. One is preventive: effective socialization inculcating a preference for accepted ways. One is curative: the reform of the deviant who abides, thereafter, by the standards of the group.* And one is tacit acknowledgement of failure in the first two processes. This is separation from the group by exile, ostracism, hospitalization, imprisonment or, the ultimate separation, death.

Deviant behavior, then, springs inevitably from personal, social, and cultural differences. And quite as invariably, human groups utilize socialization, reform, and separation to hold deviation within tolerable range. Beyond this we can conceive of deviant be-

* Reform proceeds, as does socialization, through rewards and punishments. It may be subtle, rather than of the reform school variety. For example, Spiro tells of some young men working at an Israeli kibbutz who rejected their work assignment in the dairy. In an evening skit, there was a humorous, chiding scene devoted to these conscientious objectors. The following day one of the men acknowledged its chastening and reformative effect on him. Cases of deviation may be brought up and debated at town meetings or, in serious cases, the offender may be expelled from the kibbutz (Melford Spiro, *Kibbutz, Venture in Utopia* [New York: Schocken Books, Inc., 1963], pp. 100–101).

havior as socially supportive when it generates responses that reinforce approved conduct.

From a social perspective, it is not the offending individual, but the offended group that matters. (Discussing art forgeries, the curator of prints of the Metropolitan Museum of Art is reported to have said: "It is not the integrity of the maker that matters, but the faith of the takers.") Nor, from a social standpoint, is it even the injury done a given individual that counts. Rather it is the violation of the group: the fracturing of common values and the threat implied to familiar relationships if such values are not sustained.

In a way it becomes important that there be the threat of deviation. For, as in a hydraulic lift, the great weight of customary ways can be sustained only by the publicly magnified pressure of a regular quantum of deviant behavior. It is against the counterpressure of offensive conduct that we elevate and celebrate cherished patterns of behavior.

How, then, is deviant behavior linked with social change? It appears to be an index of change when it is extraordinary, in volume or in type.

Deviance as an index of social change

Effect of change in volume

In mid-August, 1969, some 300,000 young people converged on the small town of Bethel, New York, to enjoy rock and pot. To understate the case, this was a sudden access of a type of behavior novel to Bethel and in formidable volume. As a result, public services were paralyzed—fire, transport, sanitation, postal service, police (who were almost powerless to enforce the law against sale or use of marihuana or LSD), privacy was disrupted, zoning ordinances violated. Businesses were closed, food and water were lacking, property was damaged, and one young person died and three others were hospitalized from drug overdose. Had these young people remained beyond their three or four days (doubtless Bethel residents would blanch at the thought), the social structure of the community would have changed markedly in its familial, educational, religious, economic, and political life.

We have well-known examples of a sudden input of "foreigners" inducing social change in the instant communities formed under crisis conditions of World War II. Again, the volume of the postwar baby boom had much to do with a reorganization of education—in personnel and facilities. Many of the problems facing New York city stem from the volume of Negro and Puerto Rican migration affecting family life, the economy and welfare institutions of the city, race relations, politics, and every other sector of the social order. And while volume is at issue, not deviant types, we can anticipate disruptive change in our social system as it grows by 70 to 100 million newcomers between 1970 and the year 2000.

Effect of change in type

In recent years a new deviant type has emerged as agent of social change. This is the young person who rejects the values of "the establishment," seeking as hippy or activist self-fulfillment and social justice. These young people have helped create a climate favorable to social change—a change that exploits professed ideals to alter rules and relationships.* Thus we see dramatic change in black-white relationships, and the possibility of change in civilian-military relationships, in relationships between rich and poor.

Both in the statistical and normative sense, these youth are deviants. If such deviation is an index of social change, what are the changes at work?

Deviant youth: source and symptom of social change

In past years we have seen great changes in the role of the student—or rather of that minority of vocal and influential students who have retreated from or rebelled against the establishment. The rebels are seeking to induce social change. In the process heads are cracked, students imprisoned, classes broken up, and buildings occupied; alumni, legislators, faculty, parents, and the public at large are exercised. The events are widespread: Harvard, Co-

* We need to consider the possibility of a conservative backlash that would, of course, militate against change, seeking to restore the status ante quo. Social change is the outcome of an inordinately complex set of social vectors.

† Obviously, to divide students, like all Gaul, into three parts is a device to aid analysis, not a representation of the more complex reality. Nor do I mean to suggest that there is no overlap between categories. But rebellion and retreat do seem to represent modes of protest. And the emergence of such a protest points to underlying changes in the social order.

lumbia, Cornell, SUNY campuses, Fordham, Howard, Chicago, Berkeley, San Francisco State—and abroad at the Sorbonne, the Universities of Tokyo, Prague, West Berlin, Rome, and elsewhere. (Nor does it happen only at the university level: high schools have had their sit-ins, fires, demonstrations, and vandalism.)

About such deviant behavior we can raise two questions: What are its sources? What are its consequences? Some consequences we've already seen: changes in the student role, in curriculum, in relationships between students and faculty and administrators. Some of these are likely to be enduring and hence come properly under the heading of social change. Others—effects on mass media or on legislation—are probably more ephemeral. But our interest is chiefly in the sources of this behavior. For the sociologist would certainly seek some understanding of the student revolt in conditions of the social order. To resort to our analogy with the thermostat, we might suspect that such deviant conduct is an instance of a homeostatic device, triggered when things go awry in the system. Sensitive to inconsistencies in the system (the mercury stands at a comfortable, self-satisfied 70 degrees, but the water in the glass is frozen), a few students act, attempting to eliminate the gap between *is* and *ought*.

In probing the question of this change-symptomatic behavior, let us consider the charges of rebels and retreatists, the forum in which the action occurs, and, finally, changes in the social order that are plausible sources of this behavior.

The charges against the establishment. We should be clear at the outset that we are dealing with a distinct minority who are, nonetheless, literate, vocal, and influential. Most students accept, with faith or understanding or docility, the *curriculum vitae* implicit in existing social arrangements. They find goals acceptable to them within the bounds of the establishment and conscientiously follow the curricular means to gain certification for adult roles. But flanking the agreeable majority are two other types of youth: the rebels and retreatists, activists and hippies.† The former act to change unacceptable aspects of the social order. The latter turn inward, seeking self-fulfillment quite apart from a society beyond redemption. While the former are heavily engaged in issues of education, race, and politics, the latter disengage themselves, sometimes with the use of drugs. Because they are bright, idealistic, courageous, convinced, persistent, vocal and disruptive, the rebels have found an audience for their charges. The indictments touch education, race, and politics, and are laced with moral condemnation for the common compromising of ideals.

Education is defective, students say, in the caliber of teaching, in denying students a proper voice in policy making, and in its anachronistic content indifferent to the wrongs of the world. Big, bureaucratic, and depreciating the teaching role, universities have become impersonal factories routinely grinding out a standardized, mediocre product. These young people demand some voice in matters of admissions, faculty recruitment and evaluation, financial policies, and campus rules. And they seek new courses and programs—Afro-American studies, for example—and the elimination of others—required general education courses, ROTC, and the like.

Students, of course, were the backbone of the voter-registration effort. The murders of Goodman, Schwerner, and Chaney remind us of the courage and idealism of students in the civil rights movement. More recently, on-campus blacks, seeking a distinctive racial identity, have charged that they are being educated in an inhospitable environment requiring sorts of achievement they are ill-equipped for and oriented toward adult performance in a white man's world. Hence the demand for black literature, black theology, black history, Afro-American studies.

In the realm of politics, war, poverty, and pollution have been student targets. Anti-Soviet Czech students demand a "human socialism." In Japan, the student movement sets as a long-range goal the establishment of a Communist state. In the United States, students were foremost in criticizing our military ventures. Their position on the war in Vietnam, once radical and subversive, was later echoed in the halls of Congress.

And throughout there is the allegation of hypocrisy and irrelevance. What has the higher learning to say about the poorly housed, poorly clothed, malnourished migrant crop picker? The impoverished Negro? The destitute Appalachian white living in the same society with the 27 percent oil depletion allowance, hundreds of millionaires, and a favorable market for executive sandboxes at $450? (The harassed captain of industry sits on the rosewood edge, wiggling his toes in sand which, for an extra $100, can be imported from Egypt, Mexico, or Hawaii.)[9]

The forum for dissent. Campus has been the privileged sanctuary and the university a prime target for the activists. Yet, to a degree not often approximated in other settings, the university would seem to have just those characteristics esteemed by rebellious youth. For it is an organization dedicated to reason, to democratic process, hospitable to new and diverse views and to the testing of abstract ideas against the concrete realities of life. How then account for the attacks on the university by those who are its beneficiaries?

One answer has to do with the place of higher education in the institutional structure of society. A second is based on the location of higher learning in the sequence of life cycle experiences. We find a third answer in the availability of leaders and followers who, for the time being, share a common lot.

Unlike the universally required training of the secondary schools, a liberal education has been conceived as one that stresses questioning and innovation. True, special colleges within the university have always trained professionals, simply transmitting the skills and lore of medicine, law, or engineering. But the liberation of the liberal arts requires an incessant dialectic between alternate solutions to problems of the good, the true, and the beautiful. This is what has distinguished liberal arts colleges: the free expression of novel notions, a critical assessment of the elders' traditions, a search for new forms. Among all schools, among all institutions, the college of liberal arts has offered sanctuary and freedom not found elsewhere. It is that sequestered location in the institutional structure for contained explosions, releasing energy and spleen with least destructiveness. Behind the moats of incontestably virtuous learning (nursing, dentistry, business administration) and public services (varsity athletics, out-patient clinics, in-service teacher training) the yeasty ferment of the liberal arts program carries on. This is one reason that the campus has been the vulnerable spot, in the social order, for expression of dissent.

A second reason is that, for most university students, this is the most disengaged point in the life cycle—that time when a person can think, speak, and act with a freedom never before realized and always after compromised.* Usually he is sure of bed, board, clothing, and tuition. He has no fear of jeopardizing the welfare of wife and children, his chances for promotion on the job, increases in income, or his standing in the community. Not that there are no hazards or restraints: for men, the reaction of a draft

* It may be that this period of disengagement, carrying the blessing of unusual freedoms, also carries the hazards of normlessness. This might help explain the relatively high suicide rate on college campuses, an estimated 1,000 per year among some 7 million students. This rate, about 14 per 100,000, is nearly double that for the 15–24 age group in the United States, in 1959, which was 7.4.

. . . we . . . conclude that deviance is a built-in attribute of the social order, more to be viewed as a reflection than as a cause of social change.

. . . we have seen great changes in the role of the student. . . . The rebels are seeking to induce social change. . . . events are widespread: Harvard, Columbia, . . . abroad at the Sorbonne. . . .

board, or the academic record that might compromise future job placement or graduate work.* But certainly there is freedom to probe and test and deviate to a degree not found in the adult role.

Campus is a hospitable site for deviation because it gathers together young people sharing many things in common. It offers a pool of followers and talent for leadership. Students suffer in common an often heavy study schedule, anxiety about grades, concern to establish new friendships and heterosexual relationships, the imminent possibilities of military service (for men), and, for many, moral concerns about injustices on which their academic work seems to have little bearing. In this uncertain, fluid situation, cause-oriented action comes as fulfillment and relief. Student leaders emerge, organizations are formed. Graduate students in teacher- or research-assistant roles may be especially ready to take the lead. Already thrust into the leadership role in the classroom, perhaps beguiled by the deference accorded the role, they are readier than senior faculty to extend leadership beyond the classroom. (Beyond teaching, the elders' energies are absorbed in research, committee work, and writing.)

Social sources of intergenerational conflict. There are, then objective reasons for protest: the Bay of Pigs, Vietnam, racial injustice, unequal opportunity, and poverty. And the university years provide a peculiarly appropriate time and site for protest. But we can probe further into the social sources of dissent.

One source lies in this fact: Each succeeding generation confronts a new world. Role definitions transmitted from the past may be out of phase with an ever more rapidly transformed society.† Students' grandparents knew World War I. Through them, their parents heard of Huns and trench warfare, and echoes of the Bolshevik rebellion from the Dedham courthouse that sent Sacco and Vanzetti to the chair. They marveled at the engine set on wheels, the sorcery of wireless, and man's putting screw to air to

* It's instructive to note, over a four-year period, the participation curve in student activities. It takes the shape of an inverted U, peaking in the second and third years. When graduation becomes imminent, campus participation tends to slack off as students anticipate—are concerned about—the postgraduate years. See the curve representing the course of participation in associations in Wilbert E. Moore, *Social Change* (Englewood Cliffs, N.J.: Prentice-Hall, Inc., 1963), Figure 15, p. 60.

† When social patterns lag behind changes in material culture, we have what Ogburn called "culture lag." Thus in the 19th century we saw the advent of heavy —and dangerous—industrial machinery. But we were sluggish in contriving nonmaterial adaptations, such as medical insurance or workmen's compensation. Such a gap between material and nonmaterial culture creates a tension for social change. We will touch on the culture-lag theory in the following chapter.

pull the "Spirit of St. Louis" from New York to Paris. They knew Fitzgerald's twenties, saw John Held, Jr.'s tube-shaped flappers with exposed knees. They saw, too, in the piety of prohibition, vivid testimony to the vicious outcomes of virtuous intent. In the thirties there were Steinbeck's migrants in their tired jalopies, converging on Route 66 in a stream of the anxious dispossessed. Young people joined the CCC. Under F.D.R., government was fruitful with alphabetical innovations to combat depression, and Dr. Townsend and Upton Sinclair proffered their particular nostrums for prosperity. Out of the depression and into World War II, their parents could justify unreserved commitment to a great national effort.

But for our rebels and retreatists, the world of vivid, personal meanings commences after 1945, a world without the enemy of massive poverty within, or the immediate threat of mad aggression from without. They accept most casually the mystery of hearing the inaudible, seeing the invisible. Immunized to miracles as they are to polio, they are not surprised by excursions to the Moon —or Mars. They take domestic security for granted. No generation before theirs has so felt the impact of the welfare state with more schemes to protect more people, so controlling life's unknown's, from womb to tomb. From a secure anchorage, not preoccupied with problems of getting ahead, much less survival, they can look with different eyes on the nature of the social world, some invoking Mao and Lenin for the revolution, others invoking rock and pot and pill to seek a private world, apart.

Especially in our day, the rapidity of social-cultural change may plow a gulf between generations.[10] Cultural change depends on three factors: the size of the cultural backlog, degree of contact among peoples enabling the exchange of ideas, and available techniques for analysis or manipulation of ideas. As Adam Ferguson pointed out in 1767, the cultural backlog tends constantly to grow. Each generation has what preceding generations had, *plus*.

> When nations succeed one another in the career of discoveries and inquiries the last is always the most knowing. Systems of science are gradually formed. The globe itself is traversed by degrees, and the history of every age, when past, is an accession of knowledge to those who succeed. The Romans were more knowing than the Greeks; and every scholar of modern Europe is, in this sense, more learned than the most accomplished person that ever bore either of those celebrated names.[11]

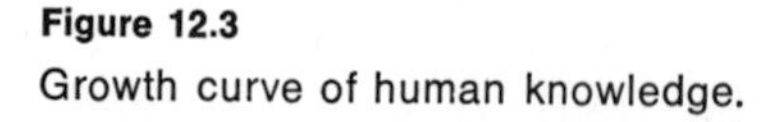
Figure 12.3
Growth curve of human knowledge.

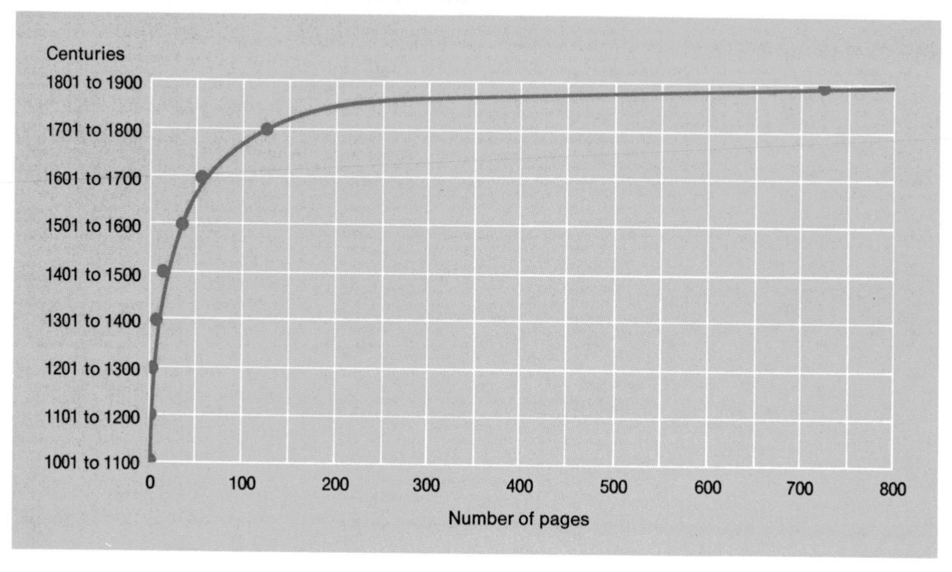

* Number of pages in Darmstädter devoted to scientific discoveries and inventions in successive centuries.

Contact and exchange have increased, especially as, through professional organizations, we have institutionalized the production of knowledge. And especially in recent years we have vastly magnified the means of manipulating ideas (through computers). So we should not be surprised at the exponential rates of growth represented by Figures 12.3 and 12.4.

And so if culture provides the meanings that inform human relationships, and if the cultural system is continuously—and ever more rapidly—altered by novel inputs, the meanings change and the network of relationships must change. When that change is great in degree and kind, the experience of succeeding generations may be so utterly different as to isolate them from the past. Never has it been so true: One cannot step twice into the same stream. So experience, tradition, and history come to seem irrelevant. This is one aspect of youth's alienation.

Perhaps this seems too obvious: when cultural evolution and social change are extraordinarily rapid, the overlap of experience between generations is minimal. Yet one might think there would

Figure 12.4
Index of cultural growth
Top curve, annual average number of publications in psychology. Bottom curve, number of publications in experimental and psysiological psychology publications.

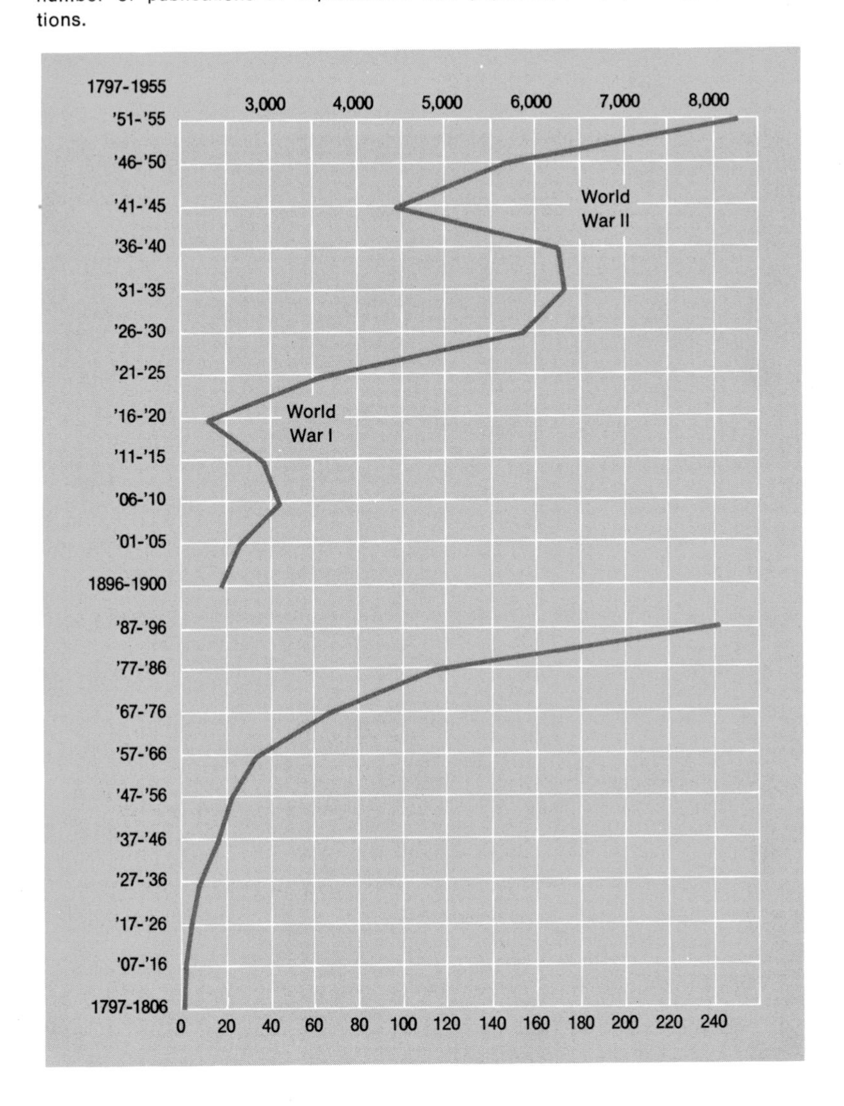

be ways of communicating past to present. But in fact there have been underlying social changes at work that have put the youthful sector of society in Coventry, isolating them from the adult world, making them privileged pariahs.[12]

This unarticulated policy of segregation is seen in the extended period of institutionalized apartheid. Over past generations, larger numbers of our apprentice adults have been put in the protective custody of schools for ever longer periods. (Recall the data in Chapter 9.) In the Middle Ages the move was virtually from infancy to adulthood. One hundred fifty years ago a period called childhood intervened before the person moved to work and marriage.[13] Now in a rich, urban-industrial society, periods of adolescence, postadolescence, and young adulthood intervene. (We search for terms to describe the period of extended dependence.)

Take the polity. In matters of politics, the general rule for the young is: Theirs not to reason why, theirs simply to comply—a structure of political participation which, except for military service and, in recent years, the Peace Corps and Vista, largely disregards young citizens. In the case of their political apartheid, as in other spheres, there is some resemblance between the exclusion of youth and the exclusion of the Negro. Both are traditional, both are ill-founded, and both today's Negroes and the young are more informed—and more sensitive to their depressed condition—than were their predecessors.

In the world of work, as in politics, youth are increasingly set apart. Young people from well-to-do families may be in their mid- or late twenties before entering the labor force. (Taken as a whole, college students would be a sizable part of the labor force were they included in it—larger than the proportion of workers in sales, or private household workers or laborers or farm workers. See Figure 12.5.) Not only are youth late to labor: they are sometimes not persuaded of its worth. The self-denial, the future orientation, the will and wit and striving to achieve—these old imperatives linked with an industrial society seem to them outmoded. They see goals and allegiances receding in the routines of large bureaucratic structures, instrumental efficiency deflecting concern from the expressive elements of life. The king of the squares is not the bigot, not even the warmonger. He is the system-sustaining hack caught up in meaningless routines, his vacuous aspirations described in *New Yorker* ads, never fully sensing that he can't take it with him.

But there is a third aspect of our social structure that may be more important in understanding the isolation of the young. This is the shifting structure of the family. Consider for a moment the isolation of the dispossessed Negro male, as documented in the Moynihan report.[14] The central fact about the lower-class black family is father-absence, mother-dominance, and the lack—especially for the boy—of a self-respecting, achieving model foreshadowing his own future. About a fourth of Negro families are headed

Figure 12.5
Position of students if included in the 1965 U.S. labor force

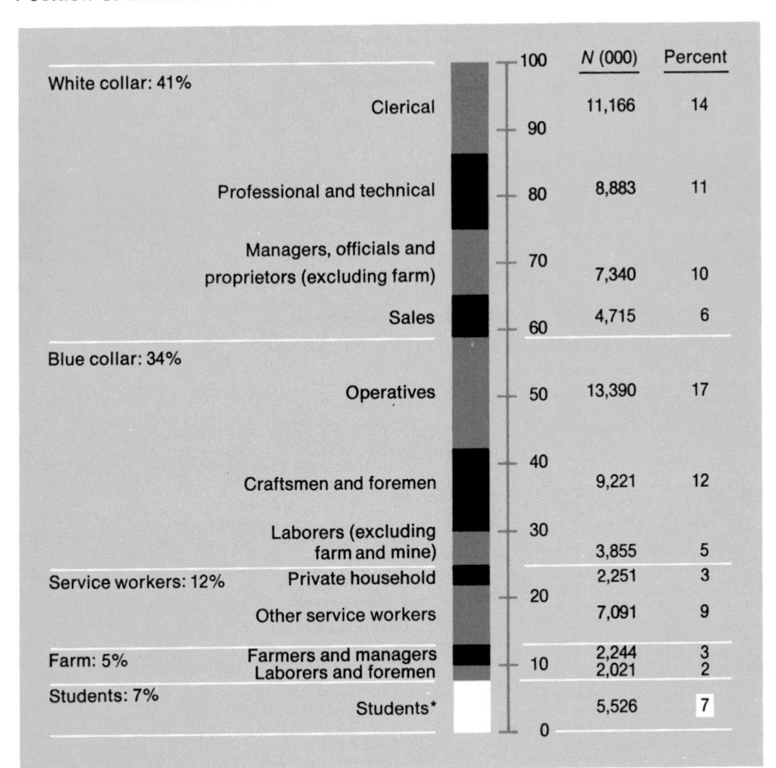

N (000)
Percent
White collar: 41%
Clerical
11,166
14
Professional and technical
8,883
11
Managers, officials and proprietors (excluding farm)
7,340
10
Sales
4,715
6
Blue collar: 34%
Operatives
13,390
17
Craftsmen and foremen
9,221
12
Laborers (excluding farm and mine)
3,855
5
Service workers: 12%
Private household
2,251
3
Other service workers
7,091
9
Farm: 5%
Farmers and managers
2,244
3
Laborers and foremen
2,021
2
Students: 7%
Students*
5,526
7
100
90
80
70
60
50
40
30
20
10
0

* All students registered for credit toward a degree in all institutions of higher education in the fall of 1965.

by a woman. In most of these families the husband is absent. Even where the husband is present and working, if someone else in the family is also working, the man is not the principal breadwinner in one out of four families. Separated spouses, husbands' unemployment, low incomes, and large families send Negro women into the labor force—56 percent of those between ages 25 and 64. The President's Committee on Equal Employment Opportunity, summarizing 1964 data, reports that "there are proportionately four times as many Negro females in significant white-collar jobs as Negro males." Since both in the home and at work the wife has the higher standing, since in the marketplace the Negro male is degraded and at home is humiliatingly dependent, we can predict that he will have destructive responses. Turned outward, they are registered in crimes of violence, against other Negroes as well as against Whitey and the symbols of his dominance—as in the gratuitous destruction of property. And perhaps the high illegitimacy rate—in 1963, 43 percent of all births in Harlem—can be seen as a sign of uncaring, exploitative aggression. Turned inward, he may withdraw self-destructively to a fantasy world induced with the help of narcotics.

Now the parallel I want to draw is not with the most depressed of white, blue-collar families, but with the middle-class families of youth in college. For here, too, the postwar pattern of relationships has changed. Consider the possibility that *un*employment for the blue-collar Negro and *over*employment for white-collar whites may have parallel effects on the children, particularly on boys. One finds some support for this notion in Keniston's study of 12 emphatically alienated Harvard students. "The young man who describes his family situation in early life as a 'father far away and a mother close at hand' summarizes for most of the rest."[15] If this is so, it may help us understand the isolation, the aloneness, the alienation of the young, the disjuncture between generations. And if isolation is felt as rejection, the response may be the repudiation, active and retreatist, that we observe in sensitive college youth.

Recent student groups have felt the impact of a peculiar set of familial influences, subtly altering husband-wife and parent-child relationships. These stem from delayed earning power, breadwinner caught in a life cycle squeeze, fathers often bodily and psychologically absent, increased dependence on mothers (themselves increasingly drawn into the labor force)—all factors posing special problems of identity and maturation for the boy.

For example, take students entering college between 1966 and 1970. Many of their fathers were, for several years, in World War II. Important years were cut out of their lives, and a few felt, additionally, the frustration of the Depression years. Some had education yet to complete. A sense of delayed earning power seems a reasonable inference. And for many, the struggle to get on must have occurred precisely at that point in the life cycle when demands were greatest, income least. A sense of relative deprivation, deferred gratifications that should now be satisfied, a drive to make up for lost time, led to heavy work commitments, making an absentee father out of the breadwinner. Several millions held more than one job.

Harold Wilensky points out that a "growing minority works very long hours while increasing millions are the reluctant victims of too much leisure." But members of this growing minority of long-working, family-absent people are not blue-collar workers. They are predominantly middle-class men who, while they spend less of their life-span working (in part because of years spent in school), yet during their working years spend longer hours on the job. For example, in Wilensky's study of a middle-class Detroit population, 38 percent worked 50 or more hours a week, and 16 percent more than 60 hours![16]

In the case of the Negro, the father's absence and the father-son estrangement stem from rejection by the establishment. For the middle-class white, the repudiation of the absentee father comes from his *being swallowed* by the establishment. This view of the distant and unfamiliar father—overworking, overstriving, supinely selling out to the system—comes through as a common theme in Keniston's study of his alienated Harvard men. Their fathers were well-to-do. They had advanced in income and standing. But as these boys talked about their fathers, the clinical psychologist detected "the tone of disappointment, the implication of 'selling out,' the unseen presence of domestic pressure, and the stated or unstated condescension of these young men for the . . . weakness of their fathers."[17] The corollary is a fix on mother and the problem, acute for the boy, of moving toward adult male identity.*

Isolation from, resentment and repudiation of, the elders are doubtless exacerbated by two other changes affecting family structure: women in the labor force, and divorce. Over a third of married women in the United States work outside the home. (Among all working women, about two thirds are married.) As to divorce, parents of today's youth have a moderately high rate of divorce (3.3 per 1,000 population in 1969). A number will have one twice-married parent. For the highest divorce rates in U.S. history were registered between 1946 and 1948.

Nor do the young exist in the anomic present only because they are isolated from their elders in forum, marketplace, and home. They are isolated from priest and teacher, as well. The parables of Protestantism do not appeal, for they often seem irrelevant, founded as they were on the theological and moral needs of archaic, pastoral communities.

* I believe this is a plausible interpretation of the situation of a minority, significant beyond its small numbers, of upper-middle-class males. It is obviously an interpretation that generalizes far beyond Keniston's nonsample of 12 Harvard students. Hence we need to run up the skeptic's warning flag.

Our schools likewise reveal youth's segregation. In James Coleman's study of 12 high schools, he finds that goals set by peers are significant, not those set by teachers. Social and athletic prowess win the day. Good students, recognizing where the kudos lie, are spun off from the dreary routines imposed by elders, winning the plaudits of their peers in sports and clubs and social life. Across the country, the collegial fellowship of the campus community is eroded. Pressure of numbers acts like a centrifuge, flinging students out to their pads in town. Campuses are ringed with satellite cells of the world remakers and retreatists, "battlers against a computerized educational system in a Jello society dominated by the military-industrial complex," as A. J. Raskin describes them in *The New York Times.* The isolation from their teachers—at least their formal faculty—is symbolized in the establishment of Free Universities, in the extension of off-campus experience, foreign and domestic, and in the burgeoning of national—even international—bodies of right-minded, like-thinking peers. Among some of these youth we find a pattern of intercampus migration, perhaps prompted by the search for self-fulfilling goals. As with many of their teachers, commitment to professional organizations (in this case, organizations of students) supersedes local campus loyalties.

The isolation of the youth sector, then, has roots in major institutions of the social order. Changes in the social order have worked, increasingly, to exclude the young from serious participation in the polity, economy, and family, in education and religion. If a policy of apartheid separates them from their elders, they will be indifferent to the past. Nor can they, from such isolation, fix on the gods and goals remotely and absurdly represented in the fathers.

Understanding movement-generated social change

We have been viewing student revolt as a type of deviance promoting and reflecting social change. We might have looked at crime rates, changes in the sex mores, dramatic and artistic themes, shifts in the labor force, or other possible indices. For example, we might have asked what changing features of our social order are implied by the fact that "most crimes, wherever they are committed, are committed by boys and young men, and that most crimes, by whomever they are committed, are committed in cities."[18] And, of course, one may look elsewhere for the sources of deviant behavior. The psychologist is likely to ask about the protest-prone personality,* using tests of rigidity-flexibility, or making distinctions between emotional and intellectual orientations. Others—for example, some of our legislators—will look for subversive leadership, especially that responding to communist influence.

The notion of scheming subversion bears on the idea that social change is to be understood as the result of a strong leader, benevolent or malevolent. Of course, this explanation of social change is diametrically opposed to the notion that human groups are so constituted as to generate a given quota of deviant behavior and that, with persistent change in social structure, there will emerge a new volume and new types of deviant behavior. We should, therefore, pause to consider this notion of the hero in history, the leader as the engine of social change. Is it plausible to explain the student movement by the leadership qualities of Mark Rudd, or Mario Savio, or Tom Hayden?

The hero as agent of social change

There is a long-standing and beguiling answer to the question of social change: the man of superior endowment shapes the course of history. What the instinct theory is to individual conduct, the great-man theory is to patterns of social action. Not so long ago, and perhaps throughout most of man's history, we interpreted

* See, for example, Kenneth Keniston's article, "The Sources of Student Dissent," in *Journal of Social Issues*, Vol. 23, No. 3 (July, 1967), p. 117. But even here, the protest-prone personality is seen as rooted in social conditions. These students' parents tend to be politically liberal, have higher incomes, more education, and are more often professionals and intellectuals than nonprotesting students' parents. Their religious background is disproportionately Unitarian or Quaker or Reform Judaism. These social factors generate intellectual interests and competence, less anxiety about social status and the like.

There is some inconsistency in the findings on student rebels. Somers, for example, found that student militants were more likely to come from blue-collar families. Likewise, Selvin and Hagstrom found that on their index of libertarianism, students from blue-collar families scored higher. These apparent inconsistencies may reflect a difference between thought and action, attitudes and a willingness to take the risks of injury and jail. See Robert H. Somers, "The Mainsprings of the Rebellion: A Survey of Berkeley Students in November, 1964," in Seymour M. Lipset and Sheldon S. Wolin (eds.), *The Berkley Student Revolt* (New York: Anchor Books, 1965). Also see, in the same volume, Hanan C. Selvin and Warren O. Hagstrom, "Determinants of Support for Civil Liberties."

individual conduct as a simple elaboration of instinctual drives. Similarly, social change was traced as the twisting path whose turns and detours are dictated by the Great Man, the Hero in History. This theory of social change errs as much in its oversimplification, in its fairy tale character, as does the instinct theory of individual development. Tolstoy spoke to this point, and tellingly, in *War and Peace:*

> The higher a man stands on the social ladder, the more people he is connected with and the more power he has over others, the more evident is the predestination and inevitability of his every action.
>
> A king is history's slave. History, that is the unconscious, general, hive life of mankind, uses every moment of the life of kings as a tool for its own purposes.
>
> In historic events, the so-called great men are labels giving names to events, and like labels, they have but the smallest connection with the event itself.
>
> Every act of theirs, which appears to them an act of their own will, is in an historical sense involuntary and is related to the whole course of history and predestined from eternity.[19]

If indeed social change is generated below the surface of society and only echoed in men's leaders, then the commonsense view is wrong. And so, when leaders act at odds with social undercurrents, their deeds should have little effect (induce little or no change). Tables 12.1 and 12.2 showing the views and actions on artificial contraception by diocean priests and the appearance of Pope Paul's encyclical *Humanae vita* (July 29, 1968) may be a striking example, if the data are adequate.*

All this is not to say that popes have no influence, that heroes don't count, or that each man's influence equals every other's. Peo-

* I say "may" because we are uncertain about the characteristics of 60 percent of this national sample of 3,750 diocesan priests who did not respond. The question is whether persons of one persuasion tend, disproportionately, to respond. One attempt to check for bias was made by inspecting postmarks. These showed a fair approximation to the actual geographic distribution of priests, by region and rural-urban distribution. But there was an overrepresentation of pastors and an underrepresentation of parish curates. Since curates more strongly favor the sometimes-permissible view of contraception, results probably underestimate this position. Data were reported in *The National Catholic Reporter*, Vol. 4, No. 49 (October 9, 1968).

Table 12.1
Percent of 1,500 diocesan priests holding and advising that artificial contraception is permissible under certain circumstances

	Before papal encyclical	After papal encyclical
Hold this view personally	51	49*
Advise this view with married Catholics	45	41†

* Plus 1 percent undecided
† Plus 2 percent undecided and 4 percent representing pro and con positions, letting couple decide.

Table 12.2
Percent holding that artificial contraception is permissible under certain circumstances, 1,500 diocesan priests, by role

	Before papal encyclical	After papal encyclical	Difference (leader's effect?)
Pastor	32.5	30.8	−1.7
Priest-teacher	60.0	56.8	−3.2
Curate	69.0	66.0	−3.0

ple do differ. And some combination of personality traits may especially suit certain social requirements.

It is to say, however, that the variance in behavior in two different roles is less to be explained in personality terms than by the differing expectation sets defining the roles. Or in a given role, despite variations in personalities of incumbents, performance will be constrained (and stabilized through time) by the set of expectations defining that role. Furthermore, the higher in the social structure, or the more central the role, the greater the limits and restraints placed upon performance in that role. "A king is history's slave." It is in such terms as these that we can understand why Republican Presidents reverse their former positions on collectivist, welfare-state innovations enacted by Democrats. Before achieving office, such legislation is anathema. From the leader's position, these laws become wise and proper.*

The movement as symptom, society as source of change

Extraordinary behavior—collective behavior is the sociologist's ambiguous term for it—is taken as a clue to the suspension of customary rules and, sometimes, the initiation of new roles and relationships. With students at the barricades, customary routines came to a halt in Paris, in 1968. Some social change ensued: student, teacher, and administrative roles were redefined through the Ministry of Education and the Chamber of Deputies.

Collective behavior embraces a variety of social actions: behavior in mobs and crowds, panics, riots, strikes, and manias.[20] We ask about the conditions, course, and consequences of reform or revolutionary movements, religious or revivalistic movements, fads and fashions.

Such behavior may be contained within the regular processes of the social order. Sometimes it has a periodicity tied to the life cycle: college boys once swallowed gold fish, or stuffed themselves in telephone booths, or, in more general terms, sowed the expected wild oats. Or unusual behaviors may be linked with seasonal changes as in New Year's celebrations, or the Mardi Gras.[21]

But repetitive ripples of deviant conduct are not social change. Social change implies a nonreversing, noncyclical shift in patterns of human relationships. Thus, with the longtime trend toward an urbanized society, we find concomitant redefinitions of relationships in every sphere of life: religious, economic, political, familial; in leisure-time activities; in crime and education; and in science, technology, and the arts.

* Some supporting evidence comes from a study by Dr. Jerome Laulicht of the Canadian Institute for Peace Research. His subjects took the roles of statesmen variously involved in the Vietnam war—Americans, Russians, North and South Vietnamese, *et al.* When these persons, acting in statesmen's roles, approached their decisions, they were advised what certain of the consequences might be—what economic costs might be entailed by such-and-such a decision, how a given decision might affect prospects of reelection, and the like.

Laulicht reported that his actor-statesmen took readily to their roles and persisted in carrying them through, consistently, in accordance with their particular national interests. He reports as "a first general finding that these acting statesmen tended automatically *to keep their decisions within a reasonable range for fear of being stripped of their power*" (Claude Monnier, special reporter at Evian, "World Congress of Sociology: From Vietnam to Project 'Camelot,'" *Journal de Geneve,* September 10, 1966. [italics mine]).

Insofar as movements stem from widespread, deep-rooted and long-standing tensions in the social order, we can reasonably interpret them as indicators of social change in process. The movement itself is seen as the crest of a wave, carried on an invisible flood tide of changes in the rules and in the conduct they govern. Simplistically put, deviant behavior, such as we have seen in the student movement, seems to represent a rejection of the old rules and relationships, and the building of new ones (participant democracy, communes, new patterns of race relations, and the like). There is a retreat from conditions deemed intolerable and a move toward some reformed future. There are frustrated aspirations (with a weakening of old ties) and a seeking for a world (and new relationships) shaped closer to the heart's desire.

Let us revert to the student protest and use it as a case to uncover generic features of change-reflecting, change-inducing movements. We can understand the change implicit in youthful revolt by fixing on four factors at work below the surface: changes in values, norms, social structure, and circumstance (precipitating and facilitating circumstances).

Values—people's conceptions of the desirable—may change as they are displaced, modified or resurrected. Each of these modes of change is represented in the student movement. The unqualified value of premarital chastity is *displaced*. The values represented by the phrase, "respect for the individual," or such terms as "individualism," or "individuality" are *modified* to stress creativity and "doing one's thing." And old values such as peace, and love, and moralistic hatred are *resurrected* and quite unconditionally applied.

Norms—the rules asserting appropriate means for achieving our values—have changed for some in the protest movement. They hold that self-fulfillment, creativity may be achieved through drugs, a practice by no means confined to those under 30. For them, love, spiritual and carnal, may be more freely expressed by virtue of the pill. New norms of conduct are seen in sit-ins, teach-ins, be-ins, in the practice of nonviolent protest on the one hand and, on the other, in norms supporting aggressive action: laudable ends justify any means.

Changes in ends and means are linked with structural changes. One central incongruity in the social structure we have already considered. This is the ostracism of a sector of the population at once more concerned and, on the whole, superior in talent and promise. Another structural feature is the typical heterogeneity of American universities. This makes it possible to draw sharper boundary lines between the "squares," the rebels, and the retreatists.* Especially for the latter two minorities, this is important. For it sustains the identity of the like-minded true believers, thus promoting interaction and the sense of distinctive mission. A third structural feature, especially for the drug-using retreatist, is his position between the incompatible claims of family and peers (see Figure 12.6). These claims tend to be resolved in favor of peers in part because of the immediate pressures exerted by those with whom he deals daily and intensely (in contrast to the remote and sporadic influence of parents). This outcome is doubtless related to another feature of our social structure, its fluidity—the considerable shifting of community and group memberships. (In the year preceding March, 1969, 35.9 million Americans changed residences—18 percent of the total population. About two-thirds of these moved within their county of residence and the rest moved farther.)[22] So for many students there have been two or more breaks: one as the family moved and a second when, as is often the case, the young person goes away to college. There is then a loss of traditional controls embedded in the requirements of familiar relationships. On the other hand, there is the immediacy and frequency of dealings with one's peers. Old bonds unravel. New ties, strongly tinctured with sentiment, are formed. (The development of strong affective ties through intensive interaction is the last requisite stage for conversion to a deviant religious perspective.)[23]

We might note, finally, another feature of our social structure: the discontinuity between the period of dependent apartheid and the ensuing stage of adult independence. The college years are a transitional time between attachment to the family of orientation and the family of procreation, with roles relatively ill-defined during this interregnum. (It's during this same, temporal no-man's land that rates of other deviant behaviors rise, subsiding, then, as the young person is drawn into adult society. See Figure 12.7.)

Of course, there are other relevant changes in social structure that might be noted. Well-to-do, permissive, intellectual, and morally sensitive parents rear children who recoil at brutal aspects of the world beyond the home (and the antiseptic, hands-off posture of the university).[24] We have noted the possible significance for

* Words help define group boundaries. Fraternity and sorority people are "Freddies and Sallies," the others "hippies," "beats," "provos," or "diggers."

Figure 12.6
Counter-demands of parents and peers

Figure 12.7
Arrests for larceny, burglary, and motor vehicle theft*

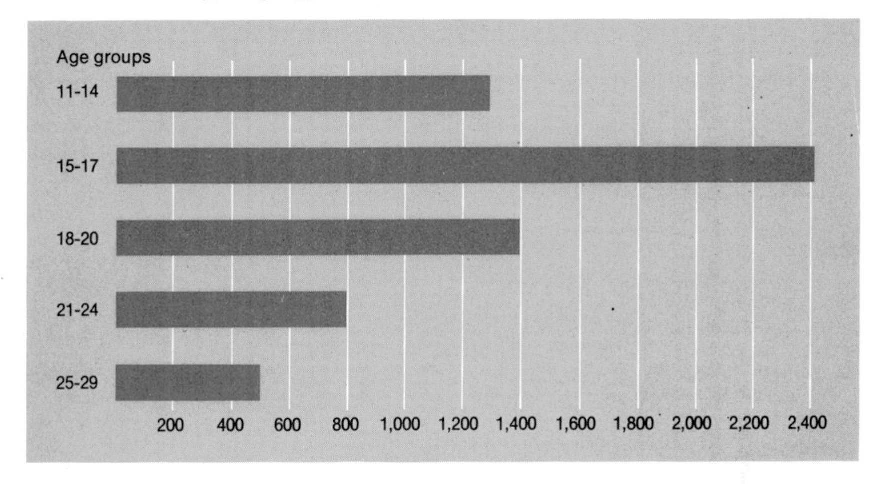

* In 1965, per 100,000 U.S. population.

male rebellion of female-headed, father-absent families (9 percent of white, 29 percent of black families in 1969).[25] There have been changes in the reward structure (family income and the distribution of wealth), in the democratization of the church and its occasional leadership in liberal causes, and in levels of literacy and the availability of mass media. But let us now move on to think about the fourth factor in social movements, the circumstances that trigger them.

Social movements seem often to be actualized by a dramatic

event, some situation that exacerbates deep-flowing discontents or holds out signal hope. Thus, to take our case again, the equality of opportunity sanctioned by the Supreme Court in its 1954 decision excited the demand for its prompt realization. Many students joined the civil rights movement and went into the South to work in voter registration drives. There was our intervention in Vietnam, not billed, originally, as a war, yet a threat to almost every male student in the country. There was, at the same time, the apparent distance between the classroom and such pressing concerns. Then came the cry for relevance in the classroom, and a share in power so as to ensure that relevance. And there are the facilitating circumstances noted before: the sanctuary of the campus and the propitious point in the person's life cycle. In addition, there are the hangers-on, the dropouts, the drug and propaganda hucksters who ring major campuses. They provide hard-core personnel and continuity at points where the demands of academic life would otherwise thin the movement. Finally, there are the police who, when uninformed and uninstructed, incite resentment in the moderate majority. Thus they may recruit new members for the movement.

Research on deviant behavior: student activists

We will conclude our discussion of deviance as an index of social change with a brief consideration of two matters. First, we will look at some research findings on the Free Speech Movement among student activitists at Berkeley. Then a brief summary will review social movements as challenge and change agents.

The student movement includes but a small part of the population. Informed estimates indicate that, at most, only 9 percent of any student body is involved in protest movements. In past years, this change-seeking minority has turned its attention chiefly to civil rights, on-campus living regulations, and Vietnam. But most students do not question current arrangements—not to the point of protest or interference with what they see as a necessary period of preparing for their own careers. In research on the activists at Berkeley, Trent and Craise studied nearly 1,500 college seniors—those among 10,000 high school graduates surveyed in 1959 who had persisted to their fourth college year in 1963.[26] Most of these seniors repeated parental patterns. Politically, they had registered or intended to register in the same party as their fathers. Only 10 called themselves socialists. Interviews revealed them as neither concerned nor sophisticated in political matters. In religion, the

Table 12.3
Arrested members of the Free Speech Movement compared with a national sample and a sample of college seniors at Berkeley on selected aspects of personality (OPI)*

Scale†	National sample (1963) ($N = 1385$)	Berkeley seniors (1965) ($N = 92$)	FSM arrested ($N = 130$)
Thought patterns			
Reflective, abstract thinking	52	55	63
Sense of complexity, ambiguity	51	54	66
Independence of thought	53	61	67
Freedom, imagination in thinking	51	54	64
Concern with beauty and form (aesthetic matters)	51	52	61
Religious liberalism	48	58	64
Lack of anxiety	52	51	48

* Omnibus Personality Inventory
† Some of the scale names have been altered to make them more immediately intelligible.

findings were similar: beliefs and a faith ascribed to parental influence. And in education, while some 30 percent felt that administration and faculty treated students more like children than adults, two thirds thought that regulations governing campus life were "sensible and necessary" and most viewed college as a place to train for a vocation.

There are, then, distinct differences in conception of, and behavior in, the student role. We have heard Keniston's suggestion about peculiarities of religious and familial background that distinguish the activists. What, now, of the personality characteristics cultivated in the socialization process and leading to activism in the student role? Trent and Craise compare 130 Berkeley student activists who were arrested in an FSM protest with a national sample and with Berkeley seniors. Findings are summarized in Table 12.3.

The investigators write:

> The highest scores obtained by the Free Speech members were on the Complexity and Autonomy [independence of thought] scales, indicating they had far more interest in intellectual inquiry, tolerance for ambiguity, objectivity, and independence of thought than the members of the other groups. But the Free Speech members compared with the other students were also marked by their much greater interest in reflective, abstract thinking in the areas of art, literature, music and philosophy, concern with esthetic mat-

ters, and freedom and imaginativeness of thinking. Their high Religious Liberalism score indicated independence from long established religious tradition . . .

The lower scores [on the Anxiety scale] indicate more anxiety than the other groups of students. This may have been a natural reflection of the stress imposed by the legal predicament the Free Speech students were in at the time they were tested. Or it may represent a price paid for the greater intellectual and social commitment they represented in contrast to other college students of their generation.[27]

This is simply a descriptive study to help answer the questions: What are student activists like and how do they differ from their peers? The data yield an ordinal scale with values ascending on the first six items as we move from the national sample, to Berkeley seniors, to the arrested FSM activists. (On the last item, lack of anxiety, the values decline.) These findings are rather at odds with the common stereotype of the thoughtless and insensitive campus activist.

A final note on social movements, deviant behavior, and social change

Student activists are one of a large class of change-inducing efforts called social movements: the labor movement, co-op movement, the women's suffrage and liberation movements, the antislavery and civil rights movements, and many others. Unlike other sorts of deviant behavior—crime, delinquency, cults aiming at personal salvation, alcoholism or drug addiction—social movements are purposive. "Change is a normal aspect [of any modern society] and the social movement is one of the most important ways through which social change is manifest[ed and] . . . produced."[28]

In a given social order, there is always some lack of fit between the complex structure with its underlying values and differentiated functions and the continuous input of traits provided through birth plus socialization and migration. Any social structure is continuously subject to change-inducing tensions—induced by differing values, beliefs, interests, and talents. When tensions between what is and what might be are felt by persons able to communicate—and thus to act in concert to achieve desired change—we have a social movement.

SDS, the civil rights movement, the Planned Parenthood Federation—all such movements build their efforts around some nucleus of values implying new norms of conduct and a rearrangement of relationships in some sector(s) of the social system. As to values, typically we pour new wine into old bottles: the old symbols are retained but reinterpreted. Equality, for example, is no longer *Plessy* vs. *Ferguson* equality (separate but equal). Separateness is seen as intrinsically imposing inequalities. Hence the term comes to mean integration. This requires new rules of conduct and a new patterning of relationships. With the student movement, a traditional value, democracy, is reinterpreted to mean "participant democracy." New rules emerge (norms of conduct): students must share in certain decisions—whom to admit, required courses, and the like. New social arrangements than are needed to implement the rules and achieve the redefined values.

The reinterpreted values animating a social movement are supported by an ideology justifying them. This justification, as Turner and Killian point out, sharpens the distinction between present evil and future good, between enemies and allies, and in the process, rewrites history in such a way as to persuade group members of the inevitability and desirability of the movement's goals.[29] Ideologies tend to freeze commitments. Differences in judgment come to be seen as telltales of treason. Occasional lapses from righteousness are viewed as sure signs of pervasive corruption in the system (thus the hyperbole of student leaders' fulminations against the establishment). In short, the ideologies of movements tend toward bivalued judgments, party lines, simplistically pitting the good guys against the bad.

A movement is organized deviance with a social mission. Clearly, not all members of the movement—converts, reformers, hangers-on—share the same sense of mission. Yet there is a social objective, and in this, movements differ from other sorts of deviance—criminal behavior, for example—which reveal personal, not social objectives.

Some evidence suggests that in a fairly stable social setting rates of individually motivated deviance are quite steady. This, you'll recall, was Erikson's thesis as he compared rates for three successive crime waves in the Massachusetts Bay Colony. And on the assumption of stability—a regular, limited, and adequately socialized input—deviant movements would also be expected to be few and far between. On the contrary, in a growing and complex society (and especially one like ours with permeable boundaries), we can predict higher rates both of personal and social deviance.

This is to suggest, then, that the rate of deviance reflects underlying and uncalculated shifts in the social order creating fault lines that fracture the social structure. These underlying social trends result from hosts of conforming and legitimate individual actions. Yet they can subtly alter the pattern of social life. And they result in unforeseen, certainly unplanned, changes in the patterning of human relationships. It is to these unplanned changes, the subtle shift from past to future, that we turn in the next chapter.

References

TEXT

1. Kai T. Erikson, *Wayward Puritans: A Study in the Sociology of Deviance* (New York: John Wiley & Sons, Inc., p. 13. The Huxley quotation is from *Prisons: The "Carceri" Etchings by Piranesi* (London: Trianon Press, 1949), p. 13.
2. See Walter Bradford Cannon, *The Wisdom of the Body* (New York: W. W. Norton & Co., Inc., 1932), especially the last chapter, and Kenneth Boulding, *The Image* (Ann Arbor: University of Michigan Press, 1956).
3. Erikson, *op. cit.*
4. Private communication from the author.
5. *Ibid.*
6. Erikson, *op. cit.*, p. 179.
7. *Ibid.*, pp. 180, 181. Italics mine.
8. These figures, and those on costs of crime come from the President's Commission on Law Enforcement and Administration of Justice, *The Challenge of Crime in a Free Society* (Washington, D.C.: U.S. Government Printing Office, 1967), pp. 18 and 33.
9. *The New York Times*, July 10, 1969.
10. See Kingsley Davis, "The Sociology of Parent-Youth Conflict," *American Sociological Review*, Vol. 5 (August, 1940), pp. 523–35.
11. Adam Ferguson, *An Essay on the History of Civil Society* (8th ed.; Philadelphia: A. Finley, Publisher, 1819), p. 48.
12. See Everett K. Wilson, "Our Privileged Pariahs," *Antioch Review*, Vol. 26, No. 3 (Fall, 1966), from which much of this argument is taken.
13. See Philippe Aries, *Centuries of Childhood: A Social History of Family Life*, trans. Robert Baldick (New York: Knopf, 1962).
14. See Office of Policy Planning and Research, U.S. Department of Labor, *The Negro Family: The Case for National Action*, (Washington, D.C.: U.S. Government Printing Office, 1965).
    This and a few following paragraphs are taken from Wilson, *op. cit.*
15. Kenneth Keniston, *The Uncommitted: Alienated Youth in American Society* (New York: Harcourt, Brace & World, Inc., 1965), p. 118.
16. Harold Wilensky, "The Uneven Distribution of Leisure," *Social Problems*, Vol. 9, No. 1 (Summer, 1961), p. 33.
17. Keniston, *op. cit.*, p. 115.
18. President's Commission on Law Enforcement and Administration of Justice, *op. cit.*, p. 5.
19. Leo Tolstoy, *War and Peace*, trans. Louise Maude and Aylmer Maude (New York: Oxford University Press, Inc.), Book 9, sec. 1.
20. See Ralph H. Turner, "Collective Behavior," in Robert E. L. Faris (ed.), *Handbook of Modern Sociology* (Skokee, Ill.: Rand McNally & Co., 1964) and, in the same volume, Lewis Killian's essay, "Social Movements." Also, Herbert Blumer, "Collective Behavior," in A. M. Lee (ed.), *New Outilne of the Principles of Sociology* (New York: Barnes & Noble, Inc., 1946), and Neil J. Smelser, *Theory of Collective Behavior* (New York: Free Press, 1963).
21. See Wilbert E. Moore, *Social Change* (Englewood Cliffs, N.J.: Prentice-Hall, Inc., 1963), p. 38, for a graphic description of different models of cyclical change.
22. U.S. Bureau of the Census, "Selected Characteristics of Persons and Families: March, 1969," *Current Population Reports*, Series P–20, No. 189 (Wash-

ington, D.C.: U.S. Government Printing Office, August 18, 1969).

23. John Lofland and Rodney Stark came to this conclusion in their study called "Becoming a World-Saver: A Theory of Conversion to A Deviant Perspective," *American Sociological Review*, Vol. 30, No. 6 (December, 1965). They divide the process of conversion into seven requisite steps. But essentially these entail a disenchantment with the past (frustrated aspirations and no solutions within the old network of relationships), then, with the attentuation of old bonds and a readiness for new ones, the development of strong affective ties to cult members through daily exposure and intensive interaction.
24. See Richard Flacks, "The Liberated Generation: An Exploration of the Roots of Student Protest," *Journal of Social Issues*, Vol. 23, No. 3 (July, 1967).
25. U.S. Bureau of the Census, *op. cit.*, p. 12.
26. James W. Trent and Judith L. Craise, "Commitment and Conformity in the American College," *Journal of Social Issues*, Vol. 23, No. 3 (July, 1967).
27. *Ibid.*, p. 40.
28. Lewis M. Killian, "Social Movements," in Faris (ed.), *op. cit.*, p. 428.
29. See Ralph H. Turner and Lewis M. Killian, *Collective Behavior* (Englewood Cliffs, N.J.: Prentice-Hall, Inc., 1957).

TABLES

12.3 James W. Trent and Judith L. Craise, "Commitment and Conformity in the American College," *Journal of Social Issues*, Vol. 23, No. 3 (July 1967), Table 1, p. 39.

FIGURES

12.1 Erikson, *op. cit.*, pp. 177, 178.

12.2 Bureau of the Census, *Historical Statistics, 1789–1957; Continuation to 1962 and Revisions*, Series A–22 and Series H–412 (Washington, D.C.: U.S. Government Printing Office, 1965), pp. 8 and 1 and pp. 217 and 33, respectively.

12.3 Based on data from Darmstädter, *Handbook of the History of The Natural Sciences and Technology.*

12.4 Joseph Ben-David and Randall Collins, "Social Factors in the Orgins of a New Science: The Case of Psychology," *American Sociological Review*, Vol. 31, No. 4 (August, 1966), based on data on p. 453.

12.5 Bureau of the Census, *Pocket Data Book, U.S., 1967* (Washington, D.C.: U.S. Government Printing Office, December, 1966), Table 133, p. 132; Office of Education, U.S. Department of Health, Education, and Welfare, *Projections of Educational Statistics to 1975–76* (Washington, D.C.: U.S. Government Printing Office, 1966), Table 4, p. 9.

12.7 President's Commission on Law Enforcement and Administration of Justice, *op. cit.*, p. 56.

chapter 13 Social change, unplanned: the subtle drift from past to future

Agriculture, which scatters men in the hinterlands,
unites them without bringing them together.
Trade, which heaps them up in cities,
brings them together without uniting them.*
Bonald, *Oeuvres*, II

If we look at society as a structure, only, we overlook its dynamic aspects. When we take a shot of a building—say Chartres cathedral—we see its structure at an instant in time: foundations, buttresses, towers, vaulting. We don't see seven centuries of decay and destruction—or of repair and rebuilding. So it is with social structures. They, too, are subject to decay, destruction, reshaping—incessantly. Human groups are always in process, changing under strains and tensions from within and without. Change alters the structure, the identity, of the group, and therefore distinctions between it and other groups. Thus social change is a boundary-altering matter. The walls that distinguish one group from another are reshaped.

* See Original Texts, Note 13.1, page 660.

Changes in the social structure

Permeable boundaries and social change

We can think of the walls of social structures as the rules defining distinctive conduct. Insuring the probable fulfillment of reciprocal expectations, they confer group identity, marking one social space off from others. But such social boundaries are permeable. From family to society, no social system is closed. There are always exchanges across the boundaries that open possibilities of social change. The replacement of losses by differently socialized infants and immigrants (Chapters 2 and 3) is a case in point. And the student movement we have just discussed is also an example of a new input into our society—one that redefines the boundaries between postadolescent youth and others. They emerge from backgrounds—familial, religious, social, and economic—different from those of their more conventional predecessors. And they cross over into other social spheres—education, politics, the economy—contributing values redefined and new rules of conduct leading to a re-forming of the social structure.

A change in the rules that mark group boundaries means a redefinition of roles—parent, child, citizen, worker, student, communicant. This entails a change in relationships: father-son, teacher-student, priest-parishioner, employer-worker, governor-governed. And this in turn means a change in that structure of relationships which is the group. Finally, at the societal level, social change implies a persisting shift in social patterns. It is not the ephemeral change of fads and fashions, or the cyclical change seen in daily, weekly, or seasonal shifts in behavior and affiliations.

Social change, then, implies the permeability of human groups, rendering traditional patterns vulnerable to challenge. Change means that the group's identity is altered as distinctions (boundaries) between it and others are redrawn. And for society, boundaries between past and present are redefined as, all unwittingly, increments of change amass, subtly altering the structure of men's relationships.

Change as the converse of group maintenance

At least since the time of Comte, social analysis has often been split into statics and dynamics. But this analytical dichotomy would be misleading were we to think that understanding the one had nothing to do with illuminating the other. Explanations of stability and change are related. To ask—and to answer—the question: How is the group sustained? is also to ask and answer its opposite: How does it change? For social change is the other side of the coin from group maintenance. If we know what holds the group together, then, other things equal, we also know what weakens the ties that bind. If isolation promotes group unity, then contact threatens its cohesion. If a range of relationships with the same others promotes social integration, then single relationships with a series of different others erodes that unity. If a strong kinship network, or the threat of an external enemy, or a distinctive language, or the pervasive influence of the sacred, dominating most of life's transactions—if these contribute to social stability, then their opposites promote change:* declining significance of the blood bond, amicable relationships with outsiders, loss of language barriers, or an increasingly secular orientation. Hence our analysis of social *structure* provides clues to the source of social *change*.

Sources of social change

The meaning of social change becomes clearer if we conceptualize a society (or a smaller group within it) as a complex mix of roles, differentiated from others by whatever is distinctive in their combination. Its boundaries being permeable, the group changes to the extent that input doesn't match output. Social change, then, is the result of a novel mix at the intersection of input and output (see Figure 13.1).

Change would not occur were there a precise replacement in every role and relationship. If input and output matched perfectly, we would have a homeostatic (steady-state) condition in the social system. For several reasons, this is never the case. Consider four.

First, the net *quantity* of input seldom if ever remains constant. As a result, frequency of interaction changes. The likelihood of fruitful (innovative) encounter changes. And patterns of organi-

* Obviously this is not to suggest that in the absence of one particular definition of the sacred (or of kinship, or of "enemy"), or in the absence of a single social mechanism for reaffirming the sacred, group cohesiveness will suffer. There *are* functional alternatives.

Figure 13.1
Change at the social crossroads

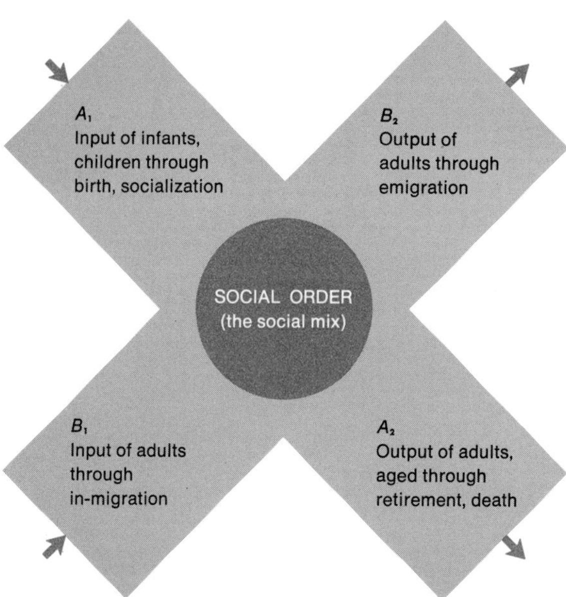

zation change. Second, *quality* of input differs from output due to inevitable differences in the socialization of newcomers, native-born or migrants. The new crew or the new shift or the new generation or the newcomers invariably differ from those they replace. Third, change-inducing tensions are regularly introduced as socialization creates *inequities in the reward structure* of the group. Inevitably, we find differences between the distribution of valued things and the distribution of worth or competence—however these are assessed by different groups. Finally, social change is stimulated as *extended education generates change-inducing tensions* through science and technology.

Since all these sources of change are maximized in urban areas, we shall conclude this chapter by looking at the city as locus and symbol of social change.

Quantity of input

Marked change in population size—growth or decline—has at least two effects. It alters the probability of change-inducing combinations of beliefs and behavior. And it affects the character of social organization. It makes a difference, both to receiving and exporting communities, that 36.5 million, nearly 1 in 5 persons, moved their place of residence between 1969 and 1970. It makes a difference that Nevada has about 4 persons per square mile and Manhattan more than 75,000. And it makes a difference that, in the decade 1950–60, Los Angeles' population increased by a quarter million blacks and 2 million whites.[1]

Increase in community size means a necessary change in the social structure.

> Never before [has it been] possible for an individual human being to come into physical contact in an hour's time, whether by walking or by riding a wheeled vehicle, with so many other individuals. And never before have the problems of organization, on the one hand, and of adjustment to the land, on the other hand, been so numerous and so difficult of solution.[2]

Other things equal, population increase means a broader range of attributes and of the chances of their encounter. Indeed, it requires the confronting of differences. Ideas are generated, the intellect is stimulated, emotion is expressed, Dewey suggested, when the smooth, ongoing tenor of life is interrupted. It is at the point of some obstacle, some intrusion, that we are faced with a problem and the need for its solution. *Large population increments guarantee a novel mix of ingredients and of the problems, challenges, and opportunities arising from them. The result is often change,* for innovation is the fruitful union of complementary elements. If all units of a system were alike, we would have that situation described by the preacher in Ecclesiastes: "The thing that hath been, it is that which shall be; and that which is done is that which shall be done: and there is no new thing under the sun."

A change-inducing lack of match between losses and replacements may be triggered from the output side. Heavy mortality in wartime affects age and sex structure for several generations. This may be reflected in altered marriage and family patterns and in the structure of the labor force. A regular decline in output through death (lowered infant mortality and extended longevity) means a change in the age composition of the group, an increase in young and old. This has happened in our society, entailing changes in preschool patterns. It has also meant problems of support of the aged and their accommodation in families now neolocal and no longer geared to embrace three generations.

Table 13.1

Traits	Possible combination							
	1	2	3	4	5	6	7	8
X	+	+	+	−	−	−	−	+
Y	+	+	−	−	−	+	+	−
Z	+	−	−	−	+	+	−	+

Quality of input

Varying input through socialization

Because of the unique socialization of each person, input and output never match. Every child is a new product. Except for the rare case of monozygotic twins, no two people are or ever were identical. Almost every person, then is a biological innovation derived from the differing but complementary germ plasm of his parents. In his organic makeup he develops unique attributes at the confluence of two genetic streams. The word *confluence*—or intersection, or conjunction—is the significant word. For inventive change is a crossroads phenomenon. And not only does the person represent a unique conjunction of genetic influences. He is a social crossroads, the conjuncture of a unique and complex set of influences.

Take as an example the unrealistically simple case where people may have, or lack, each of two traits, *X* and *Y*. A person may have both, lack both, have *X* without *Y* or *Y* without *X*. To put it differently, with two traits that may be either absent or present (with no in-between degrees), the possible combinations or varieties of traits (and, thus, of men) would be represented by 2^2. Were there three traits and, again, if each could only be present or absent, we would have the possible combinations shown in Table 13.1, with + representing the presence and − the absence of the trait. Thus with three traits, each present or absent, the possible combinations can be represented by 2^3. With 10 traits, again either present or absent, 2^{10} gives us 1,024 different sorts of persons. If this seems to exaggerate the case, since not all combinations are equally likely, we need to remember that 10 traits scarcely exhausts the attributes of a person. Using our stipulated present-absent scheme, for example, we might list such traits as: male-female, over-under age 20, U.S. citizen or not, Buddhist or not, blue-collar–white-collar, veteran-nonveteran, high school graduate or not, poor or not, Southerner or Northerner, and so on. Clearly the range of attributes is not restricted, in reality, to such simple dichotomies. Even including sex, there are intermediate grades or degrees. Human variables are typically continuous, not discrete. And, again, permutations of 10 traits do not begin to reflect the diversity of men as focuses of unique networks of social influence.

What has such diviersity got to do with social change—changes in the structure of groups? If maintenance of the group depends on the maintenance of given relationships, if these relationships depend upon like performance in roles, if the same performance in roles depends on the same socialization, if the same socialization depends upon the same social and cultural exposures, and if, finally, there is no such thing as the same social-cultural exposure, then there must be a constant erosion of group-maintaining influences.

This is the case and this is the point. Always and everywhere groups are replenished by persons whose background must differ, however slightly, from those they replace. The group's problems are continually confronted by a changing collective "mix" that makes for changing solutions. Thus there is a constant tension in the system stemming from the shifting kaleidoscope of social configurations that characterize the human input, whether through the socialization of the native-born or the varying input of attributes of the in-migrant.

Varying input through migration

The encounter of differing backgrounds, interests, and talents can lead to social change—through conflict, accommodation, and assimilation. Immigrants have not only been assimilated to patterns of American society: they have changed those patterns. (*Perspectives in American History* documents the impact of immigrant European scholars—von Neumann, Lazarsfeld, Adorno, *et al.*—on science and education in the United States.)[3] Clearly, not intellectual eminence alone, but a great range of traits among newcomers may stimulate social change: differences in language, in occupational skills, in education, in religion (even within Catholicism we have variations: Spanish, Italian, Irish), in moral positions (for example, positions on installment buying, the woman's role, the relationship of children to parents), and in politics. With high immigrant input we may find suspicion and exploitation of the vulnerable newcomers, segregation in homogeneous "alien" enclaves, so delaying assimilation and challenging customary social patterns. And, of course, rural-urban migrants have changed the social structure of the city. (Consider the case of Negro and Puerto Rican migrants to Chicago and New York.)

The significance of mobility does not lie in the mere movement of bodies through space. It resides in the contact, the intersection of differing ideas, values, standards, and behaviors. This being the case, changes in input may be impersonally conveyed through the mass media. Magazines, radio, and television have allegedly exerted, with their national coverage, a leveling influence. This suggests that there is something to be leveled, that differences exist; and indeed rural and urban, North and South, East and West do present differences. The impact of common media on a noncommon base may well generate impulses toward change. These media constitute themselves a crossroads where differing views and values intersect. Through them, urban mores penetrate the rural countryside. Through printed word, radio, and television, the more cosmopolitan coastal areas reach the hinterlands.

The mass media may move the literate young more than their elders. Patterns of parent-child relationship may be altered when the rate of change conveyed through the media is so great that the child lives in a world different from that of his parents. This is what happens with migrants when the parents are in a position of marginal people, suspended between two worlds, leaning toward the old while their children identify clearly with the new world. More generally, perhaps, this happens when the encounter of ideas promotes cultural accretion at such a rate as to transform the world between generations. From moon shots to morals, communication may be impeded, parent-child relationships altered.

The significance of migration and contact is better understood if we look at their opposites. The most effective bulwark against change is isolation, a situation in which both volume and type of input approximate output. Reflect, in passing, on one such stable, change-resisting group in which these conditions roughly hold. These are the Hutterites.

Control of input and resistance to change: the Hutterites

In his study of the Hutterites, Eaton called them "an island of stability and security in a river of change."[4] His analysis highlights the importance of isolation (and control over socialization) as conditions for matching output with input, thus inhibiting social change.

Except for 108 converts and their children, the descendants of this often-persecuted sect (originating in Switzerland around 1528) are the cultural legatees of about 50 Hutterite families who came to the United States between 1874 and 1877. In 1951, there were about 8,700 of them living in 93 communal groups, thus averaging about 94 per hamlet. From the beginning, the religion of a small, threatened minority sect has been a strong integrating factor, promoting communication within the group and inhibiting communication between its members and outsiders. They believe themselves a chosen people living in the only way that is truly Christian: simply, pacifically, communally, and, so far as they can manage it, *in isolation* from the corrupting influences of the external social order.

The economy is a communal, agrarian one, with but few possessions personally owned. Since a colony numbers fewer than 100, their dealings with one another are of the primary sort, maximizing multibonded relationships (relationships, in different roles, with the same others). The family is chiefly an affectional and procreative unit (median number of children was 10 per family around 1950), the induction of the young—their socialization—being a widely diffused community responsibility. In a way one may conceive the group as theocratically totalitarian. I use the term in a descriptive, not a derogatory sense. It means that no gross deviations from the central value system are tolerated, and that each generation is systematically indoctrinated to believe and behave in accordance with Hutterite traditions. There is little class differentiation: the range of prestige, privilege, and power is quite narrow. In everything essential, members of the group share a common lot.

Observers have remarked the serenity of their lives,[5] the rarity of crime and—although this is less certain—of mental disorder, the virtual absence of suicide or divorce or quarreling—features whose rising rates signal social change. The absence of these behaviors and the persistence of traditional ways point to an extraordinarily cohesive and stable community.

Input in this group has been almost exclusively through birth and effective socialization procedures. Social change is much less likely under these circumstances than where the input is through immigration. Contrast the situation of the Hutterite hamlet with that of New York City, where, on the zero years of the decades 1870 through 1910, inclusive, there were 0.6, 0.6, 0.9, 1.3, and 1.9

million foreign-born, respectively.[6] (Of these, in 1910, 13 percent were from Ireland, 14 percent from Germany, 17 percent from Italy, 23 percent from Russia, 12 percent from Austria-Hungary, with the rest coming from 13 other sources.)[7]

But, of course, it is almost impossible to maintain the isolation that enables a group to retain complete control over the socialization process. The Hutterites are no exception. Military service, the pressure to attend public schools and to stay longer in them, the use of farm machinery and trucks entailing contacts with outsiders, dealings with agricultural experts and other government emissaries—these are influences that compromise effectively controlled acculturation. Such influences make it impossible to match performance in the roles of departing incumbents. Social change is generated at the crossroads where Hutterite and alien ways intersect. It is at these crossroads that we confront the strange, the bizarre, the intriguing, the desirable, creating problems of choice and justification. (Five percent of the living Hutterite males over 15 years of age had chosen, as of 1950, to leave their communal groups.)

The Hutterite case is unusual. Most groups in our society are more permeable at their boundaries, less effective in their socialization. In the usual American community, open migration and booming fertility with declining mortality often mean a marked increase in the input of newcomers, straining facilities for socialization, assimilation, and maintenance. Neither home nor school, churches, social work agencies, police or other protective services, may be equipped to assimilate the newcomers and so sustain preexisting social patterns. Hence social change.

The distribution of opportunity, competence, and rewards: a source of strain toward change

Rewards are tied to roles. Power, prestige, and income vary with one's role in civic affairs, with occupational, familial, and other roles. Now one can conceive what is doubtless untrue: that some time, somewhere, there was a precise fit between competence, conscientiousness, and contributions of group members and the rewards they received. But ours is a complex social system, with thousands of occupational roles, diverse family forms, differing conceptions of civic rights and obligations, and the like. And each candidate to succeed his predecessors in these innumerable slots is like no one else who ever lived. So, in a society like ours, it is inconceivable that an appropriate match between competence, contribution, and reward could be sustained—if indeed it ever existed.

Hence we should expect to find some people comparable in competence, yet quite differently rewarded. Conversely, people differing considerably in competence and contributions may yet be given like rewards. Such discrepancies might be expected to generate tensions and stimulate change, for each entails an intimation of inequity. (If, additionally, we link race, religion, or national origins with such discrepancies, the potential for change becomes more obvious.)

But inequity takes another, virtually universal form. (It *is* inequity assuming that we take as good an equal chance in life for everyone.) In the crucial years of early life, children differ drastically in their opportunities for growth.* In the spheres of politics, work, and education, Western societies have moved slowly toward equality of opportunity. But the family remains a sacrosanct domain, whether destitute or bountifully endowed. While outright nepotism is disparaged, it is a sign of laudable parental concern that fortune and advantage should be bestowed on children of the well-to-do. But children with high potential are less likely to actualize their talents when they come from homes that can't provide the means or motivation for success in school, or work, or later family life—however success may be defined.

Therefore, there is inevitably a stratum of the able dispossessed.

We have, then, the possibility of class conflict, the conflict between categories of persons who have, in Weber's phrase, different life chances—in this case, gratuitously conferred by the accident of birth. If other affiliations or identities reinforce poverty, the potential for social change will be the greater. For change becomes more certain when we add the deprivation of minority group membership, political impotence, inferior education, menial work roles, discriminatory legislation, plus two other circumstances: awareness of the American creed with its ideal of equality of opportunity and a self-consciousness enabling people to transform a category into a militant group.

Because of this variance in motivation, aspiration, and means of growth—differences mediated by families through the sociali-

* This apparently is not the case in a kibbutz studied by Melford Spiro. Here the children, almost from the time of birth, are put under the care of nurses and teachers, all receiving the same care and nurture. See his *Children of the Kibbutz* (New York: Schocken Books, Inc., 1965).

zation process—potentials for conflict and change are inescapable aspects of Western societies. The extent, intensity, and violence of change are moderated by a number of social conditions: the extent to which education can compensate for initial deprivation in the family, legislation ruling out capricious discrimination, group memberships and identities that do *not* overlap (muting the effect of reinforcing affiliations among the deprived), and social mobility. Dahrendorf says: "There is an inverse relation between the degree of openness of classes and the intensity of class conflict. The more upward and downward mobility there is in a society, the less comprehensive and fundamental are class conflicts likely to be."[8]

Karl Marx, as we know, saw social change as stemming from antagonistic class interests. But these antithetical interests were rooted, not in inherited familial conditions, but in the social organization of work. Workers were increasingly alienated from the means of production, ever more helpless at the hands of bourgeois owners. As I indicated on page 343, Marx did not believe that evolutionary change could forestall a radical revision of the social order. The gap between the privileged and the dispossessed would grow. And as in a thunderstorm the mounting electrical charge is resolved by a stroke of lightning, so would a revolution clear away the intolerable tension between bourgeoisie and exploited proletariat. For example, Marx writes:

> The mode of production of material life determines the general character of the social, political and spiritual processes of life. It is not the consciousness of men that determines their being, but, on the contrary, their social being determines their consciousness. At a certain stage of their development, the material forces of production in society come in conflict with the existing relations of production [the increased power of bourgeois owners and the declining power of a multiplying labor force]. From forms of development of the forces of production these relations turn into their fetters. Then occurs a period of social revolution. . . . In broad outline we can designate the Asiatic, the ancient, the feudal and the modern bourgeois modes of production as progressive epochs in the economic formation of society. The bourgeois relations of production are the last antagonistic form of the social process of production; not in the sense of individual antagonisms, but of conflict arising from conditions surrounding the life of individuals in society.[9]

The Communist Manifesto stated:

> The modern bourgeois society that has sprouted from the ruins of feudal society has not done away with class antagonisms. It has but established new classes, new conditions of oppression, new forms of struggle in place of the old ones.
>
> Our epoch, the epoch of the bourgeoisie, possesses, however, this distinctive feature; it has simplified the class antagonisms. Society as a whole is more and more splitting up into two great hostile camps, into two great classes directly facing each other: Bourgeoisie and Proletariat.[10]

A century after Marx we can see that the antagonisms of bourgeoisie and proletariat have prompted change, but evolutionary rather than revolutionary. On the current scene, differing life chances determined by the accident of birth may lead to roles that are out of line with personal competence and social creed. Such differences sow the seeds of social change. But the change is slow, evolutionary, not instanter. Even revolutionary change (to say nothing of revolutionary slogans) is deceptive. A veneer of the new disguises a persisting heritage from the past.

The increase of knowledge

One theory finds social change emerging from the stress between different change rates characterizing the material and the nonmaterial culture, the former tending always to outpace the latter.[11] Especially as a result of spiraling technological developments, adaptive changes are required in the major institutional spheres: household appliances alter the wife's role and marital and parental relationships; contraceptive devices entail reconsideration of the church's doctrinal position; computers, calculators, and probability sampling have repercussions in politics.

But there are difficulties with this theory and its formulation. It is not always clear that changes in the nonmaterial sphere follow rather than precede or act concurrently with technological change. (The women's suffrage movement may have lent impetus to the invention of laborsaving devices to liberate her from a more restricted, household-anchored role.) The terms of the proposition are not coordinate: all culture, being immortal, is nonmaterial, a condition of its transmissibility from generation to generation. But what Ogburn points out is unquestionably true: when, among the interwoven aspects of the cultural fabric, some aspects change more rapidly than others, there is a strain toward adaptive social change.

But what is it that is changing when Ogburn speaks of the rapid rates of growth of material culture? Behind technology is science, and behind the rapid rate of scientific development is an immense educational system. Freed from the need to put every able-bodied person to the task of providing food, clothing, and shelter—this liberation itself being an achievement of science (knowledge) through technology—a large part of modern populations can invest their time in education, so contributing more to science and to its payoff in technology. What is changing, then, is the production of knowledge through the social mechanism of education.

Thus it becomes intelligible to say that the great increase in education in our society will have repercussions in other social spheres.* An input of knowledge, greatly altered in volume and type, has two change-inducing effects. On the negative side, it breaks the monopoly of past ways; for it reduces the assurance with which we rely on old rules and the roles they govern. On the positive side, knowledge (through technology) creates new circumstances and the rules and roles to fit them.

Challenges old certitudes

Why the paradox: with more knowledge, less certainty in knowing? It is because additional knowledge, like additional points on a scale, complicates our readings of reality. When our scale has just two values, big-little, many-few, good-bad, we can sort things, events, and persons into these categories with deceptive ease. We make relatively few mistakes in assigning to the appropriate scale point. (But, of course, when we do make a mistake it's a 100 percent error.) When, on the other hand, the scale is finely graduated,

* Most of the knowledge gained through education is tradition perpetuating and system sustaining. Yet an increasing part of the educational product has gone into the production of new knowledge. Consider, for example, these statements. "Using any reasonable definition of a scientist, we can say that 80 to 90 percent of all the scientists that have ever lived are alive now . . . any young scientist, starting now and looking back at the end of his career upon a normal life span, will find that 80 to 90 percent of all scientific work achieved by the end of the period will have taken place before his very eyes, and that only 10 to 20 percent will antedate his experience . . . if any sufficiently large segment of science is measured in any reasonable way, the normal mode of growth is exponential . . . the crude size of science, in manpower or in publications, tends to double within a period of 10 to 15 years. . . . Roughly speaking, every doubling of the population has produced at least three doublings of the number of scientists" (Derek J. deSolla Price, *Little Science, Big Science* [New York: Columbia University Press, 1963], chap. i, *passim*).

with scores of points, then we often make an inaccurate reading, although the error is unlikely to be as great.

In modern societies the rate of information exchange has so increased, the permutation of ideas has proceeded at such a rate, that precisely this development has occurred. Cognitions cannot, therefore, have the simple certainty they once enjoyed. The probability of error is greater. The size of the error is, in probability, smaller. The greater the refinement of our knowledge, the less our certainty. To put it the other way around, certainty varies directly with isolation. Isolation and its concomitant ignorance are the great bulwarks of certainty.

Uncertainty in knowing is accompanied by uncertainty in believing. If instead of the dichotomy, capitalism-socialism, we have a gradient in which the one shades imperceptibly into the other, how can our convictions be as unqualified as would otherwise be the case? (If by socialism we mean a degree of control by the public over the major productive forces in a society, then the United States is clearly socialistic to some degree and England capitalist to some extent. What shall we say of a situation like that in Canadian railways where one line is run by the government, the other operated under private auspices?) The refinement of knowledge promoted by rapid exchange of information has affected the certainty of our convictions as well as our cognitions.

This leads to the point. The ever accelerating input of knowledge shatters certainties in cognition and conviction. The expectations defining roles are clouded. And the structure of relationships built on such roles must become unstable, shifting—both symptom and source of social change.*

Promotes science, technology, and social change

While new knowledge undermines the past, it fashions a new future. The dramatic evidence lies in technology—moon shots, laser beams, controlled explosions of atomic energy. But technology stems from the more general knowledge embodied in science. Science, in turn, is nourished by an expanded system of education. And the stress on education hinges on the value we attach to transmitting and producing knowledge.

* The erosion of moral certainties (promoted in part by science's limited ability to answer the question: What *ought* to be?) has doubtless prompted many young people to seek other sources of "knowledge"—Zen Buddhism, the alleged expansion of consciousness through drugs, McLuhan, Marcuse, and lesser lights.

Table 13.2
Selected indicators of change in the United States

Item	Circa 1870	Circa 1950	Change
Population* (total, millions)	39.8	150.7	+110.9
Labor force* (total, millions)	12.9	64.7	+ 51.8
Labor input†			
Total (millions man-years)	16.5	48.0	+ 31.5
Agricultural	9.4	7.6	− 1.8
Nonagricultural	7.1	40.4	+ 33.3
Horsepower hours of energy†			
Total (billions)	27.8	410.4	+382.6
Mineral fuels and water supply	3.2	386.2	+383.0
Work animals	20.3	12.1	− 8.2
Human workers	4.3	12.1	+ 7.8
Distribution of labor force* (percent)	100.0	100.0	
Production of physical goods	75.0	46.0	− 29.0
Services	25.0	54.0	+ 29.0
Per capita gross national product*			
Current prices	$165	$1,876	+$1,711
Constant prices (1929)	$223	$1,233	+$1,010

* U.S. Bureau of the Census, *Historical Statistics of the United States, Colonial Times to 1957* (Washington D.C.:, U.S. Government Printing Office, 1960).
† Frederick Dewhurst and Associates, *America's Needs and Resources* (rev. ed.; New York: Twentieth Century Fund, 1955).

The influence, of course is reciprocal. For science stimulates, enables, and requires the production of knowledge. Extended formal education is the product of a society so organized and with such a culture base that a large sector of the population can be released from the labor force. Fifty-five million persons were enrolled in educational institutions in 1965—about 28 percent of our population—and the projected figure for 1975 is 63 million.[12] In the 50-odd years between 1910 and 1962, the number of young people between 14 and 17 years of age enrolled in school increased by 77 percent. Institutions of higher education more than doubled in number (from 951 to 2,132). Illiteracy was cut by two thirds in the same period.[13]

Advances in science and technology are implicit in most of the indices of change shown in Table 13.2. This accounts for the continuous decline in agricultural labor while farm production has steadily increased. The expansion of knowledge, registered in technology, is likewise implied by the hundredfold increase in energy production, the shift to inanimate power sources, the increase of the gross national product (per capita), and the shift in the labor force from production of physical goods to service occupations.

The city as locus, source, and symbol of change

More than any other human grouping, cities exemplify the change-inducing forces we have been discussing.* Input has not equaled output, in quantity or kind. Here the great range in man's condition is most clearly visible: cultivation and ignorance, compassion and brutality, slum squalor and sybaritic living. And it is clear that such differences in rewards are often due, not to differences in merit or potential, but to the accident of birth. Hence, given the value placed on equality of opportunity, the strong strain to alter institutions to provide compensatory opportunity. Finally, more than elsewhere, education, science, and technology flourish in the urban centers, creating impulses toward change.

To speak of the city is to imply a contrast with the country. A characteristic of the one often has its obverse in the other: in fertility, population density, relativity of standards, and the like. And as Figure 13.2 indicates, growth for one has meant relative decline for the other. Increasingly, population has clustered in metropolitan areas (65 percent in 1969). In 1890, it took something over a third of U.S. counties to embrace 75 percent of our population. In 1960, fewer than a fourth of them contained three fourths of the population.[14] Most of the population increase (80 percent) between 1960 and 1969 was in metropolitan areas.[15] Some of this was due to natural increase—births minus deaths. Some was due to immigration. But much was due to the "export" of people from rural to urban areas. Figure 13.3 shows that natural increase has been declining in the farm population and that, in the last 42 years with the exception of three, there has been a net migration loss. Large numbers of these migrants leaving farm areas have moved into the orbit of metropolitan centers.

The ever increasing prominence of "urbanism as a way of life" (the phrase is the title of an influential essay by Louis Wirth) points to a time dimension in the urban-rural contrast. For in many ways the city represents present and future, as rural areas represent the past in our society. This quantitative shift has entailed qualitative changes. For more than a century sociologists

* Take the word *city* as shorthand for urbanization, especially as seen in major metropolitan areas. We can no longer think of cities in our society as populous islands in a rural sea. Cities and contiguous areas hang together to form ever-growing metropolitan centers whose influence extends far beyond their boundaries.

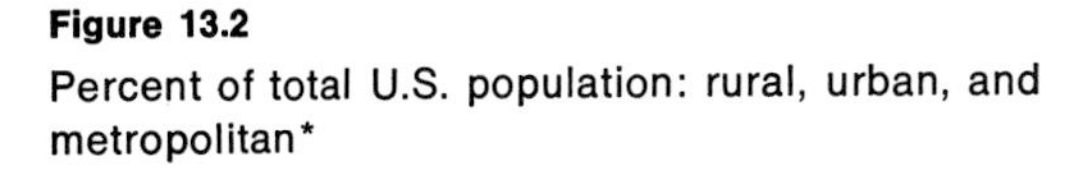

Figure 13.2
Percent of total U.S. population: rural, urban, and metropolitan*

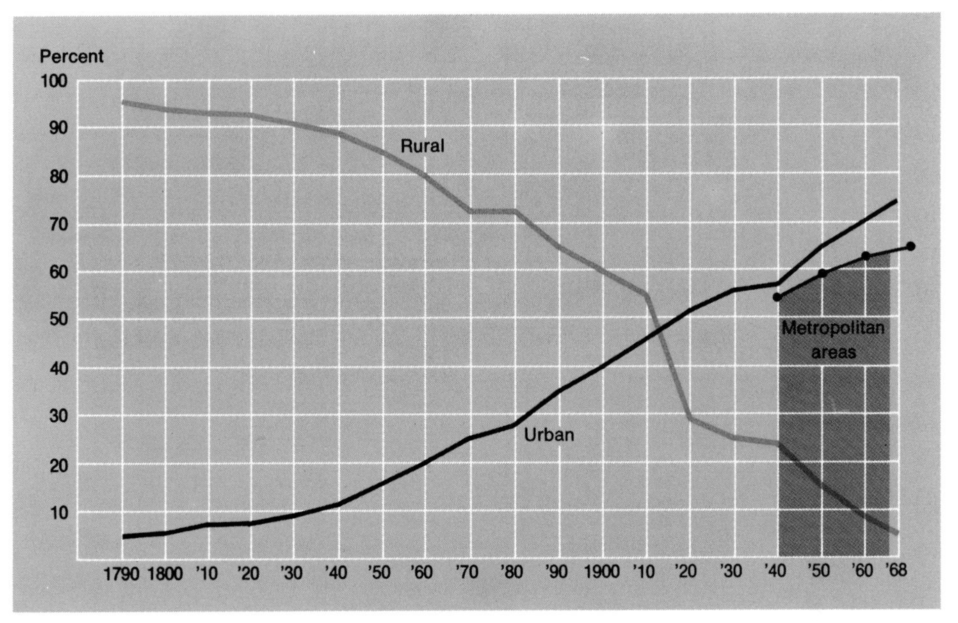

* A "Standard Metropolitan Statistical Area" (SMSA) is defined as a county, or a cluster of contiguous counties, containing at least one city—or a twin city—of 50,000 population, plus adjacent counties if they are chiefly urban and industrial in their social and economic characteristics and are integrated with the central city. Before 1950, "urban" meant incorporated places with populations of 2,500 or over. The definition of urban changes slightly for the 1950 and 1960 censuses. In 1920, a distinction was made between "rural farm" (represented in this figure) and "rural nonfarm." The 1968 figure refers to "farm population."

have tried to uncover the essential social meaning of urbanization. Herbert Spencer saw the change through time (terminating in a society represented by his London) as one from simplicity, homogeneity, and slight role differentiation to one characterized by great complexity, heterogeneity, and a highly developed division of labor. For Sir Henry Maine, the change was from a life dominated by tradition, roles being defined by ties of kin and clan, to relationships based on reciprocal interest, contractually sealed. Ferdinand Tönnies, used the terms *gemeinschaft* (community) and *gesellschaft* (society) to describe the shift from a society whose members were bound by kinship ties—a common ancestry and bonds of blood—to the great society, more individualistically oriented, with political and economic interests superseding blood ties as determinants of roles. Durkheim describes social change from a mechanical articulation of roles but little differentiated (as in simple rural settings) to a system of highly differentiated parts, bound together as in an organism. Park, Burgess, Wirth, and Redfield are among the American sociologists who have seen social change in large measure along the rural-urban axis.

Rural life, dominated by traditional rules, provided roles commonly determined by familial identity. With increased control over his destiny, man—and preeminently urban man—has rejected ascription as a basis for defining his lot in life. When his social legacy spells deprivation, he moves to alter social institutions. The broader diffusion and exponential increase of knowledge makes him more sensible, both of his present state and his possible future. Such awareness is a mainspring of social change. We see these conditions at work in the case of the urban Negro.

The city vividly exemplifies change-inducing influences in the case of the Negro. First, volume of input has been large, unbalanced by movement to rural or suburban areas. In 1969, 70 percent of the Negro population was in metropolitan areas, most living in the central cities. (Only 1 out of 25 million—4 percent—lived on farms.)[16] In regions outside the South above 90 percent of the Negro population was urban.[17] Thus any statement made about Negroes in America is a statement about an urban population—and a population most of which was recently urbanized.

Second, Negro migrants have differed markedly from most of the receiving group—in poverty, training, and vulnerability. The contrasting characteristics of this urban input are seen in every phase of life. For example:

Family

1. Broken families—23 percent of urban Negro women who have ever been married are separated or divorced or living apart from their husbands.
2. Indications are that "only a minority of Negro children reach age 18 having lived all their lives with both their parents."
3. Illegitimacy complicates parent-child relationships. Illegitimacy rates went from 3.5 percent to 9.7 percent in the period 1940 to 1968. (But while Negroes are 11 percent of the population, they have 54 percent of the illegitimate births.)

Economy

1. Unemployment is high: Among Negro men in the labor force, over a fourth are unemployed at some time during the year.

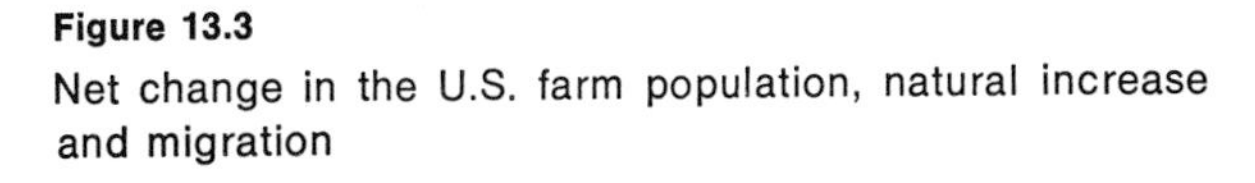

Figure 13.3
Net change in the U.S. farm population, natural increase and migration

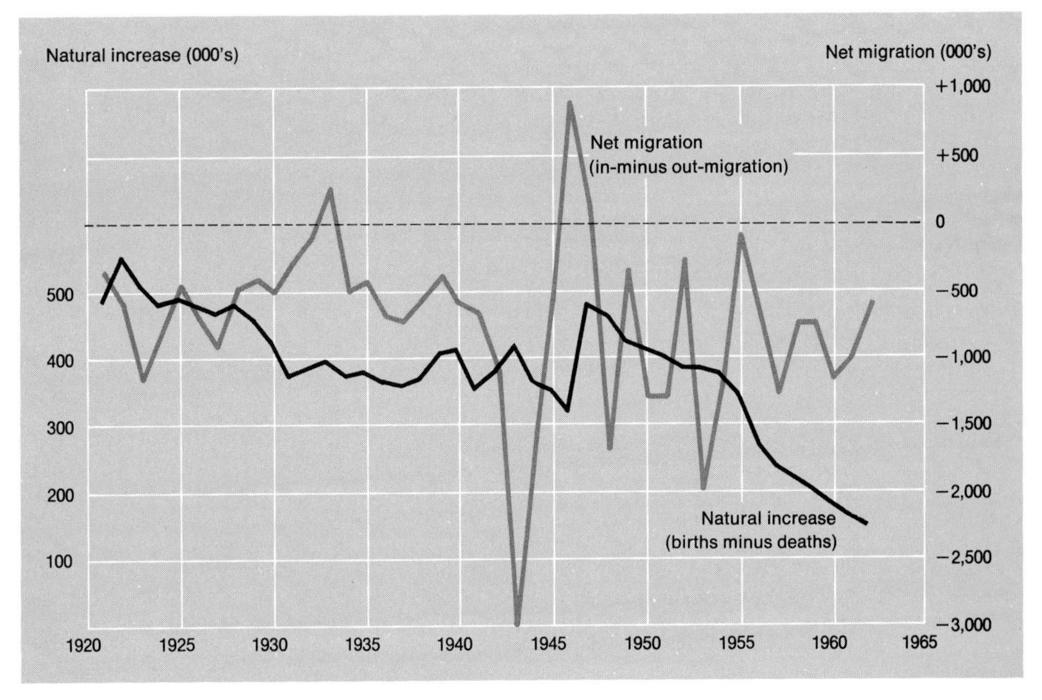

2. Income is low: The ratio of nonwhite to white median family incomes, was .60 in 1968.
3. Work and family are linked in various ways. For example, nonwhite unemployment rates vary directly with illegitimacy rates (1963 data for Washington, D.C.). And, to put it the other way around, median income varies inversely with illegitimacy rates. Family income varies inversely with number of children per nonwhite mother. In the 35–39 age category, in 1960, where the income was under $2,000, nonwhite mothers had on the average 5.3 children. When family income was $10,000 and over, average number of children was 2.9. For intermediate incomes, there was a smooth gradient from more to fewer children with income increases.

Education

1. Fewer years of schooling: Median years of school completed by nonwhites in 1964: 9.2 for males and 10.0 for females. Com-

parable figures for whites were 12.1 for both males and females. In 1969, 20 percent more whites than blacks had completed four years of high school or more.

2. Poorer performance in school. Sociologists are generally agreed that performance on I.Q. tests are heavily influenced by social conditions. "A prime index of the disadvantage of Negro youth in the United States is their consistently poor performance on the mental tests that are standard means of measuring ability and performance. . . ."
3. Intersection of institutional influences: education, economy, and family. The better educated nonwhites who have married at age 22 or later to professional or technical workers, have fewer children per woman (1.9) than their white counterparts (2.4). On the other hand, early married wives without a high school education, whose husbands are laborers have more children per woman (4.7) than their white counterparts (3.8).

Delinquency and crime

Rates are high: "The combined impact of poverty, failure, and isolation among Negro youth has had the predictable outcome in a disastrous delinquency and crime rate."

The deprivation of the Negro in urban America is pointedly brought home to us in white-nonwhite differences in longevity. At age 25 the Negro in the United States can expect to live 5.3 fewer years than the white.[18]

Third, this new element in the urban social mix presents telling evidence of inequities imposed at birth. Since the American creed ties rewards to achievements under conditions of equal opportunity, deprivation imposed by adventitious circumstance—race, birth into a poor family—is bound to be viewed as illegitimate. Thus change-generating tensions. And, again, these are found preeminently in urban centers.

For example, Gary T. Marx reports that, among respondents in a sample of over a thousand Negro adults, militancy increases with size of place (see Table 13.3). He writes:

> Today it is in the cities of the South that the traditional social structure is crumbling most rapidly. The anonymity of the city, its greater heterogeneity and mobility, its more cosmopolitan and sophisticated atmosphere and its greater integra-

Table 13.3
Negro militancy by type of community raised in

Type of community	Percent militant	*N*
Farm	15	321
Small and medium cities	28	483
Big city	37	287

Figure 13.4
Extent of Negro militancy related to measures of intellectual sophistication

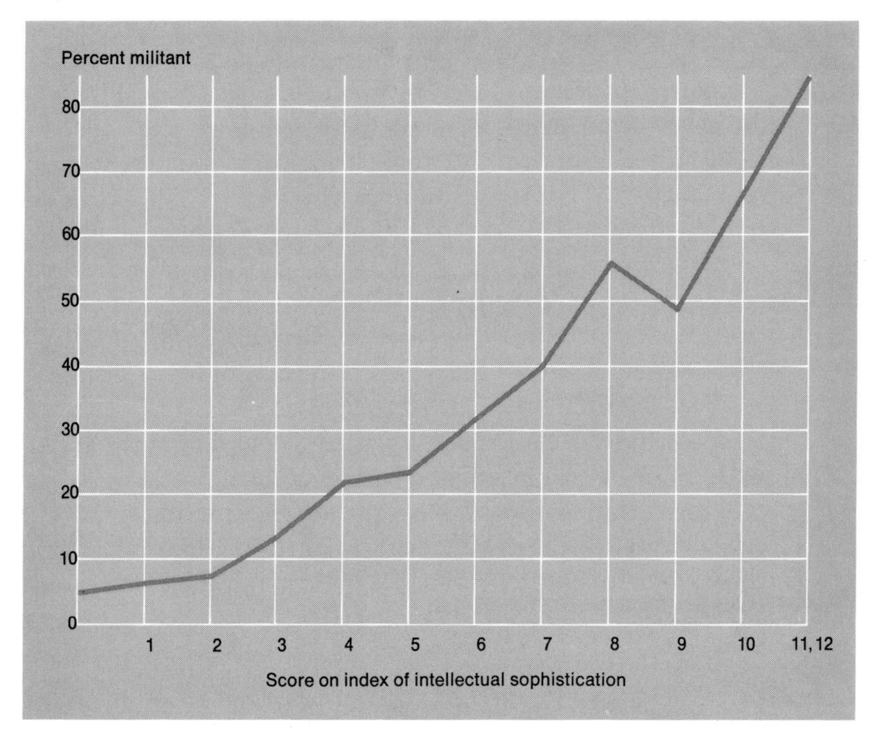

tion into the national life all militate against traditional southern patterns.[19]

Marx also relates a measure of sophistication to degree of militancy. Sophistication has often been linked with urbanism. If this is an accurate assumption, Figure 13.4 tells us something about urbanism and the disposition among Negroes to rectify inequities.*

Thus Negro input into urban centers illustrates three change-inducing influences: rapid rise in *quantity,* change in *kind* of input, and the strain to achieve *equity.* In a way the urban Negro illustrates our fourth source of change, knowledge. But it is moral knowledge that is illustrated here (conceptions of equity and democracy) and its rapid diffusion rather than the growth of knowledge itself.

For the latter, the city is the principal site for its production. In part the expansion of knowledge in urban centers is the result of the fructifying encounter of diverse ideas carried by a heterogeneous population. In part it is necessitated by a highly refined division of labor. This diversification advances very rapidly with increases in urbanization, as the left portion of Figure 13.5 indicates.† Specialization in work roles is both child and father of technological innovations that stem from science. Science, *scientia,* is knowledge. Its technological offspring is seen in scores of innovations: the internal combustion engine that so shapes life in our society, aviation, moon shots, the genetics of food production, the extension of life, artificial fibers, communications via satellite, and the like. If knowledge is a product of urban conditions, then we should expect that measures of technology, the visible index of science, would be closely related to measures of urbanism. And this is broadly confirmed by Gibbs' and Martin's findings represented in the right portion of Figure 13.5.

Change, then, is linked with the transformation of rural people, anchored to extractive industry (farming, mining, fishing, forestry) into urban dwellers. Religious, familial, and political in-

* Both *sophistication* and *militancy* are abstract terms that we commonly use and apprehend in an intuitive way. They illustrate a methodological problem often confronted by the sociologist: How translate a rather muddy abstraction into a sensible and usable index? Marx does it this way. For the "sophistication" variable he combines (1) five items from the F-Scale (originally developed to reveal rigid and authoritarian elements of personality or, conversely, breadth of viewpoint), with items testing (2) awareness of how social factors shape behavior, (3) items on acceptance of intellectual values, and (4) knowledge of Negro culture figures.

As to "militance," a respondent was so classified if he scored 6, 7, or 8 on a set of eight items such as this: "An owner of property should not have to sell to Negroes if he doesn't want to." ("Disagree" is the militant response for this item.)

† Diversification was measured by degree of spread of workers among eight major work categories. In the right portion of Figure 13.5, the level of technological development was measured by energy consumption per capita (metric tons of coal).

Figure 13.5
Measure of urbanization related to measure of industrial diversification* and to measure of technological development† in 45 countries circa 1950

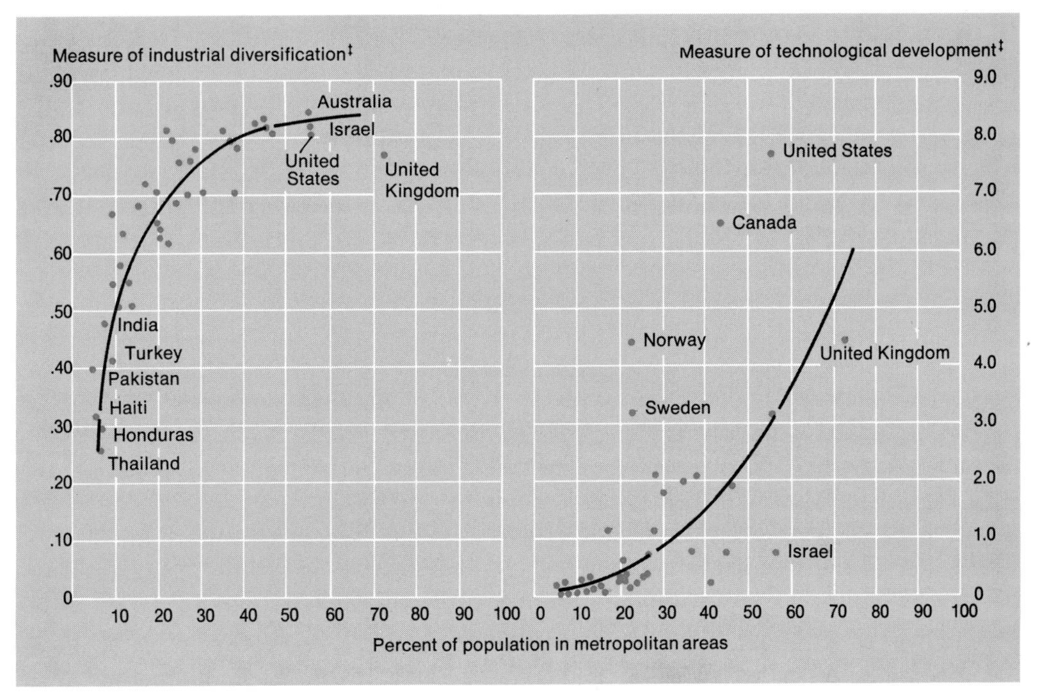

* As an index of division of labor.

† Countries low in technological development (under 0.5) and low in urbanization (under 20 percent in metropolitan areas) are as follows: Ceylon; Thailand; Malaya; India; Pakistan; Philippines; Turkey; Egypt and Portugal; and Haiti, Honduras, Costa Rica, Dominican Republic, Ecuador, El Salvador, Guatemala, Nicaragua, Paraguay, and Peru.

‡ Line is an estimate, fitted by inspection.

stitutions embodying rules given in tradition are altered under the impact of new knowledge that modifies or challenges past patterns. For example, the knowledge that brings about a dramatic decline in mortality rates will alter conceptions about required, or desired, fertility rates. Thus family patterns are changed.

Great increase in population, enormous diversity, highlighting of inequities, and ever mounting production of knowledge—these sources of social change are vividly exemplified in urban areas. We can see the city as the end point in a change process characterized by metropolitan dominance, large and dense population aggregates, heterogeneous in their traits and increasingly mobile.

Metropolitan dominance

The directives controlling the hinterlands issue from the metropolitan centers of our society. In them we find a disproportionate concentration of plants, workers, and wages—three fourths of those in the nation. Containing 63 percent of the population in 1960, metropolitan areas had 81 percent of all sales in wholesale, retail, and service establishments.[20] Metropolitan areas are the command headquarters for most complex organizations. Here are the central offices of 99 percent of U.S. business associations. Almost all manufacturing corporations having plants in two or more locations have their national headquarters in metropolitan centers. Of the 200 largest industrial corporations, 170 have national headquarters in the New York–northeast New Jersey metropolitan area. Here, too, we find a concentration of the central offices of voluntary associations: 90 percent of them located in metropolitan areas and 59 percent in just three—New York, Chicago, and Washington.[21]

Leadership is concentrated in these large urban centers. Hawley reports that, in 1960, 72 percent of all professional workers lived in and about metropolitan centers. (The figure was 62 percent in 1940.)[22] Table 13.4 shows an increasing concentration of leadership in the more populous centers—if listing in *Who's Who* can be taken as a rough index of leadership.

Leadership in various activities is indicated by Figures 13.6 and 13.7. Many such activities would be impossible without a substantial population base to provide users and patrons.

Numbers

The most obvious characteristic of the city as symbol of social change is, of course, size. Increasingly in our society population is heaped up in densely settled metropolitan areas. For example, of the nearly two thirds of our population residing in metropolitan areas, half is in two large agglomerations, one running from Boston to New York, Philadelphia, Baltimore, and Washington, and the other embracing the urbanized area that cups the southern shores of the Great Lakes from Buffalo to Chicago.

Bigness is something more than a physical fact, more than an increase in volume or external dimensions. It means a rearrangement of the component parts, a change in the nature of human relationships. We saw in Chapter 2 how the sheer number of potential bilateral relationships increases exponentially, with

Table 13.4

Percent distribution of persons listed in *Who's Who in America,* by size and type of place of residence*

Size and type of place	1920	1930	1940	1950	1960	Percent change 1920–60
Metropolitan areas	75.9	77.2	76.0	79.6	87.1	+11.2
3,000,000 and over	28.3	29.5	27.4	31.7	41.9	+13.6
1,000,000–3,000,000	15.0	15.7	16.0	21.0	21.8	+ 6.8
500,000–1,000,000	15.0	12.0	13.0	12.1	10.4	− 4.6
250,000–500,000	8.9	9.9	10.6	7.6	6.7	− 2.2
100,000–250,000	7.0	8.1	7.8	7.7	6.1	− .9
Under 100,000	1.7	2.0	1.1	0.5	0.4	− 1.3
Nonmetropolitan	24.1	22.8	24.0	19.4	12.9	−11.2
All places	100.0	100.0	100.0	100.0	100.0	100.0

* Figures are based on a 5 percent sample of *Who's Who* listings.

Figure 13.6

Percent of U.S. cities having symphony orchestras (1946), and zoos (1940)

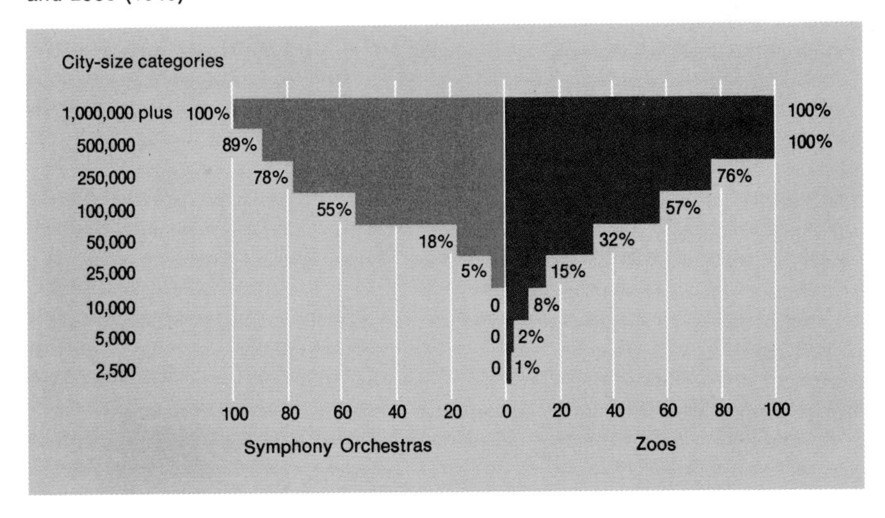

additions to the population base [where $y =$ the number of relationships and x the number of persons involved, $y = x(x-1)/2$]. Hence the impossibility of maintaining in the city the same character of human relationships as in the rural setting. In his essay "Die Grossstadt und das Geistesleben" ("The Metropolis and Mental Life") Georg Simmel has pointed out:

> If, as in a small town where one knows almost everyone and has a positive relationship to each, the city dweller were to respond inwardly and deeply to the countless others whom he encounters, he would be atomized internally, reduced to an unimaginable psychic state.*

The first few sentences of this essay suggest the contrast between past and present, a direction of social change from rural agrarian to urban industrial.

> The psychological basis of the city dweller's personality is the *intensification of nervous stimulation* flowing from the quick and uninterrupted change of external and internal impressions. . . . The metropolitan man—there are, of course, a thousand variations on the theme—develops a defense mechanism to protect himself from those crosscurrents and discrepancies in his external environment that threaten to uproot him: he reacts to them, in essence, with his head instead of his heart. . . . Thus the intellectual character of metropolitan life becomes comprehensible, in contrast with the rural pattern which is based far more on deeply felt and emotional relationships.†

Sheer mass, the bigness of the city, lends itself to a qualitatively different type of personal relationship. With the thousands of people who fall within our field of vision, contacts must be largely transitory, superficial. There is an anonymity and remoteness of relationships that has been interpreted variously as callousness, a blasé attitude, or sophistication. And so there is a tendency to convert people into things, social objects into physical objects. Clearly we cannot treat the scores whom we encounter daily with the intimacy and emotional tone characteristic of *human* relationships. People cannot be dealt with as unique and complex personalities.

Indeed, the distinguishing characteristic of a physical as over against a social object lies in the paucity, clarity, and specific utility of its attributes. Thus clues to appropriate roles are found in those symbols that define the utility of the relationship. Uniforms, badges, headgear, labels—these tell us it's the laundryman, the

* See Original Texts, Note 13.2, page 661.
† See Original Texts, Note 13.3.

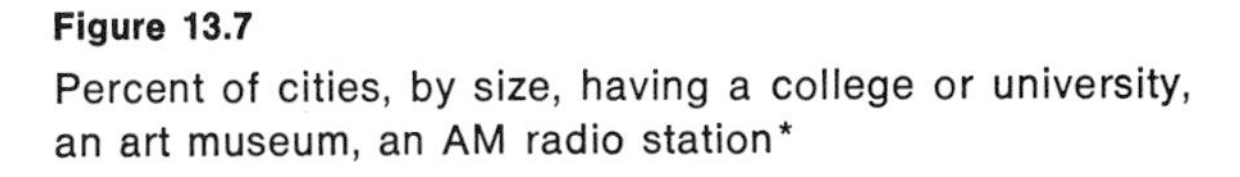

Figure 13.7
Percent of cities, by size, having a college or university, an art museum, an AM radio station*

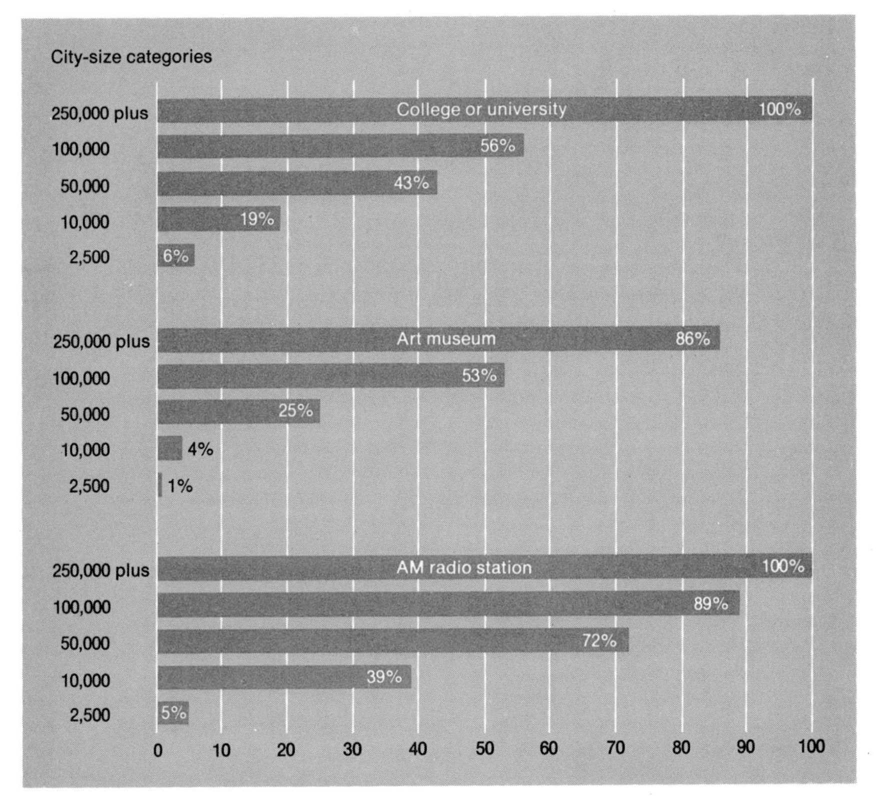

* Data are for 1940, 1938 and 1946 respectively.

milkman, the mechanic, or the people from Brinks. More than this we need not know—nor do we want to know. On the contrary, in the rural setting we will know Mr. Jones, the grocer, not merely as a food retailer, but as a neighbor whose wife has the hives; who, if his prices are sometimes exorbitant, makes recompense as deacon at the local church; and whose boy has chosen this great university on the advice of a principal who was Eta Kappa Epsilon back in '37 when a brother returned a last-minute punt 80 yards.

This change in the structure of relationships, the dealing with others in a few clearly defined aspects relevant to one's own interests entails a segmentalizing of personality, of relationships and allegiances. A deals with B on matter X, with C as to Y and with D on the matter of Z. This is obviously a concomitant of a highly refined division of labor promoting functional integration, the articulation of highly differentiated roles. Insofar as we relate ourselves to others only as they are of service to us and shrink from contact beyond a kind of contractual, *quid pro quo* relationship, others become preeminently means to our ends. To put it differently, roles tend to become instrumentally oriented.

Discussing this tendency in modern (urban) American society, Robert K. Merton points to the relative clarity and desirability of certain goals (wealth, power, winning the game) and the ambiguity, inaccessibility, or even the derogation of the institutionalized means for reaching such goals. Coupled with the calculating instrumental orientation of many urban roles and the inventive potential at the urban crossroads, this leads to the rapid increase in aberrant behavior which we regard as an index of social disorganization.

> . . . aberrant behavior may be regarded sociologically as a symptom of dissociation between culturally prescribed aspirations and socially structured avenues for realizing these aspirations.[23]
>
> The sole significant question . . . becomes, which available means is most efficient in netting the socially approved value? The technically most feasible procedure, whether legitimate or not, is preferred to the institutionally prescribed conduct. As this process continues, the integration of the society becomes tenuous and anomie ensues.[24]

Probably nowhere so much as in the city may goals of wealth and power be linked with an instrumental orientation (". . . which available means is most efficient . . .") leading to ingenious, technically efficient, but illegitimate means for reaching those goals. And this is what we would expect if indeed the city is a change-inducing crossroads: an amoral inventiveness in contriving illegitimate as well as legitimate means to one's ends.

This inventive efficiency, a preoccupation with improved techniques, is revealed in and made possible by an intellectual posture we describe as rational. This frame of mind is exactly that which assesses, preferably in quantitative and verifiable terms, the most efficient means for achieving a desired end. It is linked, again, with the inventive character of the urban crossroads; and with the requirement, where large populations are involved, of speed, careful organization, intricate timing, and new techniques to achieve success in competition. This is a feature of urban life that stands at the center of Simmel's analysis. Rationality is revealed in the quantification of things and services, especially in the elaborate network of exchange typical of great cities. The money economy is a mode of quanitification providing a common denominator for, and enabling the exchange of, quite disparate things. The central position of the marketplace, located typically at points of maximum accessibility, symbolizes the rational, calculating character of modern metropolitan life. Where land values are highest, where the most demanding hours of the day are spent —these are in the marketplace. In feudal days the cathedral dominated the community, while buying and selling went on at the city gates. In the New England village, the church occupied the focal position on the green. These positions have been significantly reversed.

This dispassionately calculating mode of dealing with men and things, is promoted by the fact that a person must deal indirectly with most of the others who affect his destiny. With vast numbers, this must necessarily be the case. People are connected by representatives and intermediaries. The law and the police, the marketplace and the ballot box, symbolize the in-between roles in which men can act with less passion, with more rationality, than any two persons immediately involved.

Finally, numbers promote rationality, since people in vast numbers must be dealt with as members of categories: as patients, clients, customers, policemen, waiters, repairmen, *et al.* The category, then, provides an impersonal definition of role and relationship, a definition based on criteria more rational than those defining an intimate, personal relationship.

Diversity and social change

Bigness is intimately related to heterogeneity. The greater the number of people, the greater the potential differentiation. The city with its diverse input is a breeding ground for new biological and cultural hybrids. It consumes people produced, or reproduced, elsewhere, either in our own rural hinterlands or in foreign lands.

There is some evidence that recent migration has contributed the top and bottom of various attributes—skills, education, occupational standing, income—to the city. In 1968, unemployed men had higher mobility rates than the employed (27.2 as over against 18.6 for the employed). The Negro and Puerto Rican migration to New York and other cities represents a disadvantaged input. At the other extreme, corporation executives and highly skilled technicians are also more mobile than most: and their destination is—other cities.

If we assume that long-distance movers—interregional migrants—usually move to cities, most recent evidence indicates that they are better educated than population resident in that region (see Table 13.5).

Thus the pull of the city on the rural hinterland tends to increase the range of any given attribute, contributing to the heterogeneity of the urban mix.

On its side, the city tolerates a diversity that rural areas do not. With its Bohemias and Bughouse Squares it provides a range of choice—and in this sense a kind of freedom—not found in the pastoral fastnesses of the more homogeneous country communities. Yet it is not a matter of mere tolerance. In fact, the city demands the diversity of tastes and services required to satisfy the needs of a motley population. The pimp and the numismatist, the gigolo and the couturier, the delicatessen owner, and the member of the Board of Public Welfare stand ready to serve. The city provides a sanctuary for the person who might elsewhere be a misfit. Here in the metropolitan complex we have the contrast between Beverly Hills, Burlingame, Brookline, and Wilmette, on the one hand, and the Harlems, the ghettos, the Little Sicily's, on the other. Here one finds a whole spectrum of religious organizations, ranging from the most esoteric sects and cults dealing in ectoplasm and Ouija boards to the great conventional churches of America. Here is the greatest diversity of voluntary associations, ranging from the *Landsmanschaften* of foreign-born groups to the loosely knit American Hoboes' Association (of whom an estimated 300,000 drift through Chicago each year).

This heterogeneity has its own consequences. When an extremely diverse population must attend the same schools, go to the same movies, listen to the same radio programs, view the same TV effusions, and read the same newspapers and magazines, there is a tendency to seek common denominators. This leveling influence is partially offset by the great variety of urban media, many of them in the language, or supporting the interests, of small, particular groups.

Differentiation also makes for segregation, especially when the variations are based on imported culture traits such as language or religion. Thus it is that the city becomes a checkered mosaic of cultural islands, a "spatial pattern and a moral order."

Table 13.5
Level of schooling completed by all U.S. residents and in-migrants 25 to 44 years old, March, 1968

Educational level	All residents	In-migrants from other regions	In-migrants exceed residents
4 years of high school	66.8%	76.3%	9.5%
1 year of college or more	25.4	42.3	16.9

Urban heterogeneity also implies a lack of common traditions. Relationships, no longer defined in custom, come to be prescribed by law. Without commonly held, internal controls built in through the socialization process, external controls must be imposed, transcending differences. This is not to suggest that the differences are suppressed. Quite to the contrary, these external, formal controls may provide occasions and channels for the expression of differences (and through their juxtaposition, the generating of innovation: through political activity, pursuit of labor union interests following the stipulations of federal and local law, and so on). But the nature of the civic relationship becomes quite different in the city. The person gains strength from the probability that there are others of like mind and interest. The contest for a favorable outcome becomes intergroup, not interpersonal. The individual's strength is multiplied because in a vast population there can always be found some with whom he can identify in promoting like interests. But his strength is limited as his group confronts others with competing interests. With some group or organization typically mediating between the person and officialdom, the distance between governor and governed must necessarily increase. Furthermore, in the contest between interest groups, the common welfare may sometimes come off second best. (Both of these circumstances favor change.)

The contest between private interest and public welfare is graphically ilustrated in Frank E. Hartung's study of the meat-packing industry in Detroit. This study tests the notion that the heterogeneity of the metropolitan social order (Durkheim's condition of "organic solidarity") weakens traditional commitments to the common cause, giving rise to an individualism, a pursuit of special interests sometimes at odds with the general welfare.[25] Hartung follows Durkheim's argument that the change in the nature of the social bond has been from mechanical to organic solidarity, from homogeneity to heterogeneity, from common interests, skills, and commitments to the complex accommodation of differences in modern urban society.

The question is whether this transformation in the social order has in fact occurred and whether, as a result, there are sometimes significant differences in response to threats to the public welfare and those to private interest. We can find out, Durkheim suggested, by looking at the rules that define men's relationships to one another, and especially by looking at the sanctions that support the rules.

These sanctions are of two kinds, retributive and restitutive. Rough parallels in contemporary law would be criminal and civil law with their respective sanctions. The first category of law (and sanctions) is invoked when generally shared commitments are violated. The second comes into play to punish violations of contract between private parties. To the extent that sanctions of the second sort increase, relative to those of the first sort, we may infer that the social order, the nature of the social bond, has changed.

Hartung makes a frontal attack on this problem. Are the sanctions of civil law linked with differentiation, with special interests? Does the public at large, in contrast to members of a special-interest group, react differently to civil and criminal violations of the law? Given a set of civil and criminal violations by a special-interest group (in this case, the wholesale meat industry in Detroit), his hypotheses were that:

1. The public should tend to disapprove both the criminal and the civil violations.
2. But public and industry should tend to differ significantly in the disapproval of civil cases, members of the industry being more indulgent of members of their own special-interest group.
3. The public and the industry should disapprove criminal violations to about the same extent.
4. The industry should differ significantly in its disapproval of criminal and civil violations.

Aside from his work on the theoretical underpinning of the study (Durkheim, Cooley, MacIver, Redfield, *et al.*), Hartung's task required: (1) Reviewing all cases of violations by the Detroit wholesale meat industry of Office of Price Administration regulations and selecting, with the help of two attorneys, five civil and five criminal cases as representing the range of violations. These 10 cases were summarized, to be presented to respondents. (2) An approval-disapproval scale, with scores ranging from maximum

Table 13.6
Mean score of degree-of disapproval test for violations of OPA regulations by the Detroit wholesale meet industry

		Criminal cases		Civil cases	
	Number of interviews	Mean	Standard deviation	Mean	Standard deviation
Public	322	21.93	2.55	20.77	3.29
Industry	40	20.68	2.90	12.98	3.85

approval (a score of 5) to maximum disapproval (a score of 25). (3) A probability sample of respondents from the industry and the public at large, the *N*'s being 40 and 322 respectively. (4) Following the interviews, analysis of the data and discussion of the findings. The bare framework of the findings is presented in Table 13.6. (A more detailed analysis holds constant the variables of age, sex, occupation, and union membership.)

Hypotheses 2 and 4 seem clearly to be confirmed. (For lack of a statement on the sampling error, we cannot be sure how safe it is to generalize to the populations as defined.) Industry goes along with the public on reactions to criminal violations; but the values of this special-interest group are markedly different from those of the public on civil violations. The public does not make the same distinction as the industry between criminal and civil violations: it disapproves of both with approximately equal strength.

The point, then, is this: the heterogeneity of the urban social order is registered in a proliferation of special-interest groups whose values may be at odds with those of the public taken as a whole. This is a significant change from the more uniform value system that, as we think, was characteristic of a more homogeneous rural society in the past. Finally, the abrasive contact of heterogeneous values at the urban crossroads is both outcome and condition of social change.

Density and social change

The density of urban populations reinforces certain of the effects of size and heterogeneity. Specialization is one such consequence. When numbers increase and area is held constant, both interests and talents are available to maximize production through an intricate division of labor. Nowhere is this characteristic of contemporary society so vividly illustrated as in our great cities. One does not simply go to the dentist: one goes to the extractionist, or

. . . Large population increments guarantee a novel mix of ingredients. . . The impact of common media on a noncommon base may well generate impulses toward change. These media constitute . . . a crossroads where differing views and values intersect.

. . . it is inconceivable that an appropriate match between competence, contribution, and reward could be sustained —if indeed it ever existed.

. . additional knowledge,
like additional points on a scale,
complicates our readings
of reality.

. . . the city . . .
current end point of change
in the social structure . . .
the effects (there) of dominance,
numbers, heterogeneity, density,
and mobility as they alter patterns
of human relationships.

the prosthetic specialist, or the X-ray technician, or the oral surgeon, or the career man in caries. Whole areas are given over to specific activities, representing a minute division of labor within the city. Often a building—a medical arts building, for example—is devoted to a certain trade or occupation. It is as though a post-medieval street on which dwelt artisans of a given trade had been upended.

Obviously, density implies close physical contacts, reinforcing the tendency to insulate one's self from the importunities of others. Thus a primary characteristic of the city is physical proximity and social distance.[26] Propinquity implies the availability of diverse skills and interests to complement one's own. Social distance implies the possibility of choice in selecting among them. Both suggest the tendency in an urban society to transform social into physical objects, to deal with others nonhumanely, instrumentally, as means to one's ends. If this is so, it is a crucial aspect of the change-inducing character of urban society.

Density also implies an intense, though rationalized, struggle for space. The minimizing of time-cost distance with car and bus and trains enables a great lateral expansion of the city. Yet there is a limit to lateral movement, and the solution is to go up. The arched contour of the city skyline roughly reflects differential land values. Maximum competition for space occurs at points of maximum accessibility to the market. Other things equal, this is at the center of the city where the main arteries of urban life converge. And here the construction of skyscrapers results from the need to get most returns from limited (lateral) space.

Mobility and social change

Both heterogeneity and density are related in a very basic way to mobility. Urban life enables one to be mobile (in a social and psychological sense) without moving (physically). For the urban dweller is exposed, willy-nilly to a great range of alternatives. Mobility in this sense is what Simmel refers to as the *Steigerung des Nervenlebens,* the intensification of nervous stimulation. The city, representing a society in flux, derives much of its change potential from this psychic and social mobility. But, of course, there is physical mobility also. There is the input of immigrants and of rural-urban migrants. There is the daily influx of shoppers and commuters. (In Chicago and New York this is a matter of hundreds of thousands, daily.) There are intercity movers and within-city shifts of residence. And there is the shifting population of our Skid Rows, thousands drifting in and out of American cities.[27]

What is the connection betwen mobility and social change? To the extent that the migrant's cultures of origin and destination differ, role definitions are at odds and relationships must change. The social order is changed for lack of stable, predictable patterns of interaction. From the perspective of the receiving group, the migrant may be ill-bred, strange in his ways, unattractive if not repulsive. He is often subject to the same sort of suspicious enmity bestowed upon the footloose person in the days of the repressive English Settlement Acts. The migrant does not know how to behave. Others do not know what to expect of him or how to respond to him. But beyond this—and as a consequence—they do not know how to control his conduct, what rewards and punishments to use to guide his behavior into appropriate channels. (In the ultimate case, where a person is sufficiently mobile, sufficiently alienated from core elements of the group's culture to endure martyrdom, he is utterly beyond control. There is some subconscious sense of the impotence of the host majority when people observe that they had better not make a martyr of someone. For this is to put him beyond their control.)[28]

We can see the matter a different way by suggesting that mobility always involves, in some degree, resocialization. And quite aside from the resistance of previously inculcated views and values, the reinduction of an adult is likely to be thought of as superfluous.

* * * *

Social change is to be understood by inverting the interpretation of social stability. Group change is the other side of the coin bearing group maintenance on its face. The matching of losses with replacements, in number and kind, makes for social stability. Shifts in the quantity or quality of input make for change. Change is generated, too, when the input of talent is at odds with available opportunity and the distribution of rewards. And we have seen how the increase in knowledge (science) produced through education and producing technological advances has generated social change.

Such influences are especially active in urban centers. The modern city is a crossroads where a shifting balance between input (birth, socialization, and in-migration) and output (death and outmigration) alters the social mix at the crossroads. Here the numbers involved require new forms of social organization, and the confrontation of differences gives rise to problems—and, when they are complementary, to innovations. The great input of Negroes at the urban crossroads has produced enormous social change, the revolution in race relations. The vastly increased input of ideas, with the aid of the mass media, professional journals, and devices like the computer have led to rapid and significant cultural change, again chiefly at the crossroads that is the city.

Finally, we have looked at the city as the current end point of change in the social structure, pointing to some of the effects of dominance, numbers, heterogeneity, density, and mobility as they alter patterns of human relationships.

In this chapter I have tried to describe social change in the structure of American society, not to evaluate it. If the reader detects a judgment, it was an unintended intrusion. Evaluation is crucial; but it is another problem.

Our concern in this chapter has been with unplanned change. We use the fuzzy word *force* to refer to unknown influences conspiring to bring about a given outcome. We have been dealing with social forces, in this sense, influences leading, all unawares, to a different social order. In the next chapter let us look, briefly, at planned social change, and its assessment by the sociologist.

References

TEXT

1. Data from Bureau of Labor Statistics, *The Negroes in the United States: Their Economic and Social Situation* (Bulletin No. 1511 [Washington, D.C.: U.S. Government Printing Office, June, 1966], Tables IA-10 and IB-1, pp. 70 and 73.
2. Amos H. Hawley, *Human Ecology: A Theory of Community Structure,* p. 102. Copyright © 1950, Ronald Press Co.
3. D. Fleming, B. Bailyn (eds.), *Perspectives in American History* (Cambridge, Mass.: Charles Warren Center for Studies in American History, 1960).
4. Joseph W. Eaton, "Controlled Acculturation: A Survival Technique of the Hutterites," *American Sociological Review,* Vol. 17, No. 3 (June, 1952).
5. See the study by Lee Emerson Deets, *The Hutterites: A Study in Social Cohesion* (Gettysburg, Pa.: Times and News Publishing Co., 1939) and his early study, "The Origin of Conflict in the Hutterische Communities," in *Publications of the American Sociological Society,* Vol. 25 (May, 1931), pp. 125–35.
6. Moses Rischin, *The Promised City* (Cambridge, Mass.: Harvard University Press, 1962), Table 2, p. 271.
7. It is important to remember that is is not the input of bodies that counts, but an input of values, skills, attitudes, knowledge, and manners that is at issue. People are their carriers (although with present means of communication, the input need not be personally transmitted. The practice of jamming radio transmission of propaganda is evidence of the power of an incorporeal, ethereal input!). For example, we get an input of occupational knowledge and specialties among East Side, largely immigrant, Jews (1890). Forty-three percent were tailors, 11 percent peddlers,

9 percent cloakmakers, 6 percent clerks, 5 percent laundry workers, 4 percent cigar workers, 3 percent hat makers, 2 percent painters, another 2 percent carpenters, and so on (*ibid.*, Table 3, p. 272). Rischin's data tell us, too, that the input of religious and political preferences as well as occupational skills, and of food and clothing habits—the input, indeed, of a way of life—by no means matched the output through retirement and death of the preestablished WASPS (white, Anglo-Saxon Protestants).

8. Ralf Dahrendorf, *Class and Class Conflict in Industrial Society* (Stanford, Calif.: Stanford University Press, 1959), p. 223c.
9. Karl Marx, *Preface to a Contribution to the Critique of Political Economy* (Chicago: Charles H. Kerr & Co., 1904), pp. 11–13, *passim.*
10. Karl Marx and Frederich Engels, *Communist Manifesto* (Chicago: Charles H. Kerr & Co., 1947), pp. 12, 13.
11. William F. Ogburn, *Social Change* (New York: Viking Press, Inc., 1938).
12. Office of Education, U.S. Department of Health, Education, and Welfare, *Projection of Educational Statistics to 1975–76* (Washington, D.C.: U.S. Government Printing Office, 1966), Table 1, p. 5.
13. Data on school enrollment and institutions of higher education are from Office of Education, *Digest of Educational Statistics, 1966* (Washington, D.C.: U.S. Government Printing Office, 1966), Tables 31 and 33, pp. 27 and 29, respectively. Data on literacy are from U.S. Bureau of the Census, *Historical Statistics of the United States, Colonial Times to 1957;* and *Continuation to 1962 and Revisions* (U.S. Government Printing Office, 1965), Series H 407, pp. 214 and 33 respectively.
14. Amos H. Hawley, *Urbanization: A Study in Human Ecology* (New York: Ronald Press, 1971), chapter 10, *passim.*
15. U.S. Bureau of the Census, *Current Population Reports,* Series P–23, No. 33, "Trends in Social and Economic Conditions in Metropolitan and Nonmetropolitan Areas," (Washington, D.C.: U.S. Government Printing Office, 1970), Table 1, p. 2.
16. "Population of the United States by Metropolitan–Nonmetropolitan Residence: 1969 and 1960." *Current Population Reports,* Series P–20, No. 197 (Washington, D.C.: U.S. Government Printing Office, 1970), Figure 1.
17. Census data taken from Office of Policy Planning and Research, U.S. Department of Labor, "The Negro Family: The Case for National Action," (Washington, D.C.: U.S. Government Printing Office, March, 1965).
18. Herman P. Miller and Dorothy K. Newman, Bureau of the Census and Bureau of Labor Statistics, "Social and Economic Conditions of Negroes in the United States," BLS Report No. 332, and Current Population Reports, Series P–23, No. 24 (Washington, D.C.: U.S. Government Printing Office, October, 1967), p. 63.
19. Gary T. Marx, *Protest and Prejudice: A Study of Belief in the Black Community* (Torchbook ed.; New York: Harper & Row, Publishers, 1969), p. 52.
20. Amos Hawley, *Urbanization: A Study in Human Ecology, op. cit.*
21. *Ibid.*
22. *Ibid.*
23. Robert K. Merton, "Social Structure and Anomie: Revisions and Extensions: (a new edition of the paper next cited), in Ruth Nanda Anshen (ed.), *The Family: Its Function and Destiny* (New York: Harper & Bros., 1949), p. 24.
24. Robert K. Merton, "Social Structure and Anomie," *American Sociological Review,* Vol. 3 (October, 1938), p. 674.
25. Frank E. Hartung, "Common and Discrete Group Values," *Journal of Social Psychology,* August, 1953, p. 3 *et seq.*

    Hartung writes: "Individualism . . . feeds upon a differentiated society. The person becomes conscious of himself as a member of groups because he is continually taking a succession of roles in *different* groups. . . . Cooley remarks that there are two kinds of individuality, one of isolation and one of choice. Modern conditions, he says, foster the latter while they efface the former."

    Speaking to the same point from the perspective of churchman and poet, T. S. Eliot asserted: ". . . when morals cease to be a matter of tradition and orthodoxy—i.e., of the habits of the community, formulated, corrected and elevated by the continuous thought and direction of the church—and when each man is free to elaborate his own, the personality becomes a thing of alarming importance" (*After Strange Gods: A Primer of Modern Heresy* [New York, 1934], p. 58).
26. See Louis Wirth, "Urbanism as a Way

of Life," *American Journal of Sociology,* Vol. 44 (July, 1938), pp. 1–24.

27. Donald J. Bogue, *Skid Row in American Cities* (Chicago: Community and Family Study Center, 1963), *passim.*

Professor Bogue distinguishes these categories of Skid Row men: physically disabled and elderly men, unskilled and daily laborers, migratory workers, transient and resident bums, criminals, and alcoholics. In 41 cities in the United States, about a third, on the average, have six or fewer years of schooling, just under half earn less than $1,500 a year. They live in city areas disproportionately male (sex ratio for the Skid Rows in these 41 cities is 172). In these same areas a fifth are nonwhite and a tenth are foreign-born.

Bogue computes a socioeconomic status score based on education and income associated with an occupation. The special character of the urban input represented by Skid Row is suggested by the following data (*ibid.*, p. 322):

Socioeconomic score	Chicago Skid Row 1958	U.S. urban males, 1950
110 and above	1.4	19.8
100 to 109	5.1	27.5
90 to 99	3.3	9.2
80 to 89	9.6	21.7
70 to 79	17.2	8.2
60 to 69	52.8	6.3
Below 60	10.6	6.3

For Bogue's method of calculating his SES score see *ibid.*, p. 317, and Appendix B., p. 516 *et seq.* He presents here a most useful discussion and solution of the problem of contriving an adequate index of social and economic status.

28. This argument is more fully developed in Everett K. Wilson, "Mobility and the Maverick," *Antioch Review,* Spring, 1957, pp. 60–71.

And from the point of view of the group he has left, the migrant may be a defector, giving allegiance to alien standards and arousing the indignation of those whose standards are, by implication, rejected.

We get some sense of this view of the expatriate in a statement by Vladimir Nabokov. "Somewhere at the back of their glands," he writes, "the authorities secreted the notion that no matter how bad a state—say, Soviet Russia—might be, any fugitive from it was intrinsically despicable since he existed outside a national administration; and therefore he was viewed with the preposterous disapproval with which certain religious groups regard a child born out of wedlock" (Vladimir Nabokov, *Speak Memory* [New York: Grosset & Dunlap, Inc., Universal Library, 1951]).

TABLES

13.2 Adapted from Philip M. Hauser, "Labor Force," in Robert E. I. Faris (ed.), *Handbook of Modern Sociology,* (Skokie, Ill.: Rand McNally & Co., 1964), Table 2, p. 168.

13.3 Gary T. Marx, *op. cit.*, Table 29, p. 52.

13.4 Amos H. Hawley, *Urbanization: A Study in Human Ecology, op. cit.*

13.5 Adapted from Bureau of the Census, "Educational Attainment; March, 1968" (errata sheet) *Current Population Reports,* Series P–20, No. 182 (Washington, D.C.: U.S. Government Printing Office, July 21, 1969).

13.6 Frank E. Hartung, "Common and Discrete Group Values," *Journal of Social Psychology,* August, 1953.

FIGURES

13.2 Urban data: Bureau of the Census, *Historical Statistics of the United States, 1789–1957,* Series A–36 and A–2 (Washington, D.C.: U.S. Government Printing Office, 1960), pp. 9 and 7 respectively; for 1960, Bureau of the Census, *Statistical Abstract of the United States, 1966.* Rural data: *Historical Statistics . . . ,* and *Continuation to 1962 and Revisions,* Series A–2, A–37, and A–38, pp. 7, 9, and 1; for 1968, Bureau of the Census, "Farm Population," *Current Population Reports,* P–27, No. 40 (July 31, 1969), p. 1. Metropolitan data: Bureau of the Census, *Pocket Data Book, U.S., 1967* (Washington, D.C.: U.S. Government Printing Office, December 1966), p. 35, and "Population Estimates and Projections," *Current Population Reports,* Series P–25, No. 427, pp. 4 and 5.

13.3 Bureau of the Census, *Historical Statistics of the United States, 1789–1957; Continuation to 1962,* Series C–74, C–75, C–76 (Washington, D.C.: U.S. Government Printing Office, 1965), pp. 47, 10.

13.4 Marx, *op. cit.*, Table 54, p. 86.

13.5 Jack Gibbs and Walter Martin, "Urbanization, Technology, and the Division of Labor: International Patterns," *American Sociological Review,*

Vol. 27, No. 5 (October, 1962), p. 671.

13.6a Figure based on data presented by Otis Dudley Duncan, "Optimum Size of Cities," Paul Hatt and Albert J. Reiss (eds.), in *Cities and Society* (New York: Free Press, 1957), p. 769. Copyright 1951, 1957 by The Free Press; reprinted with permission. Data drawn from "Symphony Orchestras in the United States and Canada," *The International Musician*, Vol. 44 (June, 1946), pp. 7–8.

13.6b *Ibid.* Data drawn from National Recreation Association, *Municipal and County Parks in the United States, 1940* (New York, 1942).

13.7 *Ibid.*, p. 768. Data drawn from: Office of Education, *Education Directory, 1941, Part III, Colleges and Universities* (Bulletin 1941, No. 1 [Washington, D.C.: U.S. Government Printing Office, 1941); and Laurence Vail Coleman, *The Museum in America* (Washington, D.C.: The American Association of Museums, 1939), Vol. III; and "Directory of Broadcasting Stations of the United States," *Broadcasting, 1946 Yearbook Number*, pp. 71–190.

chapter 14 Social change, planned

It is not enough to do good;
one must do it the right way.
John Morley, *On Compromise*

Man is a valuing animal. Always and everywhere he seeks so to modify behavior and belief as to achieve his values. A dramatic example of this was the Civil Rights Act of 1964, redefining the roles of white and Negro: the citizen role, the worker role, the customer role, and secondarily, the whole complex of roles and relationships linked with, or affected by, these. All legislation may be seen in this light: the amendments granting suffrage to women and imposing a tax on income, the minimum wage law, medicare, the draft. Indeed, this is the legislator's daily task: writing new rules, or revising old ones, and so changing the roles and relationships that constitute the social order.

But purposive change is not restricted to legislators. Social life is so shot through with efforts at planned change that we scarcely recognize them. We praise and punish, give or withhold gifts, persuade, condemn, and flatter in order to change others' behavior. Preachers, teachers, and politicians try to alter attitudes and conduct. So do salesmen and advertisers (and the businesses they represent); lawyers, courts, and congressmen; parents as they rear their young; and people pushing various causes.

Increasingly, the sociologist takes part in planned change. This is because the connections between social events are often remote and obscure. Darwin illustrated the subtle linkages of biological events when he traced the connection between cats and size of the red clover crop.* Because social connections are equally complex, Darwin's contemporary, sociologist Herbert Spencer ridiculed the naïve—which included almost all Englishmen save himself!—for the easy assumption that common sense revealed the obvious ties between social events. And over the years, sociologists have indeed turned up a number of not-so-obvious linkages between elements of the social order.

Thus Whyte notes in his study, *Street Corner Society,* that the function of police work, presumably to prevent and punish crime, is in fact not so much the enforcement of the law as the regulation of illegal activities.[1] Again, and not altogether facetiously, Peter Berger links religious and familial patterns when he suggests that an atheist is a person who has suffered a happy childhood. Over 50 years ago, Durkheim made the point that trial and punishment of an offender had its chief effect on nonoffenders, providing the occasion for group members to reaffirm their values. He notes also that the significance of the division of labor lies not so much in its productive efficiency as in the tighter weaving of the social fabric. For interdependent roles bind people together. One significant outcome of extended and improved public education is to keep an ever larger sector of the population off the labor market. We detect another unintended function of education, the university (replacing the cathedral?) as sanctuary, in the number of young men who withdrew from college after the lottery system was set up and the probability of their being called was known to be remote. Our stress on upward striving, on the virtues of competition, may have unanticipated results for some people in our society. At least, this is one possible interpretation of the finding that children living in affluent Montgomery County, Maryland—

* Red clover depends for its fertilization on bees, "humble-bees," as Darwin called them. Bees depend, if they are to thrive, on the absence of field mice that steal their food. With enough cats around, the mouse population is held down, and the bees flourish and fertilize the red clover. Since cats are found chiefly in villages and towns, clover fields nearby yield better crops than those more distant.

suburban communities having the highest median income of all counties in the United States—are nearly twice as likely to be asthmatic as children in less healthful Baltimore.[2]

Because of such distant and unexpected outcomes of social behavior, the sociologist is increasingly asked whether efforts at social change are having the intended effects, and what other, unexpected outcomes he can spot. He is asked to discover the outcomes of planned change not only because social phenomena are complex but also because people's destinies are ever more entwined. Hence the remotely ramifying outcomes of an action program may reach unknown others in unintended ways.

The very conditions that complicate planned change (and prompt practitioners to seek the sociologist's aid in program evaluation) promote planned change. The complexity of social life means an exposure to a variety of social options. Such exposure increases the likelihood that one way will be preferred to another. And preference leads to plans to achieve the preferred.

Two basic requirements for planned social change

What prompts efforts to induce change? What is basic in the notion of planned change? Two requirements underlie such efforts: first, an awareness that there are alternatives, different ways of doing things, and second, a conviction that one way is better than another. Calculated social change grows, first of all, from an awareness of differences. This means that we must have points of comparison, in space or time. If there were only one of something, it wouldn't make any difference what we called it: we couldn't discriminate between it and anything else. And there would be no question of better and worse. If there isn't any difference it doesn't make any difference.

> I was thinking the day most splendid
> till I saw what the not-day exhibited,
> I was thinking this globe enough till
> there sprang out so noiseless
> around me myriads of other globes.[3]

An awareness of differences often leads to evaluation. As between two means, one may be the more efficient and less costly way of achieving a given end. As between two ends, one may be the more ultimate, the less qualified, being therefore the more desirable or having higher priority. As between means and ends, or practice and profession, the one may not be consonant with the other.

There is something more than a mordant humor in Sarah Cleghorn's "Quatrain." She uses ironic contrast to invoke the need for change. For the difference (men play, children work) is evaluated as wrong.

> The golf links lie so near the mill
> That almost every day
> The laboring children can look out
> And watch the men at play[4]

Resistances to planned change

If there is a gap between what is and what people think ought to be, resistances to change must be implied, obstacles to closing that gap. This is the case, of course. Changes can't be made without threatening valued ways in some sector of the social order. Therefore, resistance to desirable change is inevitable. For example, to live in a peaceful society, today, would be to invite profound disruption in our economy. In a number of ways, peace would be harmful. To change our society by abiding by the Mosaic code would be to subvert great sectors of business and civic enterprise: the insurance industry, public and private police and their apparatus, the Yale & Townsend Lock Company, and so on. For an apparently modest change in England, the shift to a decimal currency with 100 pennies to the pound, the cost is estimated at a minimum of £100 million.[5] It is not merely a matter of printing and minting new money but of converting several million business machines and making a vast number of price adjustments.

Resistance to change stems from the routinizing of relationships in institutional structures. When we speak disparagingly of "the establishment," we mean that modes of behavior have become so routinized as to have lost their *raison d'être*. When roles become ritualized, preoccupation with traditional means obscures the ends sought. Organizations tend to become rigid; the structure of relationships tend to be sustained through time, safeguarded if not embalmed in printed rules, printed policies, manuals, and guides covering all imaginable contingencies. This flood of printed material may defeat itself, may result in defective communication.

> One aspect of age in the social organism is a disorder of communication, an "excess of the organ of language" attended

> by a lack of real communication, a growth of verbiage and a failure of that inner contact upon which communication depends. . . .[6]

But whatever the resistances to change (some of which induce an even greater strain toward change), we continue to plan and work toward a transformed future. That is, we contrive change. Much of this change has a quantitative air about it—we plan for more of the same thing. In this sense:

> Many of our plans are not really plans but are detailed rationalizations of the status quo, projected a bit into the future. We build more automobiles according to plan; then more highways, also according to plan; then more cars; more highways and so on ad infinitum. This may be planned change, but it is . . . in danger of becoming a synonym for rigidity and conformity and helplessness. . . .[7]

Plans to extend *what is,* as in Professor Bennett's illustration, are unlikely to meet much resistance. In the world of work, such plans are almost routine. "Better things for better living—through chemistry" or any other means, enlists the effective efforts of planners in business and industry. More for less, or newer products to accomplish the same ends more efficiently—these are ideals that prompt endless planned changes with minimum resistance. Professor March has described such ideals as limitless, represented by an upsweeping curve asymptotically approaching the vertical (Figure 14.1).[8]

But when we attempt to change the social order and its supporting culture so as to make practice more closely approximate profession, we may find that our norms are not so unqualified as might be thought. All men are created equal; but some more equal than others. Honesty is an indubitable virtue; but an excess of honesty is intolerable. Cleanliness is next to Godliness: but there is such a thing as being "mean clean." Which is to say that the optimum, the "best," may not be the most of the good or the least of the bad. Acceptable behavior and belief may lie somewhere between the best and the worst, the most and the least. March represents it as shown in Figure 14.2. Thus as we try to induce changes that shift practice closer to profession, we are likely to encounter resistances. Preventing tooth decay is good. But fluoridation is resisted. A nation's wealth is in its people and their well-being. But health insurance is resisted. Automation may reduce

Figure 14.1

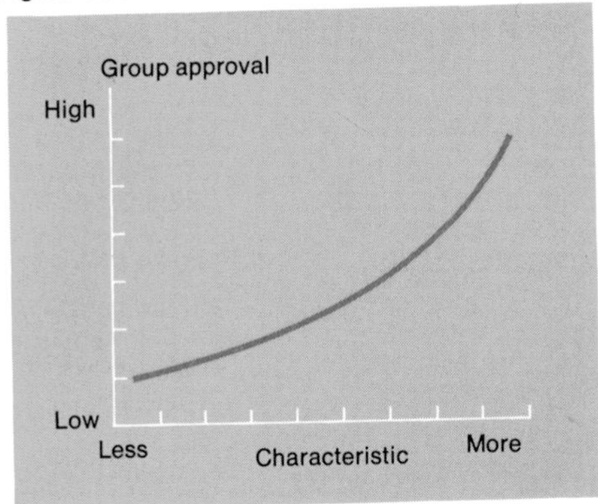

Figure 14.2

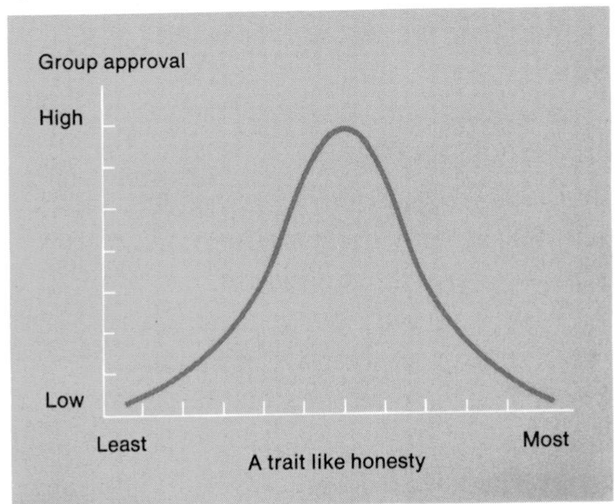

the toil invested in a product. But the displacement of workers it entails invites resistances.

Social change is complicated. This is why astute planning for change utilizes the sociologist's skills. These are used to identify the sources of resistance and measure their extent.* The costs of change must be assessed: Who will be hurt, how much? And beyond a measure of success and failure, the sociologist will antici-

* Recall the discussion of Coch and French's research, "Overcoming Resistance to Change," page 371, *et seq.*

pate a range of outcomes other than the ones planned for. Thus he allies himself with change-inducing action programs.

Action research: men of knowledge in league with men of action

Increasingly, change agents decline to work in the dark. The NAACP employs a sociologist and institutes an action research program to measure the success of its change-inducing efforts. The military ask: What are the effects on human relationships, on morale, and on efficiency when we are able, for the first time, to keep a submarine crew submerged for months at a time, or planes in the air for protracted periods? The Quakers raise the question: What in fact are we accomplishing through the program of the American Friends Service Committee workcamps as we try to educate (change) people toward the Friends' ideals? The Federal Reserve Board, through periodic national surveys, seeks information on the spending-saving habits of Americans so that it may better plan needed changes in credit policy. Perhaps the major effort in linking research with planned change is that of the U.S. Bureau of the Census. In social work and education, in business, government, and industry, the planning of new programs is ever more often linked with research to assess the extent to which professed goals are in fact achieved.

The interplay between attempted social change and its evaluation will be clearer if we consider the meaning of action research through some examples.

Here is the case of a settlement school in an isolated mountain area. It draws youngsters from poor homes to a well-equipped boarding school. Many of the children arrive with intestinal parasites. (In their initial stages, these entered the body through bare feet.) The children are wormed, shod with proper shoes, introduced to the flush toilet, taught the elements of sanitation, and given a conventional education with some emphasis on vocational training. Excepting the summer vacation, they remain at the school for a period of four to six years. Yet one might find, within weeks after graduation, that a student has undergone a fairly complete reversion. He might be barefoot again, or defecating on a slope above the well outside his family's mountain cabin. What change has ben induced by the school? Much of the honestly motivated and well-intentioned effort to induce change may come to little more than this. Not that such efforts are without consequence. But the results may be more, or less, or other than intended. It is well to ask about the adverse outcomes of well-intentioned action (and the good blown by ill winds).

Take the pattern of parole from federal prisons. These are perhaps the best of our prisons, trying to do an enlightened job in rehabilitating (inducing change in) criminals. The social workers, the chaplains, the parole officers, and a host of others combine to direct the inmate toward constructive and law-abiding behavior. Yet one of the conditions for parole has been that the prisoner return to the community he came from: often the setting, the social contacts, the influences most conducive to recidivism.

Activists are often amateurs at social change. Groaning mountains of reform sometimes deliver a very small mouse. However generously motivated, action without the check of controlled observation of consequences is likely to go far astray. Which raises one of Max Weber's questions: "whether the intrinsic value of ethical conduct—the 'pure will' or the 'conscience' as it used to be called—is sufficient for its justification, following the maxim of the Christian moralists: 'the Christian acts rightly and leaves the consequences of his action to God.' "[9] One may doubt, however, whether it's reasonable further to burden the Deity with man's inanities. It would seem the moral as well as the scientific obligation of the man of action—the teacher, the penologist, rabbi, priest, or social worker—to evaluate with all possible precision the consequences of his deeds (or misdeeds as they may turn out to be). The actions of people professionally committed to induce changes in people's behavior demand correlative research.

Turning to the last half of the term "action research," we encounter notions of lofty detachment, "purity," a desire to avoid the value-laden view. But this posture may neglect certain elementary facts in research. The data of the social sciences are infinitely numerous. It follows, then, in determining which problem is to be pursued, that we must select. And selection implies criteria, stated or not, that guide the choice. It is not a random affair: there is some purpose, perhaps more implicit than explicit in social scientists' reports.

> Probably most of the investigators who deliberately withhold a statement on the basis of their selection of data do so because they believe that this is not proper in a scientific document. Yet it is one of the basis canons of science that all steps in the collection and analysis of data be specified.[10]

To try to escape the value implications of sociological inquiry may lead, then, to the self-deception that certain kinds of research problems are value-free. But even when the value honestly espoused is the advancement of knowledge, we must ask: knowledge for what? And having stated the end, we are constrained to evaluate knowledge in contrast to alternate means to the desired end. Wherever there are differences, there are, with respect to given ends, preferences.

Again, the research purist might contend that preoccupation with action programs impedes the discovery of universal propositions or principles. Yet some first-rate research is produced by sociologists working under the auspices of applied agencies (for example, at the Bureau of Applied Social Research at Columbia University, at the Socio-Environmental Laboratory of the National Institutes of Health in Washington, D.C., and at the Bureau of the Census). And on the other hand, it is not clear that sociologists (or other scientists) enjoying the purer sanctuary of the academic groves are, in their selection of problems or means of attacking them, austerely immune to the practical immediacies of the moment, to the kudos and cash that flow from inquiries into current crises. In short, the distinction between "pure" and "applied" is less than crystal clear. Nor is it clear that research on practical problems precludes broadly generalizable findings.

In any case, two assertions seem justified. First, only as the men of action check their work against the systematic findings of research will they be able to validate their efforts. Second, only to the extent that the social scientist's predictions fit mundane experience can we place confidence in a body of propositions that claim to illuminate patterns of human relationship.

Planned change with sociologist as ally: three examples

Changes in the civic role: the encampment for citizenship

Now let us look at three instances in which men of action, attempting to induce change, collaborate with the sociologist, the latter evaluating results of the effort. One such example is an appraisal of the Encampment for Citizenship by Herbert Hyman and Charles Wright of the Bureau of Applied Social Research at Columbia University.[11] Under the auspices of the Ethical Culture Society, the Encampment aims, through its six-week summer program, to help young people identify, clarify, and understand cen-

Table 14.1

Design of the Encampment for Citizenship study

Four groups studied	Before	After: 6 weeks	After: 1 to 8 years*	Change
Experimental				
(Encampment subjects, 1955)	x_1	x_2	x_3	$x_2 - x_1 = d$
Control groups				
1. Comparable group not exposed to Encampment program	x'_1	x'_2		$x'_2 - x'_1 = d'$
2. Comparable group of American Friends Service Committee campers	x''_1	x''_2		$x''_2 - x''_1 = d''$
3. Comparable group of persons this age subject to changes normally occurring as the result of the general impact of events during a six-week period	x'''_1	x'''_2		$x'''_2 - x'''_1 = d'''$

* Encampment alumni, 1946–54.
x = measures of knowledge and attitudes characteristic of good citizenship.

$$\text{Hypotheses: } d > \begin{cases} d' \\ d'' \supseteq p < .01 \\ d''' \end{cases}$$

tral issues of our society and, in confronting them, to increase will, skill, and commitment to democratic principles.

In the summer program studied, the population (about 125 young men and women, 18 to 24 years of age) was heterogeneous in religion, race, income, education, and place of residence. While not selected for their views and values, those electing to join this group were not representative on certain attributes: in contrast to other youth, they wanted to work in the public service, and they were disposed to express their altruistic sentiments in action.

The design of this study may be translated into the scheme we have used before (see Table 14.1).

The experimental influence was, of course, the summer program of the Encampment for Citizenship. The formal program, treating economic, international, and political-social problems, consisted of lectures, discussion groups, field trips, and films. The informal influences stemmed from living with fellow members of the Encampment for six weeks, participating in the governing of the community, and in common recreational activities. Some apparently worshipped together.

What were the outcomes? ($x_2 - x_1$ or d, in contrast with d', d'' and d'''?) Eight out of ten thought the encampment experience had changed them either "moderately" or "a great deal." These perceived changes were about evenly divided four ways: greater awareness of social problems, a greater respect for and understanding of others, a decline in prejudice toward other ethnic groups, and a greater interest in social problems along with a disposition to do something about them.

The immediate effects of the encampment were an increased commitment to traditional civil rights for nonconformists and minorities. The campers also became more sanguine about solving pressing social problems through the use of established legal and social means. They did not suffer reverse prejudice, nor did they become more unrealistic or radical in their approaches to these problems. While the immediate outcome did not disclose an elitist sense, a little later, after the Encampment members returned home, there was some indication of disenchantment. There was

> . . . some increased sense that the larger society is unbound by moral imperatives (some feeling) . . . of alienation from the average American (and a) considerable attrition on the scene of action due to lack of desire to act, lack of trying despite desire, or lack of clarity in the course of action.[12]

These findings resemble those of Henry Riecken in his American Friends Service Committee–sponsored study, *The Volunteer Workcamp*,[13] a report on a Friends' summer work project in Mexico. But we should not overemphasize the slippage effect—the tendency toward reversion upon return to campers' home communities. Findings indicated a quite substantial change apparently induced by the Encampment for Citizenship, change that persisted, even among Encampment alumni who had undergone this experience from one to nine years previously. "Despite the passage of time, the alumni furthest removed show no marked lessening of sentiments on behalf of tolerance and civil liberties."[14]

A final point should be made. Although effects of the formal program and informal campus life were not separated, greatest change was induced in attitudes reinforced by the informal patterns of daily life. Thus, while there was significant change in level of tolerance and in attitudes on civil rights, there was virtually no change in political and economic orientations. It is in the former rather than the latter sphere that daily, informal intercourse with those of differing regional and ethnic backgrounds may be supposed to have had its effect. Informal peer influence apparently was potent in effecting change. There is strong evidence, the research summary states, that

> . . . the most salient feature of the total Encampment . . . what was psychologically central to the campers, was the group experience in democratic living which they enjoyed so much.[15]

Here, then, we have a good instance of contrived social change and its assessment by sociologists. First, as campers themselves changed, there was a change in the group—in the structure and strength of beliefs. ("Structure," means the way attitudes or beliefs were distributed in the group.) Then, presumably, change was induced by a different input of attitudes into their several communities as members of the Encampment returned home. Having left his home community with a constellation of attributes, x, he returns with the personality mix slightly altered (x'). Thus some slight change in the whole is induced. This kaleidoscopic process, an incessantly altered mix of attributes, goes on constantly in human communities. The thing distinctive about our example is that it is a consciously contrived process and program aimed at changing patterns of human relationship for the fuller realization of democratic values.

Changing fertility levels: the Taiwan program

Consider a second example of contrived social change, a change in all those relationships linked with rise or decline in fertility: husband-wife, parent-child, governor-governed, buyer-seller. . . . With declining mortality, especially in the new nations, and with rates of natural increase far outstripping increases in production, some have felt an urgent need to lower fertility rates. Under these circumstances we want to know (1) whether groups or governments have as official policy a reduction in the birthrate, (2) whether people do in fact desire to control the size of their families, and (3), if the answer to these questions is yes, whether "the control of fertility [can] actually be implemented on a large scale, [especially] in the developing areas."[15]

As to the first question, there are family planning programs in India, Pakistan, South Korea, Turkey, Maylaysia, Ceylon, Tunisia, the United Arab Republic, Morocco, Singapore, and Taiwan. Official agencies have encouraged family limitation to achieve a decline in the birthrate elsewhere, including Thailand, Kenya, and the United States.

. . . the legislator's daily task:
writing new rules,
or revising old ones,
and so changing the roles
and relationships that
constitute the social order.

. . . Calculated
social change
grows, first
of all, from
an awareness
of differences. . . .
An awareness
of differences
often leads
to evaluation.

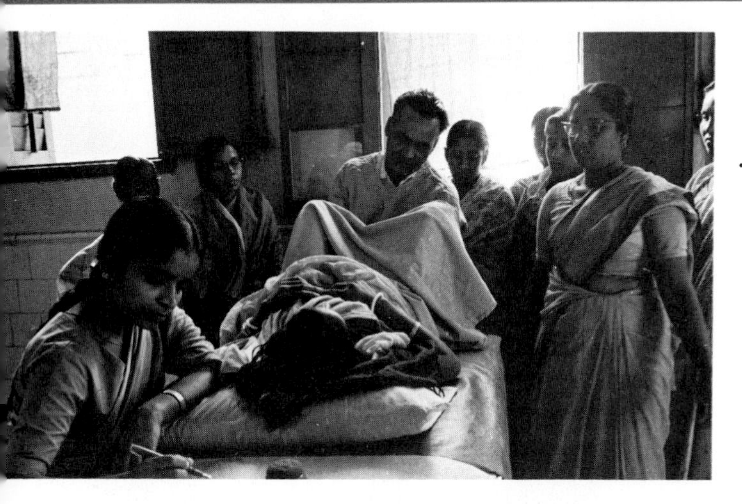

. . . man has slowly
gained control over . . .
a capriciously menacing
physical world.
. . . he seeks control
over life and birth:
new rules, new roles,
and new relationships.

. . . the most dramatic instance
of contrived change in American society
is the redefinition of the Negro's role. . . .
a change . . . quickening in recent years.

Figure 14.3
Rate of increase in Taiwan's population
Birthrate has remained high while deathrate has fallen.

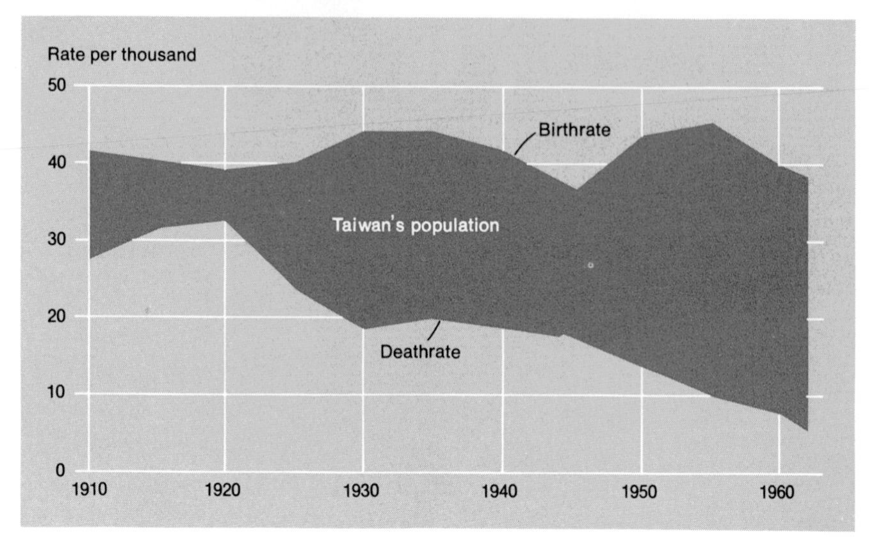

Our case of planned social change is Taiwan, where mortality rates have been dropping (to 5 per 1,000: see Figure 14.3) and where the birthrate remained high, the rate of natural increase rising to 3.5 percent (between 1951 and 1956). This would double the population in 20 years.[17] A comparison with the United States (Figure 14.4) highlights the fertility side of this natural increase.

The data show that Taichung married couples do wish to control the size of their families. Among 2,443 wives responding, 51 percent had fewer children than desired (chiefly among those with fewer than three children), 27 percent had just the number wanted, and 18 percent had more children than desired. As Figure 14.5 indicates, the larger the family, the greater the proportion of wives who said they had more children than they wanted. The longer the duration of marriage and the older the wife, the larger the percentage declaring more children than desired. Other data show that number of children wanted declined with level of education achieved and with indexes of modernization (possession of radios, bicycles, electric rice cookers, and the like). Such evidence suggests that control of family size is not a peculiarly Western inclination. At least two important influences are at work in Taiwan—and elsewhere. A declining mortality rate allows parents to achieve the desired family size without additional births. And,

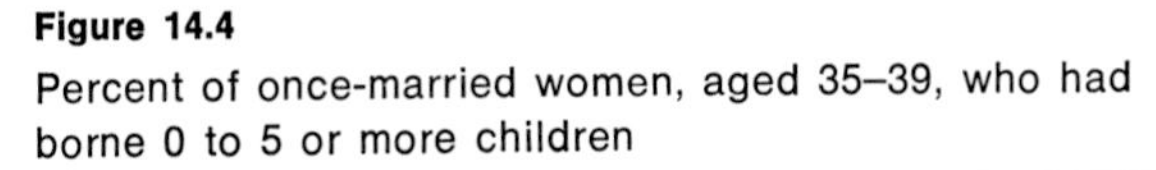

Figure 14.4
Percent of once-married women, aged 35–39, who had borne 0 to 5 or more children

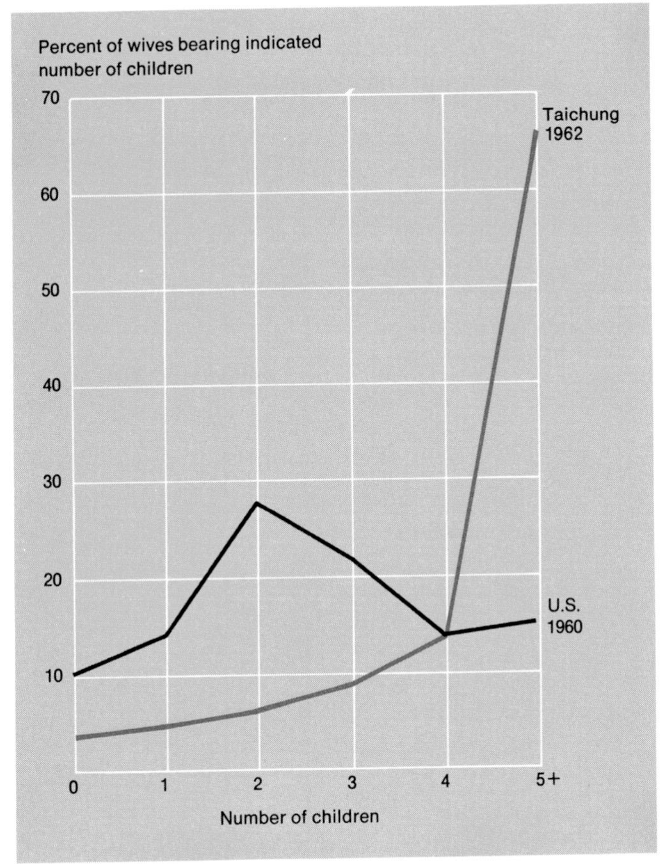

second, other desires may compete, increasingly, with that for children.

Thus, in answer to our first two questions, we have in Taiwan both an official policy favoring reduction of fertility rates and evidence that this policy accords with people's preferences. We turn, then, to the third question: How is desired change brought about? In seeking an answer we turn to "one of the most extensive and elaborate social science experiments ever carried out in a natural setting."[18]

To induce a change in family planning practices, married women 20–39 years of age (and sometimes their husbands) were treated in the ways listed in Table 14.2.[19]

Figure 14.5
Preference of number of children related to number of living children in family in Taichung sample

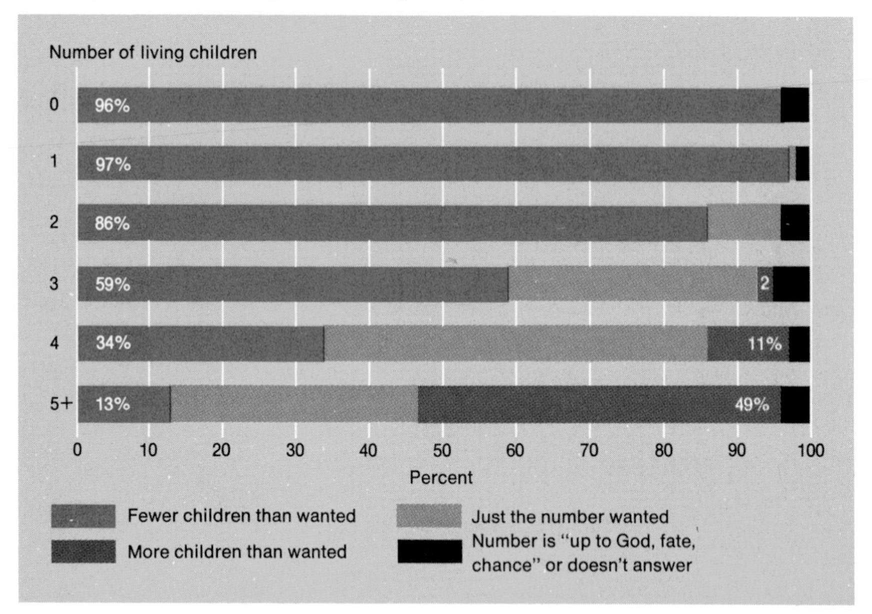

The design of the study may be represented as in Table 14.3.

Now we must ask: (1) Were changes induced? If so, to what extent were acceptance of contraception and level of fertility affected? And (2), What knowledge do we now have about ways of inducing such changes?

The evidence points to an increase in family planning and to a decline in fertility. There was a "rise in the proportion of married women 20–39 who were using contraception from 19 percent before the campaign to 26 percent at the end of nine months and to at least 33 percent within two and a half years."[20] Some of these couples might have practiced birth control in any case. (The control group gives us a measure on this point indicating that among couples intensively dealt with in the first year, about twice as many accepted contraception as among couples not given the "experimental" treatment.)[21] Even so, many would have had to resort to less satisfactory measures, such as abortion, for lack of the information and support conveyed in this program.

As to fertility, although Taichung's birth rate had already started to decline, this falling off

. . . was accelerated in the year following the experiment

Table 14.2

Treatments	Families in Experimental group #1	Experimental group #2	Experimental group #3	Control
i. Personal visits to wives and husbands by trained health workers	X			
ii. Personal visits to wives only	X	X		
iii. Neighborhood meetings	X	X		
iv. Mailings to newlyweds and to people with two or more children	X	X	X	
v. Casual indirect contact: public posters, etc.	X	X	X	X

Table 14.3
Design of the Taiwan study

	Before Feb. 1963	After Oct. 1963	Change
Receiving treatment* (Feb. through Oct. 1963)			
Experimental group 1	x_1	x_2	$x_2 - x_1 = d$
Experimental group 2	x'_1	x'_2	$x'_2 - x'_1 = d'$
Experimental group 3	x''_1	x''_2	$x''_2 - x''_1 = d''$
Control group (the "nothing" treatment)	c_1	c_2	$c_2 - c_1 = d'''$

* See Table 14.2 for descriptions of treatments.
x = some measure of fertility.
Hypothesis: d, d', and d'' will significantly exceed the magnitude of d'''.

> and for 1963–64 exceeded that of the other cities or of the province by a considerable margin. By 1965, however, Taichung's advantage was minimized, presumably because of the rapid expansion of the family planning program in other parts of the island and the continuous adoption of family planning methods outside of the program.[22]

As a result of this collaboration between sociologist and practitioner, we now know a good deal more about what measures are effective in inducing this sort of social change. We know, for example, that a campaign stressing information and service, even of short duration (nine months, in this case) can have a substantial impact. And we know that this can be carried out without the political repercussions that common sense might anticipate. We know that we can get quite exact measures and that such a pilot venture can lay the groundwork for more extensive efforts. We know that despite the fair level of literacy in Taichung, the mail campaign was not very effective. Nor was the approach to husband, as well as wife, worth the additional investment. Apparently transmission, wife to husband, can be almost as effective. And as a result of the work on Taiwan, we know that diffusion can be remarkably effective in carrying the good news from Ghent to Aix.

We have focused on the Taiwan study because it is a good example of the sociologist at work on a practical problem, not because the problem is unique to Taiwan. In American society a conservative estimate puts our population in the year 2000 40 percent higher than it was just 30 years before.[23] In our society, as in Taiwan, birth control could have two principal effects that would alter the nature of society. First, since fewer children would mean a greater investment per child, the quality of input into the system would be improved. (By quality, we mean health of body and development of mind.) And a second effect would be to alter the distribution of goods, power, beliefs, and knowledge. For there are economic problems tied to fertility patterns, problems expressed in the saying: the rich get richer and the poor get—children. And there are problems in the distribution of power—political problems. These result from the fact that excess population growth is not spread randomly across all classes, all religious, racial, and nativity groups. On the contrary, great growth is peculiar to certain sectors of the population, resulting in marked differences in need, political pressures, and political power. Religious institutions are affected too. Typically the less well educated, the religiously more fundamentalist, philosophically those most fatalist have higher fertility rates. High growth rates, then, mean a structure of beliefs weighted toward the less sophisticated end of the religious scale. And differential fertility is related to differences in education. Schools for high-fertility families suffer from inadequate resources—too few teachers, too few well qualified, ugly rooms and buildings, inadequate equipment, leading to the kind of school Jonathan Kozol wrote about in *Death at an Early Age.*

As always, there are resistances to change. Some black militants have argued that family planning is a plot to destroy Negro and Puerto Rican populations—or to keep them so small in numbers as to render them powerless in city affairs. Some believe that there are two sorts of pills: one for the wealthy, which is healthy,

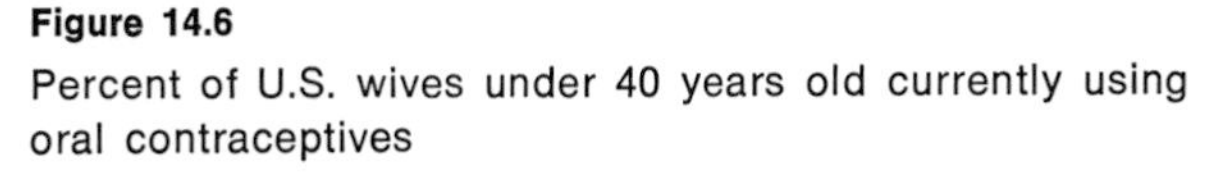

Figure 14.6
Percent of U.S. wives under 40 years old currently using oral contraceptives

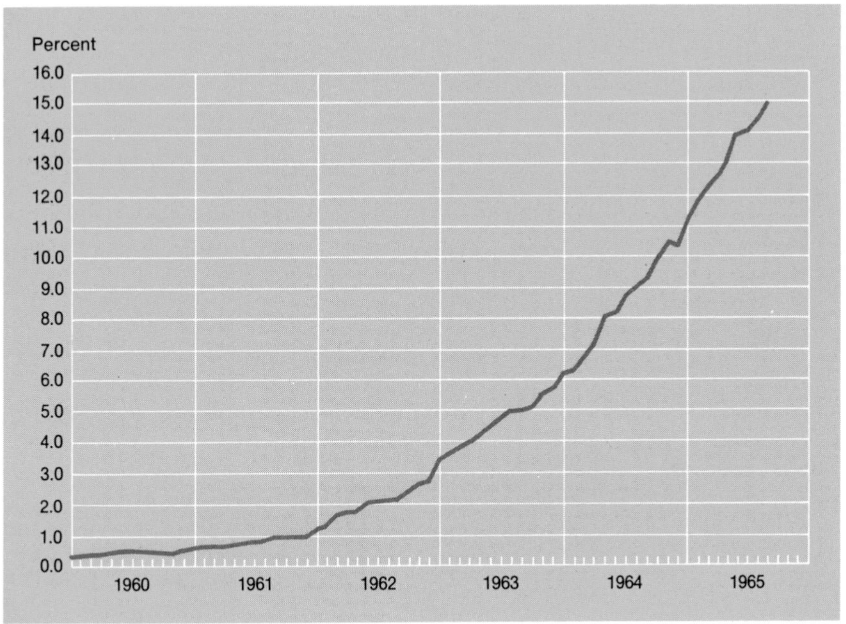

and another for the poor, which is lethal. Of course there are religious objections: the official Catholic position opposes the prevention of life through contraception. And in some instances, opposition may arise from the feeling that a failure to reproduce reflects on the husband's masculinity.

Despite resistances, it seems likely that a general sense of the need for birth control is widespread in American society. For example, Figure 14.6 indicates the rapid diffusion of a simple and effective contraceptive technique. Furthermore, population growth has become a matter of public concern and political policy. Under President Johnson's administration action was taken to help families electing to do so to limit children to a chosen number. And we see something of a landmark, acknowledging what sociologists have been thinking about for some decades, in President Nixon's Message to Congress in July, 1969. A schematic summary of this message is presented in Table 14.4. Note how much of your work in sociology bears on the issues presented in this message: demography, of course; but also the sociology of urban life, of work, of education, and of political organization.

The Taiwan study is a fair example of planned social change growing out of (1) perceived differences and (2) a preference for one alternative over the other. Over aeons man has slowly gained control over what seemed a capriciously menacing physical world. Now more knowledgeable and confident, he is no longer willing "to suffer the slings and arrows of outrageous fortune," but seeks to extend that control over his social world. Moving from increased control over illness and death, he seeks control over life and birth: new rules, new roles, and new relationships. Among these, none is more fateful in American society than planned change in Negro-white relationships.

Changing Negro-white relationships

Perhaps the most dramatic instance of contrived change in American society is the redefinition of the Negro's role, aimed at eliminating the adventitious link between race and chances for working, voting, learning, and the use of tax-supported facilities. This change is symbolized in the Supreme Court's 1954 ruling on school segregation and the 1964 Civil Rights Act. It is a change with a long ancestry and a pace slow at first but quickening in recent years.

Some indexes of slow, cumulative change are seen in the higher level of education achieved, in higher school enrollment rates (except for kindergarten and college levels),[24] a decline in illiteracy (from 95 percent in 1865 to 7.5 percent in 1959),[25] a decline in agricultural and an increase in white-collar occupations, strong rural-urban migration (a net loss from southern cities of better educated Negroes),[26] and along with the segregation of the inner city an unsuspected number of homes in integrated neighborhoods: just under a third in the Northeast, a fourth in the West, slightly over 10 percent in the North Central states and in the South.[27]

Long before Myrdal's *An American Dilemma*, sociologists had been analyzing the condition of the Negro in American society. For the most part, this research sought to find out what the situation was and why it was that way. Thus there were attempts to sort out genetic and environmental influences, to lay bare the social sources of prejudice and discrimination, to get adequate measures of bias, indexes of segregation, and the like.

While not directly related to change-inducing programs, the knowledge slowly accumulated built a foundation on which change could be more intelligently founded. Thus in 1947 we had Professor Robin Williams' monograph reviewing research on

Table 14.4

Schematic summary of President Nixon's Message to Congress on the Population Problem

Population growth	Problems: General	Problems: Specific	Solutions	Agencies
WORLD: 1830: 1 billion 1930: 2 billion 1960: 3.5 billion 1969: 3.5 billion 2000: 6–7 billion			Work to reduce rate of growth	United Nations (with which United States will collaborate)
DEVELOPING NATIONS:* Some now growing ten times as fast as they did a century ago; some will double, others triple their population in the next 30 years	Handicapped by growth rate that older, industrialized nations never had to confront	Nutrition, unemployment and underemployment, poverty, lack of medical services, lack of schools and teachers, ignorance that retards development	United States will assist countries requesting help in reducing their birthrates, when the decision to act rests ultimately with the individual	AID; Peace Corps; Departments of Agriculture; Commerce; and Health, Education, and Welfare
UNITED STATES: Growth rate about 1 percent per year (low mortality, high longevity, and an age composition favoring growth) 1917: 100 million 1967: 200 million 2000: 300 million (increase from 1967 to 2000 equivalent of building a city the size of Dayton, Tulsa or Jersey City every 30 days for the next 30 years)	Requirement of adjusting very rapidly to a growth in population that in past spread over centuries	Housing, jobs, parks and recreational facilities, water, air, plant and animal resources, education, transport and protective services, exacerbation of problems of urban life now becoming intolerable	Establish a Commission on Population Growth and the American Future to: project growth to the year 2000; make an inventory of needed resources; and specify the implications for government (National Commission on Urban Growth recommends creating ten communities of 100,000 each and ten communities of 1 million each. . . . need new architectural design, new building materials, new construction techniques, new methods of financing)	AID, OEO, Environmental Quality Council, Departments of Interior and Health, Education, and Welfare

* In Asia, Africa, Latin America.

problems of ethnic, racial, and religious group relations.[28] In addition to appraising various programs aimed at improving intergroup relations, Williams provided a list of 102 propositions on intergroup hostility and conflict, propositions based on some research evidence, selected for their probable truth and, therefore, for their usefulness in further research and action programs. Consider a study made just 20 years later on beliefs and attitudes of Negroes in certain metropolitan areas. Professor Marx found that religiousness, traditional and otherworldly in its orientation, was inversely related to militancy.[29] On the other hand, social mobility encouraged militancy. "Being removed from the values of the traditional South and having a positive self-image increase the likelihood of civil rights concern, while having a low morale and being socially isolated decrease it." Knowing what things go together we can, by increasing one, effect changes in the other. The earlier research provided a foundation for later programs of action.

With new knowledge and needs (one can't win wars, produce economically, or sustain civic harmony when falsely ascribing inferiority to a category of persons), the sociologist became increasingly engaged as an ally to the man of action. Thus it became urgent during World War II to determine conditions for amicable cooperation between white and black GI's. Such studies were undertaken, under the sociologist Samuel Stouffer, in the Research Branch of the War Department's Information and Education Division.* And more recently, we have a statement on *Social Research and the Desegregation of the U.S. Army,* reporting studies undertaken during the Korean war and instigated because of ". . . the Army's desperate need for combat manpower and its utter despair over the poor combat performance of (segregated and resentful) all-Negro units."

* Four volumes report aspects of research undertaken by this group. Volume I, *The American Soldier: Adjustment During Army Life,* Volume II, *The American Soldier: Combat and Its Aftermath,* Volume III, *Experiments on Mass Communication,* and Volume IV, *Measurement and Prediction.*

† Those who create knowledge have to face the problem of power. It is an ethical issue, for knowledge is power, and like Nobel's dynamite or Fermi's atom may be used for good or ill. These data from the Moynihan report could be used by bigots to justify the continued deprivation of the Negro. Or they could be used to support a proposal for a crash aid program to Negro families.

Perhaps the first question a sociologist must ask is whether he should stick to his last (as knowledge-creator) despite cries for relevance or the seduction of higher income. (It has been said that mathematicians and astronomers have saved more lives at sea than the lifeboat builders of all time.) Has he enough faith in the multiplier effect of big ideas to forego the popular or profitable application of trivial ones?

There are many other ethical issues that emerge when the sociologist moves toward applied fields. If he allies himself with

A more recent example of sociological research linked with policy and (recommended) program is the Moynihan report, *The Negro Family: The Case for National Action.*[31] Building on the earlier work of E. Franklin Frazier,[32] this report contends that the Negro family in urban ghettos is crumbling. In about 23 percent of urban Negro families, husbands are divorced or absent. Almost a fourth of Negro births are illegitimate (1963). Almost a fourth of Negro families are headed by women. Most Negro children, at some time, are dependent on welfare. The report states:

> . . . the Negro community has been forced into a matriarchal structure which, because it is so out of line with the rest of the American society, seriously retards the progress of the group as a whole, and imposes a crushing burden on the Negro male and, in consequence, on a great many Negro women as well.[33]
>
> [There is] a clear relation between male employment . . . and the number of welfare dependent children. Employment in turn reflects educational achievement which depends in large part on family stability, which reflects employment. Where we should break into this cycle, and how, are the most difficult domestic questions facing the United States.[34]

Here, then, we have the astonishing proposal that government somehow intervene to alter the structure of the Negro family in America!†

But let's go back to an earlier study for a rather clean example of the link between research and action on conditions of life for the Negro in American society. This was a study reported in 1951 by Morton Deutsch and Mary Evans Collins, a study of the effects

men of action in a worthy cause, can he remain a responsible scientist? Some physicists felt that government support of their discipline after World War II probably set the field back by 10 or more years—this because practical and soluble problems took precedence over scientifically significant ones.

Will the pressure to come up with an answer by next Wednesday (when next decade might be a likelier date) constrain the sociologist to offer hurried solutions with inadequate evidence?

If he gathers data as a government employee—say as a professional in the Census Bureau—is he responsible for the uses to which such data are put? Suppose his data provide the basis for astute gerrymandering of a political district, so compromising democratic process. Does the sociologist—should he—bear responsibility for this?

If you were employed by a member of the Cabinet—or by the President himself, as Moynihan was—could you resist the inclination to shade your recommendations, if not your data, so as to support the view of your employer?

A range of ethical problems touch the work of every scientist. Certainly the sociologist is not immune.

of interracial housing on the attitudes of white housewives, the base point for comparison being segregated biracial public housing. The experimental effect lay in the greater frequency of interaction characterizing integrated interracial housing.[35]

The experimental design would look somewhat as shown in Table 14.5. The aim was to test the hypotheses that the integrated interracial (in contrast to the segregated biracial) housing pattern would yield: (1) more social give and take, (2) friendlier attitudes on the part of white housewives, and (3) more equalitarian standards of behavior.

There were two projects in New York City providing low-income public housing on an integrated, interracial basis. These were matched with two projects in Newark operating on a segregated biracial basis. While the match on race of project residents was reasonably good (two-to-one Negro in New York I and Newark I, and 60–40 Negro/white in New York II compared with 50–50 in Newark II), on other factors there was marked variation. For example, there was a much higher proportion of Jews in the New York than in the Newark projects, and the New York residents tended to be more liberal than their Newark counterparts. Such differences had to be taken into account in the analysis. In short, these variables had to be controlled. For example, residents in the four projects who reported having no neighborly relations with Negroes were compared by education, religion, and political attitudes to see if these characteristics accounted for differences in white-Negro relationships. But the data show that

> . . . it seems to make little difference what type of person you are, or what kind of background you have, or what type of attitudes you possess; if you live in a segregated project, almost inevitably you will have no neighborly relations with the Negroes in the project.[36]

The figures in Table 14.6 show the consistent differences in favor of the integrated project in promoting friendly contacts (holding each of three characteristics constant). In the segregated projects, none of the 28 Catholic, politically conservative white housewives having an elementary school education had neighborly relations with Negro women. In the integrated projects, 9 out of 14 housewives, having the same attributes, had developed such relationships with Negro women.

These differences, very probably related to the occupancy pattern (propinquity and frequency of contact), were supported by different views or judgments about the housing projects and about

Table 14.5

Experimental design in the Deutsch and Collins study

	Before	Experimental treatment	After	Change
Experimental group	x_1	Admission to and living in *integrated interracial* housing	x_2	$x_2 - x_1 = d$
Control group	x'_1	Admission to and living in a *segregated biracial* housing project	x'_2	$x'_2 - x'_1 = d'$

x represents a measure describing respondents' (white housewives') attitudes toward Negroes

Hypothesis: The difference $d - d'$ will be of such a magnitude that it could not be considered a chance finding.

Table 14.6

Percent of white housewives having no neighborly relations with Negroes in project

Attributes	New York I (Integrated)	Newark I (Segregated)	Difference†	New York II (Integrated)	Newark II (Segregated)	Difference†
Political attitudes						
Liberal	36% (31)	100% (18)	64%	60% (35)	92% (26)	32%
Middle-of-road	22 (23)	100 (37)	78	59 (32)	95 (36)	36
Conservative	26 (35)	97 (45)	71	61 (31)	100 (38)	39
Education						
Only public school	39 (26)	100 (50)	61	68 (47)	93 (42)	25
Some high school	30 (30)	100 (33)	70	50 (28)	100 (34)	40
Completed high school or had some college	16 (31)	100 (14)	84	53 (15)	93 (14)	40
Religion						
Protestant	31 (16)	100 (23)	69	25 (4)	100 (16)	75
Catholic	38 (39)	98 (66)	60	58 (19)	98 (40)	40
Jew	13 (23)	100 (7)	87	67 (72)	95 (41)	28

* Figures in parentheses stand for number of cases.

† Segregated exceeds integrated in lack of neighborly contacts.

Negroes. In the segregated Newark projects, such views were more like those of the broader (extra-project) community than was the case with residents of the integrated New York projects. In the latter case, because of the greater divergence from the outside community, housewives felt more cross-pressures—as, for example, when they dealt with visitors and relatives.

When asked to recall what their attitudes toward Negroes had been before entering the project and to indicate how these attitudes had changed—if at all—the effect of occupancy pattern came out, again: "the net gain (percent of housewives reporting favorable minus the percent reporting unfavorable changes) was 56 percent and 55 percent for the integrated projects: for the segregated it was 5 percent and 20 percent."[37]

Since we are considering planned or contrived change, and the relationship between the sociologist and action agencies, the following statement by Louis Danzig, executive director of the Housing Authority of the City of Newark is apposite (the date is 1950).

> A new policy for locating tenants is now in effect in Newark's eight public housing projects. . . . As a result, the partial segregation that has characterized public housing in Newark will no longer obtain. . . .
>
> In large measure this change in fundamental policy reflects the impact of the study reported here. The study has served as a catalyst to the re-examination of our basic interracial policies in housing and as a stimulus to their change. . . . In supplying us with an objective picture of race relations in our projects . . . [the study by Deutsch and Collins] dramatically focused our attention and that of the community at large on matters which, under the press of other business, we have tended to ignore.
>
> The study did more than help to focus attention on the basic question of segregation in housing. Perhaps its most important consequence was its usefulness to those community groups concerned with intergroup relations and civil rights, such as the Essex County Intergroup Council. To such groups the study was an invaluable tool in creating the atmosphere that made it possible for the housing authority to adopt and execute a policy of non-segregation.[38]

Here we have an example of applied research in which the man of action and the man of knowledge are collaborators. While there is a difference in their roles, each contributes to the other's goal. The housing administrator has information useful to him in making decisions. And the sociologist has additional data on the effects of propinquity on interaction and the effects of interaction on prejudice.

In the case just described, we can think of the Housing Administrator as a social engineer, Deutsch and Collins as engaged in applied research. Thus, with the person engaged in pure research, we now have three categories, the characteristics of which are distinguished by Professor Hauser as shown in Table 14.7.

Table 14.7
The sociologist at work—from research, pure and applied, to social engineering

	Pure research	Applied research	Social engineering
Auspices	Organizations given to transmission and extension of knowledge: foundations, universities, and some work in government and private business	Any organization concerned with some practical problem	Any organization seeking to effect changes in behavior, in human relationships
Purpose	Extension of knowledge at the most general level possible	Knowledge immediately relevant to solution of a practical problem	To effect desired change as efficiently as possible
Manner of selecting problem	Problem grows out of antecedent research and is so selected as to promise fruitful extension of knowledge, or to resolve differences between theories yielding different predictions	Problem specified by client	Problems emerge, continuously (as in lawmaking, resolving international issues) in effort to achieve organizational ends
Procedures	Testing hypotheses to establish high-level generalizations, typically involving probability statements	Testing hypotheses to establish low-level generalizations guiding client in achieving his objectives	Formulating policy, predicting outcomes, taking into consideration uncontrollable contingencies, making decision, implementing decision in action programs
Outcomes	Another step taken in endless cycle of formulating theory, testing hypotheses, analyzing data, reformulating theory. . . . Propositions of the order: "If *a, b,* and *c* are observed in situations *L* and *M, X* will occur in situation *L, p* out of *n* times, and *Y* in situation *M*, p_1 out of *n* times, *ceteris paribus*"	Solution of immediate problem at which point work may end although findings may be relevant to pure research. . . . Propositions of the order: "Given *a* and *b* and *given* situation *M, Y* will occur *p* out of *n* times if *c* is brought into the situation, *ceteris paribus*."	Propositions of the order: "Having decided on *Y, c* is to be brought into the situation to supplement *a* and *b* in situation *M,* and situation *L* is to be avoided to preclude *X*."

* * * *

In these three illustrations we have seen how the sociologist's skills were used to determine the extent to which certain planned changes had in fact been accomplished: the development of democratic skills and attitudes, a reduction in Taichung's fertility, and, finally, friendly relationships between whites and Negroes. In such instances the sociologist is cast in the role of an outside examiner. The change agent's values may, or may not be his. His task is chiefly that of providing the methodological sophistication that will allow the change agent to answer the question: To what extent am I doing what I think I'm doing? Sometimes the sociologist may be a full-time employee of the change agent: in business, industry, government, or a private, nonprofit organization. In this case, it seems reasonable to infer that his values are those of his employer. His role is to bring knowledge and skills to bear, a facility in controlled observation and interpretation of differing patterns of human relationships, so promoting the change-inducing efforts of his organization.

In sum: By virtue of his symbol-storing and -manipulating prowess, man contrasts *then* with *now*, and *there* with *here*. Differences discerned lead to choices. He prefers one way to another. And when things valued are less than fully realized, he acts to shape the world closer to his heart's desire. His world, in its most crucial aspects, is a complex pattern of relationships. That he often bumbles in reshaping this pattern—in his efforts at planned change—testifies to the amateur in all of us. Skills in planned social change are scarcely common currency. Increasingly, the men of action seek allies among men of knowledge. In this alliance the sociologist is enlisted to help find some answers to the question: What are the outcomes of these efforts to reshape a sector of our world?

This is one facet of the sociologist's expanding role. That role merits some attention, and to that matter we now turn in a brief epilogue.

References

TEXT

1. William Foote Whyte, *Street Corner Society* (Chicago: University of Chicago Press, 1952).
2. Report in *The New York Times*, December 22, 1966, of a study by Dr. Marie Britt Ryne, a pediatrician at the Johns Hopkins hospital.
3. Walt Whitman, "Night on the Prairies," in Walt Whitman, *Complete Poetry and Selected Prose and Letters,* ed. Emory

Holloway (London: Nonesuch Press, 1938), p. 407.
4. Sarah Norcliffe Cleghorn, "Quatrain," *New York Tribune,* January 23, 1915.
5. *The New York Times,* Tuesday, September 24, 1963, p. 1 *et seq.*
6. Willard Waller, *The Sociology of Teaching* (New York: John Wiley & Sons, Inc., 1932), p. 442.
7. John W. Bennett, "Planned Change in Perspective," an introduction to a symposium on planned change, *Human Organization,* Vol. 18, No. 1 (Spring, 1959), pp. 2–4.
8. James G. March, "Group Norms and the Active Minority," *American Sociological Review,* Vol. 19, No. 6 (December, 1954), pp. 733–41.
9. Max Weber, "The Meaning of Ethical Neutrality," in *The Methodology of the Social Sciences,* trans. and ed. Edward A. Shils and Henry A. Finch (New York: Free Press, 1949), p. 16.
10. Arnold Rose, "The Selection of Problems for Research," *American Journal of Sociology,* Vol. 54, No. 3 (November, 1949), p. 219.
11. See "The Evaluators," by Charles R. Wright and Herbert H. Hyman in Phillip E. Hammond, *Sociologists at Work* (New York: Basic Books, Inc., Publishers, 1964), pp. 121–41. The initial study was conducted in 1955. In a later follow-up study, Terance K. Hopkins joined the evaluation team. These three sociologists report on their work in *Applications of Methods of Evaluation: Four Studies of the Encampment for Citizenship* (Berkeley and Los Angeles: University of California Press, 1962).
12. Encampment for Citizenship, "Summary of an Evaluation Study of the Encampment for Citizenship Made by the Bureau of Applied Social Research of Columbia University" (New York: Encampment for Citizenship, March, 1956), mimeographed, p. 9.
13. Henry Riecken, *The Volunteer Workcamp* (Reading, Mass.: Addison-Wesley Publishing Co., Inc., 1952).
14. Encampment for Citizenship, *op. cit.,* p. 12.
15. *Ibid.,* p. 6.
16. Bernard Berelson and Ronald Freedman, "A Study in Fertility Control," *Scientific American,* Vol. 210, No. 5 (May, 1964), p. 29.
17. Ronald Freedman and John Y. Takeshita, *Family Planning in Taiwan: An Experiment in Social Change* (Princeton, N.J.: Princeton University Press, 1969), p. 4.
18. Berelson and Freedman, *op. cit.,* p. 32.
19. Freedman and Takeshita, *op. cit.,* pp. 109–11.
20. *Ibid.,* p. 145.
21. *Ibid.* See Table VI–8, p. 133. Differences wash out in the succeeding two years. This is probably due to a shrinking proportion of eligibles for contraceptive practice: the more already practicing, the fewer remaining to adopt and to diffusion among those not reached in the campaign.
22. *Ibid.,* p. 147. Even with something resembling the classical design for experimentation, it is not possible to answer the question, conclusively: "What would have happened if. . .?" That is, what would have happened in the absence of the experimental intervention. Freedman and Takeshita are careful in their interpretation. But they are able to say that "approximately 60 percent of the decline in the fertility of [those accepting the intrauterine device] was the expected result of the secular trend [the ongoing, long-range decline in fertility], but 40 percent represented something else distinctive to this group." Presumably the campaign for birth control was what was "distinctive to this group." And again they say: "The acceptors in the program who initially had much higher than average fertility have much lower than average fertility in the post-insertion period, [i.e., after insertion of the intrauterine device]. There is a decline in fertility for the period of observation of about 77 percent. This is about twice as large a decline as might be expected on the basis of the normal aging effects and the secular trend in fertility for the general population." *Ibid.,* p. 302.
23. Population estimates for the year 2000 range from 266 to 321 million, depending on assumptions as to fertility. See Bureau of the Census "Projections of the Population of the United States, by Age and Sex: 1970 to 2020." *Current Population Reports,* Series P-25, No. 448 (Washington, D.C.: U.S. Government Printing Office, 1970).
24. Dorothy K. Newman, Bureau of Labor Statistics, Department of Labor, *Negroes in the United States: Their Economic and Social Situation* (Bulletin No. 1511 [Washington, D.C.: USGPO, June, 1966]), p. 24.

25. U.S. Bureau of the Census, *Pocket Data Book, U.S.A., 1967* (Washington, D.C., U.S. Government Printing Office, December, 1966), Table 169, p. 151.
26. Karl E. and Alma F. Taeuber, *Negroes in Cities* (Chicago: Aldine Publishing Co., 1965), Table 44, p. 143.
27. Seymour Sudman, Norman M. Bradburn, and Galen Gockel, "The Extent and Characteristics of Racially Integrated Housing in the United States," *Journal of Business,* Vol. 42, No. 1 (January, 1969).
28. Robin M. Williams, Jr., *The Reduction of Intergroup Tensions* (New York: Social Science Research Council, 1947).
29. Gary T. Marx, *Protest and Prejudice: A Study of Belief in the Black Community* (rev. ed.; New York: Harper Torchbook No. 1435, 1967). The following quotation is from page 215.
30. Leo Bogart (ed.), *Social Research and the Desegregation of the U.S. Army: Two Original 1951 Field Reports* (Chicago: Markham Publishing Co., 1969).
31. Issued by the Office of Policy Planning and Research, U.S. Department of Labor, March, 1965.
32. See E. Franklin Frazier, *The Negro Family in the United States* (Chicago: University of Chicago Press, 1939).
33. Office of Policy Planning, *op. cit.*, p. 29.
34. *Ibid.*, p. 47.
35. Morton Deutsch and Mary Evans Collins, *Interracial Housing* (Minneapolis: University of Minnesota Press, 1951). My comments are based on the abridged version in William Petersen (ed.), *American Social Patterns* (Garden City, New York: Doubleday, Anchor Books, 1956).
36. *Ibid.*, p. 26.
37. *Ibid.*, p. 42.
38. *Ibid.*, pp. 57, 58.

TABLES

14.6 Petersen (ed.), *op. cit.*, Table 2, pp. 26, 27.
14.7 Philip M. Hauser, "Social Science and Social Engineering," *Philosophy of Science,* Vol. 16 (July, 1949), p. 211.

FIGURES

14.3 Bernard Berelson and Ronald Freedman, "A Study in Fertility Control," *Scientific American,* Vol. 210, No. 5 (May, 1964), p. 33.
14.4 Ronald Freedman and John Y. Takeshita, *Family Planning in Taiwan: An Experiment in Social Change* (Princeton, N.J.: Princeton University Press, 1969), Table II–11, p. 49.
14.5 *Ibid.*, Table II–3, p. 41.
14.6 Norman B. Ryder and Charles F. Westoff, "The Trend of Expected Parity in the United States: 1955, 1960, 1965," Office of Population Research, Princeton University; and Population Association of America, Inc., *Population Index* (April–June, 1967), cover.

Epilogue

chapter 15 Sociology: its uses and abuses

I hold every man a debtor to his profession; from the which as men of course do seek to receive countenance and profit, so ought they of duty to endeavour themselves by way of amends to be a help and ornament thereunto.
Francis Bacon, "Preface," *Maxims of the Law*

A newcomer to the academic scene, sociology is today a flourishing, far-flung enterprise. It is always hard to pinpoint the inception of ideas, so remote and varied are their forebears. But certainly, in the United States, we cannot date the advent of sociology much before 1900.[1] We can think of a first phase of the discipline's development running from then to the end of World War I.[2] Against a background of bourgeoning industrial and urban growth, turn-of-the-century sociologists sought to build a science of society whose laws of social evolution would point to prescriptions for a better world. Many of them, religious and rural in their backgrounds, reformist in their inclinations, sought solutions to social problems: crime, poverty, alcoholism, child labor, unemployment, immigrant adjustment, and the like.[3]

Sociology in the United States: a thumbnail sketch

The early years

Using 1935 as the watershed, the Hinkles divide the years since 1918 into two periods in the development of modern sociology. World War I, they speculate, had a disenchanting effect on social scientists, who from Condorcet and Comte through Lester Ward and Albion Small had high hopes for the reformation of society, guided by the science of society. If problems then posed still revealed a concern with social issues, the central task became scientific rather than reformist. Increasingly, the task became the identification, unscrambling, and assessment of multiple causes of patterned conduct. During this period, 1918–35, there were major contributions to social psychology (Cooley, Mead, Dewey, Baldwin) and, with the contributions of Park, McKenzie, and Burgess, the field of human ecology emerged. But it has been in the years since 1935 that sociology has grown most remarkably in America. This growth can be documented in numbers, diversity and development of professional standards.

Rapid growth, high demand, short supply

In each of the two decades since 1950, the membership of the American Sociological Association has just about doubled: 1950—3,522; 1959—6,345; 1969—12,253.[4] The distribution among various categories of membership is shown in Figure 15.1. The remarkably large part of the membership who are students suggests that the field is currently attracting many young people. Rapid growth is also shown in Figure 15.2, especially in the doubling of the number of undergraduates majoring in sociology between 1960–61 and 1965–66.

The recency of sociology's growth is brought home to us by this fact. Among the 1,888 members of the Association who had doctorates in 1959, 61 percent were awarded the degree within the preceding 10 years.[5] And it appears that the profession is still short of meeting the demand for new sociology teachers. (A Labor Department report estimated in 1964 that "perhaps as many as 300 new sociology teachers will be needed each year, on the average, to fill new positions and to replace college faculty members who leave the profession."[6] Such a supply of sociologists will be hard to come by.)

How can we account for this rapid growth, high demand, and

Figure 15.1

Distribution of types of 1969 membership* of the American Sociological Association

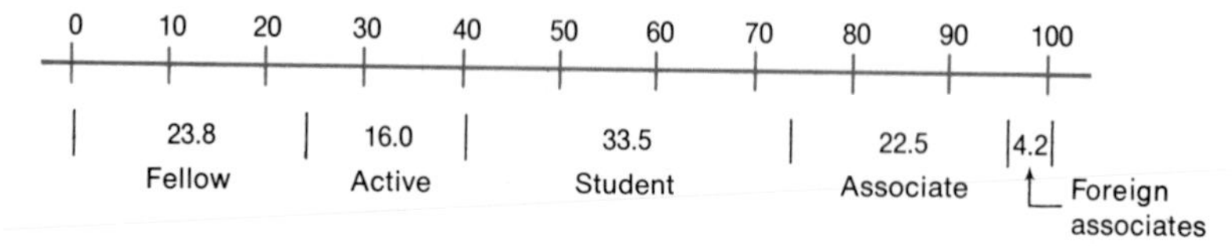

* Definitions of the first three classes of membership are these. "To be eligible for Active membership an applicant must have (*a*) a Ph.D. or equivalent professional training in Sociology or (*b*) substantial professional achievement in Sociology, or (*c*) a Ph.D., or its equivalent or substantial professional achievement in a closely related field, provided that the applicant's interest and activities have sociological emphasis or implication. . . . On completion of five years of Active membership a member shall automatically become a Fellow, provided that those whose eligibility for Active membership rested upon criterion (*c*) above shall have a major commitment to the field of Sociology. . . . Any person interested in study, teaching, research or practice in Sociology, or in closely related fields of scientific interest, may be admitted to Associate membership in the Association . . ." (Taken from *Directory—Constitution and By-laws* [Washington, D.C.: American Sociological Association, 1967], p. 317. Data provided courtesy of the Executive Office, American Sociological Association, 1001 Connecticut Ave., NW, Washington, D.C.)

short supply? It is conceivable that the complexities of our society now require that a larger proportion of all American scientists go into sociology. But the recent growth springs in large measure from the increase and changing composition of our population, swelling enrollments in colleges and universities.

Subfields: the multiplication of interests

In the house of sociology there are many mansions. For recording the specialties of its members, the American Sociological Association identifies the 33 subfields listed in Table 15.1. But the National Register of Scientific and Technical Personnel includes more than 50 specialties in sociology!

Considering this roster the reader will recognize in what a literal sense this book is an introduction to sociology.

Professionalization

The emergence of special interests, as indicated by these subfields, is one aspect of every growing intellectual discipline. But besides a proliferation of interests, there is a consolidation of interest. That is to say, the discipline establishes certain standards of competence in a given realm, stipulates the way such expertise is to be

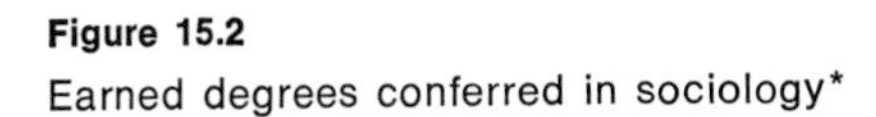

Figure 15.2
Earned degrees conferred in sociology*

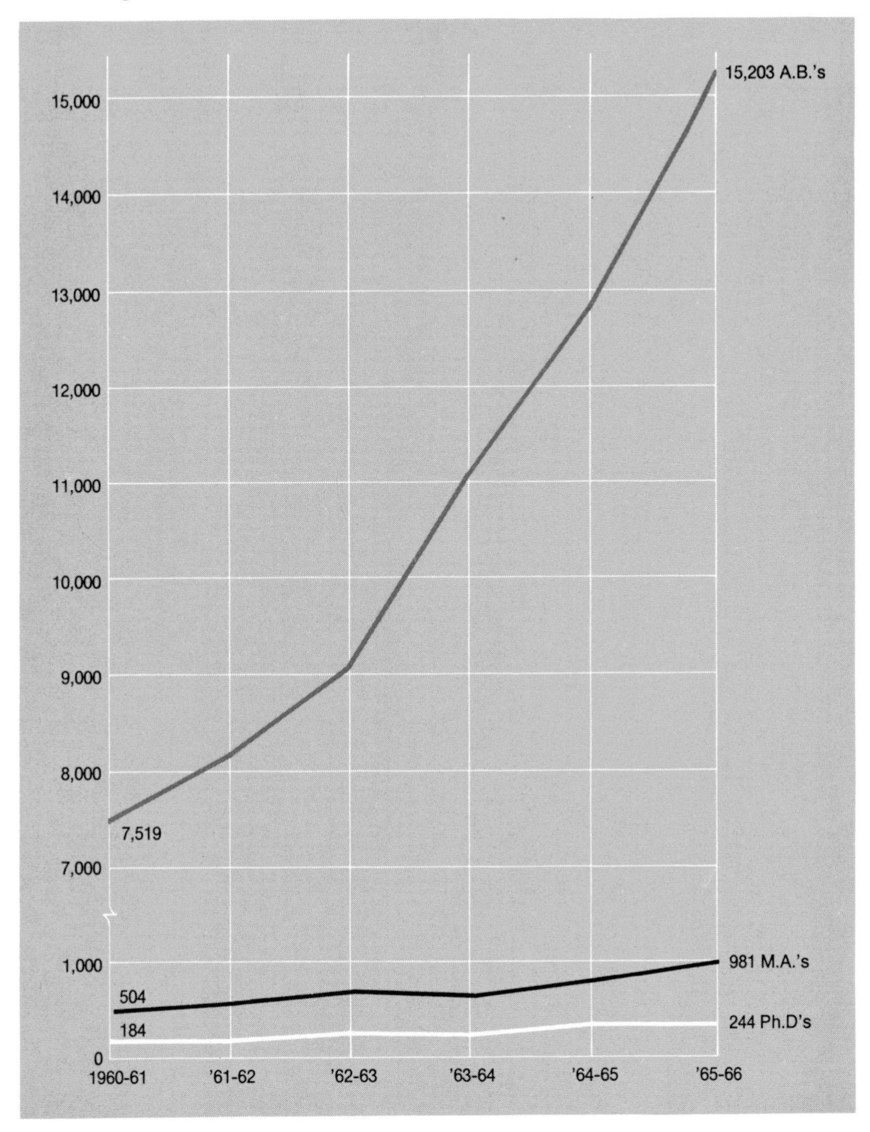

* For United States, including Canal Zone, Puerto Rico, and Virgin Islands.

achieved, arranges regular means of communication among its members, and devises codes to regulate conduct among members and toward the layman. These are parts of the professionalization process.

Table 15.1

Specialties in sociology listed by the American Sociological Association

1. Applied Sociology	16. Mathematical Sociology
2. Collective Behavior and Mass Communication	17. Medical Sociology
3. Community	18. Methodology and Statistics
4. Comparative Sociology	19. Military Sociology
5. Crime and Delinquency	20. Occupations and Professions
6. Cultural Sociology	21. Political Sociology
7. Demography	22. Race and Ethnic Relations
8. Deviant Behavior	23. Religion
9. Education	24. Rural Sociology
10. Formal and Complex Organizations	25. Small Groups
11. Human Ecology	26. Social Change
12. Industrial Sociology—Economy & Society	27. Social Control
13. Law and Society	28. Social Organization
14. Leisure, Sports, Recreation, and the Arts	29. Social Psychology
15. Marriage and the Family	30. Stratification and Mobility
	31. Sociology of Knowledge and Science
	32. Theory
	33. Urban Sociology

Their professional training takes aspiring sociologists to such schools as those listed in Table 15.2. According to our last available data, those earning doctorate are about 32 years old when it is conferred. This is 10 years after receiving the A.B. degree, although only about half this period is spent in full-time graduate study.[7] (In the social sciences—history, sociology, political science, economics, anthropology, and psychology—median years between the A.B. and Ph.D range from 9.9 to 8.4. In the life sciences the figure is 8.1 and for the physical sciences, 7.1.) Such training typically includes work in social theory, methods of research, mathematics and language, and two or three of the fields listed in Table 15.1. It culminates in a piece of research (the dissertation) that aims to make a contribution to knowledge.

In the process of professionalization, sociologists have multiplied the means of talking to one another: through publications, through local and regional organizations, and through suborganizations focused on specialties. For example, there are now five journals published by the American Sociological Association: *The American Sociological Review, Sociometry, The Journal of Health and Social Behavior, The Sociology of Education,* and *the American Sociologist.* These are in addition to more than 40 domestic journals (and many foreign ones) bearing on sociology.

Further to promote conversation, stimulation, and mutual aid there are a number of statewide associations of sociologists. But

Table 15.2

U.S. universities conferring 20 or more Ph.D.'s in sociology between 1964 and 1968

School*	Ph.D's conferred 1964–68	Graduate students in residence: Full time	Graduate students in residence: Part time	Department faculty: Full time	Department faculty: Part time†
University of Chicago	62	135	—	25	8
Michigan State University	57	82	6	12	19
University of Wisconsin‡	49	226	7	57	10
University of Minnesota	46	49	76	23	8
University California, Los Angeles	43	141	15	26	2
University California, Berkeley	39	175	—	34	10
Iowa State University	35	52	4	19	5
University of Michigan	35	144	—	29	—
Ohio State University	35	113	16	35	1
University of Washington	35	83	114	23	—
Harvard University	34	69	—	8	8
New School for Social Research	32	187	141	7	5
University Missouri	30	77	16	24	8
Washington University	30	63	3	16	1
University of North Carolina, Chapel Hill	29	75	5	23	6
Yale University	26	50	—	20	6
Northwestern	26	85	—	13	6
Indiana University	26	113	38	26	—
Florida State University	25	45	—	15	11
University of Pittsburgh	25	87	8	27	10
Purdue University	23	51	7	24	2
New York University	23	110	77	17	5
Catholic University	22	48	12	11	2
Cornell University	21	56	—	11	7
University Oregon	21	85	5	13	9
Princeton University	20	25	—	16	1
Cornell (Rural Sociology)	20	47	1	12	10
University of Texas	20	52	8	21	2
Totals	889	2,525		587	

* The first 10 universities confer 49 percent of all Ph.D's among universities in this listing. Were Cornell's Department of Rural Sociology combined with its Department of Sociology (thus displacing Berkeley), the figure would be exactly 50 percent.

† Includes faculty members with joint appointments in other departments.

‡ These are the data for two departments, the Department of Sociology and the Department of Rural Sociology. The same separation occurs at Cornell, but the data are separately reported.

these tend to be less active than such regional and special interest associations as the following:

American Catholic Sociological Society
Eastern Sociological Society
Midwest Sociological Society
Ohio Valley Sociological Association

Figure 15.3
Membership in specialty sections of the American Sociological Association as of August 1, 1969

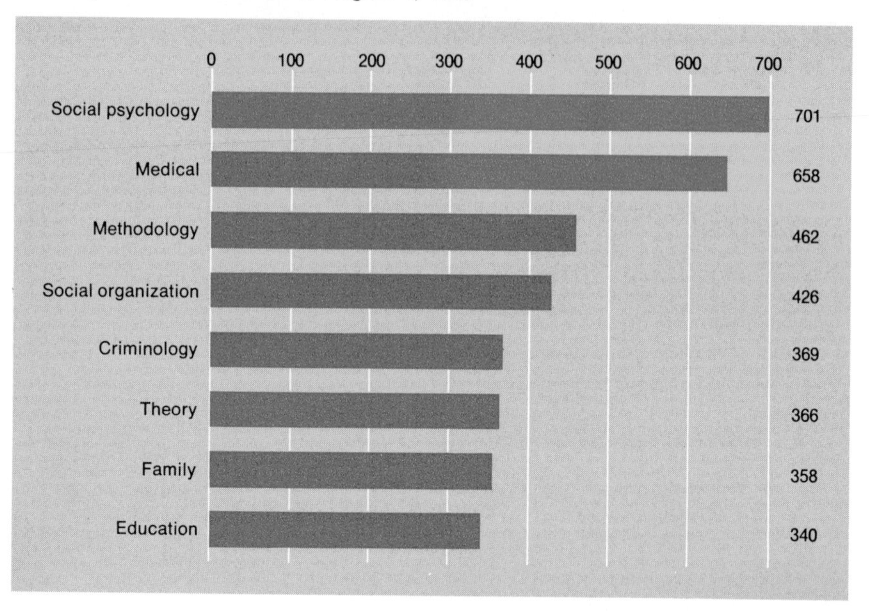

Pacific Sociological Society
Rural Sociological Society
Society for the Study of Social Problems
Southern Sociological Society

Sections of the Association emerge, formally organizing to serve special interests. Membership in the eight sections of the Association is indicated in Figure 15.3.

Not only have sociologists, and other social scientists come increasingly to share views and findings through associations and journals. They also share their data by setting up data banks, or archives. For example, Project TALENT, based at Stanford, will make available to a qualified sociologist data from a national probability sample of about 400,000 high school students. There now exists a Council of Social Science Data Archives.[8] This includes more than twenty depositories of data available for scholarly research. Data banks associated in this Council are listed in Table 15.3.

With such resources, with computer technology, with probability sampling, and with artful modes of analysis, the profession of

Table 15.3
Banks of data useful in sociological research

1. Archive on Comparative Political Elites	University of Oregon
2. Archive on political Elites in Eastern Europe	University of Pittsburg
3. Bureau of Applied Social Research	Columbia University
4. Bureau of Labor Statistics	U.S. Department of Labor
5. Carleton University Social Science Data Archives	Carleton College
6. Columbia University School of Public Health and Administrative Medicine Research Archives	Columbia University
7. Council for Inter-Societal Studies	Northwestern University
8. Graduate School of Industrial Administration	California Institute of Technology
9. Human Relations Area Files	Yale University
10. International Data Library and Reverence Service, Survey Research Center	University of California, Berkeley
11. International Development Data Bank	Michigan State University
12. Inter-University Consortium for Political Research	University of Michigan
13. Laboratory for Political Research	University of Iowa
14. Latin American Data Bank	University of Florida
15. Louis Harris Political Data Center	University of N. Carolina
16. M.I.T. Social Science Data Bank	Massachusetts Institute of Technology
17. National Opinion Research Center	University of Chicago
18. Political Science Research Library	Yale University
19. Project TALENT Data Bank	Stanford University
20. Public Opinion Survey Unit	University of Missouri
21. Roper Public Opinion Research Center	Williams College
22. Social Science Data & Program Library Service	University of Wisconsin
23. Survey Research Laboratory	University of Illinois
24. U.C.L.A. Political Behavior Archive	University of California, Los Angeles

sociology is much advanced.[9] None of these, obviously, can substitute for the imaginative posing of significant questions nor the knowledge of the wisdom literature which nourishes that imagination.

Growing knowledge is growing power. This fruit of the tree of knowledge, like dynamite, may be used for good or ill. Since malpractice by one affects the reputation—sometimes the livelihood—of all, professions commonly act to protect their members and their clients by developing a code of ethics. Rules for the role of sociologist are presented below.

Preamble

Sociological inquiry is often disturbing to many persons and groups. Its results may challenge long-established beliefs and lead to change in old taboos. In consequence such findings may create demands for the suppression or control of this inquiry or for dilution of the findings. Similarly, the results of sociological investigation may be of significant use to individuals in power—whether in government, in the private sphere, or in the universities—because such findings, suitably manipulated, may facilitate the misuse of power. Knowledge is a form of power, and in a society increasingly dependent on knowledge, the control of information creates the potential for political manipulation.

For these reasons, we affirm the autonomy of sociological inquiry. The sociologist must be responsible, first and foremost, to the truth of his investigation. Sociology must not be an instrument of any person or group who seeks to suppress or misuse knowledge. The fate of sociology as a science is dependent upon the fate of free inquiry in an open society.

At the same time this search for social truths must itself operate within constraints. Its limits arise when inquiry infringes on the rights of individuals to be treated as persons, to be considered—in the renewable phrase of Kant—as ends and not as means. Just as sociologists must not distort or manipulate truth to serve untruthful ends, so too they must not manipulate persons to serve their quest for truth. The study of society, being the study of human beings, imposes the responsibility of respecting the integrity, promoting the dignity, and maintaining the autonomy of these persons.

To fulfill these responsibilities, we, the members of the American Sociological association, affirm the following Code of Ethics:

1. *Objectivity in Research.* In his research, the sociologist must maintain scientific objectivity.

2. *Integrity in Research.* The sociologist should recognize his own limitations and, when appropriate, seek more expert assistance or decline to undertake research beyond his competence. He must not misrepresent his own abilities, or the competence of his staff to conduct a particular research project.

3. *Respect of the Research Subject's Rights to Privacy and Dignity.* Every person is entitled to the right of privacy and dignity of treatment. The sociologist must respect these rights.

4. *Protection of Subjects from Personal Harm.* All research should avoid causing personal harm to subjects used in research.

5. *Preservation of Confidentiality of Research Data.* Confidential information provided by a research subject must be treated as such by the sociologist. Even though research information is not a privileged communication under the law, the sociologist must, as far as possible, protect subjects and informants. Any promises made to such persons must be honored. However, provided that he respects the assurances he has given his subjects, the sociologist has no obligation to withhold information of misconduct of individuals or organizations.

If an informant or other subject should wish, however, he can formally release the researcher of a promise of confidentiality. The provisions of this section apply to all members of research organizations (i.e., interviewers, coders, clerical staff, etc.), and it is the responsibility of the chief investigators to see that they are instructed in the necessity and importance of maintaining the confidentiality of the data. The obligation of the sociologist includes the use and storage of original data to which a subject's name is attached. When requested, the identity of an organization or subject must be adequately disguised in publication.

6. *Presentation of Research Findings.* The sociologist must present his findings honestly and without distortion. There should be no omission of data from a research report which might significantly modify the interpretation of findings.

7. *Misuse of Research Role.* The sociologist must not use his role as a cover to obtain information for other than professional purposes.

8. *Acknowledgement of Research Collaboration and Assistance.* The sociologist must acknowledge the professional contributions or assistance of all persons who collaborated in the research.

9. *Disclosure of the Sources of Financial Support.* The sociologist must report fully all sources of financial support in his research publications and any special relations to the sponsor that might affect the interpretation of the findings.

10. *Distortion of Findings by Sponsor.* The sociologist is obliged to clarify publicly any distortion by a sponsor or client of the findings of a research project in which he has participated.

11. *Disassociation from Unethical Research Arrangements.* The sociologist must not accept such grants, contracts, or re-

search assignments as appear likely to require violation of the principles above, and must publicly terminate the work or formally disassociate himself from the research if he discovers such a violation and is unable to achieve its correction.

12. *Interpretation of Ethical Principles.* When the meaning and application of these principles are unclear, the sociologist should seek the judgment of the relevant agency or committee designated by the American Sociological Association. Such consultation, however, does not free the sociologist from his individual responsibility for decisions or from his accountability to the profession.

13. *Applicability of Principles.* In the conduct of research the principles enunciated above should apply to research in any area either within or outside the United States of America.

Sociologists: who they are and what they do

Figure 15.4 tells us that sociologists are but a small part of the total body of scientists in the United States—2 percent in 1968. From the same source* we learn that most (73 percent) are employed by educational institutions. (Eight percent work for the federal government and other governmental agencies, 5 percent for nonprofit organizations, and 2 percent in business and industry.)

But the high level of employment in education does not mean an equally high concentration in teaching. The data on sociologists' work activities are as listed in Table 15.4.

Teaching sociology does not exclude doing sociology. Often the two are combined. But "doing" is expensive. Costs of designing research, field work, programming and use of computers, and analysis and writing require major funding. This work is supported in a very modest way by university funds, more substantially by foundations and various nonprofit organizations and by government. Thirty-five percent of the sociologists on the National

* The 2 percent of all scientists in sociology represents 6,638 sociologists. How representative they are of the better than 12,000 members of the professional association is uncertain. They probably give an accurate picture of the professionals—i.e., the Fellows and Active categories—about 5,000, all told—in the membership list of the American Sociological Association.

† Forty-nine percent were not doing research on any federally funded programs. On about another 16 percent we have no information.

Figure 15.4
Fields of science in which 297,942 U.S. scientists were engaged, 1968

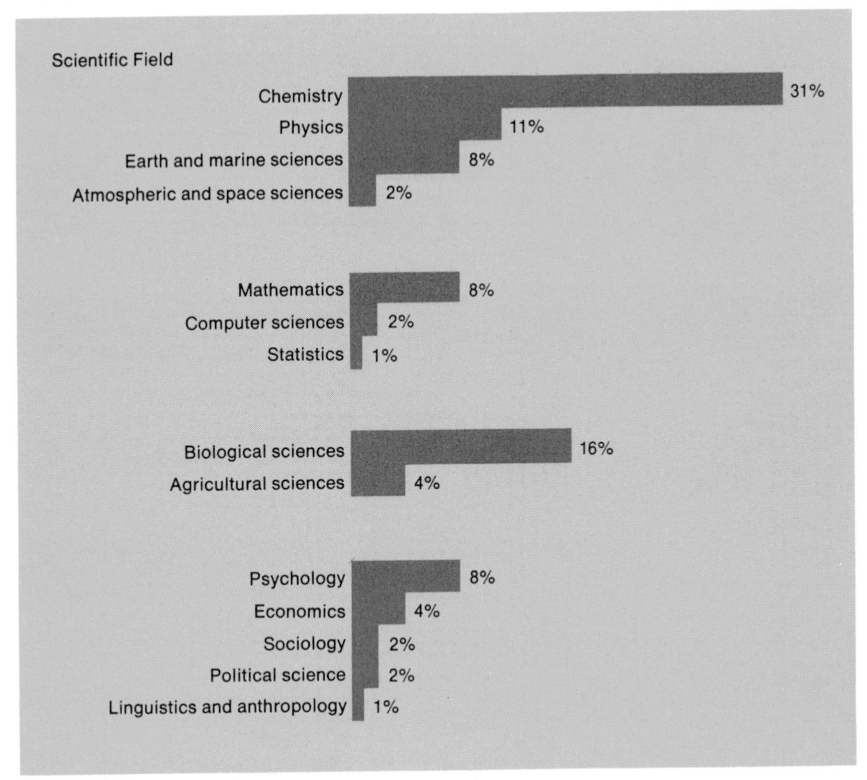

Table 15.4
Sociologists' work activities

Teaching	47%
Research and development	22
Management or administration of R.&D.	13
Not employed	8
No information	5
Other	3
Consulting, Exploration, Forecasting, and Reporting	2
	100%

Register of Scientific and Technical Personnel were getting federal funds for research in 1968, most of them in health, education, and urban development programs.† These three programs accounted for 29 percent of the total. The remaining 6 percent were working

Figure 15.5
Age distribution of 6,586 U.S. sociologists, 1968

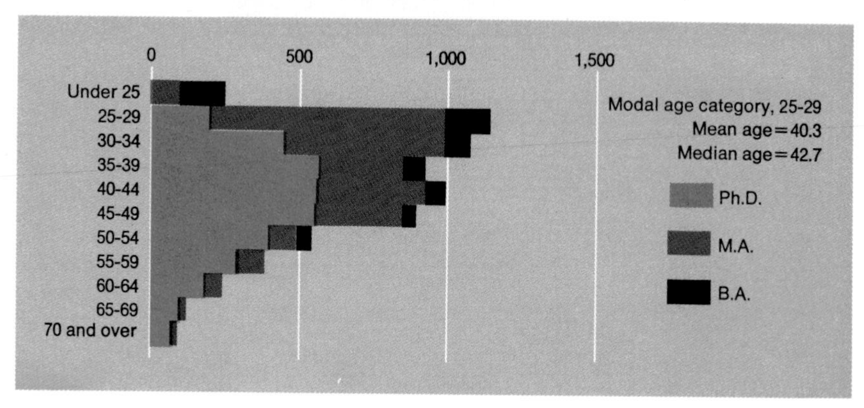

An additional 52 sociologists are not listed for want of data on age or degree.

under a variety of other governmental programs: agriculture, atomic energy, defense, housing, natural resources, public works, rural development, space, transportation, international programs, and others.

For their work, sociologists' median income in 1968 was $12,000. For those holding the doctorate, median incomes were higher: $15,000, $16,600, $18,300 and $25,000 in educational institutions (the calendar year), nonprofit organizations, the federal government, and business and industry, respectively.

To the statement of the age structure of the field made in Figure 15.5, we might add a word on the sex composition of the profession. Among all women listed in the National Register (9 percent of the 298,000 scientists), 5 percent are sociologists. (The comparable figure is 2 percent for men.) Among sociologists, however, 22 percent are women. But they are a smaller part—14 percent—among sociologists holding doctorates.

Other incidental intelligence on the species is given in Figures 15.6 and 15.7. Data are based on a sample of 429 active members and Fellows of the American Sociological Association. Figure 15.6 shows the great underrepresentation of Protestants and Catholics and the overrepresentation of Jews and those declaring some other, or no, religious preference. The data also suggest that religious identification, whatever the faith, tends to recede as sociologists advance in age.

Figure 15.6

Religious preference of sociologists' mothers and their own preference as adolescents and at time of 1967 study

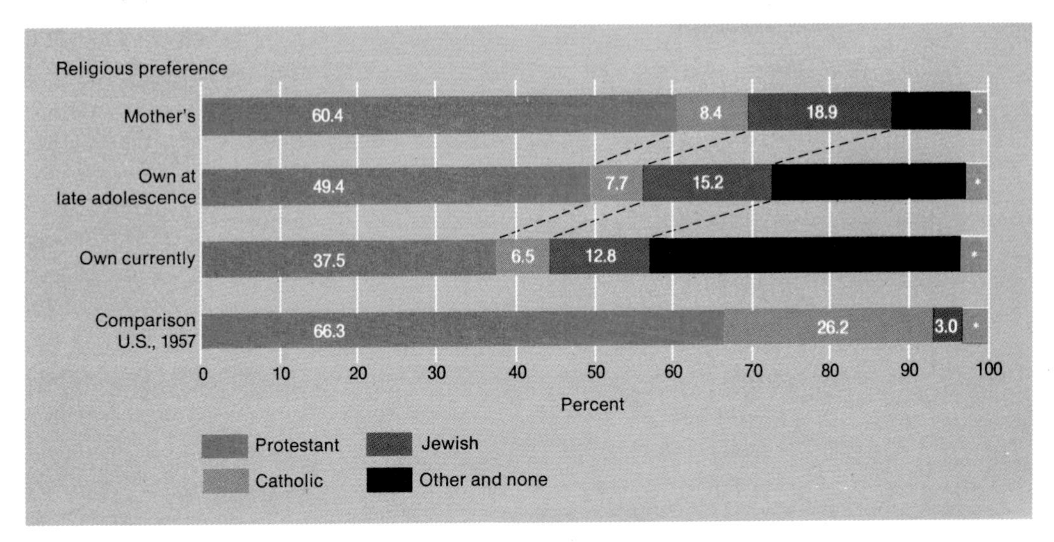

* Indicates the "no response" category.

Figure 15.7

Political orientation of sociologists' fathers and their own political inclinations as adolescents and at time of 1967 study

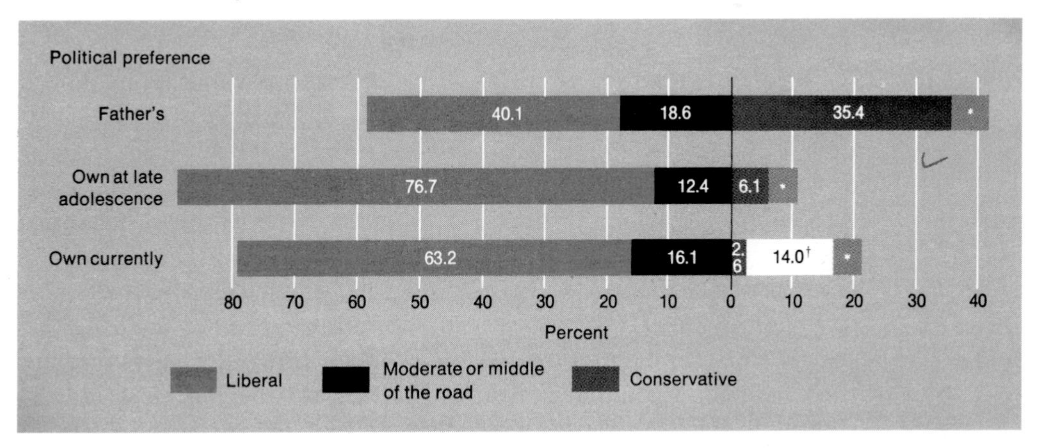

* Indicates the "no response" category.

† Other labels. Some of these reported their political orientations as "radical" or used other leftist terms. Hence the left-of-center category should be somewhat greater than the reported 63.2 percent.

Figure 15.8
Percent distribution of articles published in the 1965 and 1966 *American Sociological Review* and *American Journal of Sociology*

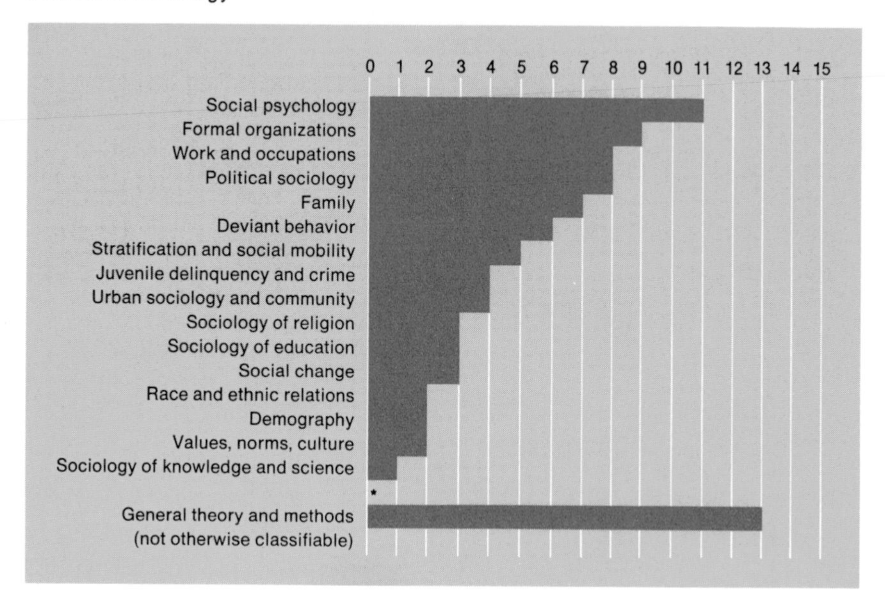

* Less than 1%: Small groups analysis, collective behavior, social ethics, communication and public opinion, sociology of medicine, of law, of war, of recreation/leisure/play.

Figure 15.7 gives us a similar picture of departure from orthodoxy when the political posture of sociologists is compared with that of their fathers. Each bar in this figure represents 100 percent.

Reverting again to what they do, we can answer this question: In what fields do they do research and report results to their fellow sociologists? Figure 15.8 gives us a tentative answer.

Comparable data for 1940–41 reveal a marked shift in research interests in the last 25 years. Over half of the articles then published in the *American Sociological Review* and the *American Journal of Sociology* were in six subfields, in this order: social psychology, urban sociology and community, family, sociology of war, demography, and social ethics. There was but a single article investigating formal organization. During this period, reported research in the sociology of work and occupations increased fivefold. Research in political sociology doubled, while inquiries into the institution of the family declined by 4 percent.

Table 15.5
Three orientations or emphases in sociology

Characteristics compared	Scientific: Theory	Scientific: Empirical research	Humanistic	Action-oriented
Role model	Natural scientist		European intellectual	Engineer
Primary goal	Social knowledge		Social criticism	Solution of social problems
Value perspective	Ethically neutral		Challenges dominant American value orientations	Guided by dominant American value orientations
Criterion for problem selection	Theoretical importance		Social importance of fundamental issues	Social importance of segmental problems
Theoretical perspective	Functionalism		Humanism	Pragmatic liberalism
Methodology	Logic and mathematics	Rigorous statistical analysis	Disciplined insight	Statistical and qualitative analysis
Criteria of adequacy	Coherence	Correspondence	Perceptiveness	Usefulness
Intellectual product	Analytical schemes	Empirical generalization	General trends and tendencies	Implications for action

Note: The second and third columns have been reversed from the original and the word "humanistic" substituted for the heading "significance."

Finally, a summary view of what sociologists do is presented in Table 15.5. It points to three somewhat different postures or orientations of the sociologist as he approaches his work. The first column, "scientific," is the orientation reflected in types of research classified in Figure 15.8. Approaches represented in the next two columns reflect emphases that we find in the "new sociology."

The new sociology

In a session on sociologists' involvement in public affairs it was reported that

Three times during the discussion some members of the audience broke into applause in response to some statement that was interpreted as a crack at fundamental, long-time, or theoretical research.

[Among sociologists in the audience] the tendency to be impatient with anything smacking of the theoretical, objective, long-time, fundamental, or purely intellectual aspects of sociology was greatly magnified.[10]

This panel discussion took place over 25 years ago. The crisis was World War II.

Some sociologists (and some observers, like *Time* magazine)[11] see the discipline taking a new direction, engagement with social problems, with the sociologist cast in the role of social prophet. Actually, the issues raised by "the new sociology" are hoary ones, and the new credo is that of sociology's founding fathers.* But the breadth and depth of disenchantment with American society is new. In 1942, the problem, its solution, the commitment of necessary resources—about these things there was little debate. The United States had been attacked, the enemy had to be vanquished, and every means, in materiel and manpower, was mobilized. Including sociology. We do not now enjoy the same consensus about the futility or immorality of the war in Vietnam, the threat of the "military-industrial complex" that President Eisenhower warned against, the evil of a double standard of living based on race, or the inequities imposed by the accident of birth (conferring wealth on some, poverty on others). But the underlying issues for sociology and sociologist remain the same.

One issue revived by the new sociology sets scholarship over against active intervention in public affairs, the stockpiling of reliable knowledge versus its application, the treatment of sociology as an end, in contrast to its use as a means for excising cancerous parts of society.

Engagement, rather than detachment, is one issue. Along with it

* To speak of the new sociology, as I do for simplicity's sake, is misleading. It is not a single voice or viewpoint. It embraces the woman's liberation movement; those who fear that the sociologist may become—for government or private employers—a hired gun; some who would define sociology in Marxist terms; others for whom sociology's main task should be achieving justice for the Negro; and some who would exploit new media, use new means, to apprehend the truth. In the following paragraphs I shall emphasize what seem to be both salient and basic issues.

go different criteria for justifying one's work: adding to a body of reliable knowledge *or* contributing to a more satisfactory society. Also related to the engagement issue is the separation of work role from civic role. The new sociology (and some of the old), sees this as a spurious split between roles. Indeed, some allege not only that it is impossible, but that it is hypocritical to pretend in one's work (research and teaching) that he has no preferences (as a citizen). For example, suppose that in his teaching the sociologist reviews the evidence for this hypothesis: variation in race is correlated with variation in achievement. A survey of responsible research leads to this conclusion: the significance of racial differentials for human conduct comes about as we take an insignificant biological fact (for example, pigmentation) and blow it up into a tremendously significant social fiction. Now shall he withhold the logical inference and the moral judgment: discrimination based on race is wrong?

The traditional answer to this question has been yes. The task of the sociologist is to distill from the evidence the best-supported factual propositions. Inferences from these propositions are the privilege of the consumer. Max Weber is often invoked in support of this traditional position:

> An unprecedented situation exists when a large number of officially accredited prophets [professors] do not do their preaching on the streets, or in churches or other public places or in sectarian conventicles, but rather feel themselves competent to enunciate their evaluations on ultimate questions "in the name of science" in governmentally privileged lecture halls in which they are neither controlled, checked by discussion, nor subject to contradiction. . . . I take the view that a "lecture" should be different from a "speech."[12]

But the new sociology takes a different position: profession, preference, and practice are fused.

Another hallmark is the emphasis on becoming, rather than being; on change, not structure; on conflict rather than harmony. To analyze adaptive social arrangements at one point in time, so some critics say, is not only to comfort the conservative who confounds what is with what, by nature, must be. It is to betray the social reality. For conflict is immanent in society, and change grows out of conflict. Furthermore, since change is desirable, its necessary agent, conflict, becomes good.

There are, then, two central themes of the new sociology.* These can be telescoped in the terms *engagement*, (or commitment) and conflict-generated *change*. If in fact they are not new in kind, the emphases are new in degree. They are forcefully stated by a zealous group who see themselves as redeeming the profession while working to transform a sick society. They would assert that sociologists have a special competence which entitles them—indeed, from a moral perspective compels them—to take authoritative positions on social issues: war, race, urban decay, poverty, and population problems. They would contend that the sociologist is delinquent if he fails to prescribe on such matters as the reallocation of power and privilege in American society. Sick societies need clinical sociologists just as the psychically disturbed need the services of clinical psychologists.

This fresh impulse in the discipline is, in fact, a return to sociology's origins—both in its value-suffused social philosophy and its commitment to doing good. (This skeleton in the closet of their background American sociologists have long disavowed. Theirs not do do and die, theirs but to verify.) It is by no means discontinuous with the sociological tradition. Furthermore, the new wave has, in a roundabout way, support from the establishment—at least in providing the data to serve as base and bench marks for change. With increasing frequency we hear the cry for adequate data so that social change may be intelligently planned and brought about. Consider some recent landmarks.

In February, 1967, Senator Mondale, along with 10 other senators, introduced S. 843, a bill proposing a "Full Opportunity and Social Accounting Act." Sections from the bill state its purpose, the creation of a Council of Social Advisers and the requirement of an annual "Social Report" by the President.

> Sec. 2. In order to promote the general welfare, the Congress declares that it is the continuing policy and responsibility of the Federal Government, consistent with the primary responsibilities of State and local governments and the pri-

* There are other corollary characteristics. One example: Assume that the task of the "old" sociology is simply to build a body of reliable knowledge. Clearly knowledge is only as reliable as the methods used to obtain it. Hence, if we are to minimize the task of acquiring knowledge we will, *ipso facto*, belittle a preoccupation with methodology. Thus Professor Flacks is reported as saying: "We'd like to do away with the obsession with methods rather than [social] problems" (*The New York Times*, January 5, 1970, p. 63).

> vate sector, to promote and encourage such conditions as will give every American the opportunity to live in decency and dignity, and to provide a clear and precise picture of whether such conditions are promoted and encouraged in such areas as health, education and training, rehabilitation, housing, vocational opportunities, the arts and humanities, and special assistance for the mentally ill and retarded, the deprived, the abandoned, and the criminal, and by measuring progress in meeting such needs.
>
> *Social Report of the President*
>
> Sec. 3. (*a*) The President shall transmit to the Congress not later than March 20 of each year a report to be known as the "social report," setting forth (1) the overall progress and effectiveness of Federal efforts designed to carry out the policy declared in section 2 . . . (2) a review of State, local, and private efforts designed to create the conditions specified in section 2; (3) current and foreseeable needs in the areas served by such efforts and the progress of development of plans to meet such needs; and (4) programs and policies for carrying out the policy declared in section 2, together with such recommendations for legislation as he may deem necessary or desirable. . . .
>
> *Council of Social Advisers to the President*
>
> Sec. 4. (4) There is created in the Executive Office of the President a Council of Social Advisers . . . composed of three members who shall be appointed by the President . . . and each of whom . . . is exceptionally qualified to appraise programs and activities of the government in the light of the policy declared in section 2, and to formulate and recommend programs to carry out such policy.

In January, 1969, the then Secertary of Health, Education, and Welfare forwarded a document to the President entitled *Toward a Social Report*. This was in response to the President's directive

> to develop the necessary social statistics and indicators to supplement those prepared by the Bureau of Labor Statistics and the Council of Economic Advisers. With these yardsticks, we can better measure the distance we have come and plan for the way ahead.[13]

Illustrating the sorts of data that might usefully serve as social indicators, this report provides tentative answers to these questions. (1) Are we becoming healthier? (2) How much opportunity is there? (Is social mobility increasing or declining?) (3) As to our physical environment, are things improving or worsening? (4) As to income and poverty, are we better, or worse off? (5) What is the impact of crime on our lives? (6) Learning, science, and art: How much are they enriching society? (7) To what extent does our society provide "congenial social relationships, a sense of belonging" and chances for constructive participation? And finally, (8) How can we do better social reporting in the future?

Just a few months later the National Academy of Sciences and the Social Science Research Council published a report making similar recommendations: a system for collecting and analyzing a broad range of social data, organized to indicate the state of the society and presented annually in a social report to, and on, the nation.[14]

Curiously enough, there had been a similar effort supported by NASA three years earlier. A book, entitled *Social Indicators,* grew out of an effort to assess the "social impact of outer space exploration."[15]

Perhaps such efforts to assess our social situation and plan for a better future simply transform sociologists into "market researchers for the welfare state," as one "new" sociologist, Alvin Gouldner, put it. Perhaps it is an effort too palliative and too slow to meet the crucial needs of American society in the 1970's. On the other hand, to some it seems "a modest plan for world conquest." This writer goes on to say: "It tends to confirm my reactionary Humanities view. Social and behavioral scientists are ambitious and expansionist. They see *their* revolution coming, and rub their hands."[16]

The revival of these old concerns has made a yeasty brew of sociology today. What does it mean? What will the outcome be?

First, it attests the field's vitality. Sociology is alive, flourishing, and contentious from Orono to Oshkosh and beyond. The creature will doubtless benefit from the exercising of its members.

Second, neither old nor new sociology will win the day. Different emphases are grounded in undebatable personal preferences and styles. But the one will serve as stimulating irritant to the other. While his failure to practice what he preaches might suggest its impracticality, there is wisdom in Chairman Mao's proclamation: "Let a thousand flowers bloom."

Third, social conditions generating the new sociology are also creating the demand for social indicators—and the sociologists who identify, gather, and analyze them. In government and elsewhere, increasing numbers of sociologists will be engaged in social accounting for the nation,* and in promoting social change.

In size and scope, then, sociology is flourishing. There may be something to Professor Talcott Parsons' statement: ". . . perhaps we may say that, ideologically, a 'sociological era' has begun to emerge, following an 'economic' and, more recently, a 'psychological' era."[17] I suspect that sociology's remarkable growth stems largely from these three factors: liberation from the soil (a once necessary preoccupation with our biophysical environment), the problems generated by large and dense populations whose activities are functionally interlocked; and traditional values imperfectly realized in contemporary social arrangements. Now the *necessary* study of mankind becomes man. The sheer survival of his social order—to say nothing of improvements in it—demands the controlled observations and interpretations that are the sociologist's task.

Some lingering fictions

Sociology as Holy Writ, social work, incantation, and common sense

There are reasons, certainly, for the fuzziness and fictions that beset the field of sociology. Outside the universities, there have been few exemplars of the discipline.† Its growth has been rapid and recent. And the imperial spread of its domain may well be mystifying. A casual survey of the subject index to the *American Sociological Review* reveals several hundred topics on which sociologists have written. These range from the Armed Forces, birth control, and bureaucracy through geophagy, lumberjacks, and music, to suicide, urbanism, war, and women. Such a welter of appar-

* See the editorial comment by Irving Louis Horowitz and Lee Rainwater. "Social Accounting for the Nation," in *Transaction,* May, 1967.

† In 1947, 23 percent of a national sample said they didn't know what a sociologist was. (This was in the NORC study of the prestige accorded various occupations. Sixteen years later, in the 1963 replication of the study, this "don't know" figure had dropped to 10 percent.)

ently disparate interests would seem reason enough for erroneous views of the nature of the field.

One such view is that sociology consists of a body of precepts. It is seen as the latter-day Holy Writ enjoining tolerant and humane relations among men. To this the sociologist would reply that his task is to inquire, not to require; to explore, not to implore. This is not to suggest that he is unconcerned with the values men live by: these constitute important data for him. (Nor should it imply that he is barred from applying his craft in a cause. See Chapter 14.) But this is altogether different from the development of a new decalogue based on the findings of social science.

Related to this misconception is the notion that sociology is social work. Here the sociologist's task is seen not so much as the specification of right belief as the reformation of wrong conditions and bad behavior. Delinquent and criminal must be made law-abiding, slum housing razed and replaced by wholesome housing, the divorce rate reduced, literacy increased, and tastes refined. No social scientist deprecates such objectives. He favors virtue. But his working hours are spent on a task only indirectly related to reform. This is the dispassionate description and analysis of patterns of human relationship as they actually are. To see him as a reformer is to confuse two roles. The scientist asks *what is.* The reformer asks *what ought to be.* Of course, the same man may ask both questions. Indeed, the Judeo-Christian ethic and our form of government demand he shall. What is more, for effective action it is imperative that the two be linked. *"Voir pour prévoir,"* said Auguste Comte a century ago. And Herbert Spencer, writing a little later, noted that hardly a law is passed that is not a law to amend an inadequate law.[18] He meant to suggest that the loftiest motivation is not enough if the law and reform are based on erroneous views of man and society. The man of knowledge and the man of action must somehow collaborate if social change is to be effective. But the social scientist must be scrupulous in distinguishing policy and preference from dispassionate analysis. The task of sociology is obscured when *what is* is confused with *what ought to be.*

Curiously enough, *sociological* is often used as an adjective synonymous with *social.* And sometimes—perhaps because it seems to carry collective connotations—sociology is identified with socialism. Certain of our congressmen apparently suffer from this delusion.

Close cousin to this error is the one which assumes that sociology develops techniques precisely for the purpose of manipulating others. The sociologist's inquiries into recurrent patterns of human conduct will enable prediction. Prediction implies control. Enter the awful specter of predictable man. It has become very fashionable to view with alarm the alleged relapse into conformity as a result of the subtle and sinister manipulations of others, including social scientists. The sociologist becomes "the hidden persuader." He is perhaps the Prince of Eggheads, cavorting through the graveyard of romance and illusion. He denies the unique in man, belittles and obscures the individual, as he discovers laws of behavior which enable manipulation.

This is shallow thinking. And it is consummate anti-intellectualism, since it asserts that knowledge which *may* be used for purposes deemed evil by some unspecified judges should be forbidden. But unfortunately this is an elementary characteristic of all knowledge. The apple of the Garden of Eden has consequences for good and evil. Indeed, the simple knowledge which allows one to discriminate between a ripe apple and a green one is weapon enough to impose diarrhea on the unwitting. All knowledge has this ambivalent character; there is no evidence that ignorance necessarily entails felicity or that perfidy invariably follows knowledge. This timid and distorted view would halt inquiry into that most significant part of nature we call *human* nature.

But what is more, such a specter obscures the very nature of man's social life. For orderly human relationships depend upon the "manipulation" and prediction of others' responses. In our daily dealings with others, we are incessantly speaking and acting in ways calculated to elicit desired and expected responses. Human life and, paradoxically, freedom itself are possible only insofar as men respond predictably. The social scientist's task is to enhance our knowledge of this order and the conditions under which it changes. Through disciplined observation and imaginative analysis he seeks a more profound and accurate understanding of man's conduct among men.

Finally, there is the view that sociology is, in fact, common sense disguised, that the sociologist ("a person who dives the deepest and comes up the muddiest") puts into incomprehensible jargon what any child of 12 knows well and states clearly. Paul Lazarsfeld, a sociologist at Columbia University, discusses this viewpoint in the following paragraphs.

When the social scientist proposes that we test our commonsense notions and beliefs, he is likely to encounter serious opposition from various segments of our society. Why spend time, money, and energy doing surveys that merely verify what is already obvious? Consider, for example, the following statements from a survey of the adjustment of servicemen to military life in World War II:

> Better educated men showed more psychoneurotic symptoms than those with less education. (The mental instability of the intellectual as compared to the more impassive psychology of the man-in-the-street has often been commented on.)
>
> Men from rural backgrounds were usually in better spirits during their Army life than soldiers from city backgrounds. (After all, they are more accustomed to hardships.)
>
> Southern soldiers were better able to stand the climate in hot South Sea Islands than Northern soldiers. (Of course, Southerners are more accustomed to hot weather.)
>
> White privates were more eager to become "noncoms" than Negroes. (Lack of ambition among Negroes is almost proverbial.)
>
> Southern Negroes preferred Southern to Northern white officers. (Isn't it well known that Southern whites have a more fatherly attitude toward their "darkies"?)
>
> As long as the fighting continued, men were more eager to be returned to the States than they were after the German surrender. (You cannot blame people for not wanting to be killed.)

We have in these examples a sample list of the simplest type of interrelationships which provide the "bricks" from which our empirical social science is being built. But, why, since they are so obvious, is so much money and energy given to establish such findings? Would it not be wiser to take them for granted and to proceed directly to a more sophisticated type of analysis? This might be so except for one interesting point about the list. Every one of these statements is the direct opposite of what was actually found. Poorly educated soldiers were more neurotic than those with high education; Southerners showed no greater ability than Northerners to

> adjust to a tropical climate; Negroes were more eager for promotion than whites; and so on.
>
> If we had mentioned the actual results of the investigation first, the reader would have labelled these "obvious" also. Obviously something is wrong with the entire argument of "obviousness." It should really be turned on its head. Since every kind of human reaction is conceivable, it is of great importance to know which reactions actually occur most frequently and under what conditions; only then will a more advanced social science develop.[19]

Sociology, then, is not a body of "correct" beliefs. Nor is it the reformation of bad behavior. Although its name suggests an interest in collectivities, it has nothing to do with collectivism or any other *ism,* including socialism. Its aim is not to develop principles for manipulating people, although to know is to predict and to predict is, sometimes, to control. As with all knowledge, it may be used well or ill. Nor can sociology be regarded as a mere restatement of commonsense knowledge. For commonsense statements typically overstate—i.e., fail to specify the limited conditions under which they *may* be true. They often contradict one another. And as in the cases above, they may be exactly contrary to scientific findings.

Fuzzy boundaries and dimensions

Flanked by the biological and physical sciences on the one side, the humanities on the other, in its intermediate no-man's land sociology is sometimes victim of the most naïve misconceptions. Perhaps the most serious of these is misconstruction or ignorance of the boundaries and units of analysis in sociology. Apparently it is hard to see that a group does not consist in a collection of people, that the sociologist is dealing with a structure of *relationships,* and their constituent roles, and that the dimensions of analysis are quite different from those used in the study of personality systems. Even thoughtful people are likely to fall into the nominalist fallacy: only the concrete individual has reality. This is reinforced by the strong position psychology has enjoyed in our intellectual tradition. It has deflected our attention from relationships *between* self and other to those *within:* emotional, cognitive, neurological. When we psychologize the social, we use dimensions

... turn-of-the-century sociologists. ... sought solutions to social problems: crime, poverty, alcoholism, child labor, unemployment, immigrant adjustment, and the like.

... (with) the new sociology ... profession, preference, and practice are fused. ... two central themes of the new sociology. ... engagement ... *and conflict-generated* change.

. . . The Sociologist's job
is the dispassionate description
and analysis of patterns
of human relationships
as they actually are.

. . . Sociology . . . deepens our sense of
the social world. . . . we cultivate
a questioning mind. . . .
Does greater contact with
persons of other races,
nationalities, and ethnic backgrounds
promote friendly attitudes?
Or does it increase hostility?
Does the work of the minister,
priest, or rabbi promote
moral behavior . . . ? Or is it
a tranquilizer . . . ?

inappropriate for group phenomena. Doing so, we reveal in a literal sense that we don't know what (realm) we're talking about.

It is precisely because of this engrained disposition to see the world as a collection of discrete individuals that we get into serious trouble. We fall into the paranoid posture of attributing social events to malevolent, unknown others—rather than to aspects of the social structure. We sometimes delude ourselves that the source of a personal predicament—especially another's—is wholly to be found in a personal defect. We can see how ludicrous this is if we imagine an American Negro taking this position. Yet this psychologized interpretation is precisely what we are wont to rely on in daily life. We are not accustomed to thinking in social dimensions.

Some insist—to cite another innocent view—that human relationships have certain ineffable qualities that resist, or are corrupted by, scientific inquiry. Science is the enemy of the humane.

> O Sweet spontaneous
> earth how often have
> the
> doting
>   fingers of
> prurient philosophers pinched
> and
> poked
> thee
> , has the naughty thumb
> of science prodded
> thy
>   beauty. . .[21]

Not only is it alleged that there are "two cultures," mutually unintelligible: they are antithetical.

This spurious split between the sciences and the humanities obscures the necessary alliance between craftsman and madman. These two are joined in scientific as well as poetic enterprise. This myopic view misses the science in art—and the art (the imaginative, creative aspect) in science. In sociology as in every fruitful scientific enterprise, there is an interplay between theory and its empirical testing, a two-way street between interpretation and observation, between imagining and knowing. "There is, it would seem, in the dimensional scale of the world, a kind of delicate meeting place between imagination and knowledge, a point arrived at by diminishing large things and enlarging small ones, that is intrinsically artistic."[22] Charles Horton Cooley spoke to the same point in his journal:

> Our common way of talking and thinking greatly exaggerates the difference between science and art. Science is nothing without an ideal—that is, a theory—which it strives to verify and perfect through facts. So art is nothing unless it is grounded in a minute study of nature. Both call for a union of patient observations and experiment with creative imagination. The difference is in the character of the ideal which is sought . . . or rather in the means through which the ideal can be realized. Art seeks a harmonious organization of emotional impressions, such as those from form, sound and color; while science seeks a more intellectual harmony, which also, in its way, appeals to emotion. It is impossible, I think, to say where science ends and art begins (*Journals* [Vol. 11, 1896], p. 57).

There are the trees and the forest, the immediate, concrete, sensible reality and the more remote, interpretive conceptualization, moving beyond perception to a higher level of abstraction. To celebrate the one by damning the other is to truncate the process of inquiry. We do not need to depreciate sociology to appreciate the humanities, or vice versa. One may indeed question whether the academic distinction between realms of inquiry makes much sense.

Man, unique, mercurial, unpredictable

In a related abuse of sociology, some assert that reliable knowledge about human behavior is impossible. Man's conduct is unpredictable, controlled, if at all by ineffable, idiosyncratic forces. "It is a rather pitiful assumption," says Congressman Reece's report, "that the springs of human behavior can be reduced to formulae."[23] This same report of a congressional committee's investigation of tax-exempt foundations (especially those supporting the social sciences) asserts:

> Human beings are motivated by a complex of factors: by goals . . . by ethical and moral concepts: by exercises of free will. Some of the social sciences seem to have wholly rejected the concept of free will.[24]

Literary people, too, often insist that the rich variety and individuality of human experience preclude the possibility—to say nothing of the propriety—of pigeon-holing and predicting. But they do not practice what they preach. As Lewis Coser's *Sociology Through Literature* clearly shows, writers offer endless insights (*and* cause-effect propositions, *and* predictions) about human relationships. And so indeed it must be. One does not discover man and his condition in a table of random numbers.

This allegation—the unpredictability of human behavior—is belied daily as we act toward others in ways that elicit predictable responses.* If we know how to anger, please or cajole it is because experience has built in us a set of unstated propositions: if this, then that. When I behave this way I can expect (predict) that sort of response. Max Weber has suggested what would happen were this not so—were man's relations with his fellows unpredictable.

> The characteristic of 'incalculability' [i.e., unpredictability] . . . is the privilege of—the insane . . . we associate the . . . feeling of freedom with those actions which we are conscious of performing rationally—that is . . . in which we pursue a clearly perceived end by means [that allow us to predict its probable attainment]. . . .[25]

This is not to suggest that Orwell's 1984 has just arrived, or that we are down on his *Animal Farm,* or that the sociologist is philosopher-king at Walden II. It is simply a reminder that human conduct is not independent of age and sex and class and race, of education, occupation and all the constraints of human relationships.

At the same time, paradoxically, the social sources of constraint (and predictability) are, in their endless permutations the sources of unique individuality. (Recall our discussion in Chapters 6 and 13.) An endlessly changing social order (none being a closed system) and infinite variety among individuals—these things go together.

* What makes gambling such a pleasant retreat from the patterns of mundane life is that it offers *un*predictable outcomes. (I mean to suggest, of course, that in daily life the outcomes are typically predictable.) Insofar as gambling is transformed so that the outcome *is* predictable, it has been converted from recreation to work, from an escape from daily life's requirements to an extension of them. It's instructive to note our tendency—a virtual mandate in business—to convert a situation in which outcomes are unknown into one where we can predict, hence control, the outcome. Control of outcome is what John Le Carré had in mind when he protested against the manipulation of the writer by "that great apparatus which was set up in order to drown the critics' protests and convert the public taste into the plaything of Hollywood and Madison Avenue. . . . It is engaged in turning the writer into an institution which will underwrite and where necessary supplement his faltering talent. *It is there in fact to take the chance out of his future.* He has become a property" (*New York Times Book Review,* June 27, 1965, p. 2. Italics mine).

There are other abuses. I pass over the once fashionable, now trite charge of jargon, a necessary characteristic of all specialties, while pointing out that among sociologists there are some superb stylists. (Indeed, Professor Bierstedt insists that their literary grace and style is a special reason for including some sociological studies in a general education program.) But let us turn to one final indictment, the issue of complexity.

Social phenomena: their inscrutable complexity

It is alleged that social phenomena are so complex that man's mind and methods of problem solution are simply inadequate. "Every adjective that may be applied to mankind is thought to denote a variable. And many other variables . . . lurk beneath the level of language proficiency. Variables are uncountable; they march in endless disarray."[26] This is a hoary chestnut, long discredited at three levels. Our daily experience, if we reflect on it, reveals how we select, from a host of social cues, those successfully predicting others' responses. First, then, we must and do cope with complexity every day. At a second level, the methodology of the social sciences suggests ways of making manageable a complex set of data. Theory isolates the crucial variables bearing on our problem. (Not all variables are relevant in understanding given behaviors.) Among these, one may be selected for study while others are controlled by means such as those discussed in Chapter 1. And occasionally we can explain much of the variance in behavior with two or three independent variables. At a third level, sophisticated mathematical techniques (now supported by computer technology) permit the manipulation of many variables simultaneously.

In short, complexity of social phenomena is not an insuperable roadblock barring solutions in sociology. Of course, there are endless ways of slicing the pie of social phenomena. The task is to discover which way of looking at the problem is fruitful, which variables, or combinations of them, make good predictors.

Some uses of sociology

Discovering the self

Certain characteristics of sociology make it an extraordinarily useful field of inquiry. Some of these, noted at the outset in Chapter 1, are worth recalling. Sociology makes a special contribution as it promotes the fuller discovery of our identity. The self is not a parthenogenetic miracle. It is a social creation. So to discover with some precision the ways in which, the extent to which, and the means by which men are socially created is to gain a fuller sense of self and society.

Discovering the world

Sociology also extends and deepens our sense of the social world. We appreciate more fully the inexhaustible variety of social life—and this even in the pedestrian experience of everyday living.* And about the commonplace range of relationships we cultivate a questioning mind. For example:

Does a class or a course enlarge us in knowledge or wisdom? Or does it discourage a tendency toward inquiry, teaching us to substitute grades for learning? Does our system of criminal justice reduce the crime rate? Or raise it? Does regularity in religious rites promote humanity in our dealings with others? Or does it certify a conviction of superiority? Does fear of demotion, of unemployment or loss of pay drive men to work? Or to evade work more artfully? Do feelings of awe, fear and reverence give rise to religion? Or is it religion that defines and elicits these emotions? Is the American Family an evolved institution best suited to breed and rear children? Or is it the chief source of blighting inequalities? And to the questioner sociology adds a warning: do not be caught by such simplistic contraries. Ask, rather, under what conditions these and other outcomes might be found.

Methodological acuity

We noted, too, that sociology profits from its position between the biophysical sciences and the humanities. It applies the wiles of science to the mysteries of the social arrangements that men contrive. Thus the field is favored in the meaning of its quest and the method of pursuit.

* As examples, consider the essay by Georg Simmel, "The Secret and the Secret Society," in *The Sociology of Georg Simmel,* trans. Kurt Wolff (Glencoe, Ill.: Free Press, 1950). Or the unravelling of some of the implications of the triad (first discussed by Simmel) in Theodore Caplow's book, *Two Against One,* (Englewood Cliffs, N.J.: Prentice-Hall, Inc., 1968). Or for new light on the ordinary world of deviant behavior, there is Kai T. Erikson's *Wayward Puritans,* alluded to in Chapter 12. Or consider the various works of Erving Goffman, commencing with *The Presentation of Self in Everyday Life.*

Reshaping the social world

As Morley put it: "It is not enough to do good; one must do it the right way." Sociology is our best chance of learning to do it the right way. We had some intimation in the last chapter of the way sociology can be put to work to provide the knowledge needed for effectively reshaping men's relationships.

Its range of relevance

Since the world is full of human relationships, the data for sociological inquiry are in good supply everywhere—in factories, on farms, in government, business, and the military, in church and school—wherever men act in concert. Its material crosscuts every walk of life and intersects the special fields of every other discipline. For example there are special sets of problems in the sociology of science, the sociology of medical organization, and the sociology of literature and aesthetic expression. The scope of sociology, cutting across all sectors of social life, means an extended range of relevance. Professor Page puts the point well when he says that undergraduate work in sociology

> is an especially appropriate educational preparation for a large number and variety of post-collegiate roles . . . sociological knowledge and sensitivity are needed more and more in public affairs, law, medicine, social work, journalism, architecture and engineering, teaching, and with its increasing semi-professionalization, a growing segment of business. . . .[27]

As liberator

Finally, let us recognize how sociology unfetters us from parochial restrictions.[28] It is especially useful in liberating the mind, the prime aim, presumably, of a liberal arts education. Excepting anthropology, sociology has no peer in opening the mind's door to the deceptively familiar world of men's social arrangements. It enables a responsible questioning of the customary. It encourages us to entertain alternatives. (Indeed, this is implied when we define the field and design our studies in terms of *differing* patterns of human relationships.) And in the process we achieve a better understanding of why what is, is. "This sort of liberation, in a world beset by provincialisms, by the ethnocentrisms of place and the temporocentrisms of time . . . is no mean . . . accomplishment."[29] A number of disciplines, of course, have the virtue of puncturing provincialisms. But sociology not only reveals, as history does, differing social structures in space and time. It transcends space and time themselves, seeking those isomorphisms characterizing groups, under specified conditions, anywhere and any time.

It liberates us, too, from the restrictions of small academic cells, mending the intellectual fissures induced by an artificial opposition of science and the humanities. Sociology is dead center in the tradition of the liberal, the liberating, arts, joining the so-called two cultures, putting together in our minds matters not meant to be disjoined. It "spans two cultures, the scientific and the humanistic, using as it does the method of science to explore the concerns and affairs of humanity."[30]

So much for a paean to sociology's virtues. Now perhaps a backward look will reveal how many of these uses have been realized.

A backward look: once over lightly

The perspective peculiar to sociology is its focus on those structures of relationships that we call groups. But men are mortal while groups, especially those institutionalized, are *im*mortal. Therefore we must have a continual replacement of losses as newcomers—infants and migrants—replace those who leave. But it is not simply a matter of replacing one body with another. The individual enters the human group, meshing his behavior with others' only as he picks up the culturally prescribed expectations transmitted to him through the socialization process. Like the musician, he joins the orchestra, comes to play his part adequately, as he learns the score. In this socialization process, self and other, individual and group are fused: the group assimilates the person as he assimilates the group.

This deceptively mundane process is, in reality, a miracle of creation. Hence we asked: How does this remarkable transmutation—seven pounds of witless protoplasm to cultivated human being—occur? So we looked into the process of induction in which the chief institutionalized agents are family and school. Kinfolk and teachers (along with his peers) are partners in the arduous task of person building. With them the newcomer engages in an intricate dialectic. The significant outcome is the elaboration of self, the realization of self through others. For we do not grow directly, but only indirectly. A person becomes an object to himself, becomes self-conscious (and so, himself, a collaborator in the process) through the responses of others. It is from their vantage point that he is able to get a fix on his position, to participate in the process of becoming a person. As others act toward him, as he estimates the judgments of him implied in their responses, his self-conception, at first wavering and uncertain, crystallizes.

Thus there is a dual outcome: both person and group are products of cultural transmission. With the creation of persons, the group is regularly rebuilt.

From the building of groups we turned our attention in Part Three to sustaining the group. Groups have a discernible structure, an arrangement of parts. To sustain a group is to maintain this arrangement. But over the years, groups are never wholly sustained, especially in a complex society such as ours. As with a physical structure, some parts wear out and replacements are never identical with their predecessors.

As we saw, one can view the social structure from several angles: the structure of its population, the moral order that is geared to a spatial pattern (ecological structure), and the structure of organizations. We stressed two other perspectives on the social structure: stratification and institutions.

Over long reaches of time and across all known human groups, we find differences in prestige, privilege, power—in style of life, reflecting differences in securing things valued by the group. The meaning of his class position for the person entering the group is suggested by research findings of sociologists: the connection between class and the extent, types, and treatment of mental illness, between class and fertility, class and longevity, class and sexual behavior, class and child-rearing patterns, class and religious conduct, class and ideology—in short, class and style of life. Class has been an effective predictor because it captures a complex cluster of variables that create

> different basic conditions of life at different levels of the social order. Members of different social classes, by virtue of enjoying (or suffering) different conditions of life, come to see the world differently—to develop different conceptions of social reality, different . . . hopes and fears, different conceptions of the desirable.[31]

In Chapters 9 through 11 we took a first look at the institutional structure. Common values, shared standards of behavior, the harmonious meshing of differentiated roles, the allocation of goods and power and authority, mating, marriage, and the rearing of newcomers to meet the group's role requirements—these things do not happen automatically or as the result of individual inclination. The group institutes behaviors, structures of relationships, to achieve these ends. And these "frozen answers to fundamental questions" we call institutions. Now the sociologist must ask: How in fact do these institutions contribute to social integration? What is the structure of roles and relationships characterizing each: family, church, economy, and polity? How do they recruit their members and officials? How does each link with the rest of the institutional structure? How does the social structure of an institution vary from place to place and time to time? What are the effects of differences in institutional arrangements? Hence the interest of the sociologist in kinship, marriage, family, and child rearing. Hence, also, the sociology of religion, of work, of political behavior, of education, of military organization, and the like.

But there would be no problem of group maintenance if all roles were played out within a narrow range of tolerance. As we saw in the just preceding chapters, this is never the case, for several reasons. Variations in socialization mean that newcomers never perform quite like those whom they replace. This is the case whether we speak of an input of infants or of migrants. And, on the quantity side, the rapidity of growth or decline exerts a stress as the structure of roles is under- or oversupplied. Change comes, too, as the group itself creates deviant behavior by institutionalizing beliefs and conduct that most would judge inequitable. Inevitably there follow efforts to reshape the social structure. And then there is the Garden of Eden effect: an input of knowledge (as well as of deviant human traits) can disrupt the structure of human relationships. Vaulting accesses of knowledge stimulate both technological and social change.

The encounter of rural with urban, immigrant with native, an encounter occurring above all in the city, suggests both locus and focus for an analysis of changes in the group. This is a principal reason for the emergence of such subfields as the sociology of rural life and the sociology of urbanism. The city is a crossroads for ideas, hence of cultural innovation. It intrigues the sociologist because such a large part of its input must be migrant; for it typically fails to replenish its ranks through natural increase. The urban order provides a perfect setting for stress and change.

Changes such as those induced by migration, or race prejudice and shortage of adequate housing (as in the development of a Harlem), are unplanned. They evolve through the reinforcing actions and decisions of many individuals. On the other hand, and perhaps especially in the city, change may be contrived. Here the sociologist plays a somewhat different part. It requires not so much an addition to the fund of reliable knowledge as an application of what he knows in order to promote a change deemed good; or he may apply his methods of inquiry in order to assess the outcomes of efforts at contrived change. As in other fields, there is an applied as well as a "pure" aspect of the sociologist's role.

Were there a way to measure it, I expect that we would find both aspects of his role more important today than ever before: the extension of knowledge and its application in the cryptic domain of the social order. It might be contended that since man's humanity stems from the fact that he is a social animal, the study of society must always have been crucially significant. But there is a difference, in degree if not in kind, in our day. Our control over land, sea, and space, over life and death, has been enormously extended. This liberates us for the effort at more effective management of our personal and social destinies. It seems clear that such management is needed. Contemporary life is more and more a matter of groups and their intertwining. While we have always had "organization men," their number, variety, and interdependence are certainly greater today than ever before. If the penalty of ignorance of history, as Santayana asserted, is to be fated to repeat it, ignorance of sociology means, at best, provincialism and at worst, disaster. For now the crucial part of nature is human nature, and human nature is preeminently social. Both woe and weal depend on our knowledge of this nature. And this knowledge must come from the controlled observation and insightful interpretation of differing patterns of human relationship: their sources and their consequences.

References

TEXT

1. The American Sociological Society (now, *Association*) was founded as recently as 1905. While the *American Journal of Sociology* first appeared in 1896, it was not until 1907 that the first official publications of the Society were issued. In 1936, the *American Sociological Review* became the official medium for interchange among sociologists.
2. I am borrowing, here, from the discussion by Roscoe C. Hinkle, Jr., and Gisela J. Hinkle, *The Development of Modern Sociology* (Garden City, N.Y.: Doubleday & Co., Inc., 1954). Origins in Europe would of course take us back to Comte or Spencer. Indeed, a case could be made for pushing back to Plato. See Alvin W. Gouldner, *Enter Plato* (New York: Basic Books, Inc., Publishers, 1965), especially Part II.
3. As to rural backgrounds, the Hinkles write: "Of the 19 presidents of the American Sociological Society who had been born prior to 1880, who had completed their graduate studies before 1910, and who had achieved some prominence before 1920, not one had experienced a typically urban childhood" (*ibid.*, p. 3). The same might be said, perhaps, of other academic disciplines, although in these—physics, for

example—the background would not have had so direct an influence on the selection of research problems.

4. Data for 1950 and 1959 are from Matilda White Riley, "Membership of the American Sociological Association, 1950–59," *American Sociological Review,* Vol. 25, No. 6 (December, 1960), p. 914. Data for 1969 come from the Executive Office of the Association, 1001 Connecticut Avenue, NW, Washington, D.C.
5. Riley, *op. cit.,* p. 920.
6. U.S. Department of Labor, Bureau of Labor Statistics, *Employment Outlook for Social Scientists* (Washington, D.C.: U.S. Government Printing Office, 1964), p. 173.
7. Elbridge Sibley, *The Education of Sociologists in the United States* (New York: Russell Sage Foundation, 1963), p. 100.
8. See "Social Science Data Archives in the United States, 1967," issued by the Council of Social Science Data Archives, William A. Glaser, Executive Director, Bureau of Applied Social Research, Columbia University.
9. See David Nasatir, "Social Science Data Libraries," *American Sociologist,* Vol. 2, No. 4 (November, 1967).
10. Carl C. Taylor, "Participation of Sociologists in National Affairs," *American Sociological Review,* Vol. 7, No. 2 (April, 1942), pp. 157–58.
11. January 5, 1970, p. 38. *The New York Times,* on the other hand, reports not so much a "new sociology" as a discipline that "is going in different directions all at once," a view expressed by Professor Neil J. Smelser. (January 5, 1970, p. 33. Sociology is becoming very newsworthy in the '70's.)
12. *The Methodology of the Social Sciences* (Glencoe, Ill.: Free Press, 1949), p. 4. Taken alone, this statement misrepresents Weber's position. He would not have denied that, given a concrete end in view, the sociologist might legitimately say, "Means$_1$ is better than means$_2$. For example, he *can* say: "If you wish to maximize your military strength, or to produce cars economically, or to produce winning football teams, then criteria of achievement (means$_1$) are better than criteria of ascription (means$_2$). On these grounds, racial discrimination is wrong."
13. U.S. Department of Health, Education, and Welfare, *Toward a Social Report* (Washington, D.C.: U.S. Government Printing Office, 1969), p. iii.
14. Raymond A. Bauer (ed.), *Social Indicators,* (Cambridge, Mass.: M.I.T. Press, 1966).
15. National Academy of Sciences and the Social Science Research Council, *The Behavioral and Social Sciences—Outlook and Needs* (New York: Prentice-Hall, Inc., 1969).
16. Reed Whittemore, "A Prejudiced View of the Social Sciences," a review of *The Behavioral and Social Sciences—Outlook and Needs* in *The New Republic,* Vol. 161, Nos. 25–26 (December 20 and 27, 1969), p. 21.
17. Talcott Parsons, "Some Problems Confronting Sociology as a Profession," *American Sociological Review,* Vol. 24, No. 4 (August, 1959), p. 553.
18. Auguste Comte, 1798–1857, Herbert Spencer, 1820–1903. The work of these men provides an important point of departure in the development of sociology. Comte coined the term *sociology* (although he would have preferred *social physics* had it not already been used in another connection), and is sometimes thought of as the father of sociology. The French phrase means: "See in order to foresee," or more adequately translated: "Know in order to predict."
19. Paul Lazarsfeld, "The American Soldier," *Public Opinion Quarterly,* Fall, 1949, pp. 279–80.
20. Jacques Barzun and Henry F. Graff, *The Modern Researcher* (New York: Harcourt, Brace & World, Inc., 1962), p. 224.
21. E. E. Cummings, "O Sweet Spontaneous Earth," in *Poems, 1923–1954* (New York: Harcourt, Brace & World, Inc., 1954).
22. Vladimir Nabokov, *Speak Memory* (New York: Grosset & Dunlap, Inc., 1951), p. 118.
23. Special Committee to Investigate Tax-Exempt Foundations and Comparable Organizations, *Report* (House of Representatives, 83rd Cong. 2d sess., House Resolution 217 [Washington, D.C.: U.S. Government Printing Office, 1954]), p. 73.
24. *Ibid.,* p. 73.
25. Max Weber, *The Methodology of the Social Sciences,* trans. and ed. Edward A. Shils and Henry A. Finch (New York: Free Press, 1949), pp. 124–25.
26. Amos H. Hawley, "Social Science and the Humanities," *Michigan Alumnus Quarterly Review,* Vol. 65, No. 21 (August 8, 1959), p. 281.
27. Charles H. Page, "Sociology as an Educational Enterprise," in *Sociology and*

Contemporary Education, ed. Charles H. Page (New York: Random House, Inc., 1964), pp. 22, 23. © 1964 by Random House, Inc. Reprinted by permission.

28. These are variations on themes suggested by Robert Bierstedt, "Sociology and General Education," in Page, *op. cit.*
29. *Ibid.*, p. 43.
30. *Ibid.*, p. 54.
31. Melvin Kohn, "Social Class and Parent-Child Relationships," *American Journal of Sociology*, Vol. 68, No. 4 (January, 1963), p. 471. See also by Kohn, *Class & Conformity* (Homewood, Ill.: Dorsey Press, 1969).

TABLES

15.2 American Sociological Association, *Guide to Graduate Departments of Sociology, 1969* (Washington, D.C.: American Sociological Association, 1969).

15.4 Adapted from Marvin Bressler, "The Conventional Wisdom of Education and Sociology," in Page (ed.), *op. cit.*, p. 99; reprinted by permission.

FIGURES

15.2 National Center for Educational Statistics, *Summary Report on Bachelor's and Higher Degrees Conferred During Year 1965–66* (and prior annual issues) (Washington, D.C.: U.S. Government Printing Office, 1968).

15.4 National Science Foundation, "National Register of Scientific and Technical Personnel," in *American Science Manpower, 1968* (Washington, D.C.: U.S. Government Printing Office, December, 1969).

15.5 National Science Foundation, *ibid.*, Appendix Table A-3, p. 52.

15.6 Norval D. Glenn and David Weiner, "Some Trends in the Social Origins of American Sociologists," *American Sociologist*, Vol. 4, No. 4 (November, 1969), Table 6, p. 297.

15.7 *Ibid.*, Table 8, p. 299, adapted.

15.8 *Ibid.*, Table 2, p. 284.

asides on methods

1. A way of controlling certain demographic observations

It is worth taking an occasional detour to sample certain elementary methods of inquiry. For our knowledge is only as sure as the methods used to get it. Here the issue is an important and recurring one in sociological inquiry, the control of variables. In this case, the variable to be controlled is age. (See page 36.)

In comparing the fertility of any two groups, age is clearly a critical variable. Youngsters and oldsters are low reproducers. Communities having disproportionate shares of their population in these categories will have low fertility rates. But fertility is also related to a number of other social variables—occupation, race, and religion, for example. Therefore, until we have eliminated the effect of age—until we control this variable—we cannot be sure that causal influence attributed to other factors, such as religion, is not spurious. As an illustration, consider two communities, Jonesville and Plainville whose CBR's are 24.6 and 8.4, respectively. Table A1.1 gives the data (fictitious).

How shall we explain this sizable difference in birthrates? Shall we examine the two communities for differences that might parallel the difference in fertility? Is Jonesville a rural-agricultural community and Plainville an urban-industrial one? Has the first community a large share of highly educated white-collar workers while the second is disproportionately blue collar? Is the first predominantly Catholic and the second heavily Jewish and Protestant?

But before we leap to such explanations we had better look at the age-specific data. Doing so, it becomes clear that much of the difference in the input of the two communities (the natural increase) is due to differences in age composition. Eighty percent of the Jonesville population is in the high-fertility, middle-aged category, while only 20 percent of the people in Plainville fall in this category.

How much of the difference in birthrates is due to these differences in the age makeup of the two communities? This we can tell very easily. For the extent to which the differences between the two CBR's would change, *were the two communities to have the*

Table A1.1

Age category	Jonesville Number of persons	Jonesville Age-specific birthrate	Jonesville Number of births	Plainville Number of persons	Plainville Age-specific birthrate	Plainville Number of births
Young	1,000	5	5	4,000	5	20
Middle-aged	8,000	30	240	2,000	30	60
Old	1,000	1	1	4,000	1	4
Total population	10,000		246	10,000		84
CBR (births per 1,000 population)			24.6			8.4

same age composition, is a measure of the influence of this variable. (How much difference would there be left, between these two birthrates, if there were no difference in age composition?) And so we can give Jonesville the same age composition as Plainville (or vice versa) and then see what the CBR's would be. In the concocted data offered here, it is clear that the two communities would then have precisely the same CBR's. *All* the difference in fertility between the two communities is, then, attributable to the difference in age composition. (The apparent difference in fertility between the two communities is in a way spurious, for it derives exclusively from differing age distributions in Jonesville and Plainville.) Now we can ask the critical question: What characteristics of these communities explain the age composition?

There is another way of controlling the variable of age in order to compare more usefully the fertility of two communities. Instead of giving community A the same age composition as community B, or vice versa, we can give them both the same age composition as that of a third community, C. We then apply the age-specific birthrates (which will differ as between the two communities rather than, as with my concocted data, above, being identical). Then, summing the births for all age categories—say, from 15–19 to 45–49, by five-year age categories and relating them to population units of 1,000, we can compare the two communities with the age variable controlled. We have, in effect, prevented its variation by holding it constant as between the two communities. When it becomes conventional for investigators to use a standard community as the base line for age composition, comparisons may then be made very generally—indeed, internationally—by many people at different times and places. Such a base "community" has been accepted. It is called the "standard million of England and Wales."

2. Three measures providing summary descriptions of group characteristics

Three measures are commonly used—mode, median, and mean—to summarize some characteristic of a group. For example, what *most* people do (or think, or feel) is the *mode*. The adjective is *modal*. Among 10 students scoring 90, 80, 70, 60, 70, 40, 30, 70, 20, and 10, the modal score is 70. To say: "In this group the modal score is 70," is to use a measure of one sort of performance to describe the group.

The *median* is the size (value) of that item which is midway in an array of values. Thus, taking the 10 student scores mentioned above and arranging them from highest to lowest, we know that the midpoint comes between the 5th and the 6th and the median will fall halfway between the values at those two points (Table A2.1).

Using this "measure of central tendency," we describe the group by saying that the median score was 65. Notice that if the top score had been 900, or 9,000, or 9 million, the median would still have been 65. Which is to say that the median is not affected by extreme scores. This is a chief reason for preferring the median when we describe the average income of a group. The median is not distorted by extreme values, as is the mean. (A few millionaires will make average income as measured by the mean, much higher than the median would indicate.)

The *mean* could be defined as that amount of something which everyone would have if each person had the same—or each unit, since groups or inanimate things might be what we're measuring. The mean ($\bar{X}$) is what we usually think of when we use the word *average*. It is the arithemetic average, the value obtained by adding all values in the distribution and dividing by the number of such values. Thus, for the 10 students' scores in our example we get, by adding them, 540. Dividing this sum by the number of such values (10) we find that the mean = 54.

Thus, in our example: The mode = 70, the median = 65, and the mean = 54.

But, of course, to say that "most people do thus-and-so" raises the question: What do we mean by most? How many others are there who don't fall in the "most" category, and how far does their behavior depart from what most do? Or to say that the median is the midpoint of a distribution of values suggests the question: How far do other values depart from that midpoint? And to say that the mean is what everyone would have if each member of

Table A2.1

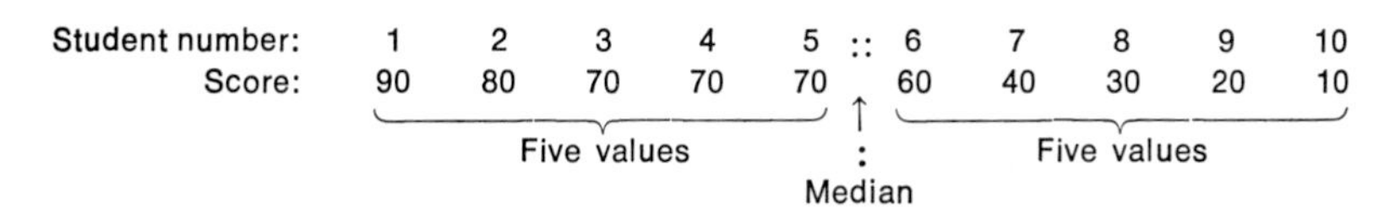

Student number:	1	2	3	4	5	::	6	7	8	9	10
Score:	90	80	70	70	70	↑	60	40	30	20	10
	Five values					Median	Five values				

the group had the same amount is surely to elicit the response: But everyone doesn't have the same amount (of wealth, income, prejudice, or whatever), and how far, in fact, do group members depart from the mean?

Used to describe a group, then, measures of central tendency do not tell us the whole truth about the group, with respect to a given trait. Indeed, they can be misleading if they are not accompanied by another measure, a *measure of dispersion.*

We can conceive of several such measures. We might simply report the range. In our case this is 80 points, the difference between lowest score (10) and highest (90). This gives us some notion of the spread within this group of students.

Or we could sum the differences between the mean and each of the 10 values in the distribution and average them. This would give us the mean deviation. In our case, the mean ($\overline{X}$) being 54, it would entail subtracting (but disregarding the sign) 54 from 90, from 80, 70, 70, 70, 60 . . . and so on, and then adding these differences and dividing by 10. We would get 232 ÷ 10, or 23.2.

Or, finally, and to shorten the story, we could average the squared differences between the mean and each value (total them and divide by N), then take the square root of this value. This is called the *standard deviation.* Its symbol is σ, and it is almost invariably the measure used to tell us how much spread there is around $\overline{X}$ (the mean). It stresses the most deviant cases, thus counteracting the fiction that the mean represents everybody in the group.

For example, in our 10 cases the $\overline{X}$ is 54, and 90 − 54, squared, gives us 36^2 or 1,296. But 70 − 54, squared, gives us only 256. The distance, then, between the mean and 90, squared, is five times the distance between the mean and 70, squared. This is, as it were, a warning (it could be an overstrong warning) not to accept the mean as a clear and unambiguous description of a group characteristic. Were everyone equally prejudiced, the mean would offer a perfect description. If not, the standard deviation tells us something about the extent to which the mean is a distorted description of the group. For the larger the σ, the greater the spread of values around the mean, the less the consensus—or the less group members' attributes are alike. σ should be fairly large for a random sample of metropolitan residents on any controversial issue. We would predict that it would be a good deal smaller for an isolated, rural community. It should be small when we are measuring attitudes on the pacifist position among professional military men, C. O.'s or members of a religious order. But we would expect σ to reveal a much greater spread in a large academic community.

And so when we read Table 2.5 (page 63), we see the mean used to measure the size of the administrative part of 428 school organizations. And in each type of school district, the average percent of school personnel in administrative roles increases with size of organization (small, medium, and large). The standard deviation (σ) is given in column 4. There appears to be less variation (σ is smaller) in size of administrative component of organizations in the unified and city school districts.

3. Using the normal distribution of sampling errors to check whether a sample finding is likely to have occurred by chance

A question raised in Chapter 3 offers an opportunity to illustrate one of the methods sociologists use to check their observations. The question was this: Does the difference in the frequency with which we find Negroes and whites among the poor allow us to draw inferences about elements of American culture? Is there such a disproportionate number of Negroes among the poor that we can conclude that our culture systematically assigns Negroes a subordinate position? Or, to put the question a third way, is the percent of the poor who are Negro (31 percent) so different from the percent of the population who are Negro (10 percent) that we can infer discrimination as an element of our culture?

Now suppose we were to take a sample of 100 poor persons. If their frequency among the poor were the same as their frequency in the population, we'd expect to draw 10 Negroes among 100 poor.* The probability, p, of drawing a black in 100 cases (n) would be 10 out of 100, or .10.

* Actually, the figure would be closer to 11. A census estimate in 1968 puts Negroes at 11.1 percent of the United States population. But to simplify our calculations, we will use the figure 10.

If we were to take a random sample of 100 from the total population of the poor, we'd expect some sampling errors. Sometimes our sample might exactly reflect the proportion of Negroes among the poor. But sometimes it would be a little larger, sometimes a little smaller than the true value for the total population of poor. The measure of sampling error for 100 such cases, randomly selected, is given by the formula: σ_s (the standard error of a sampling distribution) $= \sqrt{n\,p\,q}$, where $n = 100$ (the sample size), $p =$ the probability of drawing a Negro in this sample from the population of the poor (10 out of 100, assuming they appear with the same frequency among the poor as they do in the total population) and $q = 1 - p$ (all other possibilities). Thus $\sigma_s = \sqrt{100\,(.10)\,(.90)} = \sqrt{100\,(.09)} = \sqrt{9}$ and $\sigma_s = 3$.

Now let's back up a bit to be sure we know what's meant by saying that the standard error of this sampling distribution equals 3. The formula is derived deductively, but we can get some intuitive sense of its meaning even without deriving it. It describes the way in which the values, in a series of random samples, distribute themselves—in this case, the way in which the percent Negro would vary in a series of random samplings of a population in which 10 percent were Negro. If we took a large number of samples of the poor, for each sample plotting the proportion Negro, the distribution would take the form of a normal curve. (See Figure A3.1.) Most of the values would heap up in the middle, around the true value for the population, while a few values would range farther above and below the true value. This formula says that in a large number of samples having the characteristics of this one (100 cases, with the probability of the event—finding a Negro in the sample—equal to 10/100), we could be confident that two thirds of the time our observed value would be within the range: 10-plus-or-minus-3. Differently put, assuming 10/100 is the true statement of the frequency with which Negroes are found among the U.S. poor, sample values would fall, two thirds of the time, between 7 and 13. And a normal curve is such that in more than 9 cases out of 10, sample values would fall within the range 10-plus-or-minus-2 standard errors (σ_s)—i.e., 10-plus-or-minus-6. Figure A3.1 puts this graphically.

But what we have in fact observed (1964 data) is that 31 percent of the poor are Negro. Is such a finding likely to occur in a population in which, in fact, Negroes are 10 percent of the poor? The answer is no. Why so? How can we say no with any assurance? Because what we observe is quite far away from what we might expect were Negroes simply represented among the poor as they

Figure A3.1

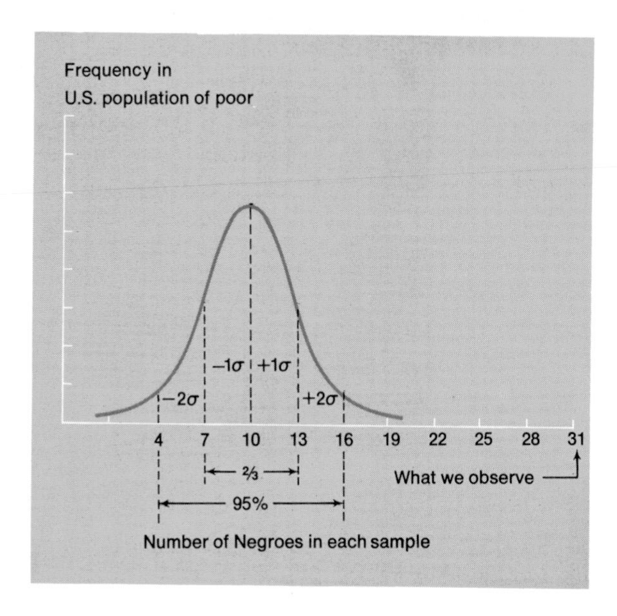

are in the U.S. population. Indeed, our finding is 7 standard errors away from what we should have found were there no difference between proportion in the general population and proportion among the poor. $\left(\frac{31 - 10}{3} = 7\right)$ Such a finding would occur by chance fewer than one in many thousand times.

We must conclude, therefore, that our finding (31 percent of the 35 million poor, in 1964, were nonwhites) is not likely to be a matter of chance. The finding in all likelihood reflects a characteristic of our culture.

4. The frequency distribution as an array of data to describe a group attribute

Arranging values—incomes, test scores, ages—for members of a group, from highest to lowest, and indicating the frequency with which each score appears is often more informative than simply reporting $\overline{X}$ and σ. (Refer to Aside on Methods: Number 2.) Sometimes it reveals things—for example, a bimodal (two modes) distribution—and raises questions that we'd otherwise miss. Fur-

Table A4.1

Grade	Frequency (number of students)
A (80–99)	10
B (60–79)	150
C (40–59)	550
D (20–39)	200
F (0–19)	90
	1,000

Note: $\bar{X} = 54$; mode = 50; median = 48.

thermore, it lends itself readily to graphic representation so that we can literally picture our findings.

Suppose we are inquiring into the adjustment of university freshmen (rather than, as in Sewell's case, young Wisconsin children). Since the aim of the organization is learning, and since grades are thought to be some indication of the extent to which this aim is achieved, we might argue that those who get good or fairish grades have made a better adjustment to the organization than those who get poor grades. So we decide to cast the grades for university freshmen in a frequency distribution. The (fictitious) results for 1,000 freshmen are shown in Table A4.1.

To get the mean, multiply the midpoint of each grade interval by the number of students receiving that grade—for example: 90×10, 70×150, etc. Sum these values and divide by N, which is 1,000.

The median (md.) is where the 500th case falls. From the top of the distribution, we find 160 students in the first two grade categories. To reach the 500th, we need therefore to move 340 units into the *C* grade interval—i.e., 340/550ths or about 0.6 of the interval of 20. This is 12 points from the lower end of the class interval just above it. Hence the median is $60 - 12$ or 48.

The mode is simply the midpoint (50) of that interval (40–59) where most students' grades fall.

As you see, this array of data reveals a peak in the middle range, with frequencies trailing off as we move toward high or low grades. Presented in what is called a histogram, these data can be telling. This is a set of perpendicular bars whose height represents frequency of occurrence and whose width represents the class interval. (While our class intervals are all the same—19.9 or approximately 20 points—if we had a class interval of 40, the base of the bar would have to be twice as wide.) The histogram representing

Figure A4.1

Distribution of grades for 1,000 university freshmen

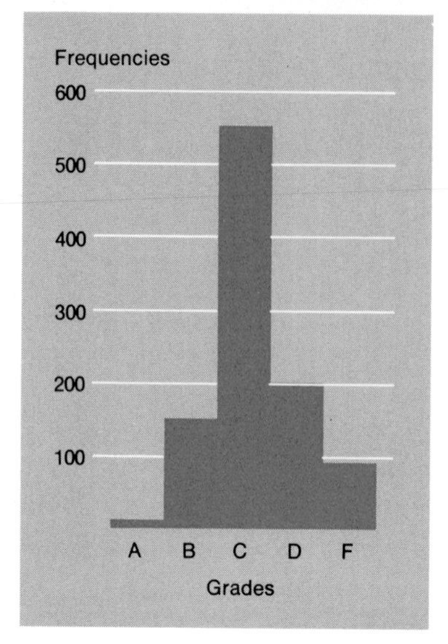

Table A4.2

Grade	Frequency	or	Frequency
A (80–99)	200		300
B (60–79)	200		175
C (40–59)	200		125
D (20–39)	200		150
F (0–19)	200		250
	1,000		1,000

the grade distribution of our 1,000 freshmen is presented in Figure A4.1.

But suppose that our findings gave us distributions like one or the other of those in Table A4.2.

The distribution with 200 grades in each category suggests an almost random assortment of grades, or some very rigid quota system based on criteria other than performance. It arouses our suspicions, for such a distribution defies our experience and our intuitive sense of the way performance tends to distribute itself.

The last distribution (see the histogram in Figure A4.2) reveals a bimodal distribution and raises some interesting and trouble-

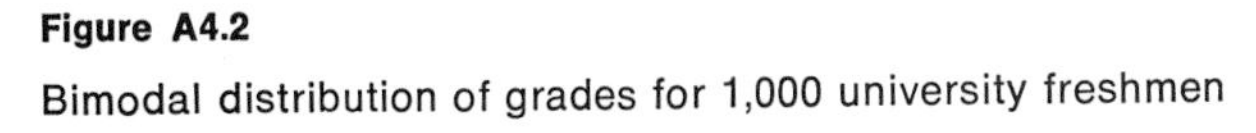

Figure A4.2

Bimodal distribution of grades for 1,000 university freshmen

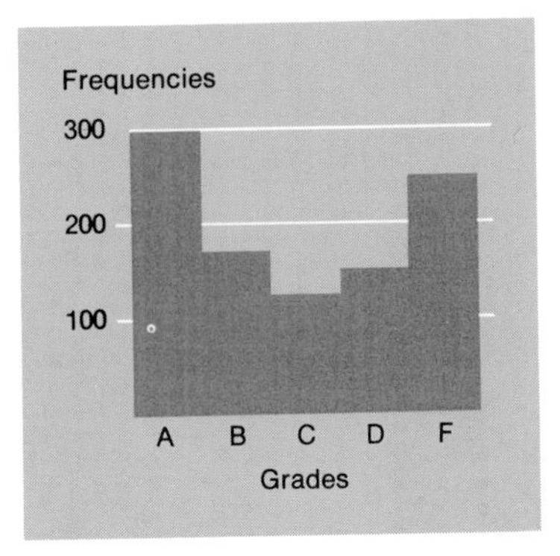

some questions. Is there a double standard for admissions? Or for grading? Are these students somehow divided into two categories, the able and the incompetent? Or those of standard, middle-class academic background and those lacking such a background? Is the school population divided into academically and vocationally oriented students? Are special programs indicated for the lagging part of the university population? Or for the other half? Does such a division indicate a source of tension and trouble?

Thus the array of data in a frequency distribution helps us to describe more fully the characteristics of a group. And as we inspect the distribution, new ideas emerge, new issues that may merit inquiry.

5. Chi-square: calculating expected frequencies to compare with observed frequencies

We use the chi-square test to answer this question. Is the frequency (f_o) with which I observe a certain relationship so different from what might be expected (f_e) if there were no relationship between the two variables, that I must conclude it can't be a matter of chance—that the variables are indeed related? In the study we are examining, the question could be put this way: Is the frequency with which we find indulgent child rearing and good adjustment going together—is this observed frequency so much greater than what we would expect to find were there no connection between

Table A5.1

Calculating expected frequencies (f_e), on the assumption of no relationship between the variables

	Indulgent	Demanding	
50	*a*	*b*	Adjustment adequate
50	*c*	*d*	Adjustment inadequate
100	50	50	

Table A5.2

Observed child-training methods and measures of adjustment

	Indulgent	Demanding	
50	*a* 40	*b* 10	Adjustment adequate
50	*c* 10	*d* 40	Adjustment inadequate
100	50	50	

them—that we can say: Good adjustment is indeed a function of lenient socialization practices?

Thus the expected frequencies (f_e) serve as a kind of bench mark from which we measure the "distance" to our actual observation (f_o). If the distance between them ($f_o - f_e$) is great, we are more confident in assuming that the observed relationship between the variables is not simply a chance affair.

Now we know what we have observed (f_o). The problem is to figure f_e—how our cases would distribute themselves if there were no relationship between indulgence-demandingness on the one hand and adequacy of adjustment on the other. Consider an example (Table A5.1) in which we have 100 children, half of them showing good adjustment, the other half bad adjustment (as we measure adjustment). Now if there's no special link between level of adjustment and level of leniency in child rearing, we would expect that cases of lenient and strict child-rearing practices would distribute themselves among the "adequate adjustment cases" (cells *a* and *b*) as they do in the general population of 100 cases. Among all our cases, 50 yield measures of demanding and 50 of indulgent socialization—i.e., half and half. Hence we would expect half of our adequate adjustment cases ($\frac{1}{2} \times 50$) to have had indulgent socialization. Thus, on the *assumption of no relationship* between the variables—this is the null hypothesis—we would expect 25 cases in cells *a* and *b*. Similarly we would expect half (25) of our *inadequate* adjustment cases to have had demanding, and half (25) indulgent mother-child relationships. So the expected frequency (f_e) in each of the four cells is 25.

χ^2 itself is a measure of the difference between observed and expected frequencies, the distance between our bench mark (f_e) and what we observe (f_o). So let us suppose we have made a study of 100 cases and that our findings fall as indicated in Table A5.2. These are our f_o's. These would be the original data. And we would take these figures—the marginals, not the figures in the cells—in order to figure expected frequencies. (We just did so.) Thus the marginals are the same in both tables. But the figures in the four cells differ. In the one case (f_o) they simply report what we have observed. In the other case (f_e) they represent the way the data would fall (using the same marginals) if there were no relationship between mode of child rearing and adequacy of adjustment.

Now, having both f_o's and f_e's, we have what we need to calculate the magnitude of the difference between them. Our measure, χ^2, is the sum of the squared differences between observed and expected frequencies expressed in each case as a fraction of the expected frequency. The formula for χ^2 is

$$\sum \frac{(f_o - f_e)^2}{f_e} .$$

To make calculation easier we can simplify this formula. Expanding the binomial we get:

$$\chi^2 = \sum \frac{(f_o^2 - 2f_of_e + f_e^2)}{f_e} \quad \text{or} \quad \sum \frac{f_o}{f_e^2} - 2\sum \frac{f_of_e}{f_e} + \sum \frac{f_e^2}{f_e}.$$

$$\text{Then } \chi^2 = \sum \frac{f_o^2}{f_e} - 2\sum f_o + \sum f_e .$$

And, since the sum of both observed and expected frequencies is the same ($N = 100$ cases in our example), i.e., $\Sigma f_o = N$, and $\Sigma f_e = N$,

$$\chi^2 = \sum \frac{f_o^2}{f_e} - 2N + N, \qquad \text{or} \qquad \chi^2 = \sum \frac{f_o^2}{f_e} - N.$$

Table A5.3

Cell	Observed frequencies (f_o)	Expected frequencies (f_e)	f_o^2	f_o^2/f_e
a	40	25	1600	64
b	10	25	100	4
c	10	25	100	4
d	40	25	1600	64
			and $\Sigma f_o^2/f_e =$	136

$$\text{Now } \chi^2 = \Sigma f_o^2/f_e - N = 136 - 100 = 36.$$

Thus, for each of the four cells we need to square f_o, dividing by f_e. We sum these four values and subtract N, the number of cases. We can arrange our data and calculate chi-square as in Table A5.3.

But what does a χ^2 value of 36 mean? Is this measure of the difference between what we observed and what we might expect (were there no relationship between the variables) large enough to permit us to say: It's not a matter of chance; the variables appear to be related? To answer this question we must take one final step. We refer to a table of chi-square values derived by mathematicians. This table will tell us how often a finding such as ours ($\chi^2 = 36$) might be expected to occur by chance with the data sorted into a table having one degree of freedom.

What does this phrase, "degree of freedom," mean? It means the number of values that are free to vary independently of one another. In this case, where we have a 2×2 table, only one of the cell values is free to vary independently; for once the marginal values are given plus the value in *one* cell, all the other values are determined. (Thus, in Table A5.2, since we have 50 cases of adequately adjusted children, 40 of whom had indulgent child rearing, the rest, falling in the "Demanding," cell *must* number 10. So, also, we can see that once the value for one cell, *a*, is given, the figures for cells *c* and *d* are likewise determined.)

Now we can turn to a chi-square table with the two necessary pieces of information: $\chi^2 = 36$ and *df* (degrees of freedom) = 1. A portion of a table of chi-square values is shown in Table A5.4.

In this table we follow the line of figures having the appropriate degrees of freedom (1), moving to the right until we find the chi-square value that comes closest to our finding (36). Then we move directly up to the top row to the figure indicating the probability (p) that such a chi-square value might occur by chance.

Table A5.4

Probability

df	.99	.98	.95	.90	.80	.70	.50	.30	.20	.10	.05	.02	.01
1	.000157	.000628	.00393	.0158	.0642	.148	.455	1.074	1.642	2.706	3.841	5.412	6.635
2	.0201	.0404	.103	.211	.446	.713	1.386	2.408	3.219	4.605	5.991	7.824	9.201
3	.115	.185	.352	.584	1.005	1.424	2.366	3.665	4.642	6.251	7.815	9.837	11.341

For our chi-square value, we move along the $df = 1$ row all the way to the right and find that 6.635 is as close as we can come to our finding ($\chi^2 = 36$). Then, moving up, we see that $p = .01$. We can put this in words by saying that the probability of finding a chi-square value as large as 6.635 in a four-celled table ($df = 1$), by chance, is one in a hundred. So it's not very likely to be a chance finding.

Now, since our chi-square value was considerably larger (36), we're even more confident that it was not a chance finding. We could write this as follows: $p < .01$, i.e., the probability is *less* than one in a hundred that the observed relationship between the variables is a chance affair. (Indeed, if we had a more complete table of chi-square values, we'd find $p < .001$.)

Hence we conclude that the observed and expected frequencies are so different that findings such as ours could be expected to occur by chance fewer than once in a thousand times. So we reject the null hypothesis of no relationship between the variables. (Note that these are concocted data. Sewell's findings were quite different.)

6. Control of variables

As we try to tease out connections between social variables, we must take care lest we fall into a spurious relationship! (Even though there's a strong relationship between the number of fire trucks sent to a burning building and the extent of damage done the building, we'd better not conclude that the more the fire department intervenes, the greater the harm done. A third variable, size of fire, accounts both for the number of fire trucks and the extent of damage.)

Suppose we were to check Durkheim's assertion that the married have significantly lower rates of suicide than do single persons. Let us get our data from 100 U.S. Communities and tally our findings in Table A6.1. What would we find?

Table A6.1

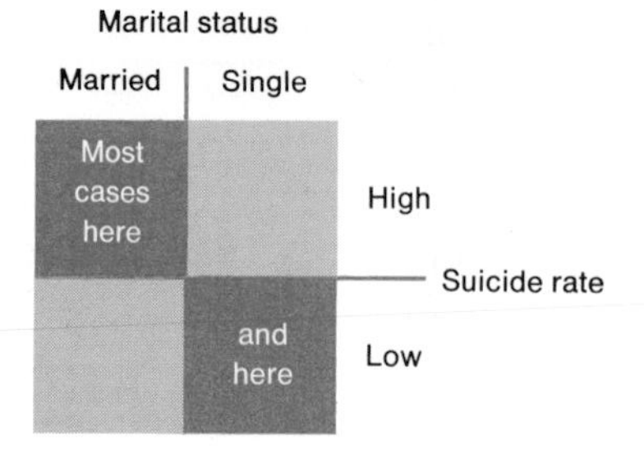

Table A6.2

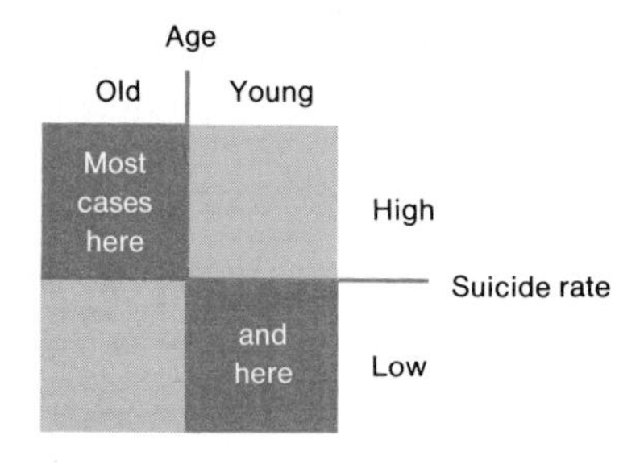

Table A6.3

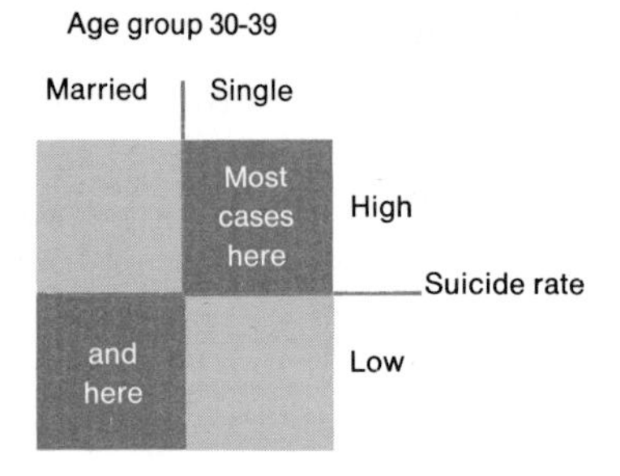

Apparently Durkheim is wrong! Or maybe his statement is too sweeping and should be restricted to Europe in the late 19th century. (Or perhaps we are wrong!) What other factors conceivably related to suicide might be disguised behind marital status? One such comes to mind immediately: the married are generally older than single persons. Is age related to suicide rate? Let us check, tallying the data in Table A6.2.

Age is, indeed, associated with suicide rates. If, then, we want to assess the influence of marital status, we had better control the variable of age. Let us eliminate most of the influence of this variable by considering only a narrow age band, say people between 30 and 39 years of age. Now our data distribute themselves as shown in Table A6.3.

And so, when married and single people *of the same age group* are compared, the apparent relation between suicide and marital status is *reversed!* Differently put: The effect of family life is to reverse the relationship which would obtain were age the only factor. Failing to control the age variable, we come up with a spurious relationship.

* * * *

Failing to take into account, and control, other variables is the way we are led, in daily life, to make spurious association between variables. "Never trust anyone over 30" links age with duplicity. Does age *cause* a person to become untrustworthy? Let us assume that oldsters often do not act with the perfect probity of the pure in heart. Conceivably, a wider experience has taught the extent to which all significant decisions are bedeviled with contingencies, making a straightforward, morally antiseptic position difficult. If this were the case, then a third variable, extent of experience, underlies both age and apparent duplicity. Or conceivably it's family—spouse and children—that inclines the elders to more conformist positions lest the family's welfare be jeopardized. In this case, a third variable, marital status, might underly both age and untrustworthiness.

Bearded beatniks are irresponsible. Does beardedness or beatnikness *cause* irresponsibility? Perhaps those persons are from well-to-do middle-class families whose wealth and permissive child-rearing practices enable the young person to explore novel life patterns. In this case, a third variable, class, might underly both the personal (beardedness) and social (indifference to conventional work patterns) variables.

If we are sensitive to the requirements of careful sociological inquiry, we can avoid some of the silly-simple, spurious, cause-effect declarations that mar our daily thinking.

7. The Pearsonian correlation coefficient

In sociology as in other sciences (physical and biological as well as social), our attention is caught by differences, variations in behavior that want describing and explaining. A first task is to document these differences. Thus Angell found that American cities differ in social integration, the extent to which their residents share and support common convictions.*

A second task goes beyond description. We try to explain such differences by relating them to some other variable, some other sort of behavior that differs in phase with the first variable. Thus Angell found that a measure of social integration (contributions to public welfare and extent of law-abidingness) varied inversely with proportion of population foreign born and Negro—this in selected American cities.

So when we do this, we are trying to understand differences in a class of behavior by discovering some other social characteristic that differs along with it—i.e., is correlated with it. We use some measure of correlation to help us move from *description* to *explanation.*

Description. Suppose we were describing the position taken by white, male university students on black militancy on American campuses. We have data from six campuses showing, in each case, the percent opposing militant action by blacks in their attempt to set up Afro-American study programs. On the campus most strongly opposed, 60 percent of all male students are against sit-ins, picket lines, and strikes. At the other end, we have one campus on which only 10 percent of the male students take this position. The other four campuses fall in between with 20, 30, 40, and 50 percent of their male populations opposed to black militancy. Along a scale, our findings would look like Figure A7.1.

Now we could *describe* these male university students' stand by figuring the average position taken on these six campuses. (We'll assume there are the same number of males on each campus, similarly distributed by year in college.) So we might calculate the mean: 10 + 20 + 30 + 40 + 50 + 60 divided by 6, giving us an average of 35 percent.

But 35 percent is not a very accurate description of male students' views on these six campuses. It's not a figure found in a single case. It is the percent that would oppose black militancy *if* each campus had the same percent opposing such actions. But

* See Robert Cooley Angell, "The Social Integration of Selected American Cities," *American Journal of Sociology,* Vol. 47, (January, 1942), and "The Social Integration of American Cities of More than 100,000 Population," *American Sociological Review,* Vol. 12, No. 3 (June, 1947).

Figure A7.1

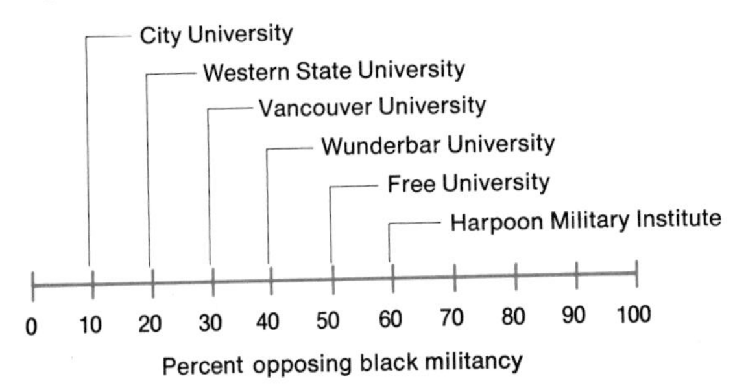

clearly that isn't the case. And the extent to which it isn't the case is the extent to which 35 percent is an erroneous statement. (If it were nearly true—if the figures were, say, 34, 33, 35, 35, 37, and 38 —then there wouldn't be much error involved in using the average. But a lot of spread, or variance, means that the mean ($\overline{X}$) isn't a very accurate statement.)

So, in describing male students' viewpoints by use of the mean, we should also add some information that would tell us how accurate, or inaccurate, the mean is. As you will recall from our second Aside on Methods, Number 2, a commonly used measure is the standard deviation, a measure of the extent to which the data spread away from the mean. To get this measure, we figure out the square root of the average squared deviations from the mean. So we take the difference between each value and the mean, square it, sum these, figure the average of these squared deviations (by dividing by N), and take the square root of the sums. As a statistical statement it would read

$$\sigma = \sqrt{\frac{\Sigma\,(x - \overline{X})^2}{N}}$$

where σ = standard deviation, x = the various values found (in our case, the values found on each of the six campuses—10, 20, 30, 40, 50 and 60), $\overline{X}$ = the mean, and N = the number of cases. In our example we need to find the sum of $(10 - 35)^2 + (20 - 35)^2 + (30 - 35)^2 + (40 - 35)^2 + (50 - 35)^2 + (60 - 35)^2$. This is 625 plus 225 plus 25 plus 25 plus 225 plus 625 or 1,750. This is, then, the sum of the squared deviations from the mean. To average them we divide by N, which is 6 in our case. Thus $1{,}750 \div 6 = 291.6$. Now the standard deviation is the square root of the average of the sum of squared deviations. So we need the square root of 291.6 which is 17.1.

Now we know that, on these six campuses, the average percent of male students opposed to black militancy is 35 percent. And we know that while this is the best single estimate we can make of the central tendency in this distribution of six cases, it is nonetheless inaccurate. For there is a wide range, or variance of opinion on this issue, a dispersion from the mean represented by the standard deviation of 17.1 percent.

Since this is a measure of the extent to which the mean ($\bar{X}$) is not true, we can regard a measure of variance as a measure of error. Crudely put, variance = error. How do we reduce the error? By gaining knowledge. How do we gain knowledge? By explaining the variance—i.e., by explaining why some campuses are high, others low in percent of males opposing black militancy. How do we explain the variance? By relating the variance to some variable, differences in which are linked with differences in opinions on black militancy.

Explanation. We have said that we want to explain the differences among these six college campuses. As soon as there are differences, there is something to explain. For unexplained differences represent ignorance.

We can begin to explain differences (the variance) in one variable by linking them with differences in another variable. Put another way, we look for some other dimension or trait that varies consistently with variations in the trait to be explained. Now the ignorance to be reduced—the variance to be explained—is in the Y variable (the dependent variable). So we're going to take the scale on page 627 and tilt it up on its side, as in Figure A7.2.

The response to black militancy on a campus is a group attribute, a characteristic of that campus. The campus climate may be sympathetic, or hostile, in varying degree, to militant actions. Our task, now, is to find out why it is more or less so. We have to find an X variable (independent variable) from whose variations we can predict to variations in the Y variable (degree of resistance to militant actions).

Suppose we were to argue that militant action on social issues will be seen as most disruptive by those who have a clear goal in sight and for whom a university education is the obvious means to its achievement. Presumably these would be persons with a strong vocational/professional orientation, those enrolled in business administration, premedicine, and the like. On the other hand, we might suppose that people enrolled in the liberal arts college

Figure A7.2

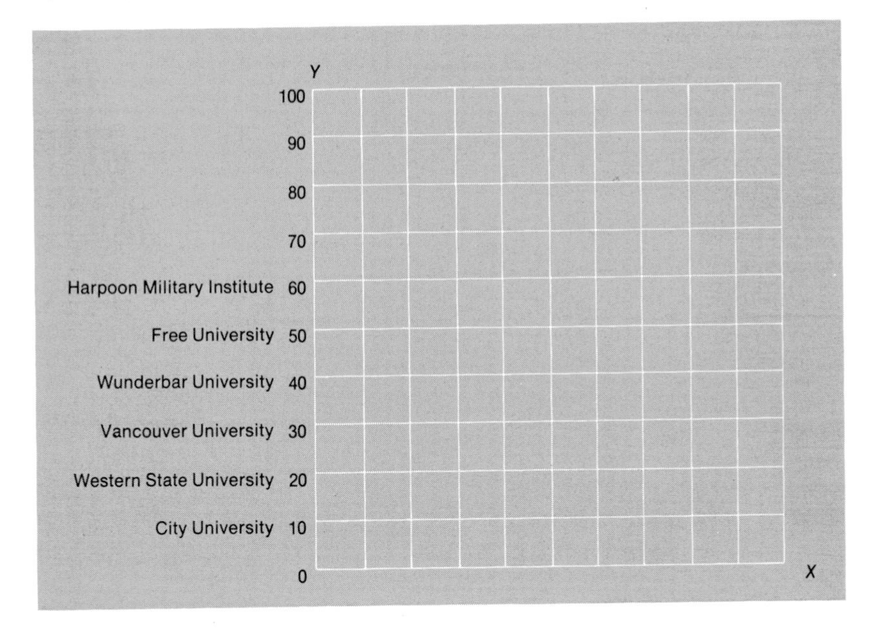

would be more responsive to public, or social issues (rather than to personal-vocational objectives). Were this the case, we would expect most resistance to militant action on those campuses most clearly committed to professional-vocational training.

We might then take for our explanatory variable another collective or group characteristic: some measure of the proportion of all resources put into professional (or preprofessional) training by a given university. If our thinking is perceptive and accurate, we come to this hypothesis: the greater the proportion of all resources (measured in personnel and/or money) put into vocational training by a given university, the greater the percent of white males who will resist militant action on a social issue.

Unlikely as it is, suppose that what we found is illustrated in Figure A7.3.

Plotting the data, we find that the six cases all fall precisely on the regression line.* We see that all our original ignorance—all the

* Note that if the relationship had been reversed—if for every unit increase in resources invested in vocational training there had been a *decrease* in percent of students opposing militant action, the direction of the line would have been reversed. (It would run from upper left to lower right, and we would call the relationship "inverse," or "negative.")

variation on Y—can now be explained by relating percent of male students opposing black militancy to another variable (X): percent of total resources allocated to professional or vocational training. The original variance ranging from 10 to 60 percent, with a standard deviation of 17.1 percent is now reduced to 0, on the regression line. (There is no variance around the line: every case falls precisely on it.) Thus we can now account perfectly for variations in percent of male students opposing black militancy. For every 10 percent increase in a school's investment in vocational curricula, there is a 10 percent increase in percent of students who are against the militant black position. So we can write:

Original ignorance (variance on the Y variable)	−	Ignorance done away with (by relating to the X variable)	= 0

or

What we wanted to find out (explanation of variation or differences in percent opposing black militancy)	−	What we have found out (with the aid of the X variable)	= 0

But this fictitious case is a little too neat. Social relationships—this time between male white and black militant students—are seldom if ever the outcomes of a single cause. It would be more realistic (although the case is still exaggerated) to find that our data fall in the fashion shown in Figure A7.4.

Now, when we plot a regression line through the data, all the cases do not fall on the line. (A regression line is mathematically calculated to strike a kind of average, or middle course, between the spread of the data.) Therefore, the relationship between the two variables does not explain all of the original variance along Y (our initial ignorance). There is still some *un*explained variance around the regression line, for five of the six cases do not fall on that line. We have reduced the range of ignorance, but we have not eliminated it.

If our original ignorance can be described by the variance around the mean of Y ($\bar{Y}$)—a range of values from 10 percent to 60 percent and a standard deviation of 17.1 percent—our remaining ignorance, after relating Y to X, can be described as the variance around the regression line.

Notice that we now have these three pieces of information:

1. What we knew originally—which was nothing. We had no explanation for the differences between students at the six campuses, the variance around $\bar{Y}$. Our ignorance was 100 percent. (We'll write this, a little later, as 1.0, representing the whole.)

Figure A7.3

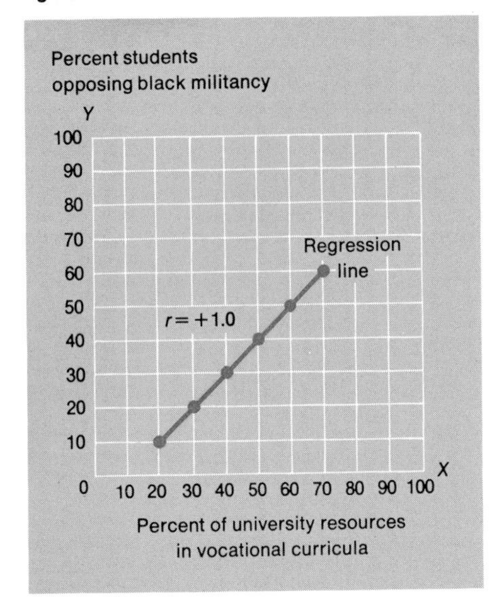

University	Percent of university resources in vocational curricula (X)	Percent of students opposing black militancy (Y)
City	20	10
Western State	30	20
Vancouver	40	30
Wunderbar	50	40
Free	60	50
Harpoon Military Institute	70	60

Figure A7.4

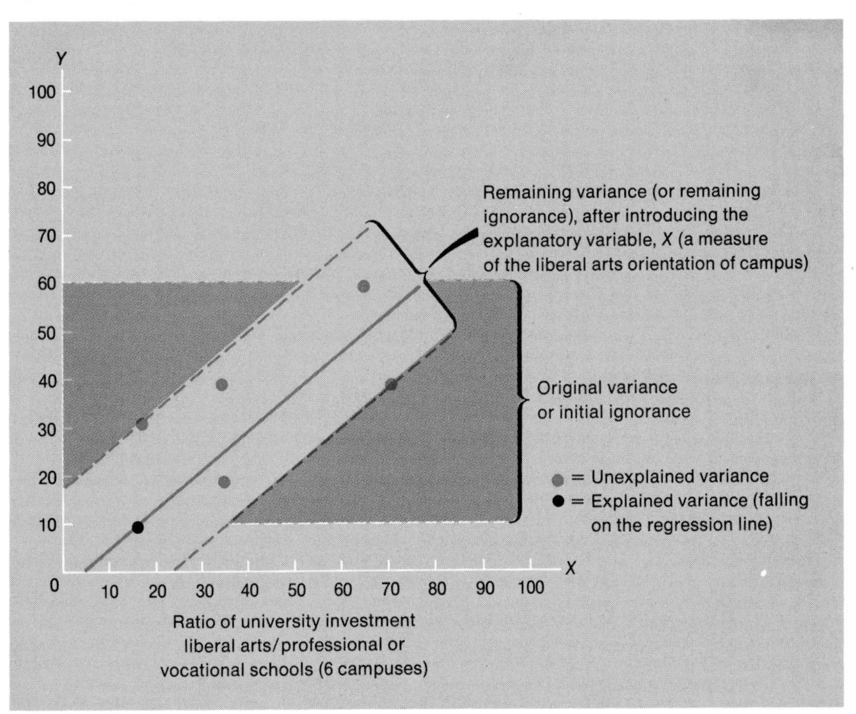

2. A part of this ignorance has been explained (by relating percent of male white population opposing militancy to percent of resources dedicated to vocational training.
3. A part has not been explained.

So we can write an equation.

Our original ignorance	=	The part that has been explained	+	The part that has not been explained (The variance remaining around the regression line)

and

Our original ignorance (100 percent or 1.0)	−	The part that has not been explained	=	What we have learned, or the part that has been explained

or

$$1.0 - \quad ? \quad = r^2$$

The question mark stands for "the-part-that-has-not-been-explained." A part is a fraction, and we can express that fraction by putting unexplained variance in the numerator and total variance in the denominator (remaining ignorance over the total, initial ignorance). It can be written:

$$\frac{\sigma^2 Y_c \text{ (variance around regression line)}}{\sigma^2 \bar{Y} \text{ (variance around the mean of } Y\text{)}}$$

And so our formula for r^2 becomes:

$$1 - \frac{\sigma^2 Y_c}{\sigma^2 Y} = r^2$$

r^2 is called the coefficient of determination. It tells us what part of the variance on Y can be explained or predicted from variance in X. Its square root, r, is the correlation coefficient. It's sometimes identified with its inventor, Karl Pearson (hence the Pearsonian correlation coefficient).

Values of r range from -1.0 (a perfect negative correlation) to $+1.0$ (a perfect position correlation). But we should note that, for any values between $+1.0$ and -1.0, r does not represent the amount of variation in Y that can be explained by variation in X. For example, $r = +.60$ should *not* be taken to mean that 60 percent of the variance in Y can be understood by referring to variance in X. Thus, where $r = +.60$, $r^2 = .36$, and about a third of the variance in Y is linked with variance in X.

To revert to our case in the text, a study was cited (page 177) in which the correlation between child's position or knowledge on moral issues and that of the parents was +.55; between children and their friends $r = +.35$; between children and their club leaders $r = +.14$; between children and public school teachers, $r = +.06$; and between children and Sunday school teachers, $r = +.002$. Now the coefficient of determination, or r^2—that is, the extent to which we can predict to Y from X—is the square of these values or, .30, .12, .02, .004, and .00004, respectively. It is important, then, that we not be misled by r into thinking the relationship between two variables is greater than in fact it is. It is also important, as you go further in sociology, to learn when it is appropriate *and when it is not* appropriate to use the correlation coefficient.

8. A simple coefficient of association between variables: Yule's *Q*

It will be worth our while to take another detour into methods, reporting on a simple coefficient of association used by Simmons —he reports 1,146 such coefficients!—to determine whether a relationship obtains between certain aspects of the role of the aged and other conditions in the social order. The device used is Yule's *Q*. It is used in fourfold tables (2×2 tables with four cells) in which, if there is a perfect positive association, all the cases fall in the upper left- and lower right-hand cells; or, if there is perfect negative association, in the other diagonal cells, lower left and upper right. Simmons finds, for example, that this measure gives him a coefficient of association of −1.00 between hunting economies and the property rights of aged men. But the relationship between herding and property rights of old men is +.76. Some of his data in a four-celled table are shown in Table A8.1. Thus an inspection of the table suggests that where herding is the main economic activity, the old men almost always have rights in property, whereas in the absence of herding, this set of expectations as to older males occurs about half the time and half of the time does not.

A perfect relationship would be one in which, wherever we found herding we would always find old men dominating property; and in the absence of herding, we would never find this characteristic in their roles. All the cases would fall in the upper-left-to-lower-right diagonal. Thus we can see in the formula for Yule's *Q*

Table A8.1

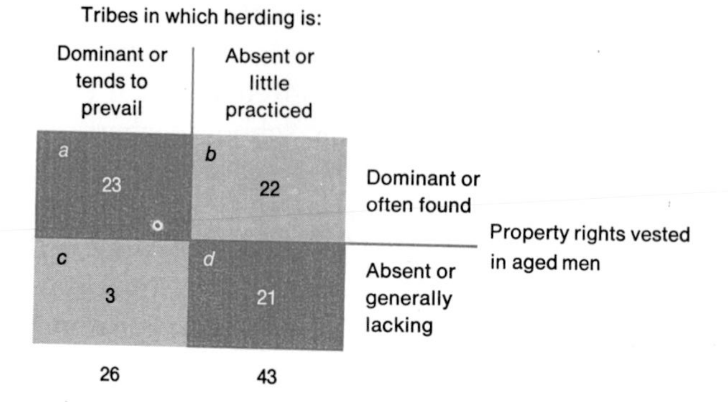

Property rights vested in aged men	Tribes in which herding is: Dominant or tends to prevail	Tribes in which herding is: Absent or little practiced
Dominant or often found	*a* 23	*b* 22
Absent or generally lacking	*c* 3	*d* 21
	26	43

Note: Data in the upper left and lower right cells supports the hypothesis: Herding, as a dominant economic activity, is associated with the vesting of property rights in the older males.

$$Q = \frac{ad - bc}{ad + bc}$$

that, for a perfect positive association, $bc = 0$ and in a perfect negative association $ad = 0$. In the usual, intermediate cases, the value of *ad* (and hence the value of a positive coefficient of association) is reduced by the extent to which we find cases falling in cells *b* and *c*.

Applying Yule's *Q* to the data provided by Simmons for herding and property rights among the aged (Table A8.1), we have the following:

$$Q = \frac{ad - bc}{ad + bc} = \frac{483 + 66}{483 - 66} = +.76\,.$$

Since the range of *Q* values is from -1.0 to $+1.0$ (0.0 indicating a lack of association) we can interpret $+.76$ as a fairly strong, positive association between the practice of herding and the vesting of property rights in old men.

9. Measuring degree of association between two sets of rank-ordered data

Measures of relationship between rank-ordered observations are especially important to the sociologist. This is because his data are often crude, preventing him from treating them as though they formed equal-interval or zero-point scales. Let me make this

Table A9.1

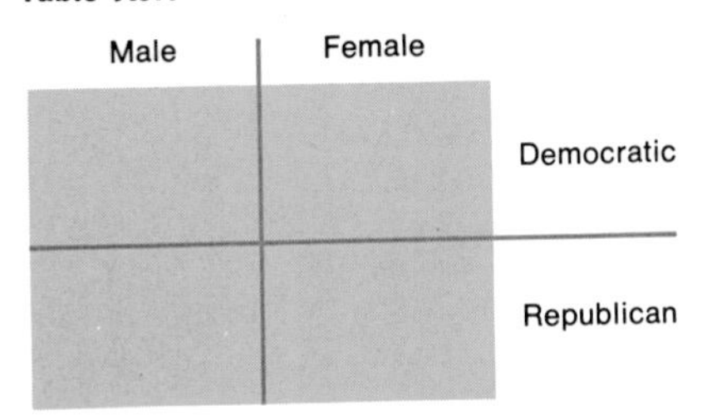

clearer. We can distinguish several sorts of scales—several ways in which data can be usefully ordered in some sort of progression. There is the nominal scale that has no inherent order, no ostensible progression. A nominal scale is one in which the points are simply labels (nominal means *name*): male-female, Democratic-Republican-Dixiecrat-Socialist-Birchite, and so on. We might, for example, wish to discover if there was any relationship between sex and voting preference, so constructing and crosscutting two nominal scales as indicated in the 2 × 2-celled table in Table A9.1.

But the ordinal scale, as its name suggests, does have an order, a succession. Thus among a group of acquaintances there can be a succession from "most liked" to "least liked."

But much less often do we have data that can be arranged so that the intervals between two points on the scale are equal. With income we know that the distance between $1,000 and $2,000 is the same as that between $17,000 and $18,000. With family size we know that the "distance" between two and three children is the same as that between four and five; and that four children is twice as many as two, just as six is twice as many as three. But to treat, say, attractiveness scores as cardinal (rather than ordinal) numbers would involve quite untenable assumptions. Can I demonstrate that I like Jones *twice as much* as Smith? Or that the two points that measure social distance ("attractiveness") between Jones and Doaks are equivalent to the equally distant points between Smith and White? Unfortunately not. But I *can* deal with them in terms of more or less, relying on *ordinal* measures.

The scheme shown in Table A9.2 may help make the distinction between nominal, ordinal, and equal-interval scales. We will use income as the variable. (Note that a variable that can be measured on an equal-interval scale can also be converted to an ordinal and nominal scale. But the reverse is not true.)

Now let us clarify the meaning of rho. (This is a measure of

Table A9.2

Type of scale: crude to complex	Characteristics	The variable	Ways of measuring
Nominal	Mutually exclusive category system	Income	A given income is either *above,* or *below* the median
Ordinal	Mutually exclusive category system + rank order (greater/ lesser)	Income	High (above $10,000) Intermediate ($5,000–$9,999) Low (0–$4,999)
Equal interval	Mutually exclusive category system + rank order + equal interval	Income	Use actual income value

Table A9.3

The (social) object: yours and your friend's acquaintances	Rank order of attractiveness of five acquaintances, by			
	You	Your friend	D	D^2
Jones	1	1	0	0
Smith	2	3	−1	1
Doaks	3	2	1	1
White	4	5	−1	1
Brown	5	4	1	1
			0	4

$$r_s = 1 - \frac{6\Sigma D^2}{N(N^2-1)} = 1 - \frac{24}{120} = 1 - .20 = .80.$$

extent of agreement, in the population studied, of two series of *rank-ordered* observations. We are working with an ordinal scale. The measure of such agreement in the sample is commonly designated as r_s, The Spearman rank correlation coefficient.)

In our illustration here (refer to page 230), we wish to know whether two persons, A and B, rank 17 others with whom they live, in the same order of attractiveness. Thus if A says Jones is his best friend (ranks highest in attractiveness), Smith his next best, and so on through the 17th person, and if B ranks these people in precisely the same order of attractiveness, r_s (or rho, if we're dealing with the whole population) = + 1.00. Perfect *dis*agreement would yield a rank-order correlation coefficient of −1.00.

The formula for calculating r_s is:

$$r_s = 1 - \frac{6\Sigma D^2}{N(N^2-1)},$$

Table A9.4

The (social) object: yours and your least-liked friend's acquaintances	Rank order of attractiveness of five acquaintances, by You	Your least-liked acquaintance	D	D^2
Jones	1	5	−4	16
Smith	2	4	−2	4
Doaks	3	3	0	0
White	4	2	2	4
Brown	5	1	4	16
			0	40

$$r_s = 1 - \frac{6\Sigma D^2}{N(N^2-1)} = 1 - \frac{6(40)}{120} = 1 - 2 = -1.$$

where N = the number of paired observations and D = the difference between the ranking assigned to each of a given pair of observations. Suppose, for example, that we were to do what Professor Newcomb did: the investigator asks you and your friend to rank the attractiveness of five acquaintances. Fictitious and oversimplified data are worked through in Table A9.3 to show the way of calculating the Spearman rank correlation coefficient.

If, on the other hand, we were calculating the rank-order correlation on extent of agreement between you and your *least* liked acquaintance, the data and outcome might be as in Table A9.4.

10. Testing whether Negro representation on South Carolina draft boards is a chance affair

Our data come from the following article in *Civil Liberties*, Monthly publication of the American Civil Liberties Union, No. 245, April, 1967, p. 1.

> *Union Asks Halt to Negro Draft*
>
> A federal suit was filed last month to enjoin the drafting of South Carolina and Georgia Negroes until they are proportionately represented on Selective Service Boards.
>
> Of the 161 persons serving on draft boards in South Carolina, 160 are white. Negroes comprise 34.8 percent of the state's population. The statistical probability that such distribution occurred by chance, according to the plaintiff's brief, is .0000000000000000000001—"less than the likelihood that in

a game of contract bridge . . . each of four players would be dealt a perfect hand . . . from a well shuffled deck of 52 playing cards."

Five out of 509 draft board members in Georgia are Negro, although the population is 28.5 percent Negro.

The ACLU contends the figures prove the systematic exclusion of Negroes from draft boards. Therefore, the induction of the plaintiff would violate the 14th Amendment equal protection guarantee.

Have we any way of telling whether some sort of selective influence is at work, resulting in the fact (we'll assume its accuracy) that only 1 out of 161 South Carolina draft board members is black in a state whose population is about 35 percent Negro?

Building a table from the available data will help us tackle this problem. If 34.8 percent of the state population is Negro we might expect, were selection random, that 34.8 percent of the 161 draft board members would be Negro. And 34.8 percent (call it 35 percent to make calculation easier) of 161 gives us 56 persons. Our summary would look like Table A10.1.

Now we ask whether a difference of this magnitude between (1 observed and 56 expected) would be likely to occur by chance. For example, if we reached randomly into a population in which 34.8 percent were Negroes, is it likely that in 161 soundings we could come up with only 1 Negro? If it is likely, there is no problem, either social or sociological. If the answer turns out to be no, then we conclude that the difference between these two figures is not a chance affair. We are then driven to find some explanation for it—*one* of which might be racial discrimination.

Perhaps simply looking at these figures might persuade you that such a difference didn't occur by chance. But oftentimes it's not easy to tell. Suppose that 20 or 25 percent of South Carolina's draft board members were Negroes. Are such figures too far away from 34.8 percent to have occurred by chance? How can we find out?

We will use the same procedure that we did in Aside on Methods: Number 3. We will ask: Where we have a sample of 161 cases* among whom 56 could be expected to be Negro, is a finding of a single Negro and 160 whites so far away from what we expected

* In fact, if the news item is accurate, we are not dealing with a sample but with the whole population of draft board members in South Carolina. But for our purposes here, we will treat it as though it were a sample.

Table A10.1

Number of whites and blacks on South Carolina draft boards

	Observed	Expected (if in same proportions as in total population)	Percentages	
			Observed	Expected
Whites	160	105	99	65.2
Negroes	1	56	1	34.8
Total	161	161	100	100.0

Figure A10.1

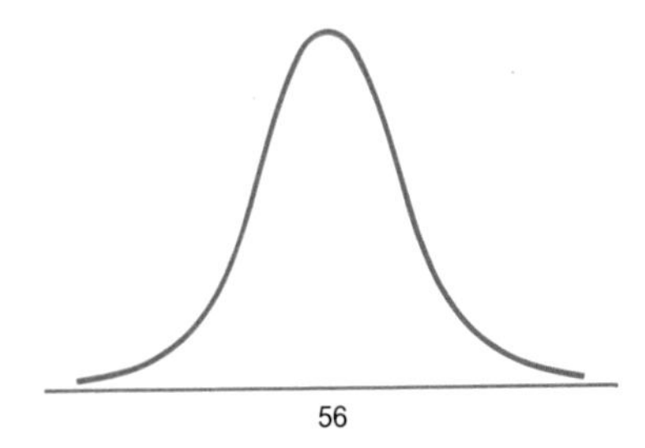

that we must attribute the finding to something other than chance?

Knowing that sampling errors follow a normal distribution, the most frequent deviations from the true population value being small ones and clustering around the mean—the true population value—we can calculate how many standard deviations away from that true population value our particular observation (one Negro among 161 draft board members) is.

Since South Carolina is 34.8 percent black and 34.8 percent of 161 draft board members gives us 56 Negroes, this would be the figure most often approached in a series of samplings *if* composition of the draft boards were unaffected by some sort of bias. So we could draw the picture shown in Figure A10.1.

In sampling we would sometimes get 57, or 55 and less often values more remote from 56. How often would we be likely to get a value of 1?

To answer this we need to know where the standard error of this sampling distribution is—in a case where:

$N = 161$

$p = .35$ (i.e., the probability of drawing a Negro from the population, randomly: the figure is rounded from 34.8 percent)

$q = 1 - p$, which is .65

Now the standard error is given by the formula $\sigma_s = \sqrt{n\ p\ q}$. In our case, evaluating the formula, we get:

$$\begin{aligned} \sigma &= \sqrt{161\ (.35)\ (.65)} \\ &= \sqrt{36.6275}, \text{ or, roughly} \\ \sigma_s &= 6. \end{aligned}$$

In a normal distribution of sample findings, two thirds of them will fall between −1 and +1 standard error: in this case, 56, plus or minus 6, or between 50 and 62. And in better than 90 percent of the cases, sample findings would fall between −2 and +2 standard errors—i.e., between 44 and 68, in our case.

But our finding, obviously, is *many more* standard errors away from the expected value, 56. Precisely, it is $56 - 1 \div 6$ standard errors distant from the value we would expect if no bias entered into the selection of draft board members. Fifty-five divided by 6 gives us 9+ standard errors, a result so far from chance that we couldn't reasonably expect it to have occurred except through some sort of nonchance influences. We can draw a picture of our findings in the fashion shown in Figure A10.2.

It might seem, given the data we had to start with and the position taken by the ACLU, that for the sociologist to tackle this issue is to belabor the obvious. But the sociologist is a skeptic. The seeming existence of a nonchance association leaves two questions unanswered. (1) What is the degree of association? and (2) How account for it?

To the first question we have an answer. (It is much the easier question.) Being black and service on draft boards are strongly (inversely) associated. The probability of a finding such as ours is much less than one time in a thousand, on a chance basis. We must reject the possibility that this is a happenstance, sampling error.

But to say that this is not a chance finding is not to say what it *is*. In search of an explanation we might have to consider a number of things. Is the 35 percent of South Carolina's population that is Negro disproportionately under age 21 and thus not eligible for draft board membership? Are draft boards set up by geographical units? And is the Negro population so clustered in small areas that their territorial concentration would make for underrepresentation on draft boards? (Are they gerrymandered?) Are fewer likely to qualify because of poor educational backgrounds when some degree of sophistication in handling symbols and paper work is required?

In short, there is a brain-cudgeling job of explanation yet to be

Figure A10.2

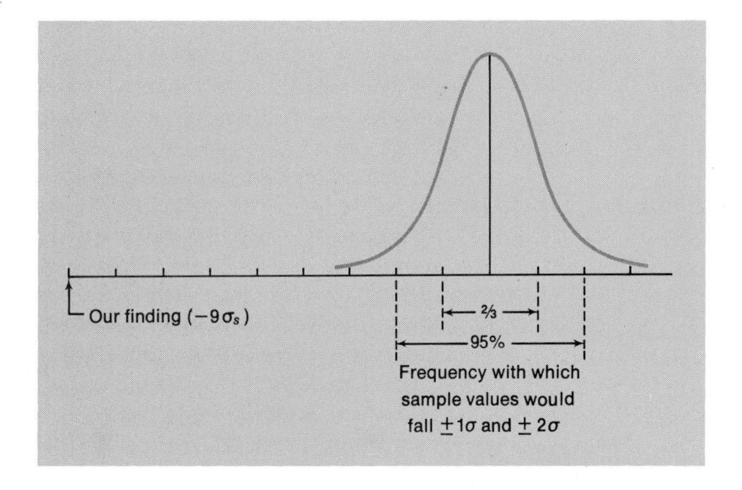

Table A10.2

Number of whites and blacks on Georgia draft boards

	Observed	Expected (if in same proportions as in total population)	Percentages Observed	Percentages Expected
Whites	504	364	99	71.5
Negroes	5	145	1	28.5
Total	509	509	100	100.0

done after we have first established the very high probability that this is not a chance affair.

Now try your hand at the Georgia data, answering the question: Could such a representation of Negroes on Georgia's Draft Boards be a matter of chance? Data are provided in Table A10.2.

11. The problem of the chemist in his own test tube: controlling interviewer effect

The reference to the Erie county research on page 421 gives us a chance to consider another methodological problem: How can we prevent the investigator from affecting the responses he gets from people? Some have suggested that sociology is greatly limited, as the biophysical sciences are not, because our data come from feeling, thinking subjects. A black respondent may provide different data for a white interviewer than he would give to another black. The respondent asked about his income bracket may link the investigator with the Internal Revenue Service and claim a pauper's pittance as his income. How can we prevent the investigator's contaminating his data? Or if he does, how can we get a measure of the error so introduced, enabling us to correct for it?

The Erie county data come from a *panel* of respondents—that is, the same persons were interviewed repeatedly—seven times in this study. This enabled the investigators to learn something about change, its extent and direction, for the same person over a period of time—and the influences accounting for change.

We have here the old problem of the chemist in his own test tube. How would repeated interviewing affect people's responses? Take J. Doaks, for example. Since the last time Joe talked with the interviewer, he has changed his mind about the candidates. But not wanting to appear inconsistent or vacillating to the interviewer, he tries to recall what he said last time so that he can repeat the views formerly expressed. It is the effect of the interviewer that introduces this distortion. How might one estimate the error introduced by this extraneous influence? The research design handled this problem in the following way.

From a visit to every fourth house in Erie County, Ohio, 3,000 respondents were chosen, closely resembling the total population in education, telephone and car ownership, age, sex, residence, and nativity. From this first group of respondents, five groups of 600 persons each were selected so that each group was "a miniature sample of the whole poll and of the county itself." Of these five groups, people in one constituted the panel and were repeatedly interviewed from May until election time in November.

But the other four groups, A, B, C, D (Table A11.1), each of them interviewed only once, served as controls for interviewer effect. A comparison of the control group with the main panel at a given point in time made it possible to estimate the effect that repeated interviewing might have on panel respondents. For assuming that the sample was properly drawn (insuring the comparability of panel and control groups), and assuming that members of each of these groups had been exposed to the same complex of influences at that time and place, the only significant difference in their experience, touching on the political campaign, was that the panel respondents had been repeatedly interviewed while the controls had not. Thus sizable differences in responses between Control D and the main panel (in October) could be taken as a measure of interviewer effect.

Table A11.1

Interview schedule and scheme to control for interview effect*

Number and month of interview	Group interviewed: Main panel (N = 600)	Control panel A (N = 600)	Control panel B (N = 600)	Control panel C (N = 600)	Control panel D (N = 600)
1 May	X	X			
2 June	X				
3 July†	X		X		
4 August‡	X			X	
5 September	X				
6 October	X				X
7 November§	X				

* Interviews of control panel B in July, control panel C in August, and control panel D in October are points of comparison of the main panel and control group responses (to compare once-interviewed with several-times-interviewed respondents) thus getting a measure of error that would be introduced by repeated exposure to the interviewer. Differences between the interviews with control panels A and B, control panels A and C, and control panels A and D give measures of any change induced by all politically relevant events *other than* repeated interviewing.

† Republican convention.

‡ Democratic convention.

§ Election.

The general scheme of the study, showing the attempt to measure (and thus control) interviewer effect, is shown in Table A11.1.

12. Causal explanations in sociology

We should note here that causal explanations in sociology require, Weber insists, both the observation of statistical regularities *and* a meaningful interpretation of such regularities. (Recall our definition of the field of sociology in Chapter 1.) Or, as the late Samuel Stouffer used to put it: to stop with a correlation coefficient—i.e., with a demonstration of statistical regularities—is an acknowledgment of defeat. In Weber's words:

> If adequacy in respect to meaning is lacking, then no matter how high the degree of uniformity and how precisely its probability can be numerically determined, it is still an incomprehensible statistical probability, whether dealing with overt or subjective processes. On the other hand, even the most perfect adequacy on the level of meaning has causal significance from a sociological point of view only in so far as there is some kind of proof for the existence of a probability that action in fact normally takes the course which has been held to be meaningful. (Max Weber, *The Theory of*

Social and Economic Organization, trans. A. M. Henderson and Talcott Parsons [New York: Oxford University Press, Inc., 1947], pp. 99, 100.)

To get at the meaningful in human conduct, that which, at the level of motive and value is at the core of recurrent patterns of conduct, Weber devises what he calls the "ideal type." The ideal type is a kind of model, expressing in a pure—and therefore unreal—form, the core characteristics of a pattern of conduct. Herbert Luethy puts it very well when he speaks of Weber's

> great and questioning mind [which was] never particularly interested in the facts of history, nor even in social and economic systems, but rather in the detection of the ultimate impulses behind man's attitudes and behaviour. What he analyzed were not the hybrid and wretched forms of an historically realised society (in which such ultimate impulses are never embodied in their purity), but rather the abstract and chemically pure "ideal types" which should provide the essences of a civilisation stripped of all the adulterations and accidents of actual history" (Herbert Luethy, "Once Again: Calvinism and Capitalism," *Encounter,* Vol. 22, No. 1 [January, 1964], p. 27).

But so "stripped of all the adulterations" of actual social life, what use can the ideal type be? It is, first of all, an attempt to state certain psychic regularities that sustain an enduring system of relationships. Second, it points out a line of inquiry and offers a target for testing. The ideal type, says Robert Redfield, referring to his own attempt to set up a conceptual model of the small, primitive society, "is there to point the way to the study of that which its use brings to notice" (*Peasant Society and Culture* [Chicago: University of Chicago Press, 1956], p. 13). Third, it provides base points from which observed behavior deviates, raising the question as to why and under what conditions such deviations obtain. And if we can measure the "distance" between the ideal type and each of two patterns of observed conduct, then we can solve for the "distance" or difference between the observed patterns, noting how they differ from elements of the ideal type. Let's illustrate this third point.

In the ideal type of bureaucratic organization, rewards are based on demonstrable capacity to perform in a work role. The preferred way of demonstrating capacity would be in actual performance or, as an approximation, on a paper and pencil test (as in the civil service).

Figure A12.1

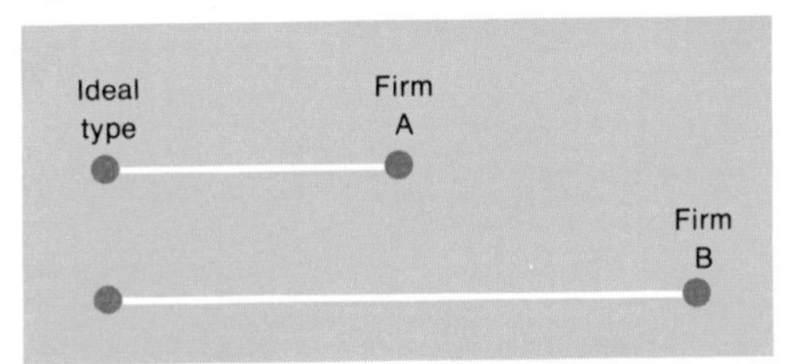

Suppose we have a work organization (Firm A) in which periodic tests of some sort are administered to determine promotion and demotion, modified by letters of recommendation in which friendship and kinship may play a part. Farther away from the ideal type is Firm B, in which age or seniority determines rewards in a family business. (The family line is a central concern.) If rational criteria—measures of achievement rather than traits automatically accruing to the person—make for greater productivity, then Firm A, other things equal, should produce more than Firm B. Deviation from the ideal type could be graphically represented as in Figure A12.1. The "distance" A–B is a measure of two things: extent to which one firm, in comparison with another, departs from the ideal-typical bench mark: and of the decline in productivity that our hypothesis asserts to be correlated with that departure from strictly rational criteria of organization.

13. The Guttman or Cornell scale

If a person gave tolerant responses on two out of three items in this fifth set, as described on pages 445–46, we can be quite sure (and by "quite sure" I mean that 96 percent of the time we would be right) that he *would do likewise in each of the other sets of questions!* How can this be so? The answer to this question promts another methodological detour to get a first acquaintance with the measure Stouffer is using here, a scale called the Guttman or Cornell scale. This sort of ordinal scale, or yardstick, has a special advantage that we call "unidimensionality." That is, it helps us deal with just one dimension at a time. This gives us more confidence in the *validity* of our measure. Now it may seem extraordinarily ingenuous for an investigator not to know what it is he is measuring, yet this is sometimes the case. What, for example, is represented by the independent variable when we find a high inverse correlation between density of population and age-specific birthrates? (The existence of a relationship may not tell us, in itself, what it is that we are measuring that accounts for the relationship.) The classic example is the intelligence test. How do we understand an inverse relationship between intelligence test scores and level of education achieved for a probability sample of Mississippi adults?

Professor Stouffer conveys very clearly the idea of the Guttman scaling procedure. Imagine, he says, a spelling test consisting of these three words: *catastrophe, cattle,* and *cat.*

> This "test" has a very special kind of built-in internal consistency. If a person can spell the hardest word, he also is very likely to be able to spell the easier words. If he can spell only two words, we know *which* two words they are. If he can spell only one, we know *which* one that is. This is called a cumulative property of a test [or measure]. When we have only a few items, we *need some such built-in property in order to know whether we are measuring a single dimension.*
>
> Unless our scale contains one dimension only, we cannot sensibly rank people in it. Consider a scale of "bigness" which mixes up both height and weight. Is a tall man who weighs 180 pounds bigger than a short fat man who weighs 200 pounds? One can rank people in terms of one *or* the other measure, but *not both on a single scale* (Stouffer, *op. cit.,* p. 262; reprinted by permission of Doubleday & Co., Inc.; last emphasis in both paragraphs mine).

The fact that we are dealing with a single scale, a single dimension, is revealed by the extent to which a given response (spells "catastrophe" correctly) implicates all others (also spells "cattle" and "cat" correctly). In the case of this tolerance-of-nonconformity scale, it is unidimensional to the extent that a person affirming two out of three tolerant responses in the fifth set, also does so in each of the four sets below. Similarly, a person who does not score as tolerant in the fifth set, but does on the fourth set of items must, if the scale is perfectly unidimensional, also give at least two out of three tolerant responses on the third, second, and first sets.

> Not everybody, of course, will be wholly consistent. The degree of consistency is measured by a coefficient of reproducibility, which, by convention, must be at least .90. The coefficient [of reproducibility, the extent to which, knowing

the person's score, we also know how he answered on each item] for this scale is a very satisfactory .96 and is exactly the same when the scale is constructed separately from the data from each of the two survey agencies. Moreover, separate tabulations by education showed that the reproducibility was approximately the same at all educational levels (*Ibid.*, p. 266).

14. Relationships pictured through scatter diagrams and regression lines

Pictures, poetry, and mathematics are kindred ways of expressing our perceptions of the world. Because of their abstract character, they have a suggestiveness that leads the mind to a range of concrete instances illuminated by that abstraction. And all three may be distinguished by precision and parsimony.

In an Aside on Methods, Number 7, we discussed a parsimonious way of stating the extent (and direction, whether positive or negative) of the relationship between two variables. We can also make a picture of such a relationship—a picture showing both the spread or scatter of the data and the central tendency, if any. Let us illustrate, using the variables discussed by Marx: extent of urbanism and degree of Negro militance. The hypothesis is this: a measure of extent of Negro militance varies positively with a measure of extent of urbanism.

This hypothesis is derived from a theory put together from a number of plausible assertions. These come from our experience and from the wisdom literature. We know, for example, that in the great cities there is a convergence of people born and reared in quite various cultures. Thus the new urban dweller is exposed to alternatives not even dreamed of in rural fastnesses. His wants and his demands will change. And here the agencies of law—the impersonal arbiters of conflicting claims—supersede the informal agencies of rural life: the articulation of traditional ways through public opinion and informal sanctions. And if the law is unresponsive, and if the values sought are legitimized in religion, or in statute and constitutional law, then people will become militant in pursuit of their claims. In some such ways our argument would run.

Now we need two series of data: one on degree of urbanism and a second on extent of militance. (*In our fictitious example we are disregarding other variables that might contribute to militance and which, therefore, should be controlled.*) For the independent variable suppose we take percent of county population living in places having 100,000 or more inhabitants. This is our measure of urbanism. And for the dependent variable, degree of militance, we will use Marx's measure. (See the footnote on page 516.) Since both variables are measured in percent, the range will be from 0 to 100 in each case.

To simplify our illustration, let us take just three counties in which the percent of population living in places having 100,000 or more people is 20, 40, and 60 percent. For these same three counties, the percent of the Negro population which is militant is 40, 60, and 80 percent, respectively. Now we can picture the data as in Figure A14.1. As we see, the relationship between the two variables can be represented by a straight line.

Now the picture of a straight line can be translated into mathematical language. The equation for a straight line is $Y = a + bX$, where $a =$ the value on the Y axis where it is intercepted by the regression line (at 20 percent in our example), and b, a second constant, tells us about the slope of the line. (This may sound a bit mysterious, but it isn't: b simply tells us how much change there is in one variable for every unit of change in the other.)

Let us take the first county, the one in which 20 percent of the population is urban (live in places having 100,000 or more people) and where 40 percent of the Negro population is militant. Plugging these data into the formula for a straight line we get:

$$Y = a + b\ (20), \text{ or}$$
$$40 = 20 + b\ (20), \text{ or}$$
$$20 = 20\ b, \text{ and}$$
$$b = 20/20 = 1.$$

The measure of slope, $b = 1$, can be translated this way. For every unit increase in X, there is 1 unit increase in Y.

If a straight line were an adequate picture of the way our data scatter on a piece of graph paper, then for any value of X, this formula would tell us what percent of the Negro population would be militant (Y). For militance would be a simple, linear function of our measure of urbanism. Suppose we were to discover a fourth county which was 75 percent urban, according to our definition of urbanism. Then $Y = a + bX$ would read: $Y = 20 + 1\ (75)$, that is to say percent of Negro population militant would be 95.

Now notice the connection between two different pictures of a linear relationship. In our example (Figure A14.2 left) a perfect linear relationship between two continuous variables is seen as a

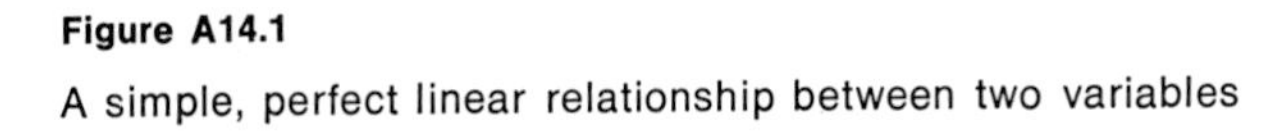

Figure A14.1

A simple, perfect linear relationship between two variables

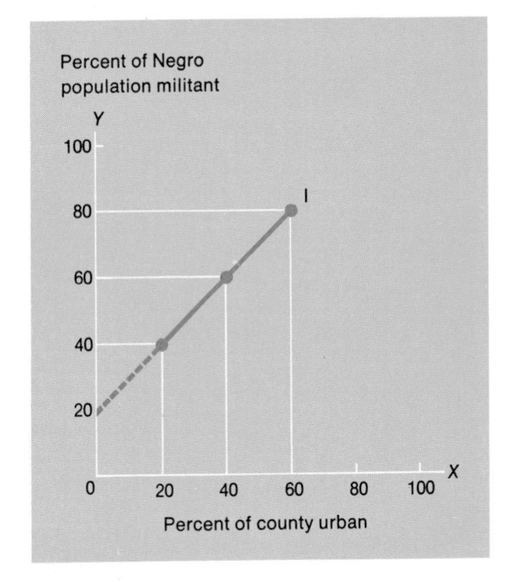

Figure A14.2

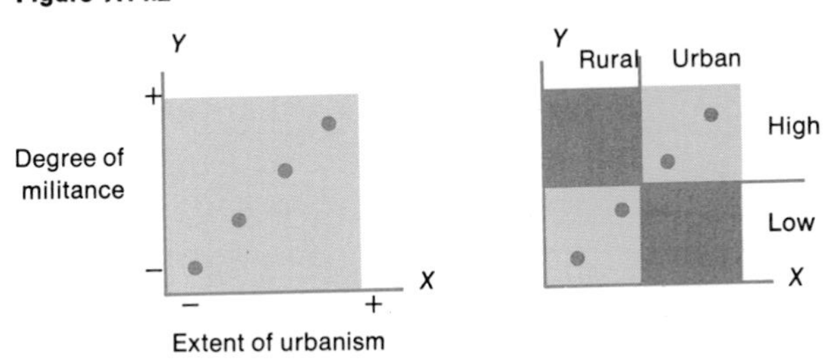

series of cases all of which fall along the diagonal. Now if we were to superimpose a four-celled table (right) to picture the relationship between two discrete variables (rural-urban and militant-nonmilitant), all of our four cases would fall in the lower left and upper right cells.

Thus our fictional case gives us two ways of picturing the same thing: a perfect relationship between the two variables. Any cases that fall *off* the diagonal, or in the upper left- or lower right-hand cells are deviant, or negative cases. They challenge our generalization or prediction, constraining us to try to discover the inadequacy of our proposition—in this case, the assertion that militance among Negroes is a linear function of extent of urbanization.

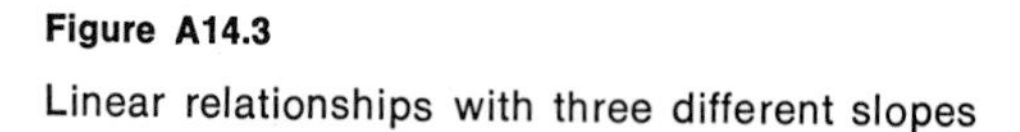

Figure A14.3

Linear relationships with three different slopes

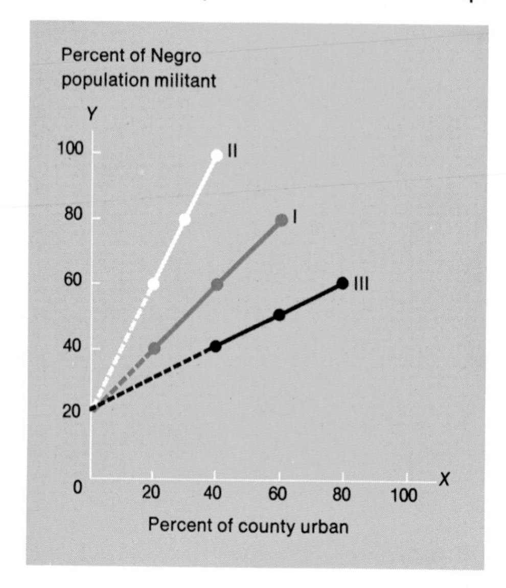

Note, finally, two other things. A straight line picturing the relationship between two variables may have various slopes—i.e., different values of *b*. And, second, either a vertical or a horizontal line would tell us that one variable was not varying: hence no relationship between the variables.

In Figure A14.3 we have three linear relationships, each with a different value for *b*. Line I we have already plotted, but we will repeat the data in Table A14.1 to enable a clearer comparison with lines II and III.

The second point could be put this way: If there isn't any difference it doesn't make any difference. (Recall the significance of this word *difference* in our definition of the field of sociology, Chapter 1.) To illustrate:

Suppose that, in three counties, the percent of Negro population militant was 20, 60, and 100, while the percent of the counties we could call urban was 40, 40, and 40. Obviously, there are no differences in extent of urbanization—no difference that helps us to understand the variance in percent of Negro population that is militant. Or put it the other way: Suppose that in our three counties the percent of population living in places having 100,000 or more people was 40, 60, and 80 and the percent of Negro population militant was 50, 50, and 50. Again, urbanization seems to

Table A14.1

Percent of county urban X	Percent of Negro population militant Y	$Y = a + bX$	Description of relationship in terms of b
Line I			
20	40	$40 = 20 + b(20)$	For every unit increase in X,
40	60	$20 = 20b$	the *same* unit increase
60	80	$b = 20/20 = 1$	in Y
Line II			
20	60	$60 = 20 + b(20)$	For every unit increase in X,
30	80	$40 = 20b$	there is *twice* that
40	100	$b = 40/20 = 2$	increase in Y
Line III			
40	40	$40 = 20 + b(40)$	For every unit increase in X,
60	50	$20 = 40b$	there is *half* that
80	60	$b = 20/40 = 0.5$	increase in Y

have nothing to do with militance and is not, therefore, a helpful variable.

Of course, variables must vary, by definition. But the point here is this: If one discovers no variance in one variable, he has nothing to help him explain variance in a second variable.

selected supplementary readings

Articles marked with an asterisk are available as reprints from the college division of the Bobbs-Merrill Company, Indianapolis, Ind.

chapter 1

* Becker, Howard S. "Problems of Inference and Proof in Participant Observation," *American Sociological Review,* 1958, pp. 652–60.

Berelson, Bernard, and Steiner, Gary A. "Methods of Inquiry," in *Human Behavior: An Inventory of Scientific Findings,* pp. 15–33. New York: Harcourt, Brace & World, Inc., 1964.

Berger, Peter L. *Invitation to Sociology: A Humanistic Perspective.* New York: Doubleday & Co., Inc., 1963.

* Bierstedt, Robert. "A Critique of Empiricism in Sociology," *American Sociological Review,* 1949, pp. 584–92.

Blalock, Hubert M., Jr. *An Introduction to Social Research.* Englewood Cliffs, N.J.: Prentice-Hall, Inc., 1970.

Campbell, Donald T., and Stanley, Julian C. "Experimental and Quasi-Experimental Designs for Research on Teaching," in N. L. Gage (ed.), *Handbook of Research on Teaching.* Skokie, Ill.: Rand McNally & Co., 1963.

* Cooley, Charles Horton. "The Roots of Social Knowledge," *American Journal of Sociology,* 1926, pp. 59–79.

Denzin, Norman K. *Sociological Methods: A Sourcebook.* Chicago: Aldine Publishing Co., 1970.

Denzin, Norman K. *The Research Act: A Theoretical Introducion to Sociological Methods.* Chicago: Aldine Publishing Co., 1970.

Faris, Robert E. L. "The Discipline of Sociology," in Robert E. L. Faris (ed.), *Handbook of Modern Sociology,* chap. i. Chicago: Rand McNally & Co., 1964.

Greenwood, Ernest. *Experimental Sociology, A Study in Method.* New York: King's Crown Press, 1949.

Hughes, Everett. "The Improper Study of Man," in Lynn White, Jr. (ed.), *Frontiers of Knowledge in the Study of Man.* New York: Harper, 1956.

International Encyclopedia of the Social Sciences.

Lazarsfeld, Paul F. "Evidence and Inference in Social Research," *Daedalus,* Vol. 87, No. 4 (Fall, 1958), pp. 99–130.

———. "Problems in Methodology," in Robert K. Merton, Leonard Broom, and Leonard S. Cottrell, Jr. (eds.), *Sociology Today,* chap. ii. New York: Harper & Row—Harper Torchbooks, 1965.

* Lundberg, George. "The Concept of Law in the Social Sciences," *Philosophy of Science,* 1938, pp. 189–203.

Merton, Robert K. "Notes on Problem-Finding in Sociology," in Merton, Broom, and Cottrell, Jr. (eds.), *op. cit.,* Vol. I, pp. ix–xxxiv.

———. "Sociological Theory," *American Journal of Sociology,* 1945, pp. 462–73.

———. "The Bearing of Empirical Research upon the Development of Social Theory," *American Sociological Review,* 1948, pp. 505–15.

Riley, Matilda White. "Sources and Types of Sociological Data," in Robert E. L. Faris (ed.), *op. cit.,* chap. xxvi.

Russett, Bruce, *et al. World Handbook of Political and Social Indicators.* New Haven: Yale University Press, 1964.

* Sewell, William H. "Some Observations on Theory Testing," *Rural Sociology,* 1956, pp. 1–12.

* Solomon, Richard L. "An Extension of Control Group Design," *Psychological Bulletin,* 1949, pp. 137–50.

Spencer, Herbert. *The Study of Sociology.* Ann Arbor: University of Michigan, 1961.

* Stouffer, Samuel A. "Some Observations on Study Design," *American Journal of Sociology*, 1950, pp. 355–61.

U.S. Bureau of the Census. Various publications available in reference libraries. Washington, D.C.: U.S. Government Printing Office.

* Weber, Max. "Science as a Vocation," in H. H. Gerth and C. Wright Mills (eds.), *From Max Weber: Essays in Sociology* (New York: Oxford University Press, Inc., 1946), pp. 128–56.

Zelditch, Morris. "Some Methodological Problems of Field Studies," *American Journal of Sociology*, 1962, pp. 566–76.

chapter 2

Berelson, Bernard, and Steiner, Gary A. "Social Demography," in *Human Behavior: An Inventory of Scientific Findings*, pp. 588–604. New York: Harcourt, Brace & World, Inc., 1964.

Bowers, David F. (ed.). *Foreign Influences in American Life.* Princeton, N.J.: Princeton University Press, 1944.

Davis, Kingsley. "Population Policy: Will Current Programs Succeed?" *Science*, 1967, pp. 530–39.

———. "The Sociology of Demographic Behavior," in Robert K. Merton, Leonard Broom, and Leonard S. Cottrell, Jr. (eds.), *Sociology Today*, chap. xiv. New York: Harper & Row—Harper Torchbooks, 1965.

* Eisenstadt, S. N. "The Process of Absorption of New Immigrants in Israel," *Human Relations*, 1952, pp. 223–46.

Freedman, Ronald (ed.). *Population: The Vital Revolution.* Garden City, N.Y.: Doubleday & Co., Inc., Anchor Books, 1964.

* Gordon, Milton M. "Assimilation in America: Theory and Reality," *Daedalus*, 1961, pp. 263–85.

Hauser, Philip M. "Labor Force," in Robert E. L. Faris, (ed.), *Handbook of Modern Sociology*, chap. v. Skokie, Ill.: Rand McNally & Co., 1964.

——— (ed.). *The Population Dilemma.* New York: Prentice-Hall, Inc., 1963.

Hutchinson, Sir Joseph (ed.). *Population and Food Supply: Essays on Human Needs and Agricultural Prospects.* Cambridge: Cambridge University Press, 1969.

Malthus, Thomas. *Population: The First Essay.* Ann Arbor: Ann Arbor Paperbacks, University of Michigan Press, 1959.

* Park, Robert E. "Human Migration and the Marginal Man," *American Journal of Sociology*, Vol. 33 (May, 1928), pp. 881–93.

Petersen, William. *Population.* New York: Macmillan Co., 1961.

* Stouffer, Samuel. "Intervening Opportunities: A Theory Relating Mobility and Distance," *American Sociological Review*, 1940, pp. 845–76.

Taeuber, Irene. "Population and Society," in Faris (ed.), *op. cit.*, chap. iii.

United Nations Demographic Yearbook and other demographic publications.

U.S. Bureau of the Census publications.

chapter 3

Barnett, James H. "The Sociology of Art," in Robert K. Merton, Leonard Broom, and Leonard S. Cottrell, Jr. (eds.), *Sociology Today*, chap. viii. New York: Harper & Row—Harper Torchbooks, 1965.

Berger, Peter L. and Luckmann, Thomas. *The Social Construction of Reality.* Garden City, N.Y.: Doubleday & Co., Inc., 1966.

Goldschmidt, Walter (ed.). *Ways of Mankind.* Boston: Beacon Press, 1954. Hear, also, the National Association of Educational Broadcasters' recordings under the same title.

Kluckhohn, Clyde. *Culture and Behavior.* New York: Free Press, 1962.

———. *Mirror For Man.* Greenwich, Conn.: Fawcett World Library, 1964; originally published in 1944.

Komarovsky, Mirra. "Culture Contradictions and Sex Roles," *American Journal of Sociology*, 1946, pp. 184–89.

Kroeber, A. L. "The Superorganic," *American Anthropologist*, 1917, pp. 163–213.

LaBarre, Weston. "The Cultural Basis of Emotions and Gestures," *Journal of Personality*, 1947, pp. 49–68.

Matza, David. "Subterranean Traditions of Youth," *Annals of the American Academy of Political and Social Science*, 1961, pp. 102–18.

McGranahan, Donald V., and Wayne, Ivor. "German and American Traits Reflected in Popular Drama," *Human Relations*, 1948, pp. 429–55.

* Miner, Horace. "Body Ritual Among the Nacirema," *American Anthropologist*, 1956, pp. 503–7.

Service, Elman R. *A Profile of Primitive Culture.* New York: Harper & Bros., 1958.

Sumner, William Graham. *Folkways.* Boston: Ginn & Co., 1906.

Weber, Max. "The Concept of Social Relationship," from *Max Weber: The Theory of Social and Economic Organi-*

zation. Trans. A. M. Henderson and Talcott Parsons. New York: Oxford University Press, Inc. 1947.

* White, Leslie A. "Culturological vs. Psychological Interpretations of Human Behavior," *American Sociological Review*, Vol. 12 (December, 1947), pp. 686–98.

Whorf, Benjamin Lee. "Science and Linguistics," in John B. Carroll (ed.), *Language, Thought and Reality: Selected Writings of Benjamin Lee Whorf*, pp. 207–19. Cambridge, Mass.: Technology Press, Massachusetts Institute of Technology, 1957.

Williams, Robin M. *American Society*. 3d ed. New York: Alfred A. Knopf, Inc., 1969.

Yinger, J. Milton. "Contraculture and Subculture," *American Sociological Review*, Vol. 25 (October, 1960), pp. 625–35.

chapter 4

* Becker, Howard S. "Becoming a Marijuana User," *American Journal of Sociology*, 1953, pp. 235–42.

* ———, and Strauss, Anselm L. "Careers, Personality, and Adult Socialization," *American Journal of Sociology*, 1956, pp. 253–63.

* Benedict, Ruth. "Continuities and Discontinuities in Cultural Conditioning," *Psychiatry*, 1938, pp. 161–67.

Berelson, Bernard, and Steiner, Gary A. "Behavioral Development," in *Human Behavior: An Inventory of Scientific Findings*, pp. 37–85. New York: Harcourt, Brace & World, Inc., 1964.

Bronfenbrenner, Urie. *Two Worlds of Childhood*. New York: Basic Books, Inc., Publishers, 1970.

Coles, Robert. *Children of Crisis, A Study of Courage and Fear*. Boston: Little, Brown & Co., 1964. See especially chaps. iii and iv.

Cooley, Charles Horton. *Human Nature and the Social Order*. New York: Schocken Books, Inc., 1964.

* Dornbusch, Sanford M. "The Military Academy as an Assimilating Institution," *Social Forces*. 1955, pp. 316–21.

Elkin, Frederick. *The Child and Society: The Process of Socialization*. New York: Random House, Inc., 1960.

Geer, Blanche; Haas, Jack; ViVona, Charles; Miller, Stephen J.; Woods, Clyde; and Becker, Howard S. "An Analysis of the Way People Learn the Ropes in a Business Machine School, a Barber College, a Training School for Nursing Assistants and a Medical Internship Program," in Irwin Deutscher and Elizabeth J. Thompson, *Among the People: Encounters with the Poor*. New York: Basic Books, Inc., Publishers, 1968.

Goslin, David A. (ed.). *Handbook of Socialization Theory and Research*. Skokie, Ill.: Rand McNally & Co., 1969.

Kohlberg, Lawrence. "Socialization," *International Encyclopedia of the Social Sciences*, Vol. 10, pp.

* Mead, George H. "The Social Self," *Journal of Philosophy*. 1913, pp. 374–80.

Shibutani, Tamotsu. *Society and Personality*. Englewood Cliffs, N.J.: Prentice-Hall, Inc., 1961.

Shuvall, Judith T. *Immigrants on the Threshold*. New York: Atherton Press, 1963.

Spiro, Melford E. *Children of the Kibbutz: A Study in Child Training and Personality*. New York: Schocken Books, Inc., 1965.

Strauss, Anselm (ed.). *The Social Psychology of George Herbert Mead*. Chicago: Phoenix Books, University of Chicago Press, 1956.

Wallace, Anthony F. C. *Culture and Personality*. New York: Random House, Inc., 1961.

chapter 5

Asch, Solomon. "Group Forces in the Modification and Distortion of Judgments," *Social Psychology*, pp. 450–500. Englewood Cliffs, N.J.: Prentice-Hall, Inc., 1952.

Biderman, Albert D. *March to Calumny*. New York: Macmillan Co., 1963.

* ———. "Social-Psychological Needs and 'Involuntary' Behavior as Illustrated by Compliance in Interrogation," *Sociometry*, 1960, pp. 120–47.

Inkeles, Alex. "Personality and Social Structure," in Robert K. Merton, Leonard Broom, and Leonard S. Cottrell, Jr. (eds.), *Sociology Today* chap. xi. New York: Harper & Row—Harper Torchbooks, 1965.

Newcomb, Theodore M.; Koenig, Kathryn E.; Flacks, Richard, and Warwick, Donald P. *Persistance and Change: Bennington College and Its Students after Twenty-five Years*. New York: John Wiley & Sons, Inc., 1967.

Rosenberg, Morris. *Society and the Adolescent Self-Image*. Princeton, N.J.: Princeton University Press, 1965.

* Schein, Edgar H. "The Chinese Indoctrination Program for Prisoners of War," *Psychiatry* (1956), pp. 140–72.

chapter 6

Banton, Michael. *Roles: An Introduction to the Study of Social Relations.* London. Tavistock Publications, 1965.

Cottrell, Leonard S., Jr. "Adjustment of the Individual to His Age and Sex Roles," *American Sociological Review,* October, 1942.

* Field, Mark G. "Structured Strain in the Role of the Soviet Physician," *American Journal of Sociology,* 1953, pp. 493–502.

Gibbs, Jack P., and Martin, Walter T. "A Theory of Status Integration and Its Relationship to Suicide," *American Sociological Review,* 1958, pp. 140–47.

* Goode, William J. "A Theory of Role Strain," *American Sociological Review,* 1960, pp. 483–96.

* Hughes, Everett C. "Dilemmas and Contradictions of Status," *American Journal of Sociology,* 1945, pp. 353–59.

* Linton, Ralph. "Age and Sex Categories," *American Sociological Review,* 1942, pp. 589–603.

Turner, Ralph H. "Role Taking, Role Standpoint, and Reference Group Behavior," *American Journal of Sociology,* 1956, pp. 316–28.

chapter 7

* Angell, Robert C. "The Social Integration of American Cities of More than 100,000 Population," *American Sociological Review,* 1947, pp. 335–42.

Berelson, Bernard, and Steiner, Gary A. "Organizations," in *Human Behavior: An Inventory of Scientific Findings,* pp. 363–80. New York: Harcourt, Brace & World, Inc., 1964.

* Blau, Peter M. "Formal Organization: Dimensions of Analysis," *American Journal of Sociology,* 1957, pp. 58–69.

* Duncan, Otis Dudley, and Schnore, Leo F. "Cultural, Behavioral, and Ecological Perspectives in the Study of Social Organization," *American Journal of Sociology,* 1959, pp. 132–46.

Durkheim, Émile. *The Division of Labor in Society.* New York: Free Press–Macmillan, 1951.

Etzioni, Amitai. *Modern Organizations.* Englewood Cliffs, N.J.: Prentice-Hall, Inc., 1964.

Firth, Raymond. *Elements of Social Organization.* Boston: Beacon Press, 1963.

Gouldner, Alvin W. "Organizational Analysis," in Robert K. Merton, Leonard Broom, and Leonard S. Cottrell, Jr. (eds.), *Sociology Today,* chap. xviii. New York: Harper & Row—Harper Torchbooks, 1965.

* Hawley, Amos H. "Ecology and Human Ecology," *Social Forces,* 1944, pp. 398–405.

* Landecker, Werner S. "Types of Integration and Their Measurement," *American Journal of Sociology,* 1951, pp. 332–40.

* Perrow, Charles. "A Framework for the Comparative Analysis of Organizations," *Americal Sociological Review,* 1967, pp. 194–208.

* Stinchcombe, Arthur L. "Social Structure and Organizations" in James G. March (ed.), *Handbook of Organizations,* pp. 142–93. Skokie, Ill.: Rand McNally & Co., 1965.

chapter 8

* Aberle, D. F.; Cohen, A. K.; Davis, A. K.; Levy, M. J., Jr.; and Sutton, F. X. "The Functional Prerequisites of a Society," *Ethics,* 1950, pp. 100–111.

Berelson, Bernard, and Steiner, Gary A. "Social Stratification," in *Human Behavior: An Inventory of Scientific Findings.* New York: Harcourt, Brace and World, Inc., 1964.

Berreman, Gerald D. "Caste in India and the United States," *American Journal of Sociology,* 1960, pp. 120–27.

Broom, Leonard. "Social Differentiation and Stratification," in Robert K. Merton, Leonard Broom, and Leonard S. Cottrell, Jr. (eds.), *Sociology Today,* chap. xix. New York: Harper & Row—Harper Torchbooks, 1965.

Dahrendorf, Ralf. *Class and Class Conflict in Industrial Society.* Stanford, Calif.: Stanford University Press, 1959.

* Davis, Kingsley, and Moore, Wilbert E. "Some Principles of Stratification," *American Sociological Review,* 1945, pp. 242–49.

* Duncan, Otis Dudley, and Duncan, Beverly. "Residential Distribution and Occupational Stratification," *American Journal of Sociology,* 1955, pp. 493–503.

Gordon, Milton M. *Social Class in American Sociology.* New York: McGraw-Hill Book Co., 1950.

Hollingshead, A. B. *Elmtown's Youth: The Impact of Social Classes on Adolescents.* New York: John Wiley & Sons, Inc., 1949.

———, and Redlich, Frederick G. *Social Class and Mental Illness.* New York: John Wiley & Sons, Inc., 1958.

* Hyman, Herbert. "The Value Systems of Different Classes: A Social Psychological Contribution to the Analysis of Stratifi-

cation," from Reinhard Bendix, and Seymour M. Lipset (eds.), *Class, Status and Power*, pp. 426–42. Glencoe, Ill.: Free Press, 1953.

* Lenski, Gerhard E. "Status Crystallization: A Non-Vertical Dimension of Social Status," *American Sociological Review*, 1954, pp. 405–13.

Liebow, Elliot. *Talley's Corner*. Boston: Little Brown & Co., 1967.

* Mills, C. Wright. "The Middle Classes in Middle-Sized Cities," *American Sociological Review*, 1946, pp. 520–29.

Mills, C. Wright. *White Collar*. (New York: Oxford Paperback Books, 1956.

Reiss, Albert J., Jr. *Occupations and Social Status*. New York: Free Press of Glencoe, Inc., 1962.

* Tumin, Melvin M. "Some Principles of Stratification: A Critical Analysis," *American Sociological Review*, 1953, pp. 387–94. (See response by Kingsley Davis and Wilbert E. Moore, "Reply" and "Comment," *American Sociological Review*, 1953, pp. 394–97.)

* Turner, Ralph H. "Sponsored and Contest Mobility and the School System," *American Sociological Review*, 1960, pp. 855–67.

chapter 9

* Clark, Burton R., and Trow, Martin. "Determinants of the Sub-Cultures of College Students: The Organizational Context," from Theodore M. Newcomb and Everett K. Wilson, (eds.), *College Peer Groups: Problems and Prospects for Research*, pp. 17–70. Chicago: Aldine Publishing Co., 1967.

* Coleman, James S. "The Adolescent Subculture and Academic Achievement," *American Journal of Sociology*, 1960, pp. 337–47.

——— (ed.). *Education and Political Development*. Princeton, N.J.: Princeton University Press, 1965.

Goode, William J. *After Divorce* (Glencoe, Ill.: Free Press, 1956.

———. *The Family* (Englewood Cliffs, N.J.: Prentice-Hall, Inc., 1964.

———. "The Sociology of the Family," in Robert K. Merton, Leonard Broom, and Leonard S. Cottrell, Jr. (eds.), *Sociology Today*, chap. vii. New York: Harper & Row—Harper Torchbooks, 1965.

Gross, Neal. "The Sociology of Education," in Merton, Broom, and Cottrell, (eds.), *op. cit.*, chap. v.

* Sewell, William H.; Marascuilo, Leonard A.; and Pfautz, Harold W. "Review Symposium on James S. Coleman *et al.*, Equality of Educational Opportunity," *American Sociological Review*, 1967, pp. 475–83.

———, and Shah, Vimal P. "Socioeconomic Status, Intelligence, and the Attainment of Higher Education," *Sociology of Education*, 1967, pp. 1–23.

Stinchcombe, Arthur L. *Rebellion in a High School*. (Chicago: Quadrangle Books, Inc., 1969.

chapter 10

Berger, Peter L. (ed.). *The Human Shape of Work*. New York: Macmillan Co., 1964.

Blauner, Robert. *Alienation and Freedom: The Factory Worker and His Industry*. Boston: Beacon Press, 1964.

* Coser, Lewis A. "The Sociology of Poverty," *Social Problems*, 1965, pp. 341–53.

* Davis, Allison. "The Motivation of the Underprivileged Worker," in William Foote Whyte (ed.), *Industry and Society*, pp. 84–106. New York: McGraw-Hill Book Co., 1946.

* Durkheim, Émile. "Some Notes on Occupational Groups," from *The Division of Labor in Society*, pp. 1–31. Trans. George Simpson. Glencoe, Ill.: Free Press, 1947.

Gouldner, Alvin. *Patterns of Industrial Bureaucracy*. New York: Free Press–Macmillan, 1964.

* Hodge, Robert W.; Siegel, Paul M.; and Rossi, Peter H. "Occupational Prestige in the United States, 1925–63," *American Journal of Sociology*, 1964, pp. 286–302.

* Inkeles, Alex. "Industrial Man: The Relation of Status to Experience, Perception, and Value," *American Journal of Sociology*, 1960, pp. 1–31.

* Polanyi, Karl. "Our Obsolete Market Mentality," *Commentary*, 1947, pp. 109–17.

Roethlisberger, Fritz J., and Dickson, William J. *Management and the Worker*. Cambridge, Mass.: Harvard University Press, 1959.

Sheppard, Harold L. *Poverty and Wealth in America*. Chicago: Quadrangle Books, Inc., 1970).

Smelser, Neil J. *The Sociology of Economic Life*. Englewood Cliffs, N.J.: Prentice-Hall, Inc., 1963.

* Stinchcombe, Arthur L. "Bureaucratic and Craft Administration of Production: A Comparative Study," *Administrative Science Quarterly*, 1959, pp. 168–87.

* Tumin, Melvin. "Business as a Social System," *Behavioral Science*, 1964, pp. 120–30.

* Udy, Stanley H., Jr. "'Bureaucracy' and

'Rationality' in Weber's Organizational Theory: An Empirical Study," *American Sociological Review*, 1959, pp. 791–95.

* Wilensky, Harold L. "The Uneven Distribution of Leisure: The Impact of Economic Growth on 'Free Time,'" *Social Problems*, 1961, pp. 32–56.

Zald, Mayer N. (ed.). *Social Welfare Institutions.* New York: John Wiley & Sons, Inc., 1965.

chapter 11

Angell, Robert Cooley. *Peace on the March: Transnational Participation.* New York: Van Nostrand, Reinhold Co., 1969.

* Bellah, Robert N. "Religious Evolution," *American Sociological Review*, 1964, pp. 358–74.

Berelson, Bernard, and Steiner, Gary A. "Military Institutions," in *Human Behavior: An Inventory of Scientific Findings*, pp. 443–49. New York: Harcourt, Brace & World, Inc., 1964.

———. "Political Institutions," in *ibid.*, pp. 417–36.

———. "Religious Institutions," in *ibid.*, pp. 384–86.

Berger, Peter L. *The Noise of Solemn Assemblies: Christian Commitment and the Religious Establishment in America.* Garden City, N.Y.: Doubleday & Co., Inc., 1961.

Berger, Peter L. *The Sacred Canopy: Elements of a Sociological Theory of Religion.* Garden City., N.Y.: Doubleday & Co., Inc., 1967.

* DeGre, Gerard. "Freedom and Social Structure," *American Sociological Review*, 1946, pp. 529–36.

Durkheim, Émile. *The Elementary Forms of the Religious Life.* New York: Free Press, of Glencoe, Inc., 1947.

* Glock, Charles Y., and Ringer, Benjamin B. "Church Policy and the Attitudes of Ministers and Parishoners on Social Issues," *American Sociological Review*, 1956, pp. 148–56.

* Gusfield, Joseph R. "Mass Society and Extremist Politics," *American Sociological Review*, 1962, pp. 19–30.

Glock, Charles. "The Sociology of Religion," in Robert K. Merton, Leonard Broom, and Leonard S. Cottrell, Jr. (eds.). *Sociology Today*, chap. vi. New York: Harper & Row—Harper Torchbooks, 1965.

Hunter, Floyd. *Community Power Structure: A Study of Decision Makers.* Chapel Hill: University of North Carolina Press, 1953.

Janowitz, Morris. *The Professional Soldier.* New York: Free Press–Macmillan, 1964.

Lenski, Gerhard. *The Religious Factor.* New York: Doubleday & Co., Inc., 1967.

* Lipset, Seymour Martin. "Democracy in Private Government: A Case Study of the International Typographical Union," *British Journal of Sociology*, 1952, pp. 47–63.

* ———. "Some Social Requisites of Democracy: Economic Development and Political Legitimacy," *American Political Science Review*, 1959, pp. 69–105.

* ———. "The Radical Right: A Problem for American Democracy," *British Journal of Sociology*, 1955, pp. 176–209.

Michels, Robert. *Political Parties*, trans. Eden and Cedar Paul. Glencoe, Ill.: Free Press, 1949.

Mills, C. Wright. *The Power Elite.* New York: Macmillan Co., 1948.

* Schneider, Louis, and Dornbusch, Sanford M. "Inspirational Religious Literature: From Latent to Manifest Functions of Religion," *American Journal of Sociology*, 1958, pp. 392–401.

Selznick, Philip. "The Sociology of Law," in Merton, Bloom, and Cottrell (eds.), *op. cit.*, chap. iv.

Weber, Max. *The Protestant Ethic and the Spirit of Capitalism.* New York: Charles Scribner's Sons, 1930 *et seq.*

———. *The Theory of Economic and Social Organization*, types of authority and bases of legitimacy, Part III. Trans A. M. Henderson and Talcott Parsons. New York: Oxford University Press, Inc., 1947.

Yinger, Milton J. *Sociology Looks at Religion.* New York: Macmillan Co., 1963.

chapter 12

* Bell, Daniel. "Crime as an American Way of Life," *Antioch Review*, 1953, pp. 131–54.

Cloward, Richard A., and Ohlin, Lloyd E. *Delinquency and Opportunity*, New York: Free Press–Macmillan, 1966.

* ———. "Illegitimate Means, Anomie, and Deviant Behavior," *American Sociological Review*, 1959, pp. 164–76.

Cohen, Albert K. *Deviance and Control.* Englewood Cliffs, N.J.: Prentice-Hall, 1966.

———. "The Study of Social Disorganization and Deviant Behavior," in Robert K. Merton, Leonard Broom, and Leonard S.

Cottrell, Jr. (eds.), *Sociology Today,* chap. xxi. New York: Harper & Row—Harper Torchbooks, 1965.

* Davis, Kingsley. "The Sociology of Parent-Youth Conflict," *American Sociological Review,* 1940, pp. 523–35.
* Eisenstadt, S. N. "Social Change, Differentiation and Evolution," *American Sociological Review,* 1964, pp. 375–86.

Feuer, Lewis. *The Conflict of Generations: The Character and Significance of Student Movements.* New York: Basic Books, Inc., Publishers, 1969.

* Fuller, Richard C., and Myers, Richard R. "The Natural History of a Social Problem," *American Sociological Review,* 1941, pp. 320–29.

King, Wendell C. *Social Movements in the United States.* New York: Random House, Inc., 1956.

* Lieberson, Stanley, and Silverman, Arnold R. "The Precipitants and Underlying Conditions of Race Riots," *American Sociological Review,* 1965, pp. 887–98.

Marx, Gary T. *Protest and Prejudice.* New York: Harper & Row, Publishers, 1969.

* Merton, Robert K. "Social Structure and Anomie," *American Sociological Review,* 1938, pp. 672–82.
* Reiss, Albert J., Jr. "The Distribution of Juvenile Delinquency in the Social Class Structure," *American Sociological Review,* 1961, pp. 720–32.

Rossi, Peter H. (ed.). *Ghetto Revolts.* Chicago: Aldine Publishing Co., 1970.

* Somers, Robert H. "The Mainsprings of the Rebellion: A Survey of Berkeley Students in November, 1964," in Seymour M. Lipset and Sheldon S. Wolin (eds.), *The Berkeley Student Revolt,* pp. 530–57. (New York: Doubleday & Co., Inc., 1965.

Tumin, Melvin M. (ed.). *Research Annual On Intergroup Relations—1970.* (Chicago: Quadrangle Books, Inc., 1970).

chapter 13

Burgess, E. W. and Bogue, Donald J. (eds.). *Urban Sociology.* Chicago: University of Chicago Press, 1967.

* Davis, Kingsley. "The Origin and Growth of Urbanization in the World," *American Journal of Sociology,* 1955, pp. 429–37.
* Duncan, Beverly; Sabagh, George; and Van Arsdol, Maurice D., Jr. "Patterns of City Growth," *American Journal of Sociology,* 1962, pp. 418–29.
* Miner, Horace. "The Folk-Urban Continuum," *American Sociological Review,* 1952, pp. 529–37.
* Ogburn, William F. "Cultural Lag as Theory," *Sociology and Social Research,* 1957, pp. 167–74.

Redfield, Robert. "The Folk Society," *American Journal of Sociology,* Vol. 12, No. 4 (January, 1947), pp. 293–308.

* Smelser, Neil. "Mechanisms of Change and Adjustment to Change," in B. F. Hoselitz and W. E. Moore (eds.), *Industrialization and Society,* pp. 32–54. Paris: UNESCO, 1966.

Vidich, Arthur, and Bensman, Joseph. *Small Town in Mass Society.* Princeton: N.J.: Princeton University Press, 1958.

* Wirth, Louis. "Urbanism as a Way of Life," *American Journal of Sociology,* 1938, pp. 1–24.

chapter 14

Empey, LaMar T., and Rabow, Jerome. "The Provo Experiment in Delinquency Rehabilitation, *American Sociological Review,* 1961, pp. 679–95.

Gouldner, Alvin W., and Miller, S. M. *Applied Sociology: Opportunities and Problems.* New York: Free Press–Macmillan, 1965.

Gross, Bertram M. (ed.). *Social Intelligence for America's Future.* Boston: Allyn & Bacon, Inc., 1969.

Gross, Bertram M. *The State of the Nation: Social Systems Accounting.* London: Tavistock Publications, 1966.

* Hauser, Philip M. "Social Science and Social Engineering," *Philosophy of Science,* 1949, pp. 209–18.

Moynihan, Daniel P. *Maximum Feasible Misunderstanding: Community Action in the War on Poverty.* New York: Free Press–Macmillan, 1969. See especially the final chapter on "Social Science and Social Policy," and Moynihan's contention that "the role of [sociology] lies not in the formulation of social policy, but in the measurement of its results."

* Sherif, Muzafer. "Superordinate Goals in the Reduction of Intergroup Conflict," *American Journal of Sociology,* 1958, pp. 349–56.

Social Science Quarterly, December, 1969, devoted to "Planned Social Intervention."

U.S. Department of Health, Education, and Welfare. *Toward A Social Report* (Washington, D.C.: U.S. Government Printing Office, 1969).

chapter 15

* Bierstedt, Robert. "Sociology and Humane Learning," *American Sociological Review*, 1960, pp. 3–9.

Cuzzort, R. P. *Humanity and Modern Sociological Thought.* New York: Holt, Rinehart & Winston, Inc., 1969. See especially, chap xvi on "The Uses of Sociological Thought."

* Deutscher, Irwin. "Words and Deeds: Social Science and Social Policy," *Social Problems*, 1966, pp. 235–54.

Freeman, Howard E., and Sherwood, Clarence C. *Social Research and Social Policy.* Englewood Cliffs, N.J.: Prentice-Hall, Inc., 1970.

Hammond, Phillip E. *Sociologists at Work.* New York: Doubleday & Co., Inc., 1964.

Lundberg, George A. *Can Science Save Us?* New York: Longmans, Green & Co., Inc., 1947.

Lynd, Robert S. *Knowledge for What?* Princeton, N.J.: Princeton University Press, 1939.

* Merton, Robert K. "The Unanticipated Consequences of Purposive Social Action," *American Sociological Review*, 1938, pp. 894–904.

Mills, C. Wright. *The Sociological Imagination.* New York: Oxford University Press, Inc., 1959.

Sibley, Elbridge. *The Education of Sociologists in the United States.* New York: Russell Sage Foundation, 1963.

Simey, T. S. *Social Science and Social Purpose.* New York: Schocken Books, Inc., 1969.

* Weber, Max. "Science as a Vocation," in H. H. Gerth, and C. Wright Mills (eds.), *From Max Weber: Essays in Sociology*, pp. 129–56. New York: Oxford University Press, Inc., 1946.

original texts

chapter 1

1. Auguste Comte, *Cours de Philosophie Positive: Discours sur l'esprit Positive*, avec une introduction et un commentaire par Ch. Le Verrier (Paris: Librairie Garnier frères, n.d.) pp. 4, 5. Comte writes:

   En étudiant . . . le développement total de l'intelligence humaine dans ses diverse sphères d'activité, depuis son premier essor le plus simple jusqu'à nos jours, je crois avoir découvert une grande loi fondamentale, à laquelle il est assujetti par une nécessité invariable . . . Cette loi consiste en ce que chacune de nos conceptions principales, chaque branche de nos connaissances, passe successivement par trois états théoriques différents: l'état théologique, ou fictif; l'état métaphysique, ou abstrait; l'état scientifique, ou positif. . . . De là, trois sortes de philosophies, ou de systèmes généraux de conceptions sur l'ensemble des phénomènes, qui s'excluent mutuellement; la première est le point de départ nécessaire de l'intelligence humaine; la troisième, son état fixe et définitif; la seconde est uniquement destinée à servir de transition.

2. *Ibid.*, pp. 14, 15 (italics mine) The original reads:

   . . . si d'un côté toute théorie positive doit nécessairement être fondée sur des observations, il est également sensible d'un autre côté, que, pour se livrer à l'observation, *notre esprit a besoin d'une théorie quelconque.* Si, en contemplant les phénomènes, nous ne les rattachions point immédiatement a quelques principes, non seulement il nous serait impossible de combiner ces observations isolées, et, par conséquent, d'en tirer aucun fruit, mais nous serions même entièrement incapables de les retenir; et, le plus souvent, les faits resteraient inaperçus sous nos yeux.

3. J. J. Maquet, *Sociologie de la Connaissance* (Louvain: Institut de Recherches Économiques et Sociales, 1949) p. 305

   Une théorie en sociologie, comme dans la plupart des autres disciplines scientifiques, est une *construction de l'esprit* qui explique la synthèse des résultats observés en postulant un principe dont on peut déduire ces résultats à titre de conséquences. Par ailleurs, elle sert de principe directeur pour les recherches ultérieures.

chapter 3

1. Karl Marx, *The Eighteenth Brumaire of Louis Napoleon* (New York: International Press, n.d.), p. 1

   In Marx's words, "Die Menschen machen ihre eigene Geschichte, aber sie machen sie nicht aus freien Stücken, nicht unter selbstgewählten, sondern unter gegebenen und überlieferten Umständen. Die Tradition aller toten Geschlechter lastet wie ein Alp auf dem Gehirn der Lebenden.

2. Émile Durkheim, *L'Éducation morale* (Paris: Librarie Felix Alcan, 1925), pp. 71, 72.

   Durkheim puts it this way: "Les générations premières, elles, sont remplacées par des générations nouvelles, et, cependant la société reste avec sa physionomie propre et son caractère personnel . . . entre la France actuelle et celle du Moyen age, il y a une identité personelle que nul ne peut songer a méconnaître. Ainsi, tandis que des générations d'individus succédaient à d'autres générations, par-dessus ce flux perpetuel des personalités particulières, il y avait quelque chose qui persistait, c'est la société avec sa conscience propre, son temperament personnel . . .

3. Marcel Mauss, "Essai sur les variations saissonières des sociétés eskimos, *Année sociologiques* (Paris: Librairie Félix Alcan, 1904–05), Vol. IX.

   The original reads as follows: En été, les membres qui le composent habitent dans des tentes et çes tentes sont dispersées; en hiver, ils habitent des maisons resserrées les unes près des autres. Tandis que la tente ne comprend qu'une famille, l'habitat d'hiver en contient normalement plusieurs . . . Tandis que l'été étend d'une manière presque illimitée le champ ouvert à la chasse et à la pêche, l'hiver, au contraire, le restreint de la manière la plus étroite . . . La religion des eskimos passe par le même rythme que leur organization. Il y a, pour ainsi dire, une religion d'été et une religion d'hiver . . . le culte privé, domestique [d'été] et l'état d'exaltation [d'hiver].

   Mais cette opposition de la vie d'hiver et de la vie d'été ne se traduit pas seulement dans les rites, dans les fêtes, dans les cérémonies religieuses de toute sort; elle affecte aussi profondement les idées, les représentations collectives, en un mot la mentalité du groupe. Dans certaines tribus, au cours d'un complexus de fêtes, on voit tous les gens du groupe se diviser en deux camps. L'un comprend tous ceux qui sont nés en hiver; dans l'autre, se trouvent tous ceux nés en été.

   Ainsi la manière même dont sont classés et les hommes et les choses porte l'empreinte de cette opposition cardinale entre les deux saisons. Chaque saison sert à définir tout un genre d'êtres et de choses. On peut dire que la notion de l'hiver et la notion de l'été sont comme deux poles autour desquels gravite le système d'idées des eskimos.

chapter 4

1. Marcel Mauss, "Mémoire et société," *L'Année sociologique,* 3rd series, Vol. I, (1940–48), (Paris: Presses Universitaires de France, 1949), pp. 3–177.

   Mauss's words are as follows: "Il n'est pas nécessaire que d'autres hommes soient là, qui se distinguent matériellement de nous: car nous portons toujours avec nous et en nous une quantité de personnes qui ne se confondent pas.

   Or, on the same theme, consider this statement of Victor Hugo's.

   > Est-ce donc la vie d'un homme? Oui, et la vie des autres hommes aussi. Nul de nous n'a l'honneur d'avoir une vie qui soit à lui. Ma vie est la vôtre, votre vie est la mienne, vous vivez ce que je vis; la destinée est une. Prenez donc ce miroir, et regardez-vous-y. On se plaint quelquefois des écrivains qui disent moi. Parlez-vous de nous, leur crie-t-on. Hélas! quand je vous parle de moi, je vous parle de vous. Comment ne le sentez-vous pas? Ah! insensé, qui crois que je ne suis pas toi!
   >
   > Flammarion, Éditeur 1856), p. 2.

   Les Contemplations (Paris: Ernest

   A translation might then run as follows: "Does this, then, speak of a man's life? Yes, and other men's lives as well. None of us has the distinction of having a life exclusively his. My life is yours, yours is mine, you experience what I do and we share the same fate. Take this mirror and look at yourself. People sometimes complain of writers who exploit personal experience. Talk to us about us [our experience] they say. But when I speak of myself I do speak of you. How is it that you can't understand that? Ah, misguided one—to think that I'm not you!"

chapter 5

1. Lucien Lévy-Bruhl, *Fonctions Mentales* (Paris: Presses Universitaires de France, 1951), p. 19.

   In Lévy-Bruhl's own words:

   > À des types sociaux différents correspondront des mentalités différentes, d'autant plus que les institutions et les moeurs mêmes ne sont au fond qu'un certain aspect des représentations collectives, que ces représentations, pour ainsi dire, considérées objectivement.

2. Émile Durkheim, *Éducation et sociologie* (Paris: Librairie Félix Alcan, 1922), p. 51.

   Durkheim writes:

   > Voilà quelle est l'oeuvre de l'éducation, et l'on en aperçoit toute la grandeur. Elle ne se borne pas à développer l'organisme individuel dans la sense marqué par sa nature, à rendre apparentes des puissances cachées qui ne demandaient qu'à se revéler. *Elle crée dans l'homme un être nouveau* (italics mine).

chapter 13

1. Louis Bonald, *Works,* II, p. 239.

   The French philosopher and Royalist wrote:

   > L'agriculture qui disperse les hommes dans les campagnes, les unit sans les rapprocher; . . . le commerce qui les entasses dans les villes, les rapproche sans les unir.

2. Published in *Die Grossstadt,* Jahrbuch der Gehe-Stiftung zu Dresden, Band IX (Dresden: v. Zahn & Jaensch, 1903), p. 195. The German reads:

   Wenn der fortwährenden äusseren Berührung mit unzähligen Menschen so viele inner Reaktionen antworten sollten, wie in der kleinen Stadt, in der man fast jedem Begegnenden kennt und so jedem ein positives Verhältnis hat, so würde man sich innerlich völlig atomisieren und in eine ganz unausdenkbareseelische Verfassung geraten.

3. Die psychologische Grundlage, auf der der Typus grosstädtischer Individualitäten sich erhebt, ist die *Steigerung des Nervenlebens,* die aus dem raschen und ununterbrochenen Wechsel äusserer und innerer Eindrücke hervorgeht . . . So schafft der Typus des Grossstädters—der natürlich von tausend individuellen Modifikationen umspielt ist—sich ein Schutzorgan gegen die Entwurzelung, mit der die Strömungen und Diskrepanzen seines äusseren Milieus ihn bedrohen: statt mit dem Gemüte reagiert er auf diese im wesentlichen mit dem Verstande . . . Daraus wird vor allem der intellektualistische Charakter des grossstädtischen Seelenlebens begreiflich, gegenüber dem kleinstädtischen, das vielmehr auf das Gemüt and gefühlsmassige Beziehungen gestellt ist.

   This whole essay, a penetrating observation on the impact of the city on mental life is beautifully translated by Kurt Wolff in Georg Simmel, *The Sociology of Georg Simmel,* trans. Kurt Wolff (New York: Free Press of Glencoe, Inc., 1950).

glossary

The word *glossary* has the same source as *gloss*, a term sometimes used (as in the phrase "to gloss over") to imply the dexterous use of the tongue to evade difficult situations. Technical terms can be difficult, especially when, as with *race*, or *culture*, or *group*, the vulgar habit is light-years away from the sociologist's usage. My intention in this glossary has been not to dodge difficulties but to clarify terms that are either difficult, or central to the text's exposition, or both. The object of the glossary is not to encourage students to memorize definitions. There is only one aim: to deepen understanding of abstract, complex terms and so to make reading and rumination more fruitful.

Over the years there have been a number of attempts to lend precision and currency to the sociologist's vocabulary. Two of the early ones were E. B. Reuter's *Handbook of Sociology* (New York: Dryden Press, 1946) and Henry Pratt Fairchild (ed.), *Dictionary of Sociology* (Totowa, N.J.: Littlefield, Adams & Co., 1955). In recent years we have had three signal contributions to the task of explicating technical terms in sociology. Among these, probably the most useful is *A Modern Dictionary of Sociology*, by George and Achilles Theodorson (New York: Thomas Y. Crowell Co., 1969). A fuller treatment, more historical and philosophical, of certain concepts will be found in the *International Encyclopedia of the Social Sciences*. For more general coverage, *A Dictionary of the Social Sciences* is a useful work. It is edited by two sociologists, Julius Gould and William Kolb, and was published by The Free Press (Macmillan) under the auspices of UNESCO.

Achievement. A criterion for role performance according to which expectations of behavior are geared to type and level of others' performance. The coach of the Green Bay Packers would not take on a halfback (or any other player) merely because his uncle happened to be Senator McCarthy. Achievement is the appropriate criterion for assignment to this role as it is to the role of doctor, lawyer, teacher, psychologist, electrician, and a host of others. In a culture celebrating efficiency, productivity, specialization and the like, ascriptive criteria (*q.v.*) are increasingly displaced by the criterion of demonstrable achievement.

Affect, affectivity. The state of being moved, hence suffused with emotion and sentiment. The opposite pole is affective neutrality. Some roles (for example, citizen, mother) are high on this dimension. Others (surgeon, businessman) may be more affectively neutral.

Aggregate. A set of individuals whose boundaries are set by their occupancy of a certain area.

Anomie. Literally, lacking a name or identity and, by extension, lacking the guides to conduct that come with an identity. In discussing anomic suicide, Durkheim uses the term to mean "de-regulation," that is, the absence of standards of conduct. Normlessness is perhaps the best definition of anomie. The reference is to a condition of the group, of society, although the term has sometimes been used to mean a disorganized state of the individual.

Ascription. A criterion for role performance leading us to anticipate behavior (and underlying subjective states) on the basis of characteristics outside the person's control. Thus age, sex, race, nativity, and class often trigger stereotypical expectations as to how a person believes and behaves. Expectations of role performance are also affected by the person's known achievements (*q.v.*). Because attributes achieved are invariably influenced by those ascribed, the distinction between these two criteria of role performance are only analytically—not empirically—distinct. Thus such ascribed traits as White, Anglo-Saxon Protestant may give the person a head start whereas Black, African-origin, and poor require a Head Start.

Association. An organized group whose members act cooperatively through differentiated roles in pursuit of a shared interest.

Association, measures of. (*See* Correlation.)

Attribute. A position on a nominal or ordinal scale. Thus Republican, Socialist, and Democrat are attributes as are upper, middle, and lower class, or married, single, widowed, and divorced, or Catholic, Protestant, and Jew, or rich and poor.

Authority. A dimension of a relationship which tells us the extent of legitimate power one person exercises over another. In contrast to the authority of the charismatic leader (*q.v.*), traditional and legal authority are tied into a given position in the social structure. Thus priest and psychiatrist have the authority to deny privileged information to police or courts, police have the authority to arrest under specified conditions, employers have the authority to fire, parents to punish, teachers to require certain performances.

Autokinetic. Literally, self-moving: the illusion that a stationary object on which one fixes his attention moves. The illusion is experimentally induced against a featureless background that offers no bench marks from which to measure movement. The experiment by Muzafer Sherif uses the autokinetic effect to study the influence of others in the formation of norms. (*Refer to* Chapter 5.)

Birthrate. A measure of a group's fertility (*q.v.*). There are a number of such measures, the most frequently used being the crude birthrate and the age-specific birthrate. The CBR is the number of live births per thousand (mid-year) population of the community concerned. The age-specific rate narrows the age band as, for example, births per thousand women aged 15–44.

Bureaucracy. A form of group organization based on the unqualified application of the principle of rationality. It is a hierarchical form of social organization rationally geared to the achievement of precisely specified objectives by means of a division of labor based on demonstrated competence.

Caste. Caste can be thought of as the freezing and formalizing of class distinctions. Determined at birth, the person's caste prescribes type of occupation, limits the range of potential marriage partners, and dictates relationships with members of other (higher and lower) castes. The term generally calls to mind the rigid, religiously legitimated system of stratification found in the past in India. A castelike pattern of stratification has been seen in the United States in Negro-white relationships.

Category. A classification of persons whose boundaries are set by the fact of sharing one or more traits in common.

Central tendency. "Measures of central tendency" is a statistical term referring to measures such as the mean, median, and mode that, in varying degree, typify some characteristic of the group. Thus we use a measure called the median to typify the income of a group or category of persons. A measure of central tendency may give us a figure not characterizing any single member of the group. But it does provide a group characteristic, a figure that comes closer to the "center" of the group than any other figure. (*See also* Mean; Median; *and* Mode.)

Charisma. The quality of being divinely favored with extraordinary capacities. Thus the charismatic leader—Father Divine, Chairman Mao, Mahatma Gandhi, Adolf Hitler—are thought to have supernatural powers.

Chi-square test. A statistical test to determine whether one's data (observations) depart so much from what might be expected were there no connection between the variables that one can infer the likelihood of a relationship. With the chi-square value (and degrees of freedom, *q.v.*) one can enter a table of chi-square values to determine the probability that a chi-square value such as that found could have occurred by chance. If the p value is quite small—e.g., $p < .001$, meaning that such a finding is likely to occur by chance fewer than once in a thousand times—we conclude that there is in fact a relationship between the variables, for reasons we think we know, or have yet to discover.

Church. (*See* Sect.)

Class. A category of attributes locating their possessors in the stratification system. (*See also* Stratification.)

Collective behavior. Since all social conduct is, literally, collective behavior, it is unfortunate to attach a special meaning to this term. But we cannot avoid it, for this is what has happened. Over many years collective behavior has come to mean a special sort of behavior minimally guided by custom, tradition, or law. Members of a collectivity fix on a common object (a lynch victim, an exit in a burning theater) but lack the internal organization of a group—i.e., differentiated but complementary roles organized to achieve some shared purpose. Collective behavior is extraordinary behavior and, therefore, behavior for which acknowledged rules are lacking. It is exemplified in crowd behavior, panics, riots, the preorganizational phases of social movements, manias, the contagion of fads and fashions, and the like.

Concept. A term for the ideas that organize our perceptions. The organization is of two general sorts: (1) classifying things—social data, in the case of the sociologist, and (2) connecting things, the cause and correlation of social phenomena, in sociology. Role, status, and class are classificatory concepts: they enable the observer to sort out what would otherwise be a wildly chaotic and incomprehensible realm of social life. They may also be used in connecting things—class, for example, with aesthetic preferences or types of mental disorder. Or, to take another example, the self-fulfilling prophecy is a concept that links anticipations with outcomes, the tendency under certain conditions for men to act in ways that confirm or promote expected results. Thus the student anticipating a course with distaste sets into motion influences that will shortly confirm this prejudgment. Concepts are the building blocks of theory, the idea-units, which, in their connections, form a body of knowledge.

Control of variables. This refers to a crucial strategy in the attempt to untangle the influence of one social factor on another. To control a variable means to eliminate its influence, or to hold it constant so that it does not intrude, unbeknownst, as the investigator assesses the relationship between independent and dependent variables (*q.v.*). Thus, in measuring the relationship between education achieved and occupational income, and knowing of the link between race and income, we know that we must eliminate the race variable (among others) if we are to measure the connection between education and income. Hence we deal *only* with whites (or blacks), thus controlling the variable of race. Randomizing, matching trait for trait in control and experimental groups, eliminating (as above) certain traits to get rid of a confounding variable—these techniques are touched on in Chapter 1. (*See also* Asides on Methods, Numbers 1, 6, and 11.)

Correlation. The extent of connectedness between measures of two variables. Various statistical measures tap various dimensions of correlation: (1) the probability that it exists, (2) the extent of the relationship, and (3) the direction of the relationship, whether positive or negative. Several such measures of relationship are touched on in this book: the Pearsonian correlation coefficient, the Spearman rank-order correlation coefficient, Yule's Q, and chi-square (all *q.v.*).

Correlation coefficient: Pearsonian. A measure of the existence, degree, and direction of relationship between two continuous variables. Its symbol is r and it varies from a perfect positive association ($r = +1.0$) to a perfect negative or inverse association ($r = -1.0$). When we have a perfect association, it means that, given the value on one variable, we then know unmistakably the value on the second variable. Perfect association of two such measures seldom if ever is found. To take an example from sociological research, Angell, in a study, "Social Integration of American Cities," found that a measure of city integration (combining measures of community welfare efforts and a reversed crime score) when related to mobility of population yielded $r = -.79$. That is to say, the greater the mobility the less the community integration. In this case, about 64% of the variation in integration scores ($.79^2$) was accounted for by the measure of mobility. (*See* Aside on Methods, Number 7.)

Correlation coefficient, Spearman rank order. A measure of the existence, direction, and extent of relationship between two ordinal variables. For example: If a social-distance scale revealed that a sample of American respondents were most favorably disposed toward the French, next the Rumanians, and third the Chinese, we might wonder whether such a rank order were reflected in the number of these nationals admitted to U.S. citizenship under our quota program. If numbers admitted fell in the same order, the Spearman rank-order correlation coefficient would give us a perfect positive association (+1.0). On the other hand if, despite American preferences, more Chinese were admitted than Rumanians and more Rumanians than French, we would have a perfect inverse rank order, and the correlation coefficient would be −1.0. (*See* Aside on Methods, Number 9.)

Correlation: Yule's Q. A measure of existence, direction, and extent of relationships between two variables when the data are cast in a 2×2 table. The difference between the (product of) cases that would confirm the hypothesis and those that would refute it is expressed as a proportion of the total (of the product of cases confirming and refuting). An example: test the hypothesis that sex is linked to political preference, women being disproportionately Democratic and men Republican. In the accompanying table, then, cells *a* and *d* confirm the hypothesis: *b* and *c* refute it.

Women	Men	
a	b	D
c	d	R

The formula is:

$$Q = \frac{ad - bc}{ad + bc}.$$

If all the cases support the hypothesis, then there are none in cells *b* and *c*, and the value of Q is +1.0. If all the cases refute the hypothesis, falling in cells *b* and *c*, then $Q = -1.0$. (*See* Aside on Methods, Number 8.)

Cult. (*See* Sect.)

Culture. What people commonly "know," both about the nature of things as they are and as they ought to be. The tangible evidence of culture is seen in people's acts and artifacts—the things they do and make. Thus the Sears-Roebuck catalog, the blueprint of a wiring circuit, a Boeing 747, the Mosaic code, a "joint," Fourth of July oratory, an atom bomb, Rock music, a corporation's table of organization, the books in a library—all these are clues to culture. Among the most important elements of culture are the standards that guide behavior. Thus culture is to conduct as rules are to roles.

Culture lag. The theory of social change developed by William F. Ogburn asserting that material culture has a faster growth rate than nonmaterial culture, the latter lagging in its adaptation to a world transformed by invention.

Degrees of freedom. A number which tells us how many values in a set of figures are free to vary independent of their relationships with other values. For example, in a four-celled table, with marginals given, only one value is independent of the rest. Consider the accompanying table.

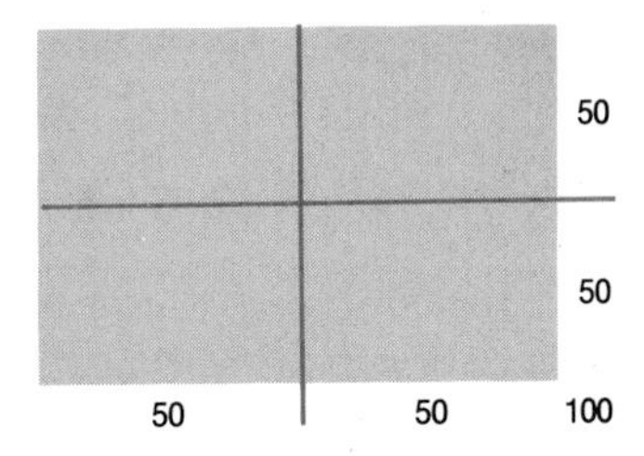

As soon as we discover the value for any single cell, the other three values are determined. If the upper-left cell contains the figure 25, we know that the upper-right cell must have 25 cases (to sum to the marginal, 50). And similarly with each column: lower-left and lower-right cells must contain 25 cases, each, to sum to 50. Using the same marginals, assume we discover that the lower-right cell contains 10 cases. Then we know the upper-right and lower-left cells must have 40 cases, and the upper-left cell will have 10 cases, since both rows and both columns must sum to 50. A number of statistical calculations are based on the assumption that the numbers dealt with are free to vary independent of one another. And values will vary depending on the degrees of freedom or independence. This is the case with chi-square. A rule-of-thumb way of figuring degrees of freedom is: (rows minus one) × (columns minus one). Thus, in our four-celled table, we have $(1) \times (1) = 1$. In a table having two columns and three rows, degrees of freedom would equal 2.

Demography. The study of population growth and composition.

Deviance. Behavior that departs in varying degree and direction from conventional norms of conduct. It can be regarded as *socially defined* (witches abound and are to be burned, Christianity is subversive and its adherents are properly lion meat), *socially engendered* (systematic criminal behavior is carefully and effectively taught, with prisons provided for remedial work with failing pupils), and *socially sanctioned.* The statistical sense of deviation warns us that we must number saints as well as sinners among the deviant.

Diffuseness. One dimension of a role (specificity is the polar opposite) referring to the range of claims one person can legitimately make of another in a given relationship. In the roles of neighbor or parent, one may respond to a wide range of initiatives from neighbor or child. On the other hand, in the world of work, the scope of performance is likely to be much more restricted. Indeed, the uniforms people wear often convey the message that claims beyond a certain restricted range are illegitimate. Along with other dimensions of role performance (achievement-ascription, affectivity-affective neutrality, universalism-particularism, *q.v.*) this term was introduced to the sociological literature by Talcott Parsons.

Dyad. A pair, hence a relationship between two parties (persons or groups) to which the German sociologist Georg Simmel called attention because of its peculiar properties. Numerically it is the first relationship, and thus the elementary social structure. It is also a vulnerable structure, since the defection or dereliction of one party suffices to destroy it. The vulnerability of the husband-wife dyad has been implicitly recognized in the institutional safeguards: husband's responsibility for breadwinning, the wife's for home maintenance, parental responsibility for children, the barriers to divorce, and so on. With the addition of one person, the triad emerges with new relational properties: the possibility of majorities and minorities, mediation, the playing of one party off against another, and the like. (*See* Chapter 2.)

Ecology, human. The study of the way man adapts himself to the conditions (human and nonhuman) of his environment through competitive and largely unwitting processes. Thus it is that unplanned *patterns* of spatial and temporal relationships emerge through time. An example of the first is the spatial pattern of economic activity: land use and values; residential districts, theater, fur, diamond, garment, retail, wholesale, and others. An example of temporal relationships is the rhythm of daily life geared to transportation schedules, eating times, play and work periods, and the like.

Empirical. Confronting the evidence of one's senses in order to test the nature of reality—that is, to see whether the terrain conforms to the map. Actually our maps, the ideas informing our lives, grow out of the daily encounters with the world through our senses. "Raw empiricism" is a pejorative term applied by those who stress theory and insight as ways of comprehending our worlds, in contrast to others who insist that knowledge never goes far beyond the tangible evidence of our senses.

Ethnocentrism. Literally, the centering on beliefs and practices peculiar to one's own ethnic group. Out of such parochialism grows the tendency to *ap*preciate the ways of one's own ethnic group and to *de*preciate others' ways.

Expected frequencies. Sometimes called "theoretical frequencies," these tell us how many cases would have such-and-such attributes *if there were no relationship between the variables.* An example: If we are testing the notion that cities, rather than rural areas are the seedbeds of movements, and if we have 50 Women's Liberation Movement persons and 50 same-age non-WLM women, and if there is no connection between urbanism and membership in the movement, then there should be as many women of urban (and rural) backgrounds among the non-WLM people as among those in the movement. Our expected frequencies on the assumption of no relationship between the variables would be 25 persons in each of four categories: WLM women having rural and urban backgrounds and non-WLM women having rural and urban backgrounds.

Fecundity. The biological capacity to reproduce.

Fertility. Observed rate of reproduction.

Folk society. A form of social organization, together with its underlying culture that stands in contrast to the urban society. Not populous, it is relatively homogeneous in the traits that characterize its members. It is likely to be isolated, outside the mainstream of contemporary affairs. Conduct will be dominated by rules given through tradition. Kinship ties will have more significance than contractual ones. It is a society described by Tönnies' *Gemeinschaft* in contrast to *Gesellschaft* (*q.v.*).

Folkways. William Graham Sumner's term for ordinary, taken-for-granted modes of behavior governed by norms whose sanctions are informal reactions of praise or blame, not the apparatus of the law.

Functional integration. (*See* Integration.)

Function. A measure of the extent to which one social variable responds to changes in another. Loosely used, it simply means that two social variables are somehow linked. Thus: level of employment is a function of military expenditures. It implies the probability that a correlation exists and that, with adequate data, changes in one variable might be specified as a mathematical function of changes in the other.

Gemeinschaft. (*See* Gesellschaft.)

Generalized other. A conception from George Herbert Mead (*Mind, Self, and Society*) suggesting that, in the socialization process, the person comes to recognize the expectations *commonly held of him* for performance in various roles. Embarrassment, shame, and humiliation are indications that we feel a sense of failure in meeting the expectations of the "generalized other."

Gesellschaft. A term introduced by the German sociologist, Ferdinand Tönnies, and usually translated "society" (in contrast to "community," or *Gemeinschaft*). It describes the nature of the social bond when people are no longer bound by the intimate ties of kin and community (relationships characteristic of the folk society, *q.v.*) but are implicated in one another's destinies formally and remotely in a network of secondary relationships. Competition, impersonality, social distance, and physical propinquity characterize the relationships of *Gesellschaft*. In contrast, *Gemeinschaftlich* relationships can be described as primary —i.e., immediate. They are intimate, founded in tradition, and conformity in role performance springs from a consensus daily reinforced through interaction with like-minded (and therefore right-thinking) others.

Group. One or more relationships whose boundaries are marked by the interlocking of differentiated roles and a common mission (distinguish from *category* and *aggregate, q.v.*).

Guttman scale. A cumulative scale that permits the ordering of persons (their traits, responses, attitudes) along one dimension, a given score indicating all the characteristics possessed (and all those not possessed) by the respondent. (*See* Chapter 11, the discussion of S. A. Stouffer's *Communism, Conformity, and Civil Liberties.*)

Heuristic. An adjective referring to a thinking tool—a device, model, or idea that stimulates or promotes our thinking—and thus our ability to solve problems. For example, there is no such thing as a stable social system, yet the notion of such a system provides a bench mark from which we can measure the degree of instability. Similarly with Weber's concept of bureaucracy, an ideal type (i.e., a distillation or caricature of reality). To the extent that a business organization or a department of government fails to exhibit bureaucratic features we predict the absence of traits (for example, productive efficiency) alleged to characterize business organizations.

Hypothesis. A statement asserting a determinate relationship between two variables under stated conditions.

Ideal type. A pattern of social conduct so described as to distill its essential character, highlighting features peculiar to it. Hence an ideal type is a caricature of reality, but a caricature consciously contrived in order to get at the roots and meaning of a pattern of behavior. Although it does not correspond to any reality, the ideal type may be used as a bench mark from which to measure reality. Thus, if we offer an ideal typification of capitalism as entailing a sense of vocation, asceticism, and a concern for better means of production, we can begin to measure the extent to which a given enterprise departs from these criteria. Thus the ideal type is essentially a heuristic device (*q.v.*).

Integration. Refers (as social integration) to the degree of unity of a human group. Integration stems from various sources. Insofar as people agree about the ends of life—on their central values—we have cultural integration. Frequency of communication, so reinforcing common ends and means, leads to what Landecker has called "communicative integration." To the extent that certain standards of behavior are commonly accepted—i.e., rules of conduct, or norms—then we have normative integration. In these ways, integration is based on people's *likenesses:* consensus as to the ends and means of life and the frequent interchange that confirms their convictions.

Another source of integration was highlighted by Durkheim, one that stresses *differences*. We call it "functional integration" and it means the unity that stems from the systemic character of human groups: the interlocking of differentiated but complementary and interdependent parts. (*See also* System.)

Institution. A way of organizing organizations—a standardized procedure (social procedure) for pursuing and achieving certain social objectives—for example, rearing children, getting officials into office, and fabricating and distributing cars or other products.

Interaction. A statistical concept pointing to the fact that the joint effect of two or more variables may be different from the effect of any of them taken separately. For example, Blau and Duncan find that size of family and sibling position interact in their effects on later occupational standing. "*Youngest* children have special advantages in *large* families . . . *oldest* children have greater advantages in *small* families. . . ." In other words, the effect of sibling position (on occupational status) depends on the size of the family. (See *The American Occupational Structure,* pp. 313 *et. seq.,* New York: John Wiley & Sons, Inc., 1967.) It becomes important, then, not only to separate the causal influence of sundry variables, but also to measure the joint, or interaction effects. (*See also* Social interaction.)

Latent function. A correlative outcome—but unintended, unrecognized, or both—of changes in other sectors of a social system. For example, government financed programs to improve the secondary school teaching of sociology have selected superior teachers who, with a master's degree, have moved out of the classroom. Thus a program to improve instruction may have had the unintended effect of worsening instruction through the selective removal of superior teachers.

Marginality. The condition in which a person does not fully belong to either (or any) of two or more groups. Standing at the intersection of two or more social circles, to borrow Simmel's term, the person may be subject to incompatible demands. To satisfy either one, he may have to compromise the other. Or his marginality may be exploited to his benefit as he plays one side off against the other.

Marginals. In a table, the sums of the rows and of the columns. (*See also* Degrees of freedom.)

Mean. A measure of central tendency which tells us what every member of a group would have—income, religiosity, tolerance, age—if each had the same amount. This is the most familiar average. It is calculated by adding all the values (scores) and dividing the sum by the number of persons. Since it is affected by extreme scores, it may give a distorted picture of the group. Thus the mean income of four persons receiving $1,000, $2,000, $3,000, and $1 million is something over $250,000, a figure hardly conveying an accurate impression of this group of four persons. For such skewed distributions the median (*q.v.*) is a better measure of central tendency.

Median. A measure of central tendency which is the mid-value in a series of values ordered from smaller to larger. Thus in the series 1, 3, 5, 7, 9 the midpoint—and the median—is 5. In the series 1, 3, 5, 7, 9, 11 the midpoint falls between the first three and the last three values. It is 6.

Because the value of the median depends on its position (the midpoint) and because it is not influenced as the mean is (*q.v.*) by extreme values, it is a preferred measure of central tendency for skewed distributions such as income.

Methodology. The study of ways of building reliable knowledge.

Mobility. A change, either vertical or horizontal, in group context. There is this important difference, however. Horizontal mobility need entail no disjunctures. It is precisely as though a left end for the Packers were to move to the Jets. Vertical mobility, on the other hand, typically requires a change in life style, as M. Jourdain discovered to his discomfort. Since social mobility implies exposure to different others, the person who reads, talks, and thinks may be more mobile than the one who moves often and far in space. Thus sociologist Louis Wirth pointed out that the schoolboy may be more mobile than the hobo.

Mode. The most frequently occurring value in a distribution. Suppose we have an instrument measuring militance of blacks, and 25 respondents score as shown in the accompanying table.

Score	Number of respondents making that score
25	/ / / / /
55	/ / / / / / / / / / / / / / /
75	/ / /
85	/ /

In this case, the mode is 55, a score made by 15 of the 25 respondents.

Norm. A rule of conduct, commonly understood (and often implicit, rather than explicit). It is linked with shared conceptions of what is good. Courteous conduct serves the value we place on the dignity of the individual. A norm is often inferred in a statistical sense —i.e., that which most often occurs suggests the influence of some generally accepted rule of conduct. Thus one whispers in church, if he must communicate. One knocks on the front door (or rings the bell) and waits, except with relatives and nearest friends. While it would have lacked alliterative clout, it would perhaps have been more precise to have entitled this book *Norms, Roles, and Relationships.* In short, a norm is a rule stipulating appropriate behavior in a given role.

Normal curve. A distribution in which most members of a group are described by intermediate values on some variable (honesty, intelligence, tolerance), the proportions displaying other values dropping off symmetrically above and below the mean. Such a distribution of test scores as this suggests the shape of a normal curve (see accompanying

Score	Number receiving that score
0–19	/
20–39	/ / /
40–59	/ / / / /
60–79	/ / /
80–99	/

table). Tilting it on its side, we have the familiar, bell-shaped curve (see accompanying drawing).

Normative integration. (*See* Integration.)

Participant observation. Making observations and gathering data while participating as a member of the group under study. Good examples are William Foote Whyte's *Street Corner Society* and Elliot Liebow's *Tally's Corner.*

Particularism. A criterion for role performance leading us to expect that something peculiar to a given relationship (he's my son, the clerk who short-changed me, my college roommate) will determine behavior. The contrasting criterion, universalism, refers to behavior expected of all persons in a given position, regardless of personal or relational qualities.

In a time of almost universal military conscription as in World War II, one sometimes found authority relations reversed: a former employee might become his employer's commanding officer. Were the CO to behave vindictively (or to show favoritism), he would run counter to the universalistic criterion stipulating that an officer must treat his men in evenhanded fashion. (*See also* Universalism.)

Pluralism, political. The situation in which a given political preference cuts across (rather than being coterminous with) a large number of social categories. For example, we have an instance of political pluralism when Democrats are found among rich and poor; Catholics, Jews, and Protestants; well educated and illiterate; and so on. A fictitious example of the opposite of political pluralism would be one in which wealth, whiteness, and Protestant religious affiliation went with political party *X*, while adherents of political party *Y* were all poor, black, and Catholic. Such an alignment of affiliations, especially when reinforced by language (the Flemish and Walloons in Belgium or the Tamils and Sinhalese in Ceylon) makes for a more volatile and vulnerable social system.

Positivism. (*See* Empiricism.)

Probability. The estimate of the likelihood that an occurrence—in sociology, a social outcome—is a chance effect. It is typically calculated on the basis of the distance between a behavioral pattern that would be produced by random influences and the behavior produced more or less systematically by cultural and social requirements. Probability theory has become an important feature of the strategy of sociological inquiry.

Relationship. Refers to the covariance of measures of two variables. If with increased values on one measure we also get higher values on the measure of the second variable, we have a positive relationship and the figure representing degree-of-relationship is preceded by a plus sign. If with increased values on one measure, values of the second decline, we have a negative or inverse relationship and the figure representing degree-of-relationship is preceded by a minus sign. Relationships between two variables may be stated algebraically (in an equation) or graphically or both. When represented graphically, a regression line is often plotted through the data. This is sometimes called a line of least mean squares, meaning that it is so plotted as to minimize the spread of the data from itself. Thus it cuts a sort of average path through the data, summarizing, as does an average, a certain characteristic of the data, the extent and direction of relationship. (*See also* Social relationship.)

Reliability. The extent to which measures (and measurers) agree in their readings of the data. Just as an elastic yardstick would be unreliable, so a questionnaire, interview schedule, or scale that changed in the hands of different users would be unreliable. Not to be confused with validity (*q.v.*).

Role. A commonly held set of expectations as to how persons occupying a given position in the social structure may be expected to perform (i.e., what the rights and duties are in that position). From a psychological perspective, the role is seen as the particular way in which the person plays his part. From a social perspective, it is the pattern of behavior peculiar to the part.

Scale. Ways of classifying and ordering social data. Nominal (name) scales simply classify the data in labeled pigeonholes: male, female, or New York, Chicago, and Los Angeles, or rural and urban. Ordinal scales arrange the data in ascending or descending order: one category has more, or less than another. When we sort indexes of class standing into upper, middle, and lower we are creating an ordinal scale. When we can say *how much more*, we are moving toward interval scales. Thus, in the case of income, we know that $2,000 is $8,000 less than $10,000. Similarly, we know that four children are three more than we have in a one-child family. A fourth sort of scale, and more refined, is the ratio scale, which has a zero point, equal intervals, and enables us to relate one value to another as a ratio. Thus $8,000 is four times as much as $2,000. But we have trouble finding social data that are amenable to ratio scaling. It is not even clear, for example, that such a quantifiable trait as number of children can be sensibly manipulated on a ratio scale. Are four children (despite differences in age and sex) twice as many as two children? And certainly, when it comes to measures of such traits as bigotry, it becomes difficult to say I have half as much as you. (*See* Aside on Methods, Number 9.)

Sect. A form of religious organization that, in contrast to the church, condemns secular society, and seeks salvation in this world and the next through adherence to Holy Writ understood as literal truth. Communicants are likely to be poor, outside the mainstream of society. Ministers are not trained but assume the role through divine appointment. Membership is not an automatically bestowed gift at birth but something achieved through confession, commitment and descent of the spirit. The sect is to be distinguished from the cult whose members seek desired ends by inducing occult powers to aid them. It obviously differs from the ecclesia, a term used to describe the church when its membership is virtually the same as the citizenry. (Medieval Catholic Europe would be an example.)

Self. That aspect of personality that, nurtured and shaped through interaction with others, confers identity. In the process of self development, the person must transform subject into object, the "I" into the "Me," seeing himself from the perspective of others. (*See also* Social self.)

Social distance. The frequency and affectivity (*q.v.*) of relationships with categories of others. A scale measuring social distance was first developed by the sociologist E. S. Bogardus. On this scale respondents indicate the most intimate relationship to which they would be willing to admit members of various racial, religious, and nationality groups. Over the years of its use (since 1933), there has been increased willingness to accept members of other groups. But the rank order of tolerance has remained remarkably constant: native Americans over Englishmen, over Italians over Negroes. . . . (among native white American respondents).

Social interaction. The communicative process through which two or more people shape one another's responses. In assessing the other's meaning and motives, the person internalizes the other. This is the psychic counterpart to the ingestion of food and, as in the case of food, the person is changed, however modestly, in the process. Because of the implication that each becomes part of the other (and this in conflict as well as more harmonious relationships), Dewey and Bentley prefer the word "transaction" to "interaction." For the latter implies something that happens *between* rather than through the people dealing with one another. Used as a verb ("Let's interact together") the word is awkward and appears pretentiously polysyllabic. Yet it persists in usage because no other word carries the complex connotations suggested above.

Socialization. The process of transmitting the group's culture to newcomers—to the child, the immigrant, the new employee, camper, candidate for church membership. . . . Formal education is the obvious mechanism in modern society. But there are many agents and mechanisms, some of them wholly unrecognized, for initiating the newcomer into the secrets of his group. From the perspective of the group, socialization is the process of group renewal as newcomers, transformed into full-fledged members, replace old-timers who move, retire, or die.

Socialization, anticipatory. The development of skills, knowledge, attitudes, and values that become useful later in roles not yet taken up. Anticipatory socialization may be consciously employed to prepare for the future. But probably most such socialization is picked up unwittingly. We learn to act appropriately as males and females long before we are full-fledged men and women. And we learn the three R's long before we apply such skills as doctors, lawyers, beggarmen, thieves.

Social relationship. The give and take between two persons or parties when the action of one elicits a highly predictable response from the other. This implies a community of interests (in fighting, or loving, or working, or whatever) and communication, either direct or indirect. Two people using mutually incomprehensible languages would find it difficult to establish a social relationship. The element of predictability is crucial in understanding a social relationship. To the extent that the other's responses are unpredictable, a relationship is uncertain, faltering. If we decided which reaction to use among the repertoire of all possible responses by referring to a table of random numbers, no social relationship could exist.

Social system. A bounded set of relationships whose unity comes from the dovetailing of differentiated but complementary and interdependent roles. Students and teacher, parents and children, two lovers, two people or groups in conflict, a Rotary club—all these and many, many more are examples of social systems. In each case, there are boundaries between one set of relationships and others. In each case, there is a differentiation of interlocking roles within the group. And in each case, an event in one part of the system generates repercussions in other parts. (*See also* System.)

Specificity. (*See* Diffuseness.)

Standard deviation. A statistical measure of the dispersion of values from the mean of a distribution. It is the square root of the variance (*q.v.*).

Standard Metropolitan Statistical Area (SMSA). One or more counties containing at least one city of 50,000 or more population, plus adjacent counties if they are chiefly urban and industrial in their social and economic characteristics and are integrated with the central city.

In 1968 nearly two thirds of the U.S. population lived in SMSA's (64%), more outside the central cities than within them. But for Negroes, the larger percentage of SMSA dwellers was within the central city. (*See* Figure 13.2, Chapter 13.)

Status. A position—where a person stands —in the group structure. Thus widowed, married, single, divorced are marital statuses. Blue collar, white collar refer to statuses in the structure of the labor force. Sometimes used interchangeably with *standing*, but this is confusing. *Rank* is preferred for this meaning.

Stratification. The hierarchical ordering of social positions (and the roles associated with those positions) along the scale of a group's values.

System. An abstract concept that points to a bounded set of elements whose unity comes from the dovetailing of differentiated but complementary and interdependent parts. Thus we speak of an ignition system (battery, starter, plugs, coil, distributor, and so on), or an educational system (taxpayers, administrators, board of trustees, teachers, students, and other positions and roles), or the solar system (the sun, the planet earth, and other bodies which, in their orbits, maintain a systematic relationship with one another). Because of the interdependence of its parts, variations in one sector of the system can be used to predict variations in other parts of the system. In a complex system, the path of influence may be long and hidden. This is a reason that, in social systems, attempts to alter human affairs often lead to unanticipated side effects. (*See also* Social system.)

Triad. (*See* Dyad *and* Chapter 2.)

Universalism. A criterion for role performance leading us to expect that *any* incumbent of a given role will, in essential respects, behave in accordance with certain standards, no matter with whom he is dealing. Thus, regardless of differences in beauty, wealth, parental background, race, and the like, students are to be treated with equal concern by the teacher, appendectomies to be performed with evenhanded concern by the physician, repairs are to be made with equal conscientiousness by the mechanic. Similarly, *all* students are expected to invest themselves in learning, *all* patients are to follow the physician's instructions, *all* customers are expected to pay their bills.

Urban. Places having a population of 2,500 or more and incorporated, or, if not incorporated, being encapsulated within a Standard Metropolitan Statistical Area (SMSA *q.v.*) or having a high density and being within the orbit of large urban areas.

In 1790, 202,000 persons (about 5% of the population) lived in urban areas. One hundred and seventy years later, 125 million persons lived in urban areas, constituting about 70% of the population. (*See* Chapter 13.)

Validity. The extent to which a measure does in fact measure—or get at—what it purports to be measuring. Thus a test for native intelligence which instead reveals differences in opportunity would be regarded as invalid. The validity of a measure is often determined by comparing the results it yields with some other, acceptable measure of the same quality. For example, the validity of a test of capacity for scientific thinking might be determined by administering it to a group of recognized scientists and to a second group of nonscientists. If the former did not score higher than those in the latter category, we would question the validity of the measure.

Values. Conceptions of the desirable and, by implication, of the undesirable. Thus the statement of a value implies a scale whose poles are the desired and undesired states. Values may be explicit in public professions like the Mosaic code, the Sermon on the Mount and the Declaration of Independence. Or they may be inferred from men's activities. Values may be thought of as social goals or ends, while norms specify the means —the rules—according to which we may legitimately achieve the ends.

Variable. In sociology, any dimension of a social relationship that can take on differing values—i.e., any attribute or characteristic that varies. A *dependent variable* is one whose differing values we wish to explain. An *independent variable* is, or represents, some causally prior influence.

Variance. A measure (σ^2) of the extent to which the values in a distribution deviate from the mean. It is the average of the squared deviations from the mean. For example, if we have 5 scores of 1, 3, 5, 7, 9, the average for the group is of course the sum of these values divided by 5—i.e., $25/5 = 5$. Now 3 and 1 deviate from the mean by 2 and 4 respectively. So do 7 and 9. Five, of course, doesn't deviate from itself at all. Now we square these deviations and take their average. This gives us $4^2 + 2^2 + 0^2 + 2^2 + 4^2$ for a total of 40 which, divided by 5 gives us a variance $(\sigma^2) = 8$. The square root of the variance, in this case about 2.8, is the most frequently used measure of dispersion. It is called the standard deviation (σ).

Such measures (variance, standard deviation) have special significance for the homogeneity-heterogeneity dimension of group life. If we compare the variance (or standard deviation) of the distribution of income for Sweden and the United States, we have an important clue to the nature of life and law in these two quite different societies.

Name index

D

E

F

G

H

Subject index

D

E

R

This book has been set in 10 point Aster, leaded 3 points. Part numbers and titles are in 18 point and chapter titles are in 12 point Helvetica Bold. Chapter numbers are in 10 point Aster. The size of the type page is 27 by 48¾ picas.

Lewis and Clark College - Watzek Library
HM51 .W48 wmain
Wilson, Everett K./Sociology: rules, rol
3 5209 00439 5816